RABBINIC TEXTS AND THE
HISTORY OF LATE-ROMAN PALESTINE

PROCEEDINGS OF THE BRITISH ACADEMY · 165

RABBINIC TEXTS
AND THE HISTORY OF
LATE-ROMAN PALESTINE

Edited by
MARTIN GOODMAN
& PHILIP ALEXANDER

Published for THE BRITISH ACADEMY
by OXFORD UNIVERSITY PRESS

Oxford University Press, Great Clarendon Street, Oxford OX2 6DP

Oxford New York

Auckland Cape Town Dar es Salaam Hong Kong Karachi
Kuala Lumpur Madrid Melbourne Mexico City Nairobi
New Delhi Shanghai Taipei Toronto

With offices in
Argentina Austria Brazil Chile Czech Republic France Greece
Guatemala Hungary Italy Japan Poland Portugal Singapore
South Korea Switzerland Thailand Turkey Ukraine Vietnam

Published in the United States
by Oxford University Press Inc., New York

© The British Academy, 2010
Database right The British Academy (maker)

First published 2010

British Library Cataloguing in Publication Data
Data available

Library of Congress Cataloging in Publication Data
Data available

Typeset by
New Leaf Design, Scarborough, North Yorkshire
Printed in Great Britain
on acid-free paper by
CPI Antony Rowe
Chippenham, Wiltshire

ISBN 978–0–19–726474–4
ISSN 0068–1202

Contents

Notes on Contributors

Philip Alexander, FBA is Professor of Post-Biblical Jewish Literature and Co-Director of the Centre for Jewish Studies in the University of Manchester. A former President of the Oxford Centre for Hebrew and Jewish Studies, he researches Jewish literature of the Second Temple and talmudic periods, especially Midrash, Targum and mystical texts, within its Graeco-Roman context. As a member of the international team tasked by the Israel Antiquities Authority to edit the Dead Sea Scrolls, he published with Geza Vermes the Cave Four fragments of the *Community Rule* in the Discoveries in the Judaean Desert series, vol. XXVI (1998). His most recent monographs are *The Targum of Canticles* (2003), *The Targum of Lamentations* (2008) and *Companions to the Dead Sea Scrolls: The Mystical Texts* (2005). He is Director of the Gaster Genizah Project at the John Rylands University Library, Manchester.

Robert Brody is Professor of Talmud in the Hebrew University of Jerusalem. His research has concentrated on rabbinic literature of the Geonic period; more recently he has been working intensively on the Babylonian Talmud. His publications in the field of Geonic literature include both detailed studies of particular texts and broader surveys, such as *The Geonim of Babylonia and the Shaping of Medieval Jewish Culture* (1998) and a biography of Saadyah Gaon, originally published in Hebrew, which is to appear in English translation in the near future.

Martin Goodman, FBA is Professor of Jewish Studies in the University of Oxford. He is a Fellow of Wolfson College and a Fellow of the Oxford Centre for Hebrew and Jewish Studies. His most recent books are *Rome and Jerusalem: The Clash of Ancient Civilizations* (2007) and *Judaism in the Roman World: Selected Essays* (2007), and he is editor of *The Oxford Handbook of Jewish Studies* (2002).

Robert Hayward is Professor of Hebrew in the Department of Theology and Religion, University of Durham. His research interests focus on Jewish Bible interpretation, with special reference to the Aramaic Targum and the Midrashim. His recent publications include *Targums and the Transmission of Scripture into Judaism and Christianity*, Studies in the Aramaic Interpretation of Scripture, 10 (2009).

Catherine Hezser is Professor of Jewish Studies in the School of Oriental and African Studies (SOAS) of the University of London. Her area of specialisation is the social history of Jews in Roman Palestine, rabbinic literature in general and the Talmud Yerushalmi in particular. She has published numerous volumes and articles in this field, among them *The Social Structure of the Rabbinic Movement in Roman Palestine* (1997), *Jewish Literacy in Roman Palestine* (2001), *Rabbinic Law in its Roman and Near Eastern Context* (2003), and *Jewish Slavery in Antiquity* (2005). She is the editor of the *Oxford Handbook of Jewish Daily Life in Roman Palestine* (2010) and has a new book on *Mobility and Communication in Ancient Judaism* forthcoming.

William Horbury, FBA is Emeritus Professor of Jewish and Early Christian Studies in the University of Cambridge, and a Fellow of Corpus Christi College. His main research interests are in Jewish history and literature of the Greek and Roman periods, early Christianity, and the history of Hebrew study and Jewish–Christian relations. Recent publications include *Messianism among Jews and Christians* (2003) and *Herodian Judaism and New Testament Study* (2006).

Richard Kalmin is Theodore R. Racoosin Professor of Rabbinic Literature in the Jewish Theological Seminary of America. He is the author of several books and numerous articles on the interpretation of rabbinic stories, ancient Jewish history and the structure and development of rabbinic literature. His most recent book, *Jewish Babylonia between Persia and Roman Palestine* (2006), was honoured by the Association for Jewish Studies as a 2009 Notable Selection in the category of Biblical Studies, Rabbinics and Archaeology. The book was also named 'Best Book of the Year on Ancient Iran' in 2007 by the Iranian Ministry of Culture.

Hayim Lapin is Professor of History and Jewish Studies and Director of the Joseph and Rebecca Meyerhoff Center for Jewish Studies in the University of Maryland. He works on the intersection of the history of Palestine as a Roman province and the development of rabbinic culture. He is currently completing a book-length study on rabbis as Roman provincials.

Moshe Lavee is a lecturer in Talmud and Midrash in the University of Haifa and the chair of the Early Judaism and Rabbinics Programme in the European Association for Biblical Studies. His studies deal with conversion to Judaism and group demarcation in rabbinic literature and with the acceptance and function of midrashic literature as documented in the Cairo Genizah.

Chaim Milikowsky is Professor of Talmud at Bar Ilan University. His work focuses on midrashic literature, specifically on the various modes of biblical interpretation prevalent in the Hellenistic–Roman period, and on rabbinic philology. His critical edition of, introduction to and commentary on Seder Olam, a rabbinic chronography, is presently in press at the Israel Academy of Sciences and Humanities.

Fergus Millar, FBA is Emeritus Professor of Ancient History in the University of Oxford, and a Senior Associate of the Oxford Centre for Hebrew and Jewish Studies. He is the author of *The Roman Near East, 31 BC–AD 337* (1993) and *A Greek Roman Empire: Power and Belief under Theodosius II* (2006), and is working on the history of the Near East under Roman rule in the fourth to sixth centuries.

Aharon Oppenheimer is the Sir Isaac Wolfson Professor of Jewish Studies at Tel Aviv University. His main research interests are Roman Palestine and Jewish Babylonia in the talmudic period. His recent publications are *Between Rome and Babylon: Studies in Jewish Leadership and Society* (2005); *Rabbi Judah ha-Nasi* (2007) [Hebrew]; 'Heilige Kriege im antiken Judentum: Monotheismus als Anlaß zum Krieg?', in *Heilige Kriege*, ed. K. Schreiner (2008); and 'Developments in the study of the Bar Kokhva Revolt during the sixty years of the State of Israel', in *Remembering and Forgetting* (= *Zion*, 74), ed. A. Baumgarten *et al.* (2009) [Hebrew].

Ronen Reichman is Professor of Talmud, Codices and Rabbinic Literature in the Hochschule für Jüdische Studien in Heidelberg. His research concerns questions related to the legal culture of rabbinic Judaism with special focus on aspects of talmudic argumentation and hermeneutics, politics and halakhah. Part of his thesis in his latest book, *Die abduktive Argumentation im talmudischen Rechtsdiskurs* (2006), is summarised in *The Talmudic Okimta and its Logical Structure: A Contribution to the Systematic Research into Talmudic Legal Hermeneutics* (= *JSQ* 2 (2005), 129–47).

Alexander Samely is Professor of Jewish Thought in the University of Manchester. His main research areas are the hermeneutic practices and literary structures of rabbinic texts from the talmudic period, on which he published *Rabbinic Interpretation of Scripture in the Mishnah* (2002) and *Forms of Rabbinic Literature and Thought* (2007). He is currently leading an AHRC-funded project devoted to developing and applying a new conceptual framework for the description of literary features of anonymous and pseudepigraphic ancient Jewish sources (www.manchester.ac.uk/ ancientjewishliterature). He also has research interests in the theory of texts more generally, as well as modern Jewish philosophy and Edmund Husserl.

Peter Schäfer, FBA is Perelman Professor of Jewish Studies and Professor of Religion and Director of the Program in Judaic Studies at Princeton University. His research fields are Jewish history in late antiquity, the literature and religion of rabbinic Judaism, Jewish mysticism, and Jewish magic. Recent publications include *Jesus in the Talmud* (2007), *The Origins of Jewish Mysticism* (2009) and *Die Geburt des Judentums aus dem Geist des Christentums. Fünf Vorlesungen zur Entstehung des rabbinischen Judentums* (2010). He is a recipient of the German Leibniz Prize and of a Distinguished Achievement Award of the Andrew W. Mellon Foundation.

Seth Schwartz is Professor of Jewish Studies in the departments of History and Classics at Columbia University. Until 2009 he taught history at the Jewish Theological Seminary in New York. He works on the social and cultural history of the Jews in the Hellenistic and Roman worlds and is author of *Imperialism and Jewish Society: 200 BCE to 640 CE* (2001) and *Were the Jews a Mediterranean Society? Reciprocity and Solidarity in Ancient Judaism* (2009).

Günter Stemberger is Professor Emeritus in the Institut für Judaistik in the University of Vienna. His main research interests are the history of rabbinic literature, the history of late-antique Palestine (up to the Muslim conquest), and Jewish–Christian relations in late antiquity. Among his recent publications are *Das klassische Judentum: Kultur und Geschichte der rabbinischen Zeit* (2009) and an annotated translation of *Die Mekhilta de-Rabbi Jishmael: Ein früher Midrasch zum Buch Exodus* (2010).

Sacha Stern is Professor of Jewish Studies at University College London. His areas of research are Jewish and general ancient history, with a particular interest in early rabbinic Judaism. He specialises in the study of calendars and time in ancient society, and is the author of *Calendar and Community: A History of the Jewish Calendar, 2nd Century BCE–10th Century CE* (2001), *Time and Process in Ancient Judaism* (2003) and *Calendars in Antiquity: Empires, States, and Societies* (forthcoming).

Amram Tropper is Lecturer in Jewish History at Ben-Gurion University. A scholar of ancient Judaism, he is the author of *Wisdom, Politics, and Historiography: Tractate Avot in the Context of the Graeco-Roman Near East* (2004), and the editor of a new edition of Elias Bickerman's classic *Studies in Jewish and Christian History*. He has also published articles on a variety of topics including ancient Jewish historiography, Jewish children and childhood in antiquity, loanwords in rabbinic literature and the formation of rabbinic sage-stories.

Wout Jac. van Bekkum is Professor of Semitics in the Department of Languages and Cultures of the Middle East, University of Groningen. His main research interests are in the field of history, religion and culture of Judaism, Hebrew and Judaeo-Arabic linguistics, medieval Jewish poetry and poetics, Karaism, modern Judaism, and Jewish Europe 1800–2000. Two recent publications are 'Pietism and poetry in thirteenth-century Baghdad: a "soul" poem by Eleazar ben Jacob ha-Bavli', *Zutot: Perspectives on Jewish Culture*, 5/1 (2008) and 'The Hebrew liturgical poetry of Byzantine Palestine', *Prooftexts*, 28 (2008).

Acknowledgements

It is fitting to acknowledge the central role in the genesis of this volume played by Fergus Millar. It was his concern to establish what valid use can and should be made by historians of the rabbinic texts of late antiquity, as he embarked on the investigation of the Roman Near East from Constantine to the beginnings of Islam which has now formed the basis of his Schweich Lectures to the Academy, which spurred the editors to organise in March 2007 a conference at the Academy, in which experts in the rabbinic literature were asked specifically to address themselves to discussion of the historical value of those texts.

We are grateful to all the participants in the conference for an exceptionally fruitful exchange of views, much of it reflected in the revised versions of the original papers which are published in this volume, and to the Academy (and especially Angela Pusey) for the flawless organisation of a large and complex meeting.

The conference has spawned also a companion volume, edited by Eyal Ben-Eliyahu, Yehudah Cohn and Fergus Millar, *Jewish Literature from late Antiquity (135–700 CE): A Handbook*, which is intended as a guide to these rabbinic materials for students of history, religion, comparative literature and other fields. We hope that the two volumes will complement each other, and we are grateful to Eyal Ben-Eliyahu and Yehudah Cohn for allowing us to make extensive use of their researches in the composition of the preliminary material in a number of the chapters in Part II of this book.

Keeping under control the large amount of material generated in the production of a multi-author volume such as this is a difficult task, and we are very grateful for all her help to Neelum Ali and to the Oxford Centre for Hebrew and Jewish Studies. We are grateful also to Susan Milligan for her expert copy-editing, not least in the standardisation of transliteration from Hebrew: for the benefit of readers unfamiliar with rabbinic texts, we have occasionally retained conventional forms which are familiar to English readers even when they do not follow precisely the main system which we have followed, which is the general simplified transliteration used by the *Encyclopaedia Judaica*.

Martin Goodman
Philip Alexander

Abbreviations

Abbreviations for rabbinic texts follow the system used in G. Stemberger, *Introduction to the Talmud and Midrash*, 2nd edn., trans. and ed. M. Bockmuehl (Edinburgh, 1996), pp. 374–6. Abbreviations for classical texts follow the system used in S. Hornblower and A. Spawforth (eds.), *Oxford Classical Dictionary*, 3rd edn. (1996), pp. xxix–liv.

AJS Review	*Association for Jewish Studies Review*
BASOR	*Bulletin of the American Schools of Oriental Research*
BSOAS	*Bulletin of the School of Oriental and African Studies*
DOP	*Dumbarton Oaks Papers*
FJB	*Frankfurter Judaistische Beiträge*
Heb.	Hebrew
HThR	*Harvard Theological Review*
JAOS	*Journal of the Americal Oriental Society*
JJS	*Journal of Jewish Studies*
JQR	*Jewish Quarterly Review*
JRS	*Journal of Roman Studies*
JSQ	*Jewish Studies Quarterly*
JSS	*Journal of Semitic Studies*
R.	rabbi
SCI	*Scripta Classica Israelica*
ZPE	*Zeitschrift für Papyrologie und Epigraphik*

Glossary of Hebrew terms

aggadah (pl. *aggadot*)	narration
amora (pl. *amora'im*)	rabbinic teacher in the talmudic period (*c.*220–530 CE)
baraita (pl. *baraitot*)	tannaitic tradition found in a later rabbinic compilation
Bavli	Babylonian Talmud
genizah	storeroom for depositing sacred objects
Geonim	heads of the rabbinic academies in Babylonia in the seventh to eleventh centuries (Geonic period)
halakhah (pl. *halakhot*)	'rule', an acceptable decision in rabbinic law
massekhet (pl. *massektot*)	tractate
midrash (pl. *midrashim*)	non-literal biblical interpretation
mishnah	teaching
perek	chapter
petiḥah	formula found at the beginning of a section in aggadic *midrashim*
piska	paragraph
piyyut (pl. *piyyutim*)	liturgical poem
seder (pl. *sedarim*)	order
shas	colloquial word for Talmud
tanna (pl. *tanna'im*)	rabbinic teacher in the first two centuries CE
targum	Aramaic translation of the Bible
Yerushalmi	Palestinian (or Jerusalem) Talmud

Introduction

MARTIN GOODMAN

THIS VOLUME, LIKE THE CONFERENCE AT THE BRITISH ACADEMY IN MARCH 2007 on which it is based, is concerned to tackle a quite specific deficiency in research into the history of the later Roman empire. Historians of the eastern Mediterranean world from the second to the seventh centuries CE are usually well aware of the existence of a large corpus of rabbinic texts, preserved within the later Jewish religious tradition, which originated in the Roman empire in the period they study, but these texts are called into service as historical evidence by non-specialists only rarely and only tentatively, and with little awareness of the issues of provenance, dating, transmission and genre which make use of this particular material particularly complex.

There are good reasons to believe that encouraging greater use of rabbinic texts by historians will be worthwhile, not least because late-Roman Palestine, from where much rabbinic evidence originated, is a province which would already be well known even without rabbinic evidence. Climate conditions unusual in the Mediterranean world have enabled the survival in some parts of the Judaean Desert and the Negev of papyri and leather documents which provide unique insights. Much of the province has been subjected to an exceptional intensity of archaeological investigation, fuelled in part by religious concerns (both Jewish and Christian), in part by a nationalist search for traces of previous Jewish inhabitants as background to the present State of Israel. A large corpus of inscriptions in Hebrew, Aramaic and Nabataean, as well as in Greek and Latin, has been, or is in the process of being, published and evaluated. The status as the Christian Holy Land of the province (or, from the fourth century, provinces) of Palestine ensured that the region bulked large in Christian texts after Constantine, from the writings of Jerome, who lived in Bethlehem, to the discussions of Church councils.

The evidence of the rabbinic texts, if properly used, should therefore be understood as a check on, and complement to, a great array of other evidence of a type more familiar in other provinces. The result should be not just that Roman Palestine should be known in a degree of detail and intimacy not possible for most of the provinces of the empire, but that the reliability of the

Proceedings of the British Academy **165**, 1–3. © The British Academy 2010.

picture of other provinces, derived from fewer types of evidence, can be better evaluated.

The reluctance of late-Romanists to engage with rabbinic texts up to now does not need to be laboured, and one striking example may suffice: it is remarkable that the relevant volumes of the *Cambridge Ancient History* (Cameron and Garnsey 1998; Cameron, Ward-Perkins and Whitby 2000) include nothing at all on the rabbinic sources. The reasons for this reluctance to engage with rabbinic material are in some ways obvious. The rabbinic texts are in Hebrew and Aramaic. They employ unfamiliar literary genres and sometimes an allusive and esoteric mode of expression. Translations into European languages have appeared only sporadically and have not always been entirely trustworthy. The marginalisation of Jews in late-Roman society may have encouraged the marginalisation of their history in the historiography about that society.

All such reasons have played their part in bringing about the current neglect of rabbinic texts by non-specialists, but two others are worth identifying here. One is that rabbinic texts differed from most other texts used by historians in the way that they were preserved in antiquity: when literary scholars struggle to identify the reading of the original text of a classical poet or Christian theologian on the basis of medieval manuscripts, they do so safe in the knowledge that there was indeed a text of some kind written down by their author at a specific time in antiquity, but for some, perhaps many, rabbinic texts, preservation may have been in oral form until the medieval period—and since they were preserved as religious texts within a living and evolving continuous tradition, some may reflect Jewish life in the Middle Ages in Europe more than conditions in late-Roman Palestine.

The second reason worth highlighting lies in the history of scholarship. Most readers of rabbinic texts before the modern era were Jews who saw them as a source of religious authority and read them essentially ahistorically. The excavation of historical information from rabbinic writings by the Wissenschaft des Judentums school in the nineteenth century was designed to demonstrate that the Jews, like other peoples, had a continuous political history throughout antiquity, an aim which not infrequently encouraged rather implausible assumptions about the underlying political rationale of rabbinic discourse. The process of charting a course between these two extremes has involved intense research and debate, especially in the past half-century, and the specialists involved in this debate, all of whom have been required first to master this complex material before discussing its possible significance, have not always been willing, or perhaps able, to transmit their findings in an accessible form to non-specialists. Of the few scholars who have made an attempt, some (notably the prolific and highly influential Jacob Neusner) have presented their own views in so partisan a manner that outsiders to the field may find it hard to distinguish between the material they can use with confidence and the material that is a product of scholarly hypothesis. It is hard to divorce entirely the esotericism of much scholarly discourse about rabbinic texts from the natural desire of a guild of experts to preserve the mystique of their profession and from the continuing role of these texts as sources of religious authority within different streams of contemporary Judaism.

This, at any rate, is the position that the present volume hopes to begin to correct. Part I lays out the context and the main issues, including the fundamental debate over whether any of these rabbinic texts existed in anything like their present form in late antiquity, a debate presented both in the classic discussion of Peter Schäfer and Chaim Milikowsky in the *Journal of Jewish Studies* in the 1980s (reprinted here in Chapters 3 and 4) and in further reflections on that debate after twenty years by the same two authors. Part II examines the differing status as historical evidence for late antiquity of different sorts of rabbinic literature, both to show the variety of genres and the difficulties involved in placing and dating this material and to illustrate the variety of modern scholarly approaches to these issues. Part III is devoted to a series of thematic studies of historical topics for which rabbinic evidence has in the past been welcomed by some as useful evidence and denied such a role by others.

This volume will have succeeded if—in conjunction with the companion volume also to be published by the Academy, *Jewish Literature from Late Antiquity (135–700 CE): A Handbook* (Ben-Eliyahu, Cohn and Millar forthcoming), which will lay out for historians in an accessible form the basic information they need to find editions, translations and other aids for use of these texts—it encourages ancient historians to begin to cite the rabbinic texts more often and with greater confidence as to how, when and where they can be used. The brief lists of Further Reading appended to each chapter are intended to facilitate this process by providing suggestions for those who wish to delve more deeply into the topics discussed.

Part I
The Issues

1

Using Rabbinic Literature as a Source for the History of Late-Roman Palestine: Problems and Issues[1]

PHILIP ALEXANDER

Introduction

To WHAT EXTENT CAN CLASSIC RABBINIC LITERATURE be used to throw light on the history of late-Roman Palestine? On the face of it, this corpus of texts has much to offer. It is very substantial, and although none of it is historiographical in genre, it is full of names of rabbis, whom we can date fairly precisely, of places we know, and of incidents and events of various kinds, some of which can be corroborated from external sources. In the past historians have quarried nuggets of 'information' from rabbinic texts and set them into grand narratives covering the history of late antiquity. The basic methodology has been straightforward, and rarely, till recently, questioned. First, use discursive histories in Greek and Latin to provide a framing narrative (having, of course, first read these closely and critically). Next, supplement, confirm, or correct this narrative with 'first-hand' information derived from archaeology, inscriptions and papyri. Then insert the rabbinic evidence in an appropriate place, usually in a supplementary fashion. Any rabbinic 'data' that does not fit into this predetermined framework is usually seen as historically questionable, and quietly ignored. This, fundamentally, is how rabbinic texts have been exploited by such eminent historians of Jewish late antiquity as Avi-Yonah (1976) and Alon (1980–84) for Palestine, and Neusner (1965–70) and Gafni (1990) for Babylonia.[2] A somewhat similar approach can be employed if one is interested in aspects of social, or economic, or political life, or even in realia. The Greek and Latin evidence forms the framing narrative, into which the 'bits' of information from the

---

[1] Scholarship on rabbinic literature seems to grow exponentially. The bibliographical references offered below are only indicative, and they are confined, in the main, to works appearing in the last twenty years. Further items may be gleaned from elsewhere in the present volume.

[2] See also: Baras *et al.* (eds. 1984), Horbury *et al.* (eds. 1999), and Katz (2006).

Proceedings of the British Academy **165**, 7–24. © The British Academy 2010.

rabbinic sources are fitted as best they can. A case in point would be Safrai's appeal to rabbinic evidence in his study of the economy of Palestine in late antiquity (Safrai 1994; see also Lapin 2001).

This approach has a long and distinguished pedigree. It is a manifestation of the school of positivist historiography which, having dominated the study of history since the Enlightenment, has come under sustained attack only in the second half of the twentieth century. History is to be reconstructed from 'bits' of fact scattered in a variety of sources. The task of the historian is to assemble the bits and fit them together like pieces of a jigsaw into a coherent and rational narrative, involving appropriate analysis of causation. This positivist historiography, it should be noted, has always had a strongly materialist bias. In many ways its classic Marxist form is its clearest incarnation. There is an easy assumption (easy because it is so easily taken for granted by post-Enlightenment minds) that economic, social and political factors drive history: they are what really counts; they are what the historian should be concerned about. Ideas are not denied but they are seen as expressions of economic, social and political forces. Any suggestion that they could arise independently in the human mind and influence events tends to be met with puzzled stares. There is a crucial point here. When asked, 'Of what use is rabbinic literature for the history of late-Roman Palestine?' we must immediately counter, 'What sort of history are you thinking of?' The rabbinic texts may be of little use, at least compared with Greek and Latin sources, for political or administrative or economic or even social history (I make no judgement on this here), but surely they are a gold mine for the study of *religious* history: they are one of the richest surviving sources from their region and their time for the history of *ideas*, and when we compare those ideas with ideas from the same time and place, documented in patristic and late pagan (e.g. Neo-Platonic and Neo-Pythagorean) sources, a flood of light is shed on the inner workings of peoples' *imaginations*, on world views which may help to explain why they behaved as they did in everyday life.[3]

The positivistic use of the rabbinic sources, domesticated within Jewish Studies by the giants of the Wissenschaft des Judentums, has been seen as increasingly problematic in the past forty years. The rest of this chapter will be devoted to considering why. I do not propose to offer an overview of the present state of scholarship on rabbinic literature: that is covered, document by document, genre by genre in the rest of the volume.[4] Rather what I propose to do is to focus on the key issues, as I see them, emerging in recent

---

[3] See Kraemer (1990) and Neusner (1991a) for interesting attempts to exploit rabbinic sources for the history of ideas.
[4] For useful overviews see Stemberger (1996, 1999, 2007); Hezser (2002); Fonrobert and Jaffee (2007).

rabbinic scholarship, which have problematised the use of rabbinic literature as a straightforward historical source, and of which anyone so using them should be aware. The first task which historians should address is surely the nature of the sources they propose to use. Until they get this straight there is a danger of misuse. It is a cardinal principle of hermeneutics that the nature and genre of a text predetermines the kind of information that can legitimately be extracted from it, and how one should set about doing so. Many of the problems raised here will come up in greater detail in the chapters that follow (and alternative solutions proposed): I shall try to stay as far as possible here on a theoretical level, and avoid raising direct historical questions, e.g. as to the *Sitz im Leben* or date of any specific text, to focus on the texts *as texts*, as they lie before us, grouping my remarks under four broad headings: (1) the rabbinic corpus; (2) the composition and transmission of the texts; (3) the languages; (4) the genres.

The Rabbinic Corpus

The first question that has to be raised is the limits of the rabbinic corpus itself. We talk of *rabbinic* literature, but what is 'in' and what is 'out'? This question was answered rather loosely but confidently until quite recently. Rabbinic literature comprises all those texts in Hebrew and Aramaic passed down to us within the rabbinic movement and its medieval successors. This 'rabbinic canon' has been defined fundamentally by great reference works starting with Zunz's *Die gottesdienstlichen Vorträge der Juden* (1892; cf. Albeck 1974) down to Stemberger's *Introduction to the Talmud and Midrash* (1996). Most recently perceptions of the 'canon' have been shaped by electronic databases such as Bar Ilan and Davka. For pragmatic reasons an inclusive approach has been adopted in the present volume, but it is important to acknowledge that this creates profound problems.

It is obvious even at a glance that the canon contains very diverse elements. The Mishnah, Tosefta, Yerushalmi and Bavli Talmuds form a strong axis within it. These are textually related in all sorts of significant ways: not only are they broadly the same type of text, but one text 'quotes' the other; the same rabbis are cited; the same leading ideas are expressed. Here, for sure, we have some sort of literary genealogy. Certain midrashim are closely aligned to this axis: the so-called tannaitic midrashim, Bereshit Rabbah, Vayyikra Rabbah, Shir Rabbah and Eikhah Rabbah, for example; but the full 'rabbinical' credentials of some midrashim are questionable. What are we to do, for example, with Pesikta Rabbati, which contains *piska*s that seem to attack the Sages?[5] Is this

---

[5] See e.g. Piska 34. Further: Goldberg (1978); Fishbane (1998).

a *rabbinic* midrash? What are we to do with the targums? Are they rabbinic? Certainly all these texts seem to have been transmitted within what might broadly be called rabbinic Judaism, but it is far from obvious that this fact alone justifies the assertion that they are 'rabbinic'. The tradition is sometimes surprisingly unreliable even about texts which it claims as its own, such as the two 'official' targums, Onqelos and Jonathan. The name 'Onqelos' appears to be an invention of the Talmud Bavli, which misunderstood a Palestinian tradition about someone called Aqilas, and which, if it is true, almost certainly referred to the *Greek* version of Aquila. The traditions ascribing the Prophetic Targum to Jonathan inspire no greater confidence (b.Meg. 3a; p.Meg. 1.9). And what are we to say about the piyyutim, or the Hekhalot texts, or the *Sefer Yeẓirah*, or *Sefer ha-Razim*, or *Harba de Mosheh*, or *Assaf ha-Rofe* (Lieber 1984, 1991), or the major prayers? Are they *rabbinic* creations, integral to the *rabbinic* 'canon'? The case of the Aramaic bowls from Babylonia is highly instructive. Hundreds of these are now known, and they date for sure from the period when the Babylonian Talmud was being composed (Levene 2003; Bohak 2008). If we were to print the surviving text continuously, it would probably cover well over one hundred A4 sides of Aramaic and Hebrew. If this amount of text had been discovered in manuscript form it would have been a sensation. Is it rabbinic, or does it attest a world of Babylonian Jewry only tangentially associated with the academies?

And does it much matter where we draw the boundaries of rabbinic literature? Arguably it does. The 'big-tent' definition of rabbinic literature has inhibited the recognition that the material passed down to us by rabbinic Judaism is highly diverse, and fostered the homogenising of it as all an expression of a *rabbinic* world view. It has also led to the imposition on the corpus of a *rabbinic* textual hierarchy which prioritises the core texts, the Talmuds and the major midrashim.[6] The working out of this hierarchy can be seen, for example, in the study of the piyyutim and the targums. When parallels have been discovered between these and core rabbinic texts it was often assumed in the past that the core rabbinic texts have priority: they are the *source* of the traditions in piyyut and targum, even that targum and piyyut are *quoting* them.[7] But why should it not be the other way round, or why should not all the texts be expressions of a rich and diverse culture that is by no means dominated by the rabbinic movement and rabbinic ideas? It is

---

[6] A. J. Heschel's *Torah min ha-Shamayim* is, *inter alia*, a sustained protest against the deeply ingrained prioritising in traditionalist circles of halakhah over aggadah in the study of rabbinic literature (Heschel 2005).

[7] e.g. Churgin (1945); Rabinowitz (1965). More nuanced are Swartz and Yahalom (2005).

important to recognise that even at the literary level the corpus of Jewish texts that has survived from late-Roman Palestine is immensely diverse, and not all of it should be seen as rabbinic in any strict sense.

We must not allow the rabbinic texts so to fill our horizon that we assume that only the rabbinic movement was religiously and textually creative in the post-70 period. We have not only the piyyutim, the targums, the Hekhalot texts, the synagogue prayers, the *Sefer Yezirah*, some of the so-called 'minor' midrashim (published by Jellinek, Wertheimer and Eisenstein), the *Midreshei Ge'ullah* and other texts of the apocalyptic revival (published, for example, by Even-Shmuel), the strict rabbinic character of which may be questioned, but we have indirect evidence from within the core rabbinic canon of a richer literary scene than has survived. The rabbis famously forbade the reading of 'outside books' (m.Sanh. 10.1). In context this designates Scripture-like writings—apocrypha (if you will)—which the rabbis wanted to make sure stayed outside the biblical canon. We can guess what sort of texts these would have been: they would have been Second Temple works like Ben Sira, and certain apocalypses, which we know were preserved, in Greek translation, within the Church. Knowledge of this sort of text surfaces in late-Amoraic and post-Amoraic Palestinian Jewish literature in *Seder Eliyahu*, *Sefer Hekhalot* (better known as 3 Enoch), *Sefer Zerubbabel*, and *Pirke de-Rabbi Eliezer*. Some have toyed with the idea that there was a rediscovery of Second Temple apocalyptic literature in rabbinic circles in the fifth/sixth centuries, perhaps mediated through Christianity, but it is just as possible that these texts were there all along. In other words, Second Temple apocrypha were preserved in Palestinian Jewish circles: they did not simply vanish, as conventional wisdom would have it, and they are precisely what the rabbis mean by 'outside books' (cf. Kalmin 2006: 61–86).

All this has profound hermeneutical implications. It affects how we read the core rabbinic texts if we see not only 'rabbinic' literature itself as internally highly diverse, but as forming only a part of a much larger body of Palestinian Jewish religious literature from late antiquity, which rabbinic Judaism has only partially preserved. We have to find a way of steering the hermeneutical barque between the Scylla of the total corpus homogenised as 'rabbinic' (a traditional approach), and thus underestimating diversity, and the Charybdis of the individual documents, each seen as presenting its own distinctive world view, and thus overestimating the extent of diversity (Neusner). To what extent this literary diversity reflects the flourishing of different Jewish sects and parties in the post-70 period, creating a complexity within Palestinian Judaism not much different from that of the Second Temple period, as some would now argue, cannot be pursued here.

The Composition and Transmission of the Texts

A second area in the study of rabbinic literature that has come to the fore in recent decades is the transmission of the texts. Many classic rabbinic texts are textually rather indeterminate, that is to say, the various manuscripts of them differ substantially as to their extent, and they exhibit substantial variant readings where they overlap. Many of them exist in different recensions or versions, which raises fundamental questions as to the redactional identity of the work in hand. It would be wrong to generalise a rule that *all* rabbinic literature is marked by textual fluidity. There is actually considerable and puzzling variation on this point. Thus while Eikhah Rabbati is attested in at least two major recensions, its sister text, Shir ha-Shirim Rabbah, though represented by a similar number of manuscripts, is relatively stable (Mandel, dissertation 1997, 2000; Kadari, dissertation 2004). This difference is, curiously, mirrored in the respective targums of these two megillot, both of which are equally well attested in the manuscripts, but whereas Targum Shir ha-Shirim is textually highly stable, Targum Eikhah, like its midrashic counterpart, is extant in two major recensions (P. S. Alexander 2002 and 2008). However, many rabbinic texts show high levels of textual fluidity and instability, and the more we probe into the manuscripts and medieval quotations, the more obvious this becomes.

The reason is broadly clear: those who copied and recopied these texts did not feel obliged to preserve them precisely as they received them. They were happy to re-create them to meet their own needs, or the perceived needs of their time. They would abbreviate sections which did not interest them; they would add material from elsewhere; they would change words which they did not like or felt were obscure. To them the texts were living and developing. Each recopying was a re-performance. This is the well-known phenomenon of the 'open book', and it is characteristic of scholastic traditions (see Alexander and Samely eds. 1994, and especially the article by Ta-Shma 1994). Broadly speaking, within rabbinic culture the fidelity with which a text was copied seems to have depended on the character of the text. Bible had to be copied with great care and precision. Halakhic works such as the Mishnah which achieved high canonic status were also copied with high levels of care, but in the case of aggadic works, the copyist felt he had considerable freedom to re-create and personalise the text as he went along.

This process of re-creation continued well into the Middle Ages, and reached a climax with the early Hebrew prints. Several of our texts, as we now have them, were, to greater or lesser degree, created by the early printers. A case in point is the highly interesting Midrash to the Psalms (Midrash Tehillim): the *editio princeps*, Constantinople *c.*1512, has comments only down to Psalm 118, but a few years later (*c.*1515) the press at Salonica reissued this text but added comments on Psalms 119–150. This fuller text was then picked up in the Venice print of 1546, in Prague 1613, and became the *textus receptus*. But the status of the comments on Psalms 119–150 remain a puzzle. The furthest any of the manuscripts goes is Psalm 119:8 (Parma 1232; Cambridge OR 786). After the first prints, the works were regarded as effectively 'closed', and people used the printed *textus recepti*, tidied up with some clever conjectural emendations (such as the Vilna Gaon's brilliant glosses to the Talmud Bavli, printed in the Romm edition), until the nineteenth century rediscovered the churning chaos that lurked beneath the calm surface. All this self-evidently complicates the use of these texts for the reconstruction of rabbinic Judaism in late antiquity, let alone for wider historical purposes. How can we tell what belongs to late antiquity, and what has been added later?

But the problem is even more deep-seated than that. Even supposing we can recover from the manuscripts a text-form that we are reasonably confident was around in late antiquity, when we examine this 'Urtext' it is often manifestly composite—a loose aggregate of units which probably come from different 'sources' and different times. It begins to dawn on us that the processes which created the 'Urtext' are rather similar to the processes by which the 'Urtext' itself was re-created in the Middle Ages. The distinction between higher and lower criticism, between source, form- and redaction-criticism on the one hand, and textual criticism on the other, becomes blurred. The 'Urtext' becomes no more than a moment of stability in the ongoing flux of tradition.[8]

These insights into the processes by which the texts that make up rabbinic literature were formed and transmitted have profound implications.

First, they raise questions as to how editions of these texts should be presented. The great editions of rabbinic texts produced by the Wissenschaft des Judentums scholars worked with a model of text-edition which prevailed in the editing of the Classics—Homer, Plato, the Athenian dramatists, Vergil, Horace, and so forth. But that model is deeply unsatisfactory when applied to many texts within the rabbinic corpus. Actually it is deeply unsatisfactory when applied to many Greek and Latin works from antiquity as well. I learned my textual criticism as a classicist from R. A. B. Mynors, and the model text we used was Lucretius. Classical text-criticism works splendidly on Lucretius, which is attested in only around ten manuscripts. The ease with which the text could be cleaned up and the 'original' Lucretius recovered was

---

[8] The source-criticism of rabbinic literature is well established. The most ambitious project in this area is David Weiss-Halivni's *Meqorot u-Masorot: Be'urim ba-Talmud* (1968, 1974, 1975, 1982, 1993), though, as the title suggests, this has as much to do with redaction-criticism as with the identification of sources. See also Becker (1999).

highly gratifying and seductive. It took me a long time to realise that this model actually worked for only a portion of Greek and Latin texts surviving from antiquity. The fact is that we lack satisfactory editions of many key texts of rabbinic literature (the absence of a critical edition of the Talmud Bavli is a case in point[9]), and so long as this is the case our use of these texts for historical purposes is going to be somewhat provisional and tentative.

Secondly, the textual fluidity of the tradition makes it highly difficult to date the texts. Without dates rabbinic literature is barely usable for historical purposes of any kind, but when we assign a rabbinic text a date we need to be clear what textual entity we are dating. That entity theoretically has to be the putative starting-point of the textual transmission documented in the manuscripts, a starting-point which may or may not be discoverable with any certainty. But that starting-point, that 'Urtext', as I have already suggested, is only a moment in the history of the tradition—a moment when certain elements, of different dates, coalesced, before being passed onward, and in some cases further heavily reworked. The date of this 'Urtext' cannot be assumed to be the date of all the elements of which it is made up, still less of all the elements recorded in the manuscripts of the work in question.

Third, the fluidity of the texts makes it difficult to establish the textual relationship between them. Older handbooks of rabbinic literature were fond of claiming that text A used text B as a source, and was itself, in turn, used by text C. Such relative chronologies look promising: they seem to offer some hope of diachronic description of the corpus, but they are highly problematic. They are based on parallels, but these parallels usually prove to be inexact, and as any student of synoptic parallelism will readily acknowledge, it is actually extremely difficult on the basis of synoptic comparison

---

[9] There are, of course, great projects under way, the first-fruits of which are beginning to appear: e.g. Friedman (1990–96). Classic text-critical editions of rabbinic texts include Horovitz (1917), Lauterbach (1933–35) and Margulies (1953–60). The synoptic approach has become common of late: e.g. Schäfer (1981); Schäfer and Becker (1991–98); Reeg (1985); Ulmer (1997–2002). The synoptic editions give the scholar the tools with which he or she can do their own text-criticism. Hayman's edition of the *Sefer Yeẓirah* not only gives the manuscripts synoptically but offers a detailed text-critical commentary mishnah by mishnah arguing his own views as to the more original readings (Hayman 2004). This gets the best of both worlds, but *Sefer Yeẓirah* is a mercifully short text, and whether we have the resources to do this for larger works is open to question. The question of resources (both human and material) has to be faced: synoptic editions, and even more so editions 'in stave', consume large quantities of both. A partial solution is to put electronic images of the manuscripts on CD or on the web. There are already digital databases available of major Talmud manuscripts (Saul Lieberman Institute for Talmudic Research at JTS; Jewish National and University Library). The digitisation of the Genizah manuscripts is well under way at Cambridge, Manchester and other centres, not to mention the Friedberg Foundation's project to create an integrated digital database. As I indicated, the problems of editing 'open book' traditions is by no means confined to rabbinic literature, but stretches right across the humanities.

alone to establish which version has priority. There are few synoptic problems in rabbinic literature which have been analysed with the intensity and care that has been devoted to the synoptic problem in the Gospels, and even if they had been, it is not certain that a consensus would have emerged, because of the intrinsic subjectivity of the whole exercise (Houtman 1996; Hayes 1997; Reichmann 1998; Cohen ed. 2000; Friedman 2002). But there is an added complication. Seeing one rabbinic text as the source of another may involve inappropriate cultural assumptions as to how these texts circulated. There was certainly in the older handbooks an unspoken assumption that the texts circulated in written form: later authors consulted earlier written texts and quoted from them. But where is the evidence that these texts circulated in written form? Was there some sort of rudimentary book market in rabbinic texts in antiquity? Certainly within the schools oral transmission played a highly significant role: what effect did that have on the transmission of the texts (Jaffee 2001, 2006; E. S. Alexander 2006)?[10]

The Languages

A third fundamental area in the study of rabbinic literature relates to languages. Here progress has certainly been made, but much still remains to be done. There are big lexical projects afoot, such as the Steve Kaufman's *Comprehensive Aramaic Lexicon* at Hebrew Union College, and the *Historical Dictionary of the Hebrew Language* of the Academy of the Hebrew Language, but these are still a long way from completion. We have also the fine corpus-based lexica of Michael Sokoloff for Palestinian Jewish and Babylonian Jewish Aramaic (Sokoloff 1992, 2002), but time and again we still find ourselves thrown back on the older dictionaries of Levy (1924) and Jastrow (1903), and even very occasionally on Kohut's mighty edition of

---

[10] The last word has certainly not been said on this problem. Most theoretical studies of orality have been based on evidence drawn from illiterate or barely literate societies, but this does not fit rabbinic Judaism. Though levels of literacy in late-Roman Palestine may not have been all that high (Hezser 2001), rabbinic communities surely qualify as literate. The rabbis' deep-seated 'scepticism towards the written word', which they shared with other scholastic communities of their day (L. Alexander 1990), was as much motivated by pedagogical and theological concerns as by the cost of reproducing written texts, or a lack of readers. The effect oral transmission had on the tradition is still wide open to debate. Claims by Gerhardsson in his classic study *Memory and Manuscript: Oral Tradition and Written Transmission in Rabbinic Judaism and Early Christianity* (1961), which echo the claims of the tradition itself, that it had little effect on the accuracy of transmission, are simply not borne out by the texts themselves. Schoeler's study (2006) of orality in early Islam relies heavily on supposed analogies to rabbinic Judaism, without fully appreciating how contested those analogies are. It should be used with great caution in contextualising rabbinic literary activity in the early Islamic period.

Nathan ben Yehi'el's *'Arukh* (1879–92)! It is easy to dismiss Jastrow nowadays, but in fact it is still the one dictionary that can be relied upon to make an attempt to explain every word, however obscure, in rabbinic literature. The proposals range from the impossible to the inspired, but at least Jastrow should be given credit for trying. I recently completed a close study of Targum Lamentations, and I was constantly frustrated at how many words in this text (the Aramaic of which is tricky in places) were not in Sokoloff, because it, and indeed the whole collection of Late Literary Jewish Aramaic Targums, did not form part of his corpus. However, I invariably found a suggestion in Jastrow.

The shortcomings of the rabbinic lexica are nowhere more obvious than in the case of loanwords—a barometer of the interaction of the rabbinic community with the outside world. There are a fair number of these, mainly derived from Greek, but also some from Latin and Persian. The most comprehensive listing of the Greek loanwords remains Krauss (1898–99). The fundamental problems of this pioneering work remain, despite fine supplementary studies by Lieberman (1962, 1965), Sperber (1982, 1984), Veltri (2002) and others. Progress has also been made in the area of grammar. The potential of the Aramaic incantation bowls for Babylonian Jewish Aramaic is considerable, despite the fact that many of these are essentially in the Onqelos-Jonathan dialect, but we still lack a truly comprehensive grammar of Babylonian Jewish Aramaic.[11]

The lack of up-to-date lexica and grammars matters because it has a direct impact on translation. Translation is a powerful analytical tool in reading difficult texts such as we find in the rabbinic corpus. But translation is also a way of opening up our discipline to other scholars working in late antiquity, whose expertise and collaboration we need, if we are to have any hope of contextualising rabbinic literature. Most of the classic rabbinic texts are now available in European languages, but there are some notable gaps: for example, we do not have an unproblematic rendering of the Talmud Yerushalmi into English.[12] And I am constantly struck in my own work how much I feel the need to 'tweak' the existing translations, either because they are inelegant, or are misleading, or occasionally because they are just wrong. Translation is a demanding art—somewhat neglected nowadays.

---

[11] Tuvia Kwasman's grammar, however, is nearing completion. Juusola (1999) provides a serviceable grammar. The basic Onqelos-Jonathan Aramaic dialect of the Jewish bowls is argued by Müller-Kessler (2001). For the relevance of the bowls for Babylonian Jewish Aramaic see Morgenstern (2004, 2005, 2007a, 2007b).

[12] Neusner's translation, by its own admission, is preliminary (Neusner ed. 1982–94). Guggenheimer (2000) should be used with some caution, but the Schottenstein translation by Malinowitz *et al.* (eds. 2005–) is proving very useful. Reliable renderings are appearing in the German series *Übersetzung des Talmud Yerushalmi* (e.g. Wewers 1980, 1981 and 1982).

Genres

Finally a word about genres. Genre, as I have already remarked, is funda-mental to hermeneutics: the way you read a text, the expectations you form of it, the questions you pose to it, and the sorts of information you deem it will yield depend heavily on the kind of text you conceive it to be. So what are the genres of rabbinic literature? Two genres of particular interest to his-torians are conspicuous by their absence: history and biography. There are, of course, ostensibly historical and biographical references within rabbinic liter-ature, but how reliable are they? Can we even say with confidence that the authors of the texts meant them as straightforward statements of fact, and not as exempla of legal or theological arguments? How do we know if it would have mattered to them whether the events they ostensibly report actu-ally happened or not? The message or argument of a novel is surely totally unaffected by whether or not what it describes is literally true.

Here unexamined cultural assumptions can be very treacherous. The Mishnah, the Talmuds and the midrashim are our primary sources for the sociology of the rabbinic movement in late antiquity, and particularly for the organisation of the schools, but to what extent is their picture soberly realistic, and to what extent is it idealised; how far is it descriptive and how far prescriptive? It surely cannot be denied that in the past historians of rabbinic Judaism have treated apparently sober statements of fact as just that, but are they any more reliable than apparently sober statements of fact in a life of a Christian saint? Applying crude criteria of reason and naturalism to sift out fact from fiction in such texts simply will not do. The Mishnah and the Talmuds contain large elements of hagiography, the primary function of which is to edify and inspire, not to inform us about facts. Averil Cameron and others have drawn attention to the role of narrative in late antiquity in encapsulating the world views of communities, and shaping their identities.[13] Though there are, as already noted, no exclusively narrative texts within the rabbinic corpus comparable to 1 Maccabees, or the Gospels, or Eusebius, there is, in fact, a great deal of story and anecdote poking here and there through the halakhah and Bible-exegesis—tales of debates and arguments between the great Sages, their acts of piety and holiness, their mighty deeds,

---

[13] Cameron (1991: 89–93): 'Christianity was a religion with a story . . . Narrative is at [its] very heart . . . at the very time when story was enjoying a prominence unusual in the ancient world . . . Christian literature . . . built up its own symbolic universe by exploiting the kind of stories that people liked to hear, and which in their turn provided a mechanism by which society at large and the real lives of individuals might be regulated. The better these stories were constructed, the better they functioned as structure-maintaining narratives the more their audiences were disposed to accept them as true.' I owe the distinction between primary and secondary myth to Loveday Alexander. Further: Fishbane (2003).

their encounters with heretics, and how they bested them, their meetings with
Roman officials and other outsiders, and occasionally stories of how they
sanctified the name of God in martyrdom. It is precisely this *narrative*
material which historians have been tempted to home in on for historical
information, but is it any more reliable than the Christian tales of the saints,
scholars and martyrs that shaped the Christian world view of the same
period? Surely it too is meant to project an idealised picture of the schools
and the Sages which encapsulates the core rabbinic values and the rabbinic
world view.[14] The mythical character of this secondary myth of rabbinic
Judaism becomes clear when we see how constantly and effortlessly it inter-
sects with the primary myth of the *Heilsgeschichte*—the biblical narrative of
the Exodus from Egypt, the giving of the Torah, the building of the Temple,
the Exile and return, and ultimately the coming of the Messiah.[15]

A number of pervasive literary features of the texts must give any serious
historian pause for thought. First, there is their extreme formalism and styl-
isation. This leads in certain cases to the reduction of *ipsissima verba* to for-
mulae, assuming the authority quoted actually did say something. And it is
being increasingly recognised that there is widespread pseudepigraphy
(Jacobs 1977; Stern 1994, 1995; Bregman 1999). Some historical figures seem
to be reduced effectively to ciphers (Hillel, Shammai, Abaye, Rava). Second,
there is the fact that much of the discourse is meta-textual, that is to say it is
primarily text about text, rather than text about the real world. This is most
obviously true of the midrashim, which are text about the Bible, but it is
equally true of the Gemara, which is text about the Mishnah, and the Mishnah
itself is, somewhat more obliquely, text about Torah (Samely 2002). The world
for these writings is first and foremost the world of the pre-existing text, into
which the 'real' world tends to intrude only in odd and angular ways.

The genres of rabbinic literature have been clarified in recent years
by painstaking analysis of their form, particularly the small forms which
constitute the building blocks out of which the rabbinic texts have been constructed.[16] This sterling work has helped us to understand the flow of the

---

[14] Hezser (1993); Kalmin (1994, 1999); Kraemer (1996); Rubenstein (1999). Rabbinic narrative
has been analysed not only from a literary but also from a folklore point of view: Yassif (1999);
Hasan-Rokem (2000, 2003). However, I am uneasy about treating rabbinic narratives as both
literature and folktale.

[15] Note, for example, how, after the famous debate over the Oven of Akhnai, Rabbi Nathan
casually meets Elijah and asks what the Holy One's reaction was to the decision of the Sages
(b.BM 59a–b).

[16] e.g. Jacobs (1991); Neusner (2002a, 2002b); Goldberg (1999); Samely (2007). Alexander
Samely, Philip Alexander and Robert Hayward are engaged in a project to devise a new way of
describing and classifying early Jewish literature (AHRC Project: Typology of Anonymous and
Pseudepigraphic Jewish Literature 200 BCE–700 CE).

argument within the texts, their structure, their coherence or lack of it, but it has done little to answer the historian's burning question: how literally does such a text intend me to take its occasional statements about the real world? We simply cannot assume as a default that every 'factual' statement is true until proved otherwise. It is far from clear how we would begin to answer this question with regard to rabbinic literature, and that in itself is deeply instructive. We would have relatively little hesitation in navigating genre-expectations with regard to the literary output in our own culture. We would also, interestingly, I think, have little problem doing the same with regard to the literary output of Greek and Roman culture. But we are assailed by doubts when we come to rabbinic literature. Whether or not this is because, as some would argue, rabbinic literature represents a radically alien mode of discourse that does not comply with dominant hermeneutical codes of the West is not a question we can discuss here.[17]

Concluding Remarks

In this chapter I have tried to draw up a rough agenda of questions which have to be tackled if we attempt to use rabbinic literature as a source for the study of late-Roman Palestine, and to hint at where current scholarship on rabbinic Judaism stands on these questions. There is now a consensus that rabbinic literature requires very heavy processing before its potential as a historical source can be realised. The extent to which scholars engaged with this literature have done the preliminary work remains patchy. There are obvious gaps in terms of editions, lexica, translations, commentaries, and analyses of genre and form. One problem is that much of the effort put in by the giants of the past, the great scholars of the Wissenschaft des Judentums, would now be seen as somewhat misdirected. They made assumptions about the nature of the texts which are questionable. They did valiant work on which we all still draw with admiration and gratitude, but between their day and ours there has been a paradigm-shift, and as a result their data now often needs reinterpretation, their findings repackaging.

I have asked questions which highlight difficulties, but I cannot close without saying that I believe there are solutions. As a historian I am an unrepentant positivist—and, in a postmodernist world, have the scars to prove it! The past is not another country to which we can no longer go. Difficulties which from a theoretical point of view look formidable turn out to be far from insurmountable, when one gets down to working on specific topics and specific texts. For me the key to solving the conundrum of rabbinic literature

---

[17] In favour of this view see Handelman (1982); Faur (1986). Against: P. S. Alexander (1990).

is precisely to contextualise it in the world of late antiquity—to start from the *assumption* that rabbinic literature and the rabbinic movement which engendered it are thoroughly at home in this world, are manifestations of cultural patterns that pervaded the Levant and the Middle East at that time. Scholars in the past found this leap curiously difficult to make, partly because of the linguistic barriers between (some) Jewish and Graeco-Roman culture in late antiquity, partly because they believed the relentless *contra mundum* rhetoric of the rabbinic texts (a rhetoric shared with Christian discourse of the period). But if this assumption is reasonable, then our best strategy for extracting useful historical information from the Jewish sources is through a rigorous dialectical process of comparison and contrast with the non-Jewish world of their time. Triangulation is the key: any phenomenon we find in rabbinic literature should be compared with similar phenomena in Christianity and paganism, and any phenomenon of Christianity or paganism should be compared with the other two points of the triangle. Many are engaged in just such a task: the fruits of their labours demonstrate that not only should historians of rabbinic Judaism be well-versed in Graeco-Roman culture, but historians of Graeco-Roman late antiquity are missing a trick if they do not acquire a competence in the Jewish texts.

Further Reading

Cohen (ed. 2000); Fishbane (1998); Jaffee (2001); Kalmin (1994); Neusner (2002a); Samely (2007); Stemberger (1996); Yassif (1999).

Bibliography

Albeck, Ch. (1974), *Ha-Derashot be-Yisra'el*, Jerusalem.
Alexander, E. S. (2006), *Transmitting Mishnah: The Shaping Influence of Oral Tradition*, Cambridge.
Alexander, L. (1990), 'The living voice: scepticism towards the written word in early Christian and Greco-Roman texts', in D. J. A. Clines, S. E. Fowl and S. E. Porter (eds.), *The Bible in Three Dimensions*, Sheffield, pp. 221–47.
Alexander, P. S. (1990), '"Quid Athenis et Hierosolymis?" Rabbinic Midrash and hermeneutics in the Graeco-Roman World', in P. R. Davies and R. T. White (eds.), *A Tribute to Geza Vermes*, Sheffield, pp. 101–24.
Alexander, P. S. (2002), *The Targum of Canticles*, Collegeville, MN.
Alexander, P. S. (2008), *The Targum of Lamentations*, Collegeville, MN.
Alexander, P. S. and Samely, A. (eds.) (1994), *Artefact and Text: The Re-creation of Jewish Literature in Medieval Hebrew Manuscripts, Proceedings of a Conference held in the University of Manchester 28–30 April 1992* (theme issue of *The Bulletin of the John Rylands University Library of Manchester*, 75.3 (1993)), Manchester.

Alon, G. (1980–84), *The Jews in their Land in the Talmudic Age: 70–640 CE*, 2 vols., Jerusalem.

Avi-Yonah, M. (1976), *The Jews of Palestine: A Political History from the Bar Kokhba War to the Arab Conquest*, Oxford.

Baras, Z., Safrai, S., Stern, M. and Tsafrir, Y. (eds.) (1984), *Eretz Israel from the Destruction of the Second Temple to the Muslim Conquest*, 2 vols., Jerusalem. [Hebrew]

Becker, H.-J. (1999), *Die grossen rabbinischen Sammelwerke Palästinas: Zur literarischen Genese von Talmud Yerushalmi und Midrasch Bereshit Rabba*, Tübingen.

Bohak, G. (2008), *Ancient Jewish Magic: A History*, Cambridge.

Bregman, M. (1999), 'Pseudepigraphy in rabbinic literature', in E. G. Chazon and M. Stone (eds.), *Pseudepigraphic Perspectives: The Apocrypha and Pseudepigrapha in the Light of the Dead Sea Scrolls*, Leiden, pp. 27–42.

Cameron, A. (1991), *Christianity and the Rhetoric of Empire: The Development of Christian Discourse*, Berkeley, CA.

Churgin, P. (1945), *The Targum to the Hagiographa*, New York. [Hebrew]

Cohen, S. J. D. (ed.) (2000), *The Synoptic Problem in Rabbinic Literature*, Providence, RI.

Faur, J. (1986), *Golden Doves with Silver Dots: Semiotics and Textuality in Rabbinic Tradition*, Bloomington, IN.

Fishbane, M. (1998), *The Exegetical Imagination: On Jewish Thought and Theology*, Cambridge, MA.

Fishbane, M. (2003), *Biblical Myth and Rabbinic Mythmaking*, Oxford.

Fonrobert, C. E. and Jaffee, M. S. (eds.) (2007), *The Cambridge Companion to the Talmud and Rabbinic Literature*, Cambridge.

Friedman, Sh. (1990–96), *Talmud 'Arukh. BT Bava Mezia VI: Critical Edition with Comprehensive Commentary*, New York and Jerusalem.

Friedman, Sh. (2002), *Tosefta Atikta: Synoptic Parallels of Mishnah and Tosefta analyzed with Introduction*, Ramat Gan.

Gafni, I. (1990), *The Jews of Babylonia in the Talmudic Era: A Social and Cultural History*, Jerusalem. [Hebrew]

Gerhardsson, B. (1961), *Memory and Manuscript: Oral Tradition and Written Transmission in Rabbinic Judaism and Early Christianity*, Lund.

Goldberg, A. (1978), *Erlösung durch Leiden: Drei rabbinische Homilien über die Trauernden Zions und den leidenden Messias Efraim (PesR 34.36.37)*, Frankfurt am Main.

Goldberg, A. (1999), *Rabbinische Texte als Gegenstand der Auslegung: Gesammelte Studien*, vol. 2, ed. M. Schlüter and P. Schäfer, Tübingen.

Guggenheimer, H. W. (2000), *The Jerusalem Talmud. First Order: Zeraim, Tractate Berakhot*, Berlin and New York.

Handelman, S. A. (1982), *The Slayers of Moses: The Emergence of Rabbinic Interpretation in Modern Literary Theory*, Albany, NY.

Hasan-Rokem, G. (2000), *The Web of Life: Folklore and Midrash in Rabbinic Literature*, Stanford, CA.

Hasan-Rokem, G. (2003), *Tales of the Neighborhood: Jewish Narrative Dialogues in Late Antiquity*, Berkeley, CA.

Hayes, C. E. (1997), *Between the Babylonian and Palestinian Talmuds: Accounting for Halakhic Difference in Selected Sugyot from Tractate Avodah Zarah*, Oxford.

Hayman, A. P. (2004), *Sefer Yesira: Edition, Translation and Text-Critical Commentary*, Tübingen.

Heschel, A. J. (2005), *Heavenly Torah as Refracted through the Generations*, ed. and trans. G. Tucker, New York and London.

Hezser, C. (1993), *Form, Function, and Historical Significance of the Rabbinic Story in Yerushalmi Neziqin*, Tübingen.

Hezser, C. (2001), *Jewish Literacy in Roman Palestine*, Tübingen.

Hezser, C. (2002), 'Classical rabbinic literature', in M. Goodman (ed.), *The Oxford Handbook to Jewish Studies*, Oxford, pp. 115–40.

Horbury, W., Davies, W. D. and Sturdy, J. (eds.) (1999), *The Cambridge History of Judaism*, vol. 3: *The Early Roman Period*, Cambridge.

Horovitz, H. S. (1917), *Siphre ad Numeros adjecto Siphre Zutta*, Frankfurt am Main.

Houtman, A. (1996), *Mishnah and Tosefta: A Synoptic Comparison of the Tractates Berakhot and Shebiit*, Tübingen.

Jacobs, L. (1977), 'How much of the Babylonian Talmud is pseudepigraphic?', *JJS* 28: 45–59.

Jacobs, L. (1991), *Structure and Form in the Babylonian Talmud*, Cambridge.

Jaffee, M. (2001), *Torah in the Mouth: Writing and Oral Tradition in Palestinian Judaism, 200 BCE–400 CE*, New York.

Jaffee, M. (2006), 'What difference does the "orality" of rabbinic writing make for the interpretation of rabbinic writings?', in S. Krauss (ed.), *New Approaches to Rabbinic Hermeneutics*, Piscataway, NJ, pp. 11–33.

Jastrow, M. (1903), *A Dictionary of the Targumim, the Talmud Babli and Yerushalmi, and the Midrashic Literature*, 2 vols., London.

Juusola, H. (1999), *Linguistic Peculiarities in the Aramaic Incantation Bowls*, Helsinki.

Kadari, T. (2004), 'On the Redaction of Midrash Shir HaSirim Rabbah', Ph.D. dissertation, Hebrew University, Jerusalem.

Kalmin, R. (1994), *Sages, Stories, Authors, and Editors in Rabbinic Babylonia*, Atlanta.

Kalmin, R. (1999), *The Sage in Jewish Society in Late Antiquity*, New York.

Kalmin, R. (2006), *Jewish Babylonia between Persia and Roman Palestine*, New York.

Katz, S. T. (2006), *The Cambridge History of Judaism*, vol. 4: *The Late Roman-Rabbinic Period*, Cambridge.

Kohut, A. (1878–92), *Aruch Completum*, 8 vols., Vienna.

Kraemer, D. C. (1990), *The Mind of the Talmud: An Intellectual History of the Bavli*, New York.

Kraemer, D. (1996), *Reading the Rabbis: The Talmud as Literature*, Oxford.

Krauss, S. (1898–99), *Griechische und lateinische Lehnwörter im Talmud, Midrasch und Targum*, 2 vols., Berlin; repr. Hildesheim, 1964.

Lapin, H. (2001), *Economy, Geography, and Provincial History in Later Roman Palestine*, Tübingen.

Lauterbach, J. Z. (1933–35), *Mekhilta de Rabbi Ishmael*, 3 vols., Philadelphia.

Levene, D. (2003), *A Corpus of Magic Bowls: Incantation Texts in Jewish Aramaic from Late Antiquity*, London.

Levy, J. (1924), *Wörterbuch über die Talmudim und Midraschim*, 3rd edn., 4 vols., Berlin and Vienna.

Lieber, E. (1984), 'Asaf's Book of Medicines: a Hebrew encyclopedia of Greek and Jewish magic, possibly compiled in Byzantium on an Indian model', *DOP* 38: 233–49.

Lieber, E. (1991), 'An ongoing mystery: the so-called Book of Medicines attributed to Assaf the Sage', *Bulletin of Judeo-Greek Studies*, 6: 18–25.

Lieberman, S. (1962), *Hellenism in Jewish Palestine*, 2nd edn., New York.

Lieberman, S. (1965), *Greek in Jewish Palestine*, 2nd edn., New York.

Malinowitz, Ch. *et al.* (eds.) (2005–), *Schottenstein Edition of the Talmudi Yerushalmi*, Brooklyn, NY.

Mandel, P. D. (1997), 'Midrash Lamentations Rabbati: Prolegomenon and a Critical Edition to the Third Parasha', Ph.D. dissertation, Hebrew University, Jerusalem. [Hebrew]

Mandel, P. D. (2000), 'Between Byzantium and Islam: the transmission of the Jewish book in the Byzantine and early Islamic periods', in Y. Elman and I. Gershoni (eds.), *Transmitting Jewish Traditions: Orality, Textuality and Cultural Diffusion*, New Haven and London, pp. 74–105.

Margulies, M. (1953–60), *Midrash Wayyikra Rabba*, 5 vols., Jerusalem; repr. 2 vols., New York and Jerusalem, 1993.

Morgenstern, M. (2004), 'Notes on a recently published magic bowl', *Aramaic Studies*, 2: 207–22.

Morgenstern, M. (2005), 'Linguistic notes on magic bowls in the Moussaieff collection', *BSOAS* 68: 349–67.

Morgenstern, M. (2007a), 'The Jewish Babylonian Aramaic magic bowl BM 91767 reconsidered', *Le Muséon*, 120: 5–27.

Morgenstern, M. (2007b), 'On some non-standard spellings in the Aramaic bowls and their linguistic significance', *JSS* 52: 245–77.

Müller-Kessler, C. (2001), 'The earliest evidence for Targum Onqelos from Babylonia and the question of its dialect and origin', *Journal for the Aramaic Bible*, 3: 181–98.

Neusner, J. (1965–70), *A History of the Jews in Babylonia*, 5 vols., Leiden.

Neusner, J. (1991a), *Judaism as Philosophy: The Method and Message of the Mishnah*, Baltimore and London.

Neusner, J. (1991b), *The Bavli's One Voice: Types and Forms of Analytical Discourses and their Fixed Order of Appearance*, Atlanta.

Neusner, J. (2002a), *How the Talmud Works*, Leiden.

Neusner, J. (2002b), *Texts without Boundaries: Protocols of Non-Documentary Writing in the Rabbinic Canon*, 4 vols., Lanham, MD.

Neusner, J. (ed.) (1982–94), *The Talmud of the Land of Israel: A Preliminary Translation and Explanation*, 35 vols., Chicago and London.

Rabinowitz, Z. M. (1965), *Halakha and Aggada in the Liturgical Poetry of Yannai: The Sources, Language and Period of the Payyetan*, New York. [Hebrew]

Reeg, G. (1985), *Die Geschichte von den Zehn Märtyren*, Tübingen.

Reichmann, R. (1998), *Mishnah und Sifra*, Tübingen.

Rubenstein, J. L. (1999), *Talmudic Stories: Narrative Art, Composition and Culture*, Baltimore and London.

Safrai, Z. (1994), *The Economy of Roman Palestine*, London.

Samely, A. (2002), *Rabbinic Interpretation of Scripture in the Mishnah*, Oxford.

Samely, A. (2007), *Forms of Rabbinic Literature and Thought: An Introduction*, Oxford.

Schäfer, P. (1981), *Synopse zur Hekhalot-Literatur*, Tübingen.

Schäfer, P. and Becker, H.-J. (1991–98), *Synopse zum Talmud Yerushalmi*, 5 vols., Tübingen.

Schoeler, G. (2006), *The Oral and the Written in Early Islam*, London.

Sokoloff, M. (1992), *A Dictionary of Palestinian Jewish Aramaic of the Byzantine Period*, Ramat Gan.

Sokoloff, M. (2002), *A Dictionary of Jewish Babylonian Aramaic of the Talmudic and Geonic Periods*, Ramat Gan.

Sperber, D. (1982), *Essays on Greek and Latin in the Mishna, Talmud and Midrashic Literature*, Jerusalem.

Sperber, D. (1984), *A Dictionary of Greek and Latin Legal Terms in Rabbinic Literature*, Ramat Gan.

Stemberger, G. (1996), *Introduction to the Talmud and Midrash*, 2nd edn., Edinburgh.

Stemberger, G. (1999), 'Rabbinic sources for historical study', in J. Neusner and A. J. Avery-Peck (eds.), *Judaism in Late Antiquity*, Part 3: *Where We Stand: Issues and Debates in Ancient Judaism*, vol. 1, Leiden, pp. 169–86.

Stemberger, G. (2007), 'Rabbinic literature: editions and studies (2004–05)', *European Journal for Jewish Studies*, 1: 157–70.

Stern, S. (1994), 'Attribution and authorship in the Babylonian Talmud', *JJS* 45: 28–51.

Stern, S. (1995), 'The concept of authorship in the Babylonian Talmud', *JJS* 46: 183–95.

Swartz, M. D. and Yahalom, J. (2005), *Avodah: Ancient Poems for Yom Kippur*, University Park, PA.

Ta-Shma, I. (1994), 'The "open book" in medieval Hebrew literature: the problem of authorized editions', in P. S. Alexander and A. Samely (eds. 1994), pp. 17–24.

Ulmer, R. (1997–2002), *A Synoptic Edition of Pesiqta Rabbati based upon all extant Manuscripts and the Editio Princeps*, 3 vols., Atlanta.

Veltri, G. (2002), 'Greek loanwords in the Palestinian Talmud: some new suggestions', *JSS* 47: 237–42.

Weiss-Halivni, D. (1968), *Meqorot u-Masorot: Be'urim ba-Talmud: Nashim*, Tel Aviv.

Weiss-Halivni, D. (1974), *Meqorot u-Masorot: Be'urim ba-Talmud: 'Eruvin u-Fesahim*, Jerusalem.

Weiss-Halivni, D. (1975), *Meqorot u-Masorot: Be'urim ba-Talmud: Mi-Yoma 'ad Hagigah*, Jerusalem.

Weiss-Halivni, D. (1982), *Meqorot u-Masorot: Be'urim ba-Talmud: Shabbat*, Jerusalem.

Weiss-Halivni, D. (1993), *Meqorot u-Masorot: Be'urim ba-Talmud: Bava Qamma*, Jerusalem.

Wewers, G. A. (1980), *Übersetzung des Talmud Yerushalmi: Avoda Zarah*, Tübingen.

Wewers, G. A. (1981), *Übersetzung des Talmud Yerushalmi: Sanhedrin*, Tübingen.

Wewers, G. A. (1982), *Übersetzung des Talmud Yerushalmi: Bavot*, Tübingen.

Yassif, E. (1999), *The Hebrew Folktale: History, Genre, Meaning*, Bloomington and Indianapolis.

Zunz, L. (1892), *Die gottesdienstlichen Vorträge der Juden historisch entwickelt*, 2nd edn., Frankfurt am Main; repr. Hildesheim, 1966.

2

The Palestinian Context of Rabbinic Judaism

FERGUS MILLAR

Introduction

THE MAP OF THE EASTERN ROMAN EMPIRE in the period between the Bar Kokhba war and the Islamic invasions left no place for a 'Land of Israel'. At the provincial level the name 'Judaea' was replaced by that of 'Syria Palaestina', while the city of Jerusalem became the site of a pagan Roman *colonia*, Aelia Capitolina. Syria Palaestina, stretching from Galilee to Idumaea, covered all the remaining areas of substantial Jewish settlement, while also extending east of the Lower Jordan and the Sea of Galilee to embrace long-established Greek cities such as Pella, Gadara and Hippos. Internally too, as we will see below, a network of Greek cities, each with a surrounding territory, expanded to cover almost all—but not quite all—of the provincial area (Avi-Yonah 2002; Millar 1993: ch. 10.4).

In the north, the neighbouring province of Phoenicia stretched south along the coast to include not only Ptolemais (Akko), but the small settlement of Porphyreon, between the southern slopes of Mt Carmel and the sea; it may or may not have ranked as a *polis* (Finkielsztejn 2005), but by the fifth century it was certainly a Christian bishopric. So also, of course, was Ptolemais, in whose territory the mosaic floor of the church at Evron has produced what is perhaps the earliest evidence for the distinctive Christian dialect and script of Aramaic known to modern scholars, somewhat paradoxically, as 'Christian Palestinian Aramaic' (see below). North of Galilee, and still within Phoenicia, lay Tyre, the *metropolis* of the province, whose territory stretched as far south-east as Kadesh (Cadasa). So the Christian churches of western Galilee surveyed by Aviam (2004: 181–204) in fact lay almost entirely within Phoenicia, in the rural territories of Ptolemais and Tyre. These questions of territory, boundaries, and religious and linguistic communities are vital to the whole question of what Jewish life was, how it was conducted, and in what context, whether wider or more localised. Provincial borders mattered too, even (and perhaps particularly) in zones

Proceedings of the British Academy **165**, 25–49. © The British Academy 2010.

where there were no obvious physical or historical boundaries. Thus
Caesarea Paneas, a Herodian foundation in whose territory Jesus had
preached, also lay in Phoenicia, and was a bishopric from at least the early
fourth century (Fedalto 1988: 722). But it is in connection with the Tetrarchic
programme of the late third century CE of establishing boundaries between
village communities that we see how in the area north-east of the Sea of
Galilee different officials were at work in the three different provinces which
met in Gaulanitis: Phoenicia, Palaestina and what the Romans called Arabia
(Ma'oz 2006). A sense of the geography of this zone, merging into the
districts of Batanea and Auranitis, is best gained from the illuminating
study, with excellent local maps, by Kropp and Mohammed (2006), locating
the small city of Dium, which lay just on the Arabian side of the border,
while Hippos, Abila and Capitolias were all within Palaestina. As we will
see, the bath and the springs of Hammat Gader on the lower Yarmouk
river offer us some of the most vivid evidence for the local co-existence of
Graeco-Roman and Jewish culture.

'Arabia' had been the name which the Romans had given to the new
province formed when the kingdom of Nabataea, with its capital at Petra,
was absorbed in 106 CE. Incorporating also two considerable Greek cities
which had not formed part of the kingdom, namely Philadelphia (Amman)
and Gerasa, Arabia then covered most of the territory of present-day Jordan
down to Aela on the Gulf of Aqaba, and stretched further south into the
Hedjaz, as well as including Sinai and the Negev.

In the Tetrarchic period, however, the imperial government, with its not
uncommon disregard of pre-existing ethnic boundaries, transferred all of
southern 'Arabia' to Palaestina, including the former Nabataean settlements
in the Negev, and all of Sinai, and the territory east of the southern half of
the Dead Sea and the Wadi Arabah, thus counting as part of 'Palaestina'
cities such as Areopolis (Rabbath Moab), Phaeno, where there were copper
mines to which Christian martyrs were sent, Petra itself, and Aela, to which
legion X was transferred from Aelia (Jerusalem). One incidental effect of this
structural change, whose reasons need not concern us here, was to bring
within Palaestina the small settlement of Zoara at the south end of the Dead
Sea. Familiar from the Babatha archive of the Bar Kokhba period, when it
lay within 'Arabia', it emerges, at least by the mid-fifth century, as a Christian
bishopric, and contained a Greek-speaking majority population and a
minority Jewish, Aramaic-speaking, one (see below).

The possible further provincial restructurings in this area which marked
the fourth century are debated (see Sipilä 2004, 2007), but what is clear is that
the southern area was detached again in the mid-century or later, to form the
province of 'Palaestina Salutaris'. It is not irrelevant that we know this from
the most important 'external' reporter on late-antique Palestine, Jerome,

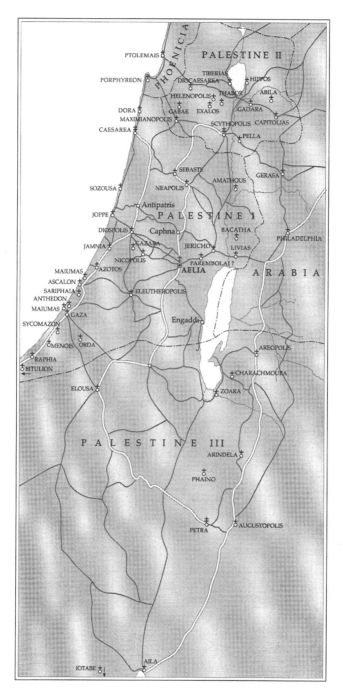

Map.   The episcopal sees of the Three Palestines in the fifth–sixth centuries

settled in Bethlehem from the mid-380s, and writing his *Hebrew Questions on Genesis* (22:33) in about 392 (see Hayward 1995: 54). Within a short period, however, a third, and in essence final, structure is found in place, first attested in 409 CE. There were from now on three separate provinces: Palaestina Prima, with its *metropolis* at Caesarea; Palaestina Secunda, in the north, with its *metropolis* at the long-established Greek city of Scythopolis; and Palaestina Tertia (sometimes still called 'Salutaris'), with its *metropolis* (paradoxically) at Petra.

This secular structure acquired a real significance for religious history when, at the Council of Chalcedon in 451, Jerusalem (Aelia) gained the status of a patriarchate (like Antioch, Alexandria, Rome and Constantinople) with supremacy over the Three Palestines. The Church of this 'greater Palestine' could function as a coherent ecclesiastical, or indeed political, body, and, as it happens, the remarkable Acts of the Church Councils in the sixth century preserve complete lists of all the bishops summoned to synods at Jerusalem in 518 and 536 (Millar 2008a; Millar 2009). The map on p. 27 combines the two lists, of thirty-four bishoprics in 518 and forty-seven in 536, partially overlapping, to produce some fifty-seven places in all. Its purpose (even if some remote places in western Sinai could not be included) is, first, to give a sense of what 'Palestine', in the terms imposed by the Christian Roman empire, now meant. Secondly, it illustrates vividly the ever-continuing diffusion of 'the Greek city'. It was certainly the norm that a bishop should be the bishop of a *polis*. Even if, as we should probably concede, the rule was not always kept, this dense network of bishoprics still reflects a very real extension of *polis* status, and the growth of sub-*polis* settlements. Thirdly, it shows graphically that Christian bishoprics were now established in southern Galilee, notably in Diocaesarea/Sepphoris and in Tiberias, and in southern Gaulanitis (Hippos and Abila). But north of that approximate line, there are no cities, and no bishoprics that we know of, until Ptolemais/Akko, Tyre and Caesarea Paneas, all of which, as we saw, lay in Phoenicia. The social and religious history of Galilee and the Golan may be of crucial importance in understanding the nature of Jewish life, and the evolution of the vast corpus of rabbinic literature.

But, firstly, we should not presume that a fully Jewish life could not be, and was not, conducted in a mixed environment, in close contiguity with other ethnic, religious and linguistic communities. Secondly, using the map of the sixth-century patriarchate, useful as it may be in offering a snapshot of Christian Palestine little more than a century before the Islamic conquest, leaves out of account the drastic changes in the wider context which had occurred since the second century.

In crude outline, in the period of almost two centuries from the Bar Kokhba war and the foundation of Aelia Capitolina to the conversion of

Constantine (312) and then his conquest of the Greek East (324), the wider environment within which Jewish life was conducted was pagan, and here the work of Belayche (2001) is of fundamental importance. Goodman's earlier study of 'state and society' (see Goodman 2000; first published 1983), based on the Mishnah, vividly illustrates the daily reality of both contact with the pagan environment in, for instance, Caesarea or Scythopolis, and of co-existence with pagans in rural communities.

Then, from 324 to approximately the end of the fourth century, comes a massive Christian impact, in the building of churches in both cities and rural communities, the extension of bishoprics, the spread of monasteries in both cities and rural locations, and the arrival of pilgrims either for visits to the holy places or as permanent settlers (Hunt 1982). Again, it is Jerome, in his *Life* of Hilarion and in his *Letter* 108, describing the journey of a rich Roman lady through Palestine in the mid-380s, who provides the most vivid testimony (see Weingarten 2005). Paganism still flourished, however, as we see in the case of Gaza, where it was only imperial intervention, procured by the still quite small Christian community, which in 401 brutally ended the public cult of the pagan gods (Grégoire and Kugener 1930).

Though we cannot overall trace the fate of pagan cults in each locality, this violent overthrow in Gaza can be taken to symbolise a new phase: after the early fifth century we encounter no further evidence of pagan cults—meaning essentially animal sacrifices directed to anthropomorphic images—being performed publicly by city officials and at communal expense. Christianity was now dominant, both as a coherent organisational structure, with links to the centres of power, as we see in the synods of 518 and 536, and as a local presence in both city and country.

Various fundamental questions thus arise. Firstly, to which of these three very distinct phases do the surviving works of rabbinic literature belong? And, if we can answer the question, does it in fact matter? In what sense, if at all, was rabbinic literature the product of reaction to, or conscious rejection of, a wider non-Jewish environment? Secondly, were there primarily 'Jewish' zones, and if so where? Or should we envisage Jewish life as being conducted to a large degree, perhaps even characteristically, by minority communities living in wider non-Jewish environments? What was it—just religious practice, or also language or writing, or culture or social organisation—that distinguished Jews from their non-Jewish neighbours? Were communal relations marked by peaceful co-existence, by rigid separation, by contact and mutual influence, or (in any direction) by the desire to induce conversion—or by destructive violence?

Before we attempt to answer any of these questions as regards Jews, it is very important to stress that Jews were not the only ethnic or religious group in Palestine who did not fit easily into the dominant model of the Christian,

Greek-speaking, city community. Firstly, even in the period after Constantine, there were Gentile pagans, who might be in violent conflict with their Christian neighbours. Secondly, there were Samaritans, concentrated in their traditional homeland around Mt Gerizim, but found also in many other places. As will be seen, as a potentially dissident ethnic-religious group, they represented, in the fifth and sixth centuries, a greater threat to the dominant Christians than Jews did. Thirdly, from the early fourth century onwards, we find an increasingly significant presence of the nomads from the steppe or desert zones whom Greek and Latin writers called 'Saracens'. As we will see, many such groups were drawn into the orbit of biblical monotheism, and converted to Christianity—and in at least some cases to the use of Greek. What is more, Christians clearly saw them as more promising material for conversion than Jews were.

Finally, to put Jewish life in context, we need to stress that all these different groups, Jews included, were marked by the combined use of Greek and of one or more Semitic languages. It is true that for Gentile pagans there is no more than occasional anecdotal evidence from Christian sources for spoken Aramaic; we have no pagan Semitic-language inscriptions or perishable documents or literature from Palestine in this period. For Christians, Aramaic appears first as a spoken language, into which spoken addresses in Greek would be translated, for instance in Scythopolis (Eusebius, *Mart. Pal.* 1.1) or later in Jerusalem (*Itinerarium Egeriae*, 47.3). But at an uncertain date (perhaps not before the fifth century) Christians in southern Phoenicia (see above), in Palestine and in the province of Arabia also began to use, in inscriptions and in religious texts, a form of Aramaic dialect and script which is distinct from Syriac, and is labelled by moderns, as we saw, 'Christian Palestinian Aramaic' (Desreumaux 1987; Müller-Kessler 1991). But in fact this is, so far as we know, a language used only for local documents and for the translation of Greek Christian works (and was not, like Syriac, the vehicle of both translations and of major original writing). This development, which might thus seem of relatively limited significance, takes on a quite new meaning if we follow the argument of Barag (2009), that the distinctive Samaritan script, a version of the Palaeo-Hebrew script (as opposed to the normal 'square' Hebrew script), came into general use (but again along with Greek) only in the later fourth century and after, and therefore in the same period as that which sees the flowering of Samaritan synagogues with mosaic floors embodying representational scenes. Barag sees both developments as reactions to the diffusion of Christianity. If so, given that all the known Jewish synagogues with representational mosaics are also now thought to date from not earlier than the later fourth century, and equally to have evolved 'in the shadow of the Church' (so Milson 2007), the conception of parallel developments clearly suggests itself—and simultaneously serves to support the main thesis of Seth Schwartz (2001) about a revival of Jewish identity in this period. Furthermore, if the Samaritan script was a new development when Jerome was in Palestine, his observations as to its distinctive character become all the more striking (*Patrologia Latina*, 28, col. 22; *Corpus Christianorum, series Latina*, 75.106).

In all these groups, Jews included, Greek was clearly current along with one or more Semitic languages. If Hebrew, as a language, was distinctive of Jews and Samaritans (and in the face of the evidence of large-scale composition in Hebrew can it really still be maintained that it had ceased to be spoken?), Aramaic was—to some degree at least—common to all, just as Greek was. Which language was most used for inter-communal communication? The dominant social and cultural force was still the Greek city—and not less so, but in fact more so, when reinforced by the dynamic force of Christian belief.

The Graeco-Roman City, and Other Settlements

A glance back at the map on p. 27 will show the truly remarkable force of the expansion of the Greek city, even if, in many cases, this must have meant simply the conferment of city status on an existing community. Many different aspects are involved, from earlier massive construction-projects under Herod the Great, at Caesarea or Sebaste, to other Herodian foundations such as Tiberias or Livias, to the grant by Vespasian of the status of Roman *colonia* to Caesarea, or his establishment in the heart of Samaritan territory of the new city of Flavia Neapolis. Here, as with 'Greek' cities in what seem to have been predominantly Jewish areas, we do not know whether to suppose a mixed population, all of whom enjoyed whatever citizen rights there were, or a dominant 'Hellenic' group and a disadvantaged population of biblical monotheists.

Whatever the social reality on the ground, it is very significant that, in the decades following the Bar Kokhba revolt (which is also the period of the formation of the Mishnah), several key places were formally re-founded as Greek cities: Sepphoris as 'Diocaesarea' (a Graeco-Latin name with pagan associations); Lydda as 'Diospolis'; Baitogabra (Beth Guvrin) as 'Eleutheropolis'; Emmaus as 'Nicopolis'. As Ben Isaac (1996, 1998) has emphasised, such renamings had a profound effect in restructuring the conceptual geography of the land. We see this best in the *Onomasticon* of Eusebius, dating probably to about 300, where villages are identified as being in the territory of a particular city, or as lying a certain number of Roman miles along a road from that city (see now the invaluable translation and presentation by Freeman-Grenville *et al.* 2003: esp. 179 f.). Thus, out of many examples, Esthemo is identified as 'a very large village of Jews in Daroma in the region of Eleutheropolis' (*Onom.* ed. Klostermann, 86.20, amply confirmed by the excavated synagogue of Estemo'a with its mosaic floor and Aramaic donor-inscription, Milson 2007: esp. 358); Iettan, in the same region, is also identified as a village of Jews, while Iether was inhabited by Christians (*Onom.* 108).

Perhaps equally significant is the fact that this information comes from one of the many works of a major Christian writer in Greek from Caesarea; it is not only that, in our conception of the culture of the region, we have to take seriously the work of Eusebius and his successors, and its implications for the educational background in these Palestinian cities. It is also that it is in essence from Eusebius onwards that a Christian Greek literature flourishes in Palestine: to name only the most obvious, there is Sozomenus, the fifth-century church historian, from the village of Bethelia near Gaza, a pagan community with temples, where his grandfather had been the first to convert (*Hist. eccl.* 5.15); then two major figures of the sixth century, Cyril of Scythopolis, the author of the nearest thing we have to a social history of Palestinian Christianity, *The Lives of the Monks of Palestine* (Price and Binns 1989), and Procopius from Caesarea, the most important secular historian from the Greek East in late antiquity.

To mention only these names is to ignore a whole school of Greek rhetoricians from Gaza in the fifth and sixth centuries, Procopius, Aeneas and Choricius (see Di Berardino ed. 2006: 253f.; C. P. Jones 2007), as well as what one may call a school of Christian ascetic writing, from the monophysite side, focused on Gaza (see esp. Hevelone-Harper 1997; Bitton-Ashkelony and Kofsky 2000, eds. 2004, 2006; Horn 2006). In this context, however, it is most important to stress the most outstanding feature of the social history of late-antique Palestine, the diffusion and expansion of small settlements (see above all Dauphin 1999; Hirschfeld 2005; and now Shatzman 2007, a major study). We may up to a point be deceived, in contrasting this period with earlier (or indeed later) ones, by the profusion of literary, papyrological and epigraphic evidence for local communities, in which inscribed records of the foundation or decoration of churches are very prominent. But it is impossible to deny the scale and wide distribution of urban-style development, from the Negev to Galilee and the Golan.

Another glance at the map will show that the spread of urbanism is most striking in the semi-desert zone south-east of Gaza, and in the neighbouring area of Palaestina Tertia (Gutwein 1981; Shereshevski 1991). Here, not only the ancient cities of Ascalon, Anthedon and Gaza itself are bishoprics, but so also are the Maiuma (or port) of both Ascalon and Gaza, as well as Menois, Sycamazon and Raphia. More striking still is the urbanisation (if with only one full *polis* and bishopric, Elousa) of the Negev in north-western

Palaestina Tertia (Lewin 2002). We may think of Sobata (Shivta), a mere village in status, but with some 170 houses, paved streets and three churches, next to one of which a mosque was inserted after the Islamic conquest; but above all of Nessana, again a mere village (*kōmē*), but with two churches, and producing 152 Greek inscriptions dating between 359 and 530 (Colt ed. 1962: 131f.), as well as literary papyri, including a bilingual glossary of the *Aeneid*, with 1,025 surviving entries, a fragment of a *codex* of the Aeneid, and the remains of a number of Greek theological works (Casson and Hettich 1950). More important still are the Greek documentary papyri, mostly written in Nessana itself, and covering nearly all of the sixth century; but one fragmentary contract is written in Elousa, while another papyrus of the early seventh century is a letter, also in Greek, from the bishop of Aila (Aqaba) (Kraemer 1958).

Though we have no positive reason to suppose the existence of Jewish communities in this area, we can never exclude the possibility. But the most important implication of the written material from Nessana is that we must acknowledge the depth of the Greek culture—at both the literary level and as used in daily life—which was carried to these marginal locations by the expansion of settlement. No Aramaic texts appear here, and while some Arabic personal names appear in Greek transliteration, no actual Arabic appears until a late group of papyri dating from after the conquest (also in Kraemer 1958; for Petra, compare now Frosén *et al.* 2002; Al-Ghul 2004, 2006).

Even in the area of high Greek culture along this section of the coast there were Jewish communities, as illustrated by the well-known synagogue mosaic from the Maiuma of Gaza, portraying King David in the style of Orpheus, with a donor-inscription of 508/9 in Greek (Ovadiah and Ovadiah 1987: no. 83, and see also Frey 1952: no. 967). Perhaps our most illuminating evidence for Christian–Jewish (and Samaritan–Jewish) interaction comes from the territory of Eleutheropolis, and we will return to this region later, in the section on inter-communal relations. But before that we will look at two 'marginal' areas, following the emphasis rightly placed by Bar (2004a, see also 2003, 2004b, 2005) on the development of the peripheral zones of Palestine. The first is Zoara, already mentioned, where a remarkable series of several hundred Christian gravestones in Greek, dating by the era of the (previous) province of Arabia, and stretching from 309 to 591 (superlatively edited by Meimaris and Kritikakou-Nikolaropoulou 2005), is matched by a much smaller group of Jewish tombstones written in Aramaic, and dating by the destruction of the Temple, which covers the period from the mid-fourth to the early sixth century (not yet fully edited, they are surveyed by Stern 2001: 87–97). One Jewish tombstone is bilingual in Greek and Aramaic— and duly uses both dating-systems (Cotton and Price 2001; Meimaris and

Kritikakou-Nikolaropoulou 2005: no. 18). Even with no help from any narrative representation of communal relations in Zoara, we could hardly ask for a more vivid reflection of a dominant Greek-speaking population, co-existing with an Aramaic-speaking Jewish minority.

If we move north, to the valley of the Yarmuk and the Gaulanitis (Golan), we find very comparable, and equally revealing, evidence in very different forms. First comes the bath-complex of Hammat Gader, as striking an example of Graeco-Roman monumental architecture adorning a resort for pleasure and healing as one could imagine. Duly equipped with a substantial series of Greek inscriptions (see Di Segni in Hirschfeld ed. 1997: 185f.), the bath-complex itself offers no hint of its belonging even in a Near Eastern, let alone a Semitic-speaking or Jewish environment. But the plan of the site (ibid., p. 3) reveals that beside the river and to the west of the baths themselves and the theatre, there lay a synagogue, the subject of a wonderfully evocative report by Sukenik (1935). What is more, there are four mosaic inscriptions in Aramaic, totalling eighteen lines, as well as fragments of two in Greek (Frey 1952: nos. 856–60). All are records of donors, and at first sight we seem to be in an entirely Jewish world, with no visible relation to a wider society. The first name to be recorded in the second inscription is 'Rab(bi) Tanhum the Levite', and there then follow acknowledgements of contributions by individuals or groups, presumably Jewish, from Susitha(?), Sepphoris, Kfar Aqabia, Capernaum and Arbela. But is it possible that the prominent personages mentioned in the first and third inscriptions are not Jews, but Gentile benefactors? If so, there was perhaps some connection between the synagogue and the grand bath-complex some 700 metres distant.

In any case Hammat Gader, as a well-known pleasure-resort, will hardly count as a typical rural settlement. But the places from which contributors are recorded as coming are evocative of a world of Jewish communities, in small towns and villages scattered across the Galilee and the Golan (see now Ben David 2006). But Gaulanitis too was, broadly, a prime example both of development on the 'periphery' and of a zone of mixed settlement, where there were both Christians and Jews, and where inscriptions in Greek form a large majority as against those in Hebrew or Aramaic. Samaritan communities might also be found east of the Sea of Galilee: Eusebius in the *Onomasticon* (102) records 'a village of Samaritans in Batanaea called Tharsila' (Freeman-Grenville *et al.* 2003: 59). Ben David (2006), however, argues that at a more local level there were distinct Jewish and Christian zones; Hippos and the Upper (eastern) Golan were Christian, while the lower (western) Golan was Jewish.

As regards Gaulanitis itself, Hippos was a bishopric by the mid-fourth century, while Gergesa/Chorsia/El Kursi, of which Origen reports in the mid-third century that it was 'shown' (evidently by Christians) as the real site from which the 'Gadarene' swine had taken off into the Sea of Galilee, reveals a pavement mosaic from the baptistery of a monastery, laid down in 585/6. But Talmudic sources indicate that there were also Jewish inhabitants there (Gregg and Urman 1996: 68–71, see also Isaac 1999). A similar picture of co-existence is revealed at Kafr Harib, south of Hippos, identified as ΚΑΠΑΡ ΗΑΡΙΒΟΥ on a Tetrarchic boundary marker, clearly the same place as the Kfar Yahrib named in Hebrew in the inscription from the synagogue at Rehov (see below), as well as in the Tosefta and the Yerushalmi, as Jewish ter-ritory, subject to the rules on tithing and the Sabbatical Year. But all of the eleven inscriptions from there are in Greek, and none is identifiably Jewish (Gregg and Urman 1996: 7–17).

A similar pattern is revealed by the archaeological and epigraphic evi-dence for the rural settlements of Gaulanitis, some very substantial (see now Urman 2006, on Rafid), which stretch north and east from the eastern shore of the Sea of Galilee. Of the inscriptions included in the survey by Gregg and Urman, 241 are in Greek, twelve in Hebrew or Aramaic, and one in Latin. Yet the fact that this was, overall, an area of mixed settlement does not in the least mean that it was not also an important centre of Jewish life.

The same in clearly true of Caesarea, a major Greek and Christian city, admittedly with a relatively modest harvest of Latin (as a *colonia*) and Greek inscriptions, which are presented, along with all the essential bibliography, by Lehman and Holum (2000; for the Greek inscriptions of the synagogue, see nos. 78–84). Equally, Diocaesarea/Sepphoris is the site of an already famous synagogue mosaic with the Binding of Isaac, a central zodiac, and symbolic representations of the Temple and its sacrifice, belonging to the earlier fifth century (Weiss 2005); but by 518 a bishop was in office there. It had probably always had a mixed population, which again represents no contradiction of its historic role as a centre of rabbinic learning. Tiberias too was a place of mixed population; it had at Hammat Tiberias a synagogue whose best-known phase, with a mosaic floor again representing a zodiac and the Temple, prob-ably belongs to the later fourth century (so Magness 2005: 8–13), while a sub-stantial church, with mosaic inscriptions in Greek, thought to be of the fourth or fifth century, is currently being excavated; and a bishop had been installed by 449. We will return to both places later. What we seem to lack so far is a detailed study of settlement, population and religious practice in the un-urbanised area of northern Galilee in late antiquity.

The prime example of the Greek and Christian city, and of monumental late-antique urbanism, which was simultaneously, both within the city and in its territory, a centre of Jewish (and Samaritan) life is Scythopolis, a Hellenistic foundation and the eventual *metropolis* of Palaestina Secunda, whose development is brilliantly surveyed by Tsafrir and Foerster (1997). In this context we can take the streets, the theatre, the hippodrome-cum-amphitheatre, the baths, the public buildings, and the churches and monasteries of Scythopolis for granted, noting only the elaborate monastery with mosaic floors founded in the sixth century by a benefactress named as 'Kyria Maria', and lying just outside the northern wall of the city (Fitzgerald 1939). What is equally significant is that we know of both a Samaritan synagogue within the city (identified as such by the Samaritan lettering, here used to transliterate Greek) and a Jewish one, thought to date to the second half of the sixth century, with floor-mosaics inscribed in Greek and Aramaic, and showing a menorah and other symbols (Ovadiah and Ovadiah 1987: nos. 29–31). More significant still, it is within the territory of this major Greek city that two of the most important of late-Roman synagogues have been found: that at Beth Alpha (Sukenik 1932), again with a mosaic representing the Binding of Isaac, a zodiac and the Temple, and with an Aramaic inscription of the sixth century; and the still not fully published synagogue of Rehov, where the long Hebrew text incorporated in its mosaic floor provides the most important documentary evidence for the currency of 'rabbinic' works within a synagogue community.

The archaeological and epigraphic material, of which only a minute selection has been alluded to here, thus provides irrefutable proof that co-existence as between different ethnic and religious communities was at least *a* characteristic social pattern in late-antique Palestine (see now Ribak 2007). What by its nature it hardly can do is to illustrate what patterns of inter-action, peaceful or violent, actually occurred. When we look finally at some items of evidence—nearly all coming from the Christian side—for inter-action, it is important to stress again that various different groups other than Jews were involved. Whether Gentiles, at first largely pagan, and later Christian, numerically outnumbered Jews or not, there is no way of telling. But it is indisputable that, at least by the later fifth century, Gentile Christians, grouped in a hierarchical structure stretching from the village church to the city bishopric, to the Patriarch in Jerusalem, and through him to the wider Church and the Emperor, were the dominant force. In the fourth century pagans could still react violently, and in the fifth and sixth centuries Samaritans on occasion posed a greater problem to the established order than Jews did. Some sense of the nature of the complex social, religious and linguistic interactions between different groups in Palestine involved is necessary if we are to see the Jewish experience—and the enormous achievement represented by rabbinic literature—in context.

Communal Relations: Pagans, Christians, Jews, Samaritans and Saracens

Overall, communal relations in late-antique Palestine show a familiar pattern of co-existence, which might be wholly peaceful for long periods, combined with latent hostility and occasional outbreaks of either localised or wide-spread violence (see now the evocative and illuminating study by Sivan 2008). It should be stressed at the outset that the practice of Judaism by Jews was never forbidden, nor was there any imperial programme of conversion. Christian relations with the other groups mentioned were in fact more frequently marked by overt conflict than those with Jews. We may begin with pagans, whom Eusebius' *Martyrs of Palestine* shows as eagerly supporting the official persecution of the early fourth century. After Constantine's conversion and victory, paganism was not forbidden, though the temple of Venus (Aphrodite) in the *colonia* of Aelia (Jerusalem) was destroyed and replaced by the Holy Sepulchre, while the Emperor ordered that pagan accretions at the oak of Mamre should be swept away, and a Christian basilica erected (Eusebius, *Life of Constantine*, 3.51–3; but see also Sozomenus, *Hist. eccl.* 2.5, who makes clear that none the less in the fifth century the site was still frequented by pagans, Jews and Christians). Pagan resentment at the subsequent spread of the Church was vividly displayed under the reign of Julian the Apostate (361–3). Again, the Emperor did not initiate any persecution. But, for instance, Sozomenus (himself coming from near Gaza, as we have seen) reports that three Christians were killed there in an act of mass pagan vengeance, their bodies buried and their remains mixed with animal bones, to prevent the institution of a cult to them as martyrs (*Hist. eccl.* 5.9). Theodoret adds that both priests and nuns were killed at Ascalon and Gaza, and that at Sebaste the tomb of John the Baptist was broken open, his bones burnt and the ashes scattered (*Hist. eccl.* 5.7).

Inevitably, the account in Mark the Deacon's *Life* of Porphyry, bishop of Gaza (Grégoire and Kugener 1930), of the destruction of the pagan temples of Gaza in 401 involves repeated acts of violence on both sides: attacks on Christian travellers by pagan inhabitants along the route from Caesarea to Diospolis and Gaza (17); a Christian assaulted while collecting money for a village church (22); then, after an imperial order has been obtained, the pagan priests barricading themselves in the great temple of Marnas, while the soldiers spend ten days destroying the other temples (65–6); finally, when after five years a new church has been built on the site of the temple of Marnas, a dispute over land between the *oikonomos* of the church and a leading pagan councillor leads to a riot in which seven people are killed, bishop Porphyry has to flee over the roof-tops to save his life, and the episcopal residence (*episkopeion*) is sacked (95–6). At various stages in the narrative, groups of pagans are described as converting, but it seems clear that even after these events the majority was still pagan (see also Rubin 1998 and Geiger 1998). In the fifth century and after, however, we no longer hear of the public, communal, practice of pagan rites in any Palestinian city.

Individual attachment to polytheism certainly continued, however, and with it, we must presume, a profound resentment of the dominant Christians. We even hear of an individual converting *to* paganism in the fifth century, in the person of a man of Samaritan origin and belief, Marinus, the author of the finest pagan biography in Greek from late antiquity, the *Life* of the great Neoplatonist philosopher Proclus. This is what said of him by Damascius (*Philosophical History*, 97, trans. Athanassiadi 1999):

> Marinus, the successor of Proclus, originated from Neapolis in Palestine, a city founded near the so-called Mount Argarizos [Gerizim]. Then the impious author blasphemously says: where there is a most sacred temple of Zeus the Most High, to whom Abraham the ancestor of the ancient Jews was conse-crated, as Marinus himself used to say. Born a Samaritan, Marinus renounced their creed (which is anyway a deviation from Abraham's religion) and embraced Hellenism.

This is not the place to attempt any account of late-antique Samaritanism (except for the highly novel views of Barag 2009, mentioned above; for the most complete modern account see Crown ed. 1987, and see now Sivan 2008: 107–42). But, to bring into focus Christian views of them, by contrast with Jews, it is worth referring to two dramatic accounts by Christian authors from Palestine, beginning with Procopius (*Aed.* 5.7.5–8, Loeb trans.), looking back from the 550s to the 480s:

> During the reign of Zeno, the Samaritans suddenly banded together and fell upon the Christians in Neapolis in the church while they were celebrating the festival called the Pentecost, and they destroyed many of them ... The Emperor Zeno ... drove out the Samaritans from Mt. Gerizim and straight-away handed it over to the Christians, and building a church on the summit he dedicated it to the Mother of God, putting a barrier, as it was made to appear, around this church, though in reality he erected only a light wall of stone. And he established a garrison of soldiers, placing a large number in the city below, but not more than ten men at the fortifications and the church.

Even more vivid and immediate is the account in Cyril of Scythopolis of the great Samaritan revolt of 529, early in his own lifetime, and relating in part to his native city (*Life* of Sabas, 70, trans. Price and Binns 1989):

> In the fourth month after Abba Theodosius' death, the Samaritans of Palestine marshalled their whole race against the Christians and performed many lawless acts: pillaging and setting fire to the churches that fell into their hands, merci-lessly killing with various tortures the Christians who fell into their hands, and setting fire to whole estates, specially in the region of Neapolis. Thereupon in

usurpation they crowned a king for themselves, one Julian of their race. Then they slaughtered bishop Mamonas of Neapolis and, seizing and butchering some priests, roasted them together with remains of holy martyrs. They performed many such acts, so that the so-called imperial highroads became unusable and impassable for the Christians. When all this came to the ears of our most pious emperor Justinian, the most glorious counts Theodore and John received orders to gather an army and march against the Samaritans; a battle ensued, in which Julian and a great mass of Samaritans with him were killed. At this juncture Silvanus, mentioned above [a prominent Samaritan], coming as if peaceably to Scythopolis without an imperial order, was seized by the Christians and burnt in the middle of the city.

As Cyril goes on to report, the petitions which Sabas subsequently presented to the Emperor on behalf of the Church of the Three Palestines asked both for a subvention for the rebuilding of churches after the Samaritan destruction, and for a fort to be constructed to protect the monasteries of the Judaean Desert against Saracen raids. Before we look briefly at the social and religious role of Saracens, it is worth noting that Cyril's *Lives*, by far the finest example of social history written in late-antique Palestine, covering from the early fifth century to the mid-sixth, make not a single concrete reference to any individual Jew, or group of Jews. This is partly because his story concerns, almost entirely, Jerusalem and the monasteries of the Judaean Desert (whose remains and history are surveyed in the masterly work of Hirschfeld 1992; see also Patrich 1995). There may indeed have been few Jews in Jerusalem or the desert; but within the area covered by the monasteries there was certainly a synagogue at Jericho, and not far from it another at Engeddi (with an extensive inscription in Hebrew and Aramaic, not yet fully published) and, to the west, others at Estemo'a (see above) and Susiya.

Cyril's subject is firstly Christian asceticism (see also Binns 1994), and secondly the impassioned struggle between those who (like himself) accepted the Council of Chalcedon of 451 and the monophysites who did not (see Perrone 1980). But it remains striking that Jews never surface in his narrative, while Samaritans and Saracens do. We first meet Saracens in Palestine early in the fourth century in the Negev, when a group of them greet the ascetic Hilarion outside Elousa, ask him, in Syriac, to bless them, and start on the path to conversion (Jerome, *Life* of Hilarion, 25; see Weingarten 2005).

In the 370s came the revolt of Mavia, the queen of those Saracens who were evidently based (as was shown by Rubin 1990) in the 'desert of the Saracens' in Sinai. It ended similarly with their accepting Christianity, and asking for a monk living in the desert to be ordained as their bishop. It is at the end of Sozomenus' account of this episode (*Hist. eccl.* 6.38) that we find the fullest expression of the conception that Saracens were descended from Hagar and Ishmael, that they had diverged subsequently from the faith of

Abraham, and that (some at least) had recently been brought back to the truth by Christians—and by Jews (see Millar 2005).

It is striking that the same theme of inherited suitability for conversion appears in Cyril's *Life* of Euthymius in connection with a quite distinct group of Saracens who deserted Persian service in the 420s, were settled in Palestine, converted to Christianity, had their leader ordained as a bishop under the name Peter, and were given an area, 'the camps' (*Parembolai*), located some-where between Jerusalem and the Jordan, to settle. It now became their bishopric, and re-appears as such in the lists of 518 and 536 (see above). As regards the original conversion, Cyril comments as follows (*Life* of Euthymius, 10, trans. Price and Binns 1989): 'He [Euthymius] . . . let them depart no longer Agarenians and Ishmaelites, but now descendants of Sarah and heirs of the promise.'

New raids by unconverted Saracens still followed, and others appear in our narratives as either workers or potentially dangerous robbers. It is enough to emphasise that in Palestine, as in Arabia, they were a constant and unstable presence, who were seen none the less as especially appropriate material for conversion.

The Jews of Palestine, so far as our Christian sources tell, followed almost consistently a less conflict-ridden course. Our sources report, briefly, one quite substantial Jewish revolt in the 350s, centred on Diocaesarea/Sepphoris, and spreading to Tiberias and Diospolis: the claim by Christian historians that Diocaesarea, as 'their' city, was now rased to the ground (e.g. Socrates, *Hist. eccl.* 2.33) does not seem to be borne out by excavation. None the less, this was one of the places, along with Tiberias, which resisted church con-struction under Constantius by the Jewish convert Joseph of Tiberias, as related in the much-quoted chapter of Epiphanius (*Panarion* 30; see Perkams 2001). A few years later Jewish leaders, from Tiberias above all (if we may believe the Syriac *Julian-Romance*), supported the Emperor Julian's abortive attempt in 363 to rebuild the Temple. Two of our, admittedly unreliable, sources relate both that there was now at least one synagogue in Jerusalem, and that many Jews there converted when signs of divine wrath stopped con-struction (Millar 2008b). It is quite unclear whether there is any truth in either report.

Even more clearly fictitious (Honigmann 1954: ch. 2) is the Syriac *Life* of the fifth-century ascetic Barsauma. Barsauma was a real person, a Syriac-speaker from near Samosata who participated in the Councils of Ephesus in 449 and of Chalcedon. But the *Life* should be seen as a Christian historical novel, probably composed between the mid-sixth and mid-seventh centuries, which offers a violent image of Christian battles against a hostile world allegedly dominated (quite unconvincingly for the fifth century) by pagans, Jews and Samaritans. Barsauma is represented as marching with his followers through Phoenicia, Arabia and Palestine, destroying the synagogues of the Jews, the meeting-places of the Samaritans and the temples of the pagans. At Areopolis (Rabbath Moab) there was allegedly a grandiose synagogue, which Barsauma's followers captured after a pitched battle and then destroyed.

We need not doubt that these images correspond to the aspirations of some Christians, and we know that attacks on synagogues did occur. But imperial policy forbade them, and our other evidence for fifth-century Palestine suggests nothing of the sort.

We may end on a somewhat more positive note, first with an episode from the *Life* (ed. Raabe 1895) of Peter the Iberian (an immigrant to the Holy Land from the Caucasus, who became a monk in the mid-fifth century). His biographer, possibly John of Maiuma, records (121, ed. Raabe 1895) that towards the end of his life he settled in a 'small town' (*polichorion*) near Iamnia. Finding that all its inhabitants were Samaritans, he and his followers promptly built a large church there, dedicated to Stephen and the martyrs. Later, however (126–7), he played a more conciliatory part, performing healings and exorcisms not only for Christians but for Jews and Samaritans living in Iamnia and its surrounding villages. Then there is another Christian Greek historical novel, perhaps, like the *Life* of Barsauma, also written in the sixth century, and allegedly relating the life of Epiphanius, the fourth-century author of the *Panarion* (it is printed in *Patrologia Graeca*, XLI, cols. 24f., and has never been edited or translated since). In this narrative Epiphanius is represented as having been Jewish by origin, coming from a poor family in the countryside round Eleutheropolis, and we encounter a remarkably positive representation of co-existing religious systems there (which the archaeology of churches and synagogues amply confirms). Trying to sell a pack-animal to raise money for his impoverished family, Epiphanius meets at a fair a Jewish trader (*pragmateutēs*), who out of solidarity insists on buying the animal and giving him cash. Then he meets a prominent Jew from Eleutheropolis named Tryphon, who owns land in his village, and is also a 'teacher of the Law' (*nomodidaskalos*), who is admirable and pious (*theosebēs*) according to the Law of Moses. Tryphon adopts Epiphanius, and teaches him diligently the precepts of the Law and the elements of Hebrew. We might begin to think that we were reading a Jewish historical novel—but Epiphanius then meets a monk named Loukianos who is generous to the poor and engages him in conversation about Judaism and Christianity. Epiphanius responds by saying that he wants to convert and become a monk, and duly does so, earning a living by accurately copying documents (*deltoi*). Then a group of forty Saracens goes past, and he effects a miraculous cure . . . But we may leave the story there, taking it, fiction as it is, as a convincing picture of the diffusion of Jewish learning in the Daroma, and (see Bar 2005) of the role of rural monks in the Christianisation of Palestine.

Conclusion

Between archaeological remains, the iconography of mosaics, whether Christian, Samaritan or Jewish, and the evidence of Christian literary sources, with all the ideological baggage which they inevitably carry, we cannot possibly claim to provide any unambiguous framework which will offer clues to the context, or contexts, in which the extraordinary corpus of rabbinic works was composed. But some basic points at least are clear. Firstly, the Christian church, rapidly expanding, was the dominant force. Secondly, there was no area of Palestine, and no group within Palestine, in which Greek was not current. Thirdly, Aramaic was also current everywhere, among Christians, Jews and Samaritans. But to compose an original religious literature in Hebrew or Aramaic was a choice, and one which only Jews made (so far as we know, there were no Samaritan authors of religious literature in the period). There was no extensive purely Jewish zone in which Jewish education could take place, and in which a Jewish literature could be composed in Hebrew or Aramaic, though there are indications that smaller areas within the Golan (Gaulanitis) and northern Galilee may have been distinctively Jewish. Overall, however, all such composition took place, and could only take place, in a society marked, both in city and countryside, by a complex interplay of beliefs, ethnic identities and languages. Rural settlements apart, three Greek cities, all of which in late antiquity had Christian bishops, Tiberias, Diocaesarea/Sepphoris and Caesarea, were the most common points of reference in Jewish religious writing. These considerations make the intellectual and spiritual achievements of Palestinian Judaism in late antiquity all the more remarkable.

Further Reading

Abel (1952); Avi-Yonah (1976); Dauphin (1999); A. H. M. Jones (1971); Millar (2006); Milson (2007); Schwartz (2001); Shatzman (2007); Sivan (2008); Stemberger (2000).

Bibliography

Abel, F. M. (1952), *Histoire de la Palestine*, vol. 2, Paris.

Al-Ghul, O. (2004), 'An early Arabic inscription from Petra carrying diacritic marks', *Syria*, 81: 105–18.

Al-Ghul, O. (2006), 'Preliminary notes on the Arabic material in the Petra Papyri', *Topoi*, 14.1: 139–69.

Amidon, P. R. (1990), *The* Panarion *of St Epiphanius, Bishop of Salamis: Selected Passages*, New York and Oxford.

Athanassiadi, P. (1999), *Damascius, the Philosophical History: Text with Translation and Notes*, Athens.

Aviam, M. (2004), 'Churches and monasteries from the Byzantine period in Western Galilee', in idem (ed.), *Jews, Pagans, and Christians in the Galilee*, Rochester, NY and Woodbridge, pp. 181–204.

Avi-Yonah, M. (1976), *The Jews of Palestine: A Political History from the Bar Kochba War to the Arab Conquest*, New York; repr. as *The Jews under Roman and Byzantine Rule*, New York, 1984.

Avi-Yonah, M. (2002), *The Holy Land: A Historical Geography from the Persian to the Arab Conquest (536 BC–AD 640)*, Jerusalem.

Bagatti, B. (2001), *Ancient Christian Villages of Galilee*, Jerusalem.

Bagatti, B. (2002), *Ancient Christian Villages of Samaria*, Jerusalem.

Bar, D. (2003), 'The Christianisation of Byzantine Palestine during late antiquity', *Journal of Ecclesiastical History*, 54: 401–21.

Bar, D. (2004a), 'Frontier and periphery in late antique Palestine', *Greek, Roman and Byzantine Studies*, 44: 69–92.

Bar, D. (2004b), 'Population, settlement and economy in Late Roman and Byzantine Palestine (70–641 AD)', *BSOAS* 67: 307–20.

Bar, D. (2005), 'Rural monasticism as a key element in the Christianization of Byzantine Palestine', *HThR* 97: 49–65.

Barag, D. (2009), 'Samaritan writing and writings', in Cotton *et al.* (eds.) (2009).

Bardy, G. (1933), 'Saint Jérôme et ses maîtres hébreux', *Revue Bénédictine*, 46: 145–64.

Belayche, N. (2001), *Iudaea-Palaestina: The Pagan Cults in Roman Palestine (Second to Fourth Century)*, Tübingen.

Ben David, Ch. (2006), 'Late antique Gaulanitis settlement patterns of Christians and Jews in rural landscape', in Lewin and Pellegrini (eds.) (2006), pp. 35–50.

Binns, J. (1994), *Ascetics and Ambassadors of Christ: The Monasteries of Palestine, 314–631*, Oxford.

Bikai, P. M. and Fiéma, Z. T. (2001), *The Petra Church*, Amman.

Bitton-Ashkelony, B. and Kofsky, A. (2000), 'Gazan monasticism in the fourth–sixth centuries: from anchoritic to cenobitic', *Proche Orient Chrétien*, 50: 14–62.

Bitton-Ashkelony, B. and Kofsky, A. (2006), *The Monastic School of Gaza*, Supplement to *Vigiliae Christianae*, 78, Leiden.

Bitton-Ashkelony, B. and Kofsky, A. (eds.) (2004), *Christian Gaza in Late Antiquity*, Leiden.

Bottini, G. C., Di Segni, L. and Alliata, E. (eds.) (1990), *Christian Archaeology in the Holy Land*, Jerusalem.

Bowersock, G. W. (1997), 'Polytheism and monotheism in Arabia and the three Palestines', *DOP* 51: 1–10.

Broshi, M. (1979), 'The population of Western Palestine in the Roman–Byzantine period', *BASOR* 236: 1–10.

Cameron, A. (1994), 'The Jews in seventh-century Palestine', *SCI* 13: 75–93.

Casson, L. and Hettich, E. L. (1950), *Excavations at Nessana*, vol. 2: *Literary Papyri*, Princeton.

Colt, H. D. (ed.) (1962), *Excavations at Nessana*, vol. 1, London.

Cotton, H. M., Hoyland, R. G., Price, J. J. and Wasserstein, D. J. (eds.) (2009), *From Hellenism to Islam: Cultural and Linguistic Change*, Cambridge.

Cotton, H. M. and Price, J. (2001), 'A bilingual tombstone from Zoʻar (Arabia)', *ZPE* 134: 277–83.

Crown, A. D. (ed.) (1987), *The Samaritans*, Tübingen.

Dauphin, C. (1999), *La Palestine byzantine: peuplements et populations*, vols. 1–3, BAR International Series 726, Oxford.

de Lange, N. R. M. (1976), *Origen and the Jews: Studies in Jewish-Christian Relations in Third-Century Palestine*, Cambridge.

Desreumaux, A. (1987), 'La naissance d'une nouvelle écriture araméenne à l'époque byzantine', *Semitica*, 37: 95–107.

Di Berardino, A. (ed.) (2006), *Patrology: The Eastern Fathers from the Council of Chalcedon (451) to John of Damascus (+750)*, Cambridge.

Di Segni, L. (1993), 'The Greek inscriptions in the Samaritan synagogue at El-Khirbe', in F. Manni and E. Alliata (eds.) (1993), pp. 231–9.

Di Segni, L. (1995), 'The involvement of local, municipal and provincial authorities in urban building in late antique Palestine and Arabia', in J. H. Humphrey (ed.), *The Roman and Byzantine Near East*, vol. 1: *Some Recent Archaeological Research*, Supplement to *Journal of Roman Archaeology*, 14, Ann Arbor, pp. 312–32.

Di Segni, L. (1999), 'Epigraphic documentation on building in the provinces of Palestina and Arabia, 4th–7th c.', in J. H. Humphrey (ed.), *The Roman and Byzantine Near East*, vol. 2: *Some Recent Archaeological Research*, Supplement to *Journal of Roman Archaeology*, 31, Portsmouth, RI, pp. 149–78.

Di Segni, L. (2004), 'The Beersheba tax edict in the light of a newly-discovered fragment', *SCI* 23: 131–58.

Di Segni, L. (2005), 'Monastery, city and village in Byzantine Gaza', *Proche Orient Chrétien*, 55: 24–50.

Di Segni, L. (2009), 'Greek inscriptions in transition from the Byzantine to the early Islamic period', in Cotton *et al.* (eds.) (2009), pp. 352–73.

Di Segni, L., Tsafrir Y. and Green, J. (1994), *Tabula Imperii Romani. Iudaea-Palaestina: Eretz Israel in the Hellenistic, Roman and Byzantine Periods. Maps and Gazetteer*, Jerusalem.

Dvorjetski, E. (2005), 'The synagogue-church at Gerasa in Jordan: a contribution to the study of ancient synagogues', *Zeitschrift des deutschen Palästina-Vereins*, 121: 140–67.

Fedalto, G. (1988), *Hierarchia Ecclesiastica Orientalis*, vol. 2, Padova.

Fiéma, Z. T. (2001), 'Byzantine Petra: a reassessment', in T. S. Burns and J. W. Eadie (eds.), *Urban Centers and Rural Contexts in Late Antiquity*, East Lansing, MI, pp. 111–31.

Fiéma, Z. T. (2006), 'City and countryside in Byzantine Palestine: prosperity in question', in Lewin and Pellegrini (eds.) (2006), pp. 67–88.

Finkielsztejn, G. (2005), 'Les mosaïques de la *komopolis* de Porphyreon du Sud (Kafr Samir; Haifa, Israel): un évêché entre village et cité', in H. Morlier (ed.), *Les mosaïques gréco-romaines*, vol. 9.1, Rome, pp. 435–51.

Fitzgerald, G. M. (1939), *A Sixth Century Monastery at Beth Shan (Scythopolis)*, Philadelphia.

Freeman-Grenville, G. S. P., Chapman, R. L. and Taylor, J. E. (2003), *Palestine in the Fourth Century AD: The Onomasticon by Eusebius of Caesarea*, Jerusalem.

Frey, J. B. (1952), *Corpus Inscriptionum Judaicarum*, vol. 2, Rome.

Frosén, J., Arjava, A. and Lehtinen, M. (2002), *The Petra Papyri*, vol. 1, Amman.

Geiger, J. (1998), 'Aspects of Palestinian paganism in late antiquity', in Kofsky and Stroumsa (eds.) (1998), pp. 3–17.

Goodman, M. (2000), *State and Society in Roman Galilee, AD 132–212*, 2nd edn., London; 1st edn., Totowa, NJ, 1983.

Gray, P. T. R. (1993), 'Palestine and Justinian's legislation on non-Christian religions', in B. Halpern and D. W. Hobson (eds.), *Law, Politics and Society in the Ancient World*, Sheffield, pp. 241–70.

Gregg, R. C. and Urman, D. (1996), *Jews, Pagans and Christians in the Golan Heights: Greek and Other Inscriptions of the Roman and Byzantine Eras*, Atlanta.

Grégoire, H. and Kugener, M.-A. (1930), *Marc le diacre, Vie de Porphyre évêque de Gaza*, Paris.

Gutwein, K. C. (1981), *Third Palestine: A Regional Study in Byzantine Urbanization*, Washington, DC.

Hayward, C. T. R. (1995), *Saint Jerome's Hebrew Questions on Genesis*, Oxford.

Hevelone-Harper, J. L. (1997), *Disciples of the Desert: Monks, Laity, and Spiritual Authority in Sixth-Century Gaza*, Baltimore.

Hirschfeld, Y. (1992), *The Judaean Desert Monasteries in the Byzantine Period*, New Haven and London.

Hirschfeld, Y. (2005), 'The expansion of rural settlement during the fourth–fifth centuries in Palestine', in J. Lefort, C. Morrisson and J.-P. Sodini (eds.), *Les Villages dans l'empire byzantin (IVe–XVe siècle)*, Paris, pp. 523–37.

Hirschfeld, Y. (ed.) (1997), *The Roman Baths of Hammat Gader: Final Report*, Jerusalem.

Honigmann, E. (1954), *Le Couvent de Barsauma et le Patriarchat jacobite d'Antioche et de Syrie*, Louvain.

Horn, C. B. (2006), *Asceticism and Christological Controversy in Fifth-Century Palestine: The Career of Peter the Iberian*, Oxford.

Hunt, E. D. (1982), *Holy Land Pilgrimage in the Later Roman Empire, AD 312–460*, Oxford.

Irshai, O. (2002), 'Confronting a Christian empire: Jewish culture in the world of Byzantium', in D. Biale (ed.), *Cultures of the Jews: A New History*, New York, pp. 180–221.

Irshai, O. (2006), 'From oblivion to fame: the history of the Palestinian church (135–303 CE)', in Limor and Stroumsa (eds.) (2006), pp. 91–139.

Isaac, B. (1996), 'Eusebius and the geography of Roman provinces', in D. Kennedy (ed.), *The Roman Army in the East*, Ann Arbor.

Isaac, B. (1998), 'Jews, Christians and others in Palestine: the evidence from Eusebius', in M. Goodman (ed.), *Jews in a Graeco-Roman World*, Oxford, pp. 65–74.

Isaac, B. (1999), 'Inscriptions and religious identity on the Golan', in J. H. Humphrey (ed.), *The Roman and Byzantine Near East*, vol. 2: *Some Recent Archaeological Research*, Supplement to *Journal of Roman Archaeology*, 31, pp. 179–88.

Jacobs, A. S. (2002), '"The most beautiful Jewesses in the land": imperial travel in the early Christian Holy Land', *Religion*, 32: 205–25.

Jacobs, A. S. (2003), 'The remains of the Jew: imperial Christian identity in the late ancient Holy Land', *Journal of Medieval and Early Modern Studies*, 33.1: 23–45.

Jones, A. H. M. (1971), *Cities of the Eastern Roman Provinces*, 2nd edn., Oxford, chs. 9–10.

Jones, C. P. (2007), 'Procopius of Gaza and the water of the Holy City', *Greek, Roman, and Byzantine Studies*, 47: 455–67.

Kelly, J. N. D. (1975), *Jerome: His Life, Writings and Controversies*, London.

Kofsky, A. (1997), 'Peter the Iberian: pilgrimage, monasticism and ecclesiastical politics in Byzantine Palestine', *Studii Biblici Franciscani Liber Annuus*, 47: 209–22.

Kofsky, A. (1998), 'Mamre: a case of regional cult?', in Kofsky and Stroumsa (eds.) (1998), pp. 19–30.

Kofsky, A. and Stroumsa, G. G. (eds.) (1998), *Sharing the Sacred: Religious Contacts and Conflicts in the Holy Land*, Jerusalem.

Kraemer, C. J. (1958), *Excavations at Nessana*, vol. 3: *Non-Literary Papyri*, Princeton.

Kropp, A. and Mohammed, Q. (2006), 'Dion of the Decapolis. *Tell al-Ash'ari* in southern Syria in the light of ancient documents and recent discoveries', *Levant*, 38: 125–44.

Lapin, H. (2001), *Economy, Geography, and Provincial History in Later Roman Palestine*, Tübingen.

Lehman, C. M. and Holum, K. G. (2000), *The Greek and Latin Inscriptions of Caesarea Maritima*, Boston.

Leibner, U. (2006), 'Settlement and demography in late Roman and Byzantine eastern Galilee', in Lewin and Pellegrini (eds.) (2006), pp. 105–31.

Levine, L. I. (ed.) (1992), *The Galilee in Late Antiquity*, New York.

Lewin, A. S. (2002), 'Il Negev dall'età nabatea all'epoca tardoantica', *Mediterraneo Antico*, 5: 319–75.

Lewin, A. S. (2007), 'The impact of the late Roman army in Palaestina and Arabia', in L. de Blois and E. Lo Cascio (eds.) (2007), *The Impact of the Roman Army: Economic, Social, Political, Religious and Cultural Aspects*, vol. 1, Leiden, pp. 463–80.

Lewin, A. S. and Pellegrini, P. (eds.) (2006), *Settlements and Demography in the Near East in Late Antiquity*, Pisa and Rome.

Lewin, A. S. and Pellegrini, P. (eds.) (2007), *The Late Roman Army in the Near East from Diocletian to the Arab Conquest*, BAR International Series 1717, Oxford.

Limor, O. and Stroumsa, G. G. (eds.) (2006), *Christians and Christianity in the Holy Land from the Origins to the Latin Kingdom*, Leuven.

Magen, Y. (1993), 'Samaritan synagogues', in Manni and Alliata (eds.) (1993), pp. 193–230.

Magness, J. (2005), 'Heaven on earth: Helios and the Zodiac cycle in ancient Palestinian synagogues', *American Journal of Archaeology*, 59: 1–52.

Manni, F. and Alliata, E. (eds.) (1993), *Early Christianity in Context: Monuments and Documents*, Jerusalem.

Ma'oz, Z. U. (2006), 'The civil reform of Diocletian in the Southern Levant', *SCI* 25: 105–20.

Maraval, P. (1997), *Le Christianisme de Constantin à la conquête arabe*, Paris.

Markschies, Chr. (1998), 'Stadt und Land: Beobachtungen zur Ausbreitung und Inkulturation des Christentums in Palästina', in H. Cancik and J. Rüpke (eds.), *Römische Reichsreligion und Provinzialreligion*, Tübingen, pp. 265–98.

Mayerson, Ph. (1994), *Monks, Martyrs, Soldiers and Saracens: Papers on the Near East in Late Antiquity (1962–1993)*, Jerusalem.

Meimaris, Y. E. (1986), *Sacred Names: Saints, Martyrs and Church Officials in the Greek Inscriptions and Papyri pertaining to the Christian Church of Palestine*, Athens.

Meimaris, Y. E. (1992), *Chronological Systems in Roman-Byzantine Palestine and Arabia: The Evidence of the Dated Greek Inscriptions*, Athens.

Meimaris, Y. E. and Kritikakou-Nikolaropoulou, K. I. (2005), *Inscriptions from Palaestina Tertia*, Ia: *The Greek Inscriptions from Ghor-es-Safi (Byzantine Zoora)*, Athens.

Millar, F. (1993), *The Roman Near East, 31 BC–AD 337*, Cambridge, MA.

Millar, F. (1998), 'Ethnic identity in the Roman Near East, 325–450: language, religion and culture', *Mediterranean Archaeology*, 11: 159–76.

Millar, F. (2005), 'The Theodosian empire (CE 408–452) and the Arabs: Saracens or Ishmaelites?', in E. Gruen (ed.), *Cultural Borrowings and Ethnic Appropriations in Antiquity*, Stuttgart, pp. 297–314.

Millar, F. (2006), 'Transformations of Judaism under Graeco-Roman rule: responses to Schwartz's *Imperialism and Jewish Society*', *JJS* 57: 139–58.

Millar, F. (2008a), 'Rome, Constantinople and the Near Eastern Church under Justinian: two synods of 536', *JRS* 97: 62–82.

Millar, F. (2008b), 'Rebuilding the Jerusalem Temple: pagan, Jewish and Christian conceptions', *Vestnik Drevnei Istorii*, 264: 19–37.

Millar, F. (2009), 'Not Israel's land then: the Church of the Three Palestines in CE 518', in H. M. Cotton, J. Geiger and G. Stiebel (eds.), *Israel's Land*, Jerusalem, pp. 147*–78*.

Miller, S. S. (1984), *Studies in the History and Traditions of Sepphoris*, Leiden.

Milson, D. (2007), *Art and Architecture of the Synagogue in Late Antique Palestine: In the Shadow of the Church*, Leiden and Boston.

Müller-Kessler, Chr. (1991), *Grammatik des Christlich-Palaestinisch Aramaischen*, I: *Schriftlehre, Lautlehre, Formenlehre*, Olms.

Negev, A. (1981), *The Greek Inscriptions from the Negev*, Jerusalem.

Ovadiah, A. (1970), *Corpus of the Byzantine Churches in the Holy Land*, Bonn.

Ovadiah, R. and Ovadiah, A. (1987), *Hellenistic, Roman and Early Byzantine Mosaic Pavements in Israel*, Rome.

Patrich, J. (1995), *Sabas, Leader of Palestinian Monasticism: A Comparative Study in Eastern Monasticism, Fourth to Seventh Centuries*, Washington DC.

Perkams, M. (2001), 'Der Comes Josef und der frühe Kirchenbau in Galiläa', *Jahrbuch für Antike und Christentum*, 44: 23–32.

Perrone, L. (1980), *La chiesa di Palestina e le controversie cristologiche: dal concilio di Efeso (431) al secondo concilio di Constantinopoli (553)*, Brescia.

Perrone, L. (1998), 'Monasticism as a factor of religious interaction in the Holy Land during the Byzantine period', in Kofsky and Stroumsa (eds.) (1998), pp. 67–95.

Price, R. M. and Binns, J. (1989), *Cyril of Scythopolis: Lives of the Monks of Palestine*, Kalamazoo, MI.

Raabe, R. (1895), *Petrus der Iberer: Ein Charakterbild zur Kirchen- und Sittengeschichte des fünften Jahrhunderts. Syrische Übersetzung einer um das Jahr 500 verfassten griechischen Biographie*, Leipzig.

Rebenich, S. (1993), 'Jerome: the "vir trilinguis" and the "hebraica veritas"', *Vigiliae Christianae*, 47: 50–77.

Ribak, E. (2007), *Religious Communities in Byzantine Palestina: The Relationship between Judaism, Christianity and Islam, AD 400–700*, BAR International Series 1646, Oxford.

Rubin, Z. (1990), 'Sinai in the Itinerarium Egeriae', *Atti del Convegno Internazionale sulla Peregrinatio Egeriae, 1987*, Arezzo, pp. 177–91.

Rubin, Z. (1998), 'Porphyrius of Gaza and the conflict between Christianity and paganism in southern Palestine', in Kofsky and Stroumsa (eds.) (1998), pp. 31–65.

Saliou, C. (ed.) (2005), *Gaza dans l'Antiquité Tardive: archéologie, rhétorique et histoire*, Salerno.

Schwartz, S. (2001), *Imperialism and Jewish Society, 200 BCE to 640 CE*, Princeton.

Shatzman, I. (2007), 'Economic conditions, security problems and the deployment of the army in later Roman Palestine. Part I: economy and population', in Lewin and Pellegrini (eds.) (2007), pp. 153–200.

Shereshevski, J. (1991), *Byzantine Urban Settlements in the Negev Desert*, Beer Sheva.

Sipilä, J. (2004), 'Roman Arabia and the provincial reorganisations of the fourth century', *Mediterraneo Antico*, 7: 317–48.

Sipilä, J. (2007), 'Fluctuating provincial borders in mid-4th century Arabia and Palestine', in Lewin and Pellegrini (eds.) (2007), pp. 201–9.

Sivan, H. (2008), *Palestine in Late Antiquity*, Oxford.

Solzbacher, R. (1989), *Mönche, Pilger und Sarazenen: Studien zum Frühchristentum auf der südlichen Sinaihalbinsel; von den Anfängen bis zum Beginn islamischer Herrschaft*, Altenberg.

Stemberger, G. (1998), 'Jewish–Christian contacts in Galilee (fifth to seventh centuries)', in Kofsky and Stroumsa (eds.) (1998), pp. 131–45.

Stemberger, G. (2000), *Jews and Christians in the Holy Land: Palestine in the Fourth Century*, Edinburgh.

Stern, E., Lewisohn-Gilboa, A. and Aviram, J. (eds.) (1993), *New Encyclopaedia of Archaeological Excavations in the Holy Land*, vols. 1–4, Jerusalem and New York.

Stern, S. (2001), *Calendar and Community: A History of the Jewish Calendar, 2nd Century BCE – 10th Century CE*, Oxford.

Stroumsa, G. G. (1988), '"Vetus Israel": Les Juifs dans la littérature hiérosolymitaine d'époque byzantine', *Revue de l'Histoire des Religions*, 205: 115–31.

Stroumsa, G. G. (1989), 'Religious contacts in Byzantine Palestine', *Numen*, 36: 16–42.

Sukenik, E. L. (1932), *The Ancient Synagogue of Beth Alpha*, Jerusalem.

Sukenik, E. L. (1935), 'The ancient synagogue of el-Hammath', *Journal of the Palestine Oriental Society*, 15: 101–80.

Taylor, Joan E. (1993), *Christians and the Holy Places*, Oxford.

Tsafrir, Y. (ed.) (1993), *Ancient Churches Revealed*, Jerusalem.

Tsafrir, Y. and Foerster, G. (1997), 'Urbanism at Scythopolis-Bet Shean in the fourth to seventh centuries', *DOP*, 51: 85–147.

Urman, D. (2006), *Rafid in the Golan: A Profile of a Late Roman and Byzantine Village*, BAR International Series 1555, Oxford.

Walker, P. W. L. (1990), *Holy City, Holy Places? Christian Attitudes to Jerusalem and the Holy Land in the Fourth Century*, Oxford.

Walmsley, A. (1996), 'Byzantine Palestine and Arabia: urban prosperity in late antiquity', in N. Christie and S. T. Loseby (eds.), *Towns in Transition: Urban Evolution in Late Antiquity and the Early Middle Ages*, Aldershot, pp. 126–58.

Weingarten, S. (2005), *The Saint's Saints: Hagiography and Geography in Jerome*, Leiden.

Weiss, Z. (2005), *The Sepphoris Synagogue: Deciphering an Ancient Message through Its Archaeological and Socio-Historical Contexts*, Jerusalem.

Wilken, R. L. (1992), *The Land called Holy: Palestine in Christian History and Thought*, New Haven and London.

Wilkinson, J. (1977), *Jerusalem Pilgrims before the Crusades*, 2nd edn., Warminster.

3

Research into Rabbinic Literature: An Attempt to Define the *Status Quaestionis*

PETER SCHÄFER

'RESEARCH INTO RABBINIC LITERATURE' in the face of advances made in recent decades alone, this is an immense topic, and it would be extremely presumptuous to wish to deal with it in a single lecture.[1] I would therefore immediately like to add that the sub-title is a more accurate description: 'An attempt to define the *status quaestionis*'. It is, that is to say, not the discussion of introductory issues in the classical sense which is of paramount importance, although the paper will naturally also touch on such matters. I would like, rather, to present the most important approaches in research on the basis of which rabbinic literature has been and is being studied. This has two implications. Firstly, such a summary cannot be comprehensive. Secondly, it will not be wholly objective. No one claiming to be involved in investigating rabbinic Judaism can possibly be impartial but will inevitably convey his personal and sometimes even overstated view of the matter.

I have divided the topic into five different research approaches and will subsequently attempt to arrive at some conclusions.

1. The first, and historically the earliest, line of research is the traditional-halakhic approach. The leading principle here is 'the Halakhah' as a superior and comprehensive construct to which all individual elements of rabbinic literature are referred, irrespective of where the work belongs. This approach is standard for classical Jewish commentary literature as well as for numerous modern introductions to rabbinic literature. A notable example of the former is S. Lieberman's famous commentary to the Tosefta (1955–73; cf. also Weiss Halivni 1968–82), and characteristic of the latter are J. N. Epstein's 'Introductions' (*Mevo'ot*; Epstein 1964, 1957, 1962), which have individual works as their foundation but are basically aimed at 'the Halakhah as such', beyond all literary boundaries.

---

[1] This contribution is the slightly revised and annotated version of a lecture given on 20 November 1984 at the University of Duisburg and on 30 May 1985 in the Oriental Institute of the University of Oxford.

Proceedings of the British Academy **165**, 51–65. © The British Academy 2010.

Commendable though these contributions are, the problem of such an approach in research is obvious. It is that the final aim and uniting bracket of all these endeavours is determined by the entity 'Halakhah', which is taken for granted and has never actually been questioned. The course of research is thus in the end systematical-theological, not historical-literary. Rabbinic literature is not really seen as literature; its literary character is of secondary importance and subordinated to a systematic principle. No one would wish to question the justifiability of such an approach but its advocates should be conscious of the methodological presuppositions and limits.

2. The next line of research, pursued *per definitionem* exclusively by Christians, I would define as *exploitative-apologetic*. This is the approach which sets for itself the acknowledged goal of using rabbinic literature as a quarry in order to draw on its isolated elements for the explanation of the New Testament. The issue here is not rabbinic literature at all, but something quite different. Rabbinic literature is merely a means to an end, the formal end being the exegesis of the New Testament, in the course of which this aim can be met with very differing results. At best, the point is to 'elucidate' the New Testament from its Jewish environment; at worst, the rabbinic parallels serve to demonstrate the superiority of the New Testament. The classic example of this research approach is the *Kommentar zum Neuen Testament aus Talmud und Midrasch* by Billerbeck (Strack and Billerbeck 1922–61). The methodological problems linked with it have been sufficiently demonstrated and are aptly classified by the term 'parallelomania'. Interesting as individual parallels may be, it is now widely accepted that isolated parallels are meaningless as long as the status of the parallel in its respective literature cannot be evaluated. This presupposes that the literature from which a parallel is taken has been analysed as a whole. Since we are far from achieving such an analysis of rabbinic literature, contributions in which a comparison is made between individual New Testament passages and individual passages in rabbinic literature are methodologically obsolete. In spite of the fact that New Testament scholars certainly do not lack methodological awareness in their own field, it is astounding how strongly the interest of New Testament scholarly journals—in so far as they are concerned with Judaism at all—is concentrated almost exclusively on this primitive methodological approach.

3. A further line of research could be described as *thematic*. Here, too, the issue is not rabbinic literature as literature but, in contrast to the approach just characterised, rabbinic Judaism is at least considered in itself and not merely as a means to an end. Mostly, theological ideas are selected as themes, for instance—to name a few examples—ideas about God, the

Holy Spirit, the Messiah or the angels.[2] This approach is (or was?) pursued, if not exclusively, then certainly to a considerable extent in Judaic studies in Germany. It involves, as a rule, collecting as many appropriate 'passages' as possible and analysing them separately but with their respective parallels. More often than not, the final result is an attempt at a synthesis of the investigated theme, in which literary and historical distinctions are taken into account as far as possible. However, most advocates of this approach decline (and rightly so) to write a 'history' of their subject, since the sources do not allow of any historical continuity.

Almost all the more recent studies in this field are aware that in each case the superordinate question (the theme) pursued is not inherent to the sources but is applied to the texts from outside. The idea of God, the idea of the Holy Spirit, of the angels, or of the Messiah, have not been made into themes in rabbinic literature; it has expressed no systematic consideration of them. The usual supposition that one need only assemble the fragments and shreds of the 'idea', 'dispersed' throughout the whole of rabbinic literature in order to 'reconstruct' a more or less uniform picture of the 'underlying' concept is only partly pertinent to the facts. The rabbis have given the themes no consideration, not because by reason of some mysterious deficiency they were unable to do so, but because they did not wish to, because they were not interested in these themes as isolated themes. This signifies in regard to the thematic approach that the identity of the object of research is not given by the sources but artificially, and this in two respects. Not only is the identity of the theme artificial, but also the identity of the material from which it is extracted. 'Rabbinic literature' in its full extent, however defined, is a fictitious entity that never existed as a *totum*.

This does not necessarily mean that the thematic approach must be altogether abandoned. The dilemma of the artificial identity of the theme cannot be avoided, but this need not constitute a fundamental objection, for it is undoubtedly possible to ask questions of the texts which they themselves do not pose. One should merely be (more than previously) aware what tradition the question has, why this particular question and no other is applied to the text. (In the case of theological themes this will mostly be an interest stemming from Christian theology and not a Jewish question, even if it can be shown that rabbinic Judaism had its own concept which differed from the Christian one or was even its precursor.)

The dilemma of the fictitious identity of the material from which the theme is extracted can be avoided to some extent if the analyses are made

---

[2] e.g. God: Kuhn (1968, 1978), Goldberg (1969); the Holy Spirit: Schäfer (1972); the Messiah: Levey (1974); the angels: Schäfer (1975).

separately work by work.[3] In this way a literary structuring of the theme is undoubtedly successful; but the extent to which a historical distinction can be connected to this presents difficulties, for the scholar immediately finds himself faced with the problem of redaction and tradition. The analysis of a separate work uncovers a theme in its chronological differentiation only at the level of the final redaction of individual writings, not at the level of the individual tradition. However, since the individual tradition is virtually impossible to date, the analysis of the work appears to be the most promising method of a thematic approach at present. I shall return later to the problem of the work concept inevitably connected with this methodological approach also.

The elaboration of a rabbinical theology is a special case within the thematic approach. The classic recent example of this is E. E. Urbach's *HZ"L. Emunot we-de'ot* (Urbach 1969; English edition: Urbach [1975] 1979). This is a very respectable attempt that could characterise both the climax and the temporary demise of its subject. J. Neusner's emphatic criticism (1984b: 115–26) of the methodological approach is, although somewhat exaggerated, basically justified, since a rabbinic theology, at whichever methodological level of reflection it may be written, intensifies the previously mentioned problems of the thematic approach: it introduces yet another general identity, namely that of 'rabbinic theology', which is no less debatable than that of the individual theme.

4. Another attempt at devising a suitable approach to rabbinic literature can be described as *biographical*. Characteristic of this are, above all, the earlier works of Jacob Neusner and his students, who make individual rabbis the objects of their investigation: Yohanan b. Zakkai, Eliezer b. Hyrcanos, Akiva, Ishmael, Yose the Galilean, Eleazar b. Azariah, Tarfon, Gamaliel II, Joshua, Meir,[4] among others. Naturally, it is not simply a matter of writing biographies of rabbis; it was clear from the outset, or became so very early, that that would be a quite unreasonable aim. Neusner's treatment of Yohanan b. Zakkai throws light on this process of thought. Whereas in 1962 he was still able to write a *Life of Yohanan ben Zakkai* (Neusner 1962), rather in the style of an imaginative biographical reconstruction, which (ironically, it must be said in retrospect) was awarded the 'Abraham Berliner Prize in Jewish History', in 1970 he completely revised his subject and published 'only' unassuming *Studies on the Traditions concerning Yohanan ben Zakkai* under the programmatic heading *Development of a Legend*.

---

[3] This is the case, for example, in Neusner (1984a).

[4] Eliezer b. Hyrcanos: Neusner (1973); Akiva: Primus (1977); Ishmael: Porton (1976–82); Yose the Galilean: Lightstone (1979); Eleazar b. Azariah: Zahavy (1977); Tarfon: Gereboff (1979); Gamaliel II: Kanter (1980); Joshua: Green (1981); Meir: Goldenberg (1978).

This title denotes the line of research of the modern biographical approach. The identity establishing the theme still has its roots in the figure of a rabbi, but this identity more and more proves itself to be fragile. It is becoming increasingly evident that virtually nothing is to be learned of the historical figure of the rabbi concerned from rabbinic sources (this is rather obvious). Neither can any coherent 'doctrine' of any chosen rabbi be discerned from an analysis of all the relevant traditions. This is the case whether we look for a structured attitude to parts of the Halakhah or, still further, for a systematic general outline of the Halakhah. The rabbis hand down the Halakhah, but beyond this purely formal function they are of no historical importance. It is an overstatement, but one might say that the only overall taxonomy reflected by a rabbi's name in rabbinic literature is the name itself, whose meaning is thus reduced to nothing.

Accordingly, the modern variant of the biographical approach has also proved itself to be, if not wrong, then certainly not very fruitful. It is significant that in 1973 Neusner himself submitted his last study concerning a rabbi (*Eliezer ben Hyrcanus*). The methodological approach makes it possible to carry out interesting individual analyses of a wide range of themes. But since the identity of the subject is based on a fictitious or ideal entity, it is in the end unsuitable for an appropriate investigation into rabbinic literature.

5.   In the light of these findings it is but consistent that the aim of research has at last moved away from tracing topics of whatever nature and is finally focusing directly on the object of the whole endeavour: rabbinic literature. In connection with this, two approaches should be distinguished, which aim at the same point from different directions.

5.1.   The first line of research to be mentioned here has been intensively pursued for several years by Arnold Goldberg and developed in his articles in *Frankfurter Judaistische Beiträge*. Goldberg probably makes the most of rabbinic literature as literature and attempts to record and describe the system of rules inherent to it. His approach might therefore possibly be described as analytical-descriptive. The identity of the subject is constituted by the common language. In a programmatic essay published in 1977 he himself called his method 'form-analytical': 'Entwurf einer formanalytischen Methode fur die Exegese der rabbinischen Traditionsliteratur' (Goldberg 1977). However, this form-*analysis* must not be confused with form- or generic *history*: 'The form-analytical method does not investigate the "Sitz im Leben" but, if the expression may be modified here, the "*Sitz in der Literatur oder in der Sprache*"', the place in literature or in language (Goldberg 1977: 2).

Proceeding from the realisation that rabbinic literature consists fundamentally of textual units the original contexts of which have been lost and which 'only' exist in newly coined (and changing) redactional connections (later he speaks of 'citemes'), the first issue is to portray the *forms* and *functions* of these smaller and larger literary units. As the most important (provisional) basic forms Goldberg names the *Midrash* (1982), the *Dictum* or *Logion*, the *Mashal* (1981), the *Ma'aseh* ('precedent'; 1974) and the *Aggadah* ('saga, legend, tale'). 'Forms of a higher order' have evolved from these basic forms according to definite structural principles, for instance the form of the *homily* (1978, 1980) or the form of the Sugya, the halakhic discussion in the Talmud.

Whereas form-analysis develops and defines individual 'citations', functional-analysis describes their 'function' within the larger redactional unit. Both aim at recording the 'message' ('Aussage') and 'meaning' ('Bedeutung') of the text, whereby Goldberg understands by the 'message' of the 'citation' that which the 'citation' itself implies (i.e. without consideration of its 'function' in the superordinate redactional unit), and by 'meaning' that which it means in the mind of the one making the citation, i.e. *within* the larger redactional unit. The analysis of the meaning must 'show the citations, reconstructed by form-analysis and portrayed as a means by functional-analysis, in their allusive and qualifying meanings over and beyond their message (sc. of the citations as such)' (Goldberg 1977: 25).

The consciously descriptive process of the depiction of the forms and functions of smaller and larger literary units in their message and meaning inevitably forgoes a diachronic (that is a historically discriminating) analysis of the texts. In his article written in 1977, Goldberg still cautiously describes a diachronic analysis of the functions as 'possibly not imperative . . . but certainly useful and therefore in no way superfluous' (1977: 20). However, in his recent article (1983), he emphasises strongly the fundamental synchronicity of the texts: 'Once it has been written, every text is exclusively synchronic, all the textual units (*textemes*) exist simultaneously, and the only diachronic relation consists in the reception of the text as a sequence of textual units whose "first" and "then" become "beforehand" and "afterwards" in the reception of the text. . . . The synchronicity of a text is . . . the simultaneous juxtaposition of various units, independent of when the units originated' (1983: 5ff.).

This emphasis on a fundamental synchronicity of the texts of rabbinic literature is completely consistent with Goldberg's methodological approach. The text, *as it stands*, is exclusively synchronic and, since we cannot go back beyond this state, there remains only the classifying description of that which is there—which should, of course, be as well considered and comprehensible as possible. A historical differentiation is deliberately excluded, because, in effect, the texts do not permit it. Whilst analysis of the forms and functions of a text makes its *system of rules* transparent, 'the comprehension of rabbinic texts through habituation and insight could be superseded by a comprehension of the rules of this discourse *as competence* (i.e. according to the rules of its production)' (1983: 45).

The question that arises here is obviously what is meant by 'text'. What is the text 'once it has been written'—*the* Babylonian Talmud, *the* Midrash, a definite Midrash, all Midrashim, or even the *whole of rabbinic literature* as a synchronic textual continuum whose inherent system of rules it is necessary to describe? Indeed, in such a description, neither the concrete text concerned, nor the form a particular textual tradition takes, needs to be important. Every text is as good—or rather as bad—as every other, the 'best' being presumably the one representing the latest redactional stage.

But this is precisely where the problem begins. Goldberg himself must finally decide on one text, and in doing so—in many cases anyway—must decide against one or several other texts. Whether he wants to or not, he inevitably faces historical questions. This problem can be elucidated by the second line of research within the 'literary' approach.

5.2. This second line of research, which has been propagated during approximately the last ten years by J. Neusner (and has superseded the biographical approach in his own research history) is that of the interpretation *immanent in the work*. Complete literary works are analysed as a whole, as literary systems so to speak, and are examined for their characteristic arguments. With admirable consistency and energy, Neusner has submitted or sent to press such analyses of the *Mishnah* and *Tosefta* (1974–77, 1979, 1979–80, 1981–83, 1983–85, 1981), as well as of the *Yerushalmi* (ed. 1982–94; 1983) and *Midrash Wayyiqra Rabbah* (1985a, 1985b), and now recently has begun work on the *Bavli* (ed. 1984–93). A new translation of the respective literary works serves as the basis for all these analyses, for Neusner proceeds from the doubtlessly correct assumption that a work in a foreign language can only be mastered via a translation.

The plane on which this research approach moves—and economically can only move—is the final redaction of the respective work, i.e. as a rule the *textus receptus*; the identity of the theme is thus constituted by the finally redacted version of a work of rabbinic literature. Two closely related problems arise from this.

The approach inevitably disregards the manuscript traditions of the work in question. But, especially in the case of rabbinic literature, this is essential. Thus, to give an example, both Vatican manuscripts of the Bereshit Rabbah (MSS Vat. Ebr. 60 and 30) represent texts which are quite different from that of the London manuscript (MS British Museum, Add. 27169) serving Theodor as a basis for his edition. The variations are sometimes so great that the redactional identity of the work is debatable.[5] Is it meaningful to speak of one work at all, or rather of various recensions of a work? But then how do these recensions relate to one another? Are they different versions of one and the same text (do they therefore presuppose an 'Urtext'), or are they autonomous to a certain extent, and is 'Bereshit Rabbah' merely an ideal or fictitious entity? What then constitutes the identity of the work 'Bereshit Rabbah'? Any preserved manuscript, or the modern 'critical' edition by Theodor-Albeck? These questions could easily be added to and applied *mutatis mutandis* to almost every text of rabbinic traditional literature.

The problem becomes more acute when the question of the boundaries of works is taken into consideration. To remain with the example of Bereshit Rabbah, the problem of what relation Bereshit Rabbah and the Yerushalmi bear to one another has been discussed since the time of Frankel (1870: 51bff.) and Zunz (1892: 185f.). The detailed comparison of numerous parallel passages by Albeck in his introduction to the critical edition of Bereshit Rabbah has made it *communis opinio* that the redactor of Bereshit Rabbah indeed used the Yerushalmi, but that this Yerushalmi was decidedly different from the Yerushalmi in existence today. How are Bereshit Rabbah and Yerushalmi related to one another in this case? Does Bereshit Rabbah quote Yerushalmi, i.e. can we regard Bereshit Rabbah and Yerushalmi at the *time of the redaction of Bereshit Rabbah* as two clearly distinguishable works, one of which (Yerushalmi) was complete and the other (Bereshit Rabbah) in the process of being completed? Did the redactor of Bereshit Rabbah therefore 'know' with what he was dealing and from what he was 'quoting'? With regard to the Yerushalmi, this conclusion is obviously unreasonable, for we immediately have to ask how the Yerushalmi of the Bereshit Rabbah is related to the Yerushalmi existent today. The Yerushalmi cannot have been 'complete' at the time of the redaction of Bereshit Rabbah since it is not identical to the one we use today.

A solution to this dilemma is offered by the temporary hypothesis whereby one speaks of various *stages* in the process of editing the Yerushalmi. There were several editorial stages, one of which (and possibly a particularly early one) is represented by the 'citations' in Bereshit Rabbah. But the problem is not thereby solved. What is the relation between stage A and stage B, and above all stage Z, the stage of the presumed final redaction? Are all the stages 'preliminary phases' leading to the one objective, the final redaction Z as the sum total of all the preceding stages? Then the predicate 'Yerushalmi' would only be added to the final redaction, and the redactor of Bereshit Rabbah would not have quoted 'the' Yerushalmi at all. But what

---

[5] The best discussion of the manuscripts of Bereshit Rabbah can be found now in Sokoloff (1982: 19ff.).

would he have quoted? A preliminary phase that did not yet merit the title 'Yerushalmi'?

Let us take another example to clarify the problem further. The question of the relation between the Mishnah and the Tosefta also has a long and highly controversial research history.[6] The realisation has long been generally accepted that simple dependence models are senseless. The Mishnah is not dependent on the Tosefta, nor is the Tosefta as a whole dependent on the Mishnah. The separate investigation of individual tractates produces a much more complicated picture. Although it can be shown that, for the main part of the material, the Tosefta presupposes the Mishnah, and is to be understood as its very first commentary,[7] this result cannot be applied to all the tractates. There appear to be Mishnah tractates which presuppose the Tosefta, and above all there are Tosefta tractates which identify it as an independent 'work' vis-à-vis the Mishnah, in which the Tosefta does not refer to the Mishnah, at least not to the one extant today. Finally certain Tosefta tractates suggest that they appeal to another (earlier?) Mishnah than the one which became normative through the final redaction.

Here, too, the question is: which entities can be compared to one another? Quite obviously these are not 'the' (one) Mishnah and 'the' (one) Tosefta, for already this quite cursory review shows that we must distinguish between three different 'Mishnahs': a postulated Mishnah which can only be 'reconstructed' from reference to it in the Tosefta; a Mishnah that has given rise to the Tosefta commentary; and a Mishnah which is by contrast to be regarded as a reaction to the Tosefta. Likewise we obtain three different 'Toseftas': a Tosefta related to an otherwise unknown Mishnah; a Tosefta appealing to the existing Mishnah; and a Tosefta completely independent of any Mishnah.

If we wished to apply the model of the various editorial stages to these findings, we would see in the postulated Mishnah the earliest form of the Mishnah, in the Mishnah expounded by Tosefta the second stage of the editorial development, and in the Mishnah based on Tosefta the final stage. The Tosefta would then be dealt with similarly, the most important decision being whether to acknowledge the Tosefta independent of the Mishnah as the earliest or the latest stage, though I am rather sure that one would tend towards the former possibility. Apart from the fact that this reconstruction of the stages would be altogether arbitrary, the question of the relation between the various stages arises here too with regard to the identity of the text investigated. Can every single stage claim the quality or identity 'Mishnah', or 'Tosefta', or only the last stage, i.e. the final redaction?

---

[6] A short résumé is provided by Strack and Stemberger (1982).

[7] This has been shown explicitly for Tohorot; cf. Neusner (1974–77: vol. 21, 247ff.).

Recent research attempts to evade the thus accentuated problem by no longer comparing 'the' Mishnah with 'the' Tosefta, but only individual Mishnah and Tosefta tractates. The relationship between Mishnah and Tosefta manifests itself differently in different tractates; accordingly, *different answers are concurrently possible*, depending on the situation of the individual tractate. Without a doubt, this is a great step forward compared with earlier research. Nevertheless, the problem is not thereby solved once and for all but is merely transferred from the level of Mishnah *versus* Tosefta to that of Mishnah tractate X *versus* Tosefta tractate X. Appeal to this level permits a more differentiated picture than that which can be conveyed by the two extremely static entities, Mishnah and Tosefta; but this picture too, referring to every tractate as a whole, remains static. Although there is, as yet, no substantially detailed investigation into the relationship between individual Mishnah and Tosefta tractates, it would hardly be too speculative to predict that the same problem will arise on the tractate level as on the level of the Mishnah as a whole *versus* the Tosefta as a whole. Even on the level of the individual tractate, *one* constant factor determining the relation will not always emerge, but the individual tractate, too, will contain different material which, *within the same tractate*, requires different models of the relation between Mishnah and Tosefta. Thus the problem of the boundaries of a work, with regard to the relationship between Mishnah and Tosefta, as well as to the extent of delimitation of the 'works' Mishnah and Tosefta, becomes more acute. We are finally referred to 'raw material', to relatively small literary units, that can only be interpreted and compared as such, and no longer as exactly determinable parts of well-defined works.

A brief reference to Hekhalot literature will constitute a last example (Schäfer 1977, 1978, 1982, 1983a, 1983b, 1984, 1985a, 1985b, 1988a). This is without doubt the prototype of a literature where the boundaries between the works are fluid. Every 'work' in this literary genre that I have investigated more closely proves to be astonishingly unstable, falls into smaller and smaller editorial units and cannot be precisely defined and delimited, either as it is or with reference to related works. This finding is of course valid with regard to the works of Hekhalot literature to a varying degree, but can be generalised as a striking characteristic feature of the whole literary genre. There is not much sense in dividing off works of any kind within Hekhalot literature and comparing them with one another as defined identities. Most of the 'works' only reached the stage of a standardising and structuring final redaction very late or not at all. Most of the manuscripts hand them down in the form of only loosely structured 'raw material', without a title (and if with a title, then with fantasy titles interchangeable almost at will), with no recognisable beginning and no recognisable end (and if with a beginning or an end, then not very uniform in the various manuscripts).

6.   It is hoped that these examples will be sufficient to draw attention to the underlying problem. The questioning of the redactional identity of the individual works of rabbinic literature inevitably also disavows the research approach to the work at the level of the final redaction.[8] The terms with which we usually work—text, 'Urtext', recension, tradition, citation, redaction, final redaction, work—prove to be fragile and hasty definitions that must be subsequently questioned. What is a 'text' in rabbinic literature? Are there texts that can be defined and clearly delimited, or are there only basically 'open' texts, which elude temporal and redactional fixation? Have there ever been 'Urtexte' of certain works, with a development that could be traced and described? How do different recensions of a 'text' relate to one another with respect to the redactional identity of the text? How should the individual tradition, the smallest literary unit, be assessed in relation to the macroform of the 'work' in which it appears? What is the meaning of the presence of parts of one 'work' in another more or less delimitable 'work'? Is this then a quotation in work X from work Y? And finally what is redaction or final redaction? Are there several 'redactions' of a 'work'—in chronological order—but only one final redaction? What distinguishes redaction from final redaction? What lends authority to the redaction? Or is the final redaction merely the more or less incidental discontinuation of the manuscript tradition?

All these questions, to which of course more could be added, point to one basic problem, namely the relation between text and time. When even the individual work of rabbinic literature—Mishnah, Tosefta, Yerushalmi, Midrashim, Bavli—is no longer a stable quantity, provides no fixed frame of reference within which closed systems can be worked out and placed in chronological relation to one another, it becomes extraordinarily difficult, if not virtually impossible, to ask adequate historical questions of the texts, and to answer them. Is then the consequence merely a return to a history of traditions in which traditions, detached from their literary contexts and more or less freely floating, are tracked down, traced and placed in relation to one another? However enlightening comparative motif research and *comparative midrash* have been, and may still be, their methods are hardly promising with respect to historical questioning. When one starts out from a diversely interwoven and in the end open text-continuum 'Rabbinic Literature', from a dynamic process that has entered into various and changing configurations and fixations, it is meaningless either to divide off finally redacted 'works' from one another and to compare them with one another, or to make pseudo-causal connections between isolated traditions.

---

[8] For another attempt to overcome the problems posed by the fluid boundaries of 'works', see now Neusner (1985c).

It appears to me that the problems thus accentuated permit of only two models offering possible solutions. One would have to be based on the fundamental synchronicity of not only one, but of all the works of rabbinic literature. If the individual text cannot be fixed in time and space, then it hardly makes sense to behave in regard to certain questions as though this were possible. We would thereby be, although at a methodologically more considered level, exactly where we started, with the 'traditional' study of rabbinic literature as a synchronic unit. This seems to follow from Goldberg's logic. His method of language- and form-analysis allows for an almost 'scientifically' precise description of the mechanisms and rules by which the corpus 'rabbinic literature' is constructed and functions; as such, it is of admirable unity and consistency. This unity and logical consistency is admittedly paid for with the final, even programmatic, renunciation of every attempt at temporal placing and historical differentiation. Legitimate and doubtless necessary as this process is, its price is very high.[9]

I would therefore favour a second model that adopts the research approach just described but goes a step further. If it is difficult to separate works from each other because on the level of their final redaction most of the works of rabbinic literature are artificial products which at best mirror the historical reality of the last redactor, and at worst, the historical reality of the modern 'critical' editor, we should reach back to the evidence in existence before the level of the final redaction: the manuscripts. Before we speak of 'works', we should analyse the manuscript traditions of the works concerned as well as the whole of rabbinic literature in its diverse relations, and compile a nomenclature of the manuscript traditions. The scholarship intent to a large degree upon constructing critical editions in the service of the 'original text' is still far from achieving this. Work on the manuscripts must rid itself of the odium of the whimsical scholar constantly in quest of the 'better' reading and finally buried under his collection of variants. It is not a matter of variants of static texts, but rather of the documentation and description of a dynamic manuscript tradition. Only when this step has been taken shall we possibly also be able to make more reliable statements about individual works of rabbinic literature and their boundaries.[10]

Study of the manuscripts also allows for more concrete historical statements. If the works of rabbinic literature cannot be fixed in time and space (because by their very nature they elude such fixation), the manuscripts

---

[9] It should be stressed, however, that Goldberg by no means considers his method as being exclusive in the sense that he allows for no other and different approaches. On the contrary, he is perfectly aware of the fact that each method requires its own set of questions, and may exclude other questions but not other methods.

[10] An important step forward in this direction seems to me the article of Sussman (1983). Cf. also Ta-Shema (1984–85).

often can. We often know from the manuscripts when, where, and by whom they were written and, in the course of time, we ought to be in a position to elicit the historical and social context from which they originate. In this way, a frame of reference of manuscripts, scribes, copyists and migrations could emerge which admittedly would not lead to the 'Urtext' (which in most cases has never existed), but which would tell us something about the history of the texts and their reception. This means that it is not 'the' text as such that is to be fixed in time and space, but rather the history of the text as reflected in the transmission of its manuscript traditions.

Note. This chapter was first published in the *Journal of Jewish Studies*, 37 (1986): P. Schäfer, 'Research into rabbinic literature: an attempt to define the *Status Quaestionis*', *JJS* 37: 139–52.

Bibliography

Epstein, J. N. H. (1957), *Mevo'ot le-sifrut ha-tanna'im*, ed. E. Z. Melamed. Jerusalem and Tel Aviv.

Epstein, J. N. H. (1962), *Mevo'ot le-sifrut ha-amora'im*, ed. E. Z. Melamed. Jerusalem and Tel Aviv.

Epstein, J. N. H. (1964), *Mavo' le-nusah ha-mishnah*, ed. E. Z. Melamed, 2 vols., Jerusalem and Tel Aviv.

Frankel, Z. (1870), *Mevo' ha-Yerushalmi*, Breslau; repr. Jerusalem, 1967.

Gereboff, G. (1979), *Rabbi Tarfon: The Tradition, the Man, and Early Rabbinic Judaism*, Missoula, MT.

Goldberg, A. (1969), *Untersuchungen über die Schekhinah in der frühen Rabbinischen Literatur*, Berlin.

Goldberg, A. (1974), 'Form und Funktion des Ma'ase in der Mischna', *FJB* 2: 1–38.

Goldberg, A. (1977), 'Entwurf einer formanalytischen Methode fur die Exegese der rabbinischen Traditionsliteratur', *FJB* 5: 1–41.

Goldberg, A. (1978), 'Die Peroratio (Ḥatima) als Kompositionsform der rabbinischen Homilie', *FJB* 6: 1–22.

Goldberg, A. (1980), 'Versuch über die hermeneutische Präsupposition der Struktur der Petiḥa', *FJB* 8: 1–59.

Goldberg, A. (1981), 'Das schriftauslegende Gleichnis im Midrasch', *FJB* 9: 1–90.

Goldberg, A. (1982), 'Die funktionale Form Midrasch', *FJB* 10: 1–45.

Goldberg, A. (1983), 'Der Diskurs im babylonischen Talmud. Anregungen für eine Diskursanalyse', *FJB* 11: 1–45.

Goldenberg, R. (1978), *The Sabbath-Law of Rabbi Meir*, Missoula, MT.

Green, W. S. (1981), *The Traditions of Joshua ben Hananiah*, Part I: *The Early Traditions*, Leiden.

Kanter, Sh. (1980), *Rabban Gamaliel II: The Legal Traditions*, Chico, CA.

Kuhn, P. (1968), *Gottes Selbsterniedrigung in der Theologie der Rabbinen*, Munich.

Kuhn, P. (1978), *Gottes Trauer und Klage in der rabbinischen Überlieferung*, Leiden.

Levey, S. H. (1974), *The Messiah: An Aramaic Interpretation. The Messianic Exegesis of the Targum*, Cincinnati.

Lieberman, S. (1955–73), *Tosefta Ki-fshuta: A Comprehensive Commentary on the Tosefta*, 9 vols., New York.

Lightstone, J. N. (1979), *Yose the Galilean*, vol. 1: *Traditions in Mishnah-Tosefta*, Leiden.

Neusner, J. (1962), *Life of Yohanan ben Zakkai*. Leiden.

Neusner, J. (1973), *Eliezer ben Hyrcanus: The Tradition and the Man*, 2 vols., Leiden.

Neusner, J. (1974–77), *A History of the Mishnaic Law of Purities*, 22 vols., Leiden.

Neusner, J. (1979), *A History of the Mishnaic Law of Holy Things*, 6 vols., Leiden.

Neusner, J. (1979–80), *A History of the Mishnaic Law of Women*, 5 vols., Leiden.

Neusner, J. (1981), *Judaism: The Evidence of the Mishnah*, Chicago.

Neusner, J. (1981–83), *A History of the Mishnaic Law of Appointed Times*, 5 vols., Leiden.

Neusner, J. (1983), *Judaism in Society: The Evidence of the Yerushalmi. Toward the Natural History of a Religion*, Chicago.

Neusner, J. (1983–85), *A History of the Mishnaic Law of Damages*, 5 vols., Leiden.

Neusner, J. (1984a), *Messiah in Context: Israel's History and Destiny in Formative Judaism*, Philadelphia.

Neusner, J. (1984b), *Ancient Judaism: Debates and Disputes*, Chico, CA.

Neusner, J. (1985a), *Judaism and Scripture: The Evidence of Leviticus Rabbah*, Chicago.

Neusner, J. (1985b), *The Integrity of Leviticus Rabbah: The Problem of the Autonomy of a Rabbinic Document*, Chicago.

Neusner, J. (1985c), 'When tales travel: the interpretation of multiple appearances of a single saying in Talmudic literature', in *Formative Judaism, V: Revisioning the Written Records of a Nascent Religion*, Chico, CA, pp. 87–103.

Neusner, J. (ed.) (1982–94), *The Talmud of the Land of Israel: A Preliminary Translation and Explanation*, 35 vols., Chicago.

Neusner, J. (ed.) (1984–93), *The Talmud of Babylonia: An American Translation*, Chico, CA.

Porton, G. (1976–82), *The Traditions of R. Ishmael*, 4 vols., Leiden.

Primus, Ch. (1977), *Aqiva's Contribution to the Law of Zera'im*, Leiden.

Schäfer, P. (1972), *Die Vorstellung vom Heiligen Geist in der Rabbinischen Literatur*, Munich.

Schäfer, P. (1975), *Rivalität zwischen Engeln und Menschen: Untersuchungen zur Rabbinischen Engelvorstellung*, Berlin and New York.

Schäfer, P. (1977), 'Prolegomena zu einer kritischen Edition und Analyse der Merkava Rabba', *FJB* 5: 65–99; repr. in idem (1988b), pp. 17–49.

Schäfer, P. (1978), 'Die Beschwörung des sar ha-panim: Kritische Edition und Übersetzung', *FJB* 6: 107–45; repr. in idem (1988b), pp. 118–53.

Schäfer, P. (1982), 'Aufbau und redaktionelle Identität der Hekhalot Zutrati', *JJS* 33: 569–82; repr. in idem (1988b), pp. 50–62.

Schäfer, P. (1983a), 'Tradition and redaction in Hekhalot literature', *JJS* 14: 172–81; repr. in idem (1988b), pp. 8–16.

Schäfer, P. (1983b), 'Handschriften zur Hekhalot-Literatur', *FJB* 11: 113–93; repr. in idem (1988b), pp. 154–233.

Schäfer, P. (1984), 'Merkavah mysticism and rabbinic Judaism', *JAOS* 104: 537–41.

Schäfer, P. (1985a), 'Zum Problem der redaktionellen Identität von Hekhalot Rabbati', *FJB* 13: 1–22.

Schäfer, P. (1985b), 'Ein neues Fragment zur Metoposkopie und Chiromantik', *FJB* 13: 61–82; repr. in idem (1988b), pp. 84–95.

Schäfer, P. (1988a), 'Shiʿur Qomah: Rezensionen und Urtext', in idem (1988b), pp. 75–103.

Schäfer, P. (1988b), *Hekhalot-Studien*, Tübingen.

Sokoloff, M. (1982), *Qiṭʿe Bereshit Rabbah min ha-Genizah*, Jerusalem.

Strack, H. and Billerbeck, P. (1922–61), *Kommentar zum Neuen Testament aus Talmud und Midrasch*, Munich.

Strack, H. L. and Stemberger, G. (1982), *Einleitung in Talmud und Midrasch*, 7th edn., Munich.

Sussman, Y. (1983), 'Masoret-limud umasoret-nusaḥ shel ha-talmud ha-yerushalmi: Leverur nusḥaʾoteha shel yerushalmi masekhet sheqalim', in *Researches in Talmudic Literature: A Study Conference in Honour of the Eightieth Birthday of Shaul Lieberman, 13–14 June 1978*, Jerusalem, pp. 12–76. [Hebrew]

Ta-Shema, I. (1984–85), 'Sifriatam shel ḥakhme Ashkenaz bene ha-meʾah ha-ʾaḥat ʿesreh', *Kiryat Sefer*, 60: 298–309.

Urbach, E. E. (1969), *HZ"L. Emunot we-deʿot*, Jerusalem.

Urbach, E. E. (1979), *The Sages: Their Concepts and Beliefs*, 2nd enlarged edn., trans. I. Abrahams, 2 vols., Jerusalem; 1st edn. 1975.

Weiss Halivni, D. (1968–82), *Meqorot umasorot*, 4 vols., Tel Aviv and Jerusalem.

Zahavy, Tz. (1977), *The Traditions of Eleazar b. Azariah*, Missoula, MT.

Zunz, L. (1892), *Die gottesdienstlichen Vorträge der Juden historisch entwickelt*, 2nd edn., Frankfurt am Main; repr. Hildesheim, 1966.

4

The *Status Quaestionis* of Research in Rabbinic Literature

CHAIM MILIKOWSKY

THE ATTEMPT BY PETER SCHÄFER[1] TO DEFINE THE STATE OF PRESENT-DAY RESEARCH into rabbinic literature is certainly commendable. The questions he raises are thought-provoking and important; indeed, all future editors of rabbinic texts will need to come to terms with his hypothesis. Notwithstanding the tentative nature of much of his argumentation, he does present a case and offer a number of conclusions. Several of these conclusions, however, must be seen as assumptions unsubstantiated by empirical evidence and it is therefore essential to delineate the problematic in his paper. It is not my intention to offer a line-by-line critique of Schäfer's article; indeed, I will barely touch upon the first half.[2]

My interest lies primarily in two subjects Schäfer discusses in a number of different contexts: (1) the text and its redaction, and (2) the question of inter-relationships between different rabbinic works. As we shall see, Schäfer considers these two questions to be different aspects of one problem and his conclusion is extreme; our perspective will be radically different.

---

[1] Schäfer (1986). The framework of this article is that of a response to Schäfer but it goes further than that in outlining some of the questions facing rabbinic research today, especially in the area of textual analysis. The article is programmatic and therefore all tangential discussions have been relegated to the notes, which are sometimes quite lengthy. References have been kept to a minimum. (Translations of Hebrew titles are used when a translated title page is available.)

[2] It must be noted, however, that his characterisation of Epstein (1957) and Epstein (1962) (see Chapter 3, pp. 51–2 above) as examples of the 'traditional-halakhic' approach, which he then defines as 'systematic-theological', is inexplicable to me. This last term, 'systematic-theological', has an exceedingly strange ring to it; its transfer from Christian theology to rabbinic literature is not successful. More importantly, though it is correct to say that Lieberman, whom Schäfer also mentions there, adopted a 'traditional-halakhic' model, this model had very critical underpinnings, as is self-evident to anyone who has used his commentaries to the Palestinian Talmud and the Tosefta, and should not be confused with a fundamentalist approach to the texts. Regarding Epstein, his books, in their rigorous attempts at source-criticism (especially true for his *Introduction to Tannaitic Literature* [in Hebrew]), have just about nothing in common with the traditional halakhic approach. (On the fascinating combination of the 'traditional' and the 'critical' in Lieberman's work, see especially the short biographical portrait by Dimitrovsky 1984.)

Proceedings of the British Academy **165**, 67–78. © The British Academy 2010.

Schafer's basic conclusions are made abundantly clear at the end. His recommendation that the research approach felicitous to rabbinic literature demands concentration on the manuscript traditions is, of course, eminently acceptable. There is just about no one in the world of rabbinic scholarship who would quarrel with this point. In fact, both Lieberman and Epstein, whose methodological presuppositions are set in contrast to modern critical scholarship by Schäfer (see n. 2), constantly emphasised the same notion: every manuscript tradition must be examined and studied closely, and the diverse traditions should not be jumbled together.

Schäfer, however, suggests (1986: 151–2) that this is necessary because 'most of the works of rabbinic literature are artificial products which at best mirror the historical reality of the last redactor, and at worst, the historical reality of the modern "critical" editor'; and further on he says, 'the *Urtext* . . . in most cases . . . never existed'. In other words, he seems to be convinced that there is no one single 'work' which can be identified as Bereshit Rabbah or as the Tosefta, rather there is only Bereshit Rabbah MS Vatican 60, Bereshit Rabbah MS Vatican 30, etc.; the differences between the various manuscripts of what is usually considered one work are simply too great to allow for this identification. This is indeed an extreme claim and one would expect it to be preceded by extensive textual analysis of at least several rabbinic works. Schäfer's argumentation is programmatic rather than analytic, and at its core appears to be based upon impressionistic assumptions which, to my mind, do not withstand careful scrutiny.[3]

Though Schäfer's allusion to the Hekhalot literature is not at all lengthy, it is clear that he views many questions concerning rabbinic literature through the prism of his work on the Hekhalot texts.[4] In those texts, he writes, the boundaries between the works are extremely fluid, and it is difficult, if not impossible, to define any specific work. However, even without entering into the question of the rabbinic origin of the Hekhalot literature, this literature is in no way prototypical for the majority of works included in the rabbinic corpus.[5]

While arguing against the validity of considering any individual rabbinic work a stable entity, Schäfer makes some very strong assertions about rabbinic literature in general: he perceives recensions everywhere and doubts

---

[3] There is going to be therefore a basic epistemological problem in much of this paper. The task facing me is disproving the existence of a three-headed cat, when no one has yet cited any evidence proving the existence of such a cat.

[4] He published a synoptic edition of these texts: Schäfer (1981). Both before this edition and since, he has published numerous articles dealing with text-criticism, all of them focusing on the Hekhalot treatises; see Chapter 3, p. 60 above.

[5] The obvious distinctions between rabbinic literature and the Hekhalot texts are summarised towards the end of the discussion.

the possibility of discerning conclusive redactorial activity. However, rabbinic textual criticism is still in its infancy, and few works have had their textual traditions analysed sufficiently for us to delineate the history of the development of the text; consequently, one should be hesitant in the conclusions one draws.[6]

The extent of major variations between the different manuscripts of early rabbinic texts does not appear to be greater than that of the Greek Bible, for example. On the contrary, it is considerably less than the extent of variation in the Septuagint with its different recensions, and very possibly even less than the New Testament.[7] There are an immense number of minor variants, but these are irrelevant to any discussion of redactional identity.[8]

Schäfer's comments concerning Bereshit Rabbah (pp. 57–9 above) are paradigmatic of his approach—'the variations [of the manuscripts] are sometimes so great that the redactional identity of the work is debatable'. Again, as already noted, no evidence is cited. My own conclusion from reading the text, utilising Theodor-Albeck's critical edition, the facsimile edition of MS Vatican 60, and Sokoloff's edition of the Genizah fragments,[9] is that there is no reason to doubt the redactional identity of the work: the variations found in the manuscripts conform to the hypothesis that there was one single work

---

[6] Among the material which should be cited in any attempt to argue for recensional variations, the following should be included: Sokoloff's dissertataion (1971: 221–66) (a list of variants between MS Vatican 60 and the other manuscripts); Sokoloff (1982: 54); Rosenthal (1964: 63). The existence of different versions of the same midrash, e.g. Eikhah Rabbah, is of course irrelevant to Schäfer's claim concerning the lack of clearly defined entities in rabbinic literature; here the differences between the versions are extensive and no one would claim they are the same work, as one does regarding Bereshit Rabbah Vatican 30 and Bereshit Rabbah Vatican 60. There are simply two separate entities known as Eikhah Rabbah, which had a complex joint history up to a certain point, though unfortunately this joint history cannot be reconstructed by philological techniques. A similar situation exists with regard to Avot d'Rabbi Natan. We have explicitly excluded the Mishnah and Talmud from our discussion; an analysis of their unique problems is beyond the limits of this paper.

[7] I am, of course, referring to the variations found in all manuscripts of the Greek Bible, not just those included in the popular critical editions, where the editors generally limit themselves with regard to the types of variants they cite.

[8] There are several factors specific to rabbinic philology which cause the number of variants to any midrashic text to balloon, but have absolutely no relevance to the text itself. One of these is the prevalence of biblical citations in the Midrash: hardly any scribe would feel himself bound by the portion of the verse cited by his *Vorlage* and each would expand or decrease the number of words cited at will. Orthographical variants and the widespread practice of abbreviating words and phrases are additional sources of countless variants which affect the text not at all. Additionally, Semitic syntax, especially in rabbinic texts, is much less structured than that of Greek, and consequently alterations in word order and the like will not necessarily be considered 'changes' by the transmitters of the texts.

[9] Theodor and Albeck (eds. 1965); *Midrash Bereshit Raba Codex Vatican 60* (1972); Sokoloff (dissertation, 1971).

known as Bereshit Rabbah, and that after its redaction it was generally considered a closed work.[10]

Furthermore, the question of recensional variation should not be identified with the question of redactional identity.[11] To the extent that recensional variations can be shown to exist among the manuscript traditions of Bereshit Rabbah—and this is certainly a possibility—one possible explanation, and not necessarily the most plausible one, would be the lack of distinctive and deliberative redactorial activity. A more probable explanation of these variations would locate them in the medieval transmission history of these texts. It is well known that some traditions of Jewish scribal activity did not hesitate to 'correct' the text by emending it and adding to it, thereby causing the text to receive the shape it—to the scribes' minds—should have had originally. This would create recensional variation, but by no means should we call this a new redaction of the text, which had already received its fixed form centuries earlier.[12]

In a very real sense, the question facing us is to define the mind set of the scholars and sages who transmitted these texts in the earliest times. Did they see them as open or closed? One of the crucial questions, therefore, pertains to the number of manuscripts exhibiting recensional variations. If the tradition is relatively stable, and only one or two manuscripts persistently contain widely divergent readings, then we should ascribe this variation to the vagaries of the scribes of these specific manuscripts. The claim that a work has no redactional unity implies that no one considered it a closed work, and so these variations should be attested in all streams of the tradition.

Of course, the first step in all of this is the analysis of the manuscript tradition of each rabbinic work, and as I noted above, this task is still in its infancy. In contrast to Schäfer's suggestion that the variations among the manuscripts are so great we must doubt the redactional identity of much of rabbinic literature, I would like to suggest that we have barely begun the groundwork which will let us decide if recensional variations exist.

---

[10] In this context reference should be made to Margulies (1972: vol. 5, Introduction, pp. xxxix–xl [in Hebrew]); his formulation is very much exaggerated.

[11] The distinction between simple variants and recensional variation is basically one of degree and extent. With regard to redaction, however, other factors, such as type of variant, date, and intent, must be considered. In other words, 'recension' is related to 'revising' while 'redaction' is related to 'editing'. Though obviously the line separating these activities is sometimes blurred, that does not mean it should be erased.

[12] Much of the evidence for this type of relatively unrestrained tampering with the text comes from Ashkenaz (northern France and Germany); see the wide-ranging study by Ta-Shma (1984–85), and our remarks concerning the text of Tosefta Sotah in MS Erfurt, below, n. 19. Ta-Shma's conclusions regarding Ashkenazic intervention in rabbinic texts need to be corrected; see my note in Milikowsky (1985–87) for further detail.

The number of rabbinic texts whose manuscript traditions have undergone rigorous stemmatic analysis is small indeed. The first publication of a stemma (though he did not call it that) by an editor of a major rabbinic text was that of L. Finkelstein (1931–32); unfortunately, it is also one of the few that have ever been published, and it has not received the attention it deserves. The reason for this state of affairs has more to do with sociology than scholarship: Finkelstein's subsequent critical edition of the Sifre on Deuteronomy was criticised extensively, for reasons which do not concern us here, by J. N. Epstein (1936–37), and more moderately by S. Lieberman (1937–38). Consequently, the theoretical basis for the edition, the previously published stemma, was also discredited, or at the very least, ignored. An excellent stemma—with copious justificat ion—was recently published by M. Kahana (dissertation 1982: 228–76; the stemma is found on p. 276). With regard to another tannaitic midrash, Professor D. Boyarin has informed me in a private communication that his researches in the text of the Mekhilta indicate that stemmatic analysis of this work is crucial for the correct understanding of the development of its manuscript tradition: very often the Urtext can be reconstructed on the basis of this analysis. In my edition of Seder Olam, I included an extensive discussion of the stemmatic relationships as well as a *stemma codicum* (Milikowsky, dissertation 1981a: 123–92; the stemma is found on p. 162). The importance of these analyses for our question cannot be over-emphasised. The very fact that the manuscript traditions of these rabbinic texts allow for stemmatic analysis indicates that we are dealing with clearly distinguishable texts, to which we can apply the accepted canons of textual criticism.

More typical, however, is the situation with regard to Bereshit Rabbah, perhaps the most important, and almost definitely the earliest, Amoraic midrashic text. Though short descriptions of the major manuscripts are found in Albeck's introduction to the Theodor-Albeck edition and excellent descriptions of the Genizah fragments in Sokoloff's publication,[13] neither of these works presents an authoritative or thorough analysis of the textual tradition. In contradistinction to the policy of editors of classical texts, where the stemmatic analysis is often one of the crucial sections of the introduction, Albeck (1960: 137) devotes exactly one page to discussing the relationships between the manuscripts. Furthermore, the stemmatic drawing presented does not especially conform to his few lines of discussion. Schäfer writes that the 'best discussion of the manuscripts of Bereshit Rabbah can now be found' in Sokoloff's work, but this is incorrect: Sokoloff's book deals with the Genizah fragments and, quite appropriately, does not include any description of the complete manuscripts of Bereshit Rabbah. (Though his Table of

---

[13] See Theodor and Albeck (eds. 1965) and Sokoloff (1982).

Contents states 'Description of MSS', this refers only to the Genizah manuscripts.) Only those manuscripts closely related to one or more Genizah fragments, such as the London and Vatican manuscripts, are mentioned, and his stemmatic drawing on page 55 includes only these manuscripts.[14]

Consequently, though a good edition of Bereshit Rabbah is available, as well as an excellent edition of the Genizah fragments, there has been no serious attempt at stemmatic analysis, or for that matter any other type of textual criticism involving analysis of the interrelationships among the primary and secondary witnesses to the text. It is my conviction, as noted above, that the stemmatic analysis of Bereshit Rabbah will lead us to the following conclusions: (1) its redactorial identity is clear-cut,[15] and (2) there is no significant recensional variation. At the very least, though, let us recognise the fact that there is a great deal of work to be done here.

This is not to say I am convinced it is possible to reconstruct the Urtext of Bereshit Rabbah; I am simply saying that I know of no evidence which leads me to believe that such an Urtext never existed. There is of course a world of difference between the claim that there was no Urtext and the claim that it is not recoverable. The inability to reconstruct the original text can result from many different factors, for example: the manuscripts preserved are of poor quality, the manuscript tradition is so contaminated it is impossible to determine the lines of transmission, or the textual analysis presents us with two hyperarchetypes, either of which can preserve the original reading. None of these difficulties have anything to do with the original redactional identity of the work.

It is worth emphasising further just how ungrounded is rabbinic textual criticism. Earlier we noted that the number of works which have undergone rigorous stemmatic analysis is small. For many of the classics of rabbinic literature, no proper edition of their entire texts, nor even lists of their *variae lectionis*, exist. A comparison to the New Testament or to classical literature indicates how embarrassing the situation is. Instead of the sanguine possibility of various editors arguing about the correct reading, as is the case with the New Testament and many works of classical literature, scholars of rabbinics consider themselves fortunate when manuscript material has been made available, even if the citations are haphazard and the method non-critical.

One finds arguments similar to those of Schäfer, and clearly influenced by him, in a recent article: 'the final texts of the Mekilta of Rabbi Ishmael

---

[14] The correct understanding of that drawing is also relevant to our discussion: it should not be taken as a technical stemma codicum, but rather as a loose representation of the relationships between the manuscripts. For example, if technically construed the stemma would imply that MSS Geniza-10, Geniza-12 and Vatican 60 (first half) form a family against MS Geniza-2, yet from the text it is clear that Sokoloff does not mean this.

[15] This is also presumably the position of Sokoloff himself, as can be inferred by the presence of the phrase 'the original Bereshit Rabbah' at the top of his stemma.

offered in Horovitz-Rabin and in Lauterbach diverge alarmingly from each other'.[16] This is an exaggeration. The divergences between these two editions do derive from the differences between the various witnesses to the text, but on the whole are not so great as to be 'alarming', nor do they prove that the Mekhilta exhibits a 'wide degree of variation between the manuscripts'.[17] No evidence is presented for the suggestion made that 'because of the wide degree of variation between the manuscripts of major rabbinic works . . . we should be talking in terms of different recensions'. As someone who uses the manuscripts of the Mekhilta and the Sifre constantly in my research, I strongly disagree with these formulations. Indeed, the amount of variation between the manuscripts of the tannaitic midrashim is considerably less than that of Bereshit Rabbah. Furthermore, as we noted above, classical stemmatic theory has proven to be eminently applicable to these texts.

To conclude this point therefore: my answer to Schäfer's question (p. 61 above), 'are there texts that can be defined and clearly delimited?', is 'yes'. The Tosefta, Mekhilta, Sifra, Sifrei, Bereshit Rabbah, Vayyikra Rabbah, and many more can be clearly delimited. The presence of variants in these texts is a function of their transmission history, not of the absence of redaction. With regard to recensional variations I am more hesitant; guessing is simply no substitute for research.

The most crucial evidence for these being clearly delimited is simply the suitability of the critical edition format for dealing with the manuscript material. In contradistinction to the Hekhalot texts, where Schäfer argued for the necessity of producing synoptic editions, there can be no doubt that the traditional format of a critical edition with a single text printed is suitable for the vast majority of rabbinic texts. Schäfer claims that the redacted treatises of Hekhalot literature studied through the course of the twentieth century 'are largely a fiction of modern scholarship',[18] and the manuscripts must

---

[16] Alexander (1983a). The influence of Schäfer's claims can be seen at the end of his n. 2 (p. 239), where he calls Schäfer's synoptic edition of Hekhalot literature (above, n. 4) 'the high-water mark of the current trend . . . in the editing of Rabbinic [!] texts'. In his review of that edition, Alexander (1983b: 103) suggests that it is a 'model for the editing of all early Rabbinic literature and . . . will put an end to the debate on how to edit Rabbinic literature'.

[17] The divergences between the editions basically stem from the fact that only Lauterbach's Mekhilta is a 'critical edition' in the sense that the term is generally used: choosing from among all the readings available, the best—based upon (1) the evidence from manuscripts and early editions and (2) the conclusions of the editor concerning the original meaning of the text. In the Horovitz-Rabin edition, the *editio princeps* was used and rarely changed; even the confluence of all the manuscripts against the printed editions was not sufficient reason to print the reading of the manuscripts. Consequently, most of the peculiar readings of the *editio princeps*, and there are many, have been retained in the Horovitz-Rabin edition. Just recently, there appeared a succinct discussion of the respective strengths and weaknesses of the two editions; see Kahana (1985–86).

[18] So P. S. Alexander summarising Schäfer's argument in his review of Schäfer's edition of the Hekhalot texts (Alexander 1983b: 105).

be presented synoptically. This is most definitely not true for rabbinic literature.[19]

Unfortunately, Schäfer does not present us with a conceptual model to explain his notion of non-delimited texts. It is surprising that no mention is made of the relevance of the oral transmission model for the understanding of the formulation of rabbinic texts. This model can offer an easy explanation of the absence of a definitive Urtext, in spite of the evidence which indicates that there was deliberate redactorial activity.

Thus, in the case of the Babylonian Talmud, it has been argued that in some sense it is improper to talk of a finished one-time redaction. Throughout the Geonic period the authoritative Talmud text was the oral one, not the written text. This allows for the possibility (though it does not necessitate it) that the deliberate redactorial activity—and about this there is no question, since there are few manuscript variations with regard to the substance of any talmudic *sugya*—was concerned with the essentials of the text and not with its exact formulation. This would mean that there was no one absolute Urtext ever in existence.[20]

---

[19] This is not to say that synoptic editions of all of rabbinic literature would not be useful; on the contrary, I am sure that all scholars of rabbinics would welcome such editions, if only because of their ease of use and their expediency in presenting the manuscript evidence to the reader. (The Saul Lieberman Institute for Talmudic Research at the Jewish Theological Seminary of America has begun a project to produce computer-generated synoptic texts (called variorum editions by the Lieberman Institute) of talmudic literature; since the variants are not inordinately great, the synopses will be arranged by line and not by column. Note also the Frankfurter Judaistische Studien editions of Pesikta Rabbati: devoting an entire volume to each chapter and having few witnesses to the text, they decided to print all the witnesses, line-under-line.) The question is rather if such an edition is the only proper way to present the text. There have been some examples of synoptic editions of rabbinic texts, but these have been justified more for simplicity of use than as necessitated by recensional variations or even by the wide disparity among the various manuscripts. See A. Goldberg's editions of Mishnah, tractate Shabbat (Goldberg 1976) and tractate Eruvin (Goldberg 1986). S. Lieberman, in his edition of the Tosefta (Lieberman 1955–73), printed much of the text of tractate Sotah in parallel columns, that is synoptically, according to MS Vienna and MS Erfurt, rather than following his usual custom of basing his text upon MS Vienna and citing the readings of MS Erfurt, together with the other variants, in the apparatus. Even though MS Vienna has generally preserved the original text of the Tosefta (see Milikowsky 1979–80), and MS Erfurt seems to have undergone that type of radical Ashkenazi revision referred to above (see n. 12), the parallel columns are justified because of Lieberman's explicit desire to delineate the lines of transmission and study through the Middle Ages. We have here, in these chapters of Tosefta Sotah, a classic case of recensional variation, where the two texts diverge sufficiently to create a need for a synoptic edition (for the reasons just noted), yet this is clearly a medieval development, and is irrelevant to any discussion of the redaction of Tosefta Sotah. Thus this synoptic edition does not support Schäfer's claim; on the contrary, it counters it. The synoptic edition of Avot d'Rabbi Natan is not relevant to our discussion; see n. 6 above.

[20] This is the basic argument of the late E. S. Rosenthal, elaborated on in several public lectures which have not yet appeared in print. [See now E. S. Rosenthal, 'The history of the text and problems of redaction in the study of the Babylonian Talmud', *Tarbiz*, 57 (1987–88), 1–36.] In a

Whether or not this understanding of the redactorial activity of the Babylonian Talmud is accepted, it is valid only because we can identify a *Sitz im Leben* for the oral redaction and transmission of this text—the academy. With regard to a text like Bereshit Rabbah, however, or other midrashic works, though obviously the vast majority of the individual passages and discourses were originally composed and transmitted orally, there is no reason to suggest that the transmission of the text as a whole was oral. Furthermore, it appears that the dimensions of manuscript variation in midrashic literature are of a different sort than those of the Babylonian Talmud. Consequently, even if one were to argue that the manuscript evidence suggests the need for an oral-redaction-and-transmission model for the Babylonian Talmud, it does not for these other texts.[21]

In my discussion up to this point, I have repeatedly stressed that this analysis applies to early rabbinic literature. When one turns to late midrashic texts—I am thinking specifically of the Tanḥuma-Yelammedenu literature—the circumstances appear to be different. It has, of course, been known for a long time that there is no one edition of Midrash Tanḥuma, and one of the dominant scholarly tendencies at present is to suggest that there never was one single edition from which all the others derive.[22] Especially important in this context is the discovery of numerous fragments belonging to this genre of midrashic literature in the Genizah.[23] Very possibly, during the period when this literature was being created, the editors-homileticists of this late type of midrash, which itself is very much based on borrowings from earlier midrashic texts, did not see the texts they produced as closed. Every scribe allowed himself the freedom to re-edit and every scholar the freedom to reformulate,[24] and it would indeed be wrongheaded to search for the original Midrash Tanḥuma.

---

forthcoming study, Dr Robert Brody of the Talmud Department at Hebrew University develops a sophisticated oral-and-written transmission model to explain the nature of variants in the direct and indirect traditions of the Babylonian Talmud. [See now Y. (R.) Brody, 'Safrut ha-ge'onim ve-ha-teqst ha-talmudi', in Y. Sussman and D. Rosenthal (eds.), *Meḥqerei Talmud*, vol. 1 (Jerusalem, 1990), pp. 237–303.]

[21] Cf. Shinan (1981). The evidence he presents does not sufficiently substantiate his claim for the continuing interplay between the oral transmission of aggadah and its written transmission, though, of course, it is theoretically feasible that scribes changed their texts under the influence of oral traditions.

[22] My formulation is a bit different from the brief but suggestive comments of E. E. Urbach (1966: 3).

[23] M. Bregman is presently preparing a dissertation on this topic, and hopefully we will all be more knowledgeable after it appears. [A slightly revised version of the dissertation is available as M. Bregman, *The Tanḥuma-Yelammedenu Literature: Studies in the Evolution of the Versions*, Piscataway, NJ [Hebrew].]

[24] An example of this freedom is presented in Milikowsky (1981b).

Let us now turn to the question of determining interrelationships between various works in the rabbinic corpus. Schäfer discusses, in relatively great detail, the relationship between the Tosefta and the Mishnah and the relationship between the Palestinian Talmud and Bereshit Rabbah. In his comments on the latter two texts, he raises the following question (or actually two questions), 'Does Bereshit Rabbah quote Yerushalmi, i.e. can we regard Bereshit Rabbah and Yerushalmi *at the time of the redaction of Bereshit Rabbah* [emphasis original] as two clearly distinguishable works . . . ?' These two questions are not at all the same. The first question in the sentence quoted leads to Schäfer's conclusion: it is incorrect to say that the redactor of Bereshit Rabbah used the Yerushalmi we have today. This, of course, is obvious. Indeed, in contrast to the supposed *communis opinio* Schäfer identifies, I would say that this approach is the dominant one in the study of rabbinics today: no one would suggest that Bereshit Rabbah used the Yerushalmi we know.

But this has nothing to do with the alleged impossibility of considering the Yerushalmi or Bereshit Rabbah as clearly defined entities. Instead of focusing on these works as a whole, the discussion of the relationship of Bereshit Rabbah and the Yerushalmi should be transferred to the small literary units themselves, as Schäfer does in his discussion of the Mishnah and the Tosefta. Important questions can be raised in this new context: what does it mean to talk of this passage being included in an earlier 'edition' of the Yerushalmi, if the only evidence for its existence is Bereshit Rabbah? Can we develop methodologically rigorous criteria which will allow us to posit the existence of an earlier non-extant text?

Let me emphasise, however, that these questions have absolutely nothing to do with the question of redaction. Some scholars have posited a proto-Yerushalmi and others have expressed their doubts, but why should the suggestion that there was an earlier form of the Yerushalmi negate the redactional identity of either the Yerushalmi we know or Bereshit Rabbah? The pre-redaction history of Bereshit Rabbah, i.e. the question of the sources used by its redactor, should not be confused with its post-redaction history, i.e. the history of its transmission, nor be relevant to the question of its redactional identity.[25]

Here again, the oral transmission model can be of crucial significance in relating to this problem. Our concern will be with the oral transmission of the various tradition-units before their inclusion in the various works.

---

[25] In order to prove that the pre-redaction history of the text is part of a continuum with the post-redaction history of the text, i.e. there was no real redaction, it would be necessary to compare the various types of variants from the different periods of the history of the text and show that there are no substantive differences.

Our model assumes that the basic form of literary transmission in the rabbinic period was oral, and that thousands of tradition-units were transmitted in this manner, both independently and as parts of literary units not preserved in the post-rabbinic period, an oral transmission that continued until, and also after, their inclusion in the various larger literary works, such as the Mishnah and the Tosefta. Very possibly, a later literary work will incorporate an earlier formulation of a tradition-unit preserved by oral transmission, while an earlier literary work could contain an evolved version of this same tradition-unit. Consequently, as is indeed assumed by Schäfer, any attempt to delineate an absolute relationship—not to speak of the claim of direct dependence—between two of the larger literary works is just about doomed to failure.[26]

This model explains therefore why there has been no resolution of the two questions Schäfer examines, and which have been discussed so often in the past: the attempt to define an absolute overall relationship (1) between the Mishnah and the Tosefta, and (2) between the Yerushalmi and Bereshit Rabbah.

This futility, however, stems from the mistaken perspective of much of the debate: analysing relationships between the tradition-units as evidence for the relationships between the finished literary works. But this problem tells us absolutely nothing about the redactional identity of any of these works nor how well-defined they are as literary works: Schäfer's juxtaposing of the two questions, as well as his general conclusions about the nature of the redactorial process in rabbinic literature, should not be accepted.

Note.   This chapter was first published in the *Journal of Jewish Studies*, 39 (1989): C. Milikowsky, 'The *status quaestionis* of research in rabbinic literature', *JJS* 39: 201–11.

Bibliography

Albeck, Ch. (1960), *Mavo la-Mishnah*, Jerusalem.

Alexander, P. S. (1983a), 'Rabbinic Judaism and the New Testament', *Zeitschrift für die Neutestamentliche Wissenschaft*, 74: 237–46.

Alexander, P. S. (1983b), '[Review of] P. Schäfer, *Synopse zur Hekhalot Literatur*', *JJS* 34: 102–6.

Dimitrovsky, H. Z. (1984), 'Mi-parshanut le-mehqar', in *Le-zikhro shel Sha'ul Lieberman*, Jerusalem, pp. 34–49.

---

[26] My conclusions about the dependence of Tosefta Sotah on Seder Olam in Milikowsky (1979–80) are to a large part dependent upon my previous conclusion that the compositional process of Seder Olam was radically different from that of rabbinic literature in general; see Milikowsky (1985: 118–19).

Epstein, J. N. (1936–37), '[Review of] L. Finkelstein (ed.), *Sifre on Deuteronomy'*, *Tarbiz*, 8: 375–92. [Hebrew]

Epstein, J. N. (1957), *Mevo'ot le-sifrut ha-tana'im*, Jerusalem and Tel Aviv. [Hebrew]

Epstein, J. N. (1962), *Mevo'ot le-sifrut ha-amora'im*, Jerusalem and Tel Aviv. [Hebrew]

Finkelstein, L. (1931–32), 'Prolegomena to an edition of the Sifre on Deuteronomy', *Proceedings of the American Academy for Jewish Research*, 3: 3–42.

Goldberg, A. (1976), *Mishna: Tractate Shabbat*, Jerusalem. [Hebrew]

Goldberg, A. (1986), *Mishna: Tractate 'Eruvin*, Jerusalem. [Hebrew]

Kahana, M. (1982), 'Prolegomena to a New Edition of the Sifre on Numbers', Ph.D. dissertation, Hebrew University, Jerusalem. [Hebrew]

Kahana, M. (1985–86), 'The critical edition[s] of Mekilta de-Rabbi Ishmael in the light of the Geniza fragments', *Tarbiz*, 55: 489–93. [Hebrew]

Lieberman, S. (1937–38), '[Review of] L. Finkelstein (ed.), *Sifre on Deuteronomy'*, *Kiryat Sefer*, 17: 323–36. [Hebrew]

Lieberman, S. (1955–73), *Tosefta*, New York.

Margulies, M. (1972), *Midrash Vayyikra Rabba*, vol. 5, Jerusalem.

Midrash Bereshit Raba Codex Vatican 60 (1972), Jerusalem.

Milikowsky, C. (1979–80), 'Seder 'Olam and the Tosefta', *Tarbiz*, 49: 246–63. [Hebrew]

Milikowsky, C. (1981a), 'Seder Olam: A Rabbinic Chronography', Ph.D. dissertation, Yale University.

Milikowsky, C. (1981b), 'The punishment of Jacob: a study in the redactorial process of Midrash Tanḥuma', *Annual of Bar Ilan University: Studies in Judaica and the Humanities*, 18–19: 144–9. [Hebrew]

Milikowsky, C. (1985), 'Seder 'Olam and Jewish chronography in the Hellenistic and Roman periods', *Proceedings of the American Academy for Jewish Research*, 52: 115–39.

Milikowsky, C. (1985–87), 'Text-types and recensions in rabbinic literature', *Kiryat Sefer*, 61: 169–70. [Hebrew]

Rosenthal, E. S. (1964), 'Ha-moreh', *Proceedings of the American Academy for Jewish Research*, 32: 1–71. [Hebrew]

Schäfer, P. (1981), *Synopse zur Hekhalot Literatur*, Texte und Studium zur Antiken Judentum 2, Tübingen.

Schäfer, P. (1986), 'Research into rabbinic literature: an attempt to define the *Status Quaestionis'*, *JJS* 37: 139–52.

Shinan, A. (1981), 'Safrut ha-aggadah: bein higgud 'al-peh u-mesoret ketuvah', in *Mehkerei Yerushalayim be-folkor yehudi*, vol. 1, Jerusalem, pp. 44–60.

Sokoloff, M. (1971), 'The Geniza Fragments of Genesis Rabba and Ms Vat. Ebr. 60 of Genesis Rabba', Ph.D. dissertation, Hebrew University, Jerusalem. [Hebrew]

Sokoloff, M. (1982), *The Geniza Fragments of Bereshit Rabba*, Jerusalem. [Hebrew]

Ta-Shma, I. (1984–85), 'Sifriyatam shel hakhmei Ashkenaz benei ha-me'ah ha'ahat esreh-ha-shtem esreh', *Kiryat Sefer*, 60: 298–309.

Theodor, J. and Albeck, Ch. (eds.) (1965), *Bereshit Rabba*, 2nd edn., 3 vols., Jerusalem.

Urbach, E. E. (1966), 'Sridei Tanḥuma Yelammedenu', in *Kobez al yad*, vol. 6 (16), Jerusalem, 3–54. [Hebrew]

5

Current Views on the Editing of the Rabbinic Texts of late Antiquity: Reflections on a Debate after Twenty Years

PETER SCHÄFER AND CHAIM MILIKOWSKY

Response by Peter Schäfer[1]

I BEGIN BY BRIEFLY EMPHASISING A COUPLE OF POINTS regarding my 1986 article (republished as Chapter 3 of this volume). First, as I wrote in my response to Chaim Milikowsky in 1989 (Schäfer 1989), the article was deliberately programmatic, subjective and polemical. I wanted to shake up our discipline with some pointed, occasionally overstated, remarks on the state of the field of rabbinic literature. And with this, as it would appear, I certainly succeeded.

Second, my article was by no means only concerned with *editing* rabbinic texts; rather, it was concerned with (and concerned about) the way we, as scholars today, approach rabbinic literature in order to learn something about the people behind this literature, their concepts and beliefs (*emunot ve-de'ot*). This should not be forgotten—despite the turn the article takes in its second part and Chaim Milikowsky's response, which focuses solely on the rabbinic text and its redaction and the question of interrelationships between different rabbinic works. Milikowsky's response (1988; Chapter 4 of this volume) has succeeded in gearing the debate here to this more limited problem, the proposition 'that manuscript variations make the search for an original form of late-antique rabbinic texts an impossible task'.

If anything, our debate has made clear that 'manuscript variations' is a mixed bag. If we mean by it just 'variant readings' (*variae lectiones*) of a certain text in different manuscripts, in most cases it would be hard to argue that

---

[1] These remarks constitute more or less unchanged the text of my address in the Academy which was presented as part of a public debate with Chaim Milikowsky on the proposition that manuscript variations make the search for an original form of late-antique rabbinic texts an impossible task.

Proceedings of the British Academy **165**, 79–88. © The British Academy 2010.

such variant readings add up to something that renders impossible the search for an original form of the text in question. But 'manuscript variations' can also mean 'recensional variations', that is, variations in the manuscript tradition of a given text that so conspicuously affect its structure and substance that they challenge or call into question what I have labelled the redactional identity of that text. It is precisely this difference between variant readings and structural-recensional variations (leading to different editions of a given text) that remains a major bone of contention between Milikowsky and me. Milikowsky not only constantly argues that *variae lectiones* normally do not affect the redactional identity of a text; he also posits that the same is true for what I call structural or recensional variations. To put it differently and more pointedly: he maintains that in most cases (at least within the formative earlier stages of the rabbinic literature) recensional variations that challenge the redactional identity of rabbinic texts simply do not exist. As I have put it in my rejoinder, Milikowsky neatly distinguishes between a pre-redactional and a post-redactional history of all rabbinic texts, firmly kept at bay by the unshakeable zero-point in between, which functions as the absolute watershed between the essentially distinct pre- and post-redactional histories of the text (Schäfer 1989: 90). With this model in mind, he assigns all variations—small and large, *variae lectiones* and recensional variations— to the medieval transmission history of these texts, claiming that various recensions of a work are always recensions of that *one* redactionally identical work originating before the enigmatic zero-point (no matter whether the manuscript evidence allows us to reconstruct it). I called—and insist on calling—this approach 'static', and I continue to believe that it fails to take into consideration the essentially dynamic and open structure of rabbinic literature. Again, I am not claiming that this latter characterisation applies to all of rabbinic literature to the same extent, but I find it methodologically more fruitful—not least with regard to the fluid boundaries between certain rabbinic works—than the rigid obsession with the one and only Urtext.

This approach has had and still has a direct bearing on the question of how to edit rabbinic texts. After the *Synopse zur Hekhalot-Literatur*, it has become almost fashionable to advocate editions that present the respective manuscripts in a synoptic or even line-by-line edition (what has been called in German a *Partiturtext*, like a musical score), and Milikowsky has directed the full force of his righteous anger against this practice (mainly in reviews in *JQR*). A case in point is his review of Rivka Ulmer's *Synoptic Edition of Pesiqta Rabbati* (Milikowsky 1999), where he distinguishes between what he calls 'transcriptional' or 'diplomatic' and 'critical' editions. According to Milikowsky, only the latter, the 'critical editions', are editions in the true sense of the word because only they '[presuppose] the use of the critical faculty of the human mind to reconstruct—or perhaps it is more fitting to write "construct"—a better text of the work than any that has been preserved in the extant documents' (by 'documents' he means here 'manuscripts') (Milikowsky 1999: 138).

This is a remarkable statement that deserves our close attention. I can live with the allegation that editors of synoptic editions do not use the 'critical faculty of the human mind', but I do have strong reservations against the telling second half of the sentence that the (desired) critical faculty of the human mind consists in constructing a better text than any that has been preserved in the manuscripts. It is precisely this claim that I programmatically and fervently wish to counter with my fondness and preference for uncritical 'transcriptional' editions.

Moreover, I am entirely baffled by Milikowsky's further claim that the 'transcriptional' editions are extremely conservative—in contrast to the truly critical editions that are progressive. My bewilderment grows when I read that this conservative tendency has its roots in late nineteenth- and early twentieth-century Germany, where 'a very conservative tendency prevailed in classical scholarship' (Milikowsky 1999: 142). It is one thing to call German classical scholarship of the nineteenth century conservative (it presumably was), yet it is quite another to hold these conservative German classicists responsible for the allegedly conservative trend in the diplomatic, transcriptional or synoptic editions of rabbinic texts. Historically, just the opposite is true. German classicists were (and many of them still are) the heroes of the *critical* edition (in Milikowsky's sense). They followed the, in my view, extremely conservative (if not arrogant) ideal of the true scholar who—sitting in his *Studierstube*, and by virtue of the critical faculty of his superb human mind—indeed constructed a better text than any of those versions preserved in his manuscripts. With my appeal to synoptic editions (in all their possible variations) I have striven to counter precisely this ideal, whether German or not, and argue for a more open, liberal and, if you wish, democratic approach to the manuscript tradition that puts the available evidence in front of the reader and allows him or her to decide as to the better reading. I would call this approach progressive (one may even want to call it postmodern). In any case, it is this approach—implicitly questioning the Urtext model—that has been followed since the late 1970s by other disciplines such as English and German literature (for example the edition of James Joyce's *Ulysses*, or editions of Hölderlin and Kafka).[2] It is no accident that the diplomatic and even facsimile editions of important German

---

[2] Joyce (1975, 1984). Incidentally, the 1984 edition was prepared with TUSTEP ('Tübingen System of Text Processing Programs'), the same word-processing program used also in the *Synopse zur Hekhalot-Literatur* of 1982. Hölderlin (1975–2008); Kafka: Reuss *et al.* (eds. 1997–).

authors at first appeared under the imprint of the Verlag Roter Stern (later Stroemfeld Verlag), with a clear reference to the Maoist red star. This is hardly an indication of their 'conservative' character.

It seems to me that the questions raised in the debate some twenty years ago have not been settled one way or the other. They are still very much alive. What has become clear, however, is the fact that the solution will not lie in the extremes but somewhere in the middle—not imposing one model on all the respective texts but taking into account the great variety of rabbinic literature.

Response by Chaim Milikowsky

In the approximately twenty years that have passed since Peter Schäfer wrote his important programmatic article on the *status quaestionis* of research into rabbinic literature and I responded to the section of the article dealing with questions of textual identity and redactorial fixation, I have returned time and time again to the fundamental questions he raised in that article.[3] Inasmuch as one of the points I make in that article is that 'rabbinic textual criticism is still in its infancy, and few works have had their textual traditions analysed sufficiently for us to delineate the history of the development of the text', I think it worthwhile to start this overview of the past twenty years by looking at some specific instances where it can fairly be claimed that at least some progress has been made.

Lamentably, it is still true that relatively few works have had the privilege of being the focus of extended textual analysis (of any sort). To paraphrase what I wrote in my original article (p. 72 above), for many of the classic works of rabbinic literature, there exists no scholarly edition of their entire texts, nor even lists of their *variae lectiones*. A comparison with Greek and Latin literature or with the New Testament indicates how embarrassing the situation is. Instead of the sanguine possibility of various editors arguing over correct readings, as is the case with the New Testament and much of classical literature, scholars of rabbinics consider themselves fortunate when manuscript material has been made available, even if the citations are haphazard and the method non-critical.

With regard to two classic early midrashic texts, Bereshit Rabbah and Vayyikra Rabbah, however, much more can be said today than was possible when my original article was published in 1988. Perhaps most importantly, a provisional synoptic edition of the entire text of Vayyikra Rabbah is available

---

[3] See Milikowsky (1999, 2002, 2006a); Milikowsky and Schlüter (1999). See also Teugels (2003, 2005); Visotzky (2005).

online.[4] On the basis of this edition I have presented detailed analyses of a number of passages in Vayyikra Rabbah (Milikowsky 2001–02, 2006b, 2008). These three articles focus on chapters 27, 28 and 30 of Vayyikra Rabbah, all three of which share two important characteristics. First of all, these three chapters, together with chapters 20 and 29, have close parallels in another rabbinic work, Pesikta de-Rab Kahana (Mandelbaum ed. 1962). Secondly, all these chapters exhibit considerably more textual variation than is the norm in Vayyikra Rabbah, textual variation that indeed seems to be recensional variation.

Regarding the first of these points, a word of explanation is necessary. In a certain sense all of rabbinic literature is a literature of parallels/borrowings/ quotations: the number of passages in the Babylonian Talmud that are paralleled in other works of the rabbinic corpus is myriad and the same is true of midrashic works such as Bereshit Rabbah and Vayyikra Rabbah. The crucial point, however, is that these parallels are generally limited to a single tradition-unit, of which all of its parts are in some manner or another connected together.[5] Since rabbinic literature is in its essence an oral-formulated and oral-transmitted literature, the presence of a parallel, even a relatively substantial one, in two works does not indicate that there is a literary relationship between the two works.[6] The passages in the works being compared may very well have had an independent existence outside of these two works and may well have continued their independent existence after their inclusion in these two works, and thus conclusions about the relationship between specific similar passages in the two works cannot be applied automatically to the works themselves.

In contradistinction to this phenomenon, the parallels between Vayyikra Rabbah and Pesikta de-Rab Kahana are of a different sort. For each of the five parallel chapters, the two works are very similar; each generally contains the same six to twelve tradition-units, arranged in more or less identical fashion. The hypothesis that as a result of independent lines of oral transmission parallel passages appear in two unrelated works can explain the parallel

---

[4] This line-under-line synoptic edition of Vayyikra Rabbah was deposited on the internet server of Bar Ilan University and is available at www.biu.ac.il/JS/midrash/VR/. It includes the entire text of all known manuscripts and of the first edition. The preparation of this edition was partially funded by the German–Israel Foundation for Scientific Research and Development (GIF) in a project directed jointly by Professor Margarete Schlüter and by me (GIF Research Grant No. I-0326-231.04/93) and partially funded by the Israel Science Foundation (ISF Grant No. 856/99-2). In this context, mention should also be made of the critical edition of Vayyikra Rabbah, edited by Mordecai Margulies (1972).

[5] This means that the specific tradition-unit can sometimes be several pages long: the crucial point is that there is a common nexus, of whatever sort, joining them.

[6] This does not, of course, exclude the possibility that there is a literary relationship between the two works; my point is simply that it cannot be presumed.

appearance of a single tradition-unit,[7] but not the phenomenon described here, where each of the parallels contains the same six to twelve tradition-units. Thus a literary relationship between the two works must be posited, and one of the questions discussed in my three articles on the subject is the nature of this relationship.

For our purposes here, my most significant conclusion in these studies is that the two characteristics noted above—(1) that these three chapters of Vayyikra Rabbah have close parallels in Pesikta de-Rab Kahana; and (2) that these chapters exhibit considerably more textual variation than is the norm in Vayyikra Rabbah—are related to each other; indeed, the second is dependent upon the first. The relatively major differences between the readings found in the various manuscripts stem from the simple fact that a number of manuscripts of Vayyikra Rabbah either contain the text of Pesikta de-Rab Kahana, and not that of Vayyikra Rabbah,[8] or were strongly influenced by the textual tradition of Pesikta de-Rab Kahana.

It is also worth pointing out that the critical assumption that underlies this series of articles is that each of the two works under discussion has its own moment of textual identity and redactorial fixation. This means that the redactor of Vayyikra Rabbah had his own intentionality when formulating the texts he included within his work, and the redactor of Pesikta de-Rab

---

[7] This is true for the classic midrashic literature corpus. I am consciously simplifying a quite complicated question here. For example, with regard to the Mishnah it is the scholarly consensus that the edited work was transmitted orally, and this would seem to argue against my claim that the hypothesis of the oral transmission of parallel passages can only explain the parallel appearance of a single tradition-unit. But this is exactly my point: it was the edited work the Mishnah which was transmitted orally and any use of that work, whether its transmissional mode was oral or written, posits a literary relationship between the Mishnah and the work that used the Mishnah. Furthermore, it is my conviction that institutional settings which explain and promote the oral transmission of entire works can only be postulated for the Mishnah and the Talmud, and not for works like Vayyikra Rabbah or Bereshit Rabbah. Cf. Mandel (2000).

[8] This claim, which sounds at first glance to be rather radical and fanciful, can be substantiated quite simply. Chapters 28–30 of Vayyikra Rabbah are just about entirely lacking in two manuscripts, and in their place is found a referral—actually three referrals, one at the beginning of each chapter—telling the reader that the passage is found in the Pesikta de-Rab Kahana (which is called simply Pesikta, the common medieval name of this midrashic work). Three other textual witnesses, belonging to the same manuscript family as these two, present a text which is just about identical to the text of Pesikta de-Rab Kahana and quite different from the text found in other manuscripts of Vayyikra Rabbah. The obvious conclusion is that the scribe of the hyperarchetype of this manuscript family decided to lighten his copying load by referring the reader to a parallel passage in another work, and the scribes of later descendants of this hyperarchetype indeed went to this other work and copied from it the relevant missing passage. Consequently, the texts of these chapters in these descendants should certainly not be used in any attempt to reconstruct the text of Vayyikra Rabbah. (The simple logic of this argument was not recognised previously because it has not been the norm in rabbinics scholarship to consider stemmatic relationships, and so it was not previously recognised that these five manuscripts stem from one hyperarchetype.)

Kahana had his own intentionality—which in our case, given the close similarity between the texts being included by the two redactors, can be sometimes identical and sometimes different than the intentionality of the redactor of Vayyikra Rabbah. Much of the work I did in these articles focused upon the reconstruction of the different intentions and ideological articulations that should be ascribed to the two redactors. While I cannot in good conscience assert that my articles demonstrate beyond doubt the textual identity and redactorial fixation of each work, I can say that such a hypothesis corresponds to the textual evidence much better than the hypothesis of free textual variation with no redactorial intentionality. And I can also say the textual evidence in no way supports this latter hypothesis.

With regard to Bereshit Rabbah, the arguments in favour of its textual identity and redactorial fixation are even stronger. I have dealt with this matter in an extended review essay (Milikowsky 2002), and will here summarise the crucial points. Most importantly, there is little major textual variation among the manuscripts of Bereshit Rabbah, and almost nothing that we would call recensional variation. An exceptional type of variation in the textual tradition of Bereshit Rabbah that does come close to what we would call recensional variation is the phenomenon seen in several manuscripts wherein their scribes inserted dozens of additional midrashic passages into the exemplars of Bereshit Rabbah that they were copying. With regard to this phenomenon two comments must be made. First of all, it is present, in various degrees, only in the later manuscripts of Bereshit Rabbah, all penned in the thirteenth century and later, and not at all in the three early manuscripts of Bereshit Rabbah.[9] This shows that what we have here is late variation, hardly relevant to any study of the rabbinic work Bereshit Rabbah. Secondly, what defines many of these sections of text that have been added is that they do not change, and indeed are often unrelated to the parts of Bereshit Rabbah that surround them. It is important to stress that the scribal mentality which permits a scribe to add to a text he is copying is not at all the same as that which permits a scribe to rework the formulation of the received text, and indeed, there is very little evidence of conscious scribal revision in these late textual witnesses.

Much of the seemingly recensional variation that can be found in the early manuscripts of Bereshit Rabbah can be explained by a fascinating phenomenon first identified by Menachem Kahana (1996). He has shown, to my mind conclusively, that the scribe of Vatican 60 often forsook the exemplar of Bereshit Rabbah that was in front of him when a parallel passage existed, and that he inserted the text of the parallel. I showed in my review essay that this phenomenon is indeed rampant in Vatican 60, but that it is

---

[9] These three early manuscripts are London MS BL Add. 27169, Vatican MS Ebr. 30, and Vatican MS Ebr. 60.

also found in the other two early manuscripts of Bereshit Rabbah.[10] Thus, an analysis of the three very different texts of Bereshit Rabbah 59:4 found in the manuscripts, one in Vatican 30, another in Vatican 60, with the third in London BL Add. 27169 and in all other manuscripts, indicates that the versions found in Vatican 30 and in Vatican 60 were generated by the insertion or strong influence of a parallel passage, and should not be considered authentic versions of this tradition.[11]

To summarise and conclude: based upon what I wrote in my original 1988 articles and what I have added here, I see no evidence of any significant recensional variation in any of the classic works of midrash, neither those included in the corpus of midrash halakhah nor those included in the corpus of midrash aggadah.[12] It must, however, be added that the question of the existence and non-existence of recensional variation is very much dependent upon the intentions of the author, the scribes and their immediate audiences. There is of course nothing immanent in classic midrashic works to preclude recensional variation: it is simply a fact that there is no such variation. And of course, there are later midrashic works that do seem to exhibit classic symptoms of recensional variation, i.e. wide, thoroughgoing textual variation that allows neither the generation of a stemmatic analysis nor the close comparison of the variant documents.[13] In a similar vein, there are specific manuscripts of classic midrashic works whose scribes revised their exemplars so thoroughly that the texts they rendered must be considered recensional variations.[14] In the final analysis, however, I can but affirm that the classic

---

[10] See n. 7. It is not found in the later manuscripts of Bereshit Rabbah.

[11] It is worth reflecting on the use of 'authentic' here. Obviously, every variant version is in some sense authentic and also important for specific scholarly purposes. However, if we focus not on the transmissional process, but on the reconstruction and presentation of rabbinic texts, then a version that can be proven to have been formulated by a medieval scribe (1) interests us barely at all; and (2) should not be considered an alternative rabbinic formulation (as Becker considers it in the book I was reviewing).

[12] For some short programmatic comments on the Babylonian Talmud, see Chapter 4 above, pp. 74–5.

[13] In the introduction to her synoptic edition of Pesikta Rabbati (a late midrashic work), Rivka Ulmer claims that 'the redactional identities of Pesiqta Rabbati are manifold and the search for one *Urtext* is futile' (Ulmer ed. 1997: p. lxiii). In my review (Milikowsky 1999: 145–7) I point out that based upon my perusal of the transcriptions available in her edition I have no hesitation in asserting that all five major text-witnesses to Pesikta Rabbati are extremely similar to each other, and that the textual variants do not justify the claim that there is any recensional variation.

[14] I am thinking here specifically of the Munich MS, Bayerische Staatsbibliothek Cod. hebr. 117, of Vayyikra Rabbah. The scribe of this manuscript (or the scribe of one of its ancestors) had in front of him at least two exemplars of Vayyikra Rabbah (and more probably three), a very full library of rabbinic literature from which he did not hesitate to borrow when formulating his own text of Vayyikra Rabbah, and a very idiosyncratic mental vision of what he thought the text of Vayyikra Rabbah should contain, which, interestingly enough, served him as an authoritative guide while going about his scribal tasks.

goal of textual criticism—the reconstruction of the most original version of the work that the extant documents allow us—is eminently suitable to the corpus of midrashic literature.[15]

Bibliography

Hölderlin, F. (1975–2008), *Sämtliche Werke* (*Frankfurter Hölderlin-Ausgabe*), ed. D. E. Sattler, 20 vols., Frankfurt am Main.

Joyce, J. (1975), *Ulysses: A Facsimile of the Manuscript*, Critical Introduction by Harry Levin, Bibliographical Preface by Clive Driver, 3 vols., London and Philadelphia.

Joyce, J. (1984), *Ulysses: A Critical and Synoptic Edition*, ed. H. W. Gabler, W. Steppe and C. Melchior, 3 vols., New York and London.

Kahana, M. (1996), 'Genesis Rabba MS Vatican 60 and its parallels', *Te'uda*, 11: 17–60. [Hebrew]

Mandel, P. (2000), 'Between Byzantium and Islam: the transmission of a Jewish book in the Byzantine and early Islamic periods', in Y. Elman and I. Gershoni (eds.), *Transmitting Jewish Traditions: Orality, Textuality, and Cultural Diffusion*, New Haven, pp. 74–106.

Mandelbaum, B. (ed.) (1962), *Pesiqta d'Rav Kahana*, 2 vols., New York.

Margulies, M. (ed.) (1972), *Vayyiqra Rabba*, 2nd printing, 3 vols., Jerusalem.

Milikowsky, C. (1988), 'The *status quaestionis* of research in rabbinic literature', *JJS* 39: 201–11; repr. as ch. 4 of this volume.

Milikowsky, C. (1996), 'On editing rabbinic texts: a review essay', *JQR* 86: 409–17.

Milikowsky, C. (1999), 'Further on editing rabbinic texts: a review-essay of *A Synoptic Edition of Pesiqta Rabbati Based upon All Extant Manuscripts and the Editio Princeps* by R. Ulmer', *JQR* 90: 137–49.

Milikowsky, C. (2001–02), 'Vayyiqra Rabba, chapter 28, sections 1–3: questions of text, redaction and affinity to Pesiqta d'Rav Kahana', *Tarbiz*, 71: 19–65. [Hebrew]

Milikowsky, C. (2002), 'On the formation and transmission of Bereshit Rabba and the Yerushalmi: questions of redaction, text-criticism and literary relationships: a review-essay of *Die grossen rabbinischen Sammelwerke Palästinas: Zur literarischen Genese von Talmud Yerushalmi und Midrash Bereshit Rabba* by H.-J. Becker', *JQR* 92: 521–67.

Milikowsky, C. (2006a), 'Reflections on the practice of textual criticism in the study of Midrash Aggada: the legitimacy, the indispensability and the feasibility of recovering and presenting the (most) original text', in C. Bakhos (ed.), *Current*

---

[15] This is not to deny that there is another very important goal of textual criticism, and that is to investigate the manuscript affiliations and the development of the tradition as a whole, allowing us to see what individual redactors, transmitters and scribes constructed from the antecedent material, and thus to trace the progression of the dynamic text as it unfolds through time. At times, this goal may be more important than the goal of reconstruction—and it is always a more feasible goal than the goal of reconstruction—but we should never make the mistake of concluding that it is the most primary and most significant goal.

Trends in the Study of Midrash, Supplement to *Journal for the Study of Judaism* 106, Leiden, pp. 79–109.

Milikowsky, C. (2006b), 'Vayyiqra Rabba chapter 30: its transmissional history, its publication history and the presentation of a new edition (to sections 1 and 2)', in Z. A. Steinfeld (ed.), *In Memory of Prof. Meyer Simcha Feldblum* (*Annual of Bar Ilan University: Studies in Judaica and the Humanities*, vols. 30–31), Ramat Gan, pp. 269–318. [Hebrew]

Milikowsky, C. (2008), 'A hitherto-unpublished Midrash on man who "Lives Forever" and on "Water in Water" (Vayyiqra Rabba 27:4): reflections on the errors of printers and editors and on rabbinic cosmogony', in U. Ehrlich, H. Kreisel and D. J. Lasker (eds.), *By the Well: Studies in Jewish Philosophy and Halakhic Thought Presented to Gerald J. Blidstein*, Beer-Sheva, pp. 303–28. [Hebrew]

Milikowsky, C. and Schlüter, M. (1999), '*Vayyiqra Rabba* through history: a project to study its textual transmission', in J. Targarona Borrás and A. Sáenz-Badillos (eds.), *Jewish Studies at the Turn of the Twentieth Century: Proceedings of the 6th EAJS Congress*, vol. 1, Leiden, pp. 311–21.

Reuss, R. *et al.* (eds.) (1997–), *Historisch-kritische Franz Kafka-Ausgabe*, Frankfurt am Main.

Schäfer, P. (1989), 'Once again the *Status Quaestionis* of research in rabbinic literature: an answer to Chaim Milikowsky', *JJS* 40: 89–94.

Teugels, L. M. (2003), 'Textual criticism of late rabbinic Midrashim: the example of Aggadat Bereshit', in W. Weren and D.-A. Koch (eds.), *Recent Developments in Textual Criticism: New Testament, Other Early Christian and Jewish Literature*, Studies in Theology and Religion 8, Assen, pp. 207–41.

Teugels, L. M. (2005), 'Textual criticism of a late rabbinic Midrash: Aggadat Bereshit', in L. Teugels and R. Ulmer (eds.), *Recent Developments in Midrash Research: Proceedings of the 2002 and 2003 SBL Consultation on Midrash*, Judaism in Context 2, Piscataway, NJ, pp. 137–53.

Ulmer, R. (ed.) (1997), *A Synoptic Edition of Pesiqta Rabbati Based upon All Extant Manuscripts and the Editio Princeps*, South Florida Studies in the History of Judaism 155, Atlanta.

Visotzky, B. L. (2005), 'On critical editions of Midrash', in Teugels and Ulmer (eds.), *Recent Developments in Midrash Research*, pp. 155–61.

Part II
The Rabbinic Texts

6

The State of Mishnah Studies

AMRAM TROPPER

1. Contents

THE MISHNAH IS PRIMARILY AN EDITED ANTHOLOGY of brief and often elliptical pronouncements on matters of Jewish law and practice, frequently providing conflicting views on the individual matters discussed. Some of these
pronouncements are attributed to a named rabbi, or group of anonymous
rabbis, while others are entirely anonymous. While the content often relates
to scripture, the form is not midrashic. The work is comprised of six 'orders'
(*seder*, pl. *sedarim*), each of which is further divided into multiple tractates
(*massekhet*, pl. *massekhtot*). The latter are further subdivided into chapters
(*perek*, pl. *perakim*) consisting of yet smaller units (*mishnah*, pl. *mishnayot*).
The titles and main subject matter of the six *sedarim* are given below. It
should, however, be borne in mind that the Mishnah frequently digresses, at
every level of organisational hierarchy, from its main topics.

1.1. Seeds (Zera'im): Eleven Tractates

Ten tractates largely deal with farming practices, tithing and other treatment
of produce. The main concern of Berakhot, the first tractate, is with prayers,
and benedictions associated with food.

1.2. Festivals (Mo'ed): Twelve Tractates

The first tractate deals with a range of Sabbath rules, and the second with a
halakhic framework for sidestepping a subset of those rules. There are individual tractates concerning the festivals Passover, Rosh Hashanah, Yom
Kippur, Sukkot and Purim. Three others cover elements of the festivals in a
more general way, and another deals with fast days. Tractate Shekalim discusses the half-shekel tax (also known from non-rabbinic sources of the
Second Temple era).

Proceedings of the British Academy **165**, 91–115. © The British Academy 2010.

1.3.   Women (Nashim): Seven Tractates

There are individual tractates dealing with betrothal, marriage, levirate marriage, divorce and suspected adulteresses. In addition, one tractate covers vows in general, and another the Nazirite vow in particular.

1.4.   Damages (Nezikin): Ten Tractates

The majority of the subject matter ranges far beyond the name given to this *seder*, which essentially refers to its first tractate only. The three opening tractates were originally one, which was split up for reasons of convenience in late antiquity. Their topic is commercial laws, and includes those involving torts, restitution for theft and robbery, found objects, borrowing and hiring, interest, sale and purchase, employment, real property and inheritance. The fourth and fifth tractates, also originally one, include laws pertaining to judicial procedure, witnesses and the imposition of punishment. Three other tractates cover oaths, idolatry and erroneous actions by authorities. A further two tractates are rather anomalous vis-à-vis the Mishnah as a whole; *Eduyot* is a list of attestations as to statements made by early masters; *Avot* contains the chain of authorities through whom the Torah was transmitted from Moses to the rabbis, as well as maxims attributed to figures ranging in date from around 200 BCE to 200 CE and anonymous ethical teachings. The entire tractate *Avot* may be a late addition to the Mishnah, and its sixth and final chapter is a late addition to the others and properly speaking is not part of the Mishnah.

1.5.   Holy Things (Kodashim): Eleven Tractates

Eight tractates cover Temple and priestly laws, including sacrifices, other offerings and dedications, and the misuse of consecrated property. Others deal with the treatment of meat that is not designated for Temple sacrifice, with the biblical penalty of extirpation (*karet*), and with the measurements and architectonics of the Temple. Some information in the latter has parallels in Josephus.

1.6.   Purities (Tohorot): Twelve Tractates

All tractates deal with the laws of purity and pollution. Among their subjects are pollution associated with utensils, foodstuffs, corpses, hands, lepers, menstrual blood and other emissions; purification, the laws of ritual baths, and the ashes of the red heifer (mentioned in Numbers 19).

2. Manuscripts

The witnesses include manuscripts of the Babylonian Talmud, in which the Mishnah is embedded, albeit in a recension that differs from the Palestinian one. The latter is largely found in manuscripts dedicated to the Mishnah alone, and evidence for both types is also found in Genizah fragments. The most important complete manuscript is MS Kaufmann (Hungarian Academy of Sciences, MS A 50), which is dated from the tenth to thirteenth centuries (it is vocalised, although this component is a later insertion). Other complete manuscripts are MS Parma (Bibliotheca Palatina 3173, De Rossi 138) and MS Cambridge (University Library Add. 470 (II)). See the *Online Treasury of Talmudic Manuscripts* of the Jewish National and University Library in Jerusalem (http://jnul.huji.ac.il/dl/talmud/).

3. Dating

While many of its traditions are much earlier, the redaction of the Mishnah is usually dated to around 200 CE, and ascribed to the Patriarch Rabbi Judah the Prince. In the Talmuds his responsibility for the work is taken for granted. Some development by others continued well into the third century.

4. Language

The Mishnah is in Hebrew, in a post-biblical form that is also known from the Dead Sea Scrolls, with considerable Aramaic influence.

5. Printed Editions

The 1492 printing by Soncino is considered the *editio princeps*, although the early seventeenth-century printing by R. Yom Tov Lipman Heller is the basis for most contemporary editions. H. Albeck's edition (with vocalisation by H. Yalon and commentary), published in Israel by Mosad Bialik / Dvir in the 1950s, has since been viewed as the standard printed edition—see below under Commentaries.

6. Translations

Single-volume translations: Danby (1933); Neusner (1988); Correns (2005). In view of the elliptical nature of the Mishnah any translation must be used with caution.

7. Commentaries

Recent commentaries, which are all in multiple volumes, include Albeck (1952–59) and Kehati (1987–96).

* * *

The Mishnah was redacted in Galilee around the year 200 CE,[1] a redaction traditionally ascribed to R. Judah haNasi.[2] After redaction, this compilation of tannaitic law quickly became a central literary composition for the amora'im of late antiquity who pored over and interpreted it in their study halls and in the Palestinian and Babylonian Talmuds.[3] In time the Babylonian Talmud replaced the Mishnah at the heart of rabbinic Judaism, and even today traditional Jews tend to interpret the Mishnah through the lens of the Babylonian Talmud. Even though the Mishnah never regained its pride of place in the life of the Jewish people, already in the Middle Ages the Mishnah re-emerged as the object of intense study and commentaries (see Sussman 1981). In the twelfth century, for example, Maimonides penned a commentary to the entire Mishnah that omits the lengthy talmudic discussions and in some cases even diverges from the Babylonian Talmud's interpretation of the Mishnah (see Kapaḥ 1963–68). Foreshadowed by some medieval and early modern precedents such as Maimonides' commentary, the modern critical study of the Mishnah seeks to interpret the Mishnah in and for itself, without recourse to the interpretations of the Talmuds. This critical approach came into its own in the nineteenth century and has continued to flourish and evolve throughout the twentieth century and into the twenty-first (see C. Gafni, dissertation 2005).

In 1990 the Jewish Theological Seminary of America published a collection of studies entitled *The State of Jewish Studies*, to which Shaye J. D. Cohen contributed 'The modern study of ancient Judaism' and Baruch M. Bokser, 'Talmudic studies'. Six years later, Günter Stemberger published a new and revised edition of his *Introduction to the Talmud and Midrash*, in

---

[1] Some additional materials were apparently incorporated into the Mishnah even after redaction as the text maintained a certain measure of fluidity for some time. See J. N. Epstein (2000: 946–79); Stemberger (1996: 133–4). It bears noting that Avot may have been redacted somewhat later than the rest of the Mishnah, though its precise date of redaction is still disputed.

[2] The 'unselfconscious attribution of mishnaic decisions' to R. Judah haNasi in the Talmuds (Stemberger 1996: 133) strongly suggests that he was responsible for the Mishnah. See also Oppenheimer (2007: 156–9).

[3] The purpose of the Mishnah is debated and it has been viewed as a collection of sources, a law code and a teaching manual (see Stemberger 1996: 135–8). For a new take on the Mishnah as a teaching manual, see Alexander (2006).

which he dedicated forty pages to the Mishnah alone.[4] Together these studies offer an extensive bibliography and excellent portrait of the state of the study of the Mishnah in the late 1980s and early 1990s. On the basis of the solid foundations established by the Mishnah scholars of the nineteenth and twentieth centuries and concisely summarised in the aforementioned studies, Mishnah studies in the last fifteen years or so have surged on, developing significant insights and innovative approaches to the study of the Mishnah. New understandings have emerged from the careful and painstaking analysis of the Mishnah within its literary and historical contexts as well as from the application of new methodologies and theories imported from other fields of study. In an attempt at penning a modest addendum to the earlier appraisals of the history and state of Mishnah scholarship, I map out below some recent developments and trends in the study of the Mishnah, focusing on new resources and editions, source criticism, the Mishnah as halakhah and the Mishnah as literature.

New Resources and Editions

Although the Mishnah was originally redacted some time around the year 200 CE, all extant manuscripts and Genizah fragments are dated to long after the third century. For example, the only three complete Mishnah manuscripts, MS Kaufmann (Hungarian Academy of Sciences, MS A 50), MS Parma (Bibliotheca Palatina 3173, De Rossi 138) and MS Cambridge (University Library Add. 470 (II)) span roughly from the tenth or eleventh to the fourteenth or fifteenth centuries. A large time gap between the date of redaction and the earliest manuscript testimony is the rule rather than the exception for early rabbinic texts and may be due in no small part to the oral medium of text transmission in late antiquity. In any event, the study of the mishnaic text rests on the analysis of the extant evidence with much weight given to the relatively early manuscripts and those which preserve the best readings. A handy new resource designed to aid scholars in this textual analysis is the *Online Treasury of Talmudic Manuscripts* (see above, p. 93), which makes excellent reproductions of important Mishnah manuscripts widely available. To date, there is still no complete critical edition of the Mishnah which collects (and evaluates) all the manuscript evidence. Critical editions of Seder Zera'im and select tractates have existed for some time now[5] and Shimon Sharvit's recent critical edition (2004) of Avot deserves special

---

[4] For surveys of Mishnah manuscripts, critical editions, commentaries and translations, see Krupp (1987); Stemberger (1996: 139–48; 2007: 157–61).

[5] See bibliography brought by Stemberger (1996: 143–4). See also Krupp (2002–06).

mention. In addition, Michael Krupp has recently edited a critical edition of the Mishnah on the basis of MS Kaufmann with a limited but useful apparatus.

There are numerous translations of the Mishnah: the English ones most frequently referenced are those by Herbert Danby (1933) and Jacob Neusner (1988) as well as the translation found in Isidore Epstein's edition (1935–52) of the Babylonian Talmud. For German, scholars have traditionally turned to the edition by Asher Sammter *et al.* (1887–1933), the so-called Giessen series edited by Georg Beer *et al.* (1912–) and Lazarus Goldschimdt's edition (1929–36) of the Babylonian Talmud. Now one may also consider the translation in Krupp's new edition (2002–06) of the Mishnah or conveniently consult the new single-volume translation by Dietrich Correns (2005).

In respect to comprehensive Mishnah commentaries, Hanoch Albeck's remains the standard edition and commentary in Hebrew as the incomplete Giessen series does in German. Pinhas Kehati's Mishnah, now also available in English, is a modern commentary in the traditional vein and the commentaries produced by Neusner and his students offer a more critical approach that highlights form-criticism in particular.[6] Shemuel, Ze'ev and Hannah Safrai's recent edition (Safrai *et al.* 2008) of Shevi'it and Shabbat deserve special mention since they are supposed to be the first volumes in a new comprehensive critical commentary of the Mishnah.

Source Criticism

Parallels to mishnaic pericopae are commonly found in the Tosefta and scholars have deployed three models in their attempts to decipher the nature of the relationship between particular mishnaic pericopae and their toseftan counterparts. The traditional model, or the 'commentary model', maintains that toseftan parallels generally postdate the Mishnah and comment upon it just as the Tosefta *in toto* was 'published' after the Mishnah.[7] In this model, the Tosefta is viewed as a commentary on the Mishnah that cites and elucidates the Mishnah, and therefore mishnaic parallels usually enjoy chronological priority. At times, however, discrepancies between parallel texts are simply too great for the toseftan parallel to be considered an expansion or elucidation of the Mishnah and in such cases, the traditional model has usually given way to an alternative model, the 'independent parallels' model. The latter model maintains that similar but non-identical texts stem from an

---

[6] Kehati (1987–96). For references to the relevant works by Neusner and his students, see Stemberger (1996: 148; 2007: 158–9).

[7] On the oral publication of the Mishnah, see Lieberman (1962: 83–99); Sussman (2005).

independent source, usually envisioned as an oral source. This common source was not preserved for posterity in writing but independent free formulations (or oral performances) ultimately derived from the common source are reflected in parallel texts. As a result, these parallels may offer fascinating comparative material but should not be plotted along a linear chronological trajectory. In tandem with the traditional model, but also on its own, the 'independent parallels' model has long been a major force in the study of Mishnah–Tosefta parallels.[8]

The third model, or the 'edited parallel' model,[9] builds on a notion already acknowledged long ago, that is, that the Tosefta may have preserved some mishnaic source material. According to the 'edited parallel' model, highly similar textual traditions tend to emerge within a single literary continuum and so rather than reflecting independent trajectories that emerged from a common source, it is likely that one of two highly similar textual traditions is a revision of the other. If the differences between highly similar texts are of an editorial nature, the 'edited parallel' model maintains that the revised text is a reworked version of a more original tradition preserved in its parallel. Proponents of this model argue that synoptic comparisons of Mishnah–Tosefta pericopae often reveal that the Mishnah reflects a later, more crystallised and reworked textual tradition, while parallel toseftan texts (and sometimes parallel baraitot cited in the Talmuds as well: see, for example, Simon-Shoshan 2007) are earlier, more pristine and original. Recently, a number of scholars have discovered that this third model sheds light on numerous Mishnah–Tosefta parallels and though the scope of its successful application still remains unclear, there seems to be a growing sense that it is quite extensive.[10]

In order to illustrate the type of insights gained from the 'edited parallel' model, let us consider a Mishnah–Tosefta parallel in which the 'edited parallel' model seems to offer a compelling interpretation of the diachronic relationship between the parallels.[11]

---

[8] For a recent illustration of this model, see Alexander (2006).

[9] The terms 'independent parallels' and 'edited parallel' were coined by Friedman (2000: 35–9).

[10] For a summary of the history of scholarship on the relationship between the Mishnah and the Tosefta, see Stemberger (1996: 149–58); Friedman (2002: 15–95); Mandel (2006: 322–8); Walfish (2005–06: 21–9). Two major proponents of the 'edited parallels' model are Friedman (2002) and Hauptman (2005). See also Houtman (1996); Felix (dissertation, 2000); Wald (2007a: 326); Kulp (2007). In attempts to develop a global approach to the Mishnah, several scholars, such as Fox (1999: 34–6) and Zeidman (1999), have offered an intertextual approach which weaves together the models discussed above. (Neusner offers a very different global approach which is unconcerned with questions of source criticism. See Neusner 1992, 2002.)

[11] Translations of mishnayot in this essay are produced on the basis of MS Kaufmann and with the aid of Danby (1933) and Jung (1938). Translations of the Tosefta are produced on the basis of Lieberman's presentation of MS Vienna (1955–88) and with the aid of Neusner (1977–86), Jung (1938) and Rabbinowitz (1938). Biblical translations are usually taken from Jewish Publication Society of America (1999).

m.Yoma 2.2

It once happened that two were even as they ran to mount the [altar-] ramp; when one of them pushed his fellow,

his leg broke.

t.Kipp. 1.12

It once happened that two priests were even as they ran to mount the [altar-] ramp; when one of them pushed his fellow within four cubits [of the altar];

The other took out a knife and thrust it into his heart. R. Zadok came and stood on the steps of the Hall and said: Our brethren of the house of Israel, hear me! Behold it says 'If one be found slain . . . and your elders and magistrates shall go out and measure' (Deut. 23:1–2). Come and let us measure (in order to determine) upon whom (rests the obligation) to bring the heifer, upon the sanctuary or upon the courts? Everyone then burst out weeping. Afterwards the father of the child came and said to them: Our brothers, May I be your atonement. My son is still writhing, so the knife has not become unclean. [His remark] comes to teach you that the uncleanness of a knife was more grievous to Israel than the shedding of blood. Thus is it also said, 'Moreover, Manasseh shed innocent blood very much, till he had filled Jerusalem from one end to the other' (2 Kings 21:16). On this basis they said: Because of the sin of murder, the presence of God was raised and the sanctuary was made unclean.

When the Court saw that they incurred danger they ordained that the Altar be cleared only by lot.

Both stories related are brought in their respective compositions in order to explain the origins of the practice of assigning priests their tasks in the temple by means of lots. Although the accounts relate a similar event and open in almost identical fashion, they part ways significantly once they reach the violent encounter at the centre of the story. According to Abraham Goldberg (1987a: 287), who deploys here the 'independent parallels' model, the Tosefta 'supplements the story about the breaking of the leg with a more tragic case' (see also b.Yoma 23a). In Goldberg's opinion, the tanna'im were familiar with two accounts of a similar tragic event and since the Mishnah cited one of them, the Tosefta complemented the Mishnah with the other. Various scholars have pointed out, however, that it seems more likely that the Mishnah's short story is a condensed and modified version of the extended story found in the Tosefta (as well as in Sifre Numbers and the Talmuds).[12] The redactor of the Mishnah was apparently unsettled by the tragic consequences of the race and the horrifying reaction of the slain priest's father in the original story, and therefore he softened the story and toned down its disquieting force (see Friedman 2002: 44–5 and his references in n. 125). Indeed, this milder version of the story is in keeping with the Mishnah's tendency to idealise Temple life (see Fraenkel 1981: 132–4). Rather than reproducing the Tosefta's highly disconcerting story, the Mishnah constructed a bare-bones version which serves its purpose in the context of the chapter, that is, it explains the origins of the Temple lots.[13]

The growing number of synoptic studies which highlight the reworked nature of the Mishnah suggests that the Mishnah is a tightly edited composition in which earlier literary materials were carefully and thoughtfully revised and rearranged. This understanding, which rests on source-critical investigations of the kind illustrated above, is highly significant in its own right, promises to shed light on the history of the halakhah (see, for example, Sabato 2004) and corroborates the results of recent literary analyses of the Mishnah described below. Moreover, the synoptic approach to tannaitic parallels holds out the promise of enriching our understanding of the Mishnah because underlying guidelines and principles that contributed to the redaction of the Mishnah are likely to emerge as we compare the Mishnah to earlier formulations it revised or rejected. These synoptic studies indicate, for example, that the Mishnah tends to condense earlier formulations, to change biblical Hebrew to Mishnaic Hebrew and to replace illustrations using Temple realia with more abstract ones (see Friedman 2002). Thus, the comparison of parallel traditions in conjunction with the higher critical study of

---

[12] See Sifre Numbers 135 (ed. H. S. Horovitz: 222); t.Shevu. 1.3–4; p.Yoma 2.2, 39d; b.Yoma 23a.

[13] The tragic murder and disconcerting force of the original story are highly appropriate in Sifre Numbers, where the story is introduced in order to illustrate the notion that murder defiles the land and drives out the presence of God. Therefore, it is likely that the Sifre preserves the earliest extant literary setting for the story. The Mishnah apparently reflects a later stage in the evolution of the story, wherein the story was refashioned in such a way that it could assume a new role, that is, to explain the origins of the Temple lots, while minimising the tragic elements that were formerly necessary but now superfluous. (It bears noting that t.Shevu. 1.3–4 also apparently borrowed our story but set it in a new context which highlights the severity of the ritual defilement of the Temple rather than that of a vicious murder in the Temple.)

the Mishnah itself should lay the groundwork for a clearer understanding of the redaction of the Mishnah.[14]

The Mishnah as Halakhah

The analysis of the halakhah in the Mishnah commenced already in tannaitic times (see Henshke 1997) and has continued unabated until today. The Talmuds and their medieval commentators are well known for their attempts to reveal and interpret the legal concepts and principles underlying mishnaic halakhah. In contrast, modern historians have sometimes interpreted mishnaic halakhah, and halakhah more generally, as responses to historical factors, such as political or socio-economic crises. A potential drawback of this historical approach to the halakhah is the risk of viewing legal concepts and reasoning as little more than *ex post facto* rationales for laws generated primarily by contemporary historical realities (see Hayes 1997: 3–9, 17–24; Soloveitchik 1978: 174–5). Seeing halakhah primarily as a response to political or socio-economic crises risks minimising the significance of internal legal considerations and ignoring the nuanced relationships of halakhah to reality, 'the patterns of resistance and response, of attentiveness and indifference' (Soloveitchik 1978: 174). Thus, contemporary studies of halakhah often seek to avoid these drawbacks in two ways: they highlight the legal reasoning and hermeneutics which justify the halakhah and refine the historical approach with methods designed to produce more compelling interpretations.

Mishnaic halakhah is presented in various forms such as precedents, enactments, edicts, customs, and, most commonly, casuistic formulations (i.e. case law). General rules also appear in the Mishnah but they are the exception as mishnaic halakhot are usually embedded in specific cases and circumstances. Since the rationales underlying the halakhot of the Mishnah are rarely stated explicitly, scholars analyse halakhot so as to expose their implicit legal basis. At times, the implied legal reasoning for a halakhah may be ad hoc and cover little more than the specific case cited, while at other times the implicit reasoning may involve a general principle with broader application. For example, one method still employed to reveal such principles

---

[14] See Wald (2007a). In addition, trends in both source criticism and literary criticism (reviewed below) suggest that the Mishnah was carefully and artfully crafted by a redactor sensitive to literary issues and these insights indicate that literary considerations may assist the text critic in selecting a preferred reading when, for example, literary considerations can determine the *lectio difficilior* and the *lectio facilior*. The analysis of manuscripts and textual witnesses along with traditional lower critical considerations will certainly continue to remain at the heart of textual criticism, but literary considerations will probably play a greater role in the textual analysis of the Mishnah in the future than they have in the past. See Walfish (dissertation, 2001: 268–9).

is comprised of the correlation of various legal positions attributed to a specific sage (or school) on the basis of a single, unified point of view.[15] Scholars
continue to debate the role of casuistic formulations and general rules in the
Mishnah and why the former appear so frequently and the latter so rarely. It
bears mentioning that Leib Moscovitz discusses at length these and related
issues in his book, *Talmudic Reasoning: From Casuistics to Conceptualization*,
a study now indispensable for the investigation of early rabbinic halakhah.[16]

Granting the importance of the analysis of the explicit and implicit rationales for halakhot, let us describe the refined historical approach mentioned
above. History, in this new approach, is not narrowly conceived along political or socio-economic lines as it was sometimes in the past, but rather history
is broadly conceived as the locus for a host of non-hermeneutic and non-
formalistic factors which impinge upon the halakhic process. Ethical, theological, economic, political and other cultural forces play a role in the
evolution of the halakhah and all these forces emerge within specific historical settings. The goal of the new approach is to reveal the traces of these
forces on the halakhah without reducing all halakhah to mere epiphenomena
of authentic, supposedly non-legal, historical activity. To accomplish this
goal, the new approach introduces external factors only when internal legal
justifications fall short. Features of the halakhah which cannot be fully
explained by internal considerations, such as uncharacteristic legal stances,
unprecedented novelties and the preference for a specific exegetical move over
another equally valid one, are viewed as traces of external historical forces
(see Soloveitchik 1978: 174; Hayes 1997: 181). Unsurprising mishnaic legal
positions rooted in unambiguous biblical law do not call for historical interpretations, whereas the atypical, the novel and the unnecessary offer the
historian a toehold and entry-point for the introduction and consideration of
historical factors.

In order to detect novelties and unnecessary or unexpected legal positions
in the Mishnah, scholars employ a comparative method. By comparing a
mishnaic halakhah to an earlier or parallel halakhah attested in pre-rabbinic
or early rabbinic literature, one may ascertain paths not taken by the
Mishnah and then, in their light, one may examine the taken path. In this
manner, for example, Moshe Halbertal (1997) has sought to demonstrate the
importance of ethical considerations in tannaitic family law, and Aharon
Shemesh (2003) has highlighted exegetical, ideological, and other historical
factors involved in the mishnaic construction of the death penalty (see also
Cohen 2007). In short, a careful analysis of internal hermeneutic and legal

---

[15] See, for example, Fisch (1997), Shapira and Fisch (1999); cf. Walfish (2003). See also
Moscovitz (2002: 65, n. 70).
[16] Moscovitz (2002); cf. Alexander (2003); Wald (2007b); Walfish (2008).

considerations alongside a comparative approach offers a promising avenue for the discovery of legal innovations in the Mishnah. Having discovered them, the historian's task is to contextualise these innovations as best as possible within an overarching historical framework (see, for example, Rosen-Zvi 2008a).

The comparative approach is potent not only because it reveals how mishnaic halakhah differs from earlier halakhah, but also because it sheds light on commonalities and correlations between halakhah and aggadah. A number of recent studies attest to a growing willingness to correlate halakhot with aggadot, or, more specifically, to view halakhah as the legal embodiment of aggadah. In the past, halakhah and aggadah were predominantly viewed as belonging to distinct domains, the halakhah comprising rabbinic prescriptions for a spiritual life and the aggadah denoting the rest of rabbinic literature including such things as wisdom sayings, stories and theological reflections. Now, however, there is a mounting trend in which halakhah is read in light of aggadah and interpreted as the legal expression of theological, spiritual or ethical positions articulated in the aggadah. Yair Lorberbaum, for example, has recently argued (2004) that a number of tannaitic halakhic positions relating to the implementation of the death penalty and the obligation to procreate were determined by aggadic readings of the biblical passage, 'And God created man in His image, in the image of God He created him' (Gen. 1:27). In a similar vein, Shlomo Naeh has interpreted R. Akiva's position in m.Ber 4.3 regarding the recitation of the daily prayer in light of the aggadic portrayal of Ḥanina ben Dosa in m.Ber 5.5. In contrast to the traditional understanding, Naeh's insightful interpretation suggests that R. Akiva did not limit the recitation of the entire daily prayer to individuals who are well versed with its blessings and remember them well. Rather, R. Akiva limited the recitation of the daily prayer to those times when the supplicant's prayer gushes forth from his mouth in religious ecstasy, in a manner akin to the free-flowing and spontaneous prayer of a mystic like Ḥanina ben Dosa.[17] In sum, studies like these demonstrate how the underlying rationale for certain halakhot may be located in aggadot.

The Mishnah as Literature

The extent to which the Mishnah's redactor employed a heavy editorial hand and reshaped the materials he received was ardently debated in the twentieth

---

[17] Naeh (1994). In response to Naeh, Walfish (1996) confirms the connection between R. Akiva's halahkic stance and Ḥanina ben Dosa's flowing prayer but interprets it differently. See also the dissertation of Nagen (Genack) (2003: 6, n. 8) for some references to earlier scholarship.

century. Comparative analyses demonstrated, on the one hand, that many mishnayot were preserved as received, thereby encouraging the notion that the redactor's editorial policy was conservative and non-interventionist. On the other hand, comparative analyses also revealed that in many other cases the Mishnah revised and reformulated its sources. From a global perspective, the truth of the matter is probably somewhere in the middle. At times, the redactor preserved his sources as he inherited them, at times he mildly altered them, and at times he significantly reshaped them. How to find the precise balance between the conservative and creative dimensions of this editorial process is still unclear, but today there is a broad consensus that the Mishnah should be viewed as a tightly edited composition (see Wald 2007a). Even if the editorial process may have been limited at times to the selection and arrangement of earlier materials, these editorial judgements are of major significance since they reflect the concerns and goals of the Mishnah's redactor/ anthologist. In short, the Mishnah is now viewed not merely as a conduit through which earlier tannaitic literary materials were preserved, but also as a composition in its own right.

Having noted contrasting dimensions of the Mishnah's redaction, let us digress for a moment in order to correct a common misconception regarding our ability to date materials in the Mishnah to periods prior to its final redaction. In light of the creative dimension of the Mishnah's redaction and a critical refusal to accept on faith the reliability of attributions to Sages in the Mishnah, the Mishnah is sometimes excluded from historical studies of first- and second-century Palestine. This is a shame because even Jacob Neusner, the scholar most identified with a highly sceptical approach to attributions, argues that many mishnaic statements with attributions truly cite positions which stem from the generation of their attributed tanna. While Neusner believes that we cannot verify whether a sage actually said or held the position attributed to him (and therefore rabbinic biographies cannot be written), he believes that we can verify if an attribution stems from the generation to which it is attributed. After applying his verification method, Neusner concluded that many an attribution may be dated roughly to the generation of its attributed tanna, a find of great significance for historians.[18] Furthermore, the existence of a great number of mishnaic statements whose dating has been verified raises the likelihood that many other mishnaic statements whose early dating cannot be verified (by Neusner's verification method or by source criticism) or falsified are probably reliably dated as well. Although we cannot test the reliability of the attributions in these materials, I believe that we are still dealing with levels of certainty common in the study of ancient history.

[18] Neusner (1981: 14–22). See also Cohen (1983: 52, 62 n. 2; 1990: 65); Maccoby (1984: 32); Poirier (1996: 75); I. M. Gafni (2001: 219); Schwartz (2001: 8).

In short, despite the strong redaction of the Mishnah, the Mishnah should still remain an important source for the legal, social and intellectual history of the first two centuries of Roman Palestine.

Extensive literary evidence for viewing the Mishnah as a carefully edited composition has been provided recently by Avraham Walfish. Walfish opens his enterprise with the recognition that though the topical and systematic arrangement of materials is the central governing principle underlying the redaction of the Mishnah, 'few tractates *consistently* follow a clear and logical pattern, and many tractates fail to display any discernible thematic development at all' (2006: 153). Many scholars have recognised literary and associative dimensions of the Mishnah on an ad hoc basis, but Walfish offers a comprehensive presentation of a few literary phenomena that recur throughout the Mishnah. His lists of anaphora, epiphora, anadiplosis, inclusio, paronomasia and keywords in the Mishnah make a strong case for the literary dimension of the Mishnah's redaction (Walfish, dissertation 2001: 323–65). Indeed, this literary dimension of the Mishnah seems to corroborate the source-critical findings described above and strengthens the argument for an active editor.[19]

In the past some have argued that what appear to us as literary features of the Mishnah were actually designed for mnemotechnical purposes. Walfish counters, however, that many of the literary phenomena he has located in the Mishnah are of questionable mnemotechnical value and, more importantly, there is no contradiction between mnemotechnical and literary-conceptual goals. 'In pre-modern texts, and particularly in oral compositions, the mnemotechnical value of a literary technique was intimately bound up with the conceptual associations with which it was linked. Hence it may be presumed that word repetitions, wordplays, and literary patterns found in the Mishnah, alongside whatever mnemotechnical value they may possess, were designed to create conceptual associations and patterns, in much the same way as they do in more overtly literary works.'[20] The Mishnah, in other words, is not just a standard legal code or textbook; rather, the Mishnah conveys spiritual, theological and ethical concepts through its presentation of halakhah. Recent studies which pursue the immanent meanings and lessons of the Mishnah beyond the prescriptive import of its laws are developing an essential element in Jacob Neusner's mishnaic programme, albeit with different tools and without necessarily viewing the Mishnah as philosophy as

---

[19] Cf. Kline, *The Structured Mishnah*. Kline's schematic structures are highly suggestive but they may not be the only way to schematise the Mishnah and possibly reflect emergent patterns produced by more basic literary techniques rather than intentional constructions. His work has yet to receive the attention and critique it deserves, though his central position, that the Mishnah is a tightly woven composition, is being corroborated by numerous other scholars.

[20] Walfish (2006: 163). See also Walfish (dissertation, 2001: 20–3; 367–84); Margalit (2000: 64–7).

Neusner proposes.[21] Whereas Neusner has produced global and systematic analyses of the Mishnah (often critiqued as impressionistic), recent literary studies of the Mishnah deploy close readings with a sensitivity to the plethora of literary cues and techniques which pervade the Mishnah.[22]

Let us illustrate the literary approach to the Mishnah with an analysis of a set of wordplays offered by Walfish.

m.Ta'an. 2.1

What is the order for fast days? They bring out the **ark** (*tevah*) into the open space of the town and put wood-ashes on the **ark** (*tevah*) and on the heads of the patriarch and the father of the court; and everyone takes [ashes] and places [them] on his head.

The **eldest** (*hazaken*) among them utters before them words of admonition:

Our brethren, it is not written of the people of Nineveh 'God saw their sackcloth and their fasting', but 'God saw what they did, how they were turning back from their evil ways' (Job 3:6) and in the Prophets it says, 'Rend your **hearts** (*levavkhem*) rather than your garments, and turn back to the Lord your God' etc. (Joel 2:13).

m.Ta'an. 2.2

They stand up in prayer and send down [as reader] before the **ark** (*hatevah*)

an **elder** (*zaken*), well versed [in prayer], who has children and whose house is empty [of food],[23] so that he might be whole-**hearted** (*libo*) in prayer. And he recites before them twenty-four benedictions: eighteen of every day and adding onto them another six.

The first two mishnayot of the second chapter of m.Ta'an. describe the two stages of the fast-day service, the admonition in 2.1 and the prayer in 2.2. In preparing for them, the ark is removed from the synagogue and placed in the central open space of the town. Ashes are placed on the ark and on the heads of the town-officials, and every individual in the community also places ash on his head. The eldest community member then admonishes the com-

---

[21] Neusner (1991). For critiques of viewing the Mishnah as philosophy, see, for example, Cohen (1983: 52–8); Sanders (1990: 313–17); Poirier (1996: 76–8); Walfish (dissertation, 2001: 30); Moscovitz (2002: 353, n. 26); Alexander (2006: 140–1, n. 56).

[22] See Neusner (1981, 1991); Walfish (dissertation, 2001: 29–31). A rather different contemporary literary approach seeks to construct a taxonomy of mishnaic functional forms by breaking down mishnaic texts into functional components which it defines and classifies, and to describe how these functional forms are combined in the creation of the mishnaic text (see Arnold Goldberg 1999; Samely 2002, 2007: 25–63). Rather than interpreting the Mishnah anew in light of its artistic literary features, this approach attempts to identify and map out the set of discrete functional tasks that appear in the Mishnah (and in rabbinic literature more generally), while also describing how they coalesce into larger literary aggregates.

[23] Cf. Ilan (2008: 26–8).

munity, reminding all that the fasting of the people of Nineveh found favour
before God only because it was an external embodiment of authentic contri-
tion and repentance. Upon the conclusion of this admonition, the community stands up for prayer and sends before the ark an elder to lead them in
prayer. The prayer-leader is supposed to be both well-versed in prayer and the
father of an impoverished family so that his prayer will be both pleasing and
sincere before God. Thus, the fast-day ritual commences with an admonition
and concludes with a public prayer session.

Walfish has pointed out three parallel terms in these mishnayot (all
printed in bold above) which structure the two-stage ritual. Both the admonition and the prayer commence with the ark, the ritual item which stands
centre-stage throughout the ritual. An elder is then called upon to perform a
leading role in the ritual and, at the end of both the admonition and the
prayer, the word 'heart' is used in the description of the elder's role. Through
these words the Mishnah draws attention to the parallel nature of the two-
stage ritual wherein the ark is the focus of attention and two elders lead the
fast-day ritual, one admonishing and the other leading in prayer. Walfish
does not refer to the parallel Tosefta in his analysis of these mishnayot, but
differences between the Tosefta and the Mishnah corroborate his reading of
the structure of these mishnayot:

> What is the order for fast days? They bring out the ark into the open space of
> the town and put ashes on the ark, and they do not switch (guards) for it, one
> sits and guards it all day long. The eldest among them utters before them words
> of admonition: My children, let a person be ashamed before his friend, but let
> a person not be ashamed for his deeds. It is better for a person to be ashamed
> before his friend, and let him and his children not swell up in hunger, and so
> Scripture says, 'Why when we fasted, did You not see? (When we starved our
> bodies,) did You pay no heed?' (Isa. 58:3) What does Scripture reply to them?
> 'Because on your fast day' etc. (Isa. 58:3), 'Because you fast in strife and con-
> tention' etc. (Isa. 58:4), 'Is such the fast I desire, a day for men to starve their
> bodies?' etc. (Isa. 58:5). Rather, what is the fast which I want? 'To unlock fetters
> of wickedness' (Isa. 58:6). If there was a dead reptile in one's hand, even if he
> immerses in the shiloah and in all the waters of creation, he will never be clean;
> (but if) he tossed the creeping thing from his hand, immersion in (only) forty
> seahs of water is effective (to cleanse him), and so Scripture says, 'he who con-
> fesses and gives them [i.e. his faults] up will find mercy' (Prov. 28:13) and says,
> 'Let us lift up our hearts with our hands' etc. (Lam. 3:41). He recites before
> them twenty-four benedictions: eighteen of every day and adding onto them
> another six. (t.Ta'an. 1.8–9)

The Tosefta, like the Mishnah, relates the two stages of the fast-day ritual,
the admonition and the prayer, but, unlike the Mishnah, the Tosefta does not
present these two stages in parallel fashion. In the Tosefta, one simply cannot
trace the 'ark–elder–heart' word order in both stages of the ritual. Moreover,

whereas the Mishnah had each stage in the ritual revolve around a different elder, the Tosefta ascribes both the admonition and the leading of the prayer to the very same elder. Thus, the toseftan parallel suggests that the mishnaic version of the ritual was carefully edited to offer a balanced portrayal of the two-stage ritual.[24]

Of the three parallel terms in our mishnayot, Walfish considers the final term, 'heart', of greatest importance because in it he perceives the literary cue for the underlying message of the text:

> Whereas the first elder exhorts the community to rend their hearts in repentance, the elder who leads the prayers is described as having an empty household so that his heart may be whole (namely: wholly concentrated) in prayer. In M. Ta. 2:1 the heart is described as being torn, but in M. Ta. 2:2 it is described as being whole and entire! There is no logical contradiction here, inasmuch as the two pericopae describe different ceremonial performances. Nonetheless, from a literary standpoint, it is unlikely that the stark contrast between the rent heart and the whole heart in two successive pericopae is accidental. . . . The Mishnah appears to suggest that the whole heart and the torn heart are not mutually exclusive but rather one and the same. According to the famous apophthegm of the Kotzker Rebbe, 'there is nothing whole in this world except for a broken heart.' In response to a broken relationship between man and God, the appropriate response is to enhance prayer by means of fasting, to rend one's heart in repentance in order to render it whole in prayer. (Walfish 2006: 188)

Focusing on the literary cues offered by the text itself, Walfish teases out what he views as the immanent meaning of the text.

The literary analysis of the Mishnah rests first and foremost on a close and careful reading of the Mishnah with particular attention given to the literary traits and structure of the text. These literary features often come more clearly into focus when the Mishnah is compared to a parallel text, as in the case just reviewed. Scholars interpret the Mishnah's literary cues via close readings but also seek to corroborate their interpretations with other sources, such as the overarching context and related aggadot. As noted above, aggadot are also employed in the interpretation of mishnaic halakhot and, in truth, 'The Mishnah as Halakhah' and 'The Mishnah as Literature' may intersect at this point. For example, Naeh's interpretation of R. Akiva's stance on prayer mentioned above under the rubric of the 'The Mishnah as Halakhah' could have been presented just as easily under the rubric of 'The Mishnah as Literature'. His interpretation is greatly enhanced by the literary structure of chapters four and five of Mishnah Berakhot, and he himself

---

[24] Components of the Tosefta may have served as the inspiration for certain components in the Mishnah. Thus, for example, the hungry children in the Tosefta may have been transformed into the prayer-leader's starving children in the Mishnah and the lifting up of hearts in prayer in the Tosefta may have inspired the whole-hearted prayer in the Mishnah. Cf. Urbach (2002: 560).

recognised that it was unclear whether he discovered the principle that originally generated R. Akiva's halakhic position or the Mishnah's reinterpretation of the position (Naeh 1994: 208, 210; Walfish 1996: 312–14). In other
words, the literary approach to the Mishnah may reveal the original rationale for halakhot or a mishnaic reinterpretation and it may also be unclear
which of the two it is doing. Consequently, it is best to consider my division
between 'The Mishnah as Halakhah' and 'The Mishnah as Literature' as a
heuristic division whose elements intersect and overlap in reality.

The literary approach just reviewed, with its focus on close and contextual readings, is significant not only for the immanent meanings it seeks to
reveal, but also for the role it plays in more historical readings of the
Mishnah. Close literary readings now serve as the springboard for historical
questions relating to the culture of the Mishnah and the ideology embedded
in its redaction. In recent historical studies of the Mishnah (often influenced
by New Historicism and cultural studies; cf., for example, Simon-Shoshan
2008), the Mishnah is viewed both as a historical artefact which reflects the
multiple settings from which it emerged and as a rhetorical treatise which
expresses the explicit platforms and implicit ideologies of its redactor. In
tandem with close readings of the Mishnah, scholars now direct their
gaze beyond the text to the culture surrounding it; to the social context of
Roman Palestine and the underlying power moves of the redactor, to the
intellectual challenges facing the tanna'im and the ambient environment of
the Greek-speaking east of the Roman empire.

Having illustrated the literary approach to the Mishnah above with a
short analysis of m.Ta'an. 2.1–2, let us return to these very same mishnayot in order to illustrate some recent trends in the historical analysis of
the Mishnah. Mishnah Ta'an. 2.1–2 presents a narrative of an elaborate
public ritual, a literary form not entirely uncommon in the Mishnah but
quite unlike the standard casuistic form of most mishnayot. The Mishnah
relates tens of ritual narratives (see Breuer 1987: 302, n. 17; cf. Rosen-Zvi
2008b: 242–8; Cohn 2008) in which traditions and materials inherited from
the past were refashioned and formalised in narrative form in accordance
with contemporary concerns of the redactor. The origins of the various
components in these rituals, as in our fast-day ritual, are to be sought in
biblical and other pre-rabbinic literature and their meanings explored
through a close reading of the ritual narrative as well as other relevant
pre-rabbinic, such as 1 Macc. 3:44–54 and Judith 4:9–15, and early rabbinic texts (Levine 2001: 66–96, 184–94). However, whereas most of the ritual narratives in the Mishnah relate to the Temple and its cult, the fast-day
ritual is not confined to Jerusalem and Temple times and takes place
instead in the open public space of any town of the tannaitic period
(Lapin 1996: 109–14).

In line with broader trends in the humanities and rabbinics, questions of power and authority are central in mishnaic studies as well, so let us consider the fast-day ritual narrative as an attempt to negotiate pressing political and social tensions or concerns. In setting the stage for the ritual, three 'characters' accompany the ark to the open space of the town: the patriarch, the father of the court and the townspeople. The patriarch presumably refers to the patriarch of the Land of Israel and not to local patriarchs of the Diaspora, but his role in the narrative should not be taken to imply that his presence was required in every town that performed the ritual. Rather, the sense of the Mishnah appears to be that prominent townspeople, such as the patriarch and father of the court, should stand centre-stage as the town's representatives. With that having been said, it is probably no coincidence that while the Tosefta makes no mention of the patriarch, the Mishnah, which is traditionally attributed to R. Judah haNasi, a patriarch, highlights the patriarch's role in the ritual. In any case, the town-leaders, like all public officers in the Mishnah, are portrayed as men, though the congregating townspeople presumably included women and children as well. In reality, women held public office in certain Jewish communities and we may imagine that, at least in such places, they also played a prominent role in local fast-day rituals (Brooten 1982). More generally, comparisons with other descriptions of the fast-day ritual in rabbinic literature may offer further insights into variations of the ritual and other possible discrepancies between the mishnaic description of the ritual and its actual implementation (Levine 2001).

The admonition of the first stage of the ritual involves quotations from the prophets and is administered by an elder, that is, a respected community member or sage. In the Bible a prophet would have admonished the people and urged them to repent, but, for the rabbis, the prophetic era ended long ago and the Sages took their place.[25] In our ritual, prophecy functions indirectly via citation by an elder, whose authority stems from knowledge and wisdom rather than prophetic revelation. In a similar vein, the prayer and the elder in the second stage of the ritual reflect the elevation of rabbinic values and institutions over other Jewish alternatives. The temple, priest and sacrificial worship have been replaced here with the open space of a town, an elder and prayer, and later on in m.Ta'an. 2.5, the Sages criticise an implementation of the fast-day ritual for being modelled too closely on Temple practice. Furthermore, the elder is not a wonder-worker like Ḥoni the Circle Drawer whose cries to God elicit rain almost magically (but are critiqued by Simeon ben Sheṭaḥ in m.Ta'an. 3.8), nor is his prayer the mystical and spiritual

---

[25] Seder Olam Rabbah 30 (ed. Ratner: 140–1); t.Sot. 13.3 (and parallels); Mekhilta de R. Simeon b. Yoḥai 20.16 (ed. Epstein-Melammed, p. 155); p.Ta'an. 2.1, 65a (and parallels). See Urbach (1945–46); Milikowsky (1994); Blenkinsopp (2004: 197–9).

eruption of Ḥanina ben Dosa. Rather, the elder's prayer is a practised and regular prayer and its authenticity and power emerge from the plight of his family rather than the holiness of his person. Ultimate religious power for our mishnah is not ecstatic, revelatory or charismatic, but stems rather from the mundane and tragic social reality in which a householder's family suffers and hungers and so he turns to God in supplication.

Ephraim Elimelech Urbach has pointed out that the positive attitude towards the Gentiles of Nineveh expressed in our ritual's admonition is rejected in later Palestinian sources. He has suggested that this post-mishnaic shift was prompted by the eventual emergence of a powerful and threatening Christian community which viewed the sincere repentance of the Gentiles of Nineveh as an admonishment to obstinate and non-repentant contemporary Jews (Urbach 2002). In the time of the Mishnah, however, the Christians were not yet deemed to be a threat and therefore the tanna'im were not troubled by the possible polemical use of the repentance of Nineveh. Urbach's contextual reading of the Mishnah's positive attitude towards Gentiles is in keeping with a growing appreciation for the importance of locating the early rabbinic movement, and Jewish society in Palestine more generally, in the political and cultural setting of the Roman Near East. Thus, the fast-day's public admonishment may be viewed in light of the popular role of public speeches in the Second Sophistic and our ritual as a whole may be fruitfully compared to similar rituals attested in Gentile and Christian sources from late antiquity. For example, Tertullian's description of a pagan ritual is highly similar to our fast-day ritual even in respect to minor details and thus suggests that our ritual is a Jewish version of a more wide-ranging cultural phenomenon.[26] Situating the fast-day ritual in a broad cultural context brings to the fore both similarities and differences between the rabbis and their Gentile contemporaries and serves as an appropriate note on which to conclude this survey, since a major feature in the recent study of the Mishnah, and rabbinic literature more generally, is the recognition that rabbinic Judaism flourished in the context of the Roman Near East. Comparing the world of the Mishnah to the ambient Roman environment thus illuminates the clash and confluence of cultures which took place in Roman Palestine.

Further Reading

Bokser (1990); Cohen (1990); Danby (1933); Hauptman (2005); Moscovitz (2002); Neusner (1981); Stemberger (1996); Zlotnick (1988).

[26] Tert. *de Jejuniis*, 16.5. See also Levine (2001: 184–214). Cf. Diamond (2004: 98).

Bibliography

Albeck, H. (1952–59), *Shishah Sidrei Mishnah*, 6 vols., Jerusalem and Tel Aviv.

Alexander, E. S. (2003), 'Casuistic elements in Mishnaic law: examples from M. Shevu'ot', *JSQ* 10: 189–243.

Alexander, E. S. (2006), *Transmitting Mishnah: The Shaping Influence of Oral Tradition*, Cambridge.

Alexander, E. S. (2008), 'Recent literary approaches to the Mishnah', *AJS Review*, 32: 225–34.

Beer, G. *et al.* (eds.) (1912–), *Die Mischna: Text, Übersetzung und ausführlich Erklärung*, Berlin.

Berkowitz, B. A. (2006), *Execution and Invention: Death Penalty Discourse in Early Rabbinic and Christian Cultures*, New York.

Blenkinsopp, J. (2004), *Treasures Old and New: Essays in the Theology of the Pentateuch*, Grand Rapids, MI and Cambridge.

Bokser, B. M. (1990), 'Talmudic studies', in S. J. D. Cohen and E. L. Greenstein (eds.), *The State of Jewish Studies*, Detroit, pp. 80–112.

Breuer, Y. (1987), 'Perfect and participle in description of ritual in the Mishnah', *Tarbiz*, 56: 299–326. [Hebrew]

Brooten, B. J. (1982), *Women Leaders in the Ancient Synagogue: Inscriptional Evidence and Background Issues*, Chico, CA.

Cohen, S. J. D. (1983), 'Jacob Neusner, Mishnah, and counter-rabbinics: a review essay', *Conservative Judaism*, 37: 48–63.

Cohen, S. J. D. (1990), 'The modern study of ancient Judaism', in S. J. D. Cohen and E. L. Greenstein (eds.), *The State of Jewish Studies*, Detroit, pp. 55–73.

Cohen, S. J. D. (2007), 'The Judaean legal tradition and the *Halakhah* of the Mishnah', in C. E. Fonrobert and M. S. Jaffee (eds.), *The Cambridge Companion to the Talmud and Rabbinic Literature*, Cambridge, pp. 121–43.

Cohn, N. S. (2008), 'The Ritual Narrative Genre in the Misnah: The Invention of the Rabbinic Past in the Representation of Temple Ritual', Ph.D. dissertation, University of Pennsylvania, Philadelphia.

Correns, D. (2005), *Die Mischna ins Deutsche übertragen, mit einer Einleitung und Anmerkungen*, Wiesbaden.

Danby, H. (1933), *The Mishnah*, Oxford.

Diamond, E. (2004), *Holy Men and Hunger Artists: Fasting and Asceticism in Rabbinic Culture*, Oxford and New York.

Elman, Y. (2004), 'Order, sequence, and selection: the Mishnah's anthological choices', in D. Stern (ed.), *The Anthology in Jewish Literature*, Oxford and New York.

Epstein, I. (ed.) (1935–52), *The Babylonian Talmud*, translated into English, 18 vols., London.

Epstein, J. N. (2000), *Introduction to the Mishnaic Text*, Jerusalem. [Hebrew]

Felix, Y. (2000), 'The Relationship of Tosefta to Mishnah in Synoptic Parallels in Tractate Kiddushin', Ph. D. dissertation, Ramat Gan. [Hebrew]

Fisch, M. (1997), *Rational Rabbis: Science and Talmudic Culture*, Bloomington, IN.

Fox (leBeit Yoreh), H. (1999), 'Introducing Tosefta: textual, intratextual and intertextual studies', in H. Fox (leBeit Yoreh) and T. Meacham (leBeit Yoreh), *Introducing Tosefta: Textual, Intratextual and Intertextual Studies*, Hoboken, NJ, pp. 1–37.

Fraenkel, Y. (1981), *Iyunim be-olamo ha-ruhhani shel sipur ha-agadah*, Tel Aviv. [Hebrew]

Friedman, S. (2000), 'Uncovering literary dependencies in the Talmudic corpus', in S. J. D. Cohen (ed.), *The Synoptic Problem in Rabbinic Literature*, Providence, RI, pp. 35–57.

Friedman, S. (2002), *Tosefta Atiqta: Pesah Rishon: Synoptic Parallels of Mishna and Tosefta Analyzed with a Methodological Introduction*, Ramat Gan. [Hebrew]

Gafni, C. (2005), 'The Emergence of Critical Scholarship on Rabbinic Literature in the Nineteenth Century: Social and Ideological Contexts', Ph.D. dissertation, Harvard University, Cambridge, MA.

Gafni, I. M. (2001), 'A generation of scholarship on Eretz Israel in the Talmudic era: achievement and reconsideration', *Cathedra*, 100: 200–26. [Hebrew]

Goldberg, A. (1987a), 'The Tosefta: companion to the Mishna', in S. Safrai and P. J. Tomson (eds.), *The Literature of the Sages*, First Part: *Oral Tora, Halakha, Mishna, Tosefta, Talmud, External Tractates*, Assen and Philadelphia, pp. 283–301.

Goldberg, A. (1987b), 'The Mishna: a study book of Halakha', in Safrai and Tomson (eds.), *The Literature of the Sages*, pp. 211–51.

Goldberg, Arnold (1999), *Rabbinische Texte als Gegenstand der Auslegung: Gesammelte Studien*, vol. 2, ed. M. Schlüter and P. Schäfer, Tübingen.

Goldschmidt, L. (1929–36), *Der babylonische Talmud*, 12 vols., Berlin.

Halbertal, M. (1997), *Interpretative Revolutions in the Making: Values as Interpretative Considerations in Midrashei Halakhah*, Jerusalem. [Hebrew]

Hauptman, J. (2005), *Rereading the Mishnah: A New Approach to Ancient Jewish Texts*, Tübingen.

Hayes, C. E. (1997), *Between the Babylonian and Palestinian Talmuds: Accounting for Halakhic Difference in Selected Sugyot from Tractate Avodah Zarah*, New York and Oxford.

Henshke, D. (1997), *The Original Mishna in the Discourse of Later Tanna'im*, Ramat Gan. [Hebrew]

Houtman, A. (1996), *Mishnah and Tosefta*, Tübingen.

Ilan, T. (2008), *Massekhet Ta'anit: Text, Translation and Commentary*, Tübingen.

Jaffee, M. S. (2001), *Torah in the Mouth: Writing and Oral Tradition in Palestinian Judaism 200 BCE–400 CE*, Oxford.

Jewish Publication Society of America (1999), *Hebrew–English Tanakh*, Philadelphia.

Jung, L. (1938), *Yoma*, in Epstein (ed.) (1935–52).

Kapah, Y. (1963–68), *Mishnah im perush Rabenu Mosheh ben Maimom: makor ve-targum*, Jerusalem. [Hebrew]

Kehati, P. (1987–96), *The Mishnah*, 24 vols., Jerusalem.

Kline, M. (n.d.), *The Structured Mishnah*, http://chaver.com/Mishnah/TheMishnah. htm.

Krupp, M. (1987), 'Manuscripts of the Mishna', in S. Safrai and P. J. Tomson (eds.), *The Literature of the Sages*, First Part: *Oral Tora, Halakha, Mishna, Tosefta, Talmud, External Tractates*, Assen and Philadelphia, pp. 252–62.

Krupp, M. (2002–06), *Die Mischna: textkritische Ausgabe mit deutscher Übersetzung und Kommentar*, Jerusalem.

Kulp, J. (2007), 'Organisational patterns in the Mishnah in light of their Toseftan parallels', *JJS* 58: 52–78.

Lapin, H. (1996), 'Rabbis and public prayers for rain in later Roman Palestine', in A. Berlin (ed.), *Religion and Politics in the Ancient Near East*, Bethesda, MD, pp. 105–29.

Levine, D. (2001), *Communal Fasts and Rabbinic Sermons: Theory and Practice in the Talmudic Period*, Bene Berak. [Hebrew]

Lieberman, S. (1955–88), *The Tosefta*, New York.

Lieberman, S. (1962), *Hellenism in Jewish Palestine*, New York.

Lorberbaum, Y. (2004), *Image of God: Halakhah and Aggadah*, Tel Aviv. [Hebrew]

Maccoby, H. (1984), 'Jacob Neusner's Mishnah', *Midstream*, 30.5: 24–32.

Mandel, P. (2006), 'The Tosefta', in S. T. Katz (ed.), *The Cambridge History of Judaism*, vol. 4: *The Late Roman-Rabbinic Period*, Cambridge, pp. 316–35.

Margalit, N. (2000), 'Not by her mouth do we live: a literary/anthropological reading of gender in Mishnah Ketubbot, Chapter 1', *Prooftexts*, 20: 61–86.

Milikowsky, C. (1994), 'The end of prophecy and the closure of the Bible in Judaism of late antiquity', *Sidra*, 10: 83–94. [Hebrew]

Moscovitz, L. (2002), *Talmudic Reasoning: From Casuistics to Conceptualization*, Tübingen.

Naeh, S. (1994), '"Creates the fruit of lips": a phenomenological study of prayer according to Mishnah *Berakhot* 4:3, 5:5', *Tarbiz*, 63: 185–218. [Hebrew]

Nagen (Genack), Y. (2003), 'Sukkot in Rabbinical Thought: Motifs in the Halacha of Sukkot in Talmudic Literature', Ph.D. dissertation, Hebrew University, Jerusalem. [Hebrew]

Nagen (Genack), Y. (2007), *The Soul of Mishnah*, Othniel. [Hebrew]

Neusner, J. (1977–86), *The Tosefta*, 6 vols., New York.

Neusner, J. (1981), *Judaism: The Evidence of the Mishnah*, Chicago.

Neusner, J. (1988), *The Mishnah: A New Translation*, New Haven.

Neusner, J. (1991), *Judaism as Philosophy: The Method and Message of the Mishnah*, Columbia, SC.

Neusner, J. (1992), *The Tosefta: An Introduction*, Atlanta.

Neusner, J. (2002), 'The Mishnah in rabbinic context: Tosefta and Sifra', in A. J. Avery-Peck and J. Neusner (eds.), *The Mishnah in Contemporary Perspective*, Part 1, Leiden, pp. 91–120.

Neusner, J. (2004), *Making God's Word Work: A Guide to the Mishnah*, New York and London.

Oppenheimer, A. (2007), *Rabbi Judah ha-Nasi*, Jerusalem. [Hebrew]

Poirier, J. C. (1996), 'Jacob Neusner, the Mishnah, and ventriloquism', *JQR* 87: 61–78.

Rabbinowitz, J. (1938), *Ta'anith*, in Epstein (ed.) (1935–52).

Reichman, R. (1998), *Mishna und Sifra: Ein literarkritischer Vergleich paralleler Überlieferungen*, Tübingen.

Rosen-Zvi, I. (2008a), *The Rite that Was Not: Temple, Midrash and Gender in Tractate Sotah*, Jerusalem. [Hebrew]

Rosen-Zvi, I. (2008b), 'Orality, narrativity, rhetoric: new directions in Mishnah research', *AJS Review*, 32: 235–49.

Sabato, M. (2004), 'Why did they say two rows in the cellar?', *Sidra*, 19: 101–16. [Hebrew]

Safrai, S., Safrai, Z. and Safrai, H. (2008), *Mishnat Eretz Yisrael*, 3 vols., Tel Aviv. [Hebrew]

Samely, A. (2002), *Rabbinic Interpretation of Scripture in the Mishnah*, Oxford.

Samely, A. (2007), *Forms of Rabbinic Literature and Thought*, Oxford.

Sammter, A. *et al.* (eds.) (1887–1933), *Mischnaioth: Die sechs Ordnungen der Mischna*, 6 vols., Berlin.

Sanders, E. P. (1990), *Jewish Law from Jesus to the Mishnah: Five Studies*, London and Philadelphia.

Schwartz, S. (2001), *Imperialism and Jewish Society: 200 BCE to 640 CE*, Princeton and Oxford.

Shapira, H. and Fisch, M. (1999), 'The debates between the Houses of Shammai and Hillel: the meta-halakhic issue', *Tel Aviv University Law Review*, 22: 461–97. [Hebrew]

Sharvit, S. (2004), *Tractate Avoth through the Ages: A Critical Edition, Prolegomena and Appendices*, Jerusalem.

Shemesh, A. (2003), *Punishments and Sins: From Scripture to the Rabbis*, Jerusalem. [Hebrew]

Simon-Shoshan, M. (2007), 'Halakhic mimesis: rhetorical and redactional strategies in Tannaitic narrative', *Diné Israel*, 24: 101–23.

Simon-Shoshan, M. (2008), 'Between philology and Foucault: new syntheses in contemporary Mishnah studies', *AJS Review*, 32: 251–62.

Soloveitchik, H. (1978), 'Can Halakhic texts talk history?', *AJS Review*, 3: 153–96.

Stemberger, G. (1996), *Introduction to the Talmud and Midrash*, 2nd edn., trans. and ed. M. Bockmuehl, Edinburgh.

Stemberger, G. (2007), 'Rabbinic literature: editions and studies', *European Journal of Jewish Studies*: 157–70.

Sussman, Y. (1981), 'Manuscripts and text traditions of the Mishnah', *Proceedings of the Seventh World Congress of Jewish Studies: Studies in Talmud, Halacha and Midrash*, vol. 3, pp. 215–50. [Hebrew]

Sussman, Y. (2005), '"Torah shebeal peh' peshutah kemashmaah"', in Y. Sussman and D. Rosenthal (eds.), *Mehqerei Talmud: Talmudic Studies Dedicated to the Memory of Professor Eliezer Shimshon Rosenthal*, vol. 3.1, Jerusalem, pp. 209–384. [Hebrew]

Tropper, A. (2004), *Wisdom, Politics, and Historiography: Tractate Avot in the Context of the Graeco-Roman Near East*, Oxford.

Urbach, E. E. (1945–46), 'Matay paskah hanevuah?', *Tarbiz*, 17: 1–11. [Hebrew]

Urbach, E. E. (2002), 'Teshuvat anshe Nineveh vehavikuah hayehudi nozri', in *The World of the Sages: Collected Studies*, Jerusalem, pp. 556–60. [Hebrew]

Wald, S. G. (2007a), 'Mishnah', in F. Skolnik and M. Berenbaum (eds.), *Encyclopaedia Judaica*, 2nd edn., Farmington Hills, MI and Jerusalem, vol. 14, pp. 319–31.

Wald, S. G. (2007b), Review of Leib Moscovitz's *Talmudic Reasoning: From Casuistics to Conceptualization*, *JQR* 97: e58–e64.

Walfish, A. (1996), 'Response: To S. Naeh, "Creates the fruit of lips"', *Tarbiz*, 65: 301–14. [Hebrew]

Walfish, A. (2001), 'The Literary Method of Redaction in Mishnah based on Tractate Rosh Hashanah', Ph.D. dissertation, Hebrew University, Jerusalem.

Walfish, A. (2003), 'Survey of publications in the field of Mishnah', *Netuim*, 10: 97–109. [Hebrew]

Walfish, A. (2005–06), 'Approaching the text and approaching God: the redaction of Mishnah and Tosefta Berkahot', *Jewish Studies*, 43: 21–79.

Walfish, A. (2006), 'The poetics of the Mishnah', in A. J. Avery-Peck and J. Neusner (eds.), *The Mishnah in Contemporary Perspective*, Part 2, Leiden and Boston, pp. 153–89.

Walfish, A. (2008), 'The nature and purpose of Mishnaic narrative: recent seminal contributions', *AJS Review*, 32: 263–89.

Zeidman, R. (1999), 'An introduction to the genesis and nature of Tosefta, the chameleon of rabbinic literature', in H. Fox (leBeit Yoreh) and T. Meacham (leBeit Yoreh), *Introducing Tosefta: Textual, Intratextual and Intertextual Studies*, Hoboken, NJ, pp. 73–97.

Zlotnick, D. (1988), *The Iron Pillar. Mishnah: Redaction, Form, and Intent*, Jerusalem.

7

The Tosefta and Its Value for Historical Research: Questioning the Historical Reliability of Case Stories

RONEN REICHMAN

1. Contents

THE TOSEFTA, LIKE THE MISHNAH, IS A COMPILATION IN HEBREW of early rabbinic legal traditions, which ostensibly date from the first to the early third century CE, the so-called tannaitic period.

2. Manuscripts

There are two main manuscripts: MS Erfurt,[1] written probably in Italy in the twelfth or possibly even the eleventh century, and MS Vienna,[2] written in Spain in the thirteenth or fourteenth century. In addition there are manuscripts in London, Bologna and Zurich, as well as numerous fragments from the Cairo Genizah in Cambridge, New York and elsewhere. The fullest text is MS Vienna, but even this is not 'complete', and the 'complete' text has to be reconstructed from different sources.

3. Editions

MS Erfurt served as the basis for M. S. Zuckermandel's classic nineteenth-century edition of the Tosefta (1880, 1882). K. H. Rengstorf's more recent edition (1967, 1983) of the same manuscript offers a more accurate transcription, but it is still incomplete. Sh. Lieberman, noting that MS Erfurt has to some degree been influenced by parallels in the two Talmuds,[3] decided to make the more independent MS Vienna the basis for his important edition,

---

[1] Oriental Department of the State Library in Berlin, Preussisches Kulturbesitz.
[2] National Library Vienna, Heb. 20, Catalogue Schwartz, No. 46.
[3] For a detailed discussion see Friedman (2002: 79ff.).

Proceedings of the British Academy **165**, 117–127. © The British Academy 2010.

despite its being later in date (Lieberman 1955–88). Both the Zuckermandel and Lieberman texts are included in the Bar Ilan Judaic Library CD. Transcriptions of MS Vienna, MS Erfurt, the Genizah fragments, and the *editio princeps* (Venice 1521) can be found on the Bar Ilan University website 'Primary Textual Witnesses to Tannaitic Literature (Prof. Shamma Friedman, Prof. Leib Moscovitz)' (www.biu.ac.il/JS/tannaim). A full critical edition of the Tosefta, which takes into account all the text witnesses (including medieval quotations) remains a desideratum.

4. Translations

The only complete translation of the Tosefta, by Jacob Neusner into English (Neusner 1977–86), has to be treated with some caution, since it is somewhat inaccurate in detail. The substantial portions available in German from a variety of hands vary in quality.[4]

5. Place and Date

Since the Tosefta quotes only Palestinian scholars and is closely related to the Mishnah, there can be no doubt that it originated in Palestine, almost certainly in one of the centres of rabbinic learning in the Galilee. Its date is bound up with its relationship to the Mishnah: if it is a 'supplement' to the Mishnah (as the name Tosefta might suggest) then it must come after that work, but some have argued that at least in some cases the Tosefta is earlier than the Mishnah (see below). It does not quote authorities later than the early third century, and this indicates that it originated then,[5] but the manuscript transmission suggests it was later quite vigorously reworked over a considerable period of time.

* * *

Since the beginning of scholarly research on the Tosefta, its normative and narrative traditions have served as an important source of knowledge and as an aid to understanding the history of Roman Palestine. The research on the Tosefta in the last twenty years, carried out especially by Shamma Friedman (2000, 2002) and Judith Hauptman (1999, 2000, 2001, 2005a, 2005b), has changed the traditional view of the Tosefta as a work that was primarily to

---

[4] e.g. the Rengstorf edition contains translation.
[5] Goldberg (1987: 293–5) dates it to the beginning of the third century, accepting the traditional view which ascribes it to R. Ḥiyya bar Abba, a student of Rabbi Judah haNasi; Stemberger (1996: 157) dates it to the end of the third century.

be considered as a commentary on the Mishnah.[6] The new findings resulting
from the synoptic comparison of the Mishnah and the Tosefta show that the
latter can be conceived as neither a response to, nor a simple continuation
and completion of the Mishnah. Much of the material in the Tosefta seems to
be the very 'stuff' from which the Mishnah was fashioned. The new findings,
and here again the work of Shamma Friedman calls for special attention, offer
insights into rabbinic legal history and are relevant for historical consideration. They stress the importance of the Tosefta for further historical research.

Thus it seems reasonable to raise some methodological considerations
about the use of this material for historical research, and, if possible, to
advance the discussion of this classical issue a step further. By doing so the
following considerations will concentrate on the use of the legal narratives
that can be found throughout the Tosefta. Although it is surely true that the
descriptive portion of the Tosefta is proportionally much smaller than its prescriptive one, in comparison to all other tannaitic texts it is much more
informative. Shaye Cohen in his survey 'The rabbi in second-century Jewish
society' (Cohen 1999) has listed the texts that describe the legal decisions rendered by rabbis as they occur in the Mishnah, Tosefta, Mekhilta, Sifra and
Sifre according to a threefold classification: type A includes cases brought
before a rabbi (or rabbis) for a decision (pp. 962ff.); type B includes stories
where the rabbis assert their authority uninvited and unasked (p. 964); and
type C includes the remaining narratives, which have a much less common
structure (p. 965). The lists are far from being complete but they nevertheless
give an impression of the proportion of the narratives in the various works.
Type A includes seventy-one cases, fifty-four being from the Tosefta; type B
includes eleven cases, of which the Tosefta documents eight; and type C
includes forty-six cases, of which twenty-two are from the Tosefta. Texts
belonging to type A have a typical form, exemplified in the following story:

> It once happened that Shema'iah, a man of the villages Otenai, had in his hand
> a jar full of purification-water, and he pushed against the door, from which the
> key, unclean with corpse-uncleanness, was suspended. And he came and asked
> Rabban Yoḥanan ben Zakkai. And he said to him: Shema'iah, go and sprinkle
> your water. (t.Parah 10.2)

Focusing on the question of the historical reliability of this sort of narrative,
it is my view that these narratives do possess significance for historical
research. Their relevance ranges from an increased understanding of the daily

---

[6] For a survey of the various traditional views that assume the dependence of the Tosefta on the
Mishnah (e.g. the views of A. Schwarz, J. H. Dünner, A. Spanier, A. Guttmann, Ch. Albeck,
J. N. Epstein, J. Neusner and A. Goldberg) see Stemberger (1996: 152–5) and Houtman (1996:
7–19). Houtman herself argues for this opinion. See ibid., pp. 230–7.

life of the Jews in Palestine and the activity of the rabbis in society, to the more precise determination of their power and position within society.

There is widespread agreement that case stories of this sort reflect historical reality, and that they should be considered as a more or less authentic report of events.[7] It is apparent that a distinction can be drawn between such stories and aggadic anecdotes that have a more strongly ideological bent. This agreement, however, has had the unfortunate consequence of reducing the demand for a full justification of the historicity of these reports, leaving the question of their historical plausibility with a distinct lack of explicit justification: either the historical significance of such reports has been taken for granted, or it has been merely asserted as if it were an already established fact. So far as is known to me, and to the extent that explicit arguments have been made on this matter, they have actually come from the opposite side and have attempted to cast various doubts on the reliability of these texts as a source for discerning historical reality.[8] This scepticism is grounded in the fact that the names of the rabbis appearing in the variant versions of these texts fluctuate (Hezser 1993: 392; 1997: 192). Furthermore, it has been argued that the highly literary and formalised patterns employed by these texts suggest a mode of composition that is apt more for oral transmission than for historical accuracy. Thus it is the distinct literary character of these texts that make them suspect with regard to their historical plausibility (Hezser 1993: 392).

An explanation of these literary traits can pursue one of two alternate paths: either these reports are highly abbreviated and redacted versions of a much more detailed account of events; or, more radically, they are pure fabrications—literary constructs that were conceived for various academic goals. Concerning the first argument, it is hard to see why such an abbreviated version of events that would include only the elementary information about the historical context and circumstances should be suspect. In fact, the opposite conclusion seems equally plausible; namely, that the reduced minimal circumstances to which the text refers do in fact reflect the historical character of events. A far more serious challenge is posed by the prospect of their being purely constructed, fictional stories. Given that it is typical for the

---

[7] Scepticism concerning the historical significance of the stories is based mainly on aggadic narratives. See the survey of Hezser (1993). As to the reliability of short halakhic stories, evaluations differ. See Hezser (1993: 391ff.; 1997: 32). See also Neusner (1983: 116): 'When Sages tell a story of an event on a particular occasion, we have no reason to believe the story, except as an account of what the storyteller wished people to believe. But when the Talmud narrates cases and precedents, we fairly assume that the character of these cases and precedents provides solid evidence about the things rabbis thought they could and could not do in their social role as judges, teachers, and holy men.' See further Neusner (1984: 16f.) and Goodman (1983: 93–4).

[8] The main representative of this line of scepticism is Catherine Hezser. Her views are set forth mainly in Hezser (1993, 1997).

rabbis to adduce preceding authorities for their halakhic pronouncements, there is a certain plausibility to the supposition that case stories are mere fabrications deserving scant historical consideration. However, in order to determine the dimension of fictionality in halakhic texts, one should take seriously the perspective in which these texts were received by the rabbis themselves. Clarifying the historical value of these texts can only be achieved when the discursive context within which these texts are embedded is thoroughly explored. The notion that texts possess inherent literary traits that would determine *prima facie* their fictionality is of questionable value. To view fictionality as an inherent quality of the text would unduly diminish the significance that the process of reception plays in shaping the meaning of the document. In fact, fictionality is not an inherent quality of any given text, but rather an interpretive judgement concerning the text. A proposition with the form 'Textual feature x is fictional' is itself dependent upon the specific social conventions governing the reception and interpretation of the interpretive community within which the proposition is proffered.[9] Indeed, the propositional approach to the problem of fictionality is not the proper way to address this problem. It is very doubtful whether texts have semantic structures that can be regarded as having the inherent quality of fictionality. There is little doubt that texts do provide more or less standardised indications of their own fictionality; but that a text is fictional in no way entails that such indicators are present. Finally, the fact that these indicators are conventionally recognised as an indication of a text's fictionality merely reinforces the conclusion that is being drawn here: even if these indications are to be integrated into the text, they must be recognised and evaluated as such in the process of their reception.

Sharing the theoretical framework proposed by literary theorists such as Siegfried J. Schmidt (1980), Achim Barsch (1997) and Gebhard Rusch (1997),[10] I would suggest that the pragmatic perspective is the correct methodological approach for exploring the fictional dimension of texts. Instead of focusing on the semantic or linguistic character of a text in order to determine its fictionality, I propose that we take a discourse-oriented approach to the problem of delimiting the border between textual fiction and historical fact. By integrating the insights that come from adopting this

---

[9] As J. Ihwe and H. Rieser have pointed out, the distinction between 'fictional' and 'non-fictional' results from a socio-cultural educational process, and there is 'simply no reason to suppose that the members of all the various cultures in existence share the same attitude to fictional discourses'. See Ihwe and Rieser (1979: esp. 75). The same also applies to the notion of 'reality', there being no such thing as 'the reality'. The reality of an object or a state of affairs, or, in other words, the truth of an assertion denoting or describing objects or states of affairs, is necessarily decided in the framework of a peculiar world-model.

[10] See also Wildekamp *et al.* (1980).

attitude, a more differentiated image of the text and its relation to historical reality comes into view.

Insofar as the legal narratives that recount the creation and initiation of legal decisions constitute the starting point of a specific halakhic discourse, it is reasonable to suppose a connection between the case story and actual events. In the context of halakhic discourse, a norm whose genesis refers back to the concrete questioning of a rabbinic authority possesses substantial normative force. It is not merely an opinion that was uttered in the academy but is directly connected to praxis and thus bears a strong degree of validity. Norms of this kind are considered as halakhah for decisions to be made in praxis, which the rabbis regarded as an important orientation for further decisions. As the baraita in Bava Batra 130b shows:

> The Halakhah may not be derived either from theoretical [opinion] or from practical [decision] unless one has been told [that] the halakhah [is to be taken as a rule] for practical decisions. [Once a person has] asked and was informed [that] a halakhah [was to be taken as a guide] for practical decisions, he may continue to give practical decisions [accordingly].

This passage serves to demonstrate the means by which the validity of norms created in this way attain authority. A pure fabrication of such cases would mean a trangression against principles that are constitutive for halakhic discourse.

By taking a discourse-oriented approach to the problem of determining the historical reliability of case stories, we also stand to gain insight into the way in which these stories accrue fictional elements in the course of their reception. Certain literary theorists speak of a 'fictionality convention' (Schmidt 1980), designating by this a particular cognitive mode in the mind of the receiver which serves as the medium for the reception of a given text. A typical case from rabbinic discourse will serve to elucidate the character of this receptive mode of cognition. For example, a narrative tradition that was presumed to have had a historical kernel subsequently undergoes explicit revision and emendation. A matter of dispute is brought before the rabbis: one side brings its opinion concerning the ruling on a halakhic issue by referring to a case story as its justification, while the other side questions the validity of the argument by raising the rhetorical question 'is there a proof from this?'[11] and by suggesting a revision of the case.

Tosefta Terumot 2.13 documents R. Judah's debate with the Sages concerning the interpretation of a case story:

---

[11] The formula *misham rea'ya* occurs several times in the Tosefta and has the same argumentative function. See t.Ter. 1.1, 2.13, 3.13; t.Eruv. 2.11; t.Suk. 2.10; t.Yev. 4.5; t.BM 4.2; t.BB 1.11; t.Sanh. 2.8.

[The laws of] *Orlah*[12] and mixed seeds in a vineyard are the same for [the field of] a Gentile in the Land of Israel, in Syria, and outside of the Land [of Israel]; however R. Judah says: A Gentile's vineyard in Syria is not subject to (the laws) of the fourth year.

Said R. Judah: 'It once happen ed (*Ma'ase*), that Sabion, the head of the synagogue at Keziv, purchased a vineyard in its fourth year from a Gentile in Syria and gave him payment. And he came and asked Rabban Gamliel, who was passing from place to place and he [Gamliel] said to him:

"Wait until we can dwell upon the law."

They said to him: "Can proof be brought from that?"

He also sent a messenger to him secretly [saying]:

"That which you have done is done, but do not do it again."'[13]

The story tells us that Rabban Gamliel, while travelling in the north, had been asked by a person named Sabion, the head of the synagogue in Keziv,[14] about permission to use grapes he bought from a Gentile who owned a vineyard in Syria in its fourth year of growth (Kerem Reva'i). Fruits of the fourth year fall into the category of commandments dependent on the Land of Israel (m.Kid. 1.9). They are consecrated and must be either brought to Jerusalem for consumption or redeemed. Ownership by a Gentile would not matter principally, but the question here referred to a vineyard located in Syria, which possesses a special status between Eretz Israel and all other foreign lands in the halakhah. This fact made answering the question difficult. One could not simply deduce the answer from the rule that holds that 'He who purchases a field in Syria is like one who purchases (a field) in the suburbs of Jerusalem.'[15] As the story was transmitted in rabbinic circles, R. Gamliel indeed left the question open. No clear decision was taken, which readily lends itself to an interpretation that R. Gamliel was offering indirectly his permission to use the fruits bought under these circumstances. Such, at any rate, was the position adopted by R. Judah. His opponents rejected this interpretation, however, making their point by supplying additional information to the case story. They point to the correspondence that took place afterwards, which reads as follows: 'He [that is, R. Gamliel] sent a messenger to him secretly, saying, "That which you have done is done, but do not do it again."' The fact that the revelation of this secret message serves as decisive refutation of R. Judah's argument should strike one as rather suspect. Had

---

[12] Orlah (literally, 'uncircumcised') entails in this context the prohibition against using and eating the fruit of trees during the first three years after their planting (Lev. 19:23).

[13] Translation according to MS Vienna.

[14] Keziv = Akhziv. The source of the name may be from Akhzav, which in Hebrew is a creek that flows only during certain times of the year. Romans called it Ecdippa or Ecdippon, which is etymologically related to the Hebrew name.

[15] See m.Ḥal. 4.11, which should be considered as an old ruling from the Second Temple period. See also in t.Kel. (BK) 1.5 and b.Git. 8a.

an answer actually been sent in secret to the head of the synagogue in Keziv, it probably would have remained a secret matter of which the Sages remained ignorant. Surely the Sages were not in possession of a better tradition than R. Judah about the details of R. Gamliel's travels around Keziv? They point only to what may have happened, to an imagined course of events 'as if' it had taken place, so that the difference between the 'real' and the 'possible' is blurred. Indeed, even R. Judah would not have been able to exclude this possibility as such, and merely noting the possibility of this addendum is sufficient to refute his argument.[16]

The argument of the opponents of R. Judah sought to make the point that postponing the answer about the use of these grapes could be, and therefore should be, interpreted as an ad hoc decision from which it is not legitimate to generalise by inferring a precedent for future decisions. The matter that concerns the disputants is R. Gamliel's indecision. What can be gained from this with regard to rulings for future cases? Referring to the correspondence secretly held between R. Gamliel and Sabion is equivalent to maintaining that postponing an answer could have consequences only with regard to the concrete situation at hand and is not to be viewed as establishing a precedent with legal force for future decisions.[17]

There are many manifestations of fictionality and there are many options to judge the truth-value of assertions that are included in a text. According to the prevailing view, a text becomes 'fictional' if readers of a text interpret or decide that some textual element is without a non-verbal, existing referent in their model of the world (world view).[18] This kind of strict dichotomy between fact and fiction does not seem to characterise the phenomenon of fictionality in the legal culture of the Sages. In this context, a text may be

---

[16] The following story in t.Suk. 2.8 repeats the same argumentative pattern: "'One should bind up the *lulav* [the palm-branch, willow-branch, myrtle-branch] only with that which is its own species.'—These are the words of R. Judah. R. Meir says: "Even with a rope [it is allowed]." Said R. Meir: "It happened that the people of Jerusalem bound up their *lulavin* with gold threads." He said to him: "Can proof be brought from that? Even they tied it up with that which is its own species underneath [the gold threads].'"

[17] The interesting point is the form in which the Sages articulate their argument. In the formulation of their answer, there is no linguistic element that shows that they were only suggesting a possibility. The only indication of the fictional character of their argument is the context of the debate, but this is enough to make it clear that the Sages, borne along by the needs of their legal reasoning, entered a realm where it makes no difference, whether, by making reference to the circumstances of a case, these circumstances are considered to be actual or possible.

[18] Schmidt (1980: 535). The application of the 'fictionality convention' would mean that 'the recipient accepts that some or all assertive statements in T have no referent in his WMO (i.e. [ortho]-world-model) because these statements bear other kinds of relevance or fulfil a need for S2 (i.e. the recipient)' (ibid., p. 540). Schmidt offers the following definition of 'ortho-world-model': 'The world-model on which a system relies in his social group I shall call ortho-world-model (i.e. WMO)' (ibid., p. 531).

considered 'fictional' in another way: namely, if the recipient, without decid-
ing that an element of the text has a non-verbal referent in his model of the
world (world view), is either not primarily interested in this decision but
rather in other features of the communication process, or is even consciously
interested in leaving matters vague to a certain degree regarding the truth-
value of the assertions at issue. Thus, the principle governing the inclusion of
a given textual element would depend less upon its historical veracity and
more upon other factors such as its normative relevance.

I suppose that students at one of the talmudic academies of the time
would have been impressed by the addendum offered by the Sages, and that
this would have been due as much to the rhetorical impact in leaving matters
vague as to the distinction between fiction and reality. This kind of rhetoric
was in fact needed to make legal arguments interesting and powerful, and to
keep the halakhic discourse as vivid and skilful as possible. Students of that
time probably did regard the end of the story as 'true' to the extent that the
normative questions constituted the focus of their interest. In this instance,
the question of fictionality would be posed within a framework not primarily
determined by historical accuracy but rather by legal argumentation.

As for us, we should maintain that R. Gamliel did visit the Jewish community in Keziv during one of his travels; that he found there a synagogue,
or something similar, led by a person named Sabion, or something similar,
who occupied himself in trade with Gentiles in the neighbouring region, and
who was familiar with the restrictions laid upon products in the fourth year
of their growth. Certainly, we should not exaggerate by drawing from this
story historical conclusions about measures taken by the centre in Yavne in
order to take control of small communities on the periphery by way of a correspondence on halakhic issues through messengers travelling between Yavne
and the north of the land in the time during which R. Gamliel occupied a
leading position in rabbinic circles.

Further Reading

Elman (1991); Fox and Meacham (eds. 1999); Friedman (2002); Neusner (1986);
Stemberger (1996).

Bibliography

Barsch, A. (1997), 'Fiktionalität in der Sicht von Rezipienten', *Studia Poetica*, 10:
93–109.
Basser, H. W. (1999), 'The antiquity of some mishnaic and toseftan decrees and

fences and the nature of the works in which they are embedded', in Fox and Meacham (eds.) (1999), pp. 241–76.

Braverman, N. (1989/90), 'Concerning the language of Mishnaic Hebrew', *Proceedings of the Tenth World Congress of Jewish Studies*, Section 4, vol. 1, Jerusalem, pp. 31–8.

Cohen, S. J. D. (1999), 'The rabbi in second-century Jewish society', in Horbury *et al.* (eds.) (1999), pp. 922–90.

Elman, Y. (1991), 'Babylonian Baraitot in the Tosefta and the "dialectology" of Middle Hebrew', *AJS Review*, 16: 1–29.

Elman, Y. (1994), *Toseftan Baraitot in Talmudic Babylonia*, New Jersey.

Fox, H. and Meacham, T. (eds.) (1999), *Introducing Tosefta: Textual, Intratextual and Intertextual Studies*, New York.

Friedheim, E. (2003), 'Who are the deities concealed behind the rabbinic expression "a nursing female image"?', *HThR* 96.2: 239–250.

Friedman, Sh. (1992–93), 'The primacy of Tosefta in Mishnah–Tosefta parallels: Shabbat 16.1—Kol Kitve ha-Kodesh', *Tarbiz*, 62: 313–38. [Hebrew]

Friedman, Sh. (1994), 'The primacy of Tosefta in Mishnah–Tosefta parallels', *Proceedings of the Eleventh World Congress of Jewish Studies*, Section 3, vol. 1, Jerusalem, pp. 15–22. [Hebrew]

Friedman, Sh. (2000), 'Uncovering literary dependencies in the talmudic corpus', in Sh. Cohen (ed.), *The Synoptic Problem in Rabbinic Literature*, Providence, RI, pp. 35–57.

Friedman, Sh. (2002), *Tosefta Atiqta Pesaḥ Rishon: Synoptic Parallels of Mishna and Tosefta Analysed with a Methodological Introduction*, Ramat Gan. [Hebrew]

Goldberg, A. (1987), 'The Tosefta: companion to the Mishna', in S. Safrai and P. J. Tomson (eds.), *The Literature of the Sages*, First Part: *Oral Tora, Halakha, Mishna, Tosefta, Talmud, External Tractates*, Assen and Philadelphia, pp. 283–302.

Goodman, M. (1983), *State and Society in Roman Galilee, AD 132–212*, Totowa, NJ.

Hauptman, J. (1999), 'Women and inheritance in rabbinic texts: identifying elements of a critical feminist impulse', in Fox and Meacham (eds.) (1999), pp. 221–40.

Hauptman, J. (2000), 'Mishnah as a response to "Tosefta"', in Sh. Cohen (ed.), *The Synoptic Problem in Rabbinic Literature*, Providence, RI, pp. 13–34.

Hauptman, J. (2001), 'Does the Tosefta precede the Mishnah? Halakhah, Aggada and narrative coherence', *Judaism*, 50: 224–40.

Hauptman, J. (2005a), *Rereading the Mishna*, Tübingen.

Hauptman, J. (2005b), 'The Tosefta as a commentary on an early Mishna', *Jewish Studies* (Internet Journal) 4: 109–32; www.biu.ac.il/JS/JSIJ/4–2005/Hauptman.pdf

Hezser, C. (1993), 'The historical significance of the stories in y. Neziqin', in *Form, Function, and Historical Significance of the Rabbinic Story in Yerushalmi Neziqin*, Tübingen, pp. 382–91.

Hezser, C. (1997), *The Social Structure of the Rabbinic Movement in Roman Palestine*, Tübingen.

Horbury, W., Davies, W. D. and Sturdy, J. (eds.) (1999), *The Cambridge History of Judaism*, vol. 3: *The Early Roman Period*, Cambridge.

Houtman, A. (1996), *Mishna and Tosefta*, Tübingen.

Ihwe, J. and Rieser, H. (1979), 'Normative and descriptive theory of fiction: some contemporary issues', *Poetics*, 8.1–2: 63–84.

Ilan, T. (1999), '"Beruriah has spoken well" (tKelim Bava Metzia 1:6). The historical Beruriah and her transformation in the rabbinic corpora', in *Integrating Women into Second Temple History*, Tübingen, pp. 175–94.

Kulp, J. (2007), 'Organisational patterns in the Mishnah in light of their Toseftan parallels', *JJS* 58.1: 52–78.

Langer, G. (1992–93), 'Zum Vermögensrecht von Frauen in der Ehe am Beispiel des Mischna- und Tosefta-Traktates Ketubbot', *Kairos*, 34–35: 27–63.

Lieberman, S. (1955–88), *The Tosefta: According to the Codex Vienna, with Variants from Codex Erfurt, Geniza Mss. and Editio Princeps (Venice 1521)*, 5 vols. (including the orders Zera'im, Mo'ed and Nashim and the three Babot of Nezikin), New York.

Neusner, J. (1977–86), *The Tosefta*, 6 vols., New York.

Neusner, J. (1983), *Judaism in Society: The Evidence of the Yerushalmi*, Chicago and London.

Neusner, J. (1984), 'Introduction: methodology in Talmudic history', in idem (ed.), *Ancient Judaism: Debates and Disputes*, Chico, CA.

Neusner, J. (1986), *The Tosefta: Its Structures and Its Sources*, Atlanta.

Porton, G. G. (1993), 'Gentiles and Israelites in Mishnah-Tosefta: a study in ethnicity', in S. F. Chyet and D. H. Ellenson (eds.), *Bits of Honey: Essays for Samson H. Levey*, Atlanta, pp. 93–111.

Porton, G. G. (1998), *Goyim: Gentiles and Israelites in Mishnah-Tosefta*, Atlanta.

Rengstorf, K. H. (ed.) (1967, 1983), *Rabbinische Text. Erste Reihe: Die Tosefta* (*Toharot*: Stuttgart 1967; *Zeraim*: Stuttgart 1983).

Rusch, G. (1997), 'Fiktionalisierung als Element von Medienhandlungsstrategien', *Studia Poetica*, 10: 134–5.

Schmidt, S. J. (1980), 'Fictionality in literary and non-literary discourse', *Poetics*, 8: 525–46.

Stemberger, G. (1996), *Introduction to the Talmud and Midrash*, 2nd edn., trans. and ed. M. Bockmuehl, Edinburgh.

Wildekamp, A., van Montfoort, I. and van Ruiswijk, W. (1980), 'Fictionality and convention', *Poetics*, 9: 547–67.

Zeidman, R. (1999), 'An introduction to the genesis and nature of Tosefta, the chameleon of rabbinic literature', in Fox and Meacham (eds.) (1999), pp. 73–97.

Zuckermandel, M. S. (1880), *Tosephta*, Pasewalk.

Zuckermandel, M. S. (1882), *Tosephta: Supplement mit Übersicht, Register und Glossar*, Pasewalk.

8

Halakhic Midrashim as Historical Sources

GÜNTER STEMBERGER

1. Contents

THE HALAKHIC MIDRASHIM ARE COMMENTARIES on the biblical books of
Exodus through Deuteronomy with a special emphasis on their importance
for the halakhah, the religious law. Because of this emphasis there is no such
midrash on the book of Genesis which contains mainly narrative, not law.
But also for the biblical books covered by halakhic midrashim, there is no
commentary on larger narrative sections as, for example, Exod. 1–11. For
each of these biblical books we have one full commentary, that is, Mekhilta
de-R. Ishmael on Exodus (Mek.), Sifra ('the book') on Leviticus, Sifre ('the
books') Numbers and Sifre Deuteronomy. Other midrashim on the same biblical books have been lost over time, but have been recovered from quotations
and fragmentary manuscripts from the Genizah of Cairo since the late nineteenth century: they are the Mekhilta de-R. Simeon ben Yoḥai on Exodus
(MRS), Sifre Zutta ('the small Sifre') on Numbers (SZ) and Midrash
Tanna'im (Midr. Tann.), also called the Mekhilta on Deuteronomy. Another
fragmentary midrash on Deuteronomy, Devarim Zutta, is known through a
number of passages (95 verses) which Kahana (2002) has excerpted from a
Karaite work; this midrash is too fragmentary to be included in our survey.

2. Manuscripts

The manuscript transmission of these works is unequal; a full description of
the available manuscripts and Genizah fragments is provided by Kahana
(1995). For the Mekhilta we have two full manuscripts, MS Oxford 151.2
from about 1291 and MS Munich, Cod. hebr. 117.1, copied in 1433. Sifra is
preserved in two very early manuscripts, belonging to two different textual
traditions: Codex Assemani 66 (Vatican) is the oldest extant rabbinic manuscript, ninth or tenth century, with a superlinear Babylonian vocalisation

Proceedings of the British Academy **165**, 129–142. © The British Academy 2010.

which attests to the quasi-canonical status of the Midrash; the end of the manuscript is not preserved. MS Vatican Ebr. 31, probably from Egypt, is dated to 1073. The earliest and most important manuscript of Sifre Numbers and Sifre Deuteronomy is MS Vatican 32, copied in the tenth or early eleventh century. For all these midrashim we also have a considerable number of fragments from the Cairo Genizah, important because many of them are earlier than the full manuscripts and in general represent an oriental textual tradition. The fragmentary midrashim have been reconstructed on the basis of quotations in two midrashic collections, the Yalkut (Europe, thirteenth century) and the Midrash ha-Gadol (Yemen, thirteenth century), and supplemented by fragments from the Genizah.[1]

3. Printed Editions and Translations

For the Mekhilta there are two critical editions, one by H. S. Horovitz and I. A. Rabin (1931), based on the *editio princeps* Venice 1545 with variants from other MSS, the other by J. Z. Lauterbach (1933–35), an eclectic edition accompanied by an English translation. Neither edition is fully satisfactory; a new critical edition of one section has been published by M. I. Kahana (1999). The full text of the manuscripts and Genizah fragments is available on the homepage of Bar Ilan University (www.biu.ac.il/JS/tannaim). The text has again been translated into English by J. Neusner (1997c), into German by J. Winter and A. Wünsche (1909) and into Spanish by T. Martínez-Sáiz (1995).

Sifra is still quoted according to the edition of I. H. Weiss (1862); the critical edition by L. Finkelstein (1983–91) remains incomplete (Lev. 1–5). The English translation by J. Neusner (1988, 1997a) is very useful, but frequently harmonised with the text of parallels in Mishnah and Tosefta.

Sifre Numbers is available in the critical edition by H. S. Horovitz (1917); a new edition according to modern standards is a desideratum (see Kahana 1986). There are translations into English by J. Neusner (1998), German by D. Börner-Klein (1997, not quite replacing the translation by K.-G. Kuhn (1959), with its very comprehensive annotation) and Spanish by M. Pérez Fernández (1989). For Sifre Deuteronomy the standard edition is by L. Finkelstein (1939); here, too, a new edition according to modern standards is desirable. Translations based on Finkelstein exist in English (R. Hammer 1986; J. Neusner 1997b), German (H. Bietenhard 1984) and Spanish (E. Cortès and T. Martínez 1989–97).

---

[1] They have been edited or re-edited by M. I. Kahana (2005). A second volume with the fragments of Sifra is still expected.

As to the fragmentary halakhic midrashim, the Mekhilta de-R. Simeon is available in the edition by J. N. Epstein and E. Z. Melamed (1955), for two-thirds of the text based on Genizah fragments; its first translation into any European language is the English–Hebrew edition by W. D. Nelson (2006). Sifre Zutta has been edited by H. S. Horovitz (1917, together with Sifre Numbers); for additional Genizah fragments one should use the edition by M. I. Kahana (2005). There is a German translation by D. Börner-Klein (2002); an English translation has been published by J. Neusner (2009). The edition of Midrash Tanna'im by D. Hoffmann (1908/9) is the least satisfactory text of all halakhic midrashim because Hoffmann for its major part had to rely on medieval quotations; a Genizah fragment not yet known to Hoffmann has been re-edited by M. I. Kahana (2005). No translation of Midrash Tanna'im exists. As to Devarim Zutta, see the edition by M. I. Kahana (2002); a translation is planned by J. Neusner.

4. Language and Place of Composition

It is unanimously accepted that all halakhic midrashim were composed in Palestine. This judgement is based on the language of these midrashim, which is Mishnaic Hebrew, the close relationship of the midrashim with Mishnah and Tosefta, and on the names of the rabbis quoted who, as far as they can be identified, are all Palestinian teachers of the mishnaic period (Tanna'im) or of the third century. This does not exclude the possibility that later stages of redaction (e.g. the insertion of additional mishnaic parallels) took place in Babylonia. B. Z. Wacholder's (1968) suggestion that the Mekhilta is a late pseudepigraphic composition, compiled in Egypt or somewhere else in North Africa, has not found supporters.

5. Date

As to the date of composition and redaction of the halakhic midrashim, there are two schools of thought. One keeps at least in part to the traditional view and regards the halakhic midrashim as more or less tannaitic writings that have their basis in the time of the Mishnah or shortly thereafter (thus roughly in the third century); the other considers them as collections of baraitot (i.e. extra-mishnaic tannaitic materials) which were redacted as literary works only at the time of the Palestinian Talmud or somewhat later (fifth century or later).

* * *

One might think that as long as we agree that the basis of these midrashim are baraitot this does not make much difference. But in reality it would make quite a difference if early materials for centuries floated in tradition as independent units or small clusters of such units, or if we can reckon with an early history as literary works. Only in the second scenario can we assume that the context of a saying has some importance beyond the external structure of the biblical book on which a midrash comments, and only in this case can we assume a rather strong stability in the tradition of the work and its units. I accept more or less the second option, although I assume a series of several redactions of which only the first one can really be considered as tannaitic. I have demonstrated this hypothesis in detail for Sifra (for a summary statement see Stemberger 2005), but I assume that *mutatis mutandis* this is true also of the other halakhic midrashim.

We need, of course, some differentiation. Midrashim which are transmitted only in fragmentary form and have been partially reconstructed on the basis of medieval quotations certainly may not claim the same degree of authority as the well-preserved and carefully transmitted midrashim like Mekhilta, Sifra and both Sifre. For the Mekhilta de-R. Simeon we do have important textual witnesses from the Genizah; to a much lesser extent this holds true also for Sifre Zutta, whereas Midrash Tanna'im to a very great extent is reconstructed and thus can be used only with the greatest caution.

I have already mentioned Wacholder's hypothesis (1968) which considers Mek. as a pseudepigraphic writing of the Islamic period. Some scholars, especially from the United States, have ever since hesitated to use the Mekhilta as an early rabbinic work.[2] It is a fact that some traits of the Mekhilta make the early origin of it somewhat problematic (first of all the fact that for so many aggadic traditions the Mekhilta is our earliest witness and finds parallels only in much later works); but there are still enough arguments to keep the traditional date with some flexibility. A systematic study of the Mekhilta is a desideratum; for the time being we can use the midrash in our context as long as we exercise the necessary caution.

Although the halakhic midrashim form a coherent group of rabbinic texts—held together by the rabbis quoted in them, their language and technical vocabulary, their general approach to the interpretation of the Torah and the high amount of syllogistic passages—they are not uniform. They are to be attributed to at least two different schools of interpretation, that of Ishmael and that of Akiva (see now Yadin 2004), a very rough differentiation that has been refined for a long time already. Practically all these midrashim

---

[2] See e.g. J. L. Moss (2004: 33): 'scholars must reckon with the evidence that the Mekhilta reached final form at a late (post-Talmudic) date.'

contain sections which come from the other school than the one to which the main body of the midrash is assigned. But even beyond this there are differences within the individual midrashim, as has been noted, for example, for the Mekhilta, and this is especially clear in Sifra. Such a differentiation may also affect the dating of the texts; but this is more important for the integration of passages from Mishnah and Tosefta and for the elaboration of the syllogistic stratum, and not so much for the simple commentary which also contains the bulk of what is of interest for the historian.

What Kind of History?

Many passages in the halakhic midrashim which contain elements of historical relevance have parallels in Mishnah and Tosefta. Where they are dependent on these works and thus later, they may be used as confirmation of the other sources or may hint at the continued relevance of earlier statements. Other elements occur in the halakhic midrashim for the first time (provided we accept the early dates of the midrashim themselves) and thus add to our knowledge.

When looking at the kind of information we can gather from halakhic midrashim, it is evident that most materials reflect inner-rabbinic history, relationships between rabbis and their special interests and halakhic views. There is also much material for the development of halakhah or ritual (e.g. Mekhilta Pisḥa 17 on tefillin (phylacteries)), which can sometimes be useful even for the reconstruction of the ritual before 70 CE. There is no need to emphasise the importance of these midrashim for understanding early rabbinic approaches to Scripture and to its interpretation. All this adds up to important insights into the religious and intellectual history of early rabbinism and is relevant for any reconstruction of the history of the rabbinic movement.

There is much less that we can learn regarding the political, economic and social history of Palestine in the tannaitic and early amoraic periods. I shall, nevertheless, try to concentrate on what may be regarded as factual history and its reflection in these midrashim.

Roman Administration

Only two Roman emperors are mentioned by name, Titus and Trajan. Titus is described as 'Titus son of the wife of Vespasian who entered the holy of holies and tore the two veils with the sword' (Sifre Deut. 328; all other variations of this story are late), thus insinuating that Vespasian's paternity is not certain; Titus' role in the destruction of the temple of Jerusalem is central for Jewish tradition.

Mek. Wayehi Beshallaḥ 3 states that God warned the Israelites not to return to Egypt; in spite of this warning they returned three times and all three times they fell: 'The third time was in the days of Trajan.' The name is spelled differently in the manuscripts and editions,[3] as is common with foreign names, but the identification is beyond doubt. The text seems to refer to the Diaspora revolt of 115–17 when the Egyptian Jewry was destroyed (Ben Zeev 2005: 103f.). He is mentioned again in Sifra Emor Perek 9.5,[4] where he is said to have killed Pappos and his brother Lulianos in Laodicea, but to have been killed himself shortly afterwards: 'They say: He had not yet departed from there before a dispatch[5] came from Rome and they knocked out his brain with clubs' (Ben Zeev 2005: 104f. sees this passage in the context of the Diaspora revolt). W. Horbury (1999) has given an excellent analysis of the story in its various versions. He sees here a Jewish martyrology; at its root 'is a second-century tradition of the execution of eminent Jews under Trajan in Syrian Laodicaea, in connection with encouragement of Jewish entry from Syria into Judaea. Here therefore, as in Josephus, martyrology is part of the ethos of resistance to Rome' (p. 293). The passage about Trajan's death might conflate the execution of Lusius Quietus, who was dismissed by Hadrian and then put to death on the way back from Judaea (*Hist. Aug. Hadrian*, 7.2–3), with Trajan's death in Cilicia during his return from Mesopotamia (Horbury 1999: 291).

This tradition is typical for the rabbinic use of historical facts. The rabbis are interested above all in what concerns Jewish history, in this case the martyrdom of the two brothers; but even they are reduced to an edifying example where the details do not matter: some texts locate the story in Lydda, not in Laodicea; it is not stated why exactly they were executed, whether in the context of the Diaspora revolt or in the aftermath of the Bar Kokhba revolt or at some other occasion. The emperor is introduced as the main person responsible, his fate mixed up with that of his representative. Any historical context has to be based on our general knowledge of Roman history; the tradition illuminates Rome's image in Jewish eyes, but offers hardly any facts not known from elsewhere. But it would be mistaken to prefer other forms of the names in the textual transmission and to refer the tradition to

---

[3] Tragianos, Traginos, Tragonos, Turninos; two Genizah fragments of the parallel in MRS 14.13 read Troginos or Trogianos.

[4] Spelled Trogianos or Troginos in the MSS. In the parallel MRS Exod. 21.13 the Genizah text reads Trionos. J. L. Moss (2004: 274) reads in Sifra Marainus, following ed. Weiss and Neusner's translation (but Neusner spells Marianos) which could refer to somebody else.

[5] Vatican 66 reads *tiple*; Vatican 31 *diupla*: Krauss (1898–99: vol. 2, 201) derives it from Greek *diploi* for Latin *duumviri*; others see in it a corruption of Latin *tabula* or *tabella*.

somebody else; this would be a kind of historical criticism not adequate for this kind of literature.[6]

Apart from them no Roman emperor or governor of Palestine or any other high Roman official is mentioned by name. The only named figure is the enigmatic Antoninus, whose contacts and dealings with Judah haNasi are first mentioned in the halakhic midrashim (see Mek. Beshallaḥ 1; Shirata 2 and 6; MRS Exod. 14.7), but are known from later sources as well. Whoever we guess to be behind the enigmatic figure of Antoninus—emperors like Marcus Aurelius or Caracalla or some combination between them and others have been suggested—these legendary stories are valuable as reflections of the relations between the Roman ruler and the leader of the rabbinic group, especially if we are prepared to date Mekhilta as early as is usual. To know how the rabbis imagined the relationship between the representatives of the Roman empire and their own leadership grants us a glimpse into the political opinions not necessarily of the Jewish people, but at least of its religious elite, at the beginning of the third century.

Of special interest are the statements about the Roman administration and the imperial court. Nearly all relevant material is found in parables on human kings and their behaviour. We are no longer prepared to exploit these parables as directly for history as Ignaz Ziegler (1903) did a century ago. We still have to develop a sophisticated approach to these parables if we want to use them as reflections of what the Palestinian people of the period really knew or thought was going on in the imperial court or at least at the courts of the provincial representatives of the Empire. All these parables occur in an exegetical context. This means that many traits of behaviour attributed to kings are developed out of the biblical text and the contrast between God's behaviour and that of human people, most frequently styled as kings. Much of what we find in these texts may be traditional and reflect earlier periods and oriental magnates; much is absolutely timeless and it takes much circumspection to find out what might reflect contemporary situations or how the normal people received and understood them. But used carefully, these parables might grant us some glimpse into the *Mentalitätsgeschichte* of the period.

Many of these parables, but also other texts, use a good number of Greek and Latin loanwords for certain offices in Roman administration and in the army or for juridical procedures. D. Sperber (1984) offers a highly valuable

---

[6] Moss (2004: 203) refers to the note in the Soncino translation of b.Ta'anit 18b that 'The identification of this name with Trajan is disputed, particularly as Trajan is known to have died a natural death.' He correctly adds that 'accuracy in facts is not a primary concern in an ideological narrative'; nevertheless, the preference of certain variants of names frequently seems to be influenced by the search for historical verisimilitude.

collection and analysis of such terms. Mek. Amalek 2, for example, mentions several degrees of authority who can revoke the decree of another:

> Said Moses before the Holy One, blessed be he, 'Lord of the age, perhaps your way is like the way of a mortal. If an *administrator* makes a decree, a *prefect* can force its revocation. If a prefect makes a decree, a *commander* can force its revocation. If a commander makes a decree, a *general* can force its revocation. When a general makes a decree, a *governor* can force him to revoke it. When a governor makes a decree, a *viceroy* can make him revoke it. When a viceroy makes a decree, the *principal ruler* can make him revoke it. For all of them are appointed, one above the next in succession: "For one higher than the high watches"'. (Koh. 5.7; translation J. Neusner)

The authorities mentioned in what seems to be an ascending order and translated by Neusner in a rather unspecific way, are in MS Oxford (and Munich with minor differences in spelling) designated by transliterations of these terms: *epitropos, chiliarchos, dekourion, hegemon, eparches, hypatikos*; only the highest authority has a Hebrew title, *moshel gadol*, 'great ruler', which might stand for *(magnus) princeps*.[7]

Instead of *chiliarchos*, the *editio princeps*, reproduced in the edition by Horovitz and Rabin, reads *klidikos*, i.e. *kleidouchos*, the official in charge of the keys, which does not fit into the hierarchy presented here. Already S. Krauss (1898–99: vol. 2, 545) who did not yet know the manuscript readings, proposed to read *chiliarchos* instead.

A Genizah fragment of this passage (Westminster College, Tal. I 112) differs to some extent from the full manuscripts, which are of European origin. It has the sequence *epitropos, chiliarchos, eparchos, hypatikos, moshel gadol*. It thus omits the *decurio* and the *hegemon*. M. I. Kahana (1999: 99) assumes that they may have been omitted because of homoioteleuton; it is unlikely that the manuscripts added these terms since there are no parallels and the word *decurio* is very rare in rabbinic texts (Sif. Deut. 322 and the parallel in Midr. Tann. Deut. 32.30). In spite of this, Kahana considers the Genizah text as preferable because the longer text does not fit the known hierarchy. The first three items reflect the scale of offices in the *ordo equester*: *epitropos = procurator, chiliarchos = tribunus militum, eparchos = praefectus*; the two further ranks are even higher, only in the *ordo senatorius*: *hypatikos = consularis, moshel gadol = (magnus) princeps*. But since this list is inconsistent insofar as the procurator is a civil office and the *tribunus militum* a purely military office, Kahana proposes to understand *epitropos* here as the equivalent of *praepositus*, the commander of a unit. But even so the sequence is not quite logical. A *decurio* should be below the *chiliarchos*, the commander of thou-

---

[7] For problems with this passage see Goodman (2000: 166f., still without MS evidence), and Kahana (1999: 98–9).

sands, and the *hegemon* should be below the *eparchos* and not above him. Kahana (1999: 100) therefore prefers the reading of the parallel in MRS, unfortunately attested only in a late textual witness, a Yemenite Yalkut. Here the sequence is *epitropos, decurio, chiliarchos, eparchos, hegemon, moshel gadol*. Here the *hegemon* is correctly above the *eparchos*, although the position of the *decurio* above the *epitropos* remains problematic.

The correct presentation of the administrative hierarchy in the Roman empire may doubtlessly indicate the degree to which authors were familiar with the workings of government in their time; it may confirm the historical reliability of a text. It is, however, somewhat problematic to use it as a text-critical criterion. Many, even well educated, citizens of the Roman world may not have been too well informed about the hierarchies of authority outside their own direct concerns. We must at least reckon with the possibility of corrections by later copyists, although it speaks for the quality of the transmission of the texts that later offices, above all that of the *dux*, are never mentioned in the halakhic midrashim.

With regard to the military world, the parable of the centurion who deserted before serving his time as *primipilus* (Sif. Num. 131) is of special interest:

> It is comparable to a centurion who had served his term but failed to enter his primipilate, to which he should have been promoted, but fled and went his way. The king sent word and brought him and imposed on him the penalty of having his head cut off. Before he was taken out to be put to death, said the king, 'Fill up for him a measure of golden denars, and bring it to him and say to him, "If you had acted as our fellows acted, you would receive this measure of gold denars, and your life would have been your own. Now you have lost your life and lost your money."' (translation J. Neusner 1998)

The parable demonstrates the familiarity of the rabbis with the Roman army, which they could observe from nearby, since Roman legions were stationed not only in Jerusalem (Aelia Capitolina), but also in Caparcotna (Legio) in Galilee. The military world is also reflected in Sif. Deut. 327–8, where we read of Israel relying on the nations of the world; they ask where their *hypatikoi* and *hegemones* are to whom they used to give *opsonia, donativa* and *salaria* (all the terms simply transcribed in the Hebrew context).

As to the proceedings of the law courts, we read of the *bema* on which the judge sits or where the advocate (*rhetor, synegor, parakletos*) stands (Sif. Deut. 343), of the false accuser (*sykophantes*), the *gradus* on which the defendant is placed, and of the executioner (Sif. Num. 91: *speculator*). Several forms of execution are mentioned, among them crucifixion (Mek. Shirata 7 and 10), which points to a situation before Constantine. The most common death sentence among Jews is said to be strangulation, described in Mek. Nezikin 5; a description of the way stoning is carried out is found in

Sif. Num. 114. Detailed discussion of compensation for damages, for medical expenses or loss of time (Mek. Nezikin 6 and 8), and other legal discussions offer interesting material for a comparative history of law.

If we can rely on Sperber's (1984) references to Greek and Latin legal terms in rabbinic literature, it is astonishing to see that only very few of the loanwords present in his Dictionary appear in these midrashim. Some of the absent words are known from Mishnah and/or Tosefta. This may be explained by the different scope of these writings and the tendency of the halakhic midrashim to keep to a large extent to the interpretation of the biblical text; most examples turn up in comparisons or in parables. One would have to check the full corpus systematically for further occurrences, but a *prima facie* evaluation suggests that most of the loanwords in this field penetrated into rabbinic language (or Palestinian Jewish language as such) only in the Byzantine period, and that the small number of such loanwords present already in the halakhic midrashim points to their early origin and the fact that, at least in this regard, the midrashim have not been subjected to a later reworking. This is especially significant for the Mekhilta because of the already mentioned hypothesis of B. Wacholder (1968) regarding its late origin.[8]

Aspects of Daily Life

The halakhic midrashim contain much information about daily life, daily co-existence with non-Jews and awareness of pagan cults, and also about converts to Judaism. There are a few reflections of negative experiences under Roman rule, such as the fiscus Judaicus (Mek. Baḥodesh 1) or memories of the repression of Jewish religious practices after the Bar Kokhba Revolt (ibid. 6), the historicity of which is very problematic. We read of insecurity in the country and the permanent threat of marauding bands and thugs (MRS 14.19, 15.10; Sif. Deut. 313: perhaps more typical of the third century than of the second).

A number of texts take for granted peaceful co-existence in daily life and even cooperation between Jews and non-Jews, for example, when discussing what kind of work a non-Jew may do for a Jew on a Sabbath (MRS 20.10). Sif. Deut. 61 deals with the circumstances in which houses which had housed idols are allowed or forbidden to Jews; a close neighbourhood of Jews and non-Jews is presupposed. That Jews and non-Jews sometimes resorted to the

---

[8] One detail might be of interest: *boule*, city council, is well known in texts such as the Yerushalmi, but never occurs in the halakhic midrashim; *bouleutes* is to be found only in Sif. Deut. 209 and in its parallel in Midr. Tann. 32.6.

same law courts may be seen in Mek. Nezikin 1, where the acceptability of Gentile courts when they apply Jewish law is discussed; according to Sif. Deut. 16, R. Yishmael served as judge between Jews and non-Jews, sometimes following Jewish law, sometimes non-Jewish law, but always to the advantage of the Jewish party.

MRS 12.16 (cf. t.Yom Tov 2.6) suggests that Jews knew how to accommodate the demands of Roman troops even on a holiday: in order to avoid a clash with them, the Jewish inhabitants of a town slaughter for them a calf, offer them food and drink and give them a place to stay overnight.

Other texts are more critical of Gentiles as, for example, in stories about red cows bought from pagans or Arabs (SZ 19.2). Criticism of pagans is also voiced in a story about the visit of Rabban Gamaliel and other rabbis in Rome (Sif. Deut. 43). But no text in the halakhic midrashim is as violent about non-Jews as Mek. Beshallaḥ 2: 'The nicest among the idolaters kill.'

General awareness of pagan religions and their practices is clear from a number of texts: Mek. Pisḥa 2 speaks of omens for pagans and Jews; Beshallaḥ 2 of the Maiuma-festival. In Amalek 3 we read of the most common practices in pagan cults—sacrificing, burning incense, making libation offerings, and bowing down to idols. Baḥodesh 6 (cf. Sif. Deut. 43) speaks of the recycling of idols: if somebody needs the metal of an idol, he melts it down and makes a cheaper idol in its stead. All the parchments in the world would not suffice to name separately all idols.

Jewish and pagan slaves are mentioned frequently and seem to have been rather common in certain strata of the population. Pagan slaves are owned by Jews and even by priests (Mek. Pisḥa 1 and 15); they pose certain problems when handling wine or on a Sabbath (Mek. Kaspa 3; cf. MRS 20.10). Hebrew slaves, including proselytes, cannot be forced to do certain things expected from a Gentile slave (Mek. Nezikin 1). A general discussion of how to deal with slaves is found in Mek. Nezikin 2.

It is perhaps surprising to see how frequently proselytes are mentioned. The reception of proselytes is dealt with in Mek. Amalek 2; MRS 12.48 mentions three necessary elements of the conversion ceremony, circumcision, immersion and offering a sacrifice, and discusses in detail what is necessary for a correct circumcision (cf. Sif. Num. 108); Mek. Pisḥa 15 speaks of the ritual bath which Valeria and her handmaidens took at conversion. Halakhic discussions concern the participation of a proselyte who converted at Pesah, at the Pesah meal (Sif. Num. 71) or the rather theoretical question whether the wife of a proselyte has to drink the bitter water in the rite of the Sotah if suspected by her husband (Sif. Num. 7). A number of texts are very positive regarding proselytes, as, for example, the saying that Abraham was circumcised only at the age of ninety-nine in order to encourage proselytes (Mek. Nezikin 18), or the demand to treat well proselytes (SZ 10.29: the text also speaks of proselytes in the Bet ha-Midrash). Other texts reveal much more critical attitudes: Mek. Nezikin 18 criticises those who mock proselytes, saying to them that yesterday they still venerated Bel, Kore and Nebo, and that they still have pork between their teeth. SZ 5.8 speaks of proselytes who induce Israel to sin, and Mek. Kaspa 2 of proselytes who relapsed. The frequency with which the topic is discussed to some extent certainly depends on the biblical texts which are commented upon; but we have to ask how frequent the phenomenon of conversion to Judaism was even after the Bar Kokhba Revolt and how far the different attitudes to proselytes depicted in the texts reflect actual problems at the time of the redaction of the halakhic midrashim. The same is true of the *minim* (Jews deviating from the norm), mentioned several times in the texts. How actual and frequent was the problem of such deviation, and whom exactly does the term designate in this context?

We could also exploit the halakhic midrashim for more mundane aspects of daily life, such as the kind of buildings common in a village, the frequency of certain cereals, fruits or vegetables, daily food or household utensils. Much of this information is to be found in Mishnah and Tosefta, too, but the halakhic midrashim frequently supplement the information found there, and thus contribute to a fuller picture of daily life at the time of the redaction of these texts.

In sum, the halakhic midrashim hardly contribute to our knowledge of political history, but they offer a lot of details regarding daily life in Palestine in the second and third centuries and the way the rabbis understood it. On the other hand, history may help us in a more precise dating of the texts or their redactional strata. In the same way that the texts offer historical knowledge, they are also illuminated by a better understanding of their historical context.

Further Reading

Ben Zeev (2005); Goodman (2000); Hadas-Lebel (2006); Kahana (2006); Neusner and Avery-Peck (eds. 1999); Stemberger (1983).

Bibliography

Ben Zeev, M. Pucci (2005), *Diaspora Judaism in Turmoil*, Leuven.
Bietenhard, H. (1984), *Der tannaitische Midrasch 'Sifre Deuteronomium'*, Bern.
Börner-Klein, D. (1997), *Sifre zu Numeri übersetzt und erklärt*, Stuttgart.
Börner-Klein, D. (2002), *Der Midrasch Sifre Zuta*, Stuttgart.
Cortès, E. and Martínez, T. (1989–97), *Sifre Deuteronomio*, 2 vols., Barcelona.
Epstein, J. N. and Melamed, E. Z. (1955), *Mekhilta d'Rabbi Sim'on b. Jochai*, Jerusalem; corrected repr., 1979.

Finkelstein, L. (1939), *Siphre ad Deuteronomium H. S. Horovitzii schedis usis cum variis lectionibus et adnotationibus*, Berlin; repr. New York, 1969.

Finkelstein, L. (1983–91), *Sifra on Leviticus according to Vatican Manuscript Assemani 66 with variants . . . and commentaries*, 5 vols., New York.

Goodman, M. (2000), *State and Society in Roman Galilee, AD 132–212*, 2nd edn., London.

Hadas-Lebel, M. (2006), *Jerusalem Against Rome*, Leuven.

Hammer, R. (1986), *Sifre: A Tannaitic Commentary on the Book of Deuteronomy*, New Haven.

Hoffmann, D. (1908/9), *Midrasch Tannaim zum Deuteronomium*, 2 fasc., Berlin; repr. Jerusalem, 1984.

Horbury, W. (1999), 'Pappus and Lulianus in Jewish resistance to Rome', in J. Targarona Borrás and A. Sáenz-Badillos (eds.), *Jewish Studies at the Turn of the Twentieth Century*, 2 vols., Leiden, vol. 1, pp. 289–95.

Horovitz, H. S. (1917), *Siphre D'be Rab. Fasciculus primus: Siphre ad Numeros adjecto Siphre zutta*, Leipzig; 2nd edn., Jerusalem, 1966.

Horovitz, H. S. and Rabin, I. A. (1931), *Mechilta d'Rabbi Ismael cum variis lectionibus et adnotationibus*, Frankfurt; 2nd edn., Jerusalem, 1960.

Kahana, M. (I.) (1986), *Prolegomena to a New Edition of the Sifre on Numbers*, Jerusalem. [Hebrew]

Kahana, M. I. (1995), *Manuscripts of the Halakhic Midrashim: An Annotated Catalogue*, Jerusalem. [Hebrew]

Kahana, M. I. (1999), *The Two Mekhiltot on the Amalek Portion: The Originality of the Version of the Mekhilta d'Rabbi Ishma'el with Respect to the Mekhilta of Rabbi Shim'on ben Yohay*, Jerusalem. [Hebrew]

Kahana, M. I. (2002), *Sifre Zuta on Deuteronomy: Citations from a New Tannaitic Midrash*, Jerusalem. [Hebrew]

Kahana, M. I. (2005), *The Genizah Fragments of the Halakhic Midrashim*, Part 1: *Mekhilta d'Rabbi Ishma'el, Mekhilta d'Rabbi Shim'on ben Yohay, Sifre Numbers, Sifre Zuta Numbers, Sifre Deuteronomy, Mekhilta Deuteronomy*, Jerusalem. [Hebrew]

Kahana, M. I. (2006), 'The Halakhic Midrashim', in S. Safrai *et al.* (eds.), *The Literature of the Sages*, Second Part: *Midrash and Targum . . .*, Assen, pp. 3–105.

Krauss, S. (1898–99), *Griechische und lateinische Lehnwörter im Talmud, Midrasch und Targum*, 2 vols., Berlin; repr. Hildesheim, 1964.

Kuhn, K.-G. (1959), *Der tannaitische Midrasch Sifre zu Numeri übersetzt und erklärt*, Stuttgart.

Lauterbach, J. Z. (1933–35), *Mekilta de Rabbi Ishmael: A critical edition on the basis of the MSS and early editions with an English translation, introduction and notes*, 3 vols., Philadelphia; repr. in 2 vols. with introduction by D. Stern, Philadelphia, 2004.

Martínez-Sáiz, T. (1995), *Mekilta de Rabbí Ismael*, Estella.

Moss, J. L. (2004), *Midrash and Legend: Historical Anecdotes in the Tannaitic Midrashim*, Piscataway, NJ.

Nelson, W. D. (2006), *Mekhilta de Rabbi Shimon bar Yohai: Translated into English, with Critical Introduction and Annotation*, Philadelphia (includes the Hebrew text).

Neusner, J. (1988), *Sifra: An Analytical Translation*, 3 vols., Atlanta (translates Finkelstein as far as available, then a traditional text); repr. as Neusner 1997a.

Neusner, J. (1997a), *The Components of the Rabbinic Documents*, I: *Sifra*, 4 vols., Atlanta.

Neusner, J. (1997b), *The Components of the Rabbinic Documents*, VII: *Sifré to Deuteronomy*, 3 vols., Atlanta.

Neusner, J. (1997c), *The Components of the Rabbinic Documents*, VIII: *Mekhilta Attributed to Rabbi Ishmael*, 3 vols., Atlanta.

Neusner, J. (1998), *The Components of the Rabbinic Documents*, XII: *Sifré to Numbers*, 4 vols., Atlanta.

Neusner, J. (2009), *Sifré Zutta to Numbers*, Lanham, MD.

Neusner, J. and Avery-Peck, A. J. (eds.) (1999), *Judaism in Late Antiquity*, Part 3: *Where We Stand: Issues and Debates in Ancient Judaism*, vol. 1, Leiden (several papers on 'Rabbinic Sources for Historical Study').

Pérez Fernández, M. (1989), *Midrás Sifre Números. Versión crítica, introducción y notas*, Valencia.

Sperber, D. (1984), *A Dictionary of Greek and Latin Legal Terms in Rabbinic Literature*, Ramat Gan.

Stemberger, G. (1983), *Die römische Herrschaft im Urteil der Juden*, Darmstadt.

Stemberger, G. (1996), *Introduction to the Talmud and Midrash*, 2nd edn., trans. and ed. M. Bockmuehl, Edinburgh.

Stemberger, G. (2005), 'Leviticus in Sifra', in J. Neusner and A. J. Avery-Peck (eds.), *Encyclopedia of Midrash: Biblical Interpretation in Formative Judaism*, 2 vols., Leiden, vol. 1, pp. 429–44.

Wacholder, B. Z. (1968), 'The date of the Mekilta de-Rabbi Ishmael', *Hebrew Union College Annual*, 39: 117–44.

Weiss, I. H. (1862), *Sifra de-be Rab hu Sefer Torat Kohanim*, Vienna; repr. New York, 1947.

Winter, J. and Wünsche, A. (1909), *Mechiltha: ein tannaitischer Midrasch zu Exodus*, Leipzig; repr. Hildesheim, 1990.

Yadin, A. (2004), *Scripture as Logos: Rabbi Ishmael and the Origins of Midrash*, Philadelphia.

Ziegler, I. (1903), *Die Königsgleichnisse des Midrasch beleuchtet durch die römische Kaiserzeit*, Breslau.

9

The Talmud Yerushalmi

SACHA STERN

1. Contents

THE PALESTINIAN TALMUD, OR TALMUD YERUSHALMI, or (here) Yerushalmi *tout court*, is one of the most important literary sources for Jewish history in Palestine of late antiquity. Yet at the same time, it is one of the least accessible sources to historians, partly because of its long-standing marginalisation in medieval and modern rabbinic tradition, and partly because of its inherent textual difficulties.[1]

The Yerushalmi is structured as a commentary and supplement to the Mishnah (hence its designation as 'Talmud'). It covers most of the Mishnah, with the exception of some chapters of some tractates, and most notably the last two orders, Kodashim and Tohorot ('Holy Things' and 'Purities'— although the first part of tractate Niddah from Tohorot is covered). It is possible that these two orders of Mishnah were ignored because of their limited relevance to post-70 CE Judaism, but this is not a very satisfactory explanation, because their inclusion in the Mishnah and Tosefta—also post-70 CE— contradicts it, and furthermore the order of Kodashim is covered by the Babylonian Talmud (or Bavli). The long-standing belief that originally the Yerushalmi covered the whole of the Mishnah, and that substantial parts were subsequently lost, is now largely discredited (Stemberger 1996: 166–8).

The Yerushalmi draws heavily on tannaitic and amoraic sources (which we call 'baraitot' and 'memrot' respectively), but these are strung together by an anonymous editor (or editors) who can be identified as the author(s) of the Yerushalmi (this anonymous layer, analogous to the *stam* of the Babylonian Talmud, is waiting to be systematically studied).[2] The Yerushalmi is earlier than the Babylonian Talmud, and therefore does not know the Babylonian Talmud as a whole, but this does not prevent it from citing Babylonian amoraic sayings from the first few generations. Note that the Babylonian Talmud, albeit later, seems also not to have known the

---

[1] For a general introduction see Bokser (1979a), Stemberger (1996).
[2] Preliminary studies in Bokser (1979b, 1990: 88).

Yerushalmi: they are thus independent works, even though they share a good deal of traditions in common (see Hayes 1997).

A distinctive feature of the Yerushalmi is the high incidence of parallel or repeated passages, that is, lengthy passages that are repeated word for word in two or sometimes three tractates. Textual errors associated with parallel passages (e.g. the recurrence of identical scribal errors, parallel passages inserted in the wrong place, beginning or end of parallel passages left out, and so on) indicate that these parallels were simply copied over from one tractate to the next, and sometimes on the contrary omitted. The phenomenon of parallel passages should therefore be attributed to early medieval scribal practice (at the level of transmission of the text) rather than to the original redaction of the Yerushalmi (insofar as there ever was an original redaction—more on this below).[3]

The contents of the Yerushalmi are halakhic and aggadic—in what proportion partly depends on the definition of 'aggadic'. Indeed, the Yerushalmi is rich in stories, mainly about amora'im, which could qualify as 'halakhic' (because of their purpose and content) as much as 'aggadic' (because their genre is story).[4] These stories, in particular, constitute an important source for the social history of the rabbinic movement and possibly of other Jews.[5] The use of the Yerushalmi as a historical source will be illustrated throughout this chapter, but addressed more systematically in the last section.

2. Authorship and Date

As in all early rabbinic works, the author(s) or editor(s) of the Yerushalmi do not identify themselves. According to Maimonides (in his introduction to the commentary on the Mishnah) the Yerushalmi was edited by R.Yoḥanan (third century), but this is impossible since much later rabbis are frequently cited (Stemberger 1996: 169–70).

It has been argued that the Yerushalmi was never redacted at any specific time, that the boundary between redaction and transmission was never determined or clear, and that the text never ceased evolving in the early medieval period.[6] I would support the view, however, that a distinction must be made between creative writing and redaction on the one hand, and editorial text-

---

[3] For an example of textual errors arising from parallel passages, see Seth Schwartz's article in this volume (Chapter 16).

[4] For a study of a type of these sources in tractate Nezikin, see Hezser (1993).

[5] On the use of Yerushalmi for the study of non-rabbis in late-antique Palestine, see Miller (2006).

[6] See in this volume the debate between Schäfer and Milikowsky (Chapters 3–5), and Stemberger (1996: 171–2).

handling and text-modification on the other. There are clear signs that the creative production of the Yerushalmi was completed in the late fourth or early fifth centuries CE (the former tends to be favoured today), after which no fresh *sugyot* (continuous passages) were composed. This date is based on the relative dating of the latest Sages mentioned in the text (amora'im of the '5th generation'), sporadic references to known historical events, and partly also on the relationship of the Yerushalmi to other Palestinian rabbinic compositions (thus the Yerushalmi is assumed to be relatively earlier than Genesis Rabbah, etc.).[7]

As Sussman (1990: 132–2) plausibly argues, the composition of the Yerushalmi cannot be much later than the latest cited amora'im, since the Yerushalmi—unlike the Bavli—does not offer extensive discussions of their opinions, and although there is an editorial layer in the Yerushalmi (see above), there are no self-standing, anonymous *sugyot* that can be distinguished from the latest Amoraic sayings as significantly later. However, the absolute dates of the latest cited amora'im, and hence (on this argument) the date of redaction of the Yerushalmi, remain somewhat uncertain.

Sussman (ibid.) also argues, not entirely successfully, that the omission of important historical events of the late fourth century indicates a mid-fourth century (or only slightly later, *c*.360 CE) dating. These events include Julian's failed attempt to rebuild the Jerusalem Temple in 363 CE, the award of honorific imperial titles to the Patriarchs in the late fourth century, and the institution of a fixed calendar by the patriarch Hillel in 359 CE. I shall consider these now in turn.

Julian's attempt to rebuild the Jerusalem Temple in 363 CE is alluded to perhaps in Genesis Rabbah (64.10), but there is no allusion in the Yerushalmi. Julian himself is hardly mentioned in the Yerushalmi: perhaps in p.Nedarim 3.2, 37d ('when emperor Lulianus [i.e. Julian?] went down there [to Babylonia], one hundred and twenty myriads went down with him'), but the parallel in p.Shevuot 3.8, 34d reads instead 'Diocletian' (which illustrates just how risky it can be to rely on these sources).

By contrast, Ursicinus (Roman general in the East and highly influential figure in the 350s CE, known from Ammianus Marcellinus 14.9–11) seems to be mentioned a few times:

> In the days of Ursicinus the king, the Sepphoreans were sought. They would put a compress on their nostrils and would not be recognised. And in the end they were denounced, and all of them were captured as a result. (p.Sotah 9.4, 23c; p.Yevamot 16.3, 15c)

---

[7] However on the complex relationship between the Yerushalmi and Genesis Rabbah, see Bokser (1979b); Becker (2000).

Reference to Ursicinus as a 'king' or 'emperor', when in fact he was only a general (at various times *magister peditum* and *magister equitum*), says something about provincial perspectives on the top ranks of the Roman imperial administration and army. But it is of course impossible to know if this passage is referring specifically to the 'Gallus revolt' of the 350s CE, even though Sepphoris—described by Jerome (*Chronicon* ad 352 CE) and later sources as one of the revolt's centres—is mentioned. The story about compresses and nostrils seems a bit outlandish, but perhaps not impossible.

> Ursicinus burned the Torah scroll of the Sennabreans. They came and asked R. Jonah and R. Yosa: 'What is [the law] regarding reading from this scroll in public?' (p.Megillah 3.1, 74a)

If this is the same Ursicinus as in Ammianus Marcellinus, this passage gives an approximate period for R. Jonah and R. Yosa (leading figures of the fifth generation of Palestinian amora'im: Stemberger 1996: 95–6), which in turn helps with the dating of the Yerushalmi as a whole.

The award of honorific imperial titles to the Patriarchs, which we know from the Codex Theodosianus at least between the years 392 and 415 CE,[8] is not referred to in the Yerushalmi—nor in fact are these later Patriarchs mentioned at all. At first sight, this may support Sussman's mid-fourth-century dating. However, these Patriarchs are similarly omitted from all other pre-Geonic rabbinic sources. This raises the question of whether the latter Patriarchs (of the later fourth to fifth centuries) were part of what is usually identified as the rabbinic movement, and whether we should expect them, therefore, to be mentioned anywhere in early rabbinic literature.

The institution of a fixed calendar by the patriarch Hillel in 359 CE is not mentioned in the Yerushalmi, but again, it is also absent in other, later rabbinic sources. In my book on the calendar (Stern 2001: 175–81), I demonstrate that this medieval tradition (attested only from the eleventh century onwards) should not be given credence. The fixed calendar was never 'instituted' at any given time, it only evolved gradually. This is why the 'event' of its institution is never mentioned in the Yerushalmi or other early sources.

However, a later dating of the Yerushalmi to the early fifth century seems also unjustified. A link between the redaction of the Yerushalmi and the end of the patriarchate in the 420s CE, which has often been assumed, is unfounded. Indeed, there is no evidence to relate the authorship of the Yerushalmi directly with the Patriarchs, and furthermore, the end of the

---

[8] Linder (1987, nos. 20, 24, 27, 32 and 41: see pp. 221–2, n. 3 and 271, n. 8).

patriarchate is not intrinsically preferable, as a historical context, to any other context or period for the redaction of this major literary work.[9] On balance, therefore, a late fourth-century dating seems reasonable.

3. Place of Redaction

Despite its name, the Yerushalmi was not composed in Jerusalem. The perspective of its authors is clearly Galilean, as is evident, for example, from the following passage:

> R. Ḥama father of R. Oshaya had a case. He asked our rabbis, and they pro-
> hibited. R. Yose asked: 'Which rabbis? The rabbis of here, or the rabbis of the
> South?' If you say the rabbis of here, it is fine. If you say the rabbis of the
> South—the great ones were before him, and he [went and] asked the small
> ones? (p.Berakhot 2.6, 5b)

By elimination, 'here' (where the rabbis are supposedly greater) can only mean the north, and more specifically Galilee. Other passages similarly exclude Caesarea (e.g. p.Shabbat 13.1, 14a, where 'here' is opposed to Caesarea). The Galilean provenance of the Yerushalmi can be narrowed further down to Tiberias, although evidence of this is more tenuous. In the following passage, the vantage point appears to be Tiberias (note that it is mentioned first, before Sepphoris), and Tiberias is given primacy:

> R. Lazar said: If one [litigant] said [let the case be heard] 'in Tiberias', and the
> other said 'in Sepphoris', the one who said 'in Tiberias' is followed.
> (p.Sanhedrin 3.2, 21a)

Tractate Nezikin (i.e. Bava Kamma, Meẓia, and Batra) differs in many respects from the rest of the Yerushalmi: it is briefer, its language is different and distinctive, and it tends to cite different Sages (or sage names—but this latter point has been disputed), which points to an entirely separate work. Lieberman argued that Yerushalmi Nezikin was composed in Caesarea ('the Talmud of Caesarea'), but Sussman (1990) and others have refuted this theory.[10] Sussman sees it as composed by another 'yeshivah' or body of rabbis, and even as representing an earlier stage in the literary evolution of Talmud, although it was not necessarily composed at an earlier time (see further Stemberger 1996: 173–5).

---

[9] Even though some have seen the Yerushalmi as hastily edited: see discussion in Stemberger (1996: 170–1).

[10] See also Wewers (1984), Bokser (1990: 90–1), and Hezser (1993: 321–77).

4. Manuscripts and other textual evidence

Manuscripts are few, reflecting the marginality of the Yerushalmi in the later medieval period. The only manuscript of the entire Yerushalmi is MS Leiden Or. 4720 (dated 1289 CE). The *editio princeps* (Venice 1523–24) was based entirely on an accurate transcription of this manuscript, supplemented with readings from other manuscripts that were physically written into the Leiden manuscript by the editors of the Venice edition. This means that the *editio princeps* has no textual value independent from the Leiden manuscript *as it now stands*. Subsequent editions were generally based on the Venice edition or its derivatives, which means they have little or no textual advantage over it, and which brings us back, again, to the single textual witness of the Leiden manuscript as it now stands.

There are a few other manuscripts for some individual tractates: MSS Vatican (order Zera'im and tractacte Sotah, thirteenth century), Escorial (tractate Nezikin, fifteenth century), and a number of 'Genizah' and other fragments (from Cairo, from various European libraries, and from book bindings especially in Italy and Germany), of which discoveries will only increase as time goes on. In addition, tractate Shekalim appears in some manuscripts of the Babylonian Talmud.[11]

Textual evidence can also be inferred from early commentaries on the Yerushalmi, in particular R. Solomon Sirillo's commentary on order Zera'im and tractate Shekalim, written in 1541–42 (some autograph manuscripts are extant). Sirillo's text differs from the Venice edition, and for tractate Berakhot at least he seems to have corrected the Venice edition on the basis of some unknown manuscript. Textual evidence can also be inferred from citations of Yerushalmi that are found in medieval (Babylonian) Talmudic commentaries (Ratner 1901–17, but this work needs updating; the distinction between citation and paraphrase in medieval secondary sources is frequently unclear).

5. Editions

There are no critical editions of the Yerushalmi, except for a few individual tractates. An annotated transcription of the Leiden MS with some restorations and corrections has been published by the Academy of the Hebrew Language (2001). A synoptic edition has been published by Schäfer and Becker (1991–2001): it includes the Venice (1523–24), Constantinople (1662), and Amsterdam (1710) editions, the Leiden and Vatican MSS, and the MSS

---

[11] For details see Stemberger (1996: 181–4).

of Sirillo. However, it is doubtful that the Constantinople and Amsterdam editions have any textual value independent of the Venice edition or Sirillo's commentary, and many textual witnesses (e.g. fragmentary MSS) have been deliberately left out of this synopsis.

Ideally a synoptic edition should include, for any given Yerushalmi passage, (1) the full range of MSS including fragments, (2) if available, the parallel texts (i.e. the same passage as repeated elsewhere in the Yerushalmi) with their own full range of manuscript evidence, and (3) if available, secondary citations of the passage (in medieval sources, up to and including Sirillo) and their own range of manuscript evidence. This is rather complicated, but achievable through modern technology in an electronic, textual database (which has the additional advantage of being upgradable, as new fragments are discovered). Yaakov Sussman has been working for decades on assembling the primary and secondary textual witnesses of the Yerushalmi; we hope this will lead to a definitive synoptic edition.

Textual variation can be substantial; it is not to be ignored by any historian (the translation of Guggenheimer—see below—has the merit of drawing attention to significant textual variation). Differences between manuscripts can lead to textual problems that will be discussed below. Some passages of particular importance to the historian have only been recovered through Genizah fragments, for example:[12]

> In the days of R. Yoḥanan, they began/allowed (*sharun*) to draw pictures on walls, and they did not object to them.
> In the days of R. Abun, they began/allowed (*sharun*) to draw pictures in mosaics, and they did not object to them. (p.Avodah Zarah 3.3, 42d)

The second sentence is absent in the Leiden manuscript, and hence in the printed editions. R. Abun, dating from the early fourth century, is just a bit too early for the late-antique proliferation of monumental mosaic floors in Galilee (which nowadays tend to be dated to the late fourth century and later). Alternatively, we may consider the reference to R. Abun unreliable: if so, the saying may rather reflect a later, fourth-century historical context. Incidentally, my hesitation whether to translate *sharun* as 'began' or 'allowed', a rather significant difference, is a good example of the obscurity of the Yerushalmi text (on which see more below).

6. Translations

The relative inaccessibility of the Yerushalmi to the modern historian has largely been due to the lack of good translations; even a Hebrew and

---

[12] Text from the Cairo Genizah, first published by Epstein (1932).

Aramaic reader will often find its text ambiguous or obscure. Fortunately, in recent years a number of English and German translations have been produced—reflecting, perhaps, renewed interest in this work. One common problem, which applies to all the new translations and reflects the length and complexity of the original text, is cost: they all come in several, expensive volumes. Another problem, this one common to the translation of all early rabbinic, halakhic works, is that of rendering the text in a readable and intelligible way.

- Schwab (1871–89): French translation, very unreliable. I mention it here because it is available online (www.objectif-transmission.org/ prefiguration/articles.php?lng=fr&pg=5), which is handy and free.
- Tübingen edition (Jerusalemer Talmud 1975–2006): text (from various sources, depending on the volume) and German translation. Most professional of all, but not immune from textual issues.
- Neusner (ed. 1982–94): English translation only, eccentric and unsatisfactory. For example, in p.Avodah Zarah 1.1, 39b Neusner translates *duqenar* as 'quaestor' (which he has obviously taken from the commentary *Penei Moshe*), when in fact the correct translation is clearly 'ducenarius'. This makes a big difference to Roman historians (Lieberman 1984: 318 and *passim*).
- Guggenheimer (ed. 2000– in progress), text (from the Leiden MS largely unemended, which can be problematic), English translation, and notes (including indications of significant manuscript variation). Reasonable but uneven quality.
- Artscroll edition (Malinowitz *et al.* eds. 2005–, in progress): text (from the Venice edition, lightly emended but only on the basis of rabbinic commentaries), some textual variants, some rabbinic commentaries (in Hebrew), and English translation interspersed with detailed elucidation. Costly not only in price, but also in shelf space, as there is more than one volume per tractate. The approach is traditional and entirely dependent on rabbinic commentaries.

7.   Commentaries

The Yerushalmi seems to have served as a primary textbook in Palestinian rabbinic circles throughout the Geonic period, but it was not used, and indeed barely known, in Geonic Babylonia until the tenth century (Brody 1997: 168–9, 240–1). It was eclipsed by the Babylonian Talmud in later medieval times, in the rabbinic centres of learning in Europe, the Mediterranean, and the Near East. As a result, there was little or no medieval tradition of commentary on the Yerushalmi (in contrast to the Bavli).

Medieval Talmudists (especially Rashi, Ravya, and the Tosafot) only comment on sporadic Yerushalmi passages, and only as part of their commentaries on the Bavli or their halakhic compendia.

Rabbinic commentaries on the Yerushalmi begin to develop from the sixteenth century onwards (e.g. Sirillo: see above). They tend to interpret the text from the perspective of the Bavli, often reading the Bavli into the Yerushalmi (e.g. Moses Margaliot, *Penei Moshe*, eighteenth century, printed in the margin of the common Vilna edition (1922), whose purpose is also to explain difficult passages in Maimonides' *Code*). The lack of a Yerushalmi-centred tradition of rabbinic commentary leaves the modern scholar more or less with a clean sheet—which has both advantages and disadvantages (see further Bokser 1979a).

Textual Problems

The text of the Yerushalmi is notoriously ridden with errors, corruption and various other difficulties. It has been remarked that these are mostly due to inadvertent scribal error, often reflecting the ignorance of medieval scribes who were not versed in the study of this text, rather than to deliberate editorial tampering (which is common in the textual transmission of the Babylonian Talmud). This may be regarded as a strength, because it is easier for modern scholars to correct scribal errors than to undo editorial tampering. Nevertheless, a lot of problems remain unresolved.

There are many types of textual errors in the Yerushalmi, which need not be surveyed here (see Lieberman 1929). They arise, for example, from the scribal insertion, omission, and/or re-insertion (sometimes with editorial adjustments) of parallel passages (Stemberger 1996: 172), babylonisation of language and spelling, accidental omission of text (e.g. tradents' names), marginal notes wrongly inserted or inserted in the wrong place, and so on.

I shall only consider in detail some of the more common textual problems that a historian using the Yerushalmi might encounter.

Variant Readings

Most relevant to the historian tend to be variant readings. This phenomenon is not unique to the Yerushalmi, but common to the whole of early rabbinic literature. Textual variation can be historically significant, as the following examples illustrate (see also the Julian passage above, and the sections on 'Manuscripts' and 'Editions', above).

אנטונינוס יהבה לר׳ תרין [אלפין] דשׂנין בארסטו

Antoninus gave Rabbi two [thousand] fields in lease. (p.Shevi'it 6.1, 36d
MS Vatican [MS Leiden])

'Antoninus' is presumably one of the Roman emperors of that name in the
second and third centuries, with whom Rabbi (Judah I) is often depicted in
close relationship. Although many of the stories within this tradition strain
the imagination (especially the collection of stories in b.Avodah Zarah
10a–11a), in this particular passage the notion of an emperor leasing out
fields to a provincial aristocrat seems quite realistic. I have argued, on the
basis of this and other passages, that Rabbi may have belonged in fact to a
local, Galilean aristocratic family (Stern 2003: 209). This argument does not
depend on assuming that the event recounted in the story actually happened;
it only assumes that stories in the Yerushalmi about Rabbi's social and economic standing were based on some historical truth. But this assumption is
open to questioning. As I have written in that same article, the history of the
rabbinic movement, which can (almost) only be inferred from rabbinic
sources, is never more than the history of the rabbis *as inferable* from these
sources (ibid., p. 194).

The textual problem with this passage is that MS Vatican omits the word
'thousand', which makes a rather big difference. The context of the passage
is an estate (or region?) called 'Yavlunah', of which the location and size are
completely unknown. I think the MS Leiden version looks more authentic,
because in this case erroneous omission is more likely than interpolation. It
may also be argued that in the context of an imperial lease, 'two' fields seem
insufficient and unlikely, whereas 'two thousand', if excessive, can be read as
a literary exaggeration.[13]

רבן גמליאל [הנשׂיא] ובית דינו התירו ...

R. Gamaliel [the Patriarch] and his court permitted . . . (p.Shevi'it 1.1, 33a MS
Leiden [MS Vatican])

In this case, there is no particular reason to favour one version over the other.
The MS Vatican version, if authentic, may be invoked as evidence that R.
Gamaliel bore the title of *nasi* (Patriarch), which for R. Gamaliel II is a con-
tentious issue. However, the passage refers almost certainly to R. Gamaliel III,
who was certainly a *nasi* and for whom this does not represent a historical
issue (Stern 2003: 198).

Note that in general, MS Vatican (cited in this and the previous passage)
is regarded as defective and flawed.

---

[13] Yet another, rather different version is attested in Sirillo's commentary, but it seems erroneous
and will not be discussed here.

Foreign Bodies

This phrase designates sections of text that appear out of place. This is a common feature of the Yerushalmi, both in halakhic and aggadic contexts, and presents a particular challenge to the interpretation of *sugyot*. The examples I shall give are chiefly halakhic, although they also contain aggadic elements with potential historical significance. In some cases the foreign body can be explained as the result of a textual error, but sometimes, as in the example that follows, it may be interpreted as a deliberate editorial decision:

> [Mishnah:] If [the rebellious son] ate [the quantity of meat required to make him liable] at a *mitzvah* gathering (*havurat mitzvah*), or at the intercalation of the month, or as second tithe in Jerusalem
> [Talmud:] ... R. Yohanan said: If they mention you for [candidature to] the *boule* (city council), let the Jordan be your frontier.
> R. Yohanan said: One may appeal to the authorities for exemption from the *boule*.
> R. Yohanan said: One may borrow at interest for a *mitzvah* gathering or for the sanctification of the month.
> R. Yohanan used to go into the synagogue in the morning, collect the crumbs, eat, and say: 'May my lot be with him who sanctified the month here [last] evening!' (p.Sanhedrin 8.2, 26a, parallel in p.Mo'ed Katan 2.3, 81b)

This passage is a string of sayings of, or stories about, R. Yohanan, but the first two—where he recommends evasion from the *boule* or exemption from it (which fits nicely with what is known about evasion from city councils in the third-century Roman empire)—seem out of context. Indeed, the *boule* sayings do not relate to any aspect of the Mishnah which this passage is supposed to comment on. This foreign body demands to be explained.[14]

The last two traditions relate very clearly to the Mishnah, as they refer to '*mitzvah* gathering' and 'sanctification of the month' (analogous, if not equivalent, to 'intercalation of the month' in the Mishnah). The story at the end suggests that R. Yohanan had somehow been excluded from a meal that had taken place, the evening before, in a synagogue; at this meal, they had 'sanctified the month'. This phrase normally refers to the declaration of the new moon or beginning of the month by an especially designated rabbinic court (e.g. m.Rosh Hashanah 2.7); yet it seems unlikely that R. Yohanan—probably the most important rabbinic sage of mid-third-century Palestine—was excluded from this rabbinic court, especially as he is mentioned elsewhere in the Yerushalmi as a member of it.[15] The *boule* sayings inserted above suggest rather that this was an assembly of the city council, that had gathered in the synagogue to hold a festive meal and sanctify the month. R. Yohanan—who

---

[14] Moskovitz (1995: 257) notes and discusses this incongruity, but remains unable to explain it.
[15] p.Rosh Hashanah 2.6, 58b; p.Sanhedrin 1.2, 18c.

earlier in this passage, paradoxically, had recommended exemption or evasion from the *boule*—regretted his exclusion from it.

I have used this passage, with this interpretation of its foreign bodies, as evidence that 'sanctification of the month' was not really the monopoly of the rabbis, as the Mishnah and later rabbinic sources generally want us to believe, but could be exercised, instead, by city councils. The inference is not from the story of R. Yoḥanan itself—on which no claim of historicity is being made—but rather from the way and particularly the context in which the story is presented in the Yerushalmi.

Another example of a foreign body of text, which I cannot explain, concerns again the calendar, although it also reveals the specifically urban perspective of the Yerushalmi and its Sages.[16] The context is the mishnaic ruling that if two witnesses differ about the date of an incident, a one-day discrepancy between them can be ignored, because people often do not know exactly when the month has begun. R. Yoḥanan suggests that such ignorance is typical of town (or 'village') dwellers:

> R. Yoḥanan says: Like those town/village dwellers.
> And the Sages say: They are nothing (*einam kelum*).
> And R. Yose says: Like me—for I have never prayed in my days the additional service [of the New Moon], because I have not known when was the [New] Moon. (p.Sanhedrin 5.3, 22d)

The Sages' saying not only makes no sense, but also is out of place, as it is clearly drawn from a tannaitic tradition (in amoraic sayings or traditions, anonymous rabbis are never designated as 'Sages', *ḥakhamim*, but rather as *rabbanan* or other such terms), whereas the other sayings are amoraic. The insertion of the Sages' saying also breaks the pattern of the amoraic sayings, which begin both with the term 'like' (*kegon*). The source of this foreign body (presumably, a longer tannaitic baraita with an attributed opinion to which the Sages respond), its original meaning there, the reason for its insertion here (erroneous or deliberate), and if deliberate, its intended meaning here, are all completely unclear.

The Yerushalmi as 'Evidence' for History

Various examples of historical use of the Yerushalmi have been presented above (see in particular my comments on the Antoninus story). In this final section, I examine historical issues (often bound up, however, with literary issues) more in detail.

---

[16] On which see most recently Miller (2006: 448–57).

Palestine and Babylonia

Comparison of parallel sources in the Yerushalmi and Bavli is a tradition that goes back to medieval talmudic commentary. Rashi (eleventh century) and the Tosafot (twelfth–thirteenth centuries), in their commentaries on the Bavli, are among the first to cite parallels from the Yerushalmi for the purpose of elucidating the meaning of the Bavli, or supplementing it, or pointing out a halakhic disagreement. As stated above, later rabbinic commentators of the Yerushalmi depend very much on the Bavli. All this is problematic because of the literary, mutual independence of both Talmuds: from a modern scholarly perspective, it makes no sense to interpret one text in terms of a completely different one.

The comparison of Yerushalmi and Bavli remains useful, however, to identify and highlight their distinctive features. It is also useful for source criticism, as it sheds light on how the same traditions (tannaitic or early amoraic) may have been transmitted and modified in different ways in Palestinian and Babylonian rabbinic/talmudic circles (see Hayes 1997). The most common and easily observable phenomenon, in this context, is the 'babylonisation' of originally Palestinian traditions, which has been widely observed in the context of the Bavli. But some cases of the reverse—'palestinisation' of Babylonian traditions—can also be identified in the Yerushalmi (Bokser 1979b).

The following example necessitates comparison of several sources, and a little more analysis than the other examples cited in this article:[17]

> Three days before the festivals of non-Jews, it is forbidden to trade with them ... R. Ishmael says: Three days before and three days after it is forbidden. (m.Avodah Zarah 1.1–2 MS Kaufman)

> Nahum the Mede says: In the Diaspora, [only] one day before their festivals is forbidden. (t.Avodah Zarah 1.1)

> Nahum the Mede says: In the Diaspora, [only] one day is forbidden.
> Why so? There, they checked and found that [the non-Jews] make their preparations in one day, and [so] they prohibited one day; but here, they checked and found that [the non-Jews] make their preparations in three days, and [so] they prohibited them [from trading for] three days. (p.Avodah Zarah 1.1, 39a MS Leiden)

> Nahum the Mede says: Only one day before their festivals is forbidden.
> They said to him: Forget this opinion (lit. let it sink) and let it not be said. (b.Avodah Zarah 7b MS Paris 1337)

---

[17] See on this Hayes (1997: 127–43), but with emphasis on other aspects of these passages.

The Mishnah prohibits trade with non-Jews three days before their festivals, and cites the opinion of R. Ishmael that is even stricter (three days before and three days after). The Tosefta, however, cites the more lenient opinion of Nahum the Mede, that prohibits only one day before their festivals; it is also cited in the Yerushalmi and the Bavli. A significant difference between these sources is that according to the Tosefta and the Yerushalmi—both Palestinian—the opinion of Nahum the Mede applies only 'in the Diaspora'; but this detail is not mentioned in the Bavli.

At first sight, it might be argued that the Bavli omits 'in the Diaspora' because it was composed in Babylonia, and a Diaspora perspective is therefore taken for granted. However, this is most unlikely, firstly because 'in the Diaspora' is an important halakhic detail which cannot be omitted without affecting the meaning and scope of Nahum the Mede's ruling, and secondly because another, similar opinion attributed to Samuel is cited in the same passage of the Bavli and *does* mention 'in the Diaspora'. Its absence in the saying of Nahum the Mede is therefore not careless or accidental.

It is far more plausible, on the contrary, that the original wording of Nahum the Mede's ruling is as preserved in the Babylonian Talmud, that is, without 'in the Diaspora', and that it is the Yerushalmi (also the Tosefta—but the history of the Tosefta and its text is outside our scope) that has added 'in the Diaspora'.[18] If so, Nahum the Mede originally intended his lenient ruling to be *universal*.

Why it was modified in the Yerushalmi can be plausibly conjectured. The opinion of Nahum the Mede seems to have met with strong opposition from the Sages of Palestine: this is evident from the unusually strong language of the baraita that is preserved in the Bavli ('let this opinion sink'), and from the complete omission of Nahum the Mede's opinion in the Mishnah. In Babylonia, however, his opinion is likely to have been well received: for there is evidence in the Bavli that in Babylonia these laws were generally applied more leniently or even completely disregarded.[19] This is also understandable given that Nahum the Mede was a Diaspora sage; although the geographical meaning of 'the Mede' remains unclear (did he actually live in Media, and if so, where exactly is this?), the Bavli considers him to be 'of our place'.[20] While the Sages of Palestine were able, at home, to reject the opinion of Nahum the Mede (as evident, for example, from its omission in the Mishnah), they may

---

[18] So Gerald Blidstein (Ph.D. thesis 1968) cited by Hayes (1997: 234, n. 12, pointing out that in the Tosefta text the word *begaluyot* appears as an interpolation).

[19] See b.Avodah Zarah 7b, 11b, and 64b–65a. In 11b, the Bavli endorses Samuel's even more lenient view, whereby in the Diaspora trade with non-Jews is forbidden only on the festival day itself.

[20] b.Avodah Zarah 7b, a little after the passage cited above.

have realised that in the Babylonian Diaspora, lenient opinions like his were prevailing. This may have led Palestinian Sages (in the Tosefta and Yerushalmi) to rephrase the saying of Nahum the Mede as applying only to the Diaspora: from a Palestinian perspective, this was a way of marginalising his opinion, and also of ensuring that it did not influence Palestinian practice. The Yerushalmi, in our passage, goes even further and works out a justification for confining his ruling to the Diaspora. The Bavli, by contrast, was happy to maintain the saying in its original, universalistic formulation.

In short, we have in this Yerushalmi passage a 'palestinisation' of Nahum the Mede's tradition. This is significant not only in literary and source-critical terms, as it accounts for the textual difference between the Yerushalmi and the Bavli, but also in historical terms, as it sheds light on the sometimes strained relationship between early, tannaitic Palestinian and Babylonian (or 'Diaspora') Sages.

Reliability of Attributions, Reliability of Sources

The example just cited also leads to the vexed question of the reliability of attributions, not specific to the Yerushalmi but relevant to the whole of early rabbinic literature. The attribution of sayings to named Sages (Nahum the Mede in our example) was traditionally used by historians as evidence for dating sayings (so, for example, Nahum the Mede is associated, in m.Nazir 5.4, with the destruction of the Temple in 70 CE) and even for the construction of rabbinic biographies. But in the 1970s the reliability of attributions came under systematic questioning (particularly through the initiative of Jacob Neusner). Scholars have remained divided on the extent to which attributions may or may not be regarded as reliable.[21]

In the last ten years, however, the question seems to have fallen out of fashion, with very few fresh scholarly contributions on the subject. I suspect this is because it has been superseded by a much broader question, implicit already in Neusner's early research: the reliability, or perhaps better 'authenticity', of the entire rabbinic saying. Recent research into the tannaitic sources preserved in the Tosefta, Mishnah, Yerushalmi and Bavli, in particular, has revealed that in many cases these sources underwent significant editorial changes—as we have seen in the example of Nahum the Mede's saying. This means not only that the attribution is no longer reliable, but indeed that the text of the whole saying, as preserved in the extant literature, is often unlikely to be original: even if Nahum the Mede did say something, we do

---

[21] The literature on this subject is vast. See the references cited in my own contribution to the debate (Stern 1994 and 1995), and add to this the summary of Hayes (1997: 11–15).

not know for sure what he said. Recent research, therefore, has shifted the question away from the reliability of attributions to that of the authenticity of early rabbinic traditions as a whole.

Some scholars (especially Jacob Neusner) despair of recovering the original text of any rabbinic tradition. Neusner (e.g. 1983) has been advocating a 'documentary' approach, according to which the rabbinic compositions that are extant (such as the Yerushalmi) should be read as reflecting only the views of their final redactors, and as obliterating all trace of their antecedent sources. However, rabbinic works such as the Yerushalmi are not sufficiently coherent for this approach to be justified: they use a variety of sometimes inconsistent sources, of which the final redactors cannot be regarded as 'authors' and which do not necessarily reflect their personal views. In actual fact, the views of the final redactors remain as elusive as of the earlier rabbinic sources. The notion that earlier sources have been completely obliterated is extreme, and as some have suggested, a form of scholarly complacency.

Most scholars at present would argue that a judicious combination of source criticism, redaction criticism, and 'documentary' approaches can lead to a plausible reconstruction of early rabbinic traditions and an understanding of how they were transmitted and edited into their present, literary forms (Cohen ed. 2000).

Talmudic Story as Literature

The historical value of Talmudic stories—which traditionally were used as prime historical 'evidence'—is now considered, by and large, to be very limited.[22] For example, from the Talmud Yerushalmi:

> A certain disciple came and asked Rabbi Joshua: 'What is [the status of] the evening prayer?' He replied: 'It is optional.' He asked Rabban Gamaliel, and he replied: 'It is obligatory.' He said: 'Tomorrow at the meeting house (*beit ha-va'ad*) rise and ask the law in this matter.'
>
> The next day, the disciple rose and asked Rabban Gamaliel: 'What is the evening prayer?' He replied: 'It is obligatory.' He said: 'But Rabbi Joshua told me it is optional!'
>
> Rabban Gamaliel said to Rabbi Joshua: 'Did you say it is optional?' He replied: 'No!' He said: 'Rise to your feet, that they may testify against you.' Rabban Gamaliel sat there expounding while Rabbi Joshua remained standing, until all the people murmured and said to Ḥuzpit the *turgeman* (expounder): 'Dismiss the people.' Then they said to Rabbi Zinon the *ḥazan* (official): 'Begin

---

[22] See in general (but almost entirely on the Bavli) Rubenstein (1999).

to recite.' He began to recite: 'For upon whom has not your wickedness passed continually? (Nahum 3:19)'

So they went and appointed Rabbi Eleazar ben Azariah to the *yeshivah*. . . . R. Akiva sat there in distress, saying: 'It is not that he [Rabbi Eleazar ben Azariah] is a greater son of the Torah than I, but he is a son of great men and I am not' . . . He [Rabbi Eleazar ben Azariah] was tenth in line from Ezra.

And how many benches were they? Rabbi Jacob b. Sisi said: 'There were eighty benches of scholars, apart from those that stood behind the barrier.' Rabbi Jose b. Avun said: 'There were 300 benches apart from those that stood behind the barrier.'

As we have learnt: 'On the day they appointed Rabbi Eleazar ben Azariah to the *yeshivah*.' We learn there: 'Rabbi Eleazar expounded this in the presence of the Sages in the vineyard at Yavneh.' Was there a vineyard there? Rather, this refers to the scholars who sat in rows like vines in a vineyard. (p.Berakhot 4.1, 7d, p.Ta'anit 4.1, 67d)

This story, where R. Gamaliel was deposed and R. Eleazar b. Azariah appointed instead as 'head of the *yeshivah*', raises the question of whether rabbinic study and instruction were already institutionalised in the tannaitic and talmudic periods. A 'meeting house' (*beit ha-va'ad*) does not necessarily imply, in itself, an institutional academy. But in many other ways, Rabban Gamaliel's meeting house shares the features of the mishnaic Sanhedrin, and more so, of the later rabbinic academies: scholars arranged in a set number of benches or rows, 'apart from those that stood behind the barrier' (disciples, or members of the general public?); officers (*turgeman*, *ḥazan*); promotion on the basis of lineage (Rabbi Eleazar ben Azariah tenth in line from Ezra—priestly lineage, in this case); and finally, the tantalising term *yeshivah*, which in this passage we should perhaps cautiously translate as 'session' or 'assembly'.

This passage is uncharacteristic of the Yerushalmi, where rabbis are otherwise never depicted as operating in academic institutions. It cannot be taken as evidence that at the time of its redaction—nor, *a fortiori*, in the period of Rabban Gamaliel (early second century)—medieval-style rabbinic academies were already in existence in Palestine.[23] What this passage demonstrates is rather the continuity of a literary, mishnaic tradition: like m.Sanhedrin, this passage looks back at the Sages of earlier periods and assumes that they operated in large-scale, Sanhedrin-like hierarchical assemblies.[24] This passage is a purely literary composition: it is not merely

[23] Rubenstein (1999: 272 and 398 n. 106). The existence of rabbinic academies in amoraic Palestine—just as in contemporary Babylonia—is highly unlikely: see Hezser (1997: 195–214).
[24] Stern (2009). The relationship between this description of Rabban Gamaliel's academy and the mishnaic account of the Sanhedrin is only implicit, but a later Palestinian source, the Midrash Shir ha-Shirim Rabbah (8.11), explicitly identifies the 'vineyard at Yavneh' and its rows of scholars with the Sanhedrin.

anachronistic (in the sense, for example, that the editors could be projecting their own experience onto an earlier period), but in fact unhistorical (the story bears no relation to any historical reality at all).

Rabbinic Perception and Historical Reality

A number of stories in the Yerushalmi are frequently cited as evidence of historical reality, when in fact it could be argued that they only reflect a sub-jective perception, i.e. the perception of the storyteller (the tradent of the story, or the talmudic editor). This raises the broader question—common to all areas of ancient history—of how literary sources are used as historical evidence. Many would argue that even if these stories are not historical real-ity, at least the perspective of their rabbinic authors—the perception that they have, or the assumptions that they make about their own society—is of historical interest. Moreover, this perception did not develop in a vacuum: it must have reflected something (but just what?) of the historical reality out there.

However, this raises in turn the general question of what is meant by 'his-torical reality'. If our perception of 'history' or 'the past' is really only a mod-ern cultural construct: that is, our own subjective perception of ancient times, then the search for historical 'reality' is flawed. The rabbinic authors' percep-tion of their historical reality—as reflected, for example, in the Yerushalmi—is only our own subjective perception of theirs. The question then becomes whether there can be a meaningful inter-subjective engagement between our-selves and our ancient sources (or their authors), and whether this inter-subjective engagement can be regarded as 'history'. As long as it is understood that history is no more than an interpretation of the past based on ancient interpretations of their own present, then there is no problem in engaging with the Yerushalmi for this purpose.

The following story, with an appeal from a small village to Rabbi Judah haNasi for provision of a local rabbi, has frequently been cited as evidence for the spread of patriarchal and/or rabbinic authority in third-century Palestinian society.[25] But has the story been accurately told, or is it just the product of rabbinic wishful thinking? Furthermore, can a halakhic-aggadic homily of this kind be used as historical evidence, or are we—modern histo-rians—attempting to read into it what its authors never intended or fath-omed? And if the latter, does it matter—does it mean that it does not qualify as 'history'?

---

[25] For a critical assessment, see Schwartz (2001: 121–3) and, with references to earlier scholar-ship, Miller (2006: 14, 202–5). My translation is adapted from Schwartz.

The people of Simonias came to Rabbi [Judah I] and said: 'We wish you to give us one person who will be a preacher, judge, *hazan*, teacher of Scripture and Mishnah, and will fulfil all our needs.' He gave them Levi bar Sisi. They made him a big *bema* and sat him upon it, and asked him: 'How does an armless woman perform the *halizah*?', and he did not answer them. 'What if she spat blood?', and he did not answer them. They said: 'Perhaps he is not a master of [legal] instruction. Let us ask him a question of *aggadah*.' . . . [a question is asked, and he does not answer] They returned to Rabbi and said to him: 'Is this the intercessor we petitioned you for?' He said: 'By your lives! I have given you a person like myself.' They called for him and asked him: . . . [the same questions as before, which he now answers]. [Rabbi] said to him: 'And why did you not answer them?' He said: 'They made me a big *bema* and sat me upon it, and my spirit swelled.' Rabbi applied to him the verse . . . [and said]: 'Who caused you to become foolish in words of Torah? It was only because you elevated yourself through them.' (p.Yevamot 12.6, 13a)

Note the distinction—critical to early rabbinic culture—between *safar*, teacher of Scripture, and *metanyan*, teacher or 'reciter' of rabbinic traditions (here rendered as 'Mishnah').

The Yerushalmi and External Sources

In a few cases, an apparent corroboration can be drawn between stories in the Yerushalmi and external, non-rabbinic sources. Some scholars extrapolate and treat these cases as evidence that the Yerushalmi is generally 'reliable'. Whatever one makes of these cases (see comments above on 'historical reality'), the corroboration is certainly interesting. It reminds us, at the very least, that the authors of the Yerushalmi belonged to a wider social context than their self-centred rabbinic circles: they belonged to Palestine, and wider still, the Roman empire.

What is the law regarding appointing elders for a limited period?
Let us hear the answer from here:
R. Hiyya b. Abba came to R. Lazar, and said to him: 'Intercede on my behalf to R. Judan the Patriarch, that he may write me a letter of recommendation, for me to go abroad and make my living.' He interceded, and he [R. Judan] wrote for him: 'Behold, I have sent you a great man. He is our envoy and stands in our stead, until he comes back to us.' (p.Hagigah 1.8, 76d)

The same R. Hiyya b. Abba is found elsewhere, in p.Megillah 3.1, 74a, collecting charity in the Syrian city of Homs—perhaps as a sequel to this story. These passages remind us of accounts in external sources (especially Epiphanius, *Panarion* 30, as well as a number of imperial letters and edicts) of fourth-century Patriarchs sending envoys to the Diaspora for the purpose of collecting 'taxes' or monies.

Finally, an epigraphic tale. A question was asked about the fair of Tyre—
to what extent was this fair associated with an *avodah zarah* (pagan cult), and
therefore forbidden to trade in? Someone was sent to find out:

> He came, and found written there:
> 'I, Emperor Diocletian, dedicated this fair of Tyre for eight days to the Fortune
> (*gad*) of Herculius my brother.' (p.Avodah Zarah 1.4, 39d)

We are not told if the inscription was originally in Greek or Latin. The reference to 'Herculius' may be a garbled reference to the god of Tyre, traditionally identified with Hercules (Millar 1993: 264–5), rather than to
Diocletian's co-regent Maximian (as commonly interpreted).[26] In any case, it
would be good if this inscription could once more be found . . .

Note. I am grateful to Robert Brody, Catherine Hezser, Leib Moskovitz and Günter
Stemberger, for their comments and assistance.

Further Reading

Bokser (1979a, 1990); Neusner (1983); Stemberger (1996).

Bibliography

Academy of the Hebrew Language (2001), *Talmud Yerushalmi according to Ms. Or.
    4720 (Scal. 3) of the Leiden University Library with Restorations and Corrections*,
    Jerusalem.
Becker, H.-J. (1999), *Die grossen rabbinischen Sammelwerke Palästinas: zur liter-
    arischen Genese von Talmud Yerushalmi und Midrash Bereshit Rabba*, Tübingen.
Becker, H.-J. (2000), 'Texts and history: the dynamic relationship between Talmud
    Yerushalmi and Genesis Rabbah', in Cohen (ed.) (2000), pp. 145–58.
Bokser, B. M. (1979a), 'An annotated bibliographical guide to the study of the
    Palestinian Talmud', in H. Temporini and W. Haase (eds.), *Aufstieg und
    Niedergang der Römischen Welt*, vol. 2.19.2, Berlin and New York, pp. 139–256.
Bokser, B. M. (1979b), 'A minor for *Zimmun* (Y.Ber. 7:2, 11c) and recensions of
    Yerushalmi', *AJS Review*, 4: 1–25.
Bokser, B. M. (1990), 'Talmudic studies', in S. J. D. Cohen and E. L. Greenstein (eds.),
    The State of Jewish Studies, Detroit, pp. 80–112.
Brody, R. (1997), *The Geonim of Babylonia and the Shaping of Medieval Jewish
    Culture*, New Haven.
Cohen, S. J. D. (ed.) (2000), *The Synoptic Problem in Rabbinic Literature*, Brown
    Judaic Studies 326, Providence, RI.
Epstein, J. N. (1932), 'Yerushalmi fragments', *Tarbiz*, 3: 15–20. [Hebrew]

---

[26] For a different interpretation see Lieberman (1974: 7–10; 1984: 318).

Guggenheimer, H. W. (ed.) (2000–), *The Jerusalem Talmud*, 12 vols. (to date), Berlin and New York.

Hayes, C. E. (1997), *Between the Babylonian and Palestinian Talmuds: Accounting for Halakhic Difference in Selected Sugyot from Tractate Avodah Zarah*, New York and Oxford.

Hezser, C. (1993), *Form, Function, and Historical Significance of the Rabbinic Story in Yerushalmi Neziqin*, Tübingen.

Hezser, C. (1997), *The Social Structure of the Rabbinic Movement in Roman Palestine*, Tübingen.

Jerusalemer Talmud (1975–2006), *Der Jerusalemer Talmud in deutscher Übersetzung*, 23 vols., Tübingen.

Lieberman, S. (1929), *Al Hayerushalmi*, Jerusalem. [Hebrew]

Lieberman, S. (1974), *Texts and Studies*, New York.

Lieberman, S. (1984), 'A tragedy or a comedy?', *JAOS* 104: 315–19.

Linder, A. (1987), *The Jews in Roman Imperial Legislation*, Detroit and Jerusalem.

Malinowitz, C., Schorr, Y. S. and Marcus, M. (eds.) (2005–), *Talmud Yerushalmi Artscroll*, Brooklyn, NY.

Milikowsky, C. (1988), 'The *status quaestionis* of research in rabbinic literature', *JJS* 39: 201–11; repr. as ch. 4 of this volume.

Millar, F. G. B. (1993), *The Roman Near East 31 BC–AD 337*, Cambridge, MA.

Miller, S. S. (2006), *Sages and Commoners in Late Antique 'Ereẓ Israel'*, Tübingen.

Moskovitz, L. (1995), 'On the aggadic "foreign bodies" in the Yerushalmi', *Tarbiz*, 64: 237–58. [Hebrew]

Neusner, J. (1983), *Judaism in Society: The Evidence of the Yerushalmi*, Chicago.

Neusner, J. (ed.) (1982–94), *The Talmud of the Land of Israel: A Preliminary Translation and Explanation*, 35 vols., Chicago.

Ratner, B. (1901–17), *Ahavat Tzion Virushalayim*, 12 vols., Vilna. [Hebrew]

Rubenstein, J. L. (1999), *Talmudic Stories: Narrative Art, Composition, and Culture*, Baltimore and London.

Schäfer, P. (1986), 'Research into rabbinic literature: an attempt to define the *status quaestionis*', *JJS* 37: 139–52; repr. as ch. 3 of this volume.

Schäfer, P. (1989), 'Once again the *status quaestionis* of research in rabbinic literature: an answer to Chaim Milikowsky', *JJS* 40: 89–94.

Schäfer, P. and Becker, H.-J. (1991–2001), *Synopse zum Talmud Yerushalmi*, 7 vols., Tübingen.

Schäfer, P. and Hezser, C. (1998–2002), *The Talmud Yerushalmi in Graeco-Roman Culture*, 3 vols., Tübingen.

Schwab, M. (1871–89), *Le Talmud de Jérusalem*, 11 vols., Paris.

Schwartz, S. (2001), *Imperialism and Jewish Society, 200 BCE to 640 CE*, Princeton.

Stemberger, G. (1996), *Introduction to the Talmud and Midrash*, 2nd edn., trans. and ed. M. Bockmuehl, Edinburgh.

Stern, S. (1994), 'Attribution and authorship in the Babylonian Talmud', *JJS* 45: 28–51.

Stern, S. (1995), 'The concept of authorship in the Babylonian Talmud', *JJS* 46: 183–95.

Stern, S. (1998), 'Dissonance and misunderstanding in Jewish–Roman Relations', in M. D. Goodman (ed.), *Jews in a Graeco-Roman World*, Oxford, pp. 241–50.

Stern, S. (2001), *Calendar and Community: A History of the Jewish Calendar, 2nd Century BCE – 10th Century CE*, Oxford.

Stern, S. (2003), 'Rabbi and the origins of the patriarchate', *JJS* 54: 193–215.

Stern, S. (2009), 'Rabbinic academies in Late Antiquity: state of current research', in H. Hugonnard-Roche (ed.), *L'Enseignement supérieur dans les mondes antiques et médiévaux*, Paris.

Sussman, Y. (1990), 'Back to Yerushalmi Neziqin', in idem and D. Rosenthal (eds.), *Meḥqerei Talmud*, vol. 1, Jerusalem, pp. 55–133. [Hebrew]

Wewers, G. (1984), *Probleme der Bavot-Traktate. Ein redaktionskritischer und theologischer Beitrag zum Talmud Yerushalmi*, Tübingen.

10

Problems in the Use of the Babylonian Talmud for the History of Late-Roman Palestine: The Example of Astrology

RICHARD KALMIN

1. Contents

THE BABYLONIAN TALMUD IS A LARGE AND COMPLEX COMMENTARY in Aramaic and Rabbinic Hebrew on the Mishnah, though only just over half of the Mishnah's tractates are actually covered, and time and again the exposition digresses into lengthy discussions of topics which are only tangentially (if at all) related to the Mishnah. It cites the Mishnah text in full, section by section, and appends to each section the Talmud's commentary, referred to in standard printed editions and translations as 'Gemara'.

2. Manuscripts

Over sixty manuscripts of the Babylonian Talmud are known, coming from all corners of the medieval Jewish world, and ranging in date from the twelfth to the seventeenth century. In addition the Cairo Genizah has yielded numerous fragments, some of which may be as early as the ninth century. Owing partly to attacks by Christian authorities in the Middle Ages (who censored and even burned the work), only one (almost) complete manuscript survives (Munich 95). The texts of the manuscripts differ from each other, generally in matters of detail, but often the differences are extremely important.

3. Editions

There is no critical edition of the whole Talmud which takes into account all the manuscripts, not to mention the extensive quotations in the Geonim and other medieval writers, though portions have been so treated. The *textus receptus* is the edition issued by the Widow and Brothers Romm, Vilna/Vilnius 1880–86 (the 'Vilna Shas', often reprinted). This is ultimately derived from the *editio princeps* printed by Daniel Bomberg in Venice (1520–23), the folio numbers of which (e.g. 59a) are still used for purposes of reference. Goldschmidt (ed. 1897–1935) conveniently gives the variant readings of the Munich manuscript. The Steinsaltz (1967–) and Schottenstein editions (1990–2005) reproduce the Vilna Shas but provide running commentaries. They are extremely useful for those trying to find their bearings for the first time in a Talmudic text.

4. Translations

The standard English translation is Epstein (ed. 1935–52; reprinted several times, including a bilingual edition which presents the English and Hebrew [= Vilna] on facing pages). The standard German translation is Goldschmidt (ed. 1897–1935, with the original text; translation also printed separately). Neusner (ed. 1984–93) offers an alternative English rendering, useful for the way it systematically clarifies the structure of the text. English versions are also provided in the Steinsaltz (1989–) and Schottenstein (1990–2005) editions, in both cases accompanying the original text.

5. Place

Though the Babylonian Talmud contains many traditions that originated in Palestine, its final editing took place in Babylonia, as its numerous statements attributed to Babylonian rabbinic authorities, and the unwavering testimony of subsequent tradition, clearly show. Its Aramaic is an eastern dialect of the language known as Babylonian Jewish Aramaic, and it evidently embodies the erudition of the Babylonian rabbinic study houses.

6. Date

Many medieval and early modern scholars claim that the Babylonian Talmud reached closure in the time of Rab Ashi (*c*.352–427), a claim based primarily on the enigmatic talmudic passage, 'Rab Ashi and Ravina are the end of *hora'ah* (practical instruction)' (b.Bava Meẓia 86a). Most contemporary scholarship is in broad agreement that a date of around 600 is probably not too wide of the mark. However, there is a major debate among experts as to the extent to which the final, anonymous editors shaped the traditions they received, a debate with direct bearing on the reliability of the work as a historical source.

* * *

Of the distinctions made by scholars in evaluating rabbinic texts for the history of late-Roman Palestine, one of the most important (and widely accepted) has been between material which derived from Palestine and material which derived from Babylonia. The history of Babylonian Jewry under Parthian rule (to the 220s) and Sassanian rule (until the rise of Islam) (Neusner 1965–70) differed markedly from that of Palestinian Jews under the sway of pagan and Christian emperors. To assume similar attitudes and ideas in two rabbinic societies in such different conditions and on so great a geographical distance would clearly be rash. It might, therefore, seem sensible to avoid making any use at all for Palestinian history of the mass of material found in the Babylonian Talmud. Such a policy would, however, be a mistake, for the Bavli contains much material which derives from Palestine and may sometimes (as this study of the example of attitudes to astrology will demonstrate) preserve Palestinian rabbinic material in a form closer to the original than is found in Palestinian compilations.

The Bavli is a vast repository of statements by and stories about the ancient rabbis, and these stories and statements are organised primarily in the form of commentaries on the Mishnah. Talmudic rabbis frequently author (1) halakhic (legal) statements; (2) aggadot (non-halakhic statements); (3) interpretations of earlier sources, for example the Bible (such statements are referred to as midrash); and objections and questions about opinions expressed by other rabbis. Rabbinic statements and stories frequently purport to derive from a variety of different times and different places, but they have been woven together in the Talmud to form a series of more or less coherent discourses.

In addition to statements by tanna'im and amora'im, the Bavli also contains substantial amounts of unattributed materials. As several scholars have noted, the anonymous sections of the Talmud are editorial in character (Feldblum 1969; Goodblatt 1981: 292–4, 314–18). They consist of an enormous commentary that analyses, explains, emends and completes the attributed statements at the editors' disposal. Their unattributed character makes them difficult to analyse, and many basic questions about them have yet to be answered. It is not known, for example, when the unattributed materials were by and large complete, with scholarly guesses ranging from the mid-sixth century until the Muslim conquest of Persia in 657 CE. Many modern scholars claim that the anonymous sections of the Talmud represent a relatively late layer of the Talmudic corpus (Friedman 1977: 296; Goodblatt 1981: 292; Halivni 2007: 5–148; Bokser 1990: 91–3; Kalmin 2006a: 840, 862–7). Even scholars who claim that composition of this anonymous material began during the period when attributed amoraic material was already being composed generally acknowledge that most of it is post-amoraic (Friedman 1996: 22–3; Brody 2008: 224–7).

M. Krupp lists sixty-three manuscripts of the Babylonian Talmud (Krupp 1987: 351–61), ranging in date from the twelfth to the seventeenth century and ranging in size from a few leaves to the entire Talmud. Some of the oldest fragments, however, are from the Cairo Genizah, some of which pre-date 1000 CE. MS Munich 95 is the only complete manuscript of the Bavli, and even it is missing a few pages. Medieval rabbinic authors are also a crucially important source of variant readings.

The best translations are in German (Goldschmidt ed. 1897–1935) and English (Epstein ed. 1935–52). J. Neusner also edited an English translation (1984–95); a French translation of several volumes appeared under the editorship of E. Munk (ed. 1972–); and A. J. Weiss translated several tractates into Spanish (1964–79).

The Saul Lieberman Institute for Talmudic Research at the Jewish Theological Seminary of America in New York maintains a computerised databank of Talmudic manuscripts and Genizah fragments. The goal of this project is to transcribe, in a searchable format, all extant manuscripts and Genizah fragments. In addition, the Jewish National and University Library in Jerusalem, and the Hebrew University's Department of Talmud, maintain an online databank of talmudic manuscripts (http://jnul.huji.ac.il/dl/talmud). Still of tremendous importance is R. Rabbinovicz (1867–97), for his sophisticated discussions of manuscript variants and of variant readings preserved in the works of medieval commentators and anthologisers of the Bavli. The Institute for the Complete Israeli Talmud is publishing a critical edition (Herschler *et al.* eds. 1972–). So far four full tractates have appeared (Ketubot; Sotah; Nedarim; Yevamot); and part of a fifth (Gittin).

In using the Bavli for the history of late-Roman Palestine, one must distinguish systematically between (1) material attributed to Babylonian rabbis in the Bavli; (2) material attributed to Palestinian rabbis in the Bavli; and (3) material attributed to Palestinian rabbis in Palestinian compilations. Careful analyses of this kind often result in surprising revisions of our understanding of the two rabbinic communities that produced the texts, since material that scholars have previously understood as an undifferentiated whole may actually be a *mélange* of different sources from different localities and different time periods. Throughout this study, unless explicitly indicated otherwise, the expression 'Palestinian rabbinic traditions' denotes statements attributed to and stories involving Palestinian rabbis in Palestinian rabbinic compilations of late antiquity. The expression 'Babylonian rabbinic traditions' denotes statements attributed to and stories involving Babylonian rabbis in the Babylonian Talmud. Statements attributed to and stories involving Palestinian rabbis in the Bavli present a particularly thorny methodological problem. On the one hand, they may be Babylonian creations, fully reflective of Babylonian attitudes and/or reality; on the other hand, they may accurately reflect the opinions or actions of the Palestinian rabbis to whom they are attributed. Such traditions also may have originated in Palestine and been subjected to greater or lesser tampering by Babylonian authors or editors during the course of their journey to and/or transmission in Babylonia. In short, such sources may belong to one of several different categories, and it would be a mistake to prejudge this material or to ignore it entirely. It is necessary to decide on a case-by-case basis whether or not a particular statement is best classified as Palestinian, Babylonian, or some combination of the two, or whether we lack a sufficient basis on which to decide the question,[1] attempting to steer a middle course between scholars who a priori tend to view all traditions in the Bavli, even those designated as tannaitic or Palestinian amoraic, as having been subjected to the heavy hand of Babylonian editors (Neusner 1989: 1–13, 19–44) and scholars who consider all material designated in the Bavli as tannaitic or Palestinian amoraic as being precisely what it purports to be.[2]

The historical value of the material in the Bavli is of course independent of its chronology or place of origin. Determining the latter is a necessary precondition for proper evaluation of a source's historicity, but Palestinian sources do not necessarily contain trustworthy evidence about Palestinian Sages and institutions, nor do early sources necessarily depict the early period more accurately than do later sources, and it is necessary to take seriously the possibility that early and later sources attest to changes in how rabbis wish to portray themselves rather than to changes in their actual behaviour, or that sources reflect different Palestinian and Babylonian desires rather than different realities in the two centres. Often the results of this (or any) study will be inconclusive but on occasion we will be in a position to advance historical hypotheses with a measure of confidence.

Astrology as a Test Case

Many modern scholars have discussed ancient rabbinic attitudes towards astrology. Scholarly discussions have been hampered in some cases, however, by a lack of familiarity with the latest tools of modern critical scholarship on rabbinic literature,[3] and at times by an inability to understand rabbinic texts

---

[1] This method has found widespread acceptance. See, for example, Goodblatt (1980); Hayes (1997: 9–17); Cohen (ed. 2000). However, it is still considered inefficacious by several leading scholars. See, for example, Stemberger (1996: 57–9).

[2] It is difficult to find scholars who utilise this approach today, but it is common in scholarly literature of past generations and is therefore influential. See, for example, Urbach (1979).

[3] For example, von Stuckrad (2000: 476–7), fails to distinguish between the Hebrew statement attributed to Rab (and paralleled in GenR 44.12 ed. Theodor/Albeck, p. 432) in b.Shab. 156a and the anonymous editorial give and take (in Aramaic) based on Rab's statement, without parallel in any Palestinian compilation. An article by Jeffrey L. Rubenstein (2007) reached me too late to incorporate into this article.

on their most basic level.[4] A fresh look at the evidence may therefore be fruitful. I confine the discussion to cases in which it is clear that the rabbis (a) divine the future based on the movements or appearance of heavenly bodies; or (b) acknowledge that heavenly bodies influence the course of events on earth. The Hebrew and Aramaic words *mazal* and *mazla* are conventionally translated as 'planet', 'constellation', 'heavenly body', 'fortune', and even 'guardian angel' (Sokoloff 2002: 653–54; cf. Sokoloff 1992: 298). Since it is impossible to capture all of these nuances with a single English word, I generally leave these words untranslated, relying on context to convey the meaning or accompanying them with an explanation.

This study is part of a wider research project into the fourth century as an important turning point in Babylonian Jewish history, a time when texts, attitudes, literary motifs, and modes of behaviour deriving from Palestine and from elsewhere in the Roman empire, particularly the eastern Roman provinces, achieved literary expression in the Bavli, often for the first time (Kalmin 2006b; idem forthcoming a), and Babylonia began increasingly to become part of the late-antique Mediterranean world. I am not suggesting that there was no exchange between Mesopotamia and the Roman empire, in both directions, prior to the fourth century, but that events of the mid-third century led to a vigorous eastern provincial Romanisation of Mesopotamia, which first achieved literary expression in Jewish and Christian sources of the fourth century, and that the exchange between the regions was largely one way, from west to east, during most of this period (Kalmin 2006b: 186; Millar 1993: 510, 516–17).

Some modern scholars have claimed that Babylonian rabbis were more enthusiastic believers in astrology than were their Palestinian counterparts thanks to Babylonia's status as the birthplace of astrology (Wächter 1969: 194–9),[5] but this claim ultimately does not stand up to critical scrutiny (von Stuckrad 2000: 564; Gafni 1990: 165), and any theory offered to explain the evidence has to take account of more nuanced distinctions and to take into consideration evidence for astrological beliefs in non-rabbinic sources in the Graeco-Roman world, according to which there was an extremely rich, albeit not uncontested, tradition of astrological practice and speculation in the Graeco-Roman world as well as in Babylonia (Charlesworth 1987: 926–30, 933–50). In addition, as we will see below, we need to take into consideration opinions attributed to Palestinian rabbis and recorded only in the Bavli, but

---

[4] Von Stuckrad (2000: 460). In addition, von Stuckrad (p. 452) uses ancient and medieval rabbinic compilations indiscriminately, leading to distortions in his accounts of the late-antique rabbinic views.

[5] Babylonia's reputation as the place of origin does seem to be deserved. See, for example, Neugebauer (1975: 5); Barton (1994: 19–29).

which attribute to Palestinian amora'im firmer conviction regarding the efficacy of astrology than anything we find in Palestinian compilations themselves.

Palestinian Amoraic Views

How can we best characterise Palestinian rabbinic attitudes towards astrology as recorded in post-tannaitic Palestinian compilations? A few traditions in post-tannaitic Palestinian compilations presuppose that astrology is unproblematically efficacious, with no hint of polemic (see below), but of great significance for the present study of the use of the Bavli for the history of Palestine is the fact that by far the most spectacular affirmations of the efficacy of astrology attributed to Palestinian amora'im are preserved in the Bavli,[6] and their Palestinian provenance is corroborated by the fact that these statements preserve striking features of Galilean Aramaic, the language of post-tannaitic Palestinian compilations (Greenfield and Sokoloff 1989: 211).

To illustrate my point about the difference between the Bavli's record of Palestinian attitudes and those preserved in Palestinian compilations, it will be helpful to quote one of the statements preserved in the Bavli, followed by its closest counterpart in a Palestinian compilation. The statement, in b.Shab. 156a, is as follows:[7]

> R. Ḥanina said: . . . A man who was born under the sun will be a proud man. He will eat from what is his, and drink from what is his, and his secrets will be revealed. If he robs, he will not succeed. A man who was born under Venus will be a rich and fornicating man. . . . A man who was born under Mercury will be an intelligent and wise man because Mercury is the scribe of the sun. A man who was born under the moon will be a man who suffers from illnesses. He builds and tears down, tears down and builds. He eats what is not his, and drinks what is not his, and his secrets are concealed. If he steals he will succeed. A man who was born under Saturn will be a man whose plans will come to naught. And some say all that people plan against him will come to naught. A man who is born under Jupiter will be a charitable man. . . . A man who is born under Mars will be a man who sheds blood.

The most significant statement in a post-tannaitic Palestinian compilation is found in GenR 10.4 (ed. Theodor/Albeck: 78–9):

---

[6] b.Shab. 156a (R. Yehoshua ben Levi and two statements by R. Ḥanina). For astrological statements attributed to Babylonian rabbis, see b.Shab. 129b (the anonymous editors); b.Eruv. 56a (Shmuel).

[7] The ellipses indicate places where the statement is interrupted by later amoraic and anonymous editorial commentary, or is set in a narrative context, none of which is relevant for my present purposes.

> Said R. Simon, There is not a blade of grass that does not have a *mazal* in the
> heavens that strikes it and says to it, 'Grow!' This is what [is written], 'Do you
> know the laws of heaven or impose its authority on earth?' (Job 38:33).

The verse from Job quoted at the conclusion of the statement teaches that
according to R. Simon, the *mazal* is an instrument of God, doing His will.

The most striking difference between the two traditions quoted above is
the fact that the tradition in the Bavli concerns human beings and the tradition in Genesis Rabbah concerns plants. Were we to have the latter tradition
without the former, we might assume that the planets controlled plant life
but had no role whatsoever in controlling human life. For reasons to be
elaborated upon below, it is unlikely that the Bavli has taken a Palestinian
tradition and transformed it according to Babylonian beliefs. Rather, the
statement appears to accurately reflect Palestinian rabbinic belief, despite the
fact that it is preserved only in the Bavli.

Most Palestinian amoraic traditions about astrology take its efficacy for
granted, but in a polemical context. This polemic can be summed up as follows: astrology is efficacious but Israelites should not engage in it since
Israel has more powerful tools at her disposal: for example, the word of God,
the holy spirit, and the covenantal relationship with God. These tools yield
certainty while astrology yields ambiguous messages that its practitioners
inevitably interpret incorrectly. This polemic has abundant parallels in
Christian and pagan sources.[8]

We find the rabbinic polemic, for example, in Pesikta de-Rab Kahana,
a post-tannaitic Palestinian compilation. This tradition emphasises the
superiority of an Israelite hero's wisdom over the wisdom of non-Israelite
astrologers:[9]

> A. It is written, 'Solomon's wisdom was greater than the wisdom of all the
> people of the East' (1 Kings 5:10). And what was the wisdom of the people of
> the East? They knew astrology and were expert in divination of the future by
> means of the calls or the flights of birds.[10]
> B. 'And all the wisdom of the Egyptians' (1 Kings 5:10). What was the wisdom
> of the Egyptians?
> You find that when Solomon wanted to build the Temple, he sent to Pharaoh
> Necho.
> [Solomon] said to him, 'Send to me skilled artisans [who I will] pay, for I want
> to build the Temple.'

---

[8] See, for example, Origen, cited in Eusebius, *Praeparatio Evangelica*, 6.11, and *Philocalia*,
12.1–21. See also Denzey (2003: 212–19).
[9] PRK 4.3 ed. Mandelbaum, p. 60 (= EcclR 7.1.23).
[10] Mandelbaum, ibid.

What did [Pharaoh] do? He gathered together all of his astrologers and they examined [the heavens] and saw people who would die that year and he sent them to him. When they came to Solomon, he saw by the holy spirit that they would die that year. He gave them burial shrouds and sent them [back] to [Pharaoh]. And he sent and wrote to him, saying, 'You didn't have shrouds to bury your dead? Here they are and here are their shrouds.'

According to part B, Solomon outsmarts Pharaoh because he is inspired by the holy spirit. Part A asserts that Solomon's wisdom was greater than the astrology of the people of the East (the Babylonians?), without stating explicitly that the source of Solomon's wisdom was divine. Nevertheless, the proximity of part B, together with the fact that generally in Palestinian rabbinic literature it is through God's help that the Israelite heroes best non-Israelite astrologers, raises the likelihood that we are to understand part A along these lines as well.

We find a variation of these themes in GenR 44.10 (ed. Theodor/Albeck, p. 432). In this tradition the biblical hero, Abram, is the astrologer. God Himself, rather than the Israelite hero, demonstrates that astrology yields only partial truth, which leads to error when it is not supplemented by divine insight. Abram fills the role of the non-Israelite astrologer, since his encounter with God takes place before God changed Abram's name, before God commanded him to circumcise himself, and before Isaac inherited God's promise to Abraham.

None of these texts addresses the issue of what Jews are to do in the here and now, when prophecy has ceased. Evidently, the question of what to do in the here and now is not their concern. These traditions pick up the threads of Second-Temple apologetic literature, and evidently they are addressed to rabbis (or rabbis in training) and/or to non-rabbinic Jews, to instil in them pride in Israel's glorious past, more glorious than that of any other people, past or present. Perhaps their unstated implication is that God's direct communication to Jewish heroes will resume some time in the future.

One of the most straightforwardly negative Palestinian amoraic traditions about astrology is preserved in p.Shab. 6.10, 8d. The message of this story is not that astrology is a mode of access to the correct prediction of the future, which, however, yields only partial insight and therefore leads to error. Rather, the message here is that astrology is something that Israel must not engage in because of its status as a holy nation. God punishes Jews who trust in astrology and rewards those who trust in God, the two being incompatible. When a Jew does engage in it, that Jew is marginal—for example, a convert. Significantly, this story relates an event that ostensibly took place in the rabbinic present and not in the biblical past:

R. Huna told this story:

A convert was an astrologer.[11] One time he wanted to go out.

He said, 'Should one go out now?'

He then said, 'Why have I cleaved to this holy nation? Is it not to separate from these things?'

He went out in the name of the Creator. He approached a tax house and his donkey kicked him and made him fall. His donkey went on along [and so saved him from the tax].[12]

Why did he fall? Because he thought about [relying on astrology]. Why was he saved? Because he relied on his Creator.

A story even more hostile to astrology is recorded in p.AZ 2.2, 41a:

A convert was a barber and an astrologer. He saw in his horoscope that Jews would spill his blood. But it was only because they converted him.[13]

Whenever a Jew went, wanting to get a haircut with him, he killed him.

How many did he kill?

R. Lazar bar Yosi said, 'Eighty.'

R. Yosi bei R. Bun said, 'Three hundred.'

Finally they prayed about him and he returned to his idolatrous ways.

As in the previous story, the astrologer in this story is a convert to Judaism. In this story, however, the convert actually engages in astrology and is responsible for the murder of many Jews. The gulf between Judaism and astrology is reinforced by the fact that the convert ends up leaving Judaism, showing that he was not a legitimate Jew in the first place. The Palestinian rabbinic claim that astrology was incompatible with being Jewish is clearly a rabbinic fantasy, since it is unlikely that the only Palestinian Jews who engaged in astrology were converts. It is interesting that the two most negative depictions in post-tannaitic Palestinian compilations are both found in the Yerushalmi. Perhaps this is linked to the fact that the Yerushalmi, a non-midrashic work, deals with astrology in the rabbinic present rather than in the remote biblical past. The goal in the midrashic texts was not to condemn but to belittle astrology, and also to glorify biblical heroes. The stories in the Yerushalmi, in contrast, have as their primary motive the condemnation of astrology in the present, insofar as it threatened to be or in fact was a practice that Jews engaged in. The ferocity of the condemnation is proportional to the rabbis' perception of the seriousness of the threat.

---

[11] Lieberman (1934: 114–15).

[12] Ibid., pp. 115–16.

[13] Cf. Sokoloff (1992: 127).

Babylonian Amoraic Views

In this section, we examine Babylonian rabbinic attitudes towards astrology and attempt to show that post-tannaitic Babylonians, unlike their Palestinian counterparts, did not polemicise against astrology, and were not preoccupied with erecting clear boundaries between astrology and Judaism. We will tentatively suggest an explanation for the differing Palestinian and Babylonian rabbinic statements about astrology in the conclusion, below, where we will also expand upon our claim that the Bavli is an important source for the history of late-Roman Palestine.

The ensuing discussion argues that the Bavli, in sharp contrast to Palestinian compilations, always depicts astrologers as fully correct in their predictions. In addition, the Bavli sometimes depicts the predictions of astrologers as conforming to the will of God. The Bavli has no difficulty depicting righteous Jews, including rabbis, getting close enough to astrologers to be informed by them of their predictions for the future. It is not even made clear in any of the Bavli's accounts whether astrologers are Jews or non-Jews, since the term 'Chaldean', which typically denotes 'astrologer' in the Bavli, 'could denote an astrologer of any ethnicity' (Barton 1994: 9; Reed 2004: 125). A narrative in b.Shab. 119a illustrates several of these points:

> Yosef Who Honours the Sabbath, there was a certain non-Jew in his neighbourhood who had a lot of property.
> Chaldeans said to him, 'Yosef Who Honours the Sabbath will consume all of your property.'
> [The non-Jew] went and sold all of his property and bought with it a precious gem. He put it in his cap.[14] When he was crossing a bridge, a wind caused it to fly away and threw it into the water. A fish swallowed it. Someone lifted it up and brought [the fish] towards evening before the arrival of the Sabbath.
> They said, 'Who will buy this now?'
> They said to them, 'Go and bring it to Yosef Who Honours the Sabbath, who is accustomed to buying [things just before the Sabbath].'
> They brought it to him, he bought it and tore it open, and found in it the precious gem. He sold it for 13 measures[15] of golden dinars.
> A certain elder encountered him.
> He said, 'He who borrows [for the Sabbath],[16] the Sabbath pays him.'

Based on the conclusion of this story, it is clear that Yosef receives the precious gem as a divine reward for honouring the Sabbath. The last two

[14] Sokoloff (2002: 802).
[15] Ibid., p. 855.
[16] Rabbinovicz (1867–97: n. ḥet).

sentences are missing in several versions[17] and are therefore suspect as a later addition, but even without them the message is clear, first from Yosef's sobriquet ('Who Honours the Sabbath'), and second from his practice of buying expensive, perishable foods just before the Sabbath for the sole purpose of honouring the Sabbath. So apparently God is active behind the scenes, arranging for Yosef to be rewarded for his devotion to the Sabbath. The fact that there is conformity between the prediction of the astrologers and God's will serves to distinguish the Bavli's story from stories in Palestinian compilations.

Along the same lines, a story in b.Shab. 156b involving Rab Naḥman bar Yiẓhak portrays Chaldeans as correct in their prediction regarding the fate of a Babylonian rabbi:

> The mother of Rab Naḥman bar Yiẓhak, Chaldeans said to her, 'Your son will be a thief.'
> She said to [her son], 'Cover your head so that the fear of heaven will be upon you, and ask for mercy [i.e. pray].'
> He did not know why she said this to him. One day he was sitting and studying under a palm tree. The garment fell from his head. He lifted up his eyes and saw the palm tree. His inclination overpowered him,[18] he ascended [the tree] and cut off the cluster [of dates] with his teeth.[19]

According to this story, astrology has power. So much so that even though Rab Naḥman bar Yiẓhak is studying (at the time!) and even though he regularly prays, when his head is accidentally uncovered and he is distracted from his studies, his 'impulse' overcomes him and the prediction of the astrologers comes true.

Examination of the term *mazla* in the Bavli further suggests that Babylonian rabbis tend not to polemicise against astrology or to portray it as irreconcilable with Judaism. In addition, examination of this term reveals a transformation in its meaning from the mid-fourth century, unattested in earlier layers of the Bavli but with echoes in Palestinian rabbinic literature, and, surprisingly, much stronger parallels in non-rabbinic and even non-Jewish literature deriving from elsewhere in the Roman empire, supporting the notion that the mid-fourth century was a turning point in the development of the literature and culture of Jewish Babylonia. We will discuss in the conclusion below why this evidence further supports our claim regarding the importance of the Bavli for the study of late-Roman Palestine.

---

[17] See Sheiltot 1 ed. Mirsky, p. 15; Midrash Aseret ha-Dibrot (see *Beit ha-Midrash*, ed. Adolph Jellinek (1853–77; repr. Jerusalem, Wahrmann Books, 1967), vol. 1, p. 75); MSS Oxford, JTS ENA 2990.5–11; JTS ENA 2825.21; Aggadot ha-Talmud.
[18] Sokoloff (2002: 135).
[19] Ibid., p. 1009.

It will be helpful to preface this discussion with a few words of definition. The ensuing discussion focuses on the term *mazla* when it designates a heavenly body that has a special connection to a particular individual, often serving to protect that individual from harm. The fates of the *mazla* and the individual are inextricably intertwined, such that the *mazla* becomes 'impaired' or 'lowered' when the individual suffers a reversal, and vice versa: the person suffers when his *mazla* loses potency. An individual's *mazla* can experience things on his behalf, producing an effect on the individual as if he had the experiences himself. A person's *mazla* comes into being when he is born, and although this is not stated explicitly, presumably it disappears when the person dies.

For example, we read in b.MK 28a:

> Rab Se'orim the brother of Rava sat before Rava. He saw that [Rava] was dying.[20]
> [Rava] said to [Rab Se'orim], 'Let the master tell [the angel of death] not to cause us pain.'
> [Rab Se'orim] said to [Rava], 'Is not the master his close friend?'[21]
> [Rava] said to him, 'Since my *mazla* has been lowered,[22] he pays no attention to me.'
> [Rab Se'orim] said to him, 'Appear to me [after your death].'
> He appeared to him.
> [Rab Se'orim] said to him, 'Did the master have any pain?'
> [Rava] said to him, 'Like the incision of a scalpel.'[23]

This story, involving Babylonian amora'im of the mid-fourth century, supports my claim that a rabbi's *mazla* is closely linked to his personal fate. Once Rava's *mazla* has been 'lowered', presumably via his sickness, Rava no longer has any influence over the angel of death. The descent of the rabbi and his *mazla* occur simultaneously and mutually reinforce one another.

Important information is also revealed in b.BK 2b:

> A. What is the difference between [the verb used to describe the goring of] a person, where it is written, 'When an ox gores (*Ki Yigah*) [a man or a woman to death]' (Exod. 21:28), and a beast, where it is written, 'When [an] ox gores (*Ki Yigof*) [his neighbor's ox and it dies]' (Exod. 21:35)?
> B. [Regarding] a person, who has *mazla*, it is written *Ki Yigah*. [Regarding] an animal, that has no *mazla*, it is written *Ki Yigof*. And [scripture] informs us in an incidental manner that [a beast that] has the presumption of goring a human being also has the presumption of goring a beast, but [a beast that] has the presumption of goring a beast does not have the presumption of goring a human being.

---

[20] Sokoloff (2002: 737).
[21] Ibid., p. 1125.
[22] Ibid., p. 693.
[23] Ibid., p. 1072.

This anonymous discussion informs us that a human being has *mazla* but a beast does not, and that as a result, a beast is more likely to kill another beast than to kill a human being. *Mazla* confers protection on a creature that is unavailable to one without *mazla*.

A discussion in b.Pes. 2b provides additional information:

> A. What is [the meaning of] *Or* [a term used in the Mishnah]?
> B. Rab Huna said, 'Day.'
> C. Rab Judah said, 'Night.'
> D. They objected [based on a source of higher authority], 'Perish the day on which I was born. . . . May its twilight stars remain dark. May it hope for *Or* and have none. May it not see the glimmerings of the dawn' (Job 3:3, 9). Since scripture says, 'May it hope for *Or* and have none', this proves that *Or* is day.
> E. In that case [i.e. in Job 3:3, 9], Job is cursing his *mazla*, saying, 'May it be [God's] will that I[24] look for [a source of] light but not find it.'[25]

According to the anonymous editors (section E in this passage), Job's *mazla* becomes his on the day of his birth.

All of the texts surveyed above derive from the mid-fourth century or later.[26] As noted, a few traditions in post-tannaitic Palestinian compilations reflect a similar conception of *mazla*,[27] although we find significantly closer parallels in non-rabbinic literature. The first-century CE Roman author Pliny the Elder asserts that every person has his or her own star, which rises with them at birth and falls with them at death, and varies in brightness corresponding to the person's fate in life.[28] In addition, according to the *Book of Hermes Addressed to Ammon*, a star causes an individual's illness 'because it has suffered negative influences itself', and the star therefore needs strengthening by means of 'sympathetic energy'.[29] In addition, 'In the *Sacred Book of Hermes Addressed to Asclepius*, the medical recipes clearly envisage strengthening the decan responsible for causing disease in a particular part of the body' (Barton 1994: 190–1).[30] Barton characterises the belief that each person had his or her own star as widespread throughout the Roman empire (ibid., p. 113). The significance of these Western parallels, much closer to the Bavli's usage than to anything in a Palestinian rabbinic compilation, will be discussed in the conclusion, below.

[24] Literally, 'that man', a circumlocution.

[25] See Rashi, s.v. *Le-Nehora*. Here, *Or* means neither night nor day.

[26] See also b.Ber. 55b; b.Shab. 61b, 145b–146a; b.Meg. 3a; b.Ḥag. 4b–5a; b.BB 12a–b. See also the discussion of b.BB 98a; b.Bek. 8b in Kalmin forthcoming b.

[27] For one example, see GenR 10.4 ed. Theodor/Albeck, pp. 78–9 (pp. 171–2 above).

[28] See *Natural History*, 2.5.23. See also *Sefer ha-Razim*, 1:161–67.

[29] See *Physici et medici Graeci minores*, vol. 1, ed. Ideler, pp. 387 and 430.

[30] See C. E. Ruelle, 'Hermès Trismégiste, le livre sacré sur les décans', *Revue de Philologie*, 32 (1908), 252–3 and 258–9. Already Plato, *Timaeus*, 41D–E attests to this idea.

Summary and Conclusions

To summarise, the Bavli's understanding of *mazla*, attested in Babylonian traditions dating from the mid-fourth century and later, was a commonplace in the Roman empire but had only faint echoes in Palestinian rabbinic literature. The fact that a notion well-attested in the Graeco-Roman world and in the Bavli has only faint echoes in Palestinian rabbinic literature shows the Bavli's importance for the study of Roman Palestine. The weak attestation of this notion in Palestinian rabbinic literature is probably an accident of transmission, since it is unlikely that Palestinian rabbis were surrounded on all sides by people familiar with this notion but were unaware of it themselves.

It is also possible that the absence of this notion from Palestinian rabbinic compilations is the result of deliberate editorial activity, namely the post-tannaitic Palestinian rabbinic suppression of traditions favourable to astrology. As noted, three crucially important astrological traditions were authored, or reported, by early Palestinian amora'im, but are preserved only in the Bavli,[31] and their Palestinian origin is corroborated by their formulation in Galilean Aramaic, the language of Palestinian rabbinic compilations but not of the Bavli. In addition, a lengthy astrological tradition recorded in two tannaitic compilations (t.Suk. 2.5; Mek. ed. Horowitz, p. 7) has a lengthy parallel in the Bavli (b.Suk. 29a–b) but is not recorded in the Yerushalmi. Similarly, the only Palestinian tradition that portrays Abraham favourably as an astrologer is found in a tannaitic compilation and the Bavli, but once again it is without parallel in a post-tannaitic Palestinian compilation (Harari 2006: 562–3).[32] While one should be wary of placing too much weight on an argument from silence, it is difficult to believe that post-tannaitic Palestinian compilations were ignorant of all of these traditions, since the Bavli knew them all. It is likely, although by no means certain, that the Palestinian compilations were aware of at least some of this material but suppressed it because of later Palestinian rabbinic opposition to astrology. As we saw above, it is revealing that Palestinian compilations are willing to depict Jews as practising astrologers in the rabbinic present only when those Jews are marginal.

We thus have further indication of the importance of the Bavli for study of late-antique Roman Palestine. Without the Bavli, we would have no idea that third-century Palestinian rabbis authored (or reported) astrological statements linking the fate of individual human beings to the regnant planets

---

[31] b.Shab. 156a (R. Yehoshua ben Levi and R. Ḥanina (twice)). See the discussion above.

[32] See t.Kid. 5.17; b.BB 16b. See also b.Yoma 28b.

at the days or hours of their birth, statements otherwise unattested in Palestinian rabbinic literature.

Finally, we found that Palestinian rabbis were substantially more concerned than their Babylonian counterparts (prior to the mid-fourth century) with polemicising against astrology and with stigmatising it as a non-Jewish practice. Babylonian rabbis, in contrast, tended to depict astrological forces and the predictions of astrologers as unproblematically efficacious, even in conformity with God's will, and as having an important impact on the lives of important rabbis, without a hint of polemics.

At present the reason for these distinctions between Palestinian and Babylonian rabbis is not entirely clear, but it is at least possible to hazard a guess, building on (a) conclusions in earlier research that Babylonian rabbis, to a greater extent than Palestinian rabbis, worked to build strong boundaries between *themselves* and *other Jews*; and (b) Isaiah Gafni's insight that it was more important to Palestinian than to Babylonian rabbis to build strong barriers between *Jews* and *Gentiles* (Gafni 1990: 124). Astrology, therefore, might have served Palestinian rabbis as simply one of many practices that they claimed distinguished Jews from non-Jews. Babylonian rabbis, in contrast, did not seize upon astrology as a means of distinguishing between themselves and other Jews, perhaps for the simple reason that astrology was not a marker of non-rabbinic Jewish identity in Babylonia, where it was instead firmly rooted in the indigenous, non-Jewish culture. In addition, perhaps the relative strength and security of the Jewish community in Babylonia contributed to the Babylonian rabbis' lack of an urgent need to erect firm boundaries separating Jews from Gentiles, in contrast to the Palestinian Jewish community's greater vulnerability in pagan Roman and later Christian Palestine.

Obviously it is necessary to examine the full range of evidence, for example the Babylonian magic bowls, and the abundant archaeological and epigraphic record in Palestine, to better evaluate this hypothesis. The issue of the extent to which and the consistency with which Babylonian rabbis did not construct firm boundaries between Jews and Gentiles, finally, is complex (Hayes 1997: 127–81, 233–49), and a fresh look at the evidence is necessary before final conclusions are drawn.

Further Reading

Boyarin (1993); Friedman (1993); Gafni (1990); Hayes (1997); Kalmin (1994, 2006b); Levine (1989); Schäfer (2007); Vidas (2008); Zellentin (2007).

Bibliography

Barton, T. (1994), *Ancient Astrology*, London.

Bokser, B. M. (1990), 'Talmudic studies', in S. J. D. Cohen and E. L. Greenstein (eds.), *The State of Jewish Studies*, Detroit, pp. 80–112.

Boyarin, D. (1993), *Carnal Israel: Reading Sex in Talmudic Culture*, Berkeley.

Brody, R. (2008), 'The anonymous Talmud and Amoraic dicta', in B. Schwartz *et al.* (eds.), *Selected Papers in Jewish Studies*, vol. 1: *The Bible and Its World*, Jerusalem, pp. 213–32. [Hebrew]

Charlesworth, J. (1987), 'Jewish interest in astrology during the Hellenistic and Roman periods', in H. Temporini and W. Haase (eds.), *Aufstieg und Niedergang der Römischen Welt*, vol. 2.20.2, pp. 926–50.

Cohen, S. J. D. (ed.) (2000), *The Synoptic Problem in Rabbinic Literature*, Providence, RI.

Denzey, N. (2003), 'A new star on the horizon: astral Christologies and stellar debates in early Christian discourse', in S. Noegel *et al.* (eds.), *Prayer, Magic, and the Stars in the Ancient and Late Antique World*, University Park, PA.

Epstein, I. (ed.) (1935–52), *The Babylonian Talmud*, 35 vols., London.

Feldblum, M. (1969), 'The impact of the "Anonymous Sugya" on Halakic concepts', *Proceedings of the American Academy for Jewish Research*, 37: 19–28.

Friedman, S. (1977), 'A critical study of *Yevamot* X with a methodological introduction', in *Texts and Studies. Analecta Judaica*, 1, New York, pp. 275–441. [Hebrew]

Friedman, S. (1993), 'On the historical Aggadah in the Babylonian Talmud', in idem (ed.), *Saul Lieberman Memorial Volume*, Jerusalem, pp. 119–64. [Hebrew]

Friedman, S. (1996), *Talmud Arukh: Bava Meẓi'a, VI: Text. Critical Edition with Comprehensive Commentary*, New York. [Hebrew]

Gafni, Y. (1990), *The Jews of Babylonia in the Talmudic Era: A Social and Cultural History*, Jerusalem. [Hebrew]

Goldschmidt, L. (ed.) (1897–1935), *Der Babylonische Talmud.* 9 vols., Berlin; Index volume, ed. R. Edelmann, Copenhagen, 1959; repr., 1980–81.

Goodblatt, D. (1980), 'Towards the rehabilitation of Talmudic history', in B. M. Bokser (ed.), *History of Judaism: The Next Ten Years*, Chico, CA, pp. 31–44.

Goodblatt, D. (1981), 'The Babylonian Talmud', in J. Neusner (ed.), *Approaches to Ancient Judaism*, vol. 2: *The Palestinian and Babylonian Talmuds*, New York, pp. 257–336.

Greenfield, J. C. and Sokoloff, M. (1989), 'Astrological and related omen texts in Jewish Palestinian Aramaic', *Journal of Ancient Near Eastern Studies*, 48: 201–14.

Halivni, D. (2007), *Sources and Traditions: A Source Critical Commentary on the Talmud, Tractate Baba Bathra*, Jerusalem. [Hebrew]

Harari, Y. (2006), 'The Sages and the occult', in S. Safrai *et al.* (eds.), *The Literature of the Sages*, Second Part: *Midrash and Targum* . . ., Assen, pp. 521–64.

Hayes, C. E. (1997), *Between the Babylonian and Palestinian Talmuds: Accounting for Halakhic Difference in Selected Sugyot from Tractate Avodah Zarah*, New York.

Herschler, M. *et al.* (eds.) (1972–), *The Babylonian Talmud, with Variant Readings*, Jerusalem. [Hebrew]

Kalmin, R. (1994), 'Christians and heretics in rabbinic literature of late antiquity', *HThR* 87: 155–69.

Kalmin, R. (2006a), 'The formation and character of the Babylonian Talmud', in S. T. Katz (ed.), *The Cambridge History of Judaism*, vol. 4: *The Late Roman-Rabbinic Period*, Cambridge, pp. 840–76.

Kalmin, R. (2006b), *Jewish Babylonia Between Persia and Roman Palestine*, New York.

Kalmin, R. (forthcoming a), 'The miracle of the Septuagint', in Z. Weiss *et al.* (eds.), *The Lee Levine Jubilee Volume*, New York.

Kalmin, R. (forthcoming b), 'Astrology in rabbinic literature of late antiquity', in S. Fine *et al.* (eds.), *Shoshanat Yaakov: Ancient Jewish and Iranian Studies in Honor of Professor Yaakov Elman*, Leiden.

Krupp, M. (1987), 'Manuscripts of the Babylonian Talmud', in S. Safrai and P. J. Tomson (eds.), *The Literature of the Sages*, First Part: *Oral Tora, Halakha, Mishna, Tosefta, Talmud, External Tractates*, Assen and Philadelphia, pp. 346–66.

Levine, L. I. (1989), *The Rabbinic Class of Roman Palestine in Late Antiquity*, Jerusalem.

Lieberman, S. (1934), *Ha-Yerushalmi ki-Feshuto*, Jerusalem. [Hebrew]

Millar, F. (1993), *The Roman Near East, 31 BC–AD 337*, Cambridge, MA.

Munk, E. (ed.) (1972–), *La Guemara: le Talmud de Babylone*, Paris.

Neugebauer, O. (1975), *A History of Ancient Mathematical Astronomy*, New York.

Neusner, J. (1965–70), *A History of the Jews in Babylonia*, 5 vols., Leiden.

Neusner, J. (1989), *Making the Classics in Judaism*, Atlanta.

Neusner, J. (ed.) (1984–95), *The Talmud of Babylonia: An American Translation*, Chico, CA.

Rabbinovicz, R. (1867–97), *Diqduqe Soferim: Variae Lectiones in Mischnam et in Talmud Babylonicum*, 12 vols., Munich; repr. 2001–02, Jerusalem. [Hebrew]

Reed, A. Y. (2004), 'Abraham as Chaldean scientist and Father of the Jews: Josephus, *Ant.* 1.154–168, and the Greco-Roman discourse about astronomy/astrology', *Journal for the Study of Judaism*, 35: 119–58.

Rubenstein, J. L. (2007), 'Talmudic astrology: *Bavli Šabbat* 156a–b', *Hebrew Union College Annual*, 78: 109–48.

Schäfer, P. (2007), *Jesus in the Talmud*, Princeton.

Schottenstein Edition (1990–2005), *Talmud Bavli* (numerous volumes by different translators and editors), ArtScroll/Mesorah, New York ('The ArtScroll Talmud').

Sokoloff, M. (1992), *A Dictionary of Palestinian Jewish Aramaic*, Ramat Gan.

Sokoloff, M. (2002), *A Dictionary of Babylonian Jewish Aramaic*, Ramat Gan.

Steinsaltz, A. (1967–), *Talmud Bavli*, numerous volumes, Israel Institute for Talmudic Publications, Jerusalem ('The Steinsaltz Talmud, Hebrew Edition').

Steinsaltz, A. (1989–), *The Babylonian Talmud*, numerous volumes, Random House, New York ('The Steinsaltz Talmud, English Edition').

Stemberger, G. (1996), *Introduction to the Talmud and Midrash*, 2nd edn., trans. and ed. M. Bockmuehl, Edinburgh.

Urbach, E. E. (1979), *The Sages: Their Concepts and Beliefs*, 2nd edn., trans. I. Abrahams, Jerusalem.

Vidas, M. (2008), 'The Bavli's discussion of genealogy in *Qiddushin* IV', in G. Gardner and K. L. Osterloh (eds.), *Antiquity in Antiquity: Jewish and Christian Pasts in the Greco-Roman World*, Tübingen.

von Stuckrad, K. (2000), *Das Ringen um die Astrologie: Jüdische und Christliche Beiträge zum Antiken Zeitverständnis*, Berlin.

Wächter, L. (1969), 'Astrologie und Schicksalsglaube in rabbinischen Judentum', *Kairos*, 11: 181–200.

Weiss, A. J. (ed.) (1964), *El Talmud de Babilonia*, Buenos Aires.

Zellentin, H. M. (2007), 'Late Antiquity Upside-Down: Rabbinic Parodies of Jewish and Christian Literature', Ph.D. dissertation, Princeton University.

Zolli, E. (1958), *Il Talmud babilonese*, Italian translation (only tractate Berakhot), Bari; repr. Rome, 1968 as *Il trattato delle Benedizioni del Talmud babilonese*, with introduction by S. Covalletti.

11

Literary Structures and Historical Reconstruction: The Example of an Amoraic Midrash (Leviticus Rabbah)

ALEXANDER SAMELY

1. Contents

LEVITICUS RABBAH IS A COMMENTARY ON THE BOOK OF LEVITICUS which now forms part of Midrash Rabbah, a great collection of commentaries of various dates on the Pentateuch and the Five Scrolls or Megillot (Lamentations, Song of Songs, Ruth, Ecclesiastes and Esther), put together for the first time by sixteenth-century Hebrew printers as a sort of encyclopaedia of midrash (Midrash Rabbah to the Pentateuch: Constantinople 1512; Midrash Rabbah to the Five Scrolls: Pesaro 1519; Midrash Rabbah to the Pentateuch and Five Scrolls: Venice 1545). It is commonly classified as one of the 'amoraic midrashim'—an extensive group of both exegetical and homiletic Bible commentaries, which quote from the amora'im, scholars of the third to sixth centuries CE who are quoted also in the Gemara of the Palestinian and Babylonian Talmuds. The amoraic midrashim are implicitly contrasted with the tannaitic (or halakhic) midrashim, which quote only scholars of the tannaitic era (first to early third centuries CE), the period of the Mishnah.

2. Manuscripts

Leviticus Rabbah is typical of the amoraic midrashim. It is now attested only in medieval manuscripts—ten more or less complete (of which British Library Add. 27169, Vatican Ebr. 32, and Munich heb. 117 are particularly important), and some forty fragments mainly from the Cairo Genizah (most of which are now in Cambridge and Oxford).

Proceedings of the British Academy **165**, 185–215. © The British Academy 2010.

3. Editions

The *textus receptus*, together with traditional commentaries and glosses, can be found in the Vilna edition of Midrash Rabbah (2 vols. folio, Vilna 1878, often reprinted). Essentially the same text is more readably presented in the editions of Mirkin (1956–67) and Halevi (1956–63). Margolioth (1953–60) offers a scholarly, critical text, with *apparatus criticus* and short but useful notes citing parallels in other rabbinic literature. Most comprehensive and useful of all, however, is Chaim Milikowsky and Margarete Schlüter's synoptic edition of almost all the surviving manuscripts and fragments, hosted on the Bar Ilan website (www.biu.ac.il/JS/midrash/VR/editionData.htm).

4. Translations

J. Israelstam and J. J. Slotki offer a generally sound English translation of the *textus receptus* in volume 4 of the Soncino Midrash Rabbah (volume 2 of the compact edition; Freedman and Simon eds. 1977). Jacob Neusner's English version (1986a) is also worth consulting, not least because its helpful layout makes much clearer the structure of the text. The old German translation by Wünsche (1884) in the Bibliotheca Rabbinica series adds nothing to these.

5. Place

That Leviticus Rabbah was composed somewhere in the Galilee is shown by the fact that portions of it are in the Galilean dialect of Aramaic. Its frequent use of Greek loanwords and its citation of Palestinian scholars, mainly of the third and fourth centuries CE, confirm its Palestinian provenance.

6. Date

The question of its date is complicated by the problem of its relationship to other amoraic compositions, notably Genesis Rabbah, Pesikta de-Rab Kahana, the Palestinian Talmud, and to the early synagogue poets (the Payyetanim, especially Yannai). All the evidence taken together suggests that Leviticus Rabbah was compiled in the fifth century, but, like many other rabbinic writings, subsequent copyists felt free to 'improve' its text.

* * *

This chapter has three parts. In the first I present ten theses about the special problems which the literary structures of rabbinic texts pose for the historian. In the second I examine a section of the amoraic work Leviticus Rabbah to describe some of those literary structures. The third part provides some speculative thoughts on what the message of these structures might be.[1]

The key point of the first part will be that we cannot yet explain how the textuality of rabbinic sources worked, and that this lack of clarity affects our use of them as historical sources.

The second part will claim that it is characteristic for many rabbinic works, and certainly for Leviticus Rabbah and its homilies, that they fill the same 'functional position' in a text *more than once*. There is more than one occupant for the same textual ('syntagmatic') slot, and these occupants are not thematically subordinated to each other, nor does the multiplication of a slot create a form of a higher order. Rather, the multiple occupants of the same slot are merely adjacent, creating a repetition of the slot itself (a 'paradigmatic' structure). In describing this feature in more detail, I attempt to clarify one manifestation of what scholars might mean when they speak of a rabbinic text as 'collection', 'compilation' or 'anthology'.[2] I will argue that such terms, where used to suggest that the texts present themselves merely as 'storage'[3] of otherwise self-contained earlier 'traditions', are reductionist. This is true even if it were conceded that the texts are to some extent the result of accidental redactional decisions, that is, decisions which do not respect a specific thematic focus or formal consistency. Because even if the presence and placement of *some* of their specific contents are governed by automatisms of, say, 'association' (whatever exactly is meant by this term), the multiplication of functional slots must still be explored in its own right as a sustained *building principle* of texts. For it is not an exceptional and accidental but a regular feature of those texts.

The third part will make a tentative attempt to populate this literary structure with some historical possibilities, prominent among them the idea that they could have had a 'training effect' for habits of thought.

---

[1] The wider context for the analysis here presented is the AHRC project 'Typology of Anonymous and Pseudepigraphic Jewish Literature in Antiquity' (www.manchester.ac.uk/ ancientjewishliterature).

[2] On the wider question see the articles in Stern (ed. 1997).

[3] Cf. for instance Jaffee (2007: 34).

A. Rabbinic Literary Structures in Modern Academic Historiography

It appears to me that an empirical and theoretically informed investigation of the literary character of rabbinic texts is important for any kind of historical enquiry into rabbinic Judaism. In order to contextualise such an investigation, of which part B of my chapter is a tranche, I here present some thoughts on the relationship between the texts and (a certain kind of) modern historiography in rabbinic studies.

Ten Theses on the Relationship between Historical Reconstruction and Literary Analysis

1. Historians use texts as sources. Texts have meaning structures beyond the level of the single sentence. The meaning emerging from the placement and sequence of sentences within a text therefore influences the meaning of the individual sentences occurring in them, for example, by narrowing down the topic these sentences are meant to speak about (cf. Samely 2009c).
2. Historians analyse the history of the texts they use as sources for a number of reasons, including:
    a. in order to test the texts' veracity (questions of bias, corruption);
    b. in order to understand the information content of the texts and to determine what topic they provide historical evidence for;
    c. in order to find out whether the whole of the text testifies to one and the same historical context, or whether there are parts of it which reflect a different historical context (and thus perhaps author, ideology, purpose, etc.);
    d. the genesis of documents can also provide information about the wider culture from which the sources emerged, for example, the role of orality versus literacy, questions of social institutions, etc.
3. Every diachronic hypothesis on how a text might have come about in an *unplanned* manner (that is, producing relationships between text parts that were not intended) inevitably also makes implicit claims about the literary structures *as they now are*. This is unavoidable, for two reasons:
    a. The starting point for any conclusion that an unplanned intervention (by an editor, scribe, etc.) took place is almost always an interpretation of the current text surface, as being in some way

conspicuous, and thus evidence for 'higher criticism'. Often this conspicuousness is a coherence problem relating to the *meaning* of the text, e.g. Gen. 1–3. In that sense, diachronic analysis presupposes an interpretation of the literary structures as they are. From this appears to follow a methodological postulate:

> *Postulate 1*
> Any diachronic hypothesis of text growth based on internal evidence should be tied to an explicit statement of how the coherence problem arises which the diachronic hypothesis is meant to explain. The coherence issue should be placed into the context of the whole of the text and its overall literary character. That overall literary character should not be taken for granted and treated in silence, as it reveals just what assumptions the scholar makes about textuality and coherence in rabbinic times.

b. A diachronic hypothesis involves a judgement on whether the text has become unusable (say, incomprehensible) by the introduction of those unplanned textual relationships. Where that is *not* thought to be the case, for example, because it is clear that a text has survived in active use for a long time after its current shape was reached, there appears to follow a second methodological postulate:

> *Postulate 2*
> Consideration ought to be given to how the text structures, *after the unplanned intervention*, could continue to be meaningful to later audiences (in the reconstructive understanding of the modern historian). This modern account of the meaningfulness of the text as it has been since the time of the unplanned intervention will effectively become an alternative solution, at least for a certain context of text reception, to the coherence issue which motivated the modern scholar to a diachronic separation of text parts in the first place.
>
> Even where the later use of the text is one of selective appropriation (using it like a 'quarry'), that too ought to be translated back into a literary characterisation. For this too ascribes to the document a kind of textuality, namely one which allows selective use in a manner that would be frowned upon in other traditions of textuality (including that of the modern scholar). That is in itself a distinctive feature worth pinning down, and would be quite different from any modern concept of 'anthology'.

4. Any assumption that a text forms a unity is a self-fulfilling prophecy for rabbinic literature, because rabbinic texts do not claim such a unity.

   By not claiming a specific kind of limited unity (thematic, formal, didactic, procedural, etc.), most rabbinic texts appear to empower the reader to look for unifying structures on any level and for any thematic angle. That makes it almost impossible to *disprove*, on entirely literary grounds, claims that the text forms a unity. This explains why both traditional reading and some modern critical readings (e.g. Neusner 1986b) of rabbinic sources can find strong overall work coherence where many scholars see only partial coherence.

5. The scholarly assumption of the disunity of a text is equally a self-fulfilling prophecy for rabbinic texts. This is again because they do not claim any unity, and also because they have structures of multiplication (see below) which invite a diachronic reading that separates 'traditions' within the text flow.

6. Given the potentially radical difference between rabbinic practices of textuality on the one hand, and textual practices governing modernity (and thus our scholarly habits) on the other, it is likely that we do not yet know what counted as a unified 'text' in rabbinic Judaism. But we can find out: by empirically studying the literary structures, in the first instance *as they are* in real text shapes as attested by physical evidence.

7. There is no one-to-one, predictable relationship between literary form on the one hand, and historical origin, purpose and use (e.g. *Sitz im Leben*) on the other. To be a literary form means: to be *imitable* in new circumstances, or for different purposes, and to be capable of being put to new uses. Analysing the literary form alone therefore can only suggest *possibilities* of historical origin and purpose. That is the nature of the beast, 'form'.

8. We know almost nothing certain about the regularities of oral transmission which many scholars believe account for rabbinic text structures, except what we ascertain through an empirical analysis of *how those texts work as texts*.

9. In addition to the well-known parallels of thematic substance found across rabbinic works, suggesting a common source for a certain idea (or 'tradition'), there are *functional parallels* within the same rabbinic text. One might say parallels are of two types: those where the same substance occurs in different texts, and those where different substance occurs in the same text. The latter parallels arise when the same textual position (say, the supporting argument for a

rabbinic statement) is filled with more than one thematic substance (say, more than one biblical proof text). These functional parallels within the same text help to create the impression that these texts are 'mere' collections just as much as the frequently discussed parallels of substance across different texts.[4]

10. The display of such functional parallels within many rabbinic texts requires to be appreciated as an important literary structure. It is capable of conveying implied messages, and of adding an extra dimension to the explicit meanings of the sentences in a text. This will be illustrated in the remainder of this chapter.

I shall now go over some of the same ground in more detail, and analyse an example of functional multiplicity taken from Leviticus Rabbah, one of the key works in the group usually referred to as amoraic midrash. It may be useful, before making the transition to literary analysis, to stress the following. Literary analysis of the type suggested here does not take place in a vacuum. Even as it tries to make the most of the evidence that is on the page—for example, the structural relationships between words and texts parts—it relies on generic assumptions about historical context, and these narrow down the theoretically possible meanings to what is manageable and relevant. In our case, for example, it is part of the background assumptions I make that we are analysing texts from antiquity, that Hebrew or Aramaic is their original language (not a translation language) and that these texts are in some sense 'Jewish' or even 'rabbinic' (and thus are likely to have links to other texts also 'rabbinic'). In that sense, a general historical picture of the text's origin always already makes a contribution to apparently ahistorical analyses of textual structures—but also the other way round. Methodologically speaking, the crucial thing is for the scholar to remain aware of all these factors: how do the historical assumptions effectively create what for the literary analysis are initial prejudices; and how do certain unchallenged assumptions of how the text works create certain historical pictures of its context?

B. What Sort of a Text is a Homily in Leviticus Rabbah?

As modern critical historians, we are used to distinguishing unitary ancient documents from composite ones. If there is no specific external evidence for

---

[4] Thus Heinemann's use of 'collect' and 'collection' throughout Heinemann (1971) shows that what is uppermost in his mind is the angle of a common pool of ideas available to the maker of Leviticus Rabbah as 'raw material'; but he also intuits that there is something about the manner in which they are put together which is noteworthy (see the quotation on p. 209 below). Cf. also Visotzky (2003: 14); on the problem of substantive parallels more generally, see Cohen (ed. 2000).

early text growth, as in the case of most rabbinic texts, we rely on methods of internal literary analysis to examine the unity. These methods investigate in particular propositional and stylistic coherence in comparison with other works. This is—relatively—straightforward in the case of narrative, and the modern separation of sources within Genesis 1–3 is a paradigm case of this. It is not so easy for discursive texts, that is, texts whose contents are not presented as being ordered on a time line (as the events in a story). Since there is no time line available as default principle of ordering, the text maker has to impose thematic coherence, or some external criterion of sequence, so as to provide order to the linear sequence of parts (e.g. sentences). Thematic-discursive texts tend to be subjected to the same scholarly methodology as narrative texts. Where we encounter problems with propositional and stylistic coherence, or other kinds of inconsistencies, we divide the document until we have smaller continuous units within which the coherence from sentence to sentence works well again. The point at which the modern scholar surmises that one pre-existing 'source' ends, and another such 'source' or the editorial framework begins, is then precisely the boundary between one continuous coherence-unit and the next, as constituted by the modern interpreter.

Do rabbinic documents conform to a basic expectation of fairly strong and even coherence from sentence to sentence, which would allow us to find the fault lines, if any, by locating the point at which there is an abrupt transition? The answer is no. For there is often a very marked difference in rabbinic texts between the strength by which each sentence and small form hangs together internally, and the comparative weakness with which adjacent sentences and small-form units hang together. It is natural for there to be a marked difference between these two types of cohesive force within a text: for example, the sentences hang together with each other by indirect force of ideas (supported by linguistic means of cohesion), while the words hang together with each other in the sentence by direct force of grammar. But in the case of rabbinic literature that difference is markedly greater than it is for other thematic-discursive texts of antiquity from outside the rabbinic culture, such as, say, Gaius' *Institutions* or Aristotle's *Metaphysics*; and, indeed, also greater than it is for narrative texts, even those inside rabbinic culture. This poses grave problems for any methodology which separates sources by degrees of coherence, in particular if the underlying coherence expectations are not spelled out by the methodology.

Scholars using rabbinic documents often assume that the small-scale units with strong coherence were single 'traditions', that is, single sentences, single utterances or brief mini-texts (e.g. m.Meg. 1.4ff.), and that they pre-existed not just the earliest rabbinic documents as we now have them, but were transmitted *outside any textual order* before they came together in the long and complex texts we now have (whether the latter are being envisaged as oral or written, does not affect the argument here). They are envisaged as floating freely. If this were accurate (and it is unlikely), it would leave the crucial transition from 'single item of information/recollection' to 'order of a plurality of sentences' unexplained. Yet often the assumption of free-floating 'traditions' is taken to *account* for rabbinic textual structures. The gap between single tradition and textual aggregate is bridged, so some scholars feel, by unexplained ideas such as 'association' and by reference to mnemonics. Both really reflect the assumption that rabbinic texts do not actually embody any *decisions* on thematic order and literary form: they just come about. This attitude is promoted by the rabbinic documents themselves, insofar as they do not even acknowledge their own existence as texts,[5] and their makers generally play down their own presence in the text. The scholarly reader trained in diachronic distinctions is prepared to perceive 'tradition at work' in such texts, but much less prepared to take note of the 'here I am' of the text itself.[6] Much literary analysis therefore only searches for traces of text history, for instance, probable scenarios and mechanisms of oral tradition. To such an approach it may appear as if the text allowed its own history to be directly perceived, without involving the scholar in judgements on the *literary* structures. This is an illusion. Rabbinic texts can provide no such transparent access to their own history. No *text* can. Rather on the contrary, rabbinic documents often make their apparent (or real!) text history the object of a display, and 'stage' their origins. They thus become manifestations of the opposite of the unselfconscious mechanisms of collection which some scholars assume. They turn the 'origin' into an artifice.

One of the key methods of displaying what looks at first like the text's 'past' is the *juxtaposition of passages that fulfil the same function*.[7] This is a way for a text to repeat itself, not by repeating information, but by filling with *variant* information functionally equivalent slots. If pre-existing passages are assembled in these texts, then they are assembled in such a way that, by that very placement, they are turned into functional equivalents or substitutes of each other, by performing the same discursive or literary move in the wider literary context.

I will now illustrate this phenomenon by examining the 'rabbinic homily'. This complex literary form is known to us from Leviticus Rabbah and from other so-called 'homiletical midrashim', that is, works which are collections

---

[5] For a rare rabbinic example of what such an acknowledgment looks like, see Mishnah Tamid 7.3: '*This* is the order (*seder*) of the Tamid of the service of the House of our God', where 'this' is an implicit self-reference to the text as such.

[6] A propos a passage in the Bavli (b.Meg. 3a), W. Smelik (2005: 28) puts it like this: 'There is perhaps something irresistible in the assumption that some oral traditions were thrown in, in order to preserve them, or as an associative digression.' (He goes on to resist.)

[7] For juxtaposition in rabbinic texts more generally, see Samely (2007).

of rabbinic homilies according to varying principles of selection and order.[8] The homily is practically the only rabbinic example of an extended literary form that is constituted hierarchically. Its constitutive 'functional forms' (Goldberg 1999; Lenhard 1998) relate to each other in a meaning-shaping manner, together creating a formally definable whole on a higher level of form, the rabbinic homily. The core functional forms which make up the homily are named in recent scholarship as the Petiḥah (in certain types of homily preceded by another unit, the Yelammedenu), followed by the Inyan (sometimes preceded by the unit Semikhah), followed by the Hatimah.[9] The functional interdependency between these is simple, but provides an effective network of relations. The Petiḥah section leads the reader from the quotation and explanation of a biblical verse, at first appearing to be randomly chosen, to the topic of a second verse, the opening ('Seder') verse of a different biblical passage altogether; the Inyan section stays with that Seder verse by interpreting successive lemmata from it or its immediate co-text; and the Hatimah leads away from the Seder verse to some new verse used as a closure, providing a message of comfort or of eschatological hope.[10]

Since the Petiḥah (plural, Petiḥot) is of particular importance for our topic, it may be useful to summarise what I consider to be the key features of (many) Petiḥot found in rabbinic literature. I shall concentrate on the narrative Petiḥah here (see Samely 2007: 75f., 185f.). The list below aims to include regularly occurring features, but many Petiḥot do not have all of these. Which of these features one considers as defining the 'essential' formal components of the Petiḥah depends to some extent on the modern scholar's context and purpose, and does not need to detain us at the moment.

---

[8] See Goldberg (1999: 107–11), for a distinction between 'compositional' and 'distributive' forms; the homily is an example of the former, Leviticus Rabbah an example of the latter.

[9] Petiḥah: literally, 'opening'. For a definition see p. xv. Yelammedenu: from the stereotypical opening words of the unit, *yelammedenu rabbeynu*, meaning, 'May [our rabbis] teach us.' Inyan means 'subject' or 'topic', and refers in the present context to a section of the homily which consists of a word-by-word or verse-by-verse commentary on that biblical passage which is the main theme of the rabbinic homily, opening with the Seder verse. Semikhah indicates the relationship of lying next to something (*samakh*) and is here used as a technical term for a unit in the homily which deals with one or more verses from the *preceding co-text* of the Seder verse in Scripture. Hatimah: literally, 'seal/signature/closure', used as modern scholarly term for the final part of the rabbinic homily.

[10] Cf. Visotzky (2003). Not all homilies in Leviticus Rabbah have the full Petiḥah-Inyan-Hatimah structure of the Goldbergian homily: several appear to have no Hatimot (cf. Neusner 1985, Visotzky 2003), which is an important lack.

1. Hermeneutic Features of the Narrative Petiḥah

1.1. The Petiḥah verse is employed in expressive use,[11] so as to speak generically about an event which is reported directly in the narrative verse (the 'Seder' verse). This employment identifies the event as *illustrating* a general truth *expressed* in the Petiḥah verse. Petiḥah verse and Seder verse do not come from the same narrative framework, and usually the Petiḥah verse is entirely generic, poetic or proverbial, coming from appropriate biblical books.

1.2. It is this application of the Petiḥah verse to some happening (or person, object) which the Seder verse speaks about, that 'fulfils' the Petiḥah verse, thereby also determining tacitly the meaning of the Seder verse's words in certain ways.

1.3. Generally speaking, the Petiḥah will highlight a verbal overlap between the Petiḥah verse and the Seder verse, that is, point to a meta-linguistic relationship between the wordings of the two verses. (Note that the 'application' movement just described in 1.1 and 1.2 is not, in itself, meta-linguistic.) This is usually manifest in the subsidiary employment of midrashic units as components in the Petiḥah which explicitly thematise the meaning of certain verbal expressions.

2. Literary Features of the Narrative Petiḥah

2.1. The Petiḥah *introduces* the Seder verse (or the narrative verse) by approaching it from a 'distant' theme, namely from the prima facie topic of the quoted Petiḥah verse (which is then developed in an unexpected direction). The Petiḥah then shows the theme of the Seder verse, (usually but not always) cited towards the end, to be relevant to the theme of the Petiḥah verse cited at the beginning.

2.2. The Petiḥah introduces thematic sidetracks into this approach to the Seder verse from the 'distant' Petiḥah verse which further delay the resolution of the tension of the Petiḥah. It does so by duplicating functionally equivalent parts, or by the inclusion of Petiḥah verse explanations which do not lead to the Seder verse at all (both illustrated below). This can heighten the effect of surprise when the Seder verse event is finally linked to the Petiḥah verse, an effect that may have been part of a rhetorical function of the Petiḥah.

---

[11] This means that the rabbinic speaker (or text voice) utters, in actual use, what is a pre-existing biblical wording (similar to the way one uses a proverb); see Samely (2002: 417) and search online for 'expressive-use' in Samely (2003) to view 264 mishnaic occurrences in English translation (the search rubric is 'formal features').

2.3. The Petiḥah is capable of being a functional (and necessary) component in the higher-order form, 'rabbinic homily', in which its Seder verse becomes, in its own right, the focus of the Inyan-part of the homily, and is subsequently linked to a Ḥatimah verse. But the Petiḥah also occurs outside rabbinic homilies, as for instance in Genesis Rabbah.

This list of features allows us, among other things, to distinguish the occurrences of Petiḥot (or Petiḥah-like units) in works such as Genesis Rabbah, Lamentations Rabbah and Ruth Rabbah, where 2.3 is not realised at all, from occurrences in works like Leviticus Rabbah and Tanḥuma (where it usually is realised).

In the larger context of this awareness of the overarching form 'homily', what exactly does one find when examining the progression from sentence to sentence, and from literary unit to literary unit within a Leviticus Rabbah homily? We find that the propositional and thematic unity of the homily is left entirely implicit. In fact, although the intermediary forms of the homily—Petiḥah, Inyan, Ḥatimah—are recognisable as such in many cases, and constitute a larger whole, these intermediary forms are in turn shaped from the use of stereotypical smaller forms: midrashic units, speech reports, *meshalim* (parables), disputes, formulaic dialogues, and so on. These small forms are shared between texts that have homiletic form and other kinds of texts in rabbinic literature. But outside the rabbinic homily, the small forms tend to be used in an open-ended recursive manner, and thus precisely not to be bounded by a higher form.[12]

The other result of examining the progress from unit to unit is that whole Petiḥot or functional parts of Petiḥot can be found juxtaposed to each other in the same rabbinic homily. In other words, we encounter the proliferation of functionally equivalent literary units in each other's co-text.

This phenomenon of multiplication arises in other genres of rabbinic literature as well (see below), but it is particularly conspicuous for the Petiḥah because of its strong literary-thematic definition and its formal-functional contribution to the homily as a whole. To understand this phenomenon of multiplication better, it may be useful to draw upon the somewhat analogous case of a sentence. We can construct an (ungrammatical) sentence in which the same syntactic slot is filled several times, when there should really be only one occupant, as in the following case:

> *I did my shopping yesterday today a week ago.*

'Yesterday', 'today' and 'a week ago' are all members of the paradigm of expressions which can occur in the slot 'adverbial time' as defined by a sentence syntagma, for example the following one:

---

[12] Samely (2007) addresses the recursive use of small forms as typical of most rabbinic genres.

[some person/agent] [did/does something] [at time X].

In our example sentence, the slot labelled [at time X] is filled by three members from that paradigm, not just one. They are contradictory,[13] and they certainly modify (or distort) the syntagma. It may be helpful to use this manner of speaking of syntagma and paradigm to analyse what happens in rabbinic homilies when there are multiple Petiḥot. One could present the syntagma of the rabbinic homily in its fullest form as follows:

[+/– Yelammedenu part] [Petiḥah part] [+/– Semikhah part] [Inyan part] [Ḥatimah part][14]

It is clear that, if a rabbinic homily contains *more than one Petiḥah*, the syntagma 'rabbinic homily' is expanded, distorted, undermined, or put into abeyance in some way. This happens in probably most rabbinic homilies. But something similar also happens to parts within the Petiḥah itself, as our example below will illustrate. As a result, such texts delay or destroy the thematic and formal progress modern scholarly readers most naturally expect from a coherent text. Deviations of this sort are not really lapses, as they are in the case of the grammatical form of the non-poetic sentence, but rather a variation of form, or the creation of a new form—or at least that must be our initial approach, if we are to avoid reductionism. The idea of a 'grammar', and therefore of grammatical correctness, is ultimately not applicable to texts (see Samely 2005), although it is still possible to define a 'syntagma' for any text. So what is happening in passages of the homily where the same functional part occurs more than once?

As a first approximation, we might say that there is a clear literary structure on the macro-level (the rabbinic homily), but that it appears that certain other literary features interfere with it. My claim is now that this can be profitably understood as the *multiplication of functionally equivalent units in continuous text*. Such units can be marked out, by their contents as well as sometimes by their form, as being in some sense *variations of each other*. Typically, the reader encountering such variations is left without guidance whether to take these as mutually exclusive or as complementary (see Heinemann 1971). A similar ambiguity can be found in most other,

---

[13] This is not necessarily always the case: one could have a multiplication of the same syntagmatic slot which combines propositionally compatible information, such as 'I did my shopping earlier three hours ago a while ago.' 'Earlier', 'three hours ago' and 'a while ago' can be taken to designate the same actual time slot, and thus there is no problem of contradiction. But this is still an extension or distortion of the syntactic shape. It is different from a modification of the syntagma which adds a new functionality, such as 'I did my shopping earlier *in town*', or which adds conjunctions such as 'three hours ago *or* a while ago'.

[14] The plus-minus sign is meant to indicate parts which are not necessary to establish the most basic form of the syntagma, but are optional.

non-homiletic, rabbinic texts, and for basically the same structural reasons. It is also this juxtaposition of functionally repetitive units to which modern scholars respond most strongly with the idea that a rabbinic text merely 'collects', for purposes of preservation, 'traditions'.

To illustrate the analysis of such a multiplicity in a specific literary co-text, I am now going to present a translation and subsequent interpretation (Table 11.1) of the two Petiḥot of Leviticus Rabbah's homily number 7.

Translation of LevR 7 Petiḥot (ed. Margolioth, vol. 2, pp. 147–53)

§1 [First Petiḥah]

Command Aaron (Lev. 6:2). [This instantiates the truth of:] *Hatred stirs up judgements* (or *strife*); *but love covers all sins* (Prov. 10:12). [*Hatred stirs up judgements* means:] The hatred which Israel [at the time of the golden calf] put between themselves and their heavenly father, *stirs up judgements,* [that is,] stirs up against them many judgements. Said R. Ishmael bar R. Neḥemiah: For almost nine hundred years the hatred between Israel and their heavenly father was suppressed, [namely] from when they went out from Egypt until Ezekiel arose. This is what [is meant when] it says: *And I said to them: Cast away everyone the detestable things that you are drawn to [and do not defile yourselves with the idols of Egypt. I am the Lord your God. But they defied me and refused to listen to me. They did not cast away the detestable things they were drawn to, nor did they give up the idols of Egypt. Then I resolved to pour out my fury upon them, to vent all my anger upon them there, in the land of Egypt]* (Ezek. 20:7–9). But I dealt with them for the sake of my great Name, so that it not be defiled. This is what [is meant when] it says: *But I acted for the sake of my Name, that it might not be profaned in the sight of the nations among whom they were* (Ezek. 20:9). *But love covers all sins* (= second half of Prov. 10:12) [means]: The love with which the Holy One loved Israel, [namely] *I have loved you, said the Lord* (Mal. 1:2).

Another interpretation (*davar aḥer*) [of Prov. 10:12]:
Hatred stirs up judgements—The hatred which Aaron put between Israel and their heavenly father, *stirs up judgements*—stirs up against them many judgements. Said R. Assi: This teaches that he took a hammer and opened it [i.e. the golden calf] before them [i.e. the Israelites] and said to them: See that there is no reality in this [thereby making their sin worse]. And this is what the Holy One, Blessed be He, said to Moses: *The one who sins against me, I shall blot him out from my book* (Exod. 32:33) [said after the incident of the golden calf; taken to mean that Aaron will not be mentioned in some parts of the Pentateuch]. This is what is written [see Table 11.1, note b, below]: *And*

against Aaron the Lord was angry enough to destroy him, [so I also interceded for Aaron at that time] (Deut. 9:20, Moses speaking). R. Yehoshua de-Sikhnin [said] in the name of R. Levi: The language of 'destruction' which is written here really means the extinction of sons and daughters, as you may cite,[15] *And I destroyed his fruit from above [and his root from beneath]* (Amos 2:9).

But love covers all sins (= second half of Prov. 10:12) [then means:] The prayer which Moses prayed on his [i.e. Aaron's] behalf. And what did he pray on his behalf? R. Mani de-She'ab and R. Yehoshua de-Sikhnin [said] in the name of R. Levi: From the beginning of the book [of Leviticus] until here [Lev. 6] is written, *And the sons of Aaron, [the priests,] shall offer* (Lev. 1:5), *And the sons of Aaron [the priest] shall put* (Lev. 1:7), *And the sons of Aaron, [the priests], shall lay out* (Lev. 1:8), *And the sons of Aaron shall burn* (Lev. 3:5). Moses said before the Holy One, Blessed be He: 'Master of the Universe, is the well hated and its water beloved? [Also,] you have accorded honour to a tree for the sake of its offspring [i.e. fruit], as we have learned [in the Mishnah]: "All kinds of tree may be used for the altar fire, except for the olive and the vine" (m.Tamid 2:3). And will you not to Aaron accord honour for the sake of his sons?' The Holy One, Blessed be He, said to him: 'By your life, because of your prayer I am bringing him near. And not only that, but I make him the core and his sons the periphery [by saying]: *Command Aaron and his sons, saying . . .*' (Lev. 6:2 = the Seder verse, whose event—Aaron being addressed again by God—is now explained as instantiating the truth of the Petiḥah verse, Prov. 10:12).

§2 [Second Petiḥah]

Command Aaron (Lev. 6:2). [This instantiates the truth of:] *The sacrifices of God are a broken spirit* (Ps. 51:19–21). Zabdi b. Levi and R. Yosi ben Petros and the Rabbis [provided interpretations]. One of them said: David said before the Holy One, Blessed be He [i.e. what now follows presupposes the repentance expressed earlier in the Davidic Ps. 51]: 'Master of the Universe, if you have received me in [my] repentance, I shall know that my son Solomon will build the Temple and build the altar and offer upon it all the offerings of the Torah.'—[this] from this verse:[16] *The sacrifices of God are a broken spirit; [a broken and contrite heart, O God, you will not despise. May it please you to make Zion prosper; build the walls of Jerusalem. Then you will delight in sacrifices of righteousness, burnt and whole offerings, then bulls will be offered on*

---

[15] For this way of translating the Aramaic phrase literally meaning, 'as you may say', see Bacher (1905: vol. 2, 11).

[16] This phrase, as some others, is in Aramaic rather than Hebrew.

your altar] (Ps. 51:19–21). The other [Rabbi] said: Whence [do we know] that
to the one who has performed repentance it is reckoned as if he had gone up
to Jerusalem and built the sanctuary and built the altar and offered upon it
all the offerings that are in the Torah? From this verse: *The sacrifices of God
are a broken spirit . . .* (Ps. 51:19–21). And the Rabbis said: Whence [do we
know] that the one who goes in front of the ark [of the synagogue, to say the
Eighteen Benedictions prayer] is required to bow after having mentioned the
sanctuary? [Namely] after/from[17] the Benediction 'Take pleasure, O Lord our
God, and dwell in Zion your city . . .' Some wish to hear this [meaning] from
the following: *The sacrifices of God are a broken spirit . . .* (Ps. 51:19–21).

R. Abba bar Yudan said: Everything that He declared invalid in animals
He declared valid in humans. What did He declare invalid in animals? *Blind,
or broken, or maimed, or with a wen* (Lev. 22:22). [That] He declared valid in
humans: *A broken and contrite heart, O God, you will not despise* (Ps. 51:19b).
R. Alexandri said: The non-priest, if he uses a broken vessel, it is a disgrace
to him. But the Holy One, Blessed be He—all the vessels that he uses are broken, as it is written: *The Lord is close to those of a broken heart* (Ps. 34:19), *He
who heals those of broken heart* (Ps. 147:3), *Yet with the contrite and the lowly
in spirit—reviving the spirits of the lowly and reviving the hearts of the contrite*
(Is. 57:15)—*A broken and contrite heart, O God, you will not despise* (Ps.
51:19b). R. Abba bar Yudan said: [This may be compared] to a king whom
his friend honoured with a jar of wine and a basket of figs. Said to him the
king: This is [your] gift? He [the friend] said to him: My lord king, according
to this hour I have honoured you. But when you enter your palace you will
know how I [truly] honour you. Thus the Holy One, Blessed be He, said to
Moses: *This is the law of the burnt offering—is this [really] the burnt offering?* [= the continuation of the Seder verse Lev. 6:2, with its repetition being
read as rhetorical question to Moses]. He [Moses] said before Him [in
response]: Master of the Universe, according to this hour have I offered this
before you, but when *it pleases you to make Zion prosper, build the walls of
Jerusalem, then you will delight in sacrifices of righteousness, burnt and whole
offerings . . .* [Ps. 51:19–21, the expanded Petiḥah-verse whose transition from

---

[17] Literally, 'from this Benediction' (again, in Aramaic), but the text then cited is not functionally a prooftext of the statement (which would be rare for a prayer text anyway), but rather the
opening words of the Benediction that mentions the Temple service (with its wording echoing Ps.
51:20). It is, however, possible that the version of the Benediction which is being alluded to here
(the ancient Palestinian one, rather than the Babylonian one in modern use) contained an explicit
mention of 'bowing' (see the note in Margolioth 1953–60: vol. 2, pp. 151–2). This would then
make the biblical verse Ps. 51:19 an *additional* prooftext, which is what the subsequent Aramaic
words 'some wish to hear this [meaning] from the following' are most naturally also implying.
See also Freedman and Simon (eds. 1977: 91 f., n. 6).

'broken spirit' sacrifices to real sacrifices is interpreted generically and then applied to the case of Moses at Lev. 6:2 being contrite in the desert situation].

Analysis of LevR 7 Petiḥot

The text is clearly quite complex, even in an English translation incorporating a number of explanatory comments in brackets. I shall now present the sequence of its literary units in the form of a table. I have segmented the continuous text into thematic units (other segmentations are sometimes equally possible), and analysed them with regard to their mutual relationship. These two steps of analysis go hand in hand. Table 11.1 thus has two columns. On the left I present a summary of the continuous segments, assigned to functional levels by capital letters and by indentation, thus:

Levels of discourse distinguished by indentation:

0 = Seder verse (as lemmatic point of reference of the whole homily)
    A = Petiḥah section leading to an explicitly (re-)quoted Seder verse
       B = level of the Petiḥah or Seder verse quotation, or its interpretation
          C, D, E, F = subsidiary steps of interpretation or quotation of rabbis

On the right I identify and number the functional repetitions according to each level. The table shows that, for the Petiḥot of homily 7 in Leviticus Rabbah, the multiplication of versions of 'the same' is a central strategy of composition. As the right-hand column records, this text is full of bifurcations, doublings and alternatives. A very high proportion of adjacent passages have *alternative meaning but equivalent function*. Although each is specific in contents, they are clearly all manifestations of a more general trend in structuring this homily, namely the multiplication of its syntagmatic or functional slots. Thus, the two columns of Table 11.1 provide an overview of the text's structure, as well as a record of the appearance of alternatives on any of its levels.

Table 11.1. Sample analysis of the Petiḥot of Leviticus Rabbah 7 (ed. Margolioth, vol. 2, pp. 147–53)

Summary of segments of text	Repetitions and alternatives
0 Thematic verse: Lev. 6:2	
A The Petiḥah section of the homily	*A alternative 1*: first functional unit 'Petiḥah'
[§1] 1. Petiḥah	
B Petiḥah verse	*B alternative 1*: choice of Petiḥah verse Prov. 10:12[a]
I. Prov. 10:12: 'Hatred stirs up judgements / love covers up sins.'	
C Theme:	*C alternative 1*: a thematic focus for Prov. 10:12 [*this does not lead to the Seder verse*]
(a) The hatred which Israel put between themselves and their heavenly father (golden calf incident) stirred up many 'judgements' (punishments) against them . . .	
(b) R. Ishmael said: 900 years . . . then in the days of Ezekiel (*hadahu dikhtiv*: Ezek. 20:7–9) . . .	
(c): 'but love covers all sins' (Pet. verse) (+ Mal. 1:2)	
II. *davar aher* (= another interpretation) of Prov. 10:12	*C alternative 2*: another thematic focus for Prov. 10:12, and a close variation of I(a)
C Theme:	
(a) The hatred which Aaron put between Israel and their heavenly father stirred up many 'judgements' (punishments) against them . . .	
(b) R. Assi: This teaches (*melamed*) that Aaron showed Israel what the golden calf really was (thus increasing their guilt).	
D	
(i) and this is (*we-hu she-. . . amar*) what God said, that he 'blots out' from 'my book' (Exod. 32:33) (= i.e. does not mention Aaron), up to this verse, Lev. 6:2:	**D** *Alternative 1 for a biblical lemma expressing Aaron's punishment*
(ii) *hadahu dikhtiv*:[b] This is what is written, Deut. 9:20 'to destroy Aaron': R. Yehoshua de-Sikhnin: 'destroy' means: destruction of all children (*heykh de-at amar* + Amos 2:9) (cf. Nadab and Abihu in Lev. 10:1–2');	**D** *Alternative 2 for a biblical lemma expressing Aaron's punishment*

(c) 'but love covers all sins' (Petihah verse): the prayer which Moses prayed for Aaron, mentioned in Deut. 9:20.

D

(i) And what did he pray? R. Mani / Yehoshua de-Sikhnin: up to this point in Lev. only the sons of Aaron are addressed (1:5, 7, 8; 3:5) — Moses asked in in to reinstate Aaron to the honour due to him through his sons (by in in Aaron), using two similes:

E

well (= father) and its water

tree (= father) and its fruit

    F as we have learned (*ke-de-tenan*): quote of Mishnah Tamid 2:3 for E Alternative 2

(d) So that God reinstated Aaron to being an addressee, and relegated his sons to a subsidiary role: Seder verse Lev. 6:2: 'Command Aaron and his sons . . .' (i.e. Aaron addressed, and mentioned first)

[= end of the first Petihah, suggesting that Lev. 6:2 points to Aaron's being reinstated as God's addressee, and that this event is an instance of the maxim in Prov. 10:12]

    A The Petihah section of the homily

[§ 2] 2. Petihah

    B Petihah verse

I. Ps. 51:19: 'The sacrifices of God are a broken spirit . . .'

    C Theme

Dispute between R. Zabdi / R. Yose / Rabbanan

(a) One says: David's *teshuvah* (= 'broken spirit') led to God allowing Solomon to build the Temple and to bring all sacrifices of the Torah — from this (*min ha-deyn*) verse: Ps. 51:19 (+20)

(b) The other says: Everyone who performs *teshuvah* is considered by God as if he had built the Temple and brought all sacrifices of the Torah — from this verse: Ps. 51:19

E Alternatives 1 and 2: two similes in argument function

A alternative 2: 2nd functional unit 'Petihah'

B alternative 2: choice of Petihah verse Ps. 51:19

C alternative 1: thematic focus for Ps. 51:19

C alternative 2: another thematic focus for Ps. 51:19 and variation for (a)

Table 11.1. Continued.

Summary of segments of text	Repetitions and alternatives
(c) Rabbanan: the reciter of the Eighteen Benedictions must bow down [show 'broken spirit'] after reciting the blessing '*Retseh* . . .' which mentions the Temple service—from this [verse]: Ps. 51:19ᶜ	**C alternative 3**: another thematic focus for Ps. 51:19
(d) R. Abba b. Yudan: Everything that he declared invalid in an animal he declared valid in man . . . 'broken' (+Lev. 22:22)—'broken heart' is acceptable: Ps. 51:19b	**C alternative 4**
(e) R. Alexandri: contrastive comparison (man/God): the latter, all he uses are *broken* vessels: **D** +Ps. 34:19; Ps. 147:3, Is. 57:15—then: Ps. 51:19 (Petiḥah verse)	**C alternative 5** **D several alternative warrants**
(f) R. Abba b. Yudan: parable of a king in the desert, asking, 'this is your gift?' —so God: 'This is the law of the burnt offering—is this [really] the burnt offering?' (Lev. 6:2 = Seder verse)	**C alternative 6**
[= main point of the second Petiḥah: the Seder verse shows God pointing to the poverty of the animal offering he asks for, implying the 'broken spirit' of the Petiḥah verse as the real sacrifice]	
(g) As in the parable, Moses answers: for the time being, but when 'it pleases you to make Zion prosper . . . then you will delight in sacrifices of righteousness, burnt and whole offerings'—Ps. 51:20–21.	**C alternative 7** (but integrated with the parable which also delivers alternative 6)
[= actual end of the second Petiḥah, extending the hermeneutic work to the co-text of the Petiḥah verse (20, 21)]	

[a] The two levels A and B are here intimately connected, effectively arising together: they do not constitute two different 'alternatives', but only one. However, it is important to separate them, in order to mark the possibility that *the same* Petiḥah verse is functionally used twice (as leading to the same Seder verse in the same homily), but constituting two separate Petiḥot, e.g. because of a different thematic take, and thus interpretation.

[b] The introductory formula *hadahu dikhtiv* ('this is what is written: . . .') marks out the subsequent biblical quotation as reinforcing the immediately preceding position. This should be presented in the table as moving the discourse to a level 'down' from D, namely to E, making this an E passage. But the actual content of the section II(b)(ii) appears not to reinforce the idea that Aaron was punished by not being mentioned (which is also the idea that ultimately leads to the Seder verse in II(d)). Instead, it seems to provide an alternative way to construct Aaron's punishment altogether. I am grateful to Chaim Milikowsky for discussing this passage with me at the London meeting, and rightly insisting on the force of the introductory formula. I am not convinced, however, that II(b)(ii) can be read as reinforcing II(b)(i), and thus become reconciled with its introductory formula, without importing too much information of which there is no trace in its actual wording. It is conceivable that the tension arises precisely from two text-building principles here at work: functional *subordination* of adjacent text parts, which is required for the rabbinic homily as an overarching structure, and the multiplication of functionally *equivalent* units. There is no reason to think the formula a later scribal addition, as Margolioth (1953–60: vol. 1, 149) records its absence only from the first print of *Yalkut Shimoni*; while the sources in Milikowsky and Schlüter's *Synoptic Edition* all have it.

[c] A somewhat problematic passage; see note 17 above.

Of the units substantially distinguished in Table 11.1, sixteen have an indication in the right-hand column that there is an *adjacent* functional equivalent for them on one of several possible levels. Specifically, juxtaposition of this type can be observed on the following levels:

a. The level of literary function and form—multiple Petiḥot.

b. The level of the choice of Petiḥah verse, as leading towards Lev. 6:2 (Prov. 10:12 in 1, Ps. 51:19 in 2).

c. The level of the theme which is assigned to a Petiḥah verse already determined: 1.I(a) and II(a); 2.I(a)–(c), (d) and (e). Some of these themes are operative for the transition to the Seder verse, others are not. Sometimes the ideas are presented as being variations of each other through overlaps in wording (e.g. Israel awakening the punishments versus Aaron awakening the punishments, I(a) versus II(a)).

d. The level of the subordinate biblical quotations which support the theme assigned to the Petiḥah verse (1.II(b)(i) and (ii) and 2.I(e) level D).

e. The level of supporting arguments, proof texts, warrants, reasons or comparisons (can overlap in one case with item d above), e.g. 1.II(c)(i) level E (well/tree).[18]

f. The level of the whole homily, as defined by the choice of Seder verse location from the biblical book treated (thus defining the location of the Inyan-part).[19] On the level of Inyan passages, each homily in Leviticus Rabbah is a functional equivalent of every other.

g. The level of the character mentioned in the text as speaker of a particular utterance delineating a theme of the homily (insofar as themes are not presented anonymously). These multiple slots of 'R. X said' are, in a very abstract sense, functionally equivalent to each other, but they make no contribution to larger functional relationships within the homily. They thus constitute a different topic from the one treated in this chapter, but are worth noting here.

The juxtaposition (as opposed to the subordination) of themes *emphasises* the plurality. The succession of passages thus highlights the fact that there is a multiplicity of messages. At the same time the text offers no explanation for this multiplicity in mere juxtaposition, and no common denominator for the themes. In addition to the basic phenomenon of adjacent

---

[18] In other literary rabbinic contexts such explanations can be offered with a dialectical formula of selection, e.g. *we-iba'et, ema* in the Bavli (e.g. b.Suk. 2a).

[19] This is the selection level on which the composition of the whole of Leviticus Rabbah comes into view, in respect of whether or not it follows some predetermined segmentation of Leviticus into weekly public reading portions and, if it does, which segmentation exactly.

multiplication of function, four other literary structures contribute to this emphasis on the functional equivalence of what, in its propositional content, is different from each other:

i.   The text contains 'blind alleys' which do not lead to what turns out (with hindsight) to be the next higher goal of the text. For example, interpretations are presented for the Petiḥah verse which do not lead to the Seder verse; in other words, the Petiḥah verse is, for those interpretations, not a Petiḥah verse, as it has no functional relationship with the Seder verse (e.g. in Petiḥah 1.I(a) in comparison with II(a)). Yet in respect of being interpretations of the same verse, these units are functionally equivalent and thus alternatives of each other.

ii. These blind alley passages, by constituting 'dummy runs' of those interpretations that actually lead to the Seder verse, also show that they could fulfil the Petiḥah function *in some other* homily (with another Seder verse). By not creating the functional link here, yet having the same form and position as the units which do, they illustrate the functional versatility of *all* units of this form.

iii. The text juxtaposes passages which are immediately apparent as variations of 'the same' idea, because they contain prominent verbal repetition, as between 1.I(a) and 1.II(a). Verbatim overlap in adjacent units is immensely conspicuous, creating a display of differences embedded in similarities. This is also a very common phenomenon in exegetical—as opposed to homiletical—midrash.[20]

iv. There are a number of signals of segmentation which give prominence to the functional duplication. These include the repetition of a biblical lemma, the use of *davar aḥer* ('another interpretation') and the introduction of a new (or the same) speaker in a new speech report. This underscores the 'separateness' of these adjacent units,[21] and displays their mutual difference in contents, while showing up their equivalence in function.

This display of difference, through repeated functionality in adjacent position, is part of a much larger phenomenon in rabbinic texts, one which sets this literature apart from other kinds of ancient Jewish literature. It can be generically defined as follows:

---

[20] See Samely (2007). To mention just one example: GenR 55.4 contains three alternatives for the event that might have happened just before God commanded Abraham to offer his son; two (in MS Vatican 30, three) of these are largely identical with each other word for word.

[21] There are some phenomena in mishnaic discourse which are related to such a segmentation, including the occurrence of 'afterthought' information. See Samely (2009c).

A text contains contiguous segments which are functionally equivalent to each other in conspicuous ways, while offering different themes or contents. Such segments may fulfil the same literary, evidential, hermeneutic, or narrative function as adjacent segments without the text's governing voice explicitly integrating them into a unified topic or overall argument. In meaning, these functional alternatives usually oscillate (or are ambiguous) between mutual exclusion and complementation.

Using this definition, one can define a number of other manifestations of multiplied functionality. Arising from a large-scale investigation of the text genres of Jewish antiquity at Manchester and Durham Universities,[22] here is a preliminary list (almost certain to be incomplete), several of whose items are illustrated in the Leviticus Rabbah 7 table above:

Types of Multiplied Functionality in Adjacent Text Position

1. There is more than one midrashic unit for the same biblical lemma, whether or not introduced by *davar aher* in continuous text.
2. There is more than one biblical quotation for the same rabbinic statement within a single midrashic unit.
3. There is more than one Petihah for the same rabbinic homily in continuous text.
4. There is more than one *mashal* (parable) or simile for the same location and/or discursive juncture in continuous text.
5. There is more than one version of a rabbinic quotation in continuous text.
6. There is more than one reason clause for the same rabbinic statement in continuous text.
7. There is more than one version of a tannaitic dispute in continuous text (e.g. in the Gemara of the Babylonian Talmud).
8. There is more than one version of the same *ma'aseh* (understood as a narrative instantiating a legal ruling by a rabbi) in continuous text.
9. There is more than one version of events within the *same* narrative account (e.g. reports introduced by 'and some say . . .').
10. There is more than one narrative or report in continuous text presenting identical or very similar events but using different characters (e.g. Tosefta Yom ha-Kippurim 2.5f.).

---

[22] What follows is an excerpt from a draft *Inventory of Literary Features* of the Project mentioned in n. 1. For an overview of the main divisions of this *Inventory*, see my paper presented at the 2008 British Association for Jewish Studies meeting in Manchester (Samely 2008). The excerpt above reflects section 9.9 of *Inventory* version-391 of October 2008. The current *Inventory* will in due course become available from the website given in n. 1 above.

As this enumeration shows, there are many phenomena in rabbinic literature which can be understood as multiplying functional slots for adjacent
passages—the topic of this chapter with respect to the rabbinic homily. Most
of them are well known in principle but usually only considered from the
angle of literary history. They can be very different in nature from each other.
One key difference is whether there is any acknowledgement of the multiplication (e.g. through a *davar aḥer*) or not; another, whether there is an explanation offered for the multiplication (e.g. as a historical alternative). Yet it is
clear that, taken as an abstract *strategy of text building*, the phenomenon is
very widespread. Our Leviticus Rabbah 7 passage, while likely to have a characteristic 'Leviticus Rabbah' way of implementing this strategy, is therefore
part of a much larger trend in rabbinic documents.

C. Possible Contexts

What all this amounts to is that the text *displays* the multiplicity of its
parts. Placing in adjacent position functionally similar units emphasises the
'differential' between them. That which separates the neighbouring units
becomes a focus for the reader or listener, because of a tendency to expect
that a new textual slot will also bring new information. In a different
scholarly paradigm, Joseph Heinemann reflected on this aspect of the
construction of Leviticus Rabbah as follows:

> The most outstanding feature of the composition of this *midrash* is the ten-
> dency of the author to present his themes in all their complexity and with all
> their manifold implications. He does not see any virtue in simplification, still
> less in over-simplification; he looks upon his subjects not just from one angle,
> but from all possible angles; he likes to bring out contrasts and emphasize
> opposites. What we might term his 'dialectical approach' is manifest through-
> out the work in a variety of ways. For one thing *when he is obliged to use het-
> erogeneous material for building up one of his homilies* [my emphasis], he often
> achieves integration by stressing the contrast between different interpretations
> and thus creates a relationship between them of thesis and antithesis . . .
>
> Often the emphasis on contrast and opposites is first and foremost a stylistic
> device for knitting together more closely the different *aggadot* making up the
> constituent parts of the homily . . .
>
> There are many more passages where we find this tendency of emphasising
> contrasts and opposites, of presenting contradictory or conflicting viewpoints.
> Some of these may, of course, have been inherent in the traditional material of
> which the author of Leviticus Rabbah made use. But even so, had he wished to
> do so, he could easily have avoided a good many of the 'contradictions' con-
> tained in his work, harmonized opposing ideas or omitted them. Far from
> doing so, he appears to delight in demonstrating to his readers the complexity
> of the Torah, which may be expounded 'by adducing forty-nine reasons for

declaring a thing unclean and forty-nine for declaring it clean' (XXVI.2), and in making manifest the many facets of the one divine truth. For, in spite of all seeming contradictions, 'Both these and those are the words of the living God' (b.Eruvin 13b). (Heinemann 1971: 149f.)

Heinemann considers the text from the angle of how themes and assertions, that is 'contents', are presented in Leviticus Rabbah. This is a different perspective to my attempt in this chapter to forge an analytical tool which identifies the functional–formal structures of the text and allocates literary units to the same or different levels of functionality, quite independently of whether the contents are seen as mutually contradictory or not. Yet Heinemann clearly addresses a closely related issue. In doing so, he effectively suggests ways of seeking out a unifying 'higher' level of meaning in the composition. Even assuming, as he does, that the text collects diverse material, he still sees the text as setting out to 'demonstrate' something, and thus follow a complex idea of unity. In this I agree with Heinemann,[23] because the literary structures as highlighted in this paper point in precisely that direction: the juxtaposition of functionally equivalent units is a recurrent strategy of creating textuality. Following those structural clues, we are invited to look for a unity of a higher order, necessarily more abstract than any straightforward unity of directly expressed ideas. We then postulate (or at least allow for) the existence of *non-thematic* contents in the text, or the sort of contents which would only become thematic if the text were ever to speak about itself as a text, which it does not. (For example, by saying: 'I have here collected *everything I could find* on the topic of Lev. 6:2.'[24])

I will now present some possibilities of how such texts were used, and thereby also reasons why someone might actually construct them in this way. I deliberately include some possibilities here that are, on the face of it, historically implausible. I wish thereby to illustrate just how open are the contextual possibilities of literary forms in rabbinic literature. Since so much of our picture of the 'historical context' of the documents is in fact extrapolated from textual structures and contents in the first place, because of the paucity of direct information on their provenance and historical context, it seems prudent to keep in play a wide range of possibilities.

1. The juxtaposition of functionally equivalent parts is effectively a kind of repetition, and may have had the effect of reinforcing a very general message that underlies the units in all their mutual differentiation. Regardless of whether the user is expected to 'read' this repetition, it could have constituted a constant reinforcement of some

---

[23] See Thesis number 3b in part A above.
[24] This is my paraphrase of a tentative suggestion in Visotzky (2003: 14).

underlying idea, e.g. 'God cares for Israel'. The multiple occupation of the same functional slots could have had an affective and intellectual impact without being analysed by the user.

2. The user is in fact expected to perceive and sort out the repeated functionality, in one of a number of different ways. For example, the user combines neighbouring units where possible, and otherwise ignores them, thus building up a consistent literary *Gestalt* of one possible and functional homily in stops and starts; or, the user checks out more systematically the different single homilies that can be construed from the multiple units in Leviticus Rabbah 7 (e.g. one homily with only Petiḥah 1, another homily with only Petiḥah 2, etc.).

3. The user does not perceive the structural multiplicity as such, yet relishes the flow of midrashic units, that is, pairings of biblical quotations with rabbinic statements in constant mutual reinforcement. These repeated pairings are affecting and reassuring in their very monotony, even without any synthesis of a concrete idea (although this option can be combined with option 1). One might call this model the 'bathing in midrash' or 'trance of tradition' model, and its affective power could have been strengthened in communal settings.

4. The multiplication of functional slots amounts to a massive repetition of a limited set of *moves of thought*. The text displays what may be the same procedures of analysis, the same approach to the biblical wording and/or extra-biblical problems, again and again. Without any need for an explication of these moves and of the fact that they are repeated, the user can become trained in certain habits of thought. This would be compatible with a broadly pedagogical aim of the text, teaching the user certain intellectual skills and cultural habits through constantly repeated exposure, rather than through explanation. This could initiate the audience, by implicit means, into the 'right' way to construct new experiences.[25]

5. Perhaps alongside one of the other scenarios, the preservation of traditional information might also be part of the point of this construction. The accumulation of similar material in functional slots alone would not contribute to the meaning of a whole, but undermine it. Yet on the back of one of the text-unifying user options above, anticipated by the text maker, the text could *also* serve the function of 'preserving' such non-functional information, as a thematic 'surplus'.

---

[25] This kind of explanation is, I believe, also important for the Babylonian Gemara, another document which frequently juxtaposes functionally equivalent passages (in different ways from Leviticus Rabbah, to be sure).

6. There is also another scenario, as possible corollary to option 4 above and in contrast to 5. The repetition of functional slots may have served to *liberate* the users from the confines of any specific traditional contents. The ability to *vary* the contents, while retaining (albeit also distending) the form, opens up the avenue of creating new units from scratch. And even where the information integrated into the structure pre-existed the text, its multiplicity renders each specific content less important than the structure in which it appears. If the repetition is there to teach a process, then it is not primarily there to teach the specific ideas. To some extent they cancel out each other's authority by the very fact of being presented side by side as functional substitutes for each other, even without being marked as mutually contradictory. The unique idea, image, parable, halakhah in its precious status as coming from a master of the tradition would then not be the focus at all (and neither would be its preservation), but rather its inter-changeability with many others.

In this last scenario, the rabbinic text makers are projected as having a very different outlook and goal from the master rabbis to whom they refer in their texts. They would transform into a tangential topic what for those master rabbis in their own historical contexts (be they contemporary with the text maker or earlier) may have been the main goal, say, getting things *right* for a *specific* halakhic or hermeneutic question. In doing so the text makers would implicitly characterise themselves (as the persona that speaks through the text) as *not a rabbi*, though perhaps a meta-rabbi. They would then, by their texts, create in the first place that homogeneous image of 'the' rabbi which, for modern scholarship and other users of these texts, defines much of our idea of *rabbinic* Judaism. For when it comes to the historical reality of rabbis, we have no other substantial evidence than 'rabbinic'—*texts*.

So these are some—to be sure, generic—historical contexts which historical imagination can supply to match the multiplication of functionally equivalent slots in texts. But as Thesis number 7 in part A above emphasises, there is no one-to-one correspondence between literary structures on the one hand, and historical scenarios on the other, such that we could draw a reliable inference from the former to the latter. The relationship between text and context is very malleable. The 'meaning' of a particular literary configuration can change from one cultural-historical context to another quite dramatically—both for new texts created at a later stage and for already existing texts transmitted into a new context. One partial safeguard for keeping constant the wide open implicit messages of literary structures is explicit announcements of the theme, purpose, main point, key parts, intended audience, authorship, and so on within the same text. Such announcements, and thus this safeguard, are absent from rabbinic documents. This includes the question of whether the texts even wish to be taken as unified in the first place, and in what dimension (Theses number 4 and 5 in part A). How then can one gain a measure of certainty in such questions? Obviously, it is always vital to use such external evidence as exists for the historical context of rabbinic texts, and to use it judiciously without committing trivial errors of circularity. Moreover, certain quite generic assumptions about a text's origin play a role from the start in any apparently 'pure' literary analysis, as I said above. Nevertheless, the use of literary structures for reconstructing historical contexts is also necessary in the study of rabbinic history. Confidence can be restored to this kind of reconstruction by a large-scale empirical description of rabbinic text structures, on a level of detail comparable to the description in part B above, and with conceptual tools of roughly that order. In particular when it comes to firmly excluding certain scenarios (any of the above numbers 1 to 6, for example), our reconstructions really need as firm a foothold in the literary structures as possible. This requires a critical mass of empirical analysis across all rabbinic texts, which makes them visible as they actually are (not their ghostly past as 'traditions'), and uses concepts that do not take too much for granted and therefore have a greater comparative reach.

Note. The vital support provided by the Arts and Humanities Research Council (UK) for research on the project 'Typology of Anonymous and Pseudepigraphic Jewish Literature in Antiquity' is hereby gratefully acknowledged. I am indebted to my Project colleagues Philip Alexander, Rocco Bernasconi and Robert Hayward for our discussions on literary structures in general and the ones addressed in this paper in particular. I am grateful to colleagues' responses to this paper in two other contexts: a lecture and workshop at the Hochschule für Jüdische Studien Heidelberg, where I presented parts of these results in February 2008, and had the opportunity to discuss them with Ronen Reichman and graduate students; and the British Academy meeting at which the other papers in this volume were also presented, where I benefited from advice given by Chaim Milikowsky and Joanna Weinberg in particular.

Further Reading

Cohen (ed. 2000); Goldberg (1999); Lenhard (1998); Samely (2007); Stemberger (1996, 2008).

Bibliography

Bacher, W. (1905), *Die exegetische Terminologie der jüdischen Traditionsliteratur*, 2 vols., Leipzig.

Bregman, M. (2003), *The Tanḥuma-Yelammedenu Literature: Studies in the Evolution of the Versions*, Piscataway, NJ. [Hebrew]

Cohen, S. J. D. (ed.) (2000), *The Synoptic Problem in Rabbinic Literature*, Providence, RI.

Fraade, S. D. (1987), 'Interpreting Midrash 1: Midrash and the history of Judaism', *Prooftexts*, 7: 179–94.

Freedman, H. and Simon, M. (eds.) (1977), *The Midrash Rabbah*, compact edition, vol. 2 (Exodus and Leviticus), London, Jerusalem and New York (contains English translation of Leviticus Rabbah).

Friedman, S. (2004), 'A good story deserves retelling: the unfolding of the Akiva legend', *Jewish Studies* (*Internet Journal*), 3: 55–93; www.biu.ac.il/JS/JSIJ/3–2004/Friedman.pdf (accessed May 2008).

Goldberg, Arnold (1999), *Rabbinische Texte als Gegenstand der Auslegung. Gesammelte Studien*, vol. 2, ed. M. Schlüter and P. Schäfer, Tübingen.

Halevi, F. E. (1956–63), *Midrash Rabbah*, 8 vols., Tel Aviv.

Heinemann, J. (1971), 'Profile of a Midrash: the art of composition in Leviticus Rabba', *Journal of the American Academy of Religion*, 31: 141–50.

Jaffee, M. (2007), 'Rabbinic authorship as a collective enterprise', in C. Elisheva Fonrobert and Martin S. Jaffee (eds.), *Cambridge Companion to the Talmud and Rabbinic Literature*, Cambridge, pp. 17–37.

Lenhard, D. (1998), *Die Rabbinische Homilie: Ein formanalytischer Index*, Frankfurt.

Margolioth, M. (1953–60), *Midrash Wayyikra Rabbah: A Critical Edition based on Manuscripts and Genizah Fragments with Variants and Notes*, 5 vols., Jerusalem.

Milikowksy, Ch. and Schlüter, M. (1999), '*Vayyikra Rabba* through history: a project to study its textual transmission', in J. T. Borrás and A. Sáenz-Badillos (eds.), *Jewish Studies at the Turn of the Twentieth Century*, vol. 1: *Proceedings of the 6th EAJS Congress Toledo 1998*, Leiden, pp. 311–21.

Milikowsky, Ch. and Schlüter, M. (n. d.), *Synoptic Edition of Wayyiqra Rabbah*, www.biu.ac.il/JS/midrash/VR/editionData.htm (accessed December 2007). [Hebrew]

Mirkin, M. A. (1956–67), *Midrash Rabbah*, 11 vols., Yavneh and Tel Aviv.

Neusner, J. (1985), *The Integrity of Leviticus Rabbah: The Problem of the Autonomy of a Rabbinic Document*, Chico, CA.

Neusner, J. (1986a), *Judaism and Scripture: The Evidence of Leviticus Rabbah*, Chicago.

Neusner, J. (1986b), *Comparative Midrash: The Plan and Program of Genesis Rabbah and Leviticus Rabbah*, Atlanta.

Neusner, J. (1986c), 'The synoptic problem in rabbinic literature: the cases of the Mishna, Tosephta, Sipra and Leviticus Rabba', *Journal of Biblical Literature*, 105: 499–507.

Samely, A. (2002), *Rabbinic Interpretation of Scripture in the Mishnah*, Oxford.

Samely, A. (2003), *Database of Midrashic Units in the Mishnah*, http://mishnah.llc.manchester.ac.uk/home.aspx (accessed September 2008).

Samely, A. (2005), 'Observations on the activity of reading', in G. Banham (ed.), *Husserl and the Logic of Experience*, Basingstoke and New York, pp. 131–59.

Samely, A. (2007), *Forms of Rabbinic Literature and Thought: An Introduction*, Oxford.

Samely, A. (2008), 'A first report to the British Association for Jewish Studies on the project "Typology of Anonymous and Pseudepigraphic Jewish Literature in Antiquity"', available from: www.llc.manchester.ac.uk/research/projects/ancient-jewishliterature/background/bajspaper/ (accessed September 2008).

Samely, A. (2009a), 'Gattungen/Jüdische Bibelhermeneutik', in O. Wischmeyer *et al.* (eds.), *Lexikon der Bibelhermeneutik*, Berlin and New York, pp. 190–1.

Samely, A. (2009b), 'Kommentar/Jüdische Bibelhermeneutik', in Wischmeyer *et al.* (eds.), *Lexikon der Bibelhermeneutik*, pp. 331–2.

Samely, A. (2009c), 'Notes on the sequencing of information in Mishnah tractates', *FJB* 35: 19–64.

Sarason, R. S. (1982), 'The Petihot in Leviticus Rabba: "oral homilies" or redactional constructions?', *JJS*, 33 (= G. Vermes and J. Neusner (eds.), *Essays in Honour of Yigael Yadin*, Totowa, NJ), pp. 557–67.

Smelik, W. (2005), 'Translation and innovation in BT Meg 3a', in L. Teugels and R. Ulmer (eds.), *Recent Developments in Midrash Research: Proceedings of the 2002 and 2003 SBL Consultation on Midrash*, Piscataway, NJ.

Stemberger, G. (1996), *Introduction to the Talmud and Midrash*, 2nd edn., trans. and ed. M. Bockmuehl, Edinburgh.

Stemberger, G. (2001), 'The formation of rabbinic Judaism, 70–640 CE' (part G, 67–70), in A. J. Avery-Peck and J. Neusner (eds.), *The Blackwell Reader in Judaism*, Oxford, pp. 78–92.

Stemberger, G. (2008), 'The Derashah in rabbinic times', in A. Deeg, W. Homolka and H.-G. Schöttler (eds.), *Preaching in Judaism and Christianity: Encounters and Developments from Biblical Times to Modernity*, Berlin, pp. 7–21.

Stern, D. (ed.) (1997), *The Jewish Anthological Imagination*, vol. 1, Special Issue of *Prooftexts*, 17/1.

Ta-Shma, I. (1993), 'The "open book" in medieval Hebrew literature: the problem of authorized editions', in P. S. Alexander and A. Samely (eds.), *Artefact and Text: The Re-creation of Jewish Literature in Medieval Hebrew Manuscripts. Proceedings of a Conference held in the University of Manchester 28–30 April 1992* (= theme issue of the *Bulletin of the John Rylands University Library of Manchester*, 75/3 (1993)); Manchester, pp. 17–24.

Visotzky, B. (2003), *Golden Bells and Pomegranates: Studies in Midrash Leviticus Rabbah*, Tübingen.

Wünsche, A. (1884), *Der Midrasch Wajikra Rabba*, Leipzig; repr. Hildesheim, 1967.

12

The Future of Ancient Piyyut

WOUT JAC. VAN BEKKUM

1. Contents

PIYYUT IS LITURGICAL POETRY (FROM THE GREEK ποίησις, POETRY, POEM), that was composed to replace or serve as an alternative to prayers in the synagogue, mainly on Sabbaths and festivals and special occasions such as circumcisions and weddings.

2. Manuscripts

Most of the piyyutim from the Byzantine period are preserved in the Cairo Genizah. Another source is MSS of prayer books from central and southern Europe, from the medieval period.

3. Dating

Pre-classical piyyutim are generally dated to the fourth and fifth centuries. Dating is based on commonalities of language, a typical rhythm and a basic style that did not employ rhyme. The authors of the pre-classical piyyutim are unknown. This is why scholars tend to use the term 'the Anonymous Era'. The only known composer from this period is Yose ben Yose, though he may have belonged to a later group. However, it is impossible to situate him precisely in terms of dates or locality. The classical period of the piyyutim that flourished in Byzantine Palestine up to and during the period of the Arab conquest includes such authors as Yannai, Shimon Bar Megas, Yehudah, Hadutahu and Eleazar birabbi Kallir. The mentions of Arabs in the piyyutim are a key indicator that they belong to the Arab period. The first mention of historical composers of piyyutim comes from Saadyah Gaon (882–942), and is found in the Arabic introduction to his *Sefer ha-Egron*. He lists the five earliest synagogue poets: Yose b. Yose, Yannai, Eleazar (Kallir), Joshua (haKohen) and Pinḥas (haKohen). Joshua and Pinḥas date to the Arab period (starting in 640 CE).

Proceedings of the British Academy **165**, 217–233. © The British Academy 2010.

4. Languages

Piyyutim are mainly in Hebrew, with a few Greek words. Another corpus that dates to the end of the Byzantine period is in Palestinian Aramaic. The authors of the piyyutim adapted and modified Hebrew to their poetic requirements, and hence created a unique language that did not always obey the classical norms of Hebrew grammar.

5. Printed Editions

Please see the Bibliography below. Yahalom and Sokoloff (1999) contains works in Aramaic by anonymous composers. Most editions are of the works of individual authors.

6. Translations

Out of the huge number of piyyutim from this period, only a few have been translated into English. A few examples can be found in Weinberger (1998). There are also translations in Carmi (1981) and Swartz and Yahalom (2005).

7. Commentaries

Hollender (2005).

What is Piyyut?

Piyyut or synagogue hymnography is distinctive in both its volume and its focus from biblical psalmody and poetry. This type of poetry was produced from the late-Roman period in Jewish communities and congregations where poetry was allowed to embellish Jewish liturgy. Such compositions were preferably written for Sabbath and festival, when statutory prayers were supposed to have a link with the theme of the day. The majority of Jewish liturgical poems (piyyutim) for the Sabbath relate to biblical topics or address ways of exegesis with regard to biblical themes, whereas festival compositions extensively deal with the aspects of the holiday involved. Tens of thousands of liturgical poems have been handed down in prayer books and manuscripts. Israel Davidson's epoch-making *Thesaurus of Mediaeval Hebrew Poetry* listed in the 1920s and 1930s every printed Hebrew liturgical poem composed after the canonisation of the Hebrew Bible until the end of the eighteenth century. Sometimes he extended his entries to the manuscripts when the compositions involved great names like Solomon ibn Gabirol, Yehudah Halevi, Moses ibn Ezra and Israel Najara. Davidson could not have fully realised to what extent the discovery of the Genizah, a large manuscript collection from Cairo, was about to change modern scholarly understanding of piyyut. Since the early twentieth century, many piyyutim have been collected from the Genizah manuscripts, deciphered, reconstructed and edited in critical editions, with great results in particular for our knowledge of Byzantine-Jewish and Babylonian-Jewish liturgy and hymnology. The study of piyyut and Hebrew poetry in general was to gain the most from these new or better texts from the Genizah collection, of which some 40 per cent consists of poems.

By virtue of these textual studies names and works of long-forgotten synagogue poets (paytanim) in different temporal and regional settings have been added to the corpus, leading to great progress in knowledge about distinct piyyutic genres and forms. We would not have known otherwise about the significance and growth of the early *kinot* (threnodies), *selihot* (penitential hymns), *avodot* (compositions for the Day of Atonement), *kedushta'ot* or *yozrot* (multi-part hymns for the Sabbath and festival morning service), nor would we have been acquainted with the names of great hymnists who have been crucial for the tradition of piyyut. Although the quantity of publications has been quite considerable since the days of Davidson, the attempts to offer a synthetic history of piyyut, a comprehensive literary analysis of its poetics, or a comparison with Greek, Syriac and Latin Christian hymnology have been few. Leon J. Weinberger's *Jewish Hymnography: A Literary History* is informative in the sections about medieval centres of (Karaite) piyyut in south-eastern Europe, particularly the Balkans, but other sections like those concerning the early piyyut of Byzantine Palestine, Sephardi piyyut, or Ashkenazi piyyut do not have the same quality. Obviously, future research will have to accomplish some of the vital desiderata of the field, as we will see in the following paragraphs.[1]

Piyyut Scholarship: From Zunz to Zulay and After

The title 'From Zunz to Zulay' indicates that piyyut scholarship primarily developed in Germany, and continued in Jerusalem and to a lesser extent in New York. One could argue that piyyut in the hands of Wolf Heidenheim

---

[1] See Davidson ([1924–34], 1970); Weinberger (1998); van Bekkum (1998a, 1988b).

(1757–1832) and Leopold Zunz (1794–1886) underwent a 'liturgical down-fall' and an 'annexation' by scholarship. The change of approach towards piyyut as an object of research can be described as a form of 'secularisation' of religious items. This term can be used in either a purely descriptive fashion or with a deprecatory implication. When used derogatorily, it usually indicates that a secular approach to Jewish studies involves the destruction of the normative character of Jewish religious tradition. This is not necessarily true. However, Modern Judaism, in its formative and reformative period, was ambiguous about the legacy of the past. This ambivalence led in two directions. On the one hand, the scientific study of piyyut 'secularised' the hymns, divorcing them from the religious domain; on the other, piyyutim remained part of the Jewish liturgy. Today, the contradiction between traditional respect and actual use is manifested in the fact that many festival piyyutim are still printed in whatever (truncated) form in festival prayer books but are hardly ever completely recited or really sung, not even in orthodox synagogues.

An outstanding scholarly example is Menahem Zulay (1901–54), whose personal biography exemplifies the transition of piyyut research from Germany to Palestine-Israel and whose work on the Palestinian hymnists Yehudah and Yannai is normative for this period. Nowadays a majority of the Genizah poetic texts have been catalogued and most hitherto unknown collections of piyyutim have been described or edited. The present situation is to some extent comparable to the state of research of Qumran hymns: the pioneering work is done, but now further analysis, explanation and contextualisation of piyyut is needed. The Genizah research focus is now on the disclosure of Firkovicz fragments from St Petersburg, much more pertaining to Andalusian and Karaite Hebrew hymnology and the poetry of the Islamic East.[2]

Piyyut Research from Generation to Generation

One of the prominent scholars in Jerusalem after Zulay was Ezra Fleischer (1928–2006), whose achievement it was to offer a survey of the entire field

[2] See van Bekkum (1998a, 2007); S. Elizur (2004, 2007); Löffler (2008); Mirsky (1977); Rabinovitz (1985–87); Rand (2005); Schirmann (1965); Swartz (2004); Yahalom (1984, 1996); Yahalom and Löffler (2006); Zulay (1933). Zulay's thesis (1933) was supervised by the famous Hebraist and Semitist Paul Kahle, who wrote important studies of Hebrew vocalisation systems in his *Masoreten des Westens* and *Masoreten des Ostens*. Zulay's main focus concerned an unknown composer named Yehudah, whose works were partly transmitted in a sequence of Babylonian *parashot*. However, Zulay's suggestion that this Yehudah was an early poet 'not too distant from Yannai' has proved to be right. Subsequent studies of this paytan have occasionally been ignored by researchers, who have erroneously categorised him in the 'post-classical' period; Zulay (1938): one of the finest editions that has ever appeared in the study of ancient piyyut; Zulay (1995); Zunz (1855–59, 1865–89).

of early Jewish liturgy and hymnography. Fleischer accomplished in 1975 a fundamental volume on Jewish hymnography with much attention for structural-poetic features of the different piyyutic genres. He can be considered as a representative of the Israeli school of researchers whose interest in Palestinian-Jewish liturgical poetry is linked with the desire to reconstruct an 'authentic' literary corpus, historically attached to the land of Israel. A fine example of an American researcher of similar status is Shalom Spiegel from New York. However, his major aim, to create a corpus of all liturgical poetic texts from Palestine in the ancient period and to write a history of its literary values, was not fulfilled. Fleischer's periodisation of Jewish liturgical poetry according to time and place has been commonly accepted by modern scholars in the field,[3] but fundamental questions with regard to the suitability of his terminology remain. Qualifications such as 'pre-classical', 'classical', 'post-classical', and especially 'Late Eastern' do not always justify a proper categorisation of a given piyyut or a meaningful classification of a given individual paytan.

Periodisation according to Ezra Fleischer

1. The pre-classical period of anonymous paytanim and the one composer of *avodot* known by name: Yose ben Yose (*circa* fourth–sixth centuries).
2. The classical period of paytanim flourishing in Byzantine Palestine until and in the period of the Arab conquest: among them are Yannai, Shimon bar Megas, Yehudah, Eleazar birabbi Kallir, Yohanan haKohen and Pinhas haKohen (*circa* sixth–eighth centuries).
3. The post-classical or Late Eastern period: the centre of piyyut shifted from Palestine to Babylonia (Iraq) in the East (*circa* ninth–eleventh centuries).
4. The Spanish school (*circa* tenth–thirteenth centuries).
5. The Italian-Ashkenazic-Tsarfatic school (*circa* tenth–thirteenth centuries).

Piyyut in Context

Two Jerusalem scholars, Ezra Fleischer and Joseph Yahalom, represent in my opinion a crucially distinct approach towards piyyut in its historical and

---

[3] See Fleischer (1975). A large part of Fleischer's bibliography can be found in S. Elizur *et al.* (eds. 1994: 379–89). See also Spiegel (1996); Hollender (2001); Reif (2000).

cultural contexts. The following quotations are illustrative of the opposing trends in their thought. Today it is generally not considered sufficient to focus piyyut studies exclusively on the internal evolution of hymnology and liturgy in Jewish communities while leaving out any relation to their social, historical and cultural setting.

I offer first a quotation from Ezra Fleischer's article in *De'ot*:

> Paytanut is a culture, not a religion, a minor culture under pressure of persecution, but a culture of great meaning for the communities of Israel with an internal transmission of models and contents from one hymnist to the other, from one community to another. Paytanic verse was an independent unit among the contemporary cultures of poetry. (Fleischer 2006a: 19)

The following is by Fleischer in *Compendia Rerum Iudaicarum ad Novum Testamentum*, 2006 edition:

> The rise of paytanic verse was an immanent development of public worship in early Palestinian communities. Piyyut was created in order to offer a poetic alternative for the wording of public synagogue service, especially on Sabbath and holidays. . . . The *qedushta*, the oldest and most central genre of Piyyut, was meant to embellish *'amidah* prayers in which a *qedushah* is said. The *qedushah* is also known to be central to most of the extant poetical fragments from the Hekhalot literature. But the link between the ecstatic Hekhalot poetry and the poetics of the *qedushtaot* is very slight indeed. The poetry of paytanut is 'orthodox' by nature and has a marked aversion to esoteric topics. (Fleischer 2006b: 366)

Lastly, a quotation from Joseph Yahalom in *Compendia Rerum Iudaicarum ad Novum Testamentum*, 2006 edition:

> It is not always justified to barricade oneself behind fortified lines in areas that should be viewed as open, connected with one another, and complementary. That is true of the distinction that is made between literary and documentary material from the early medieval manuscripts preserved in the Cairo Genizah. The Jews of that society wrote highly personal letters and preserved them like the apple of their eye, until they ultimately found their way into the welter of documents in the Genizah, and Jews from that very society often wrote horribly conventional poetry, which the community also preserved for some reason. Furthermore, the absolute distinction between the formal aspect and the thematic aspect, which often fails to receive true attention, is problematic. (Yahalom 2006: 375)

Piyyut in Cultural Context ('Jew and Greek')

The term piyyut is derived from Greek *poiesis*, whereas the paytan or hymnist is occasionally called a *paytas*, very similar to the Greek noun ποιητής.

Piyyut as a phenomenon in Jewish culture and literature deserves further investigation concerning its interaction with surrounding cultures and religions. Themes and motifs are not exclusively versified reworkings of rabbinic-midrashic materials, but also draw upon other non-canonical and non-rabbinic sources or can be considered as intrinsically paytanic. Piyyut language is a fascinating combination of biblical, rabbinic, 'jargonic-piyyutic' grammar and vocabulary, at times mixed with elements from Aramaic and Greek. The language and idiom of liturgical verse already intrigued the medieval Jewish grammarians and linguists, who considered piyyut vocabulary as a part of a 'national' literary heritage. The tradition of poetic texts for the sake of synagogue liturgy evokes questions about the socio-religious position of their composers-performers and their audience. Recent research highlights the status and activity of the cantor-poets, whose influence in the case of the enigmatic hymnist Eleazar birabbi Kallir (or Killir) upon Jewish liturgy could be felt for centuries and could often be found in the *maḥzorim* (festival prayer books) of medieval Europe (as has been demonstrated by Daniel Goldschmidt and Yona Fraenkel in their superb edition of Kallir's compositions in the Ashkenazi *maḥzor*). This type of research is for a large part true work in progress.[4]

Piyyut in Translation ('Poetry to the People')

The translation of piyyutic texts into European languages is an unending struggle. What can be 'saved' from poetic beauty and lyrical expressivity alongside a correct rendering of the intentions of the verses and strophes? An interesting attempt is the edition of *Avodah* compositions by Michael Swartz and Joseph Yahalom (2005).

Another point might be the exercise in intertextuality. Every piyyutic text contains the language of the composer interspersed with previously

---

[4] See van Bekkum (2002, 2008a); E. Elizur (1994). In this gratulatory article for Ezra Fleischer, Elizur observes distinctions within the *kedushta* hymn with respect to the density and obscurity of the midrashic treatment of the week's scriptural reading. She argues that the design of the tri-partite classical *kedushta* and the different ways of versifying the same biblical and midrashic motifs, occasionally reinforced by the repetition of keywords or additional responses, were functional for addressing distinctive social groups within the audience. This assumption seems rather far-fetched because it raises crucial questions of a practical nature about the actual performance of the cantor-poet within the context of Sabbath liturgy and communal worship. It is difficult to conceive that one and the same composer would deliver his work to different segments of audience according to a certain intellectual division. See Fraenkel (1993, 2000); Goldschmidt (1970a, 1970b); Goldschmidt and Fraenkel (1981); Hezser (1997); Kalmin and Schwartz (eds. 2003); Lapin (2001); Levine (ed. 2004); Rand (2001); Schirmann (1979); Schwartz (2001), with review in Miller (2007); Yahalom (1999), with review in van Bekkum (2001); Yahalom (2008a, 2008b).

formed words and expressions, predominantly from Bible, Midrash, or earlier piyyutim, or any other less current source. Most allusions to subtexts or sources will be difficult to perceive in translation. The translator of piyyutim will have to deal with a designation of the level on which he wants to involve the results of his own investigation and judgement. An early specimen of Jewish Palestinian-Aramaic poetry in translation will serve here as a useful example.[5]

1. *The Bible as the Main Source of Piyyut*

A dramatic moment before the crossing of the sea by the Israelites is described in the book of Exodus, chapter 14, specifically verses 15–16: 'Then God said to Moses: "Why are you crying out to me? Tell the Israelites to move on. You will lift up your staff and stretch out your hand over the sea to divide the water so that the Israelites can go through the sea on dry ground."' It is worth examining how this episode is treated differently in a midrash from the end of the first millennium CE and in a piyyut from late-Roman Palestine.

2. *Midrash alongside Piyyut: The Other Side of the Coin*

Exodus Rabbah 21.6: You will lift up your staff (Exod. 14:15). Moses said to the Holy One, Blessed be He: 'You command me to divide the sea and to convert it into dry ground; but have you not written, "Who have placed the sand for the bound of the sea (Jer. 5:22), and did You not swear that You will never divide it?"' R. Eleazar haKappar said: 'Moses asked God: "Did You not promise that the sea would not be changed into dry land, for it says: 'Who have placed the sand for the bound of the sea?' (Jer. 5:22), and does it not say, 'Or who shut up the sea with doors?' (Job 38:8)."' The divine reply was: 'Did

---

[5] See Tanenbaum (2001); Hakohen (2006); Heinemann (1973); Kasher (2004); Katsumata (1998, 2002a, 2002b, 2008); Münz-Manor (2007a): this article specifically focuses on hymns no. 32 and 33 in the collection of Palestinian Aramaic Poems edited by J. Yahalom and M. Sokoloff (1999: 196–219). Kister (2007: 161–2, n. 302) casts serious doubts on Münz-Manor's conclusions with regard to the intentions of these hymns. Rand (2007a); Rodrigues Pereira (1997); Sáenz-Badillos (1993); Siesling (2006); Swartz and Yahalom (2005), with reviews in Reif (2007) and Schmelzer (2007); Yahalom (1978a, 1985); Yahalom and Sokoloff (1999) with reviews in Fassberg (2002) and van Bekkum (2004); Kister (2007): in the sixth part of this important review article Kister demonstrates with regard to a number of versions of the Aramaic hymn cited above that some major motifs go back to early traditions preserved in Greek, Syriac, Hebrew and Islamic literature, whereas an early common source is suggested for later midrashim such as *Midrash Wayyosha* and *Midrash Hallel* and other descriptions of the splitting of the Sea extant in Jewish Aramaic poetry. Kister is conspicuously hesitant about these hymns as sources of original traditions in later midrashic literature, cf. p. 147: 'It seems assumable that the much later *Midrash Wayyosha'* and *Midrash Hallel* derived materials from Aramaic poetry. However, grammatical analysis will prove that what has been clearly outlined in the midrashim, has been obscured in their poetic formulation.'

you not read the Torah from the beginning, where it is written: "And God said: 'Let the waters under the heaven be gathered together [. . . and let the dry land appear]'" (Gen. 1:9). It was I who made a condition at the very beginning that I would one day divide it, for it says: "And the sea returned to its strength when the morning appeared" (Exod. 14:27), that is, in accordance with the condition which I made with it at its creation.' Moses immediately hearkened to God and went to divide the sea, but the sea refused to comply, exclaiming: 'What, before you shall I divide? Am I not greater than you? I was created on the third day and you on the sixth.' When Moses heard this, he went and reported to God, 'The sea refuses to be divided.' What did God do? He placed His right hand upon the right hand of Moses, as it says, 'That caused His glorious arm to go at the right hand of Moses that divided the water before them' (Isa. 63:12). When [the sea] beheld God, it fled, as it says, 'The sea saw it, and fled' (Ps. 114:3). What did it see? It saw God's right hand placed upon Moses, and it could no longer delay, but fled at once.

3. *A Piyyut in Palestinian Jewish Aramaic Dialect: The Continuity of Traditions*

> Go Moses, and stand at the sea, / tell the sea: 'Move from before me';
> In My name you shall go and tell the sea: / 'I am the messenger of the Creator of the beginning;
> Give (your) way a brief while, / so that the redeemed of the Lord will go forward in the midst of you;
> The tribes of Jacob are in trouble, / their enemies chase after them;
> Behold, you are blocking in front of them, / and the wicked Pharaoh comes behind them.'
> And Moses went and stood at the sea, / and he said unto the sea: 'Move from before me [Moses].'
> The sea went aside before Moses, / when he saw the staff-of-miracles in his hand;
> Anger and fury arose in the sea, / and he arrogantly tried to turn back:
> 'You are making a mistake, son of Amram, / you are not my ruler or senior to me;
> I am three days older than you, / because I was created on the third day and you on the sixth.'
> When Moses saw the sea refusing, / and its waves boasting to him, God shouted and said: 'Stop it:
> This is not the time of judgement, / Israel is in trouble!'
> Moses said unto the sea again: / 'I am the messenger of the Creator of the beginning.'
> The sea turned around when he heard his word, / to act on the request of the Lord of heaven;
> Finally the sea said unto Moses: / 'To one born of woman I will not yield.'

Moses replied to the sea: / 'The One greater than me and you will subdue
   you.'
Moses opened his mouth in singing, / and this is how he sang his praises:
A prayer of Moses rose up in petition, / and in supplications he expressed
   his word:
'The word you said to me in the book of the Torah: Now you will see
   what I will do to Pharaoh!
Lord of the world, do not deliver your people / into the hands of the
   wicked Pharaoh!'
The sea hearkened to the voice of the Holy Spirit, / speaking to Moses
   from amidst the fire;
The sea drew back from its waves, / and the Israelites went forward into
   the midst of it.

Other Aspects of Piyyut

Piyyut and Liturgy

It goes without saying that the advances in piyyut research have quite a few
repercussions for modern insights into the development of Jewish liturgy in
the early synagogue. Piyyut collections of earlier and later paytanim have
shed much light on the traditions of Bible-reading customs on Sabbaths
and festivals in the synagogues of Palestine and Babylonia. The piyyut
genres are intrinsically connected with the fluctuation of liturgical trends,
only to be standardised to some extent in the period of the Babylonian
Geonim. Exploration of piyyutic conventions and innovations is worthy of
attention for liturgical origins, developments, variant prayer texts, synagogue ritual, Greek parallels, and the status and influence of rabbis (or the
lack thereof).[6]

Piyyut and Codicology ('Past and Present')

Codicological and palaeographical aspects of the Genizah findings are not a
core business in piyyut research, but the descriptions of manuscripts and
their physical characteristics lead to surprising conclusions with regard to the
existence of scattered *maḥzor* codices and the use of later choral refrains
within earlier compositions, so that one can extract arguments from this

---

[6] See S. Elizur (2006a); Fine (2005); Fleischer (1988, 1998); Gerhards (2007); Heinemann and
Petuchowski (2006); van der Horst and Newman (2008); Kalmin (2004); Langer (2004, 2007);
Reif (1993, 2004); Shmidman (2006, 2007, 2008); Tabory (ed. 1999).

evidence for a more accurate chronology of paytanim and the status of their oeuvres.[7]

Piyyut and Poetics ('the Younger Generation')

The exploration of linguistic, literary and prosodic values of early piyyut and paytanut is strikingly recent, leading to interesting publications. Most researchers would now agree upon a larger detachment of piyyut from midrashic models and motifs, as has been proposed by Aharon Mirsky and recently by Shulamit Elizur.[8]

Piyyut in Contemporary Context ('from Prayerbook to Website')

Piyyut has a future when it comes to digitalisation of words, phrases, verses and compositions. A *Dictionary of Early Medieval Byzantine and Late Eastern Piyyut* is in preparation, questioning the tricky issue of what belongs or does not belong to the piyyutic corpus according to time and place (see the periodisation of Fleischer, above). An important new branch of piyyut research is the extensive listing performed by Elisabeth Hollender from Cologne (Germany) in the form of a key or a catalogue of hundreds of piyyut commentaries from medieval Europe. These commentaries add to our understanding of the reception history and the variant readings of early (often Kalliri) piyyutim in later (mostly Ashkenazi-Tsarfatic) traditions.[9]

---

[7] See Fleischer (1974); Löffler (2002: esp. 166, n. 41); Yahalom (1978a); Yahalom and Engel (1987): a second facsimile edition of a reconstructed *Maḥzor Eretz Israel* by J. Yahalom in collaboration with B. Löffler is forthcoming.

[8] See S. Elizur (2006b): Elizur's description of the 'analogous sermon'—whatever the term 'analogy' may signify here—is basically an elaboration of Aharon Mirsky's approach towards midrashic hermeneutical concepts—such as *mah maẓinu, middah ke-neged middah, davar we-hippukho* or *gezerah shawah* (or *ma'al*)—as the source for various piyyutic forms: cf. Mirsky (1985). However, Yahalom has already demonstrated in his earlier studies to what extent paytanic originality and inventiveness in both structure and contents destined the genres of Jewish liturgical verse. A first assumption to be made in modern research of piyyut is to what extent the cantor-poets themselves created new poetic devices and forms by which prose homilies from the realm of Midrash can be transferred into an original sense and meaning. For instance, every two rhyming hemistichs within a given piyyutic verse establish a play of symmetry (a much better term than analogy) between meaningful sounds and sounding meanings, very often reflecting independent paytanic interpretations. The paytanic contribution to the midrashic corpus should not be underestimated, cf. Yahalom (1999: esp. 137–72; 1984: esp. 28–45); Münz-Manor (2006, 2007b); Novick (2008); Rand (2006, 2007b, 2007c); Rosen and Yassif (2002: 265–70); Yahalom (2004).

[9] See the Academy of the Hebrew Language: online Historical Dictionary—*MA'AGARIM*; Bar-Ilan University: online Responsa Project Judaic Library Database; Davidson ([1924–34], 1970); Ehrlich (undated): Prayer in Rabbinic Literature: A Developing Database; Hollender (2005, 2007a, 2007b, 2008).

Conclusions

Over the past couple of decades there has been a striking growth of interest in the study of piyyut inside and outside the Jerusalem school of research. Since Fleischer's *Hebrew Poetry in the Middle Ages*, scholars have published a substantial number of texts and studies in journals and have started to produce several translations. Beyond these, a plethora of articles and monographs has appeared as evaluations of piyyutim and piyyutic traditions from the ancient and medieval world. The observations and issues presented here do not therefore reflect an exhaustive picture of current research themes and perspectives, but the matters provided here disclose a preliminary 'state of the art' in piyyut studies. The fascinating topic of piyyut is attracting an increasing amount of fresh attention from scholars and students whose positive contributions question some of the traditional ways of describing and defining piyyut. Applying ideas of historical and literary comparison, we may conclude that many of the scholars represented in the field are now suggesting new means of viewing piyyutic and paytanic values. Future studies of ancient piyyut will have to pay much attention to a proper designation of appropriate criteria for the discussion of Jewish hymnography amidst a wide range of adjacent disciplines.

Further Reading

Van Bekkum (1998a, 2008b); Yahalom (1999).

Bibliography

Carmi, T. (1981), *The Penguin Book of Hebrew Verse*, Harmondsworth.
Davidson, I. ([1924–1934], 1970), *Thesaurus of Mediaeval Hebrew Poetry*, New York. [Hebrew]
Ehrlich, U. (undated), *Prayer in Rabbinic Literature: A Developing Database.*
Elizur, E. (1994), 'The congregation in the synagogue and the ancient *Qedushta*', in S. Elizur *et al.* (eds.) (1994), pp. 171–90. [Hebrew]
Elizur, S. (2004), *The Liturgical Poems of Rabbi Pinhas Ha-Kohen*, Jerusalem. [Hebrew]
Elizur, S. (2006a), 'The use of biblical verses in Hebrew liturgical poetry', in J. L. Kugel (ed.), *Prayers That Cite Scripture*, Cambridge, MA and London, pp. 83–100.
Elizur, S. (2006b), 'On the ways of design of the analogous sermon in the *Piyyutim*', in J. Levinson *et al.* (eds.), *Higayon L'Yona: New Aspects in the Study of Midrash, Aggadah and Piyut in Honor of Professor Yona Fraenkel*, Jerusalem, pp. 499–528. [Hebrew]

Elizur, S. (2007), 'Fifty years of research in the path of Menahem Zulay', in S. Elizur and J. Levinson (eds.), *Essays in Memory of Menahem Zulay*, Jerusalem Studies in Hebrew Literature 21, pp. 1–18. [Hebrew]

Elizur, S. (2009), 'Series of biblical verses in Hebrew prayers and liturgical poetry', *Ginzei Qedem: Genizah Research Annual*, 5: 9–63. [Hebrew]

Elizur, S. et al. (eds.) (1994), *Knesset Ezra: Literature and Life in the Synagogue. Studies Presented to Ezra Fleischer*, Jerusalem. [Hebrew]

Fassberg, S. (2002), Review of *Jewish Palestinian Aramaic Poetry from Late Antiquity*, *Leshonenu* 64: 159–64.

Fine, S. (2005), 'Between liturgy and social history: priestly power in late antique Palestinian synagogues?', *JJS* 56.1: 1–9.

Fleischer, E. (1974), *The Pizmonim of the Anonymous*, Jerusalem. [Hebrew]

Fleischer, E. (1975), *Hebrew Poetry in the Middle Ages*. Supplemented and annotated by S. Elizur and T. Beeri, Jerusalem, 2007. [Hebrew]

Fleischer, E. (1988), *Eretz-Israel Prayer and Prayer Rituals As Portrayed in the Geniza Documents*, Jerusalem. [Hebrew]

Fleischer, E. (1998), 'The *Qedushah* of the *'Amidah* (and other *Qedushot*): historical, liturgical, and ideological perspectives', *Tarbiz*, 67: 301–50. [Hebrew]

Fleischer, E. (2006a), 'Ancient Hebrew poetry in the Cairo Genizah', *De'ot* 25: 19–21.

Fleischer, E. (2006b), 'Piyyut', in S. Safrai et al. (eds.), *The Literature of the Sages, Second Part: Midrash and Targum . . .*, Assen, pp. 363–74.

Fraenkel, Y. (1993), *Mahzor Ashkenaz le-Pesah*, Jerusalem.

Fraenkel, Y. (2000), *Mahzor Ashkenaz le-Shavu'ot*, Jerusalem.

Gerhards, A. (2007), 'Crossing borders: the Kedusha and the Sanctus: a case study of the convergence of Jewish and Christian liturgy', in A. Gerhards and C. Leonhard (eds.), *Jewish and Christian Liturgy and Worship: New Insights into its History and Interaction*, Jewish and Christian Perspectives Series 15, Leiden and Boston, pp. 27–40.

Goldschmidt, D. (1970a), *Mahzor Ashkenaz le-Yamim ha-Nora'im*, I: *Rosh Hashana*, Jerusalem.

Goldschmidt, D. (1970b), *Mahzor Ashkenaz le-Yamim ha-Nora'im*, II: *Yom Kippur*, Jerusalem.

Goldschmidt, D. and Fraenkel, Y. (1981), *Mahzor Ashkenaz le-Sukkot, Shemini Azeret we-Simhat Torah*, Jerusalem.

Hakohen, E. (2006), 'Studies of the dialogue form in the liturgical poetry of ancient Israel and the sources of dialogue poems for Purim', *Jerusalem Studies in Hebrew Literature*, 20: 97–171. [Hebrew]

Heinemann, J. (1973), 'Remnants of piyyutic creativeness by early translators', *Ha-Sifrut*, 4: 362–75. [Hebrew]

Heinemann, J. and Petuchowski, J. (2006), *Literature of the Synagogue*, Jewish Studies Classics 4, Piscataway, NJ.

Hezser, C. (1997), *The Social Structure of the Rabbinic Movement in Roman Palestine*, Tübingen.

Hollender, E. (2001), Review of *The Fathers of Piyyut: Texts and Studies toward a History of the Piyyut in Eretz Yisrael*, *Prooftexts*, 21/2: 229–37.

Hollender, E. (2005), *Clavis Commentariorum of Hebrew Liturgical Poetry in Manuscript*, Clavis Commentariorum Antiquitatis et Medii Aevi 4, Leiden and Boston.

Hollender, E. (2007a), 'Commentary on a "lost" Piyyut: considering the transmission of teachings and texts in Rashi's Bet Midrash', in D. Krochmalnik, R. Reichmann and H. Liss (eds.), *Raschi und sein Erbe, Internationale Tagung der Hochschule für Jüdische Studien mit der Stadt Worms*, Heidelberg, pp. 47–63.

Hollender, E. (2007b), 'Parashat "Asser Te'asser" in Piyyut and Piyyut commentary', in A. Gerhards and C. Leonhard (eds.), *Jewish and Christian Liturgy and Worship: New Insights into its History and Interaction*, Jewish and Christian Perspectives Series 15, Leiden and Boston, pp. 91–107.

Hollender, E. (2008), *Piyyut Commentary in Medieval Ashkenaz*, Studia Judaica, Forschungen zur Wissenschaft des Judentums 42, Berlin.

Kalmin, R. (2004), 'Holy men and rabbis in late antiquity', in L. I. Levine (ed.) (2004), pp. 210–32.

Kalmin, R. and Schwartz, S. (eds.) (2003), *Jewish Culture and Society under the Christian Roman Empire*, Leuven.

Kasher, R. (2004), 'The beliefs of synagogue *Meturgemanim* and their audience', in Levine (ed.) (2004), pp. 420–42. [Hebrew]

Katsumata, N. (1998), *Sidre 'Avodah for the Day of Atonement from the Generation of Sa'adia Gaon*, Jerusalem. [Hebrew]

Katsumata, N. (2002a), 'An additional Seder 'Avodah for Yom Kippur by Shelomo Suleiman Al-Sinjari', *FJB* 29: 1–56.

Katsumata, N. (2002b), *The Liturgical Poetry of Nehemiah ben Shelomoh ben Heiman ha-Nasi: A Critical Edition*, Hebrew Language and Literature Series 2, Leiden, pp. 76–153. [Hebrew]

Katsumata, N. (2008), *Seder Avodah by Shelomoh Suleiman*, Texts and Studies in Medieval and Early Modern Judaism, Tübingen.

Kister, M. (2007), 'Jewish Aramaic poems from Byzantine Palestine and their setting', review of *Jewish Palestinian Aramaic Poetry from Late Antiquity*, *Tarbiz*, 76: 105–84. [Hebrew]

Langer, R. (2004), 'Early rabbinic liturgy in its Palestinian milieu: did non-rabbis know the '*Amidah*?', in A. J. Avery-Peck, D. Harrington and J. Neusner (eds.), *When Judaism and Christianity Began: Essays in Memory of Anthony J. Saldarini*, vol. 2: *Judaism and Christianity in the Beginning*, Leiden and Boston, pp. 423–39.

Langer, R (2007), 'Biblical texts in Jewish prayers: their history and function', in A. Gerhards and C. Leonhard (eds.), *Jewish and Christian Liturgy and Worship: New Insights into its History and Interaction*, Jewish and Christian Perspectives Series 15, Leiden and Boston, pp. 63–90.

Lapin, H. (2001), *Economy, Geography, and Provincial History in Later Roman Palestine*, Tübingen.

Levine, L. I. (ed.) (2004), *Continuity and Renewal: Jews and Judaism in Byzantine-Christian Palestine*, Jerusalem and New York.

Löffler, B. (2002), 'We-Nosaph 'Od: additions to the Supplements of *Maḥzor Yannai*', *Asuppot: Annual for Jewish Studies*, 14: 155–216, 376. [Hebrew]

Löffler, B. (2008), 'Qedushta le-Shabbat Wayyassa' le-Rabbi El'azar berabbi Qilir', *Yerushaseinu: The Annual Journal of Toras Ashkenaz. Research, Review, and Recollections of Ashkenaz Heritage and Customs*, 2: 223–58. [Hebrew]

Miller, S. S. (2007), Review of *Imperialism and Jewish Society 200 BCE to 640 CE*, *AJS Review*, 31.2: 329–62.

Mirsky, A. (1977), *Yosse ben Yosse: Poems*, Jerusalem. [Hebrew]

Mirsky, A. (1985), *The Origin of Forms of Early Hebrew Poetry*, Jerusalem.

Münz-Manor, O. (2006), 'All about Sarah: questions of gender in Yannai's poems on Sarah's (and Abraham's) barrenness', *Prooftexts*, 26: 344–74.

Münz-Manor, O. (2007a), '"Voices of others": Haman, Jesus and the question of representations of the "other" in hymns for Purim from Byzantine Palestine', in Y. Shapira, O. Herzog and Tamar Hess (eds.), *Popular and Canonical: Literary Dialogues*, Tel-Aviv, pp. 69–79, 217–23. [Hebrew]

Münz-Manor, O. (2007b), 'Structural ornamentations and figurative language in the ancient Piyyut', in S. Elizur and J. Levinson (eds.), *Essays in Memory of Menahem Zulay*, Jerusalem Studies in Hebrew Literature 21, pp. 19–38. [Hebrew]

Münz-Manor, O. (2009), '"As the apple among fruits, so the priest when he emerges": poetic similes in pre-classical poems of the "how lovely" genre', *Ginzei Qedem: Genizah Research Annual*, 5: 165–88.

Novick, T. (2008), 'Praying with the Bible: speech situation in the *Qedushta'ot* of Yannai and Bar Megas', *Masoret ha-Piyyut*, 4: 7–39.

Rabinovitz, Z. M. (1985–87), *The Liturgical Poems of Rabbi Yannai according to the Triennial Cycle of the Pentateuch and the Holidays*, Jerusalem. [Hebrew]

Rand, M. (2001), 'Metathesis as a poetic technique in *Hodayot* poetry and its relevance to the development of Hebrew rhyme', *Dead Sea Discoveries*, 8.1: 51–66.

Rand, M. (2005), 'The Seder Beriyot in Byzantine-era Piyyut', *JQR* 95.4: 667–83.

Rand, M. (2006), *Introduction to the Grammar of Hebrew Poetry in Byzantine Palestine*, Piscataway, NJ.

Rand, M. (2007a), 'Observations on the relationship between JPA poetry and the Hebrew Piyyut tradition: the case of the *Kinot*', in A. Gerhards and C. Leonhard (eds.), *Jewish and Christian Liturgy and Worship: New Insights into its History and Interaction*, Jewish and Christian Perspectives Series 15, Leiden and Boston, pp. 127–44.

Rand, M. (2007b), 'Marginal notes on the Qillirian rhyme system', in S. Elizur and J. Levinson (eds.), *Essays in Memory of Menahem Zulay*, Jerusalem Studies in Hebrew Literature 21, pp. 39–45.

Rand, M. (2007c), 'Liturgical compositions for Shemini 'Atzeret by Eleazar be-rabbi Qillir', *Ginzei Qedem: Genizah Research Annual*, 3: 9–99.

Rand, M. (2009), 'More on the Seder Beriyot', *JSQ* 16/2: 183–209.

Reif, S. C. (1993), *Judaism and Hebrew Prayer*, Cambridge.

Reif, S. C. (2000), Review of *The Fathers of Piyyut: Texts and Studies toward a History of the Piyyut in Eretz Yisrael*, *JSS* 45: 196–8.

Reif, S. C. (2004), 'Jewish prayers in their literary and cultural contexts during the Roman-Byzantine period', in L. I. Levine (ed.) (2004), pp. 389–401.

Reif, S. C. (2007), Review of *Avodah: An Anthology of Ancient Poems for Yom Kippur*, *JSS* 52.2: 401–3.

Rodrigues Pereira, A. S. (1997), *Studies in Aramaic Poetry (c.100 BCE—c.600 CE)*, Assen, pp. 88–102, 397–401.

Rosen, T. and Yassif, E. (2002), 'The study of Hebrew literature of the Middle Ages: major trends and goals', in M. Goodman (ed.), *The Oxford Handbook of Jewish Studies*, Oxford, pp. 241–94.

Sáenz-Badillos, A. (1993), *A History of the Hebrew Language*, Cambridge, pp. 202–19.

Sáenz-Badillos, A. (1999), Review of *Jewish Hymnography: A Literary History*, *JQR* n.s. 90.1/2: 227–9.

Schirmann, J. (1965), *New Hebrew Poems from the Genizah*, Jerusalem. [Hebrew]

Schirmann, J. (1979), *Studies in the History of Hebrew Poetry and Drama*, Jerusalem. [Hebrew]

Schmelzer, M. (2007), Review of *Avodah: An Anthology of Ancient Poems for Yom Kippur*, *AJS Review*, 31: 178–80.

Schwartz, S. (2001), *Imperialism and Jewish Society 200 BCE to 640 CE*, Princeton, NJ.

Shmidman, A. (2006), 'The liturgical function of poetic versions of the grace after meals', *Ginzei Qedem: Genizah Research Annual*, 2: 45–102. [Hebrew]

Shmidman, A. (2007), 'Developments within the statutory text of the *Birkat ha-Mazon* in light of its poetic counterparts', in A. Gerhards and C. Leonhard (eds.), *Jewish and Christian Liturgy and Worship: New Insights into its History and Interaction*, Jewish and Christian Perspectives Series 15, Leiden and Boston, pp. 109–26.

Shmidman, A. (2008), 'On the destination of poetic versions of the grace after meals for the Day of Atonement', *Ginzei Qedem: Genizah Research Annual*, 4: 61–90. [Hebrew]

Siesling, H. (2006), '"Go, Moses, and stand by the sea": an acrostic poem from the Cairo Genizah to Exodus 14:30', in R. Roukema *et al.* (eds.), *The Interpretation of Exodus: Studies in Honour of Cornelis Houtman*, Louvain, pp. 139–54.

Spiegel, S. (1996), *The Fathers of Piyyut: Texts and Studies toward a History of the Piyyut in Eretz Yisrael*, selected from his literary estate and edited by M. H. Schmelzer, New York and Jerusalem.

Swartz, M. D. (2004), 'The power and role of Hebrew poetry in late antiquity', in L. I. Levine (ed.) (2004), pp. 452–62.

Swartz, M. D. and Yahalom, J. (2005), *Avodah: An Anthology of Ancient Poems for Yom Kippur*, University Park, PA.

Tabory, J. (ed.) (1999), *From Qumran to Cairo: Studies in the History of Prayer*, Jerusalem.

Tanenbaum, A. (2001), 'On translating medieval Hebrew poetry', in N. de Lange (ed.), *Hebrew Scholarship and the Medieval World*, Cambridge, pp. 171–85.

van Bekkum, W. J. (1998a), *Hebrew Poetry from Late Antiquity: Liturgical Poems of Yehudah*, Leiden, Boston and Köln.

van Bekkum, W. J. (1998b), Review of *Jewish Hymnography: A Literary History*, *JJS* 49.1: 168–70.

van Bekkum, W. J. (2001), Review of *Poetry and Society in Jewish Galilee of Late Antiquity*, *Journal for the Study of Judaism*, 32: 113–15.

van Bekkum, W. J. (2002), 'Hearing and understanding Piyyut in the liturgy of the synagogue', *Zutot: Perspectives on Jewish Culture*, 2: 58–63.

van Bekkum, W. J. (2004), Review of *Jewish Palestinian Aramaic Poetry from Late Antiquity*, *Bibliotheca Orientalis*, 61.1–2: 194–6.

van Bekkum, W. J. (2007), 'Some thoughts on the "secularization" of Hebrew liturgical poetry in pre-modern and modern times', in R. Fontaine, A. Schatz and I. Zwiep (eds.), *Sepharad in Ashkenaz: Medieval Knowledge and Eighteenth-Century Enlightened Jewish Discourse*, Amsterdam, pp. 235–47.

van Bekkum, W. J. (2008a), 'Qumran hymnology and Piyyut: contrast and comparison', *Revue de Qumran*, 91.23: 341–56.

van Bekkum, W. J. (2008b), 'The Hebrew liturgical poetry of Byzantine Palestine: recent research and new perspectives', *Prooftexts*, 28/2: 232–46.

van der Horst, P. W. and Newman, J. (2008), *Early Jewish Prayers in Greek: A Commentary*, Commentaries on Early Jewish Literature Series, Berlin.

Weinberger, L. (1998), *Jewish Hymnography: A Literary History*, London.

Yahalom, J. (1978a), *A Collection of Geniza Fragments of Piyyute Yannai*, Jerusalem (facsimile edition). [Hebrew]

Yahalom, J. (1978b), 'Ezel Moshe according to the Berlin Papyrus', *Tarbiz*, 47: 173–84. [Hebrew]

Yahalom, J. (1984), *Liturgical Poems of Shim'on bar Megas*, Jerusalem. [Hebrew]

Yahalom, J. (1985), *Poetic Language in the Early Piyyut*, Jerusalem. [Hebrew]

Yahalom, J. and Engel, E. (1987), *Mahzor Eretz Israel: A Geniza Codex*, Jerusalem. [Hebrew]

Yahalom, J. (1996), *Priestly Palestinian Poetry: A Narrative Liturgy for the Day of Atonement*, Jerusalem. [Hebrew]

Yahalom, J. (1999), *Poetry and Society in Jewish Galilee of Late Antiquity*, Tel Aviv. [Hebrew]

Yahalom, J. (2004), 'Poet-performer in the synagogue of the Byzantine period', in L. I. Levine (ed.) (2004), pp. 443–62. [Hebrew]

Yahalom, J. (2006), '"Syriac for dirges, Hebrew for speech": ancient Jewish poetry in Aramaic and Hebrew', in S. Safrai *et al.* (eds.), *The Literature of the Sages*, Second Part: *Midrash and Targum . . .*, Assen, pp. 375–91.

Yahalom, J. (2008a), 'The idiom of the nation: passages from ancient poetry enlisted as prooftexts', *Leshonenu*, 70: 399–411. [Hebrew]

Yahalom, J. (2008b), 'Piyyut in Byzantium: a few remarks', in R. Bonfil *et al.* (eds.), *The Jews of Byzantium: Dynamics of Minority and Majority Cultures*, Jerusalem Studies in Religion and Culture, Leiden and Boston.

Yahalom, J. and Löffler, B. (2006), '*Mi Lo Yira'akha Melekh* [Who Shall Not Fear You, O King]: a lost *Siluk* by Kallir for Rosh Hashanah', in E. Hazan and J. Yahalom (eds.), *Studies in Hebrew Poetry and Jewish Heritage in Memory of Aharon Mirsky*, Ramat Gan, pp. 127–58. [Hebrew]

Yahalom, J. and Sokoloff, M. (1999), *Jewish Palestinian Aramaic Poetry from Late Antiquity*, Jerusalem. [Hebrew]

Zulay, M. (1933), *Zur Liturgie der babylonischen Juden*, Bonner Orientalistische Studien, Heft 2, Stuttgart.

Zulay, M. (1938), *Piyyute Yannai: Liturgical Poems of Yannai Collected from Geniza-Manuscripts and Other Sources*, Berlin. [Hebrew]

Zulay, M. (1995), *Eretz Israel and Its Poetry: Studies in Piyyutim from the Cairo Geniza*, ed. E. Hazan (reprints of various articles), Jerusalem. [Hebrew]

Zunz, L. (1855–59), *Die synagogale Poesie des Mittelalters*, I & II: *Die Ritus des synagogalen Gottesdienstes*, Berlin.

Zunz, L. (1865–89), *Literaturgeschichte der synagogalen Poesie*, Berlin.

13

Targum

ROBERT HAYWARD

1. Contents of the Texts

TARGUM ('TRANSLATION, INTERPRETATION') IS A TERM USED TO DESCRIBE the ancient Aramaic versions of books of the Hebrew Bible which, along with translation of the Hebrew base-text into Aramaic, incorporate in varying degrees explanations of the biblical text, along with exegetical insertions.

2. Manuscripts

The manuscripts of the various Targumim present many complexities, most conveniently described by L. Díez Merino (1994). Differences between Yemenite, Babylonian and Western traditions in the transmission of Targum are evident, and there is still much research to be done on the manuscripts themselves. What follows aims to give only some principal witnesses to the Targumim, and is in no way exhaustive.

Targums of the Pentateuch include the following:

1. *Targum Onkelos* (TO): its best witness is generally agreed to be Vatican Library MS Ebr. 448, dating to the mid-eleventh century CE. This has Tiberian punctuation superimposed on Babylonian supralinear pointing (the printed edition closely related to the witness of this MS is *Biblia Hebraica*, Sabbioneta, 1557). At least thirty other manuscripts of TO are extant.
2. *Targum Pseudo-Jonathan* (PJ) is represented by the single British Library MS Add. 27031 of sixteenth-century date; and by the *editio princeps*, prepared from a MS belonging to the Foa family of Reggio, which is no longer extant: it was published at Venice in 1591 by Juan Bragadin.
3. *Targum Neofiti 1* (TN) survives in a single MS of the Vatican Library. Numbered 39 in a list of works donated to the Pia Domus Neophytorum in Rome, it was described as *Aparafrasi Caldea sopra al Pentateuco scritta a mano in carta pecora*, and was given to the

Vatican Library, where it was wrongly catalogued as Targum Onkelos. Its identity was discovered in 1956 by Alejandro Díez Macho. The colophon to the MS gives its date as 5264/1504. Many glosses, both marginal and interlinear, characterise this MS. Written in at least ten different hands, they very often agree with other known Targumim.

4. *Fragment Targums* (FT): (a) Paris, Bibliothèque Nationale hébr. 110, folios 1–16, of fifteenth-century date. (b) Vatican Library, Ebr. 440, folios 198–227, of thirteenth-century date. (c) Nürnberg, Stadtbibliothek Solger 2.2⁰, folios 119–47, of thirteenth-century date. Moscow, Günzberg 3 is probably a copy of this manuscript. (d) Leipzig, Universitätsbibliothek B. H., folio 1, of thirteenth- to fourteenth-century date. (e) New York, Jewish Theological Seminary (Lutzki) 605 (E. N. Adler 2587), folios 6 and 7, probably of thirteenth-century date. (f) Sassoon 264, folios 225–67, of seventeenth-century date. (g) British Library MS Or. 10794, of eleventh- to thirteenth-century date. (h) Cambridge University Library T-S AS 72.75–77, of ninth- to eleventh-century date.

5. *Targum from the Cairo Genizah* (CG): Palestinian Targum in manuscripts ranging in date from the eighth to the fourteenth centuries, presenting (a) Targum with continuous text (MSS designated A, B, C, D, E, Z); (b) Fragment Targum (MSS Br, DD and J); (c) Targum-Lectionaries (MSS f, G, Y, LL, W, U, S, Q, H, K, AA, BB, HH, GG, KK, MM, NN and PP); and (d) Hebrew Maḥzorim with some Aramaic Targum (MSS T, JJ, vv). For detailed description of these, and other Genizah MSS, see Glessmer (1995: 105–19, 128–57).

6. *Tosefta Targum*, i.e. additional Targum to discrete passages of the Pentateuch, represented by Cairo Genizah MSS R, M, RR, I, X, FF and EE; papyrus Berlin 8498 (fourth–fifth century CE); and other witnesses listed by Glessmer (1995: 177–81).

Targums of the Prophets: for the Former Prophets, Sperber used British Library MS Or. 2210 representing the Yemenite tradition as the base text, and listed ten other manuscripts. A list of manuscripts of Targum Jonathan of Former Prophets, with description, is given by Smelik (1995: 118–29), to which should be added further witnesses recorded by van Staalduine-Sulman (2002). For the Latter Prophets, Sperber utilised British Library MS Or. 2211, listing six further MSS. See also below, under 'Available Editions'. For both Former and Latter Prophets, Codex Reuchlinianus and its marginal glosses is of special importance: it differs considerably from the Yemenite tradition preferred by Sperber.

Targums of the Writings: for Job, the best witness is Cambridge University Library MS Ee5.9, with at least thirteen other manuscripts extant. Multiple translation whereby single verses are given two, or even three renderings, is a feature of this Targum, as also (but less frequently) in Targum of Psalms, for which MS 116-Z-40 of the Complutensian University, Madrid has been critically edited by L. Díez Merino (1982). For Targum of Lamentations there are two MS recensions, one Western and best represented by Vatican Library MS Urb. Ebr. 1 (Codex Urbinas 1), the other Yemenite, preserved in British Library MS Or. 1476; 2375; and 2377. A similar situation is apparent for Targum of Canticles, with a Western recension to be found (e.g.) in Codex Urbinas 1, and a Yemenite recension extant in British Library MS Or. 1302 and some other witnesses. Ruth, too, has a Targum showing Yemenite (e.g. British Library MS Or. 2375, MS Or. 9906) and Western (e.g. Rome, Biblioteca Angelica MS N.72) recensions. At least eleven MSS of Targum Kohelet are known, including Codex Urbinas 1; Targum of Chronicles, however, is known only in three MSS of the thirteenth–fourteenth centuries (Vatican, Codex Urbinas 1; Cambridge, University Libray MS Or. Ee5.9; and Berlin, Deutsche Staatsbibliothek MS Or. fol. 1210 and 1211). Of Esther, there are certainly two Targums, and most likely a third which was printed in the Antwerp Polyglot (1569–72): the first and the second Targums are represented in Yemenite (e.g. British Library MS Or. 2375) and Western (e.g. Paris, Bibliothèque Nationale Ms. héb. 110) recensions.

3. Date and Place of Origin

Targum Onkelos is widely held to have originated in the late first or early second century CE in the Land of Israel, from where it was taken to Babylonia. There it seems to have undergone revision, which resulted (in the fourth or fifth century CE) in the production of a standard text approved by rabbinic authority: this eventually included a Masorah. This account of TO's origins is suggested by the fact that its non-legal traditions are paralleled mostly in Palestinian documents, and its language is predominantly West Aramaic. But its legal rulings agree with the Mishnah as interpreted by Babylonian Sages, who called it 'Our Targum' (b.Kid. 49a), and it displays traces of East Aramaic forms. A similar process, taking place at more or less the same time, seems to lie behind the present form of Targum Jonathan of the Prophets. For a recent critique of this consensus, however, see Müller-Kessler (2001).

It is likewise commonly believed that most of the remaining Targumim probably originated in a Palestinian setting, although some (e.g. Targum Canticles) may have originated in Babylonia, and the several forms in which others have reached us in some cases betray Babylonian influence. Their dates, however, are often problematic and uncertain. Pseudo-Jonathan contains some very early, possibly pre-Christian material, along with traditions which can only be dated to the Islamic period. Targum Neofiti 1 dates most probably from the third or fourth century CE, although dates both much earlier and much later have been proposed (Alexander 1992: 323). The dates of composition of the Fragment Targums, Tosefta Targums, and Targums from the Cairo Genizah are almost impossible to determine, given the nature of the material. Targums of the Writings are particularly difficult to date, and dates proposed for them are often mere possibilities. Thus Targum Psalms may be of fourth-century date (or later); Targum Job fourth or fifth century, with some earlier material included; Targum Lamentations may derive from the seventh century; Targum Canticles from the seventh or eighth century; Targum Chronicles from the eighth or ninth century. The dates of the Targums of Proverbs, Ruth, Kohelet and Esther may well lie within the same general time frame proposed for the other Targums of the Writings, that is, from the fourth to the ninth centuries CE.

4. Available Editions

The Pentateuch

TO: A. Sperber, *The Bible in Aramaic*, I: *The Pentateuch according to Targum Onkelos* (Leiden: Brill, 1959). A second impression (1992) has a foreword by Robert Gordon signalling limitations of this edition. Chief among these was Sperber's failure to utilise MS Vat. Ebr. 448 as his base text, choosing instead British Library MS Or. 2363 (and, where this was defective, MSS Or. 2228; 2229; and 1467); and a highly unsatisfactory arrangement of the textual Apparatus.

PJ: most reliable is the edition of E. G. Clarke, with W. E. Aufrecht, J. C. Hurd and F. Spitzer, *Targum Pseudo-Jonathan of the Pentateuch: Text and Concordance* (Hoboken, NJ: Ktav, 1984).

TN: A. Díez Macho, *Ms. Neophyti 1*, in 5 volumes as follows: *Tomo I Génesis*; *Tomo II Exodo*; *Tomo III Levítico* (Madrid-Barcelona: Consejo Superior de Investigaciones Científicas [CSIC], 1968, 1970, 1971); *Tomo IV Números*; *Tomo V Deuteronomio* (Madrid: CSIC, 1974, 1978).

FT: M. L. Klein, *The Fragment Targums of the Pentateuch according to their Extant Sources*, 2 vols. (Rome: Biblical Institute Press, 1980).

CG: P. Kahle, *Masoreten des Westens*, vol. 2 (Stuttgart: Kohlhammer, 1930; repr. Hildesheim, 1967); M. L. Klein, *Genizah Manuscripts of Palestinian Targum to the Pentateuch*, 2 vols. (Cincinnati: Hebrew Union College Press, 1986).

The Prophets

A. Sperber, *The Bible in Aramaic*, II: *The Former Prophets according to Targum Jonathan*; *The Bible in Aramaic*, III: *The Latter Prophets according to Targum Jonathan* (Leiden: Brill, 1959, 1962). For the difficulties presented by the edition, see Barthélemy (1992: pp. ccix–ccxi). For individual books, see E. Martínez Borobio, *Targum Jonatán de los Profetas Primeros en tradición babilónica*, vol. II: *I–II Samuel* (Madrid: CSIC, 1987); J. Ribera Florit, *Targum Jonatán de los Profetas Posteriores en tradicion babilónica. Isaías* and *Jeremías* (Madrid: CSIC, 1988, 1992).

The Writings

For the complete corpus, P. de Lagarde, *Hagiographa Chaldaice* (repr. Osnabrück: O. Zeller, 1967) is still invaluable. Recent critical editions of individual books include D. M. Stec, *The Text of the Targum of Job: An Introduction and Critical Edition* (Leiden: Brill, 1994); L. Díez Merino, *Targum de Qohelet* (Madrid: CSIC, 1987); R. H. Melamed, *The Targum to Canticles according to Six Yemen MSS, compared with the 'Textus Receptus'*, ed. P. de Lagarde (Philadelphia: Dropsie College, 1921); C. A. Fontela, *El Targum al Cantar de los Cantares (Edición Crítica)*, Colección Tesis Doctorales, No. 92/87 (Madrid: Editorial de la Universidad Complutense de Madrid, 1987); and A. van der Heide, *The Yemenite Tradition of the Targum of Lamentations: Critical Text and Analysis of the Variant Readings* (Leiden: Brill, 1981).

5. Translations

For an English translation of the Aramaic Targums, see K. Cathcart, M. Maher and M. McNamara (eds.), *The Aramaic Bible*, 22 vols. (Collegeville: Liturgical Press; Edinburgh: T. and T. Clark, 1987–2007).

* * *

The type of literature represented by the extant Aramaic Targumim has been succinctly classified as 'Aramaic paraphrase of the biblical text in dependence on its wording' (Samely 1992: 180), the paraphrastic elements being well known for their inclusion of exegetical comment on the biblical verse being rendered into Aramaic.[1] One particular aspect of that exegetical comment

---

[1] For discussion of the principal characteristics of Targum and the methods of translations and interpretation employed by the Meturgemanim, see Taradach (1991: 51–62); Alexander (1992).

which has frequently been observed is the willingness of Targumists to relate particular biblical verses more or less directly to the social and political realities of their own time, thus as it were 'modernising' the biblical text and emphasising just how apposite it might be for hearers or readers of Targum.[2] Accordingly, biblical references to places are often updated, to represent their contemporary designations: we may here record, among many instances which could be listed, the appearance of Constantinople and Caesarea at PJ of Num. 24:19 to define the unnamed 'city' of the Hebrew text of that verse;[3] the identification of the biblical Shur at TN of Gen. 16:7 as Halusa, the Nabataean Elousa;[4] and the elucidation of biblical Argob as Trachonitis at TN of Deut. 3:4.[5]

Accompanying this 'modernisation' of the Bible's words, students have often found in the Targumim direct or indirect allusions to historical events of differing kinds. For example, PJ of Exod. 29:30 follows the Hebrew text in its instruction that the priests from among Aaron's sons are to wear designated vestments, but adds the note that such personnel are to be 'not from among the Levites'. This ruling on the Targum's part seems almost certain to relate to events in the days of King Agrippa II who, according to Josephus, *AJ* 20.216–17, persuaded the Sanhedrin to permit Levites to assume priestly garments, contrary to ancestral tradition (see further Büchler 1895: 153–4; Mortensen 2006: vol. 1, 110–11). Similarly, the Targum of 1 Sam. 15:4 elucidates an obscurity in the Hebrew text in such a way as to inform us that King Saul enumerated his armed forces by counting the Passover lambs, an interpretation of the verse which recalls the means adopted by Cestius Gallus, Roman Governor of Syria at the time of the First Revolt, to count the Jewish population.[6] The Roman governor's procedure is described in detail by Josephus, *BJ* 6.422–7.

---

[2] On the social and religious settings of Targum, see especially Fraade (1992).

[3] The Hebrew 'the remnant of the city' PJ interprets twice, as signifying 'the remnant which was left from Constantinople the sinful city . . . and . . . the rebellious city of Caesarea the stronghold of the cities of the Gentiles'. For textual details, see le Déaut (1979: 237). FTP and FTV of this verse identify the 'city' as Rome. Constantinople features also along with Rome and Edom at Tg. Psalms 108:11, for the historical implications of which see Stec (2004: 200). For contemporisation of place names in the Palestinian Targumim of Numbers, see McNamara and Clarke (1995: 8–21).

[4] TN offers the same identification at Gen. 20:1; 25:18 (so also PJ); Exod. 15:22 (so also PJ). Halusa also represents biblical Bered at TN and PJ of Gen. 16:14. For the Nabataean Elousa, see Josephus, *AJ* 14.18. Further discussion of these identifications may be found in R. le Déaut (1978: 176–7); McNamara (1972: 195).

[5] See also PJ and TO of this verse, and all three Targumim of Deut. 3:13, 14; and further discussion on Tg. 1 Kings 4:13 in Dray (2006: 33).

[6] The Hebrew reports that Saul mustered the people *battla'im*, often construed as referring to a place, 'in Tela'im'. The Targum, however, has understood the expression via Aramaic *talya*, Hebrew *taleh*, 'lamb'. See van Staalduine-Sulman (2002: 39, 322). The matter was discussed earlier, with reference to other rabbinic interpretations of the verse, by Smolar and Aberbach (1983: 69).

It must be admitted, however, that in these and many other similar cases, the presence of historical allusions in the Targum can be discerned only with the help of other, *datable*, non-targumic sources. We might, indeed, reasonably deduce from PJ of Exod. 29:30 that there might have been persons who at some time or other held the opinion that Levites might legitimately don priestly garb; but this would remain a hypothetical view held by hypothetical individuals, if we did not have in our hands the report of Josephus concerning Agrippa II. Similarly, the Targum's report that Saul numbered his troops with reference to Passover lambs might justifiably be taken as arising solely from a typically targumic exegesis of an unusual Hebrew word, were it not for our knowledge of what Cestius Gallus had done. This state of affairs must be borne constantly in mind, as we examine examples of what are likely to be reports of historical events preserved by the Targumim. Here we have space to discuss only three instances of targumic exegesis which appear to be related to historical events, instances which have attracted detailed scholarly investigation during the last fifteen years. All three represent the potential value and problems which the whole targumic corpus offers to the historian.[7]

Targum of Judges 5 and the Second Revolt against Rome

Events which took place before, during, and after the Second Revolt against Rome (132–5 CE) appear to have left their mark on targumic interpretations of the Song of Deborah. The difficult opening words of the poem, *bifro'a prao't byisrael*, which have been translated in such diverse ways as 'when locks [of hair] go untrimmed in Israel', or 'when leaders lead in Israel',[8] called forth no fewer than three interpretations in the Aramaic Targum, of which the second and third read as follows in Willem Smelik's translation:

> Thus, because of the retribution of Sisera's shattering and that of his army, and because of the miracle and the redemption that was performed for the sake of Israel—when the Sages sat down openly in the synagogues again and taught the people the words of the law—therefore bless and give thanks before the Lord. (Smelik 1995: 394–5)

The Aramaic expression rendered 'openly', Smelik observes, refers to the steadfast attitude of the Sages who continued publicly to study and teach Torah during the Hadrianic persecution which, according to rabbinic

---

[7] For an attempt systematically to collect and evaluate historical allusions in the Targum of the Prophets, see Smolar and Aberbach (1983: 63–128). For a systematic critique of their work, see van Staalduine-Sulman (2002: 39–43).

[8] For the first of these translations, see Berlin and Brettler (eds. 1999: 519); for the second, see RV and RSV.

tradition, involved a complete ban on these activities. Further targumic expansions of the Hebrew text appear to confirm this. Thus at Targum Judg. 5:7 we hear of unwalled cities, which had once been inhabited, now standing waste and desolate following the expulsion of their inhabitants. As Smelik remarks, following the failure of the Second Revolt, many Jewish settlements vanished completely, and the Jewish population went into decline. Indeed, the demographical consequences of the Jewish defeat were most marked (Smelik 1995: 432–4). The likely historical situation delineated in Targum of Judg. 5:2 seems to make another appearance in the Targum of 5:9, which represents Deborah as praising the scribes of Israel, who

> when this distress occurred, did not cease to expound the law and who, when it was proper for them, sat down openly in the synagogues and taught the people the words of the law and blessed and gave thanks before the Lord. (Translated Smelik: 443)

The following verse also (Targum of Judg. 5:10) speaks of these same scribes who gave up their occupations and travelled through the Land of Israel to administer justice, a necessary emergency arrangement following the chaos unleashed by the Second Revolt (Smelik 1995: 445).

While it might seem a priori possible that the Targum refers to events known to those for whom the Second Revolt was still a recent memory, matters are in fact not quite so straightforward. With Smelik, we may note that the words 'this distress' in Targum of Judg. 5:9 seem elsewhere in Targum of the Prophets to refer to the First Revolt, when the Temple was destroyed. After that event, rabbinic tradition records that the Sanhedrin moved from place to place; and the reference to 'scribes' in Targum of 5:9, rather than to 'Sages', might suggest a period before the Second Revolt and closer to times described by the New Testament, when scribes appear to have been fairly prominent in Jewish affairs.[9] These observations inevitably raise the question of the date of Targum of Judges in its final form. Smelik, who offers the most detailed and sustained treatment of the Targum available at present, notes inconsistencies both in the Targum's halakhic stance and its translations. These inconsistencies, in his view, point to a not entirely systematic revision of an earlier proto-Targum, which in its turn led to the production of the bulk of the present targumic text some time in the second half of the second century CE. If this be the case, then references within targumic expansion to aspects of the Second Revolt and the period following might be expected.

---

[9] See Smelik (1995: 443–6), who records (p. 444, n. 645) my suggestion that 'this distress' might refer to the persecution of Antiochus IV. Herein lies the difficulty: targumic information is often so vague that it might be reasonably understood to refer to quite differing times, places, and circumstances.

Even so, Smelik's suggestion that the extant text of Targum Jonathan of Judges represents a revision of a proto-Targum inevitably creates uncertainty, he himself indicating that a number of apparent allusions to the Second Revolt might have once have referred to the First, and have been later updated to accommodate more recent historical perspectives.[10] A similar uncertainty hangs over our second example, which presents complications of a different kind.

The Song of the Lamb and the First and Second Revolts

Eveline van Staalduine-Sulman's recently published commentary on the Targum of Samuel has once more drawn attention to a body of targumic exegesis which she and Johannes de Moor had identified in the early 1990s as comprising part of a lost poetic composition, The Song of the Lamb.[11] The Song is of interest not least because the two scholars have identified it largely on the basis of Tosefta Targum of 1 Sam. 17:43 and 17:8, with Targum Jonathan of 2 Sam. 23:8 representing a third component. The material in the Tosefta Targum, to which we shall confine discussion, includes a conversation between David, portrayed as a lamb, and Goliath 'the bear' before they engage in the fight which ends in Goliath's death. Of particular interest is the Tosefta Targum of 1 Sam. 17:43, which puts into Goliath's mouth a series of pleas to David to think twice before he embarks on his foolhardy enterprise. Thus the giant encourages David to think of his youth and his lack of experience in military affairs: he is not yet married, and will forfeit the joys of marriage if he ends up as a corpse. He will also forfeit a kingdom, for Goliath perceives that he will succeed Saul. He is encouraged to think of his grieving parents, his own good looks, and of his prospects for the future, all of which will be ruined if he falls victim to the Philistine. In short, Goliath urges the lad to use his common sense. David refuses, with the unquestioning certainty and confidence of youth:

> David said to Goliath: The Word of My God who has come with me, He will save the lamb from the mouth of the bear. Repose is what belongs to me: but wrath belongs to you. You [act] in the name of the idol, but I in the name of the Lord of Hosts. As for your sword, which is sharp, I will cut off your head with it.

[10] So in all his discussion of the verse selected here. In the case of one verse in the Song of Deborah (Targum of 5:24) he notes a fairly clear agreement with amoraic tradition (see Smelik 1995: 471–3).

[11] For her commentary, see above, n. 6: the Song is discussed chiefly at pp. 351–4, 364–83, 682–6. A convenient summary of the texts involved, and suggested interpretation, is given in de Moor and van Staalduine-Sulman (1993). A much fuller treatment may be found in van Staalduine-Sulman (1993).

Smolar and Aberbach had already suggested that the dialogue between Goliath and David might be understood as a targumic re-presentation of 'the arguments used by the protagonists of peace and war during the Roman–Jewish war of 66–70 CE'.[12] Specifically, they singled out the crucial role which Josephus (*BJ* 2.267, 290, 303, 409; 4.121–8) attributes to hotheaded youth in stirring up the nation to take arms against Rome, a topic which has since been investigated in greater depth by Martin Goodman (1987: 210–14). The words of David in the Tosefta Targum of 1 Sam. 17:43 seem to echo the attitudes of these youths. Even more striking are the similarities between the warnings put into Goliath's mouth, and the caution which Josephus reports King Agrippa II as urging on those bent on confrontation with Rome. Like Goliath in the Tosefta Targum, the King emphasises the youth and lack of military experience of the would-be freedom-fighters (*BJ* 2.346) and its inevitable consequences, for no nation can stand against the might of Rome (especially *BJ* 2.365–87). As the Tosefta Targum makes Goliath boast, 'there is no lamb that can stand up against a bear'; and David should seek no help from God, since God is on Goliath's side: 'as for your heart which has been exalted, the Lord will bring it low'. We may note a similar progression in Agrippa's speech. No nation can stand against Rome, and the Jews should not imagine that God will help, since his alliance is with the Romans (*BJ* 2.390).[13]

To all this, van Staalduine-Sulman brings additional material particularly from Pseudo-Philo's *Liber Antiquitatum Biblicarum*, a work most likely dating in its present form from the late first or early second century CE.[14] Chapter 61 of this book presents Goliath as the one responsible for the capture of the Ark, its transfer to the house of Dagon, and the slaughter of Israelite priests, items which also feature in the Tosefta Targum of 1 Sam. 17:8 and, more or less incidentally, in a speech of Josephus to the Jewish fighters (*BJ* 5.384–5: van Staalduine-Sulman 1993: 285). There is no denying the dramatic force of the two Tosefta Targums which de Moor and van Staalduine-Sulman have highlighted, and the affinities between these Targumim and the stances adopted by different groups at the time of the First Revolt are noteworthy. Yet it must be admitted that, if the writings of Josephus and Pseudo-Philo were not extant, it would be no easy matter to relate the dialogue between Goliath and David specifically to the First Revolt. Other plausible historical

---

[12] Smolar and Aberbach (1983: 72). For what follows, see their analysis of the Tosefta Targum of 1 Sam. 17:43 at pp. 72–4 of their monograph.

[13] This last argument is, in truth, a favourite in the mouth of Josephus, and is starkly expressed at *BJ* 5.412, 'God has fled from the holy places, I believe, and now stands alongside those whom you fight'; see also *BJ* 6.110.

[14] For the date of the *LAB*, see Schürer (1986: 328–9), and for the book's ideas about Israel's leaders, see Mendels (1992).

settings for the speeches might be envisaged (indeed they might be imagined in any event), not least since, according to the Tosefta Targum, David (the Jews) neither takes Goliath's (Agrippa's) advice, nor does he fail in his aim, but is resoundingly victorious with divine help over a foe much stronger than he. And matters are made no less complicated by our inability to ascribe any firm date to the Tosefta Targums of these verses.[15]

Even if some relationship between these targumic traditions and the troubled times preceding the First Revolt be admitted, little in the way of historical information can be derived from them in respect of the course of events or of the destinies of those who held the opinions ascribed to Goliath and David. The exegesis of biblical material in these passages, however, is illuminating when considered in a broader perspective, as presenting us with a picture of an ideal Jewish leader in the face of an apparently insuperable enemy; that leader's trust in the Almighty; and the ultimate vanity of naked power and strength. What stays in the mind, and suggests that the Targum may here have preserved views of those opposed to the First Revolt in particular, is the oddly irenic tone of Goliath's words to David which, set alongside the pleas of Agrippa II, still have resonance.

The Targum of the Twelve Prophets

While it is possible to bring forward evidence suggesting that the Targum of Judges 5 and the Tosefta Targums of 1 Sam. 17:8, 43 may have been shaped, in ways still discernible, by historical events attendant on the First and Second Revolts against Rome, the situation relative to material in the Targum of the Twelve Prophets is somewhat different. Until the early 1990s, students of this Targum seemed confident of identifying verses which clearly evoked episodes in Jewish history, among them Targum of Nah. 1:9 with its apparent references to the First and Second Revolts; Targum of Hab. 3:17, which seemingly treats of Roman taxes levied in the Land of Israel; and Targum of Mal. 1:11, which seems to envisage a time after the destruction of the Temple and to offer some theological reflection on it. A detailed study by Robert Gordon of these and other verses in this Targum which may preserve historical allusions from the Roman period, however, clearly exposes the dangers of assuming too readily that hard information can be gathered from the texts.[16]

---

[15] For commentary on the Aramaic text of the relevant verses, see Kasher (1996: 106–7, 109–11); and his studies of the homiletic aspects of Tosefta Targum in Kasher (2000).

[16] See Gordon (1994: 41–5 (on Nah. 1:9), 45–9 (on Hab. 3:17), 56–8 (on Mal. 1:11)), to which reference should be made for arguments summarised in our discussion here. In this chapter devoted to historical allusions in this Targum (pp. 40–61), Gordon deals also with Targum of Zeph. 3:18; Zech. 11:1; 12:11; and Mal. 3:6.

A brief account of some of his most telling remarks on these verses will be useful at this point.

The Targum of Nah. 1:9 follows directly a striking pronouncement in the Targum of the preceding verse: God will make an end of those nations which destroyed the Temple, and will hand over his enemies to Gehinnom. Arriving at verse 9, the Targumist interprets the Hebrew to mean that 'relief after affliction will not be established twice for you as for the house of Israel'. Mention of the Temple's destruction in the preceding verse suggests that, by the time we reach verse 9, Israel has already experienced two destructions of the Temple, and that the Targumist is thus referring to a time after 70 CE. Indeed, the noun 'affliction' seems to refer to the events of 70 elsewhere in targumic interpretation: Gordon cites Targum of Isa. 51:19, which most probably refers to the two destructions of the Temple in 586 BCE and 70 CE. So far, so good; but Gordon notes a shorter reading of Targum Nah. 1:9 preserved in the Antwerp Polyglot, which declares merely that 'trouble shall not be established twice in the house of Israel'. He offers convincing arguments for the originality of this shorter text, which are sufficiently strong to suggest that the longer text represents a later reworking of the Targum. Indeed, the shorter text need have no reference at all to the events of 70. The uncertainty surrounding the targumic text in this instance, therefore, renders its potential as a witness to historical events so limited as to be almost useless.

The Targum of Hab. 3:17 offers a different set of problems. Here, the Romans are mentioned by name, and some scholars have also felt moved to recognise a reference to their taxes imposed on the Jewish people. Gordon translates as follows:

> For the kingdom of Babylon will not endure nor exercise suzerainty over Israel, the kings of Media will be killed, and the warriors from Greece will not prosper; the Romans will be destroyed and will not collect *qyswm'* from (var. 'in') Jerusalem.

Serious difficulty lies in the word *qyswm'*, which Pinkhos Churgin had understood as 'tribute', and had happily related to the census undertaken by Quirinius in 6–7 CE. But this word, as Gordon observes, is an 'otherwise unattested vocable', and his extended description of attempts by earlier scholars to define it tells its own tale. Buxtorf had noted that his predecessors could throw no light on it: he himself linked it with the Latin *census*.[17] Levy, on the other hand, sought an explanation in the verbal root *qsm*, 'cut, decide': *qyswm'* is thus what the ruler *decides* in the way of tribute.[18] Kohut invoked

---

[17] See Gordon (1994: 46), quoting Buxtorf's entry for the word: *Elias scribit, se ignorare quid sit. Aruch adducit, sed non explicat.*

[18] See Gordon (1994: 46–7) for Levy's invocation of Targum 1 Kings 10:25. It is difficult to see how this verse might support Levy's argument.

the Arabic *qasama*, 'divide, distribute', in favour of the meaning 'tribute', whereas Krauss discerned a Greek loan word κηνσωμα.[19] Radically differing from all these explanations, Jastrow drew attention to the Aramaic word *qysm*, a 'chip' or 'fragment', and proceeded to vocalise the word as *qîssûmâ* with the collective sense of 'rakings'. The verse would then mean that the Romans would not gather Jerusalem's rakings: that is, they would not enjoy the city's destruction. Little help in solving these problems is afforded by the verb describing what the Romans will not do: the Aramaic is *wl' ygbwn*, and may offer us the root *gby* or *gb'*, which often refers to the collection of tribute and taxes. However, the Aramaic consonants may be vocalised such that the verbal root is *gbb*, 'rake', a meaning which neatly supports Jastrow's explanation of *qyswm*.

This brief summary of the linguistic problems is enough to demonstrate the near intractable problems in this verse, even without the added complication of its specific mention of Jerusalem rather than the whole of Israel (Gordon 1994: 48–9). Any attempt to derive precise historical information from this verse is clearly hazardous.

The Targum of Mal. 1:11 offers information less complex, though nonetheless awkward to interpret. It might seem, prima facie, to refer to worship offered by Jews of the Diaspora, by converts to Judaism, or even by non-Jews, a matter pursued in some detail by J. G. Baldwin (1972). Gordon's translation of the verse runs as follows:

> For from the rising of the sun even to its setting my name is great among the nations, and on every occasion when you fulfil my will I hear your prayer and my great name is hallowed because of you, and your prayer is like a pure offering before me; for my name is great among the nations, says the Lord of Hosts. (Gordon 1994: 56)

As Gordon demonstrates, it is very difficult to locate the origins of this Targum to one time or place: while Justin Martyr (*Dialogue* 1.10–12) is a witness that there were Jews in the mid-second century CE who understood the verse in the manner of the Targum, there are no definite grounds for arguing that the Targum originated then. Even though Churgin had insisted that the Targum was to be dated after the end of sacrifice and the fall of the Temple, Gordon is right to point out that the Bible itself in several places grants to prayer a value equivalent to sacrifice.[20] In truth, the Targum of Mal. 1:11 may have originated at any time before the final redaction of our present text. It

---

[19] For details, see Gordon (1994: 47), listing others who favoured this interpretation including Dalman. See also Dray (2006: 24).

[20] See Gordon (1994: 57), citing Pss. 50:13–14, 141:2, along with post-biblical writings and rabbinic sources. To the biblical texts may be added the powerful voice of Ps. 69:30–1 (song and thanksgiving are more pleasing to God than ox or bull).

contains nothing which might necessitate an origin in any particular time and place. And we may add to Gordon's remarks a further observation: what the Targum certainly achieves is the complete elimination of any reference to the offering of incense outside the confines of the Temple, which the original prophecy of Malachi might seem to permit. Given that severe penalties were prescribed for those who attempted to burn Temple incense outside the Sanctuary and its service, the Targum takes on a rather different colour, and becomes less susceptible to historical interpretation.[21] With this example, we may sum up the section in Gordon's words:

> In short, 'historical' references in the Targums can be extremely difficult to pin down in a precise chronological way, and those that do comply, or that seem to comply, indicate an extended period of development before Tg Prophets crystallized in something like its present form. (Gordon 1994: 61)

Some Evidence from other Targumim

This brief survey has so far concentrated on the so-called 'historical books' and some prophetical writings, attempting to draw attention to items which might relate to the later Roman period. If the results have seemed disappointing for the earlier historical books, they are even more meagre for the books of Kings. Carol Dray's recently published study, which opens with chapters devoted to targumic contemporisation of biblical texts and toponymy, has scant reference to the Roman period. True, the Roman *denarius* receives a mention at 2 Kings 5:5 (Dray 2006: 18), and there is a reference to the destruction of the Temple in the targumic version of 1 Kings 9:8 which may, as Dray observes (p. 20), relate either to the First or the Second Temple. She does not, however, attempt to relate specific verses of the Targum to historical events in the Roman period.

If we turn to Targum of the Writings, the situation seems equally unfavourable. Given what Philip Alexander (2003: 13) has called the 'strikingly coherent reading of Canticles' which the Targum of that book presents, we might expect some historical material to make itself felt. This is not least because Targum of Canticles systematically interprets its parent Hebrew text with reference to three extended historical periods, the first from Israel's servitude in Egypt to the time of Solomon; the second from the Babylonian exile to the time of the Hasmoneans; and the third from the exile of Edom,

---

[21] Thus the Lord says to Malachi: 'in every place incense is brought near to My Name'; but the rules for the composition of the incense (Exod. 30:34–7) are followed by the note (Exod. 30:38) that anyone attempting to make incense like it is subject to *karet*. See further b.Ker. 5a.

as it is called in Targum Canticles 7:2, to the coming of King Messiah.[22] In this third period some reference to events in the Roman period might be expected, but none is found. Alexander (2003: 57–8, 84, 169, 185–6), indeed, notes historical allusions within the Targum; but these seem to belong in the Islamic period, and are discussed in that context. Similar observations might be made about the Targum of Psalms, the study of which has been considerably advanced by David Stec's recent work on the manuscript tradition and exegetical stance of the Targum. Instructive here is the list of foreign loan words which Stec has compiled, where Latin features hardly at all; and there is just one direct reference to Rome.[23]

Conclusion

Recent scholarly work on the Aramaic Targumim has shown itself less willing than earlier research to identify historical information preserved in the extant texts, and to make use of that information either to comment on the date and provenance of the Targumim, or to supplement our historical knowledge. We may usefully contrast the classic work of Smolar and Aberbach on Targum Jonathan of the Prophets, which quite confidently lists targumic passages and relates them to the history of the Jews in Hellenistic and Roman times, with the more measured and reticent approach of Robert Gordon. Both approaches have briefly been recorded here; and it should be clearly understood that Gordon's caution arises not from any unwillingness on his part to perceive historical material in the Targumim, nor from any preconceptions he may bring to those texts. His concern is grounded in the difficulties which targumic texts so often pose for interpreters, which are often difficult, if not impossible, to resolve. Most other students of Targum would find themselves in agreement with him. That said, the Targumim are rather more informative in matters of social custom and religious observance which, though not direct witnesses to major historical events of their times, nonetheless convey to us significant information which, critically appraised, can be utilised along with other sources to construct a picture of Jewish life in the Land of Israel in the later Roman period (Shinan 1992).

At the outset, we noted how the identification of historical material in the Targumim may itself depend on our access to other historical sources which we are able to date with some degree of precision. These can offer

---

[22] For details, and for the literary structure of each of these three periods, see Alexander (2003: 13–18).

[23] Stec (2004: 20–1) on loan words, and (2004: 200) for the Targum's reference to Rome and Constantinople at Ps. 108:11, already recorded above, n. 3.

information which, judiciously applied to the Targumim, may reveal historical details which might otherwise escape our notice. Thus we noted the case
of the Levites and the priestly garments signalled by Targum Pseudo-
Jonathan, and the census of Israel through the Passover lambs recorded in
the Targum of 1 Samuel. Without the corresponding evidence found in
Josephus' writings, we would be hard pressed to account for the targumic
passages in any detail. Once the latter are identified and given their proper
historical setting, however, they can illuminate social and religious dimensions about which Josephus is silent. This itself is valuable, and can certainly
be exploited by the historian; but its limitations will be evident.

Where the Targumim might reasonably be supposed to report or comment upon historical events, we face a further difficulty, in that what they may
have to tell us is almost always piecemeal. They do not present us with historical narrative, with events selected and set out in chronological order and
duly analysed. If they were to offer any such thing, it would almost certainly
stand at the very beginning of any scholarly Introduction to Targum! For the
dating of the Targumim, and of the individual traditions which they preserve,
is notoriously difficult; and historical material in the Targumim, whenever it
might be available, is commonly seized upon by students in an attempt to
locate the Targum in place and time. In other words, students of Targum tend
to look to historical material to help with interpretation of their texts, rather
than to mine the Targumim for information about Jewish history as such. As
we have seen, their researches in this area need to be conducted with caution,
and without undue expectations of definite results.

Further Reading

Alexander (1990, 1999); Flesher (1995); Kugel (1994); le Déaut (1988); Levine (1988);
Shinan (2006); Stemberger (1996); Vermes (1973, 1975).

Bibliography

Alexander, P. S. (1990), 'Jewish Aramaic translation of Hebrew scriptures', in M. J.
    Mulder and H. Sysling (eds.), *Mikra: Text, Translation, Reading and Interpretation
    of the Hebrew Bible in Ancient Judaism and Early Christianity*, Minneapolis,
    pp. 217–54.
Alexander, P. S. (1992), 'Targum, Targumim', in D. N. Freedman (ed.), *The Anchor
    Bible Dictionary*, vol. 6, New York, pp. 320–31.
Alexander, P. S. (1999), 'How did the rabbis learn Hebrew?', in W. Horbury (ed.),
    Hebrew Study from Ezra to Ben Yehuda, London, pp. 71–89.
Alexander, P. S. (2003), *The Targum of Canticles*, The Aramaic Bible 17a, Edinburgh.

Baldwin, J. G. (1972), 'Malachi 1:11 and the worship of the nations in the Old Testament', *Tyndale Bulletin*, 23: 117–24.

Barthélemy, D. (1992), *Critique Textuelle de l'Ancien Testament*, III: *Ezéchiel, Daniel et les 12 Prophètes*, Göttingen.

Berlin, A. and Brettler, M. Z. (eds.) (1999), *The Jewish Study Bible*, Oxford.

Büchler, A. (1895), *Die Priester und der Cultus im letzten Jahrzeit des jeruschalmischen Tempels*, Vienna.

de Moor, J. C. and van Staalduine-Sulman, E. (1993), 'The Aramaic Song of the Lamb', *Journal for the Study of Judaism*, 24: 266–79.

Díez Merino, L. (1994), 'Targum manuscripts and critical editions', in D. R. G. Beattie and N. J. McNamara (eds.), *The Aramaic Bible: Targums in their Historical Context*, Journal for the Study of the Old Testament suppl. series 166, Sheffield, pp. 51–91.

Dray, C. (2006), *Translation and Interpretation in the Targum to the Books of Kings*, Leiden.

Flesher, P. V. M. (1995), 'The *Targumim*', in J. Neusner (ed.), *Judaism in Late Antiquity*, Part 1: *The Literary and Archaeological Sources*, Handbuch der Orientalistik 16, Leiden, pp. 40–63.

Fraade, S. D. (1992), 'Rabbinic views on the practice of Targum and multilingualism in the Jewish Galilee of the third–sixth centuries', in L. I. Levine (ed.), *The Galilee in Late Antiquity*, New York, pp. 253–86.

Glessmer, U. (1995), *Einleitung in die Targume zum Pentateuch*, Tübingen.

Goodman, M. (1987), *The Ruling Class of Judaea: The Origins of the Jewish Revolt against Rome AD 66–70*, Cambridge.

Gordon, R. P. (1992), Foreword to reprint of A. Sperber, *The Bible in Aramaic*, 4 vols., Leiden, vol. 1 beginning, pages not numbered.

Gordon, R. P. (1994), *Studies in the Targum of the Twelve Prophets from Nahum to Malachi*, Leiden.

Kasher, R. (1996), *Toseftot of Targum to the Prophets*, Sources for the Study of Jewish Culture 2, Jerusalem. [Hebrew]

Kasher, R. (2000), 'Eschatological ideas in the Toseftot Targum to the Prophets', *Journal for the Aramaic Bible*, 2: 25–59.

Kugel, J. L. (1994), *In Potiphar's House: The Interpretive Life of Biblical Text*, Cambridge, MA.

le Déaut, R. (1978), *Targum du Pentateuque*, I: *Genèse*, Sources Chrétiennes 245, Paris.

le Déaut, R. (1979), *Targum du Pentateuque*, III: *Nombres*, Sources Chrétiennes 261, Paris.

le Déaut, R. (1988), *Introduction à la littérature targumique*, Rome.

Levine, E. (1988), *The Aramaic Version of the Bible: Contents and Context*, Beihefte zur Zeitschrift für die alttestamentliche Wissenschaft 174, Berlin.

McNamara, M. (1972), *Targum and Testament*, Shannon, Ireland.

McNamara, M. and Clarke, E. G. (1995), *Targum Neofiti, 1. Numbers and Targum Pseudo-Jonathan: Numbers*, The Aramaic Bible 4, London.

Mendels, D. (1992), 'Pseudo-Philo's *Biblical Antiquities*, the Fourth Philosophy, and the political messianism of the first century CE', in J. H. Charlesworth (ed.), *The Messiah: Developments in Earliest Judaism and Christianity*, Minneapolis, pp. 261–75.

Mortensen, B. (2006), *The Priesthood in Targum Pseudo-Jonathan*, Studies in the Aramaic Interpretation of Scripture, 2 vols., Leiden.

Müller-Kessler, C. (2001), 'The earliest evidence for Targum Onqelos from Babylonia and the question of its dialect and origin', *Journal for the Aramaic Bible*, 3: 181–98.

Samely, A. (1992), *The Interpretation of Speech in the Pentateuchal Targums*, Tübingen.

Schürer, E. (1986), *The History of the Jewish People in the Age of Jesus Christ*, vol. 3.1, revised and ed. G. Vermes, F. Millar and M. Goodman, Edinburgh.

Shinan, A. (1992), 'The Aramaic Targum as a mirror of Galilean Jewry', in L. I. Levine (ed.), *The Galilee in Late Antiquity*, New York, pp. 241–51.

Shinan, A. (2006), 'The late Midrashic, Paytanic, and Targumic literature', in S. T. Katz (ed.), *The Cambridge History of Judaism*, vol. 4: *The Late Roman-Rabbinic Period*, Cambridge, pp. 678–98.

Smelik, W. (1995), *The Targum of Judges*, Oudtestamentische Studiën 36, Leiden.

Smolar, L. and Aberbach M. (1983), *Studies in Targum Jonathan to the Prophets, and Targum Jonathan to the Prophets by Pinkhos Churgin*, New York and Baltimore.

Stec, D. (2004), *The Targum of Psalms*, The Aramaic Bible 16, London.

Stemberger, G. (1996), *Introduction to the Talmud and Midrash*, 2nd edn., trans. and ed. M. Bockmuehl, Edinburgh.

Taradach, M. (1991), *Le Midrash: Introduction à la littérature midrashique*, La Monde de la Bible 22, Geneva.

van Staalduine-Sulman, E. (1993), 'The Aramaic Song of the Lamb', in J. C. de Moor and W. G. E. Watson (eds.), *Verse in Ancient Near Eastern Prose*, Alter Orient und Altes Testament 42, Neukirchen, pp. 265–92.

van Staalduine-Sulman, E. (2002), *The Targum of Samuel*, Studies in the Aramaic Interpretation of Scripture 1, Leiden.

Vermes, G. (1973), *Scripture and Tradition in Judaism*, 2nd revised edn., Leiden.

Vermes, G. (1975), *Post-Biblical Jewish Studies*, Leiden, pp. 59–165.

14

The Epistle of Sherira Gaon

ROBERT BRODY

THE EPISTLE OF SHERIRA GAON, WRITTEN IN 986 OR 987,[1] is an extraordinary instance of the genre of Geonic responsa. From at least the middle of the eighth century until the middle of the eleventh, one of the most important and characteristic activities of the leading talmudic academies of Babylonia, associated with the cities of Sura and Pumbedita (although eventually both relocated to Baghdad), was the composition of written responses to questions sent by individuals and communities scattered throughout the Jewish world of the time, but especially in North Africa and Spain. These questions could cover a considerable range of topics, but the overwhelming majority dealt either with talmudic exegesis or practical halakhic issues, or with a combination of the two. The responsa were issued by the Gaon or head of the academy on behalf of its senior scholars, although the extent of their actual input is unknown and probably varied according to circumstances. The collective nature of these writings is reflected *inter alia* in the convention which decreed that they be phrased in the plural, even when they contain personal references to the Gaon.[2]

Sherira's Epistle is exceptional both in terms of its length (approximately 15,000 words) and in terms of its subject matter. In fact it might be more accurate to describe it as a series of closely related responsa than as a single responsum. It addresses a number of questions formulated by Rabbi Nissim b. Jacob ibn Shahin on behalf of the scholars of Qayrawan (in present-day Tunisia), one of the most important Jewish communities and intellectual centres of the time. Most of the questions deal with talmudic literary history. These pay particular attention to the Mishnah, the central work of the rabbinic literary corpus, and to the interplay of tradition and redaction in the creation of this work, and then deal more concisely with other collections of tannaitic literature and with the Babylonian Talmud. Post-tannaitic

---

[1] The Epistle is dated to 1298 or 1299 of the Seleucid era, which began in 312 BCE (this system is also used for all the dates given within the text); see Lewin (1921: 2, 4 and n. 5 on p. 4).

[2] For a more detailed treatment of this genre see Brody (1998: 185–201) (and for Sherira's Epistle ibid., pp. 19–25).

Palestinian writings, including the Palestinian Talmud and many midrashim, are ignored. It is worth noting that the various elements of talmudic literature are conceived by the questioners, apparently quite unselfconsciously, as written works, and so the questions take the form: 'How was the Mishnah written? . . . and the Talmud—how was it written?' The final question is devoted primarily to the history of the post-talmudic period: 'and the Savoraic rabbis—how were they ordered after Ravina, and which heads of academies reigned after them, and how many years did they reign, from that time until now?' (Lewin 1921: 5–6). The nature of the questions reflects the intellectual breadth and curiosity which characterised the scholarly community of Qayrawan; some scholars have contended that these questions arose in the context of a Karaite challenge to rabbinic authority, but this is probably incorrect.[3]

The Epistle written in response to these questions conforms to Geonic convention and is written in the first person plural, but is primarily if not exclusively Sherira's work; at its very end it includes personal references to his own appointment as Gaon (in 968) and his appointment of his own son as deputy head of the academy two years before the composition of the Epistle. The structure of the answers is rather different from that of the questions which generated them: Almost half of the Epistle is devoted to the single, tersely worded question concerning post-talmudic history. Furthermore, the author saw fit to expand his response to this question beyond what had been asked, and begin his prosopographical survey with the beginnings of the period which saw the creation of the Babylonian Talmud rather than with its end, explaining: 'we have seen fit to explain the roots of this matter, and how the leadership of Israel was [organised] previously, and how the two academies separated, because there is erroneous information [circulating] with regard to this matter.'[4] The work is written primarily in Aramaic but some passages are in Hebrew, in addition to many citations in Hebrew from classical rabbinic literature.

Sherira's Epistle circulated widely in the Middle Ages and served as a central source for historians and others interested in the development of talmudic literature and the history of rabbinic learning in Babylonia in the talmudic and Geonic periods.[5] Surviving manuscripts belong to two distinct

---

[3] For the Karaite theory see Lewin (1921: pp. v–x). In fact it appears there was no Karaite presence in Qayrawan at this time, but there was considerable intellectual curiosity; see Ben-Sasson (1996: 41–6).

[4] Lewin (1921: 72). The answers to the questions concerning literary history occupy pp. 7–71 of this edition while the answer to the final question occupies pp. 72–122.

[5] Other influential works dealing with these periods are largely dependent on the Epistle and have very little independent value, see e.g. Brody (1998: 12 (with nn. 39–40), 31). The major exception (for the talmudic period only, and with very little on the Savora'im) is *Seder Tanna'im ve-Amora'im*; see pp. 257–8 and n. 15 below.

recensions; in addition to numerous minor differences in wording and the like, there are quite substantial differences between them in many passages. The most striking and well-known difference concerns the issue of oral versus written transmission of rabbinic literature. As noted above, the questioners assume that the various works of talmudic literature were written *ab initio*. The two recensions of the response differ in this regard: one preserves many of the references to writing, while the other consistently discusses the redaction and transmission of the rabbinic corpora in language which does not imply the use of writing. Halberstam and Hazzan, writing about 1860, developed an elaborate theory according to which the versions of the Epistle which speak of written texts represent a 'Spanish recension', which is to be preferred to the 'French recension' found in the other versions; in this they were followed by Lewin in his edition of the Epistle.[6] However, there is now a clear scholarly consensus that this assessment is incorrect, and the so-called French recension is generally preferable to the so-called Spanish recension. In fact, neither of these designations is appropriate in terms of the provenance of the manuscripts; the earlier theory was based on very shaky assumptions about the versions of the Epistle which were consulted by medieval writers in these lands. All known Genizah fragments of the Epistle belong to the 'French' recension, while the 'Spanish' version is clearly derivative at many points (and sometimes based on a misunderstanding of the original), as well as being inconsistent on the issue of oral versus written transmission of Talmudic texts, as outlined above.[7] In a few places the 'Spanish' version appears prima facie to be preferable; these require further investigation but do not affect issues of substance.[8]

Leaving aside late manuscripts which were probably copied from printed editions, there are eight or nine known manuscripts which contain all, or at least very substantial parts, of the Epistle, as well as the *editio princeps* (Constantinople 1566).[9] Probably the earliest of these, and one of the most

---

[6] See Schlüter (1993: 17 and nn. 5–6); Lewin (1921: pp. xlvii–lxxi).

[7] See Elbogen (1929); Epstein (1962: 610–15); Lewin (1921: p. xliv) and (on the issue of oral and written transmission) especially ibid., pp. 71–2, and Abramson (1989).

[8] For cases in which the 'Spanish' recension is prima facie to be preferred to the 'French' recension see e.g. Lewin (1921: p. 14 lines 12–13, p. 15 lines 5–8, p. 45 lines 11–12, and p. 67 line 21–p. 68 line 1). In a few instances it appears that both recensions display the same erroneous reading, suggesting that they derive from a common ancestor later than the original text. See ibid., p. 106 line 9, with Lewin's n. 2 ad loc. (the 'Spanish' recension seems to have made several changes to the text in the next few lines in an attempt to deal with the resulting difficulties); ibid., p. 31 and n. 3; and cf. p. 257 and n. 12 below.

[9] For descriptions of the *editio princeps* and the manuscripts see Lewin (1921: pp. xvii–xliv) and Schlüter (1993: 24–9) (facsimiles of MS Berlin and the *editio princeps* are published ibid., pp. 4*–70*). In addition to these manuscripts, the computerised catalogue of the Institute of Microfilmed Hebrew Manuscripts at the Jewish National and University Library (Jerusalem) lists two very late manuscripts: Jewish Theological Seminary (New York) 1806, dated to the

reliable, is Berlin MS Or. Qu. 685, in a tenth- or eleventh-century German or Italian hand, which includes the Epistle in a *mélange* of texts including many other Geonic responsa. Most of the other manuscripts probably date to the thirteenth to seventeenth centuries; their provenance ranges from Spain to Franco-Germany. There are also more than fifteen fragments in various Genizah collections, some of which may be sorted into groups deriving from single manuscripts; their probable dates range from the eleventh to the thirteenth century.[10]

All previous editions of the Epistle were superseded by Lewin's edition of 1921, which has been reproduced several times. This is the only edition to date which can be described as critical, although the text certainly deserves to be re-edited. Lewin made use of all the known larger manuscripts and most of the known Genizah fragments, and presented the text in parallel columns representing the 'French' and 'Spanish' recensions, choosing the *editio princeps* as the base text for the 'Spanish' version and MS Aleppo, a sixteenth-century Spanish manuscript now owned by the Jewish National and University Library of Jerusalem, as the basis for the 'French' version. Nevertheless, both recensions are presented in eclectic versions; some of the editor's corrections are indicated by the use of brackets and parentheses while others are indicated only in his notes. There are some problems with the assignment of particular manuscripts to one or the other recension (see Epstein 1962: 615) and other difficulties with regard to the presentation of manuscript readings, in addition to the fact that not all the Genizah fragments were utilised. Probably the most serious shortcoming of this edition, however, is its editor's adherence to the now discredited theory that the 'Spanish' recension is generally to be preferred, which led him astray in quite a few of his notes, despite his vast erudition in Geonic and rabbinic literature.

Translations of the Epistle into Hebrew and Latin, each based on a single manuscript, were published in the mid-nineteenth century.[11] There are three relatively recent translations: N. D. Rabinowich published an English translation based on Lewin's 'Spanish recension' (Rabinowich 1988) and followed this with a Hebrew translation based on Lewin's 'French recension' (Rabinowich 1991). The English translation, in addition to being based on an inferior version of the original, is quite periphrastic and betrays a failure to

---

seventeenth or eighteenth century, and London Or. 10242 of the nineteenth century, which is described as copied from a printed edition.

[10] See Lewin (1921: pp. xliv–xlv); Schlüter (1993: 28); and Brody (2000: 76, n. 8). On the basis of the catalogue mentioned in the previous note we may add two fragments from the John Rylands Library (Manchester) Genizah collection: A 1152 and B 4573.

[11] See Lewin (1921: pp. xxv–xxviii) and Schlüter (1993: 21–3) who also describes an abridged Hebrew version of the earlier twentieth century, a French translation (1904) and several translations of excerpts into English.

understand the author's Aramaic idiom in a number of places; the subsequent Hebrew version corrects the most egregious errors of the English translation and is based on a sounder Aramaic text, but still leaves a good deal to be desired. A scrupulously careful German translation, which presents the two recensions in parallel columns and notes many variant readings, is included in Schlüter (1993: 43–282).

Sherira made use of a variety of sources in composing his Epistle, and not all of these can be identified with confidence. We will touch briefly on four types of source material which he utilised. (1) Talmudic sources, primarily selections from the Babylonian Talmud, figure very prominently throughout most of the Epistle (excluding the last sections which deal with the Savoraic and Geonic periods). Sometimes the author identifies the tractate, and sometimes the chapter, from which a given passage is cited; on other occasions he does not (and on some of these occasions copyists or the editor of the first edition provided more detailed references). Several citations are abbreviated in similar fashion in all available texts of the Epistle; these abbreviations may go back to the author himself or to a very early copyist.[12] Once Sherira cites the Palestinian Talmud, without informing his readers of his source; this citation gave rise to a later question addressed to him, asking what source he had quoted.[13] (The questioners' imperfect knowledge of the Palestinian Talmud, as contrasted with their impressive familiarity with the Babylonian Talmud, accords well with the fact noted above, that their questions on the development of talmudic literature completely ignore the Palestinian Talmud as well as contemporaneous and later works of Palestinian rabbinic literature, and refer to the Babylonian Talmud as 'the Talmud' pure and simple.) (2) Sherira clearly depended to a large extent on non-talmudic chronological (and perhaps historical?) sources, especially to provide the backbone of the second, prosopographical half of his essay. He only refers explicitly to his use of written sources twice, with regard to a single event in the fifth century and a brief survey of events in the early sixth century CE.[14] However, it is abundantly clear that he depends on similar records for the chronology of the amoraic and Geonic periods; elsewhere I have attempted to show that his chief source for the chronology of the amoraic period, which was utilised also (in a different copy) by the somewhat earlier work known as *Seder Tanna'im ve-Amora'im*, consisted primarily of a list of the death dates of prominent rabbis, with occasional references to other events which affected the Jewish community of Bablyonia, and offered some conjectures as to the

---

[12] Lewin (1921: 23, 55, 63, 66 and cf. 21, 46).

[13] See ibid., pp. 76–7 and pp. xi–xii of the appendices. For a possible second citation of the Palestinian Talmud see ibid., p. 20 and n. 8.

[14] Ibid., pp. 96 and 97–9 (including what appears to be a verbatim citation from the beginning of p. 98 to the beginning of p. 99).

provenance of this source.[15] (3) Sherira made use on a number of occasions
of oral traditions of various sorts; some of these were apparently current in
Babylonian (perhaps specifically in Pumbeditan) academic circles, while others were part of his family lore. As we shall see below, a central conundrum
with regard to the Epistle is the extent to which its author may have been
dependent on such oral traditions in other passages in which he makes no
explicit mention of them. It is worth noting that although Sherira mentions
such traditions only a few times, he uses a variety of expressions in doing so,
and it appears that some of these are chosen in order to distance himself
from particular traditions and hint at some scepticism about their contents,
while other traditions are cited without qualification.[16] (4) Finally, Sherira
refers a number of times to data which were apparently common knowledge
(or at least common belief) in his milieu, especially with regard to the location of buildings associated with various amora'im, for example, 'we have
heard ... that ... Rab Huna bar Ḥiyya reigned in Pumbedita, and he now
has a large house of study there.'[17]

Sherira's Epistle has served for the last millennium as a point of depar-
ture for virtually all investigations of talmudic literary history and of the history of the Jews of Babylonia from the third through the tenth centuries, but
questions of various sorts have been raised as to its reliability. On the one
hand, Sherira shows a laudable degree of caution in his approach—not only
does he hint at his reservations concerning the accuracy of some of the traditions he cites, as noted above; sometimes he explicitly admits the limits of
his knowledge. For example, he states that the Tosefta was obviously redacted
after the publication of the Mishnah, but 'we are not certain' whether during
the lifetime of Rabbi Judah the Patriarch or after his death; and on a broader
scale, he states that he has only fragmentary information as to the history of
the Sura academy in the earlier part of the Geonic period: 'And in all these
years, the Geonim who were in Meḥasia—we do not know them clearly and
in order' (Lewin 1921: 105). On the other hand, the Epistle contains a few
rather clear errors, both with regard to literary history and to
institutional/prosopographical history;[18] Sherira was of course not a 'profes-

[15] Brody (2000); the best available edition of *Seder Tanna'im ve-Amora'im* is Kahan (1935). A
new edition is long overdue and some central questions concerning the text have yet to be
resolved; see Brody (1998: 274–7).
[16] See Lewin (1921: 60, 71 (twice), 83–4, 86, 92–3 (clearly a family tradition although not explicitly labelled as such), 98, 99), and cf. pp. 261–2 below.
[17] Ibid., p. 86; cf. ibid., pp. 73, 84. For more purely geographic knowledge, see ibid., pp. 70, 71,
73, 89.
[18] With regard to literary history see Albeck (1969: 21–4), and compare Epstein (1948: 983–8) as
contrasted with the strained explanations offered by Sherira, Lewin (1921: 33). For examples of
chronological errors see Brody (1987; 2000: 84–6). On the other hand, I believe some scholars
have been far too sceptical towards the chronological data contained in the Epistle; in my

sional' historian, and his work can certainly not be taken as an unimpeachable guide to talmudic or Geonic history, despite its author's credentials and bona fides.

Furthermore, one should take note of a number of apologetic tendencies which find expression in the Epistle. Sherira goes to considerable lengths to present an idealised portrait of the state of rabbinic learning during the Second Temple period, which is described as a golden age of nearly total consensus and widespread knowledge, while the manifold disputes which are such a characteristic element of rabbinic literature are said to reflect a process of decline. Even if Sherira's questioners were untroubled by Karaite critiques of rabbinic tradition and authority, Sherira was sensitive to the threat presented by the Karaite challenge and took this opportunity to engage in tacit polemics. Similarly, he lays great stress at several points on the antiquity of rabbinic learning and tradition in Babylonia, in a way which almost certainly reflects the ongoing struggle between the Palestinian and Babylonian centres for influence in the Jewish world, which had not been completely resolved in his day, as well as the threat to the dominant position of the Babylonian academies presented by the emergence of important centres of rabbinic learning remote from Babylonia and Palestine. Furthermore, within the world of Babylonian rabbinic Jewry there are clear indications of Sherira's identification specifically with the academy of Pumbedita, as against the competing institutions of the exilarchate and the Sura academy, both of which, according to Sherira, were essentially defunct by the time he wrote his Epistle. And finally, even when he is describing internal conflicts within one or the other Geonic academy, Sherira's preferences are usually clear.[19]

Leaving aside these issues of authorial *Tendenz* which it is relatively easy to isolate, questions arise both in terms of identifying the sources underlying Sherira's history and with regard to his use of these sources. Despite the fact that his non-talmudic chronological sources are not extant, and that some of his chronological data have been questioned on the basis of other sources, I believe that it is possible to reconstruct Sherira's main source for amoraic

---

opinion Gafni (1987) convincingly refutes the approach taken by Neusner (1965–70) and Goodblatt (1975); see especially the formulation of Goodblatt's position ibid., pp. 38–9, cited by Gafni (1987: 2–3, n. 10), and with regard to a later period see Brody (1986: 290–4).

[19] The antiquity of the Oral Law and the idea that the need to provide official formulations of its contents reflects a process of decay figure prominently in the first part of the Epistle, see especially Lewin (1921: 7–11, 21–3, 68–9). For the antiquity and importance of Babylonia as a centre of rabbinic learning see especially ibid., pp. 40–1, 72–4, and more subtly ibid., pp. 47, 59, 76–9. For Sherira's Pumbeditan bias see Brody (1998: 25 and n. 23); for the (temporary) demise of the Sura academy see Lewin (1921: 116–18); and for the competition between the academies and the exilarchate see Brody (1998: 75–82). For Sherira's expressions of a preference for one faction or another within a Geonic academy, see Lewin (1921: 109, 113, 119–21), and cf. ibid., p. 118.

chronology and to argue convincingly that this was a contemporary and quite reliable source, despite occasional errors in its transmission.[20] Similarly, there is no reason to question the accuracy of the chronological sources which Sherira utilised for later periods, with very few exceptions, and some of his data may be confirmed from other sources.[21]

More troubling questions arise with respect to Sherira's use of talmudic sources and oral traditions. In particular, to what extent is his presentation of talmudic literary history and the history of the talmudic period dependent on the talmudic sources which he cites? To what extent, if any, did he possess genuine extra-talmudic traditions concerning the talmudic period? In a somewhat paradoxical formulation one might say that the evidentiary weight of Sherira's statements is almost inversely proportional to the extent to which they are supported by the Talmud itself: when Sherira repeats an explicit talmudic datum, it seems quite likely that he derived it from the obvious talmudic source and his citation adds nothing; but when he makes a claim which cannot possibly have been derived from talmudic sources (for example, with regard to the date of death of an amora) we are forced to believe that he is dependent on other sources of information to which we have no direct access. The difficulty is in assessing the grey areas which lie somewhere on the spectrum spanning these extremes: that is, cases in which Sherira could conceivably have arrived at a given position by a particular understanding of talmudic sources but this understanding is not entirely straightforward. Is it better in such cases to assume that we are able to identify Sherira's talmudic source and his use of it, which we may then accept or reject, or to suppose that he had at his disposal other sources which are not available to us and which we probably lack the means to critique? This question arises even in cases in which Sherira cites a talmudic source—it is possible, as argued especially by Abramson, that many of Sherira's talmudic sources are cited for rhetorical purposes, for example, to buttress his positions by reference to sources with which his readers were familiar and which they considered authoritative, but in actual fact the positions he took were based on academic traditions and not on these literary sources.

Sometimes it is clear that a talmudic source which Sherira cites functions only as a sort of decorative flourish or at most a partial confirmation of statements which are actually based on other sources. For example, consider the following passage (Lewin 1921: 89–90, citing b.Shevuot 48b):

[20] See n. 18 above and Brody (2000: esp. 84–6).

[21] For an isolated example of a chronological error, and a suggested explanation, see Brody (1987). Sherira's data on the chronology of events during the Geonic period can be confirmed, directly or indirectly, in several instances. See especially Mann (1921), and cf. Brody (1986: 304–5).

And after R. Naḥman b. Isaac there reigned several Geonim: Rab Ḥama in Nehardea, and he died in the year 688 [Seleucid = 376/7 CE]. And this is what we say in [the Talmudic chapter] 'all who swear': A certain judge acted in accordance with the opinion of R. Elazar. There was a disciple of the rabbis in his place. He said to him: I will go to the academy and bring a letter [stating] that the law does not follow R. Elazar. He came before Rab Ḥama . . .

Sherira might have deduced from the talmudic passage he cites that a certain Rab Ḥama, who lived no earlier than R. Elazar, was the head of an academy, and Rab Ḥama's connection with Nehardea is clear from other talmudic passages, as is the approximate time of his floruit, but the passage cited says nothing about his date or location, and there is no conceivable way of concluding on the basis of any talmudic passage that he died in 376/7. Sherira merely asserts that this talmudic passage refers to the same Rab Ḥama about whom he knows certain facts from other sources. There are other instances in which Sherira makes a statement about a particular sage, invoking neither a talmudic source nor a tradition, in which it seems overwhelmingly likely that he was dependent on extra-talmudic tradition, for example, when he asserts that the primary scene of Rab Sheshet's activity was the village of Shilḥi.[22]

Furthermore, it appears that Sherira was well aware of the pitfalls of deriving historical information from talmudic sources in a simplistic manner, as illustrated by the following case (Lewin 1921: 34–5, citing b.Ḥagigah 3a):

And as for the Tosefta, certainly R. Ḥiyya arranged it, but we are not certain whether [he did so] in the days of Rabbi [Judah the Patriarch] or after him . . . but the rabbis say that [the?] baraitot were arranged in the days of Rabbi and they were taught in his house of study, from this [story related in tractate] Ḥagigah, that there were certain mutes in Rabbi's neighborhood . . . whenever Rabbi entered the house of study they would enter and sit before him and their lips would move. Rabbi sought mercy [i.e. prayed] for them and they were cured, and it was found that they had learned laws, Sifra, Sifre, Tosefta, and Talmud.

Sherira dissociates himself from those rabbis (were they his predecessors or contemporaries?) who took this story as evidence that the collections of tannaitic sources named here were actually compiled during the lifetime of Rabbi Judah the Patriarch. Perhaps he was dissuaded by the fact that this story also claims the men in question had learned Talmud, although Sherira asserts (correctly) that when the term 'Talmud' appears in the Talmud it

---

[22] See Lewin (1921: 82) and Albeck (1969: 312) (although of course it is not inconceivable that Sherira was familiar with a version of some talmudic passage which gave this information). Cf. the assertion that Rab Dimi was originally Babylonian (Lewin 1921: 61 and Albeck 1969: 358). Consider also the assertion (Lewin 1921: 78) that Rab was many years older than Samuel: this could be a conjecture based on the talmudic passage cited ibid., pp. 78–9 and on the fact (ibid., pp. 81–2) that Rab died seven years before Samuel, but I find this explanation somewhat implausible.

cannot refer to this literary work, but rather to a genre which existed much before the compilation of 'the Talmud'. On the other hand, it seems clear that Sherira's scholarly caution did not grant him immunity against similar pitfalls, as when he states that 'the head of the rabbis in Babylonia was called *resh sidra* [. . .] and he [Rab] was called *resh sidra*, as R. Yoḥanan said to Asi b. Hani: who is the *resh sidra* in Babylonia? He said to him: Abba Arikha' (Lewin 1921: 78, 80 based on b.Hullin 137b). In fact this was, in all probability, a Palestinian term which R. Yoḥanan the Palestinian used in asking about the situation in Babylonia.[23]

Ultimately it seems to me that in many instances we have no way of determining for certain whether what Sherira has to say reflects his interpretation of talmudic sources or his use of independent sources, presumably oral traditions; nor of assessing the reliability of any such traditions which he may have had.[24] I will conclude with an example which illustrates this quandary and bears on a much debated topic:[25]

> And they, Rab and Samuel, had two academies, for we say in [the chapter] 'one who brings a writ of divorce': Babylonia—Rab says it is like the land of Israel with regard to writs of divorce, and Samuel says—like the diaspora. And we explain that Rab thought that since there are academies, [witnesses] are to be found, but Samuel thought that the [scholars of the] academies are preoccupied with their recitations.

Did Sherira have other reasons for believing that Rab and Samuel served as the heads of academies, implying that such institutions (whatever their precise structure may have been) existed already in their generation? Or did he naively accept the interpretation of the anonymous voice in the talmudic passage as conveying historical facts, while ignoring the possibility of anachronism? I believe that in this and many other instances there is no way to know for sure; historians must exercise their best judgement but consensus will be difficult if not impossible to attain.

[23] See Goodblatt (1975: 41–2) and the literature cited there.

[24] It seems to me there is no good reason to question some of the traditions which he cites explicitly, while Sherira himself hints at his lack of faith in others. See above, p. 258 and n. 16, p. 261 and n. 22.

[25] Lewin (1921: 81), based on b.Gittin 6a; cf. Gafni (2008). For the possibility that Sherira hinted at his own doubts on this question, and some relevant talmudic data, see Brody (2000: 104–7); for the most recent treatment of issues relating to the existence of academies in the talmudic period, with bibliography and a summary of scholarly discussions of these topics, see Goodblatt (2006).

Further Reading

Beer (1967); Brody (1987, 2000); Lewin (1921); Schlüter (1993).

Bibliography

Abramson, Sh. (1989), 'Writing the Mishnah (according to the *Geonim* and *Rishonim*)', in M. Ben-Sasson, R. Bonfil and J. R. Hacker (eds.), *Culture and Society in Medieval Jewry: Studies Dedicated to the Memory of Haim Hillel Ben-Sasson*, Jerusalem. [Hebrew]

Abramson, Sh. (forthcoming), *Studies in Geonic Literature*, Jerusalem. [Hebrew]

Albeck, Ch. (1969), *Introduction to the Talmud: Babli and Yerushalmi*, Tel Aviv. [Hebrew]

Beer, M. (1967), 'The sources of Rav Sherira Gaon's Igeret', *Bar-Ilan Annual*, 4–5: 181–96. [Hebrew]

Ben-Sasson, M. (1996), *The Emergence of the Local Jewish Community in the Muslim World: Qayrawan, 800–1057*, Jerusalem. [Hebrew]

Brody, R. (1986), 'Were the Geonim legislators?', *Shenaton ha-Mishpat ha-Ivri*, 11–12: 279–315. [Hebrew]

Brody, R. (1987), 'Amram bar Sheshna: Gaon of Sura?', *Tarbiz*, 56: 327–45. [Hebrew]

Brody, R. (1998), *The Geonim of Babylonia and the Shaping of Medieval Jewish Culture*, New Haven and London.

Brody, R. (2000), 'On the sources for the chronology of the Talmudic period', *Tarbiz*, 70: 75–107. [Hebrew]

Elbogen, I. (1929), 'Wie steht es um die zwei Rezensionen des Scherira-Briefes?', in *Festschrift zum 75 jährigen Bestehen des jüdisch-theologischen Seminars*, Breslau, II, Deutscher Teil, pp. 61–84.

Epstein, J. N. (1948), *Introduction to the Text of the Mishnah*, Jerusalem. [Hebrew]

Epstein, J. N. (1962), *Introduction to Amoraic Literature: Babylonian Talmud and Yerushalmi*, Jerusalem and Tel Aviv.

Gafni, I. (1987), 'On the Talmudic chronology in *Iggeret Rav Sherira Gaon*', *Zion*, 52: 1–24. [Hebrew]

Gafni, I. (2008), 'Talmudic historiography in the Epistle of Rav Sherira Gaon: between tradition and creation', *Zion*, 73: 271–96.

Goodblatt, D. M. (1975), *Rabbinic Instruction in Sasanian Babylonia*, Leiden.

Goodblatt, D. (2006), 'The history of the Babylonian academies', in S. T. Katz (ed.), *The Cambridge History of Judaism*, vol. 4: *The Late Roman-Rabbinic Period*, Cambridge, pp. 821–39.

Kahan, K. (1935), *Seder Tannaim we-Amoraim . . ., bearbeitet, übersetzt, mit Einleitung und erklärenden Noten versehen*, Frankfurt am Main.

Lewin, B. M. (1909), 'Das Sendschreiben des Rabbi Scherira Gaon', *Jahrbuch der Jüdisch-Literarischen Gesellschaft*, 7: 226–92.

Lewin, B. M. (1921), *Iggeret Rav Sherira Gaon*, Haifa. [Hebrew]

Mann, J. (1921), 'A Fihrist of Sa'adya's works', *JQR* n.s. 11: 423–8.

Neusner, J. (1965–70), *A History of the Jews in Babylonia*, Leiden.

Rabinowich, N. D. (1988), *The Iggeres of Rav Sherira Gaon*, Jerusalem.

Rabinowich, N. D. (1991), *The Iggeres of Rav Sherira Gaon*, Jerusalem. [Hebrew]
Schlüter, M. (1993), *Auf welche Weise wurde die Mishna geschrieben? Das Antwortschreiben des Rav Sherira Gaon*, Tübingen.

15

Hekhalot Literature and the Origins of Jewish Mysticism

PETER SCHÄFER

WITH THE TERM MERKAVAH MYSTICISM, scholars refer to that unique and enigmatic complex of traditions that revolve around God's divine chariot (*merkavah*) and focus on the ascent of a mystic[1] through the seven heavens and heavenly palaces to God's throne. The individual undertaking the ascent is designated *yored (la-) merkavah*, that is, literally, one who 'descends to the Merkavah'.[2] The literature in which these traditions are preserved is called Hekhalot literature, a term that alludes, not coincidentally, to the architecture of the earthly Temple (where the *hekhal* refers to the entrance hall to the Holy of Holies). A genre all its own, this literature presents an extremely fluctuating and complex set of different, competing, and even conflicting ideas that cannot and must not be forced into the Procrustean bed of a harmonious synthesis. Only at a later stage was it developed into more or less fixed 'works' with fancy (and varying) titles assigned to them.[3]

The most important 'works' or 'macroforms' are—in the order that best expresses the most likely internal chronological sequence of the Hekhalot literature—Hekhalot Rabbati ('The Greater Hekhalot'), Hekhalot Zutarti ('The Lesser Hekhalot'), Ma'aseh Merkavah ('The Work of the Merkavah'), Merkavah Rabbah ('The Great Merkavah'), and 3 Enoch (Schäfer 1992: 7ff.). Macroforms whose affiliation with the Hekhalot literature in the strict sense of the word is contested are *Re'uyyot Yehezkel* ('The Visions of Ezekiel') and *Massekhet Hekhalot* ('The Tractate of the Hekhalot'). Much of this literature contains not only ascent accounts of the Merkavah mystics but also eminently magical sections in which angels are adjured by magical tools; moreover, even the ascent accounts are often peppered with magical adjurations.

---

[1] I am using the words 'mysticism' and 'mystic' continuously in imagined quotation marks.

[2] On the reversed terminology—one would expect 'ascend' instead of 'descend'—see Kuyt (1995); Schäfer (1992: 2f., n. 4); Wolfson (1993; 1994a: 82–5).

[3] I have suggested avoiding the term 'work' and instead using the terms 'macroforms' and 'microforms' (Schäfer 1988: 199ff.; 1992: 6, n. 14).

Proceedings of the British Academy **165**, 265–280. © The British Academy 2010.

Numerous Hekhalot manuscripts have survived, with a clear predominance of the macroforms Hekhalot Rabbati and 3 Enoch.[4] The seven most important Hekhalot manuscripts (i.e. manuscripts that contain more than just one macroform) are published in the *Synopse zur Hekhalot-Literatur*; the Genizah fragments known until 1984 are published in *Geniza-Fragmente zur Hekhalot-Literatur*. Most of the comprehensive Hekhalot manuscripts are of German (Ashkenazi) provenance and were filtered through a rather aggressive editorial process (Ta-Shma 1985; Dan 1987). The oldest comprehensive manuscript is the Ashkenazi manuscript Oxford 1531 (early fourteenth century?) (Schäfer ed. 1981: p. ix); the oldest known Genizah fragment is T.-S. K 21.95.S (before the ninth century CE).[5] MS New York 8128 (around 1500) merits particular attention (and caution) because it was submitted to a notably vigorous magical redaction by Ashkenazi scholars (Herrmann and Rohrbacher-Sticker 1989, 1992).

The *Synopse zur Hekhalot-Literatur* (Schäfer ed. 1981) and the *Geniza-Fragmente zur Hekhalot-Literatur* (Schäfer ed. 1984) have become the standard editions of the Hekhalot literature;[6] on the methodology involved, see Schäfer (ed. 1981: pp. v–vi); Halperin (1984); Davila (1994); Abrams (1996); Boustan (2007a: 147ff.). The only complete translation available is in German (Schäfer, Herrmann 1987–95); for a concordance, see Schäfer (ed. 1986–88). A comprehensive English translation of the Hekhalot corpus is in preparation.

The date and provenance of the Hekhalot literature is still a highly contested matter, with views ranging from the early rabbinic (tannaitic) period to the late rabbinic or even post-rabbinic era. Most scholars agree, however, that the *circles* of mystics behind the literature originated in Palestine, whereas the Hekhalot *literature* took shape in talmudic and post-talmudic Babylonia (Schäfer 1992: 160; Boustan 2007b: 18ff.). The relationship of the Hekhalot literature's heroes with the rabbis is disputed, though scholars who opt for an early origin of the 'movement' are inclined to identify certain rabbis (Ishmael, Akiva, Neḥunyah b. ha-Kanah) as the earliest propagators of Merkavah mysticism (Scholem 1974: 40ff.; 1965: 14ff.), whereas scholars who opt for a later origin regard the rabbinic attributions as pseudepigraphic (Schäfer 1986; 1988: 293; 1992: 159). Attempts to uncover the original mystical circles behind the literature (e.g. Halperin 1988: 437ff.; Swartz 1996: 209ff.; Davila

---

[4] For a comprehensive catalogue of the Hekhalot manuscripts, see Schäfer (1983, 1988); Herrmann (1994: 22–65).

[5] Schäfer (ed. 1984: 10). Some of the Genizah fragments antedate the mid-eleventh century, but many of them are considerably later.

[6] The standard editions of *Re'uyyot Yeḥezkel* and *Massekhet Hekhalot* are Gruenwald (1972) and Herrmann (1994).

2001) have not led us very far. The practitioners of the ascent and the socio-historical grounding of their 'experiences' have largely eluded us.[7]

The Hekhalot literature, with its peculiar literary character, fails to provide us with any reliable information regarding the history of Roman Palestine. What has been extensively discussed, however, is the question as to whether Merkavah mysticism can be regarded as the first phase of Jewish mysticism and hence a precursor of early Christian and later medieval Jewish mysticism (Kabbalah). In what follows I will briefly discuss certain definitions of mysticism and then address the question of ancient Jewish mysticism by surveying the various stages of that alleged first phase of Jewish mysticism. I will begin with Merkavah mysticism and move backward through rabbinic Judaism to Qumran and the apocalyptic literature.[8]

Definitions

Any attempt to find a generally acceptable definition of 'mysticism' is hopeless. There is no such thing as a universally recognised definition of mysticism, just as there is no such thing as a universally recognised phenomenon of mysticism or notion of mystical experience. Mystical experiences differ widely from culture to culture; the particular cultural and religious conventions within which a mystic lives make his or her mystical experience culturally specific.

For heuristic purposes, I will present two definitions that are highly characteristic and useful for our purpose. The first is by Gershom Scholem, the founding father of the academic discipline 'Jewish Mysticism', and the second is the most recent one by Philip Alexander. Scholem, in the introductory chapter to his soon to become famous *Major Trends in Jewish Mysticism* (first published in 1941) asks, almost despairingly: '[W]hat is Jewish mysticism? What precisely is meant by this term? Is there such a thing, and if so, what distinguishes it from other kinds of mystical experience?' (Scholem 1974: 3). To answer, he first summarises what we know about mysticism in general and then rejects two of the major presuppositions of many definitions of mysticism. The first is the notion of *unio mystica*, the individual's mystical union with God. This term, he posits, 'has no particular significance' in mysticism in general and in Jewish mysticism in particular: 'Numerous mystics, Jews as well as non-Jews, have by no means represented the essence

---

[7] For an excellent survey of current research on Hekhalot literature and Merkavah mysticism in general, see the introduction in Boustan (Abusch) (2005: 1ff.), and the updated summary in Boustan (2007a: 130ff.).

[8] These remarks are a condensed summary of some of the results presented in my book *The Origins of Jewish Mysticism*, Tübingen, 2009.

of their ecstatic experience, the tremendous uprush and soaring of the soul to its highest plane, as a union with God' (Scholem 1974: 5). The second rather useless presupposition is the assumption that 'the whole of what we call mysticism is identical with that personal experience which is realized in the state of ecstasy or ecstatic meditation' (Scholem ibid.). So, although within certain strands of mysticism we do find mystical union and ecstasy, they are useless as parameters in defining mysticism and Jewish mysticism alike. What remains is mysticism as a historical phenomenon, to be described and analysed within the framework of other religious phenomena and, moreover, in different and changing historical contexts (Scholem 1974: 5f.). Hence, ultimately, according to Scholem, there is not much to be gained from definitions of mysticism. Everything depends on the concrete historical circumstances of certain phenomena.

Philip Alexander has been somewhat more forthcoming. He believes that, '[a]lthough there is no mysticism per se, it is possible to isolate a number of abstract ideas which seem to be shared by the different concrete mystical traditions'—the most important of which are the following:

1. Mysticism arises from the religious *experience* of a transcendent divine presence beyond and behind the visible, material world and called 'God' in the monotheistic religions.
2. The mystic, who becomes aware of this transcendent presence, is filled with a desire for a closer relationship with it. In theistic systems this desire is described as *communion*, whereas in pantheistic systems it is described as *union*.
3. Mysticism always demands a *via mystica*, a way by which the mystic sets out to achieve union/communion with the divine (Alexander 2006: 8f.).

There is much to be said in favour of such a broad definition—though it is not without its problems. First, we immediately notice Alexander's emphasis on the *experience* of the mystic and his or her *mystical union* with the divine, precisely the two aspects that Scholem singled out but found not particularly useful in determining the essence of mysticism. Yet Alexander introduces a very important distinction between 'union' and 'communion' with the divine, the former being reserved for pantheistic and the latter for theistic systems. But by adding that, 'In actual fact the language of union in the strictest sense is common also in the theisms' (Alexander 2006: 8), he blurs that distinction. In other words, he wishes to keep that cherished *unio mystica* as the ultimate determinant of all three monotheistic religions, including Judaism.

Second, the broadness of Alexander's definition is both its strength and its weakness. For what then distinguishes 'mysticism' from 'religion'? Isn't the experience of a transcendent divine presence and the desire for a closer relationship with it characteristic of religion in general, and not just its mystical offshoot? So doesn't such a sweeping definition of mysticism in fact run the risk of confusing religion with mysticism? It would seem that indeed the question of mystical union in the strict sense of the word—not just as communion—constitutes the bone of contention for determining the mystical character of a religion. For mystical union of a human being with the divine, unlike communion, entails a transformation of the human self that ultimately brings about the absorption or even dissolution of the human in the divine, in other words, his or her divinisation. There can be no doubt that the desire for a mystical union of the human with the divine becomes manifest in medieval Christianity (in particular Christian monasticism) and probably also penetrates certain strands of the Kabbalah (Abraham Abulafia); but the problem remains whether it is legitimate to use this category for ancient and late-antique Judaism or whether it reads back into ancient Judaism aspects of mysticism for which the earliest evidence is in fact medieval.

Ancient Jewish Mysticism

The problem of conflating later characteristics of mysticism with ancient Judaism notwithstanding, Scholem and all his contemporary followers are convinced that Jewish mysticism indeed begins in antiquity. In *Major Trends in Jewish Mysticism*, Scholem opens his broad survey of the topic with a chapter on Merkavah mysticism. For him, Merkavah mysticism is the first fully-fledged mystical system in Judaism, originating in Palestine in the second century CE and developing over several centuries. It did not come out of the blue, however, but had its roots in early rabbinic Judaism (the period of the tanna'im, in particular R. Ishmael and R. Akiva) and in the apocalyptic literature of Second Temple Judaism (Scholem 1974: 40ff.). Scholem's legacy has been programmatically taken up by Rachel Elior, who sets out to fill the conspicuous gap left by Scholem—the literature of the Qumran community, which wasn't yet available when Scholem wrote his *Major Trends*—and who wishes to see in that peculiar amalgam of Enochic and Qumranic literature (less so rabbinic Judaism) the hotbed from which Jewish mysticism grew (Elior 2004). Recently Philip Alexander has categorically declared: 'There *was* mysticism at Qumran. . . . This mysticism was the historical forerunner of later Jewish Heikhalot mysticism, and should now be integrated into the history of Jewish mysticism' (Alexander 2006: p. vii; Alexander's emphasis).

Merkavah Mysticism

In determining what might be mystical about Merkavah mysticism, scholars point to the ascent of the mystic to the divine throne in the seventh heaven with the vision of God on his throne as the climax of the ascent. Yet the reader who follows the long, convoluted, and in many cases fragmentary ascent accounts, narratives, hymns and prayers in the Hekhalot literature is not rewarded with a description of God;[9] instead, he observes the mystic as he participates in the heavenly liturgy of the angels. I have coined for this experience the term *unio liturgica* ('liturgical union'),[10] in deliberate contrast to the problematic term *unio mystica* ('mystical union'). This is not to say that there is no vision in Merkavah mysticism—there may well be, but unfortunately the authors and editors of the Hekhalot literature did not bother to communicate the contents of such a vision. Moreover, except for the Third Book of Enoch, we find no traces in the Hekhalot literature of the mystic's physical transformation into an angel (that is, of his angelification, *unio angelica*). The liturgical communion of the mystic with the angels and also, to some degree, with God—which occurs during the angels' and the mystic's joint praise of God—does not lead to the mystic's angelification. And even less does the mystic's vision and praise of God lead to a process of his deification or quasi-deification. The attempts made by Elliot Wolfson to read into the alleged 'enthronement' of the mystic—following his vision of God—the mystic's deification, are not convincing (Wolfson 1993: 22ff.; 1994b: 194). It is only Enoch's transformation into the highest angel Metatron and Metatron's enthronement in 3 Enoch as the *YHWH ha-katan* (the 'Lesser YHWH') that can be justifiably termed angelification and that even borders on deification. But 3 Enoch is the latest offshoot of Hekhalot literature, and it may well be that the idea of Enoch-Metatron's transformation and enthronement is a *response* to the Christian claim of Jesus' elevation into heaven rather than early, pre-Christian evidence of a Jewish binitarian tradition (*pace* Boyarin 2001, 2004; 2005: 62f.).

Furthermore, the vision—or better, the 'empty vision'—in the ascent accounts does not benefit or serve the needs of the mystic as an individual; rather, it serves the needs of the earthly community: the mystic is expected to return to his fellow Jews on earth and to assure them of God's continuous love for his people after the destruction of the (Second) Temple. So the ultimate message of (much of) the Hekhalot literature is that God still cares for

---

[9] The claim made by Scholem (Scholem 1965: 36ff.) and his followers that the description of the Shi'ur Komah, the bodily dimensions of God, contains the essence of the mystic's vision is not supported by the textual evidence.

[10] More precisely, it is a liturgical communion of angels and human beings which, however, can turn into a union—if the human being becomes an angel.

his people of Israel. Such a message obviously presupposes not only the destroyed Temple but also the admission that this deplorable situation may continue for the foreseeable future—and beyond. If we take seriously the late formation of the Hekhalot literature towards the end of the rabbinic or even during the post-rabbinic period, we arrive at a historical context that is deeply impressed by the claim of a Christian Church firmly establishing itself in Palestine as the predominant power. This applies similarly to the Jews of Palestine and the Jews of Babylonia, and it does not matter, therefore, where we choose to locate our Merkavah mystical texts. The Temple was lost to the Christians, who claimed that they were the new Israel and the new spiritual Temple—a claim that made rebuilding the Temple and resuming its sacrifices superfluous. It is under these historical circumstances that the Merkavah mystics set out on their journey into the heavenly Temple, to rediscover their God there, to unite with the angels in the heavenly liturgy, and then to return to their earthly community with the divine assurance of love and redemption.

The Rabbis

Research on the alleged mystical implications of rabbinic Judaism has focused on a number of well-defined texts that deal with the Merkavah. The earliest of these sources understand by 'Merkavah' the chapter with Ezekiel's vision in the biblical book of Ezekiel (Ezek. 1 and 10), where Ezekiel beholds the divine chariot (although *kisse*, 'throne', is used there for the divine chariot rather than the technical term *merkavah*). These texts, therefore, focus on the proper reading and expounding of the Torah, in this case of Ezek. 1. Whereas in the Tosefta (Megillah 3 [4]:28) the *public* exposition of the Merkavah, that is, of Ezek. 1 and 10—captured by the phrase *lisdrosh ba-merkavah* ('to expound the Merkavah')—is taken for granted, the Mishnah adopts a stricter position and prohibits the use of Ezek. 1 as Haftarah in the synagogue service (Megillah 4:10).[11] This more restrained and cautious approach of the Mishnah is reinforced by the famous Mishnah in m.Ḥagigah 2.1, according to which the 'Merkavah' (i.e. again Ezek. 1) 'may not be expounded by an individual,[12] unless he is wise (i.e. a scholar) and understands on his own'. Shifting the focus from the public synagogue setting to a private teacher–student relationship, the Mishnah turns the successful exposition of the 'Merkavah' into an esoteric discipline reserved for an elite few.

---

[11] Parallels t.Meg. 3(4), 31–8; b.Meg. 25a–b.
[12] So in all Mishnah manuscripts, except MS Cambridge, which reads 'to an individual' (Halperin 1980: 11, n. 3).

As the continuation of m.Ḥagigah makes clear, the Mishnah is concerned with the improper and unbridled exegesis of Ezek. 1 (as well as of Gen. 1).[13]

A cycle of seven stories preserved in the Tosefta, with parallels in the Yerushalmi and Bavli, illustrates the mishnaic principle of not expounding the 'creation' of Gen. 1 and the 'Merkavah' of Ezek. 1.[14] It provides

1. an example of that highly exceptional individual who successfully expounds the Merkavah—because he is 'wise and understands on his own'—in front of his teacher (Eleazar b. Arakh, student of Yoḥanan b. Zakkai);[15]
2. a very short list of some other students;[16]
3. the famous story of the four rabbis (Ben Azzai, Ben Zoma, Aḥer and R. Akiva) who entered the 'garden' (*pardes*) of dangerous biblical exegeses (i.e. Ezek. 1), only R. Akiva surviving unharmed;[17]
4. a parable of someone who looks at the marvels of a king's 'garden'—most likely again a metaphor for certain difficult passages in the Bible;[18]
5. another parable meant again as a caveat against the improper preoccupation with particularly dangerous biblical passages;[19]
6. a story about Ben Zoma and the dangers of expounding Gen. 1;[20]
7. a story that illustrates the Mishnah's prohibition on dealing with matters of cosmology.[21]

All seven units collected in this cycle aim at illuminating the Mishnah's harsh prohibition and warn the reader against misusing the two most difficult and dangerous passages in the Bible: Gen. 1 (the 'work of creation' according to rabbinic terminology) and Ezek. 1 (the 'work of the Merkavah'). Originally, they were all concerned with the *exegesis* of these passages as an *esoteric* discipline and not with a heavenly journey of some mystics to the divine throne. It is only in the Bavli version of certain of these stories that we

---

[13] According to the Church Father Origen of Caesarea, Gen. 1 and Ezek. 1 are among those biblical passages that the Jews exclude from the standard curriculum of young students (Origen, *Commentarium in Cant. Canticorum Prologus*, in *Patrologia Graeca*, ed. Migne, vol. 13, Paris 1857, cols. 63f.).

[14] Carefully and convincingly analysed by Halperin (1980).

[15] t.Ḥag. 2.1; p.Ḥag. 2.1/9f., 77a; b.Ḥag. 14b.

[16] t.Ḥag. 2.2; p.Ḥag. 2.1/14, 77b; b.Ḥag. 14b.

[17] t.Ḥag. 2.3f.; p.Ḥag. 2.1/15 and 2.1/18, 77b; b.Ḥag. 14b, 15a, 15b. On the interpretation of this notorious text, see in particular Halperin (1980: 88ff.); Schäfer (1984); Morray-Jones (1993a and 1993b).

[18] t.Ḥag. 2.6; p.Ḥag. 2.1/42, 77c.

[19] t.Ḥag. ibid.; p.Ḥag. 2.1/8, 77a.

[20] t.Ḥag. 2.5; p.Ḥag. 2.1/13, 77a/b, b.Ḥag. 15a; GenR 2.4.

[21] t.Ḥag. 2.7; p.Ḥag. 2.1/33f., 77c; b.Ḥag. 11b.

find traces of Merkavah mystical (in the technical sense of the word) elements which, however, were often neutralised and re-rabbinised by the Bavli editor. It has been argued against the overall exegetical make-up of the rabbinic attitude towards the Merkavah that, if we take into consideration the 'experiential' aspect of rabbinic exegesis, we are ultimately able to rescue the mystical character of rabbinic Merkavah exegesis (Wolfson 1994a: 121ff.). This is an avenue that may be worth further exploration, but for the time being the experiential element of rabbinic Merkavah exegesis remains very vague (to say the least).

Qumran

The Qumran library consists of a large number of quite diverse writings, some of which are clearly sectarian in the sense that they originated in the Qumran community, whereas others are equally clearly writings that originated outside the community and just happened to be part of its library; and with regard to still others scholars disagree whether they belong to the former or to the latter category. Of the many Qumranic writings, the *Songs of the Sabbath Sacrifice* and the so-called *Self-Glorification Hymn* play a crucial role in the discussion of the Qumranic origins of Jewish mysticism. It is on the basis of these texts in particular that scholars like Rachel Elior and Philip Alexander have concluded that the Qumranic form of mysticism was the 'historical forerunner of later Jewish Heikhalot mysticism' (Alexander 2006: p. vii). The *Songs of the Sabbath Sacrifice*, a cycle of thirteen songs altogether, which were apparently composed for performance during the first Sabbaths of the year, number among those writings whose provenance is unclear; but because of the sheer quantity of fragments found in Qumran and the many parallels between the *Songs* and other Qumranic texts, most scholars agree that they were of paramount importance to the Qumran sectarians (Newsom 1985: 4; 1990: 184; Boustan 2004: 198, n. 11). The *Self-Glorification Hymn*—a unique text composed by an unknown author, who boasts himself of having been elevated among and above the angels and of having been seated on a throne in heaven—belongs most likely to the sectarian Qumranic texts (Eshel 1996).

If we scrutinise the Qumran writings with regard to the ascent of the mystic(s) to the divine throne, a subsequent vision of God, and the possible angelification and/or divinisation of the mystic(s), the result is rather bleak. As for the ascent, only the author of the *Self-Glorification Hymn* envisions himself as being elevated to heaven—but we do not learn how he got there; his actual ascent plays no role. Furthermore, the Qumran texts betray even less concern for the vision. The visionary element in the *Songs* focuses on the animated architecture of the Temple and on the angels (Boustan 2004). Even in the *Self-Glorification Hymn* there is no trace whatsoever of the author's desire to see God; he is completely satisfied with his place among the angels. In the liturgical texts (the *Hodayot* and the *Songs of the Sabbath Sacrifice* in particular), the human sectarians enter into a liturgical union—or better yet communion—with the angels ((*comm*)*unio liturgica*); that is, both humans and angels praise God in joint worship. But wherever this communion takes place (in heaven or on earth), the earthly community does not (physically) ascend to heaven. Some scholars choose to read the *Songs* as a kind of performative act during which the Qumran sectarians ascend to heaven in order to unite with the angels (Morray-Jones 1998), but this 'unitarian' aspect is by no means clear: rather than to record the *content* of the actual praises, the main purpose of the *Songs* is merely to *invite* the angels to praise God (Nitzan 1994: 183–9, 195–200; Boustan 2003: 225). The only explicit case of an angelification (*unio angelica*) of a human being is the *Self-Glorification Hymn*.

Yet neither the liturgical (comm)union of the mystics with the angels nor the transformation of a mystic into an angel must be confused with their transformation into God (divinisation).[22] Hence, if we take divinisation (*unio mystica*) as the yardstick of mysticism, the Qumran texts cannot be included in that precious category—and accordingly lose their favoured role as the historical trail-blazer of Merkavah mysticism. Alexander's attempts to nevertheless rescue that function—at least with regard to the hero of the *Self-Glorification Hymn* (Alexander 2006: 90) and despite his own definition (ibid., p. 8)—are open to question.

The Ascent Apocalypses

The ascent apocalypses of the Second Temple period take up and further develop elements from Ezekiel's vision (Ezek. 1 and 10) and the vision of the Son of Man in Daniel (Dan. 7). Whereas Ezekiel sees the heavens open and the figure of God seated on a throne carried by four enigmatic creatures, the seers in the ascent apocalypses ascend to heaven in order to approach God on his throne in the highest heaven. These ascents are, as a rule, fraught with the customary horror and fear on the part of the seer, by which he responds to the extraordinary experience imposed on him.

---

[22] As Alexander aptly summarises: 'Where does Qumran stand on this issue [the question of a mystical union with God]? The position there seems to be unequivocal: there is no absorption into God. The highest transformation that the mystic can undergo is into an *angel*, not into *God*, and angels are definitely not God' (Alexander 2006: 105).

Some apocalypses, however, go further and describe the transformation of the seer into an angelic being—that is, his angelification—as the ultimate climax of the ascent experience. This trend begins with the Enoch of the Similitudes (late first century BCE / early first century CE), where Enoch is transformed into something new that isn't yet fully spelled out but is presumably an angel (1 Enoch ch. 71). The Enoch of the Second Book of Enoch (2 Enoch, first century CE) discovers to his astonishment that he, following his vision of God, has become like one of the angels with 'no observable difference' (2 Enoch 22:10). Similarly, the prophet Isaiah in the Ascension of Isaiah (chs. 6–11, early second century CE)[23] not only enters into a *unio liturgica* with the angels of the sixth heaven; reaching the seventh heaven and being stripped of his 'garment' of flesh, he even becomes like an angel (9:30). This transformation, however, is only temporary, since he must return to his garments of flesh—that is, his bodily existence—until his death (11:35). This final stage is attained by the hero of the Apocalypse of Zephaniah (late first or early second century CE), who, having arrived at the place of the deceased righteous souls, dons an angelic garment—that is, is transformed into an angel (8:3), this transformation enabling him to understand the language of the angels and to join in with their heavenly praise (8:4).[24] Ultimately, however, all the ascent apocalypses retain the distance between the visionary and his God; again, angelification must not be confused with *unio mystica* and the seer's deification (*pace* Morray-Jones 1992: 13ff.; Chester 2007: 80).

The vision itself that the seer encounters at the peak of his ascent is a remarkably subdued experience—if a vision is conveyed at all. Most apocalypses emphasise the aspect of fire and brightness surrounding that enigmatic human-like figure of God seated on his throne (influenced by Ezek. 1). According to the Book of the Watchers (late third or early second century BCE), God's raiment veiled in fire is the object of Enoch's desire (1 Enoch 14:20–22); the Enoch of the Second Book of Enoch sees the face of God 'like iron made burning hot in a fire and brought out, and it emits sparks and is incandescent' (2 Enoch 22:1); and the author of the Apocalypse of John describes God on his throne in terms of brilliant jewels (Rev. 4:3). What is more important to the authors of all the ascent apocalypses is that the function and purpose of the vision revolve around the future history of the people of Israel in general and the unavoidable destruction of the Temple in particular. The seer and his earthly community are assured—despite the

---

[23] Chapters 6–11 of the Ascension of Isaiah, an ascent apocalypse, are no doubt of Christian origin but in all likelihood depend on a Jewish source (Himmelfarb 1985: 136f., 156, n. 56; 1993: 55, 135, n. 30); chapters 1–5, an account of Isaiah's martyrdom, are of Jewish provenance.

[24] The Apocalypse of John, an unmistakably Christian apocalypse (written towards the end of the first century CE) that draws, however, on traditional Jewish material, is not concerned with the fate of the visionary.

bleak outlook on the future—that God is still residing in his heavenly Temple and that the gap between God and his human creatures can still be bridged—even after the destruction of the Temple.

The question as to whether the preserved texts are to be regarded as literary constructs, that is, as fiction, or rather as genuine (mystical) experience, has been addressed most acutely to the ascent apocalypses. Christopher Rowland, in particular, tries to liberate modern scholarship from the sterile alternative of fiction versus experience by proposing a 'dynamic imaginative activity in which the details of Ezekiel's vision were understood by a *complex interweaving of vision and textual networking*' (Rowland *et al.* 2006: 48, my emphasis; Rowland 1982). Seen in this way, he argues, the apocalypses of Second Temple Judaism may provide 'examples of those moments when human experience moves beyond what is apparent to physical perception to open up perceptions of other dimensions of existence . . . *different from a purely analytical or rational approach* to texts or received wisdom' (Rowland *et al.* 2006: 55, my emphasis). Unfortunately, what our texts in fact reveal of Rowland's 'complex interweaving of vision and textual networking' is little more than the 'textual networking'; or, to put it differently, the 'vision' consists of the 'textual networking'. Hence, Rowland's proposition fails to lead us out of the impasse of fiction versus experience.

Mysticism

This survey yields two main results. First, it does not confirm that trend in modern scholarship which locates the origins of Jewish mysticism in the Qumran literature and wishes to see an unbroken chain of distinctly mystical ideas leading from Qumran through rabbinic Judaism to the Hekhalot literature. Such models of linear development are methodologically highly problematic—whether they claim to reconstruct 'history' or 'only' to describe ideas that are 'phenomenologically' related (Idel 1988: pp. xviii–xix; Elior 2004). If we insist on establishing literary and conceptual connections between the Hekhalot literature and earlier Second Temple literatures, the ascent apocalypses may turn out to open up more promising avenues for future research than the Qumran literature.

Second, the category of mysticism has proved to be a dubious one. In their desire to rescue the category of mysticism for ancient Judaism, scholars tend to equate 'union' with 'communion', 'angelification' with 'deification', or in some other way to sneak the notion of *unio mystica* into the ancient texts. If we do not want to impose later concepts on ancient Judaism—and if we do not want to render the category of mysticism meaningless by confusing mysticism with religion—we may come to the conclusion that mysticism is not a particularly useful category for any historically sound description of the ideals, aspirations, and goals propagated in ancient Judaism.

Further Reading

Alexander (1983, 2006); Boustan (2007a); Halperin (1988); Himmelfarb (1993); Schäfer (ed. 1981, 1988, 1992, 2009); Schäfer *et al.* (1987–95); Scholem (1965); Swartz (1996).

Bibliography

Abrams, D. (1996), 'Critical and post-critical textual scholarship of Jewish mystical literature: notes on the history and development of modern editing techniques', *Kabbalah*, 1: 17–71.

Alexander, P. S. (1977), 'The historical setting of the Hebrew Book of Enoch', *JJS* 28: 156–80.

Alexander, P. S. (1983), '3 (Hebrew Apocalypse of) Enoch', in J. H. Charlesworth (ed.), *The Old Testament Pseudepigrapha*, vol. 1: *Apocalyptic Literature and Testaments*, New York etc., pp. 223–315.

Alexander, P. S. (1984), 'Comparing Merkavah mysticism and Gnosticism: an essay in method', *JJS* 35: 1–18.

Alexander, P. S. (1987), '3 Enoch and the Talmud', *Journal for the Study of Judaism*, 18: 40–68.

Alexander, P. S. (2006), *The Mystical Texts: Songs of the Sabbath Sacrifice and Related Manuscripts*, London and New York.

Boustan, R. S. (2003), 'Sevenfold hymns in the Songs of the Sabbath Sacrifice and the Hekhalot literature: formalism, hierarchy and the limits of human participation', in J. Davila (ed.), *The Dead Sea Scrolls as Background to Postbiblical Judaism and Early Christianity: Papers from an International Conference at St. Andrews in 2001*, Leiden and Boston, pp. 220–47.

Boustan, R. S. (2004), 'Angels in the architecture: temple art and the poetics of praise in the *Songs of the Sabbath Sacrifice*', in R. S. Boustan and A. Yoshiko Reed (eds.), *Heavenly Realms and Earthly Realities in Late Antique Religions*, Cambridge and New York.

Boustan, R. S. (2005), *From Martyr to Mystic: Rabbinic Martyrology and the Making of Merkavah Mysticism*, Tübingen.

Boustan, R. S. (2007a), 'The study of Heikhalot literature: between mystical experience and textual artifact', *Currents in Biblical Research*, 6: 130–60.

Boustan, R. S. (2007b), 'The emergence of pseudonymous attribution in Hekhalot literature', *JSQ* 14: 18–38.

Boyarin, D. (2001), 'The Gospel of the Memra: Jewish binitarianism and the Prologue to John', *HThR* 94: 243–84.

Boyarin, D. (2004), 'Two powers in Heaven; or, The making of a heresy', in

H. Najman and J. H. Newman (eds.), *The Idea of Biblical Interpretation: Essays in Honor of James L. Kugel*, Leiden, pp. 331–70.

Boyarin, D. (2005), 'The parables of Enoch and the foundation of the rabbinic sect: a hypothesis', in M. Perani (ed.), *'The Words of a Wise Man's Mouth Are Gracious' (Qoh 10,12): Festschrift for Günter Stemberger on the Occasion of his 65th Birthday*, Berlin and New York, pp. 53–72.

Chester, A. (2007), *Messiah and Exaltation: Jewish Messianic and Visionary Traditions and New Testament Christology*, Tübingen.

Cohen, M. S. (1983), *The Shi'ur Qomah: Liturgy and Theurgy in Pre-Kabbalistic Jewish Mysticism*, Lanham, MD.

Cohen, M. S. (1985), *The Shi'ur Qomah: Texts and Recensions*, Tübingen.

Dan, J. (1987), 'Hidden Hekhalot', *Tarbiz*, 36: 433–7. [Hebrew]

Dan, J. (1993), *The Ancient Jewish Mysticism*, Tel Aviv.

Dan, J. (2009), *History of Jewish Mysticism and Esotericism: Ancient Times*, 3 vols., Zalman Shazar Center, Jerusalem. [Hebrew]

Davila, J. R. (1994), 'Prolegomena to a critical edition of Hekhalot Rabbati', *JJS* 45: 208–26.

Davila, J. R. (1999), 'The Dead Sea Scrolls and Merkavah mysticism', in T. H. Lim (ed.), *The Dead Sea Scrolls in their Historical Context*, Edinburgh, pp. 246–64.

Davila, J. R. (2001), *Descenders to the Chariot: The People behind the Hekhalot Literature*, Leiden, Boston and Köln.

Deutsch, N. (1999), *Guardians of the Gate: Angelic Vice Regency in Late Antiquity*, Leiden.

Elior, R. (2004), *The Three Temples: On the Emergence of Jewish Mysticism*, Oxford; originally in Hebrew, Jerusalem, 2002.

Eshel, E. (1996), '4Q471B: a self-glorification hymn', *Revue de Qumran*, 17/65–68: 175–203.

Eshel, E., Eshel, H., Newsom, C., Nitzan, B., Schuller, E. and Yardeni, A. (1998), *Qumran Cave 4*, VI: *Poetical and Liturgical Texts*, Part 1, Oxford.

Gruenwald, I. (1972), 'Re'uyyot Yehezqel', *Temirin*, 1: 101–39.

Gruenwald, I. (1980), *Apocalyptic and Merkavah Mysticism*, Leiden.

Halperin, D. J. (1980), *The Merkabah in Rabbinic Literature*, New Haven.

Halperin, D. J. (1984), 'A new edition of the Hekhalot literature', *JAOS* 104: 543–52.

Halperin, D. J. (1988), *The Faces of the Chariot: Early Jewish Responses to Ezekiel's Vision*, Tübingen.

Hamacher, E. (1996), 'Die Sabbatopferlieder im Streit um Ursprung und Anfänge der jüdischen Mystik', *Journal for the Study of Judaism*, 27: 119–54.

Herrmann, K. (1994), *Massekhet Hekhalot: Traktat von den himmlischen Palästen*, Tübingen.

Herrmann, K. and Rohrbacher-Sticker, C. (1989), 'Magische Traditionen der New Yorker Hekhalot-Handschrift JTS 8128 im Kontext ihrer Gesamtredaktion', *FJB* 17: 101–49.

Herrmann, K. and Rohrbacher-Sticker, C. (1992), 'Magische Traditionen der Oxforder Hekhalot-Handschrift Michael 9 in ihrem Verhältnis zu MS New York JTS 8128', *FJB* 19: 169–83.

Himmelfarb, M. (1985), *Tours of Hell: An Apocalyptic Form in Jewish and Christian Literature*, Philadelphia.

Himmelfarb, M. (1988), 'Heavenly ascent and the relationship of the Apocalypses and the Hekhalot literature', *Hebrew Union College Annual*, 59: 73–100.

Himmelfarb, M. (1993), *Ascent to Heaven in Jewish and Christian Apocalypses*, New York and Oxford.

Himmelfarb, M. (1995), 'The practice of ascent in the ancient Mediterranean world', in J. J. Collins and M. A. Fishbane (eds.), *Death, Ecstasy and Other Worldly Journeys*, Albany, NY, pp. 123–37.

Idel, M. (1988), *Kabbalah: New Perspectives*, New Haven.

Kuyt, A. (1995), *The 'Descent' to the Chariot: Towards a Description of the Terminology, Place, Function and Nature of the Yeridah in Hekhalot Literature*, Tübingen.

Lesses, R. M. (1998), *Ritual Practices to Gain Power: Angels, Incantations, and Revelation in Early Jewish Mysticism*, Harrisburg, PA.

Morray-Jones, C. R. A. (1992), 'Transformational mysticism in the Apocalyptic-Merkabah tradition', *JJS* 43: 1–31.

Morray-Jones, C. R. A. (1993a), 'Paradise Revisited (2 Cor. 12:1–12): the Jewish mystical background of Paul's apostolate. Part 1: The Jewish sources', *HThR* 86: 177–217.

Morray-Jones, C. R. A. (1993b), 'Part 2: Paul's heavenly ascent and its significance', *HThR* 86: 265–92.

Morray-Jones, C. R. A. (1998), 'The temple within: the embodied divine image and its worship in the Dead Sea Scrolls and other early Jewish and Christian sources', *Society of Biblical Literature Seminar Papers*, 37, pp. 400–31.

Morray-Jones, C. R. A. (2002), *A Transparent Illusion: The Dangerous Vision of Water in Hekhalot Mysticism*, Leiden.

Newsom, C. (1985), *Songs of the Sabbath Sacrifice: A Critical Edition*, Atlanta.

Newsom, C. (1990), '"Sectually explicit" literature from Qumran', in W. Propp, B. Halpern and D. Freedman (eds.), *The Hebrew Bible and Its Interpreters*, Winona Lake, IN.

Nitzan, B. (1994), *Qumran Prayer and Religious Poetry*, Leiden.

Orlov, A. A. (2005), *The Enoch-Metatron Tradition*, Tübingen.

Orlov, A. A. (2007), *From Apocalypticism to Merkabah Mysticism: Studies in the Slavonic Pseudepigrapha*, Leiden and Boston.

Reed, A. Yoshiko (2005), *Fallen Angels and the History of Judaism and Christianity: The Reception of Enochic Literature*, New York.

Rowland, Ch. (1982), *The Open Heaven: A Study of Apocalyptic in Judaism and Early Christianity*, London.

Rowland, Ch. with Gibbons, P. and Dobroruka, V. (2006), 'Visionary experience in ancient Judaism and Christianity', in A. D. DeConick (ed.), *Paradise Now: Essays on Early Jewish and Christian Mysticism*, Atlanta, pp. 41–56.

Schäfer, P. (1983), 'Handschriften zur Hekhalot-Literatur', *FJB* 11: 113–93; repr. in Schäfer (1988), pp. 154–233.

Schäfer, P. (1984), 'New Testament and Hekhalot literature: the journey into heaven in Paul and Merkavah mysticism', *JJS* 35: 19–35; repr. in Schäfer (1988), pp. 234–49.

Schäfer, P. (1986), *Gershom Scholem Reconsidered: The Aim and Purpose of Early Jewish Mysticism*, 12th Sacks Lecture, Oxford; repr. in Schäfer (1988), pp. 277–95.

Schäfer, P. (1988), *Hekhalot-Studien*, Tübingen.

Schäfer, P. (1992), *The Hidden and Manifest God: Some Major Themes in Early Jewish Mysticism*, trans. A. Pomerance, Albany, NY.

Schäfer, P. (2009), *The Origins of Jewish Mysticism*, Tübingen.

Schäfer, P. (ed.) (1981), *Synopse zur Hekhalot-Literatur*, in collaboration with M. Schlüter and H. G. von Mutius, Tübingen.

Schäfer, P. (ed.) (1984), *Geniza-Fragmente zur Hekhalot-Literatur*, Tübingen.

Schäfer, P. (ed.) (1986–88), *Konkordanz zur Hekhalot-Literatur*, in collaboration with G. Reeg, 2 vols., Tübingen.

Schäfer, P. *et al.* (1987–95), *Übersetzung der Hekhalot-Literatur*, 4 vols., Tübingen.

Scholem, G. (1974), *Major Trends in Jewish Mysticism*, 3rd revised edn., Jerusalem and New York; first published 1941.

Scholem, G. (1965), *Jewish Gnosticism, Merkabah Mysticism, and Talmudic Tradition*, New York.

Swartz, M. D. (1996), *Scholastic Magic: Ritual and Revelation in Early Jewish Mysticism*, Princeton.

Swartz, M. D. (2001), 'The Dead Sea Scrolls and later Jewish magic and mysticism', *Dead Sea Discoveries*, 8: 182–93.

Ta-Shma, I. (1985), 'The library of the Ashkenazi Sages in the eleventh and twelfth centuries', *Kiryat Sefer*, 60: 298–309. [Hebrew]

Wolfson, E. (1993), '*Yeridah la-Merkavah*: typology of ecstasy and enthronement in ancient Jewish mysticism', in R. A. Herrera (ed.), *Mystics of the Book: Themes, Topics, and Typologies*, New York, pp. 13–44.

Wolfson, E. (1994a), *Through a Speculum that Shines: Vision and Imagination in Medieval Jewish Mysticism*, Princeton.

Wolfson, E. (1994b), 'Mysticism and the poetic-liturgical compositions from Qumran: a response to Bilhah Nitzan', *JQR* 85: 185–202.

Part III
History

Part 01
History

16

'Rabbinic Culture' and Roman Culture

SETH SCHWARTZ

GIVEN HOW FRAUGHT AND CONTROVERSIAL THE IDEA OF 'CULTURE' HAS BECOME,[1] it will be best to start with some brief theoretical reflections by way of ground-clearing; it will be necessary to perform the same operation on the more specific 'rabbinic culture', a phrase frequently uttered but rarely subjected to analytic scrutiny, as also the question underlying this paper (what can rabbinic literature teach us about Roman imperial culture), which *could be* understood to posit the rabbis or Jews as the Romans' proximate other, rather than as an interestingly unusual subspecies of 'Roman'—so that rabbinic literature actually constitutes part of Roman culture.

The most progressive theoretical positions nowadays tend to regard 'culture' as one of those totalising constructs symptomatic of European imperialism and therefore to be rejected in favour of a view of social behaviour as the completely contingent consequence of more or less unfettered human agency.[2] In this view, to designate any aggregation of behavioural stuff as 'culture' is to engage in an aggressive act of reductive schematisation: it arbitrarily domesticates a literally unruly phenomenon. It is a political paradox that the strongest opposition to this view comes from Marxists who believe that not only is culture a real entity but that it is a completely predictable epiphenomenon of a society's economic relations. An intermediate position, which I embrace, avoids both the determinism and oversimplification of the Marxist position and the aporetic character of the postmodern one. Culture is human behaviour, often baffling when viewed in close-up—and so not explicable in Marxist (or indeed structuralist) terms simply as the inscription in practice of social and economic structures—but never simply the consequence of unmediated and unconstrained human agency. In my view it is a useful thing about which to talk and think, but the project of writing

---

[1] See, for example, the editor's Introduction and most of the essays in Ortner (ed. 1999).
[2] Basic discussion in Burke (2005: 127–40, 172–82). And note Smith (1982: 18), citing F. E. Williams's characterisation of culture as a 'heap of rubbish', a 'tangle' and a 'hotch-potch'. I refer to this position as 'postmodern' for the sake of convenience: in fact, if viewed as a descendant of individualism, it has a long pedigree.

Proceedings of the British Academy **165**, 283–299. © The British Academy 2010.

especially about the culture of a long-dead world is something that must be done with precision, analytic rigour and a self-consciousness that I confess I have only rarely seen in writing about the ancient Jews.

Rabbinic Culture

Let me start by tackling 'rabbinic culture'—a discussion necessary if we wish to determine what in cultural terms we are reading when we read rabbinic texts. 'Rabbinic culture' probably got its start as an expression of methodological caution and scepticism. Scholars before Neusner might write about the specifically rabbinic professional culture of the study house, for example, or might recognise that stories of rabbinic behaviour reflected not the general cultural attitudes of the Jews but the supererogatory piety of the stories' rabbinic protagonists. But on the whole, older scholarship regarded rabbinic texts as a repository of evidence of almost archival character about the Jews, who were assumed to share rabbinic norms even if they did not always live up to them.

The Neusnerian revolution's main valid consequences have been to force us to recognise the textuality of rabbinic texts, and the social, political and cultural specificity of their rabbinic authors. In retrospect, the earlier tendency to read rabbinic texts as the national archives of the Jewish people was unnatural. These aspects, at least, of the Neusnerian revolution have been effective because they conform in so obvious a way to what the rabbinic texts actually are: rabbinic texts. But once that has been established, the texts cease to serve in any simple way as evidence for the Jews in general and—at least if one was a relatively cautious interpreter—could now be said to provide evidence for the ideals, attitudes and behaviour—the culture—primarily of the rabbis alone.

But this position is less intuitively obvious than it first appears. To be sure, the rabbis were humans who acted and interacted and thus can be said to have possessed a culture, not to mention, in theory, corporate political and social interests. But is the designation of this culture as rabbinic actually the more cautious, sceptical position? Is it justified at all? Of whose culture, precisely, are rabbinic texts an artefact? This is less certain. When we specify a culture by adding an adjective to it we are normally positing that the body to whom we are attributing the culture has some meaningful integrity as a society. This is why it is actually very controversial to speak about Roman culture (to mean something more than the culture of the metropolitan imperial centre) because there is wide disagreement over whether the Roman empire was meaningfully integrated. Another possibility is to suppose that rabbinic literature reflects the *institutional* or *professional culture* of the rabbis. It is normally understood that these are very different sorts of entities than, say, national cultures. Professional cultures are not totalising, as national cultures ostensibly are, but rather are subcultures. The 'culture' of stockbrokers, Columbia University professors, or Manhattan drycleaners (pardon the parochial nature of my examples), is highly compartmental—it governs only interaction amongst themselves and their clients, and even that often in quite limited circumstances. Columbia professors might behave one way towards one another if they meet at a restaurant and quite differently if they meet in the reading room of Butler Library. Institutional cultures are not totalising enough to exist on their own: their practitioners possess simultaneously other sorts of cultural identity. If it is this sort of cultural situation that rabbinic literature reflects, then we would have to determine on a case-by-case basis whether the pericope being analysed reflects the corporate subculture of the rabbis, the as yet undefined culture of the Jews, or the broader culture of Roman subjects/citizens.

Another possibility is to see the rabbis as a *counterculture*, a small, highly integrated and rigorously bounded group who set themselves up in self-conscious opposition to broader social norms (both Jewish and Roman)—not a society, then, but a group possessing a 'culture' which may be quite as distinctive and totalising as that of a larger-scale society. It too, however, relies on the existence of a general normative culture, but not in the same way as an institutional culture, which may be merely a compartmentalised component of the general culture. A counterculture needs the general culture because opposition to it is what gives the counterculture its moral urgency. (Of course countercultures can become routinised or domesticated, in which case they might lose some of their self-consciousness; but to the extent that its constituents continue living non-normative lives in normative society, even the most traditional counterculture—think of the Jews in Polish-Lithuanian market towns in the eighteenth century—never sheds it completely: see Rosman 2007: 82–110.)

In what sense then did the rabbis have a culture? Were they a society, an institution, or a counterculture, or some combination? While it is not unusual for scholars to write quite unselfconsciously about 'rabbinic society', it is obvious that this characterisation cannot withstand critical scrutiny (e.g. Rubenstein 2003: 11, and *passim*). There were never more than a few dozen rabbis alive at any one time—and those were geographically scattered—and even if we suppose that their students and closest followers raise the tally of rabbis and rabbi-types to a few hundred at a time, there is no meaningful way to regard this loose corporation (or whatever precisely it was) as a society. In my view this renders projects like Jeffrey Rubenstein's, of producing an ethnography of the rabbis, or at least an inventory of some of their central cultural norms (the norms extrapolated through a close reading of talmudic narratives, and the centrality of those norms posited on the basis of anthropological tradition), deeply problematic a priori, because this sort of scholarship never stops to consider the implications of precisely what kind of group the rabbis were; it tends to treat the rabbis as conventional ethnographic subjects, possessing a totalising, unselfconsciously embraced, depoliticised culture, and their writings as field notes. It could be said to collude in the rabbis' self-representation. It is some consolation that such projects are in truth often less concerned with producing a history or an ethnography than with using some historical hypotheses and anthropological concepts as tools for reading texts—a method which is not per se objectionable as long as one avoids the temptation to reify one's hermeneutical constructs (as Rubenstein did not). And even so, such models should be used much more cautiously than they usually are.

The remaining hypotheses—rabbinic culture as institutional culture, or as counterculture—I think both contain partial truths about the Palestinian rabbis of the third and fourth centuries. By the third century the rabbis were indubitably emerging as some sort of professional group who were clearly beginning to cultivate certain unusual norms of in-group interaction which are best understood as aspects of a professional culture. Lee Levine (1989) collected the evidence for this but unfortunately most of it came from the Bavli, which allowed the more rigorous Catherine Hezser (1997) to dismiss it. Yet the Yerushalmi provides evidence for the existence of such group norms among the Palestinian rabbis, even if they were somewhat different and less elaborate than those practised by the Babylonians. The locus classicus for this is p.Bikurim 3.3, part of which was famously studied by Gedalya Alon (1977). Here the Talmud spends several pages quite anxiously probing the value of norms of in-group deference, and of the specific types of address, clothing and deportment typical of *hakhamim*. One reason for the anxiety is that the rabbis knew and resented the fact that they shared this culture with non-rabbinic patriarchal judicial appointees, 'those appointed for money', in the rabbis' polemical formulation. But another reason is that the Palestinian rabbis were not after all fully committed to the idea of a rank-based hierarchy and sometimes manifested discomfort with the very idea of honour.

This brings us to the countercultural aspect of rabbinic behaviour. In the first place, rabbinic literature itself is as a whole a deeply countercultural artefact, manifestly self-conscious in its oppositional stance. It seems to constitute a thorough and radical rejection of the cultural norms of the environment in which it was written, the urban Roman East. I will not say much more about this, to save space and because I discuss the issue fully in a forthcoming publication. In brief, the rabbis seem to reject the language, the laws, a remarkable amount of the practice (in Bourdieu's sense), and finally the most basic political legitimacy, of their imperial rulers. No one should think this is self-explanatory—in fact such thorough-going opposition to the ruling power is rarely attested in the history of Jewish subjection. And rabbinic rejection extended even, in many cases, to Judaised versions of Roman practice already domesticated by the rabbis' contemporaries—for example, the modified euergetism which constituted the economic and cultural foundation of the local Jewish religious community.

It hardly needs to be argued that one reason the rabbis were hostile to Roman culture was because the Romans had long before abrogated the agreement that the Jews had traditionally maintained with their rulers, and which the Babylonian rabbis continued to maintain with the Sasanian Empire: if the state supported the Jews' right to follow their own laws, the Jews would recognise the state's right to intervene in their lives in limited ways, by collecting taxes, for example. But the Romans had destroyed the Temple, disempowered the priests, and suspended the Jews' autonomy, so the rabbis reciprocated by failing to acknowledge the legitimacy of the Roman state.

But there is a more profound reason for the rabbis' rejection not simply of the authority of the Roman state, but of Roman cultural norms also. The rabbis were the embodiment of Torah, and the Torah was itself a countercultural document. To abbreviate drastically a point I have argued at length elsewhere (Schwartz 2009), the Torah envisions Israelite society as egalitarian, self-enclosed, and bound together not through the pulsation of goods, benefits, and cultural capital through the nation in a way potentially constitutive of social integration, but through unconditional solidarity and love based on shared dependency on the God of Israel. Reciprocity is eschewed as a value: one must treat one's fellow Israelites fairly and compassionately whether or not they return the favour. Indeed, reciprocity is regarded as resulting inexorably in inequality and oppression, which are to be avoided in the community of Israel. Israelites are to possess no aristocracy, only a clergy, which is partly privileged and partly disadvantaged. A corollary of this is that honour, often a by-product of hierarchical systems of social dependency, has no real place among humans. Just as the sole fully legitimate relationship of social dependency outside the family is with God, so too the only creature who truly possesses honour is God. This social vision self-consciously rejects the alternative one in which people are thought to be bound together by institutionalised reciprocity and exchange, and so it constructs itself as countercultural. But the Romans embraced reciprocity as a fundamental principle of social and political integration: the importance of such reciprocity-based institutions as patronage and friendship hardly requires demonstration, and it has recently been argued that honour, too, played a fundamental role in the functioning of the Roman state (Saller 1982; Wallace-Hadrill ed. 1989; Lendon 1997). So the rabbis not only hated the Romans for their violence against and oppression of the Jews, but they also, inasmuch as they embraced the values of the Torah, rejected the core political and social values of Rome. Or so one might think.

But this is not the end of the story. The rabbis were Romans, after all, however paradoxical. In the wake of three disastrous revolts, no Jew can have been unaware of the cost of uncompromising rejection of Roman norms. For this reason it is often possible to detect a surprising strain of ambivalence or even accommodation under the surface of rabbinic opposition. In what follows I will illustrate the peculiar combination of opposition, accommodation and appropriation characteristic of the Palestinian rabbis' approach to Roman practices and values by analysing two relevant short pericopae from the Talmud Yerushalmi. I will conclude by arguing that in the aggregate such stories, when compared with what we know of the behaviour of other literate provincials, can tell us a lot about different patterns of subjection to Roman rule (and can be used to criticise and refine a model of imperial Greek culture advocated most influentially by Greg Woolf and adopted by many other Cambridge colleagues).[3] They also show that rabbinic culture, poised somewhere between subculture and counterculture, can never be fully understood without reference to the norms and practices of the broader culture in which it was so ambivalently embedded, with which it was so thoroughly entangled. At least as far as the texts indicate, the rabbis understood themselves, *qua* embodiments of Torah, to be living and acting in a state of exquisite tension with Roman values.

Sympotika

The first pericope is a brief but surprisingly intricate story about rabbis' treatment of their dependants at dinner parties. At one level the story concerns the rabbinic—and presumably the generally Jewish—appropriation of the norms and practices of the Roman *convivium*; but at a deeper level it concerns the rabbis' struggles with the Roman values of honour, precedence and hierarchy, and their conflict with the rabbis' premier value, Torah. It may be worth saying here that while the classical Greek *symposion* ideally was a celebration of the egalitarian amity of the aristocratic *hetaireia*, or in its public, civic manifestation, a symbolic expression of the democratic solidarity of the citizen body, the Roman *convivium*, while continuing to value traditional *parrhesia* in a limited way, was much more explicitly a ritualised enactment of

---

[3] See Woolf (1994); this model informs the views of the editor of and many of the contributors to Goldhill (ed. 2001).

hierarchy and social dependency; as such, it could be, as many texts, both Jewish and Roman, remind us, a highly fraught event:[4]

> The tutor of the son of Rabbi Hoshayya Rabbah was a blind man,[5] and he was accustomed to dine with his master daily. One time Rabbi Hoshayya had guests and did not ask the tutor to eat with him. That evening Rabbi Hoshayya went to the tutor and said, 'Let my lord not be angry at me; I had guests and did not wish to injure my lord's honour. For this reason I did not dine with you today.' The tutor responded, 'You have apologised to the one who is seen but does not see; may the One Who sees but is not seen accept your apology.' Rabbi Hoshayya asked, 'Where did you learn this expression?' The tutor responded, 'From Rabbi Eliezer ben Jacob, for once upon a time a blind man came to Rabbi Eliezer ben Jacob's village, and the rabbi sat below the man [on the couch at dinner], so that the guests said, "if he were not a great man Rabbi Eliezer ben Jacob would not have sat below him", and so they provided for the blind man an honourable maintenance. The blind man said to them, "Why have you done this for me?" They responded, "Rabbi Eliezer ben Jacob sat below you." And so the man offered the following prayer on the rabbi's behalf: "You have performed a deed of mercy for one who is seen but does not see; may the One Who sees but is not seen perform a deed of mercy for you!"'

This story juxtaposes and contrasts the two value-systems discussed above: Rabbi Hoshayya Rabbah seems at first to act as if he thinks that Torah is the only real value, that it overcomes the normative rules of precedence and honour, and so he happily dines daily with the blind man who teaches his son Torah. But this turns out to be true only when the rabbi is dining in private. When he has guests, the blind tutor reverts to his servile or subordinate status: he is not invited. The rabbi then tries to appease the tutor with words which crudely (so I believe we are meant to read it) invert the correct rank of the protagonists. Hence the rabbi addresses the tutor repeatedly as 'my lord' and insists that by not inviting him he was preserving rather than wounding his honour. The tutor's response I take as a clever variant of 'Go to hell'. Not only is Rabbi Hoshayya's declaration that the tutor outranks him, and is honourable, appearances to the contrary, sternly rejected, but the tutor takes the opportunity to extend the reproach by telling the rabbi a story which illustrates true generosity. (It may also be meant to prove that the tutor, who has rabbinic teachings at his fingertips, is actually a *talmid ḥakham* after all, and so fully his master's equal.[6])

---

[4] The story appears in the Palestinian Talmud in two slightly different versions, one in Pe'ah 8.9, 21b, the other in Shekalim 5.5, 49b. I follow the former here. The differences are inconsequential. On the Greek public feast, see Schmitt Pantel (1992). On the history and ideology of the archaic and classical symposium see Levine (1985); Murray (1990); on the Roman *convivium*, see D'Arms (1990); Bradley (1998); Dunbabin (2003); Roller (2006).

[5] *Sagya nehora*, literally, 'filled with light', a familiar euphemism for blindness in rabbinic Aramaic.

[6] I am indebted to Richard Kalmin for this suggestion.

The story's setting, the vulnerability of the tutor to insult—exacerbated or indeed generated by the fact that he is not usually treated like a slave—and the very ambiguity of his position in the story, in broad terms are reminiscent of a long section of Lucian of Samosata's essay, *De mercede conductis potentium familiaribus* ('On salaried posts in great houses'), in which the author offers advice to a young man who is about to take a job as a tutor in the household of a wealthy Roman. Much of the essay concerns the perils which await the young man at dinner parties. Both in the Talmud and in Lucian's essay, banquets are regarded as occasions when social unease is particularly heightened—though in Lucian's essay it is possible to detect a hint of nostalgia for the refinements of the authentic *symposion*, absent in the Yerushalmi. Both texts reflect the 'status dissonance' of figures like tutors—servile even if not actually slaves, but by definition well-educated, possibly more so than their employers, and so bearing at least one diagnostic marker of social distinction. Both texts also reflect the importance of the *convivium* as an arena for social competition, not only in the metropolitan centre of the Roman empire, but among the grandees—even the relatively modest ones, like the rabbis—of its eastern peripheries (see Dunbabin 2003: 68–71).

If Rabbi Hoshayya pretends to consider the anti-reciprocal values of the Torah supreme but in reality values honour more, a fact merely highlighted by his unconvincing attempt to appease the tutor, Rabbi Eliezer ben Jacob engages in the inverse dissimulation. He pretends to value the rules of hierarchy and precedence—this is why his guests interpret his seating plan (the description of which, like many rabbinic stories and laws, takes for granted the seating arrangement characteristic of *symposia*, adopted in the Roman *convivium*)[7] as they do: the rabbi's decision to sit below the blind guest would not have been meaningful if he were not thought normally to respect social convention, according to which the 'greatest' man present reclines at the head of the central couch. In fact, though, Rabbi Eliezer only conforms with conventions, exploiting them in order to accomplish his true goal, which is the bestowal of a favour on a needy man in a way actually meant to preclude reciprocation. He tricks his friends into providing benefits for the blind wanderer, rather than offering a gift himself, hoping in this way to avoid embroiling the man in a relationship of social dependency with an individual patron. So Rabbi Eliezer plays along with socially competitive conviviality, but truly embraces the values of the Torah. The blind man reciprocates anyway, with a prayer to God to bestow benefits on Rabbi Eliezer. The words of his prayer,

---

[7] The excellent archaeological evidence that these rules were followed in prosperous households in Palestine (the situation of the couches is frequently marked in triclinium mosaics) is surveyed in Talgam and Weiss (2003).

used to express gratitude to a righteous benefactor, the blind tutor of Rabbi Hoshayya uses to shame his false benefactor.

Euergetism

In the second passage I wish to discuss, honour, deference and precedence also play an important role, but the issue I will focus on is the text's appropriation, with crucial changes, of aspects of exchange and memorialisation typical of the Roman practice of euergetism. Let me first emphasise that the Talmud wasted little breath condemning actual Roman-style municipal euergetism: it thought nothing of the practice and took it for granted that many of its products—temples, theatres, public statuary—either were unacceptable, or were simply a neutral part of the urban landscape. This is an aspect of the Talmud's countercultural pose. The rabbis certainly liked baths, and to some extent gardens, but unless these were part of a temple complex, were uninterested in how they happened to be funded or maintained.[8] They *did*, however, notice and address the version of euergetism that was beginning, in the third and fourth centuries, to be naturalised in local Jewish religious communities, discussing in some detail the status of items dedicated to synagogues or communities by private benefactors (m.Megillah 3; t.Megillah 4; p.Megillah 3). But some stories and comments make it clear that they regarded the monumental synagogue—the most important product of Jewish communal euergetism—as a waste of money. The rabbis were happy to exploit Jewish euergetism in order to manipulate Jews into supporting Torah study, or performing the *mitzvah* of supporting the poor, but they clearly did not fully approve of it. Yet, once again, on closer examination, matters prove far more complex and interesting:[9]

---

[8] On rabbis and bathhouses, see Jacobs (1998). As usual, though, matters were really not quite so simple, as the ample literature on m.Avodah Zarah 3.4 demonstrates: see Yadin (2006), including citations of earlier scholarship.

[9] There are partial parallels to the pericope in p.Berakhot 2.1, 4b, p.Shekalim 2.6, 47a and b.Yevamot 96b–97a. In Shekalim the pericope is used to illustrate the following *baraita*: Rabbi Shimon ben Gamliel says, 'They do not make funerary monuments (*nefashot*) for righteous men, for their words are their memorial.' Helpful as this juxtaposition is for my purposes, it is secondary since the *sugya* is surely not original to its context in Shekalim: it appears neither in the Leiden manuscript nor in the Genizah fragments. The Shekalim text has furthermore been revised to bring it into line with b.Yevamot. To be sure, Ginzberg appears to have argued that all versions of the pericope were influenced by, or 'taken from', the Bavli, at least in part, but this is manifestly untrue of the version provided in Mo'ed Katan. On the problems created by this passage, see Epstein (1962: 536); Ginzberg (1941: 235, with n. 7); Sussman (1983: 48). I am most grateful to Richard Kalmin and Shlomo Naeh for their comments.

Rabbi Yoḥanan walked about while leaning on Rabbi Jacob bar Idi,[10] and Rabbi Lazar saw Rabbi Yoḥanan and hid. Rabbi Yoḥanan said, 'This Babylonian committed two wrongs against me, one that he did not greet me, and another that he did not recite a teaching in my name.' Rabbi Jacob bar Idi said to him, 'This is the custom among them [the Babylonians], that a lesser man does not greet a greater man, since they are accustomed to observe the verse, "Youths saw me and hid, elders arose and stood"' (Job 29:8).[11]

As they were walking they saw a study house. Rabbi Jacob bar Idi said to Rabbi Yoḥanan, 'Here Rabbi Meir would sit and expound, and recite teachings in the name of Rabbi Ishmael, but not in the name of Rabbi Akiva.' He responded, 'Everyone knew that Rabbi Meir was the student of Rabbi Akiva [and so it would have been superfluous to cite him by name].' Rabbi Jacob responded, 'And everyone knows that Rabbi Lazar is the student of Rabbi Yoḥanan!'

Rabbi Jacob said to Rabbi Yoḥanan, 'Is it permitted to pass before the image of Adori?'[12] He responded, 'Do you show honour to him? Pass before him and ignore him!'[13] He responded, 'Then Rabbi Lazar acted properly when he did not pass before you!'

---

[10] So also in p.Berakhot; in p.Shekalim, Rabbi Ḥiyya bar Ba.

[11] We could say, in Goffmanian terms, that the Babylonians treated their masters with greater deference than the Palestinians did since their rituals of avoidance, their maintenance of 'ceremonial distance', took a more extreme form (see the seminal discussion of Goffman 1956). Characteristically, though, the distinction is presented as one of biblical exegesis. Bar Idi's response takes it for granted that among the Palestinians, it is the younger parties, or the students, who stand, in accordance with the verse, 'Before the hoary head shalt thou rise' (Lev. 19.32).

[12] Following Sokoloff s.v., who follows the reading at p.Avodah Zarah 3.8, 43b. The meaning is uncertain (Adonis (unlikely), Adados? And why is it *de-Aduri ẓilma* and not *ẓilma de-Aduri?*) though the statue is mentioned several times in the Talmud and seems to have been a well-known landmark perhaps in Tiberias. The suggested explanations of the words in the standard scholarship (S. Klein: Aduri = Adrianos; S. Krauss, Ad/ruri = Arueris, allegedly an Egyptian deity) are unconvincing, but Krauss reports a reading in the Midrash Shmuel (*harodim*) which may suggest that the statue portrayed Herod (Antipas? Antipas was the founder of the city in 19 CE). See Klein (1967: 99–100), Krauss (1897: 345), Friedheim (2006: 100, n. 343). I thank Emmanuel Friedheim for his learned comments to me on this subject. Qorban Ha'edah on the p.Shekalim parallel interprets the story as an attempt to justify Rabbi Lazar's decision to hide: Rabbi Yoḥanan's response to the question about the idol demonstrates that to walk by something/someone without acknowledging it is to dishonour it/him, so Rabbi Lazar had to hide at Rabbi Yoḥanan's approach since if he had not done so, given his Babylonian aversion to greeting his elder, he would have dishonoured Rabbi Yoḥanan. I would add that the story in implicitly comparing Rabbi Yoḥanan to an idol contains a hint of a reproach at what it may see as the rabbi's self-aggrandisement.

[13] *sami eynoyi*—literally, 'blind his eye'; see Sokoloff s.v. *smy*. The idiom is not uncommon. This episode is complicatedly related to the string of halakhic anecdotes at p.Avodah Zarah 3.8, 43b: Gamaliel Zuga was leaning on Rabbi Shimon ben Lakish when they arrived at the Stele [*tavnita*; presumably another well-known idolatrous monument in Tiberias, *vel sim.*]. He said, 'What is the law about passing before it?' He responded, 'Pass before it and ignore it!' Rabbi Isaac bar Matnah was leaning on Rabbi Yoḥanan when they arrived at the statue of [at] the *Boule*. He said, 'What is the law about passing before it?' He responded, 'Pass before it and ignore it!' Rabbi

He said to him, 'Rabbi Jacob bar Idi, you truly know how to pacify!'

And why was Rabbi Yoḥanan so insistent that they report teachings in his name? Even David sought mercy on this point, as it is written, 'I shall dwell in Your tent forever' (Ps. 61:4). Rabbi Pinḥas in the name of Rabbi Yirmiyah said in the name of Rabbi Yoḥanan, 'Did David really think that he would live forever? Rather, David said as follows, "May I merit that my words be said in synagogues and study houses."'

How did it benefit him? Bar Tira [?Nazira?] said, 'Someone who recites a teaching in the name of its sayer, his lips move along with it in the grave, as it is written, "gliding over sleepers' lips" (Song 7:9)—just like a shrunken mass of grapes[14] which flows of its own accord.'

Rabbi Ḥinena bar Papa and Rabbi Simon dispute this point. One says, 'He is like one who drinks spiced wine.' The other says, 'He is like one who drinks old wine: even though he has already drunk it its taste remains in his mouth.'

No generation lacks scoffers: In David's generation what did the libertines do? They would walk by David's windows and say, 'David, David, when will the Temple be built? When will we go to the Lord's house?' And he would say, 'Although they intend to anger me, I swear that I rejoice in my heart', as it is written, 'I was glad when they said to me, Let us go to the house of the Lord' (Ps. 122:1). 'And it came to pass when your days were fulfilled and you lay with your fathers' (1 Chr. 17:11): Rabbi Samuel bar Naḥman said, 'The Holy One said to David, "David, I am counting out for you full days, not deficient ones; is not your son Solomon building the Temple to offer sacrifices? But more beloved to me than sacrifices are the justice and righteousness which you perform."' As it is written, etc. (p.Mo'ed Katan 3.7, 83c)

Like many of the Yerushalmi's stories about rabbis, this one has as one of its themes honour and deference; I will not address these issues in detail here. Rabbi Yoḥanan, unfamiliar as he is either with alleged Babylonian practice— and it is possible that the Talmud itself believes Rabbi Jacob bar Idi has invented it in order to pacify his master—or with the sociology of deference, is offended by a student's apparent failure to pay him appropriate respect. It is very hard to know whether the Talmudic storyteller sympathises with Rabbi Yoḥanan. Certainly there is at least a hint of reproach, a sense conveyed by the tone of the story that the storytellers thought Rabbi Yoḥanan's

---

Jacob bar Idi was leaning on Rabbi Joshua ben Levi when they arrived at the statue of Adori. He said to him, 'Naḥum of the Holy of Holies [renowned for his aversion to images] used to pass by it and you will not? Pass before it and ignore it!' On the relationship between the passages see especially the brief comments of Moskowitz (1990: 28–30).

[14] So Jastrow, s.v. *kumra*; Even-Shoshan translates *kumar* as 'fruit whose ripening is completed by heating it in soil'. Both translations seem speculative/approximate. The rabbinic exegete appears to understand the word *dbb* in the biblical prooftext not as 'gliding over' but as 'causing to murmur'.

behaviour excessive ('Why was he was he so insistent . . .?').[15] I will return to this issue below.

However, the second half of the pericope argues that the practice of reciting teachings in the name of the teachers is not only a matter of honour, or may indeed not be a matter of honour at all. Rather, Rabbi Yoḥanan was so concerned about the correct citation of his teachings because, like David, he felt it would secure his immortality, or his eternal memorialisation: just as David hoped that he would live for ever through the recitation and study of his Psalms in synagogues and study houses, so too Rabbi Yoḥanan thought the perpetuation of his teachings would secure his immortality. The medieval scribe who copied this pericope into p.Shekalim 2.6, 47a, there to serve as commentary on the tannaitic teaching that the righteous need no funerary monuments, since 'their words are their memorial', understood its gist correctly. (The material which follows immediately seems to argue that the dead secure tangible benefit from the repetition of their teachings. This to some extent subverts the point that precedes it in that it de-emphasises the theme of memorialisation). This is a completely perspicuous rabbinisation of what Josephus presents as the traditional Jewish view about memorialisation (Schwartz 2008); it also conforms with the implications of p.Pe'ah 8.7, 21a,[16] that inscription in a text (even in what was perhaps still a purely 'oral' text like the Mishnah: see Sussman 2005) constitutes an appropriate type of memorialisation.

These considerations may also help explain the conclusion of the pericope, which otherwise seems irrelevant (as Neusner in his translation claimed it was, though it appears also in all parallels except that in b.Yevamot). The story of David and the scoffers first of all offers consolation to those living without a temple. But it may also be setting up an antithesis between two modes of memorialisation, monumental/material and moral/cognitive. God certainly approves of the idea of a temple, which performs a public service in helping to expiate the sins of the people of Israel, but prefers David's righteous behaviour. His virtues will live on in people's memories at least as long

---

[15] Cf. p.Sanhedrin 2.6(5), 20c: '[Rabbi Yoḥanan] saw Rabbi Ḥaninah bar Sisi splitting logs. He said to him, "Rabbi, this dishonours you [*let hu mi-kevodakh*]." Rabbi Ḥaninah responded, "What can I do? I have no one to serve me (i.e. a disciple, or, less likely, a slave)." Rabbi Yoḥanan responded, "If you have no one to serve you then you should not have accepted *minui*!"' Here, too, it is difficult to say whether the storyteller agrees with Rabbi Yoḥanan.

[16] Rabbi Yosi went to Kifra (on the outskirts of Tiberias) in order to appoint *parnasim* (charity administrators) for the inhabitants. But they (the people appointed) refused to accept the appointment. Rabbi Yosi came and said to them, 'Ben Bevai was in charge of the gourd' [m.Shekalim 5.1—a list of functionaries in the Jerusalem Temple; Ben Bevai's job was the manufacture of lampwicks from plants]. If the man who was in charge of wicks nevertheless deserved to be counted among the great men of his generation, how much the more so will you, who are being put in charge of people's lives, be so remembered!'

as his son's great building project—in fact, the talmudic storyteller may expect us to see, much, much longer. I would suggest with some diffidence that there is a hint here of the Josephan contrast between honour and piety, between memorialisation in plastic form, and in the preferable form of repetition of stories about the deceased's righteous acts.

The Yerushalmi understood the relationship between the rabbi and the students in his study house as a characteristic euergetistic exchange, though with the sorts of Judaising adaptations already familiar to Josephus. The master bestowed on his students the benefit of his Torah, and the students reciprocated by deferring to and honouring their master, and also by perpetuating his memory, not in the form of inscriptions,[17] statuary, or monumental construction, but by reciting teachings in his name. Thus, at the very institutional and ideological core of rabbinic corporate culture, Roman values, however peculiarly modulated, were somewhat ambivalently embraced—the ambivalence reflected not only in the hint of editorial disapproval of Rabbi Yoḥanan's zeal here, but much more profoundly and systematically in p.Bikurim 3.3's critique of the practice of deferring to and honouring recipients of *minui* (judicial appointment, which was, in Palestine, what made rabbis rabbis). Notwithstanding the ambivalence, honour and memorialisation served—or were meant to serve—as a kind of political currency among rabbis just as they did among Roman elites. The emerging institutional culture of the rabbis in third- and fourth-century Palestine, mirrored, with some distortion, that of the retainers of the Roman state. How are we to understand this?

Conclusion: Roman and Rabbinic Culture

Rabbinic texts tell satisfyingly complex stories about Roman culture and its reception. At the simplest level, both stories analysed here attested to a relatively unfraught process of 'romanisation'. The norms of the Roman *convivium* are taken for granted, not only here but in general in rabbinic rules about meals in the Tosefta and the Yerushalmi, which remarkably adopt rules familiar to us from the elder Pliny, Plutarch and Athenaeus as the halakhic standard (t.Berakhot 5.5ff.; p.Berakhot ad loc.).[18] Somewhat less

---

[17] The well-known Hebrew inscription from Dabbura in the Golan Heights (date unknown) marking the *bet midrash* of Rabbi Eliezer ha-Kapar probably does not constitute an exception to this rule: see Naveh (1978: 25–6, no. 6).

[18] Saul Lieberman denied in a revealingly emphatic way that this was intended as halakhah (my translation): 'This passage describes the customary conduct of feasts in antiquity among the Jewish elites. It includes several details from which no legal conclusions should be drawn, because they originate in the local customs, and not in Jewish law. Generally, the order of the

directly, the second story reflects rabbinic embrace of norms of honour, deference and memorialisation likewise ultimately of Graeco-Roman origin.

But this simple tale of appropriation is complicated by all sorts of contextual issues. The first of these is the rabbis' *ostensible* rejection of Rome, and of *romanitas* in all its manifestations. The second is the fact that both of these Roman norms—the *convivium* and euergetism—had themselves been borrowed by the Romans from Greek praxis, and in fact already had a long—and interesting—history among the Jews by the high and later Roman empire. In the early second century BCE Ben Sira had already devoted sustained attention to sympotic etiquette in a way which shows that well-to-do Jews like their incipiently Hellenising Roman contemporaries had already transformed the symposium from a celebration of solidarity into an arena for social competition (Ben Sira 34(31).12–35(32).13). In the early first century, Philo, paradoxically reclaiming some of the original function of the symposium in the course of a hilariously hostile parody of its contemporary practice, celebrates instead the dignified, silent, and truly egalitarian feasts of the Therapeutae (*De vita contemplativa*, 40–91). As for euergetism, there is some unimpressive evidence for its appropriation by the Jews of Palestine in the middle of the Hellenistic period (assembled by Gardner 2007), but it became a major issue under Herod, whose efforts at mediating between Jewish and Roman interests included serious experimentation with the Graeco-Roman style of benefaction. Josephus declared the experiment a failure but he surely exaggerated. At any rate he himself endorsed a peculiar adaptation of it, in which euergetism and charity were conflated and expressions of gratitude to benefactors assumed an oral rather than a material form.

Another complicating factor is that, if we may trust the evidence both of rabbinic literature itself and of archaeology, Palestinian Jews outside rabbinic circles, or at least the relatively prosperous ones, had appropriated far more eastern Roman culture than the rabbis thought proper. Many talmudic stories portray rabbis behaving as they do in the first story here—manipulating Roman norms so as to trick apparently romanised Jews into following Jewish norms. The Talmud thus admits that rabbis had accommodated to Roman culture, but with the crucial reservation that they simultaneously adhered to and slyly promoted a set of norms they knew to be subversive of the Roman ones.

Still another complicating factor—and one which needs a far more detailed investigation than I have been able to undertake—is that the rabbis seem not to have distinguished strongly between local Greeks and Romans

---

feast conforms with Roman and late Greek practice; there is no *law* of the feast here' (Lieberman 1955: 62). The Passover seder has also been adduced as an example of the adoption, or rather appropriation, of the *convivium* or symposium by the Jews: see Stein (1957).

(though they certainly distinguished between the Greek and Latin languages). I cannot find any indication that the rabbis knew or cared about the cultural lineage of the *convivium* or of public municipal benefaction, or about the discomfort of Greek intellectuals in the face of Roman hegemony. And here is where a reconsideration of Greg Woolf's model (Woolf 1994), and its more thorough assimilation to postcolonial theory adumbrated in Goldhill (ed. 2001), enters the picture. The bits of Hellenic culture the rabbis struggled with they necessarily saw not as sites of resistance to Roman hegemony, but as that hegemony's very essence. Rabbinic literature is important to students of Roman culture because, like Christian literature but in a different way, it gives a stronger indication of what was really at stake for anyone—other than the Roman knight Plutarch and the Roman consul Cassius Dio—trying to resist not just the cruder elements of *romanitas*, but Roman power itself.

Further Reading

Hezser (1997); Jaffee (2000); L. Levine (1989); Lieberman (1994); Ortner (ed. 1999); Rosman (2007); Rubenstein (2003); Schwartz (2002, 2009).

Bibliography

Alon, G. (1977), 'Those appointed for money', in idem, *Jews, Judaism and the Classical World*, Jerusalem.

Bradley, K. (1998), 'The Roman family at dinner', in I. Nielsen and H. S. Nielsen (eds.), *Meals in a Social Context: Aspects of the Communal Meal in the Hellenistic and Roman World*, Aarhus, pp. 36–55.

Burke, P. (2005), *History and Social Theory*, 2nd edn., Ithaca.

D'Arms, J. (1990), 'The Roman convivium and the idea of equality', in O. Murray (ed.), *Sympotica*, pp. 308–20.

Dunbabin, K. (2003), *The Roman Banquet: Images of Conviviality*, Cambridge.

Epstein, J. N. (1962), *Prolegomena ad Litteras Amoraiticas*, ed. E. Z. Melamed, Jerusalem. [Hebrew]

Friedheim, E. (2006), *Rabbinisme et paganisme en Palestine romaine: Étude historique des realia talmudiques (Ier–IVeme siècles)*, Leiden.

Gardner, G. (2007), 'Jewish leadership and Hellenistic civic benefaction in the second century BCE', *Journal of Biblical Literature*, 126: 327–43.

Ginzberg, L. (1941), *A Commentary on the Palestinian Talmud*, vol. 1, New York.

Goffman, E. (1956), 'The nature of deference and demeanor', *American Anthropologist*, 58: 473–502.

Goldhill, S. (ed.) (2001), *Being Greek under Rome: Cultural Identity, the Second Sophistic and the Development of Empire*, Cambridge.

Hezser, C. (1997), *The Social Structure of the Rabbinic Movement in Roman Palestine*, Tübingen.

Jacobs, M. (1998), 'Römische Thermenkultur im Spiegel des Talmud Yerushalmi', in P. Schäfer (ed.), *The Talmud Yerushalmi and Greco-Roman Culture*, vol. 1, Tübingen, pp. 219–311.

Jaffee, M. (2000), *Torah in the Mouth: Writing and Oral Tradition in Palestinian Judaism, 200 BCE–400 CE*, New York.

Klein, S. (1967), *Galilee: Geography and History of Galilee from the Return from Babylonia to the Conclusion of the Talmud*, 2nd edn., Jerusalem.

Krauss, S. (1897), 'Ägyptische und syrische Götternamen im Talmud', in G. A. Kohut (ed.), *Semitic Studies in Memory of Rev. Dr. Alexander Kohut*, Berlin, pp. 339–53.

Lendon, J. E. (1997), *Empire of Honor: The Art of Government in the Roman World*, Oxford.

Levine, D. (1985), 'Symposium and the polis', in T. Figueira and G. Nagy (eds.), *Theognis of Megara: Poetry and the Polis*, Baltimore, pp. 176–96.

Levine, L. (1989), *The Rabbinic Class of Roman Palestine in Late Antiquity*, Jerusalem and New York.

Lieberman, S. (1955), *Tosefta Kifshutah*, vol. 1, New York. [Hebrew]

Lieberman, S. (1994), *Greek in Jewish Palestine; Hellenism in Jewish Palestine*, with a new introduction by D. Zlotnick, New York.

Moskowitz, L. (1990), '*Sugyot Muhlafot* in the Talmud Yerushalmi', *Tarbiz*, 60: 19–66. [Hebrew]

Murray, O. (1990), 'Sympotic history', in idem (ed.), *Sympotica: A Symposium on the Symposion*, Oxford, pp. 3–13.

Naveh, J. (1978), *On Stone and Mosaic: The Hebrew and Aramaic Inscriptions from Ancient Synagogues*, Jerusalem.

Ortner, S. (ed.) (1999), *The Fate of 'Culture': Geertz and Beyond*, Berkeley.

Roller, M. (2006), *Dining Posture in Ancient Rome: Bodies, Values, and Status*, Princeton.

Rosman, M. (2007), *How Jewish is Jewish History?*, Oxford.

Rubenstein, J. (2003), *The Culture of the Babylonian Talmud*, Baltimore.

Saller, R. (1982), *Personal Patronage under the Early Empire*, Cambridge.

Schmitt Pantel, P. (1992), *La Cité au banquet: Histoire des répas publics dans les cités grecques*, Rome.

Schwartz, S. (2002), 'Historiography on the Jews in the Talmudic period', in M. Goodman (ed.), *The Oxford Handbook of Jewish Studies*, Oxford, pp. 79–114.

Schwartz, S. (2008), 'Euergetism in Josephus and the epigraphic culture of first-century Jerusalem', in H. Cotton, J. Price and D. Wasserstein (eds.), *From Hellenism to Islam: Cultural and Linguistic Change in the Roman Near East*, Cambridge.

Schwartz, S. (2009), *Were the Jews a Mediterranean Society? Reciprocity and Solidarity in Ancient Judaism*, Princeton.

Smith, J. Z. (1982), *Imagining Religion: From Babylon to Jonestown*, Chicago.

Stein, S. (1957), 'The influence of symposia literature on the literary form of the Pesah Haggadah', *JJS* 8: 13–44.

Sussman, Y. (1983), 'Mesoret limud u-mesoret nusah shel ha-talmud ha-yerushalmi: Le-verur nusha'otehah shel yerushalmi masekhet sheqalim', in *Researches in*

Talmudic Literature: A Study Conference in Honour of the Eightieth Birthday of Sha'ul Lieberman, 13–14 June 1978 (no editor), Jerusalem, pp. 12–76. [Hebrew]

Sussman, Y. (2005), '"Torah she-be'al peh' peshutah ke-mashma'ah: koho shel qutzo shel yod', in Y. Sussman and D. Rosenthal (eds.), *Meḥqerei Talmud: Talmudic Studies Dedicated to the Memory of Professor Eliezer Shimshon Rosenthal*, vol. 3.1, Jerusalem, pp. 209–384. [Hebrew]

Talgam, R. and Weiss, Z. (2003), *The Mosaics of the House of Dionysos at Sepphoris*, Jerusalem.

Wallace-Hadrill, A. (ed.) (1989), *Patronage in Ancient Society*, London.

Woolf, G. (1994), 'Becoming Roman, staying Greek: culture, identity and the civilizing process in the Roman East', *Proceedings of the Cambridge Philological Society*, 40: 116–43.

Yadin, A. (2006), 'Rabban Gamliel, Aphrodite's bath, and the question of pagan monotheism', *JQR* 96: 149–79.

17

Material Culture and Daily Life

CATHERINE HEZSER

DURING THE LAST DECADES SCHOLARSHIP HAS SEEN MAJOR CHANGES in the analysis of rabbinic literature and in the assessment of the impact of rabbis on ancient Jewish society and culture. At the same time archaeologists have extended the scope of their interest beyond synagogues and burial places to private houses and the various remnants and artefacts of daily life. One of the main problems of research on material culture and daily life, perceived by talmudists, historians and archaeologists alike, is the establishment of a proper relationship between rabbinic literary references and archaeological data, between text and object. How and to what extent can rabbinic sources be used to elucidate the excavated material? Or, looked at from the perspective of the student of the text: what is the benefit of archaeological material for the interpretation of a textual passage? As we shall see in the following discussion, these complex problems are still unresolved. It will be suggested in the following that these issues should be approached on the basis of a historical-critical study of rabbinic sources in a broad interdisciplinary framework, which takes account of archaeological research within the Graeco-Roman and early Byzantine context and which uses tools, methods and models developed by the social sciences.

Methodological Issues

Whereas in the past scholars would talk about rabbinic literature and 'realia', nowadays the study of 'material culture' has become fashionable not only as far as ancient Judaism is concerned. A simple search on the internet leads to a number of definitions of 'material culture', for example: 'the buildings, tools, and other artefacts that include any material item that has had cultural meaning ascribed to it, past and present'; 'the material means by which humans adapt to the world'; 'the material objects that are used to: (1) help determine a sequence of events and dates, (2) formulate a reconstruction of many ways of life, and (3) help to provide us some understanding of why human culture has changed through time'. These formulations already show that 'material culture' has a much broader meaning than 'realia': in the study of material culture the respective 'realia' are seen within their wider social and cultural context. The objects no longer remain isolated fragments and artefacts which are mute and disconnected; they rather receive meaning and significance through their use by members of a particular culture and social group. The study of the material culture of the Jewish inhabitants of Roman Palestine must therefore be conducted in the context of an interdisciplinary cultural studies approach, which requires the cooperation of archaeologists, classicists, talmudists, historians, and scholars of paganism and ancient Christianity.

The traditional study of 'realia' often went hand in hand with a positivistic approach to rabbinic literature. The goal was to find archaeological evidence of phenomena mentioned in rabbinic sources or, vice versa, to interpret excavated finds on the basis of a simplistic literal reading of rabbinic sources which took the texts at face value as historical records of ancient Jewish life and practice. Differences between early and late, and between Palestinian and Babylonian traditions were often not taken into account. The entire body of rabbinic literature was rather seen as a vast treasure trove of bits and pieces of information on almost all aspects of daily life. The resulting studies arranged this information thematically, explained terminology, and tried to harmonise as best as possible between rabbinic references and the 'hard evidence' which archaeologists provided (see, for example, Krauss's monumental work, originally published 1910–12, republished in 1966). In cases where archaeological support could not be found, Krauss referred to Arab life in Mandate Palestine as the framework for interpreting some of the practices of ancient Jewish daily life.

In the last three decades scholarship on rabbinic literature and society has undergone major changes, changes which challenge rabbinic literature's value as the major framework for interpreting archaeological finds and which make a re-evaluation of the relationship between literary and material remains mandatory.

Firstly, rabbinic texts are no longer seen as historically trustworthy depictions of events and practices in ancient Jewish society: that is, the direct link between literary depiction and social reality, which was traditionally taken for granted, has been severed. Jacob Neusner has been most outspoken in maintaining that rabbinic literature merely allows us to reconstruct rabbinic ideology, theology, and halakhic theory rather than reflecting ancient Jews' real life (see, for example, Neusner 1980, 1984, and 1988). Since rabbinic traditions were transmitted orally for decades or even centuries before they were written down and constantly changed and adapted during the transmission period, the written sources do not necessarily provide evidence of practices or views held prior to the editors' own time. That rabbinic references to so-called realia reflected real life cannot be assumed at the outset but needs to be investigated for each text individually (see Goodblatt 1980). Since rabbis were interested in such 'trivia' as garments, jewellery or cooking vessels only as far as they were relevant for the discussion of certain halakhic issues, such references are scarce and sporadic. We have to reckon with inaccurate and/or typological descriptions and standardisations, not to mention the large gaps left by certain aspects of everyday life not mentioned at all.

Secondly, rabbinic opinions and practices are no longer seen as representative of Palestinian Jewish society at large. It can now be considered *communis opinio* that rabbis were not the officially appointed leaders of communities who controlled other Jews' daily lives. They rather formed a widespread network of like-minded Torah scholars whose influence on their contemporaries was based on personal ties and persuasion only (Hezser 1997: esp. 228–39, 450–66). Some scholars therefore see their impact on ancient Jewish society as rather limited and circumscribed.[1]

On the basis of these new directions which rabbinic and historical scholarship have taken, the relationship between rabbinic texts and archaeological remains becomes much more complex and complicated than perceived in the past: if we cannot assume that rabbinic literature provides historically accurate information on the so-called 'realia', how can these texts be used to interpret the excavated material which remains mute without other evidence? If rabbinic literature reflects the perspective of the rabbis only, how can these texts be used to make any assumptions about ancient Jewish life in general? Can this literature serve as the proper framework for interpreting buildings and artefacts on whose existence and function rabbis would not have had any influence? If rabbinic sources lose at least part of their interpretative value, which other contexts and frameworks are available to make sense of the material traces of non- or extra-rabbinic Judaism that survive?

These questions and problems are linked to another important aspect of the investigation of ancient Jewish material culture: How can we separate a 'Jewish' material culture from the broader Graeco-Roman and Byzantine material culture of the Land of Israel? What lets us assume that a certain building or artefact or inscription or image is Jewish rather than Graeco-Roman or Christian? In the past, when 'Jewish' was considered identical with 'rabbinic' such issues were much easier to decide. Now that we lack this direct connection and are much more aware of the varieties of ancient Jewish life and practice, we have to assume that blurred boundaries between Jewish, Christian and pagan culture existed. The criteria which are commonly used

---

[1] S. Schwartz (2001: 103–28); see also Miller (2006: 464): 'The rabbis were largely speaking, studying, and teaching among themselves and their households.'

to identify realia as Jewish obviously provide evidence for one type of Jewish culture only through identifiably Jewish symbols, names, and Hebrew as the 'holy language'.[2] We have to reckon with the possibility that many or even the majority of Jews did not even feel the need to identify themselves, their buildings, clothes and lifestyles as Jewish, especially if they lived in the Land of Israel, the Jewish homeland, where Graeco-Roman customs and images and architectural styles may not have been considered as much a threat as in the Diaspora, as the lack of pagan images in Diaspora Jewish art in comparison to Jewish art in Palestine suggests (see below).

How can we, then, approach the challenge of interpreting the material remains of Roman Palestine, given that rabbinic documents constitute the major Jewish literary source for the time and area under investigation? First of all, it is necessary to be more open-minded than some previous scholars were: to reckon with the possibility that Jewish material culture may not have differed from pagan or Christian material culture in many aspects of daily life (see also Friedheim 2006, who even reckons with Jewish participation in pagan rituals) and that various types of agglomeration and adaptation existed. Even rabbis themselves accommodated to Graeco-Roman culture (see S. Schwartz 1998), so that Goodenough's hypothesis (Goodenough 1953, see the discussion below) of a strict division between rabbinic and popular culture does not provide a satisfactory solution either, although it is still championed by some contemporary scholars.

Secondly, other frameworks of interpretation besides the rabbinic one need to be explored. Such frameworks are provided by Graeco-Roman and early Christian architecture and art, literature and mythology. For example, for many architectural features of ancient synagogues church architecture provides the appropriate explanatory base (Fine 2005: 88; Milson 2006). The many theatres excavated in Roman Palestine can be understood properly only in the context of late-antique performances and plays (Weiss, thesis 1995; Hezser 2005). This approach often requires a knowledge and expertise beyond the respective scholar's field of specialisation, and interdisciplinary cooperation is thus necessary. The study of the material remains of ancient Jews needs to move away from the investigation of mere 'realia' towards a much more integrated, cultural-historical approach which views the excavated objects as traces of the religious, cultural and everyday life practices of ancient Jews. For example, it is no longer sufficient merely to describe the architectural forms of buildings such as bathhouses and to provide an analysis of rabbinic references to these institutions; rather, both the material and literary evidence need to be evaluated in the social and cultural context of the

---

[2] See the criteria mentioned by van der Horst (1991) to identify Jewish inscriptions; see also Lapin (1999a).

bathing culture of late antiquity (cf. Jacobs 1998a; Eliav 2000). In this connection rabbinic sources may provide important supplementary information to the material finds, providing traces and allusions to ways in which the buildings were used. For such a more comprehensive analysis, methods and models developed by sociologists, anthropologists and cultural historians may be helpful.

Public Architecture and Infrastructure

Cities such as Caesarea and Beth She'an/Scythopolis, but also Sepphoris and Tiberias, were constructed like Roman cities with the *cardo* and *decumanus* as the main intersecting streets, lined by Roman institutions such as theatres, bathhouses, and basilica-style buildings. Whereas earlier scholarship viewed archaeological remains in the context of rabbinic references to Caesarea (Levine 1975), more recent interdisciplinary studies have analysed the city and its harbour within the much wider scope of the Roman empire at large (Raban and Holum 1996). The rabbinic connection to Caesarea is only one aspect of this approach, and Caesarean rabbis are correctly viewed within the context of other late-antique intellectual movements (see Lapin in Raban and Holum 1996: 496–514). It is hoped that such interdisciplinary studies will also be devoted to other cities of Roman Palestine in the future.

Historical scholarship on ancient Judaism has mainly been concerned with the issue of rabbis' greater presence in cities in the third and fourth centuries, in comparison with the earlier tannaitic period. Lapin has not only studied the literary evidence (Lapin 1999b) but also the consequences and significance of rabbis as late-antique city dwellers (Lapin 2000). Rabbinic sources also abound with references linking rabbis to villages, however, and interactions between cities, smaller towns, and the countryside need to be explored more. Romans were interested in expanding the city territories into the countryside. The Roman road system created a vast network of interlinked settlements (see Roll 1995), of which rabbis seem to have taken advantage. Like other late-Roman intellectuals, rabbis present themselves as very mobile. A connection between the improved infrastructure of Roman Palestine and relationships amongst the geographically dispersed and decentralised rabbinic movement may be assumed.

Studies of public buildings of Roman Palestine usually distinguish between Graeco-Roman (theatres, bathhouses, temples, basilicas), Jewish (synagogues, cemeteries) and Christian (churches, monasteries) institutions. Yet recent studies have shown that many architectural features were shared: late-antique synagogues and churches followed the Graeco-Roman basilica model; the *bema* (elevated platform) of the late-antique synagogues and churches resembles the theatre stage (Hezser: 2005: 293–4); synagogues seem to have taken over architectural features from churches (see Fine 2005: 88, 92; Milson 2006) and some were eventually transformed into churches in the Byzantine period. Similarities in building styles and the lack of Jewish identity markers make it often difficult, if not impossible, to identify the nature and function of a space. It is no longer persuasive to argue that a large basilica building such as the one recently excavated in Tiberias should be considered the seat of the Sanhedrin, and the identification of some of the first-century rectangular halls at Masada, Gamla, Herodion and Jericho as synagogues in the sense of religious communal centres has become questionable (S. Schwartz 2001: 225).

The larger Graeco-Roman (provincial) context constitutes the framework in which these buildings need to be analysed. It is interesting, for example, that guest quarters or hostels were part of or associated with both pagan and Christian religious institutions in antiquity. A hostel is also mentioned in the Theodotus synagogue inscription from Jerusalem (Levine 2000: 55) and rabbinic sources mention dining rooms in synagogues (see, for example, p.Ber. 2:9, 5d: R. Issa and R. Shmuel b. R. Yiẓhak eat in a room above a synagogue). This shows that hypotheses about the functions of certain rooms can be made on the basis of the literary and epigraphic sources and comparative architectural evidence only.

Schools (*batei sefer*) and study houses (*batei midrash*) are examples of institutions mentioned in rabbinic sources for which no archaeological evidence exists (with the exception of one well-known lintel inscription from the Golan). In contrast to the Sanhedrin, the evidence for whose post-70 existence has been successfully dismantled by David Goodblatt (1994), scholars agree that study houses existed and that (informal) elementary teaching took place as well. The places where these activities took place cannot be identified, however, since they could have taken place in any private or public room or building—which may have been used for other purposes at other times (the same is true for elementary schools in Graeco-Roman society). Thus, it is imaginable that rooms in synagogue complexes as well as elementary teachers' private homes could function as 'schools' (see Hezser 2001: 51–4), and this consideration applies to study houses as well (see Hezser 1997: 205–14).

Rabbinic literature juxtaposes synagogues and study houses with theatres and circuses but does not tell us much about the latter, besides rabbis' critical attitude towards them (see Jacobs 1998b; Hezser 2005). Rabbinic literature therefore does not serve as a very good interpretative context for the many theatres, amphitheatres and stadia excavated in the Land of Israel. Similarities to the rabbinic attitude towards these Roman entertainment institutions can also be found amongst pagan and Christian intellectuals. The negative view must be considered a minority attitude, however, which would not have reflected the views of ancient Jews at large. Rabbinic admonitions rather imply that many Jews were attracted to the performances offered at these locales, and they may even have travelled from the countryside to the city to attend them, as Greeks and Romans did. Information on the nature of the performances and the attraction they had for the Italian and provincial population can be found in Graeco-Roman sources. In order to understand properly what was going on at the theatres of Roman Palestine, non-Jewish literary sources are therefore much more relevant than Jewish ones, which are relatively mute on this topic and reflect religious functionaries' views only.

The case of bathhouses is different because rabbis obviously liked these institutions and frequented them themselves.[3] An analysis of rabbinic literature can reveal how these institutions were used by a particular provincial intellectual group in late antiquity. Obviously, the bathhouse stories cannot be taken literally as historical evidence for these institutions. Rabbis were most interested in the halakhic issues involved, but some literary details fit the picture which archaeological excavations and Graeco-Roman literary sources provide. What is most interesting is the bathhouse culture which seems to have been a common late-antique phenomenon, perhaps with the exception of Christian clergy who condemned the nudity and frivolity associated with these institutions. It would be interesting to see how Roman Palestine compares with other Roman provinces in this regard, at least until the fourth century CE.

Scholarly debate concerning the Zodiac motif on the mosaic floors of late-antique synagogues continues (for an introduction to the debate see Hachlili 1977; Levine 2000: 200ff., 572ff.). The Zodiac cycle representing the twelve months of the year surrounds Helios, whom Greeks and Romans worshipped as Sol Invictus. Helios appears as the sun or a figure driving a chariot. Personifications of the four seasons are usually part of this complex, which is accompanied by biblical salvation scenes such as the binding of Isaac and Daniel in the lion's den. The Jewish depiction differs from the pagan and Christian use of the motif in a number of regards, but the very phenomenon that Jews could represent Helios in the religious context of the synagogue has struck scholars for decades. In the 1950s Erwin R. Goodenough had tried to explain the phenomenon by distinguishing between an 'orthodox' aniconic rabbinic Judaism, which he believed would not have tolerated such images, and a popular syncretistic and mystical

---

[3] Accordingly, Jacobs (1998a) on bathhouses is much more voluminous than his article on theatres, Jacobs (1998b); see also Eliav (2000).

Judaism which adopted them from the surrounding culture in a liberal and deliberate way.[4]

Nowadays hardly any scholar would share such a harsh opposition between 'the rabbis' and 'the people' in late-Roman Palestine. Rabbis are mentioned as donors in synagogue inscriptions (Hezser 2001: 403–6). Shaye Cohen's view that these 'epigraphical rabbis' could not have been Torah scholars and should therefore be distinguished from the 'literary rabbis' is hardly convincing and not accepted by most scholars nowadays (see Cohen 1981–82; Hezser 1997: 119–23; Miller 2004). The so-called 'literary rabbis' did not form a homogeneous group but differed amongst themselves. Rabbinic literature therefore presents ambiguous information on rabbis' relationship to images (see, for example, the discussions in p.AZ 3, 42b–43d). Their relation to (pagan) images therefore needs to be re-examined. Literary references to symbols (e.g. in Midrash and liturgy) have to be studied together with the archaeological material (see Neusner 1991; Miller 2004), a task which has not yet been undertaken in a comprehensive and historical-critical way.

The explanations offered range from associating the Zodiac-Helios complex with priests, considering it an expression of the Jewish God's power over creation, and viewing it in the context of the calendar, astrology and Jewish liturgy.[5] Again, the proper significance of the imagery in the Jewish context can be established only on the basis of a comparison with similar depictions in Graeco-Roman paganism and early Byzantine Christian art. There may have been certain aspects of ancient mythology which were sufficiently open and 'universal' to be shared by Jews, Christians and pagans but given different meanings in different contexts (see Hezser 2005). The same is true for the biblical motifs and scenes which appear in both synagogues and churches of the fifth and sixth centuries CE and can be combined with the Zodiac imagery. The issue of Jews and 'pagan' art is a much wider topic — pagan images appear not only in synagogues but also in private houses (e.g. in Sepphoris) and cemeteries (e.g. in Beth She'arim) — which, again, leads us to the necessity of an interdisciplinary approach which integrates the expertise gained by talmudists, archaeologists, classicists, art historians and scholars of early Christianity.

---

[4] Goodenough (1953: vols. 1–3), abbreviated version by Neusner (ed. 1988); for a collection of Goodenough's articles see Neusner and Frerichs (eds. 1986).
[5] For recent discussions of the issue see S. Schwartz (2000); A. Cohen (2001); Goodman (2003); Levine (2003); Magness (2003); Fine (2005: 199–205).

Domestic Architecture and Daily Life

In contrast to public buildings, and foremost amongst them synagogues, ancient Jewish private architecture has not received much attention amongst either archaeologists or scholars of rabbinic literature so far (on public–private distinctions in rabbinic literature see Hezser 1998). Understandably, scholars have been more interested in the origins and development of important contemporary Jewish institutions than in the details of daily life in antiquity, which have been considered inconsequential and unextraordinary. Two further reasons may be adduced for the lack of academic attention to 'daily life' issues since Krauss's monumental *Talmudische Archäologie* was written a hundred years ago. Historians of Graeco-Roman antiquity have begun investigating everyday life in depth since the 1970s and 1980s, after Fernand Braudel (1902–85) and the so-called *Annales* School began to stress the significance of the social sciences, anthropology and economic history. One could argue that if the daily life of Jews, especially as far as material culture is concerned, did not differ much from that of Greeks and Romans in antiquity, it would not require detailed analysis.

Yizhar Hirschfeld and Katharina Galor are the only archaeologists who have excavated and studied the domestic architecture of Roman Palestine in a comprehensive way (Hirschfeld 1995; Galor 2000, 2003). In his book Hirschfeld differentiates between a number of different types of houses according to their architectural features (especially so-called simple dwellings and courtyard houses) and compares them with Arab houses in the Middle East. The typology seems too complex and disparate to be useful, however (for example, the courtyard is a feature not only of the so-called courtyard houses), and Roman (provincial) domestic architecture may provide a more appropriate framework for analysing the buildings than modern Arab building styles. In particular, the Roman *insulae*, multi-unit apartment buildings, which are also found prominently both in cities (e.g. Sepphoris) and in villages (e.g. Korazim) of Roman Palestine, are not given sufficient attention. Furthermore, rabbinic references to the use of rooms and the halakhic issues involved in shared apartment buildings are not evaluated critically. Rabbinic literature contains numerous discussions of domestic legal problems (for example, damages to shared buildings, disturbance by noise or fumes, trouble with the trees of neighbours overreaching one's property), which need to be discussed in conjunction with the archaeological material and in the context of Graeco-Roman archaeological and literary evidence properly to assess ancient Jewish living conditions.[6]

---

[6] See Hezser (1998: 481–577) for a discussion of neighbourly disputes and domestic architecture in the Talmud Yerushalmi.

An issue relating to domestic architecture is the question whether certain pits, which are found in the *insula* quarters of Sepphoris and elsewhere, should be identified as Jewish ritual baths or *mikva'ot*, which are also discussed in rabbinic sources. Even though these cavities sometimes do not fulfil the halakhic requirements of *mikva'ot* prescribed by rabbis, some scholars believe that they nevertheless served ritual purity purposes (E. Meyers 2002; Reich 2002). Others have questioned this view and suggested several other explanations (Eshel 1997; Miller 2007), such as freshwater reservoirs, storage pits, bathtubs. It is necessary to distinguish between the various finds according to their features and contexts rather than applying the 'mikvah' label to all of them (see Jacobs 1998a: 221–3). The various suggested functions also need not have been mutually exclusive. This is a good example of archaeological finds remaining mute without a literary context, but also of the danger of using literature to read something into excavated material. Obviously the issue has a much larger significance beyond the mere identification of archaeological remains. Was purity observance common amongst non-rabbinic Jews? Did the Jewish populace follow rabbinic recommendations? How does ritual purity relate to ordinary baths and the bathhouses of Roman Palestine?

Shops and workshops are other types of buildings which form part of the private sphere of daily life. They were often part of domestic buildings, occupying (part) of the ground floor of buildings and opening either into the (shared) internal courtyard or into the alleyway or street (see Peskowitz 1993). The connection between workshops and private quarters already indicates that for the less wealthy members of the lower and middle strata of society a strict distinction between private and public could not be maintained. Furthermore, gender divisions in the use and allocation of space break down in the case of (work)shops: in contrast to upper-class women, working women's lives could not be confined to the private sphere (see Peskowitz 1997a). They had to work alongside men in workshops, attend to customers in shops, and go to the market themselves. This brings up the issue of gender in the study of material culture and daily life. Not enough attention has been paid to differences between Jewish men and women in the use of the various types of public and private buildings and in regard to material culture in general.[7] The gender-conscious approach, which Carol Meyers has carried out for biblical archaeology (see Meyers 2003, 2004), needs to be applied to the material culture of Roman-Byzantine Palestine as well.[8]

Other material aspects of daily life concern shoes and clothing, jewellery, household vessels, food, and burial practices. Not much work has been done

[7] For gender issues and Palestinian archaeology see Sawicki (1994) and the reply of Peskowitz (1997b); Edwards and McCollough (eds. 2007). See also Baker (2002).

[8] For general introductions to Jewish women's studies see Ilan (1996, 2002).

on these topics yet (*The Oxford Handbook of Jewish Daily Life in Roman Palestine*, which I have edited, will be published in 2010). Tziona Grossmark has completed a doctoral thesis on rabbinic references to jewellery (Grossmark 1994) and she has published a few articles on particular details, such as rabbinic laws regarding idolatry and jewellery (Grossmark 2005). At Bar Ilan University Dafna Shlezinger-Katsman is currently working on a Ph.D. thesis on ancient Jewish clothing under the guidance of Joshua Schwartz, who has published an article on the issue (Schwartz 2004). The literary evidence needs to be integrated with the archaeological remains of clothing and jewellery found in Roman Palestine, and all of these data have to be studied within the context of clothing and jewellery in the Roman empire at large. It seems that, in general, Jews did not wear particular clothes or ornaments which separated them from non-Jews, so the issue of whether a certain item belonged to and was used by a Jew or non-Jew is complicated and depends on the specific context in which it was found.

Household vessels were produced in a variety of materials, amongst them clay, stone and glass. The production of pottery vessels has been investigated by David Adan-Bayewitz (1993) from a regional archaeological point of view and in the context of Galilean local trade. On the basis of excavated stone vessels Roland Deines (1993) has argued that large numbers of the Jewish population of the early first century CE adhered to Pharisaic purity ideals, which he reconstructs from rabbinic halakhah. There are a number of problems with this argument, which are similar to those already mentioned in connection with the alleged *mikva'ot* (see also Miller 2003; Regev 2006). There is no archaeological evidence which would suggest that the stone vessels were used specifically for purity purposes. The rabbinic sources cited in support of Pharisaic positions were compiled and edited after the first century and cannot be considered historically reliable.

The food, food preparation, and meals of Jews in Roman Palestine constitute another important issue of everyday life which has not yet received sufficient attention. Susan Weingarten has devoted a number of articles to this topic (2003, 2005) and David Kraemer has recently published a book on *Jewish Eating and Identity Through the Ages* (2007). Israeli archaeologists have dealt with this issue, too, and viewed Jewish eating and drinking habits in the context of the Mediterranean and/or Roman diet (see e.g. Reich 2003; Borowski 2004; Broshi 2007). Again, archaeological and literary evidence has to be correlated, but not harmonised, to create a more integrated picture of ancient Jewish dietary customs. The issue of food is closely related to meals and banquets, and these institutions have to be seen in the context of social contacts and socialising in antiquity (see e.g. Vana 1997). Rabbinic literature contains numerous stories about rabbis sharing meals with each other and other people, discussions about ritually proper food preparation and festival meals, problems with non-kosher food offered to Jews, and parables about royal banquets. All of this material needs to be evaluated together and seen in the context of studies of Roman and early Christian ordinary and ritual meals.

Since human life ends with death and burial, this is a proper topic to be mentioned at the end of this survey. The material remains consist of graves, cemeteries, and burial inscriptions (on Jewish epigraphic practices, see Hezser 2001: 364–97), whereas rabbinic literature mainly deals with deathbed scenes and mourning practices (Saldarini 1977; Neusner 1986). Issues of afterlife seem to have been of minor importance to rabbis but may have been the basis of the Herodian-period practice of secondary burial in ossuaries (Fine 2000). Various forms of the title 'Rabbi' appear in funerary contexts, even at Beth She'arim, the alleged burial place of the patriarch R. Judah haNasi, where many sarcophagi have pagan images (see S. J. D. Cohen 1981–82). Interestingly, at Beth She'arim rabbis are mostly commemorated in Hebrew or Aramaic and bilingual inscriptions and buried in sarcophagi without figural images, so that even in this quite Hellenised context certain distinctions were maintained (see Hezser 2001: 385–7). Although family burials were common, women are clearly under-represented in both ossuary and sarcophagus inscriptions and usually mentioned in relation to named male individuals only (see Hezser 2001: 368–9, 379, 388). An issue which has puzzled scholars is the frequent mention of the foreign origins of the deceased at Beth She'arim and elsewhere. The question whether these individuals were Diaspora immigrants, or brought to the Land of Israel for burial only, remains unresolved (Gafni 1981; 1997: 79–95; Rajak 1998).

Further Reading

The classical statement on ancient Jewish 'realia' is Krauss (1910–12). The following studies provide good introductions into the topic of ancient Jewish material culture and the methodological issues involved: Goodblatt (1980), Eliav (2002), Fine (2006), J. Schwartz (2006). On the investigation of non-rabbinic 'popular' culture see Hezser (2005). On the relationship between Jewish and Graeco-Roman culture see Goodman (2007). For a good example of an interdisciplinary approach, see Raban and Holum (1996).

Bibliography

Adan-Bayewitz, D. (1993), *Common Pottery in Roman Galilee: A Study of Local Trade*, Ramat Gan.

Baker, C. M. (2002), *Rebuilding the House of Israel: Architectures of Gender in Jewish Antiquity*, Stanford, CA.

Borowski, O. (2004), 'Eat, drink, and be merry: the Mediterranean diet', *Near Eastern Archaeology*, 62: 96–107.

Broshi, M. (2007), 'Date beer and date wine in antiquity', *Palestine Exploration Journal Quarterly*, 139: 55–9.

Cohen, A. (2001), 'The celestial host, the calendar, and Jewish art', in I. Fishof with A. Cohen and M. Idel, *Written in the Stars: Art and Symbolism of the Zodiac*, Israel Museum, Jerusalem, pp. 11–18.

Cohen, S. J. D. (1981–82), 'Epigraphical rabbis', *JQR* 72: 1–17.

Deines, R. (1993), *Jüdische Steingefässe und pharisäische Frömmigkeit. Ein archäologisch-historischer Beitrag zum Verständnis von Johannes 2,6 und der jüdischen Reinheitshalacha zur Zeit Jesu*, Tübingen.

Edwards, D. R. (ed.) (2004), *Religion and Society in Roman Palestine: Old Questions, New Approaches*, London.

Edwards, D. R. and McCollough, C. T. (eds.) (2007), *The Archaeology of Difference: Gender, Ethnicity, Class and the 'Other' in Antiquity: Studies in Honor of Eric M. Meyers*, Boston.

Eliav, Y. Z. (2000), 'The Roman bath as a Jewish institution: another look at the encounter between Judaism and the Greco-Roman culture', *Journal for the Study of Judaism*, 31: 416–54.

Eliav, Y. Z. (2002), '"Realia", daily life, and the transmission of local stories during the Talmudic period', in L. V. Rutgers (ed.), *What Athens Has To Do With Jerusalem: Essays on Classical, Jewish, and Early Christian Art and Archaeology in Honor of Gideon Foerster*, Leuven, pp. 235–65.

Eshel, H. (1997), 'A note on "Miqvaot" at Sepphoris', in D. R. Edwards and C. T. McCollough (eds.), *Archaeology and the Galilee: Texts and Contexts in the Graeco-Roman and Byzantine Periods*, Atlanta, pp. 131–3.

Fine, S. (2000), 'A note on ossuary burial and the resurrection of the dead in first-century Jerusalem', *JJS* 51: 69–76.

Fine, S. (2005), *Art and Judaism in the Graeco-Roman World: Towards a New Jewish Archaeology*, Cambridge.

Fine, S. (2006), 'Archaeology and the interpretation of rabbinic literature: some thoughts', in M. Kraus (ed.), *How Should Rabbinic Literature Be Read in the Modern World?*, Piscataway, NJ, pp. 199–217.

Friedheim, E. (2006), *Rabbanisme et paganisme en Palestine romaine*, Leiden.

Gafni, I. (1981), 'Reinterment in the Land of Israel: Notes on the origin and development of the custom', *Jerusalem Cathedra*, 1: 96–104.

Gafni, I. (1997), *Land, Center and Diaspora: Jewish Constructs in Late Antiquity*, Sheffield.

Galor, K. (2000), 'The Roman-Byzantine dwelling in the Galilee and the Golan: "house" or "apartment"?', *Archaeologia Transatlantica*, 18: 17–34.

Galor, K. (2003), 'Domestic architecture in Roman and Byzantine Galilee and Golan', *Near Eastern Archaeology*, 66: 44–57.

Goodblatt, D. (1980), 'Towards the rehabilitation of Talmudic history', in B. M. Bokser (ed.), *History of Judaism: The Next Ten Years*, Chico, CA, pp. 31–44.

Goodblatt, D. (1994), *The Monarchic Principle: Studies in Jewish Self-Government in Antiquity*, Tübingen.

Goodenough, E. R. (1953), *Jewish Symbols in the Graeco-Roman Period*, 3 vols., New York.

Goodman, M. (2003), 'The Jewish image of God in late antiquity', in R. Kalmin and S. Schwartz (eds.), *Jewish Culture and Society under the Christian Roman Empire*, Leuven, pp. 133–45.

Goodman, M. (2007), *Rome and Jerusalem: The Clash of Ancient Civilizations*, London.

Grossmark, T. (1994), 'Jewelry and Jewelry-Making in the Land of Israel at the Time of the Mishnah and Talmud', Ph.D. thesis, Tel Aviv University. [Hebrew]

Grossmark, T. (2005), 'Laws regarding idolatry in jewelry as a mirror image of Jewish–Gentile relations in the Land of Israel during Mishnaic and Talmudic times', *JSQ* 12: 213–26.

Hachlili, R. (1977), 'The zodiac in ancient Jewish art: representation and significance', *BASOR* 228: 61–77.

Hezser, C. (1997), *The Social Structure of the Rabbinic Movement in Roman Palestine*, Tübingen.

Hezser, C. (1998), '"Privat" und "öffentlich" im Talmud Yerushalmi und in der griechisch-römischen Antike', in P. Schäfer (ed.), *The Talmud Yerushalmi and Graeco-Roman Culture*, vol. 1, Tübingen, pp. 424–579.

Hezser, C. (2001), *Jewish Literacy in Roman Palestine*, Tübingen.

Hezser, C. (2005), 'Toward the study of Jewish popular culture in Roman Palestine', in M. Perani (ed.), *The Words of a Wise Man's Mouth Are Gracious (Qoh. 10,12): Festschrift for Günter Stemberger on the Occasion of his 65th Birthday*, Berlin and New York, pp. 267–97.

Hezser, C. (ed.) (2010), *The Oxford Handbook of Jewish Daily Life in Roman Palestine*, Oxford.

Hirschfeld, Y. (1995), *The Palestinian Dwelling in the Roman-Byzantine Period*, Jerusalem.

Ilan, T. (1996), 'Gender studies and Jewish studies: when and where do they meet?', *JSQ* 3: 162–73.

Ilan, T. (2002), 'Jewish women's studies', in M. Goodman (ed.), *The Oxford Handbook of Jewish Studies*, Oxford, pp. 770–6.

Jacobs, M. (1998a), 'Römische Thermenkultur im Spiegel des Talmud Yerushalmi', in P. Schäfer (ed.), *The Talmud Yerushalmi and Graeco-Roman Culture*, vol. 1, Tübingen, pp. 219–311.

Jacobs, M. (1998b), 'Theatres and performances as reflected in the Talmud Yerushalmi', in P. Schäfer (ed.), *The Talmud Yerushalmi and Graeco-Roman Culture*, vol. 1, Tübingen, pp. 327–47.

Jacobs, M. (2000), 'Pagane Tempel in Palästina: rabbinische Aussagen im Vergleich mit archäologischen Funden', in P. Schäfer and C. Hezser (eds.), *The Talmud Yerushalmi and Graeco-Roman Culture*, vol. 2, Tübingen, pp. 139–59.

Kraemer, D. C. (2007), *Jewish Eating and Identity Through the Ages*, New York and London.

Krauss, S. (1910–12), *Talmudische Archäologie*, 3 vols., Leipzig; repr. Hildesheim, 1966.

Lapin, H. (1999a), 'Palestinian inscriptions and Jewish ethnicity in late antiquity', in E. M. Meyers (ed.), *Galilee Through the Centuries: Confluence of Cultures*, Winona Lake, IN, pp. 239–68.

Lapin, H. (1999b), 'Rabbis and cities in later Roman Palestine: the literary evidence', *JJS* 50: 187–207.

Lapin, H. (2000), 'Rabbis and cities: some aspects of the rabbinic movement in its Graeco-Roman environment', in P. Schäfer and C. Hezser (eds.), *The Talmud Yerushalmi and Graeco-Roman Culture*, vol. 2, Tübingen, pp. 51–80.

Levine, L. I. (1975), *Caesarea Under Roman Rule*, Leiden.

Levine, L. I. (2000), *The Ancient Synagogue: The First Thousand Years*, New Haven.

Levine, L. I. (2003), 'Contextualizing Jewish art: the synagogues at Hammat Tiberias and Sepphoris', in R. Kalmin and S. Schwartz (eds.), *Jewish Culture and Society under the Christian Roman Empire*, Leuven, pp. 91–131.

Magness, J. (2003), 'Helios and the Zodiac cycle in ancient Palestinian synagogues', in W. G. Dever and S. Gitin (eds.), *Symbiosis, Symbolism, and the Power of the Past: Canaan, Ancient Israel, and Their Neighbors from the Late Bronze Age through Roman Palaestina*, Winona Lake, IN, pp. 363–89.

Meyers, C. (2003), 'Engendering Syro-Palestinian archaeology: reasons and resources', *Near Eastern Archaeology*, 66: 185–97.

Meyers, C. (2004), 'Where the girls are: archaeology and women's lives in Ancient Israel', in M. C. Moreland (ed.), *Between Text and Artifact: Integrating Archaeology in Biblical Studies Teaching*, Leiden, pp. 31–51.

Meyers, E. (2002), 'Aspects of everyday life in Roman Palestine with special reference to private domiciles and ritual baths', in J. R. Bartlett (ed.), *Jews in the Hellenistic and Roman Cities*, New York, pp. 193–220.

Miller, S. S. (2003), 'Some observations on stone vessel finds and ritual purity in light of Talmudic sources', in S. Alkier and J. Zangenberg (eds.), *Zeichen aus Text und Stein: Studien auf dem Weg zu einer Archäologie des Neuen Testaments*, Tübingen, pp. 402–19.

Miller, S. S. (2004), '"Epigraphical" rabbis, Helios, and Psalm 19: were the synagogues of archaeology and the synagogues of the Sages one and the same?', *JQR* 94: 27–76.

Miller, S. S. (2006), *Sages and Commoners in Late Antique 'Ereẓ Israel: A Philological Inquiry into Local Traditions in Talmud Yerushalmi*, Tübingen.

Miller, S. S. (2007), 'Stepped pools and the non-existent monolithic "Miqveh"', in Edwards and McCollough (eds.) (2007), pp. 215–34.

Milson, D. (2006), *Art and Architecture of the Synagogue in Late Antique Palestine: In the Shadow of the Church*, Leiden.

Neusner, J. (1980), 'Story as history in ancient Judaism: formulating fresh questions', in B. M. Bokser (ed.), *History of Judaism: The Next Ten Years*, Chico, CA, pp. 3–29.

Neusner, J. (1984), 'Introduction: methodology in Talmudic history', in idem (ed.), *Ancient Judaism: Debates and Disputes*, Chico, CA, pp. 5–24.

Neusner, J. (1986), 'Death-scenes and farewell stories: an aspect of the master-disciple relationship in Mark and in some Talmudic tales', *HThR* 79: 187–97.

Neusner, J. (1988), 'Judaic uses of history in Talmudic times', *History and Theory*, 27: 12–39.

Neusner, J. (1991), *Symbol and Theology in Early Judaism*, Minneapolis.

Neusner, J. (ed.) (1988), *Goodenough's Jewish Symbols: An Abridged Edition*, Princeton.

Neusner, J. and Frerichs, E. S. (eds.) (1986), *Goodenough on History of Religion and on Judaism*, Atlanta.

Peskowitz, M. B. (1993), '"Family/ies" in antiquity: evidence from Tannaitic literature and Roman Galilean architecture', in S. J. D. Cohen (ed.), *The Jewish Family in Antiquity*, Atlanta, pp. 9–36.

Peskowitz, M. B. (1997a), *Spinning Fantasies: Rabbis, Gender, and History*, Berkeley.

Peskowitz, M. B. (1997b), 'Empty fields and the romance of the Holy Land: a response to Marianne Sawicki's "Archaeology" of Judaism, gender, and class', *Method & Theory in the Study of Religion*, 9: 259–82.

Raban, A. and Holum, K. G. (1996), *Caesarea Maritima: A Retrospective After Two Millennia*, Leiden.

Rajak, T. (1998), 'The rabbinic dead and the diaspora dead at Beth She'arim', in P. Schäfer (ed.), *The Talmud Yerushalmi and Graeco-Roman Culture*, vol. 1, Tübingen, pp. 349–66.

Regev, E. (2006), 'Archaeology and the Mishnah's halakhic tradition: the case of stone vessels and ritual baths', in A. J. Avery-Peck and J. Neusner (eds.), *The Mishnah in Contemporary Perspective*, Part 2, Leiden, pp. 136–52.

Reich, R. (2002), 'They are ritual baths: immerse yourself in the ongoing Sepphoris Mikveh debate', *Biblical Archaeology Review*, 28: 50–5.

Reich, R. (2003), 'Baking and cooking at Massada', *Zeitschrift des Deutschen Palästina Vereins*, 119: 140–58.

Roll, I. (1995), 'Roads and transportation in the Holy Land in the early Christian and Byzantine times', *Jahrbuch für Antike und Christentum*, Ergänzungsband 20: 1166–70.

Saldarini, A. (1977), 'Last words and deathbed scenes in rabbinic literature', *JQR* 68: 28–45.

Sawicki, M. (1994), 'Archaeology as space technology: digging for gender and class in Holy Land', *Method & Theory in the Study of Religion*, 6: 319–48.

Schwartz, J. (2004), 'Material culture in the Land of Israel: monks and rabbis on clothing and dress in the Byzantine period', in M. Poorthuis and J. Schwartz (eds.), *Saints and Role Models in Judaism and Christianity*, Leiden, pp. 121–37.

Schwartz, J. (2006), 'The material realities of Jewish life in the Land of Israel, *c.*235–638', in S. T. Katz (ed.), *The Cambridge History of Judaism*, vol. 4: *The Late Roman-Rabbinic Period*, Cambridge, pp. 431–56.

Schwartz, S. (1998), 'Gamaliel in Aphrodite's bath: Palestinian Judaism and urban culture in the third and fourth centuries', in P. Schäfer (ed.), *The Talmud Yerushalmi and Graeco-Roman Culture*, vol. 1, Tübingen, pp. 203–17.

Schwartz, S. (2000), 'On the program and reception of the synagogue mosaics', in L. I. Levine and Z. Weiss (eds.), *From Dura to Sepphoris: Studies in Jewish Art and Society in Late Antiquity*, Portsmouth, RI, pp. 165–81.

Schwartz, S. (2001), *Imperialism and Jewish Society, 200 BCE to 640 CE*, Princeton.

Vana, L. (1997), 'Les relations sociales entre Juifs et païens à l'époque de la Mishna: La question du banquet privé ("mishteh shel goyim")', *Revue des Sciences Religieuses*, 71: 147–70.

van der Horst, P. W. (1991), *Ancient Jewish Epitaphs*, Kampen.

Weingarten, S. (2003), 'A feast for the eyes: women and baking in the Talmudic literature', in M. Shilo (ed.), *To Be a Jewish Woman. Proceedings of the Second International Conference: Woman and Her Judaism*, Jerusalem, pp. 45–54.

Weingarten, S. (2005), 'Children's food in the Talmudic literature', in W. Mayer and S. Trzcionka (eds.), *Feast, Fast or Famine: Food and Drink in Byzantium*, Brisbane, pp. 147–60.

Weiss, Z. (1995), 'Games and Spectacles in Roman Palestine and their Reflection in Talmudic Literature', unpublished Ph.D. thesis, Hebrew University of Jerusalem. [Hebrew]

18

Rabbinic Literature and the History of Judaism in Late Antiquity: Challenges, Methodologies and New Approaches

MOSHE LAVEE

RABBINIC LITERATURE EXHIBITS A PARADOXICAL GAP. On the one hand, it is our richest literary source about Judaism of late-Roman Palestine; on the other hand, there are immense uncertainties about its validity and reliability for the reconstruction of Judaism as it was at the time. This chapter is divided into four parts. In the first part I will present a sketchy outline of Judaism as presented in rabbinic literature. In the second I will point out the difficulties in utilising these sources to create a firm historical reconstruction. Recent methodological strategies that have been used to cope with these challenges are presented in the third part. The last part includes a few examples demonstrating some issues in assessing the historical applicability of rabbinic literature.

Judaism as Portrayed by the Rabbis

Rabbinic literature presents the life of the Jews, according to the rabbis, in a prolific and detailed manner. It covers an impressive scope of religious life, including concepts, beliefs[1] and practices. It outlines a Jewish way of life, structured by what later came to be known as 'halakhah' (see Urbach 1986), the rabbinic legal system, which covers such topics as liturgy,[2] the purity laws,[3] life-cycle events like birth, marriage and death,[4] and the Sabbath and

---

[1] See Urbach (1975). See the discussion of the work below, p. 331.

[2] For liturgy see the comprehensive bibliography by Tabory (1993); Levine (2005: ch. 16); Kimelman (2006). For debate about the development of obligatory prayer, see Example 1, p. 336 below. For physical gestures in rabbinic prayers see Ehrlich (2004).

[3] Recent studies on the topic focus on early rabbinic literature and its relation to Second Temple customs: see Noam (2007); Klawans (2000); Hayes (2002a).

[4] Life-cycle rituals: on circumcision see Cohen (2003, 2005); Boyarin (2003: 24–58); Rubin (1995, 2003). In this book and in subsequent related works listed below, Rubin took a sociological

Proceedings of the British Academy **165**, 319–351. © The British Academy 2010.

holidays (see Tabory 1995, 2006a). Civil law is included as part and parcel of the system and ascribed the same degree of religious importance.[5]

Rabbinic literature constitutes a literary system comprised of a dual canon. The written and the oral law, with the Hebrew Bible (and especially the Pentateuch), constitute the primary canon, while the works of the Sages, especially the Mishnah, are the secondary canon.[6] The dual-canon system can be reflected in the very structure of the rabbinic literary heritage, including works organised around the Bible (midrashic works), and works following the mishnaic order (the Tosefta and Talmuds). Literary works arranged according to different organisational models reappeared only in the Muslim era. The curriculum of rabbinic studies, mentioned many times in rabbinic sources, perpetuated the dual structure by having the reading of Torah and the reciting of the Mishnah at the core of the rabbinic ideal of Torah study.[7] This literary dualism is also expressed in the linguistic fabric of rabbinic works, which interweave two distinct linguistic layers: (1) biblical quotations and (2) rabbinic statements, discussions and commentaries in Mishnaic Hebrew and Aramaic.

Thus, rabbinic literature presents a Judaism focused around the Scriptures and regards the rabbis as its valid interpreters. The Hebrew Bible is considered the source for the various convictions, commandments, year-cycle events, and the perception of the past (see Gafni 2007; Bohak 2002). The liturgy developed in the rabbinic era (see Example 1 below, p. 336) frequently alludes to and develops biblical themes, and includes substantial biblical

---

approach, in some cases at the expense of careful examination of the historical context of rabbinic sources. On mourning see Rubin (1997). On marriage see Gafni (1989); Satlow (2001); Schremer (2003); Rubin (2004).

[5] For a helpful handbook, see Elon (1994). Being written for lawyers, as part of an effort to incorporate rabbinic law into the contemporary Israeli legal system, the work supplies a comprehensive survey of sources, and includes some insights on the development of various Jewish legal customs, but is not designed to support the perspective of historians. For a recent effort to discuss rabbinic civil law in historical context, see Lapin (1995).

[6] Schiffman (2003) refers to the Mishnah as 'the new scriptures'. For medieval tensions regarding the social role and importance of the two corpora see Halbertal (1997). The conceptual framework offered in this work is very helpful for explaining the relations between the biblical canon and its new rival adherent—rabbinic literature. Also relevant is the question of the (in)dependence of the structure of the Mishnah from that of the Talmud. See Neusner's view cited by Hezser (2001: 207–8). The Mishnah presents itself as an independent text, but demonstrates quite frequently its dependence on Bible-based categories.

[7] For a recent discussion of the ideology of the study of Torah see Hirshman (2006a); Elman (2005) discusses the tension between prayer and study, a tension intensified (if not invented) in the Babylonian Talmud; Satlow (2003) argues that the value of study was 'a Graeco-Roman form of spirituality, expressed, of course, in a uniquely Jewish idiom' (p. 224). For the question of elementary education see Hezser (2001: 40–89); see Levine (2005: 398–404) on the role of the synagogue as a study place. See Hirshman (2006b: 122–3) for an assessment of the place of aggadic midrash in elementary education.

portions such as the recitation of Shema and the chanting of the Hallel (Psalms 113–18).[8] The role and significance of the Hebrew Bible is also evident in the centrality of homilies, sermons and exegetical activity reflected in midrashic works,[9] as well as in the importance attached to the physical scroll (see Goodman 1990a; Friedman 1993a). However, this centrality of Scriptures is subject to rabbinic mediation. The Bible serves in these roles as specifically interpreted, understood, and in some cases manipulated by the rabbis.[10]

Rabbinic literature presents a Judaism preoccupied with the memory of the Temple and its destruction, as evidenced by the extensive halakhic discussion of Temple-related issues, such as sacrifices, tithing, purity laws and various Temple rituals.[11] Similarly, non-legal materials frequently refer to the Temple, its destruction and its location (the Temple Mount).[12] At the same time, rabbinic literature is part of a project that offered an alternative to Second Temple Judaism, as exemplified in the structuring of prayers in relation to the Temple sacrifices and the substitution of the Seder night for the sacrifices of the Paschal lamb (see Safrai and Safrai 1998; Kulp 2005; Tabory 2006b). The positioning of rabbinic Judaism as an alternative was in the past considered as a conscious and deliberate act of the Sages of the first decades after the Destruction, associated with the figure of R. Yoḥanan b. Zakkai in Yavneh, but recent studies see it as a prolonged and gradual development, which ripened over centuries and was only retrospectively ascribed to the early and foundational years following the Destruction.[13] Similarly, the shift

[8] For an introductory survey see Reif (2004). For the place of the Bible in liturgy see Shinan (2004). For the Shema see Levine (2005: 550–4); Kimelman (2001).

[9] The abundant scholarship about midrashic literature will illuminate this aspect of the presence of the Bible in rabbinic culture. See Boyarin (1990); Kugel (1998, 2006); Hirshman (2006a, 2006b); Bakhos (2006a).

[10] And thus, for example, biblical figures are portrayed as Sages occupied with the study of the Torah: see Gafni (2007: 305). For a different assessment of the relation of rabbinic versus biblical authority see Yadin (2004).

[11] It is not clear whether these materials are traditions from an earlier time or speculative fantasies about the past. In any case, they are presented as if they are a living part of a continuous present. See Rosen-Zvi (2008). While not rejecting the existence of a sotah (adulterous woman) rite during the Temple period, Rosen-Zvi suggests that the rite as presented in the Mishnah is a new construction, inspired by both biblical and Roman models of public punishment.

[12] See Eliav (dissertation 1998). He pointed to the rabbinic emphasis of the idiom 'Temple Mount', and offered its affinity to the role of the Temple Mount in the Jewish-Christian followers of Jacob, the brother of Jesus.

[13] See Aderet (1998); Bokser (1983). The perception of Yavneh as a foundational period of establishing rabbinic Judaism as a post-Temple Judaism is exemplified in the title of Aderet's book: *From Destruction to Restoration: The Mode of Yavneh in Re-establishment of the Jewish People.* The challenges of this view are demonstrated in Hezser (1997: 66–7): '[T]he story . . . cannot be considered a trustworthy record of what really happened. It serves as the foundation legend of the rabbinic movement, tracing it back to the alleged re-organization of Judaism by Yochanan

from the plurality of Jewish sects and groups in the Second Temple days to the alleged uniformity of rabbinic Judaism is now perceived as a gradual and complicated process.[14]

Judaism, as presented in rabbinic literature, is not only a system of beliefs and practices, but a profound system that defines a certain group—'Israel'—and regulates belonging to this group. In that respect the use of the term 'Judaism' is slightly problematic since it implies a system of doctrines and practices, yet minimises the nature of Judaism as perceived by the rabbis as a group ('Israel') with an imagined ethnic origin based on shared ancestry (see Boyarin 2004a: 202–26; 2004b; Satlow 2005: 159). Accordingly, rabbinic literature is heavily preoccupied with the construction of Jewish identity and the demarcation of its boundaries. A variety of legislation regulates Jewish–Gentile relations[15] by instituting a separation between them or accommodating limited contact through laws about intermarriage and status (see Cohen 1999a: 241–305; Hayes 2002b; 2002a: 68–103, 143–98), by defining Gentiles in relation to the rabbinic purity system,[16] and so on. The setting of boundaries is also achieved through regulating relations with liminal groups, like the Samaritans[17] and the establishment of a conversion proce-

---

b. Zakkai after 70 CE.' Neusner ascribed the intention of developing a post-Temple Judaism to the Mishnah as a whole and not only to Yavneh. See Neusner (1983). Recent studies noticed that the narrative materials about this period, especially in the Bavli, were heavily reworked by late transmitters/redactors, creating the 'Yavneh legends', as part of creation of later rabbinic 'historiography', or even 'the invention of rabbinism' as put by Boyarin. See Boyarin (2000; 2004a: 151–201; 2005); Schremer (2005).

[14] For a recent presentation of the former view see Meyers (2002: 162–5). For a rejection of the identification of rabbis and Pharisees see Cohen (1984: 36–8); Hezser (1997: 69). For Essenes and Sadducees after the destruction of the Temple see Goodman (1994a). Another support might be found in Kalmin (2005), who argued for relative neutrality towards the Sadducees in Palestinian traditions (compared with the Bavli). Jaffee (1997: 18) summarised: 'Many of the Judaic worlds of Second Temple Judea and the Hellenistic Diaspora persisted for quite some time into the post-70 CE period and influenced Rabbinic Judaism dramatically.' Within this context we should mention the growing attention to halakhic aspects of Qumran literature. See Sussman (1989); Schiffman (1983); Fraade *et al.* eds. (2006); Noam (2005, 2006).

[15] A recent summary of current research is provided by Hayes (2007: 244–55). She suggested a helpful distinction between non-Jew as a religious other and as an ethnic other. Relevant sources in the tractate Avodah Zarah (Idolatry) were surveyed by Schäfer (2002: 335–52). For a helpful description of concepts see Stern (1994a: 1–86). For an intensive survey of tannaitic sources see Porton (1988). Feldman (1993) discusses some of the relevant rabbinic sources, mainly in the context of earlier periods, and is less interested in the construction of rabbinic concepts in late-Roman Palestine (with the exception of his discussion of proselytising—see below). See also the various papers in Mor *et al.* (eds. 2003).

[16] See esp. Hayes (2002a) and the literature listed above, n. 3.

[17] Rabbinic literature presents a gradual shift towards separation of Jews and Samaritans: see Stern (1994a: 99–105); Schiffman (1985a). This tendency is intensified in the Bavli, where they are decreed as 'absolute non-Jews', and the idea about their false conversion in the past is constantly repeated, and ascribed to early Sages. See my forthcoming 'The Samaritan may be

dure.[18] The demarcation of identity is also common in aggadic materials, mainly in exegetical deliberations referring to biblical figures and nations as archetypes for contemporary identities.[19]

Challenges and Difficulties

Despite the abundant information offered in rabbinic literature, constructing a detailed and reliable depiction of Jewish life in late-Roman Palestine is fraught with difficulty. Firstly, while the central role of rabbinic literature in constituting Judaism in the centuries following the production of the literature is well established, there are doubts concerning the extent to which rabbinic literature represents Judaism, or the varieties of Judaisms, in late antiquity.[20] Many scholars doubt the role of the Sages as the leading class of Jewish society at the time and, in consequence, the commonly held perception of their literature as a faithful representation of the way of life of the majority of the Jews.[21] They criticised earlier historiography that positioned the

---

included: the status of Samaritans in talmudic literature', in M. Mor (ed.), *Proceedings of the 2004 Conference of the Samaritan Research Society.* For a recent assessment of the historical significance of relevant sources in the Yerushalmi, see Lehnardt (2002). He argued that narrative material might imply actual contacts (and competition) between rabbis and Samaritans, presenting Samaritans' customs and their reservations about rabbinic rites.

[18] Earlier sources only hint at components of the procedure. A full account is found only in the Babylonian Talumd and the external tractate Gerim. For an intensive survey of sources see Porton (1994); for a discussion of the rabbinic conversion procedure see Cohen (1999a: esp. ch. 7); Goodman (1990b). Cf. Schiffman (1985b). For the late institutionalisation of the procedure and the role of Babylonian tendencies in it see Kulp (2004) and my forthcoming 'The Tractate of Conversion'. For the adjacent issue of proselytising in rabbinic literature see Goodman (1994b); Cohen (1992a); Feldman (1993), and his reconsideration in Feldman (2003). For the image of Abraham in this context see Hayward (1999). While in the past such sources were read as reminiscent of massive Jewish proselytising in the Second Temple period, recent assessments consider later developments in the rabbinic approach towards the idea, though not necessarily towards active proselytising.

[19] See Goodblatt (2006: 28–48). Many recent studies are devoted to the perception of certain biblical figures and their social function. See for example Bakhos (2006b) on Ishmael (discussing also Esau); Yuval (2006) on Esau and Jacob; Baskin (1983) on Balaam, Jethro and Job. For a thorough discussion of the literary mechanisms of identity discourse in exegetical narratives see Levinson (2000).

[20] For the concept of plurality of Judaisms in antiquity see for example Neusner (1994: 18): 'There never was, in real, social terms, that single Judaism, there were only infinite and diverse Judaic systems, as various social entities gave expression to their way of life, worldview, and theory of the social entity that they formed'; Visotzky (1989: 48): 'We have learned to speak of ancient Judaisms and ancient Christianities'; Boccaccini (2002). Cf. Schiffman (2003).

[21] See Goodman (1983); Hezser (1997: esp. 353–404, 450–66); S. Schwartz (2001), and the bibliography in Satlow (2005: 155–6 and n. 4). For a defence of the view ascribing a ruling status to the Sages see Safrai and Safrai (2005).

rabbis in conjunction with the Patriarchate as the ruling class of the Jews[22] and questioned whether the rabbis held a sufficient degree of institutionalisation and administration to facilitate such governance.[23] According to such criticism, rabbinic literature eventually became foundational for later Judaism, yet the extent to which it reflects the standard Judaism of its time remains unclear (see, for example, Goodman 2005).

Even if we accept the centrality of the rabbis, rabbinic literature is an elusive historical source. Rabbinic works are collections of legal, exegetical and narrative materials that were not designed to portray a coherent historical portrait of their times, nor do they adhere to any standards, ethos or rhetoric of commitment to accurately describe the past. The texts avoid coherent reports about their own literary nature and the context in which they were produced. Thus the literature does not easily lend itself to detailed and accurate reconstruction of historical reality or depict clearly and consistently distinctions between various schools, their geography and their development over time, as I will discuss below.

Chronology

The use of rabbinic literature to chart the chronological developments of ideas, institutions, practices, and so on, needs to take into account the complicated history of the rabbinic works as a collective literature that evolved

---

[22] For recent surveys of this scholarly shift see Miller (2006: 7–17); S. Schwartz (2002); Siverstev (2002: 1–7). Scholars in the 1980s and early 1990s challenged some components of rabbinic authority or institutionalisation, and postdate them to the third century, emphasising the significance of Rabbi Judah's patriarchate in this process (typical representatives are the works of Levine 1989 and Goodblatt 1994; Cohen 1999a; see also S. Schwartz 2001: 112–14). In more recent studies the influence of the rabbis is even further doubted; the rabbinic movement is perceived as an 'informal network of relationships which constituted a personal alliance system' (Hezser 1997: 493), and depicted as a marginal, though not totally insignificant group. See S. Schwartz (2001: 110–28).

[23] That rabbis functioned as officials in the Patriarch's administrations and established academies in various localities is still held and defended by some scholars today. See the arguments put forward by Safrai (1995: 18ff.). See also Oppenheimer (2001); Habas-Rubin (1999). For a mediating view see Miller (2006: 446–66). In some cases this view seems to be the 'official view' held in rabbinic sources; see ibid., p. 467; 'The rabbis took it for granted that their view of the world was normative for all Israel, but such a view can quite well persist regardless of reality' (Goodman 2005: 179). For source-based examples see Fraade (2002: 328): 'The Yerushalmi . . . extends the rules for the king, and especially considerations for his honour, to the Rabbinic patriarch as well as to Rabbinic judicial and academic appointment'; for recent surveys on institutionalisation of the rabbinic movement see Rubenstein (2007: 58–65); S. Schwartz (2002); Hezser (1997: 185–227); Lapin (2000: 57–68). See also S. Schwartz (2004). The role and status, co-existence and tensions of the patriarchate in relation to the rabbis in this process are discussed in many works. See Levine (1989: 134–61); Milikowsky (1991); Goodman (1992); S. Schwartz (1999); Levine (2001); Fraade (2002); Siverstev (2002: 19–94); Stern (2003).

gradually over a period of centuries during which there was a varied degree of creative redaction and flexible transmission. Later generations reworked, interpreted and contextualised earlier materials and situated them in new literary structures, which prevents us in some cases from directly accessing the earlier rabbinic stratum. Every rabbinic work, and sometimes even different segments of a given work, has its own story of evolution and transmission.[24] Indeed, during the long period of evolution-through-creative-transmission of rabbinic compositions, various redactors and transmitters contributed to the shaping, wording and presentation of traditions ascribed to earlier Sages. Consequently, various rabbinic works present a slightly different chronological prism.[25] The dating of ideas, legislation and events on the basis of one work might collide with that which stems from another. However, there are also numerous examples in which quotations appear verbatim in different works, apparently reflecting the rabbinic ideology of accurate transmission of traditions. Thus historians face the task of distinguishing the words of the Sages from new formulations which reflect the tendencies of later redactors and transmitters.[26] It is often possible to date practices and opinions based on their attribution to specific scholars, as well as on other, more sophisticated means.[27] Nonetheless, scholars have raised concerns regarding the reliability of such attributions.[28]

[24] A few examples: (1) Tractate Nezikin of the Palestinian Talmud was originated in a different redaction than other tractates of the Talmud; see below n. 36. (2) A similar assessment is suggested regarding tractates Nedarim, Nazir, Keritot, Me'ilah and Temurah of the Babylonian Talmud. (3) Autonomous midrashic works on various biblical books were compiled in late medieval manuscripts to become the most canonical midrashic collection of the print era, Midrash Rabbah. Among them we can find works which consist of two different parts from two different redactions, such as ExodR and NumR. (4) Pesikta Rabbati organised materials of classical (5th–6th century) and late (7th–9th) midrashic works according to a redactional organisation established in the classical work Pesikta de-Rab Kahana.

[25] Thus, for example, a statement in the tannaitic Midrash is attributed to an amora of a later Midrash; a justification of a tannaitic view is presented as part of the saying of a tanna himself in the Tosefta, and as a late Aramaic anonymous addition to his view in the Bavli, and so on. However, the use of the term 'Pseudepigraphy' in this context is misleading as we are speaking here about a complex situation in which original materials were reworked during transmission in a manner that created biases, rather than invention of new works intentionally ascribed to and written as works of earlier authorities. See Jaffee (2007) for the question of authorship in rabbinic literature.

[26] Most of this process was conducted by oral transmission. See Sussman (2005); cf. Jaffee (1998, 2001); Alexander (2007); for the transition from oral to written transmission, see Mandel (2000). Even during the period of written transmission, various works were still subject to modifications with a variable degree of flexibility.

[27] With some modification, the method is still widely used, esp. by Israeli scholars. For a nice demonstration of its use, see Schiffman (1985a).

[28] See the discussion of these sceptical views in Stern (1994b). See also Stern (1995); Jacobs (1971, 1991); Kraemer (1989); Neusner (1984), and the vast bibliography offered by Bregman (1999).

This flexible transmission affected various literary genres, including legal dicta and deliberations, and homilies and exegesis. It is particularly significant for historians with regard to narrative materials, which were most readily used to reconstruct rabbinic history prior to criticism of this approach in the last two generations of scholarship. Scholars have now developed strategies of literary analysis for use with rabbinic narrative materials, which have brought into question their historical authenticity and emphasised their anachronistic tendencies.[29]

These general textual challenges are intensified in the Babylonian Talmud, which constitutes one of the most pronounced products of creative transmission and reworking of former materials; furthermore, the Babylonian Talmud was redacted in a distant place, later period, and different cultural and political milieu than late-Roman Palestine.[30] The implications are far-reaching, since from early medieval times the Bavli has functioned as the prevailing, if not canonical, rabbinic work, and its influence on our perception of the past is still immense.[31] Contemporary scholars tend to turn only to Palestinian sources or, if they rely on the Bavli, read it with a critical eye, which has repeatedly led to new examples which demonstrate how our knowledge and perception of the past is based on, and indeed biased by, Babylonian prisms, conceptual frameworks and perspectives.[32]

---

[29] Historians who noticed the non-historical nature of the material concurrently raised such concerns regarding rabbinic narratives. A leading voice in this criticism was Neusner. Scholars of the literary approach raised the same concerns when they explored the literary features of rabbinic narratives (esp. Frankel 1981; 1991: ch. 9; 2001; see also the recent appraisal of his work by Newman 2006). This was also at issue among scholars who examined the process of redaction and formation of collections of narratives (Friedman 1987, 1993b; see also Rubenstein 1999; Hezser 1993: 288–91; Boyarin 2004a: 45–9). On literary redaction of other kinds of rabbinic materials see the following: on the Mishnah see Walfish (dissertation 2001; 2006); for the talmudic Sugiah see Valler (2001); for midrashic compilations see the bibliography in Visotzky (2005: 11, n. 6); Kahana (2006). These studies apply the reading strategies developed in the analysis of rabbinic narratives to halakhic and hermeneutic materials.

[30] Once again, recent scholars have demonstrated how former studies were based on Jewish laws, customs and institutions as legislated or depicted in the Bavli. See, for example, the discussions of Am-Ha'arez, Samaritans, Yavneh, and the question of the divine image in this chapter. Positivist historians commented about the biases of the Bavli; see the summary and bibliography in Levine (1989: 20). Recent developments in the study of the Bavli have pointed to the significance of the latest phases of its transmission in the shaping of its content, including narrative materials about and statements attributed to early generations. For an updated survey see Rubenstein (ed. 2005: 1–20). See also Stern (1994b); Hayes (1997); Rubenstein (1999, 2003); Kalmin (1999: 12 n. 3, 87–110, 142, 213–16).

[31] See Schiffman (2003: 378–82); I am using the term 'canon' in this context with some reservations. See Halbertal (1997).

[32] See, for example, my comments about Yavneh, n. 13.

Geography

Rabbinic literature is limited to a sketchy description of the geographical spread of the rabbis and their influence. Once in a while, the locale of the rabbis or of certain events is mentioned, and this data has been used by scholars for geographical depictions of the rabbinic movement,[33] as well as discussions of the urbanisation of Roman Palestine and studies of the rural population.[34] Such sources have proved helpful in depicting the various centres of rabbinic activity in the Galilee and the southern plain,[35] and in some cases have enabled the depiction of unique characteristics of certain communities.[36] However, the distinctions between rabbinic cultures of various localities are not profound, and do not exceed the relatively uniform cultural framework of rabbinic literature. As suggested by Hirshman (1996: 470) in a slightly different context, '[G]iven the anthological nature of rabbinic literature, an attempt to draw the spiritual profile of a specific community is extremely difficult, if not impossible.'[37]

[33] The most comprehensive collection of sources is still Klein (1977). For recent studies, see Hezser (1997: 157–65); Rosenfeld (1998). See also the discussion of late attribution of localities to the rabbis in Lapin (1999). For a comparison with archeological findings, see Levine (1997: 169).

[34] The urbanisation of Palestine is considered to have had certain significance for the consolidation of the rabbis into an influential social factor, and maybe even on their literary production. Many studies considered the period between the second and the third centuries as an influential time of accelerated urbanisation. See Levine (1989: 25–33); Oppenheimer (1992: 114–15); Oppenheimer (1996a); Cohen (1992b; 1999b: 941–76). For the role of urbanisation in the formation of rabbinic literature, see Lightstone (2002: 190–200). Hezser (1997: 157–65) argued that the process of urbanisation was gradual and prolonged, from the first to the fourth centuries, and the urbanisation of the rabbinic movement was not parallel to it. See also Rosenfeld (1998). For recent efforts to reassess the degree of urbanisation following Hezser's critique, see Lapin (1999, 2000); Miller (2006: 13–17 and his summary at pp. 446–66). S. Schwartz (1998) pointed to the role of urbanisation in shaping the rabbinic response to paganism. For a survey of rural localities see Rosenfeld (1998: 69–89).

[35] For studies of specific areas and places see the following (partial) list: on the Galilee see Goodman (1983); Oppenheimer (1991); Miller (2007). For a comprehensive survey of Sepphoris traditions in the Yerushalmi, see Miller (2006: 33–106). See also Miller (1984, 1987, 1993), Rosenfeld (1998: 62–5). For Tiberias see Miller (2006: 107–17); Rosenfeld (1998: 66–9). For Caesarea, see below. For Lydda, see Oppenheimer (1988); J. J. Schwartz (1991); Rosenfeld (1997). For Bene-Brak, see Oppenheimer (1996b). For Yavneh, see Oppenheimer (1977b). For echoes of regional cultures in rabbinic literature see Reiner (1998). He began his study with medieval regional traditions, and claimed that they shed light on some rabbinic sources, enabling the portrayal of regional cultures, which is usually overlooked in rabbinic literary documentation.

[36] As in the case of Caesarea, see Levine (1989: 83–91; 171–8); Hirshman (1996); Lapin (1996). Also related is the question of the redaction of tractate Nezikin of the Yerushalmi in Caesarea. For updated and helpful surveys see Hirshman (1996: 469); Lapin (1996: 499); Hezser (1993: 362–77).

[37] On the differences between Judaea and the Galilee, see Goodman (1999).

Geographical considerations of international relations are mainly occupied with the question of the relationship between the two Jewish centres in Palestine and Babylon, and the scarcity of evidence for travels to and contact with Rome or other places within the Graeco-Roman milieu. Future study may address questions about the implications of rabbinic literature for our understanding of geo-political and geo-cultural processes in the eastern borders of the Roman empire in late antiquity. The Jewish community provides an example of a provincial ethnic/religious group, dispersed across the political boundaries of the Roman and Persian regimes. Rabbinic literature might warrant examination of the nature and extent of cultural transference between the East and the West, the affinities between cultural and political borders, and how means of traffic and communication enabled the diffusion of ideas across political borders. Rabbinic sources demonstrate a divergent degree of the extent of knowledge and idea transfer between Babylon and Palestine. Can this data serve the study of contacts and communication across the borders of the Empire? Such studies will in turn support our understanding of the rabbinic movement and its final development into a leading factor in shaping medieval Judaism. Did the location of the eastern border of the Roman empire play a role in the emergence of the rabbis in a leadership position? Is it accidental that the evolution of the Babylonian Talmud coincides with the rule of the Sasanian dynasty (Gafni 1997, 2004; Kalmin 2006)?

Distinctions between Various Segments of Society

The use of rabbinic literature to portray non-rabbinic ideas, views and practices and to describe non-rabbinic social elements poses further difficulties. Firstly we must acknowledge the presence of the non-rabbinic within the rabbinic literature, which often engages with non-rabbinic segments of society. It defines the status of the 'internal other', those who might be part of a rabbinic household, but are not rabbis, such as women,[38] slaves (see Hezser 2002a, 2005), and minors;[39] it is occupied with those who represent competing elements of society not part of rabbinic circles, such as *minim* (heretics) and *ame'i ha'arez*, literally 'the people of the land', who did not adhere to certain rabbinic practices.

---

[38] Considering the importance of and growing interest in gender studies, the subject deserves a survey of its own, and I can only point here to some of the prominent writings on the topic during the last decade, such as Ilan (1997), Hauptman (1999), Baskin (2002), Fonrobert (2000), Boyarin (1993a, 2000), Hasan-Rokem (2000, 2003), Peskowitz (1997), Valler (2001) and Satlow (2002). For a wider literary survey see Rosen-Zvi (2008).

[39] For a recent discussion of 'the internal other' see Hayes (2007).

Our ability to present a portrayal of such social groups on the basis of rabbinic literature is limited, since we only have the solipsistic viewpoint of the rabbis (see Stern 1994a: 199–223). On the other hand, the anthological and multivalent nature of rabbinic literature,[40] including literary genres such as stories, parables and proverbs that tend to give voice to marginal components of society, makes it open to subversive readings, reading 'against the grain', and extracting or retrieving the voices of other elements of society.[41] This view was clearly expressed by Levinson (2005: 380), discussing the latest stratum of the Talmud: 'This polyphonic aspect . . . creates, as Bakhtin said, a "plurality or co-presence of independent but interconnected and unmerged voices".'

Let me exemplify some of these difficulties in relation to the categories of *minim* and *am ha'arez*. Recent studies have shown that it is very difficult to accept these categories as representations of identifiable and well-defined social elements. The term 'minim' is found as a general name for a variety of non-rabbinic groups, and probably cannot be perceived as a named group such as early Christians or Judaeo-Christians.[42] As such, the term is used to mark the 'other' and at the same time to present rabbinic Judaism as the one and only acceptable Jewish path.[43] The term 'am ha'arez' is used to refer to people who do not partake in certain components of the rabbinic system of practices and habits. These individuals are contrasted with 'haver', a category which is only partially congruent with the rabbis (Hezser 1997: 74–5). The rabbinic approach towards the *am ha'arez* became in the last decade one of the most prominent examples of the difficulties in reconstruction of the history of Judaism on the basis of rabbinic literature. Dated attributions suggest that there was a development in the rabbis' negative attitude towards the *am ha'arez* between the second and third centuries, but recent studies have undermined

---

[40] On the anthological nature of rabbinic literature see also Jaffee (2006: 19); Visotzky (2005).

[41] This approach seems appropriate for the study of collective literature, and was mainly applied in gender studies, as exemplified in the works of Hasan-Rokem, who also supplied a theoretical framework for it. See Hasan-Rokem (2000; 2003: 1–27).

[42] For this former perspective see the comments and bibliography in Stern (1994a: 110); Miller (1993: 378, nn. 5–6); Visotzky (1995: 68–70, 144–5). Boyarin (2004a: 55). For the new perception see Miller (1993: 377). They are identified with 'Sadducees, Baitousin, Zealots, Samaritans and Jewish Christians' in Sussman (1989: 54, n. 176).

[43] Goodman (1996); Janowitz (1998); Boyarin (2004a: 54–61) discussed the use of *minim* as a parallel phenomenon to heresy in Christianity. Both featured mechanisms involved in the process of the parting of the Jewish and Christian ways. See also Hayes (2007: 258–9). It seems that rabbinic literature would not permit the portrayal of any specific social group of *minim*, as Miller concluded in his survey of *minim* in Sepphoris in rabbinic narratives: 'To extrapolate from these few instances cohesive groups, movements, or distinct communities of like-minded *minim* at Sepphoris is to go beyond the evidence' (Miller 1993: 400). Scholars also have pointed to avoidance of contact with *minim* as reflective of the rabbis' strategy towards them. See Goodman (1996: 505); Kalmin (1999: 68; 1994a). Kalmin distinguished between relevant Palestinian and Babylonian sources. For an additional reading on *minim* see Schiffman (1985b: 41–9); Bohak (2003); Kimelman (1999). For the blessing of *minim* see Ehrlich and Langer (2005); Teppler (2007).

such perception, pointing to the fact that it is utterly based on Babylonian representations of the topic.[44] It is possible that the search for representations of non-rabbinic masses should not focus on this rabbinic category, but should instead highlight rabbinic attitudes towards the common people, such as traditions about the customs of people of certain localities (Miller 2006).

Distinctions between Different Concepts

The collective, multigenerational and anthological nature of rabbinic literature has dual implications when considering it as a source for depiction of rabbinic views and beliefs. Rabbinic literature gives us access to a variety of views and perceptions. It preserves disputes arising from within the limited circles of the rabbis. Recently scholars have pointed at conceptual distinctions between the Akiva and Ishmael schools, which were first distinguished only in terms of their terminology and different hermeneutics.[45] However, the sources also convey polemical materials that give voice to other groups in the rabbis' cultural surroundings (albeit always through the lenses of rabbinic representation). As such, rabbinic literature preserves evidence of a variety of religious tendencies that probably were not regarded or accepted as mainstream within rabbinic literature.

The presence of non-mainstream tendencies is evident in the portrayal of some rabbis in rabbinic literature not only as scholars and experts of the law, but also as holy men, charismatic pious figures, and healers[46] and by the dearth of materials that would hint at mystical traditions (see Chernus 1982), sorcery,[47] angelology, asceticism,[48] and so on. Nonetheless, the infrequent

---

[44] The most comprehensive and influential work in the field is Oppenheimer (1977b). See also Levine (1989: 112–27). For recent surveys see Stern (1994a: 114–19); Hayes (2007: 259, and the bibliography on p. 302, n. 3). The critique of this view is based on the literary analysis of Babylonian materials, which challenged this perception as it seems to be heavily based on Babylonian literary constructs that project much later views, and attribute them to earlier tannaitic generations. See Wald (2000: 211–51); Cohen (1992b: 165–7); Kalmin (1999: 45); Rubenstein (2003: 123–42); Miller (2006: 304, n. 8, 302–27); Gafni (2001: 218); Hayes (2007: 260–2). See Oppenheimer (2007: 98) for a re-evaluation of his views in this regard.

[45] For example, see Hirshman (1999), who pointed to a universal tendency of R. Ishmael's school which perceived the Torah as offered to the nations and not only to Israel; Lorberbaum (2004) offered a distinction between Akiva's circle's tendency towards anthropomorphism in contrast to R. Eliezer's view.

[46] See, for example, the literature about Ḥanina b. Dosa (enlisted in Avery-Peck 2006; Bokser 1985). While he was a first-century figure, most sources about him are much later, and probably indicate the relevance of such figures within later rabbinic circles.

[47] See Harari (2006); Harari criticised Urbach and Lieberman for ascribing rabbinic materials on the issue to the masses, while presenting the rabbis as elitists who at best tried to reconcile such practices with their intellectual views and moral perceptions.

[48] See Satlow (2003), and the bibliography he provides.

representation of these topics in rabbinic literature cannot be regarded as indicating that they were uncommon in Jewish society of the time, and even in rabbinic circles, nor can it justify claims that these issues were rejected by the rabbis. It is possible that the rabbis intentionally avoided documentation of these aspects of their religiosity.

Although the views documented in rabbinic literature are broad and varied, historical contextualisation can be elusive or impossible. The sources do not provide a coherent and consistent theology. The collective and fragmentary nature of the literature prevents a reconstruction of systematic theology, and brings into question whether such coherence existed at the time. Rabbinic literature features clusters of concepts and ideas that lack coherent definition and applicability, are intermingled with one another, and in some cases are contradictory.[49] Views on any given topic are scattered throughout numerous sources, and in most cases are expressed only implicitly through exegesis of biblical sources or in narratives and parables.

Due to these circumstances there is no satisfactory handbook of rabbinic ideas, beliefs and practices in late-antique Palestine. Comprehensive works of former generations, such as *Judaism* by Moore, or *The Sages*[50] by Urbach, fail to satisfy our current methodological awareness and other considerations that have been raised in the last forty years, as outlined in this chapter, although Urbach's is indeed an encompassing work, providing a helpful collection of rabbinic sources organised around an immense variety of topics, and frequently discussing rabbinic concepts against the background of other cultural elements in the Persian and the Graeco-Roman milieus. These earlier works have not yet been replaced or revised.

A meaningful effort to cover a wide range of topics is, nonetheless, reflected in the numerous works produced by Neusner and some of his students. They address a variety of topics discussed in rabbinic literature, and thereby provide helpful access to sources and translations albeit of debated

---

[49] More than fifty years ago Kadushin offered an interesting framework to present rabbinic values and concepts. Albeit ahistorical, his approach is helpful in certain cases. Many of his writings were reprinted in 2001 (see Kadushin 2001a, 2001b, 2001c; for an appraisal of his contribution, see Neusner 2001).

[50] Moore (1927–30); Urbach (1975); see also the collections of his essays, Urbach (2002; 1998: vol. 2, Section B). This is still the most comprehensive body of works that offers a well-organised collection of relevant materials on various subjects, organised according to helpful categories, which sheds light on their historical context and illuminates the cultural surrounding of the Sages. However, it was written more than thirty years ago, and Urbach did not cope with many of the difficulties that have been raised since and presented here. He did not take into *systematic* account the divergent prisms of various works, nor consult the redaction context and the use of literary devices in his appraisal of materials. However, many of his comments, scattered throughout his analysis, do show awareness of these issues. For an appraisal of his work see Sussman (1993).

quality. A comprehensive critical survey of this body of literature demands much more than one paragraph can supply, hence in my following description of Neusner's project, I am constrained to approach his huge body of writings with a broad brush. Many of the sceptical observations provided in this chapter are in debt to Neusner: the questions he posed, and the doubts he raised in his early works, as in his studies about R. Eliezer (Neusner 1973), played an important role in our re-examination of the research models used in the study of rabbinic literature as a source for history. Pointing to the variation of traditions and the unique angle provided in different works, he taught us how cautious we should be with rabbinic sources. However, in the following decades, he turned to models of study which seem to oversimplify the solutions to the problems he raised. He surveyed topics using the documentary approach (see below p. 333); he then moved to emphasising the conceptual undertow of the redactors of works, as identified on the basis of the structuring of the works, the themes selected or neglected, and so on. The danger with such an approach is that it may create a fictional redactor and attribute to him, in some cases, a philosophical mind set for which there is no direct evidence. It is true that many rabbinic works do have a unique voice, but this unique voice may well be the product of layers of contributions of the transmitters and redactors reflecting the unique *Sitz im Leben* of the evolution of each work, and should not necessarily be treated as the intentional work of a redactor.[51] Some of Neusner's observations inspired by structuralism are insightful, but not always for historians of the late-Roman period: they are helpful for those interested in identifying the cultural work of rabbinic literature as a literary canon in the centuries following the time of the rabbis, but should not necessarily therefore be used as a means for reconstructing editorial tendencies of late antiquity, particularly since the impressionistic hand, picturing the 'landscape' of the rabbinic treatment of a topic, may reflect less the ancient editor than Neusner himself presenting sources sorted out in a manner that fits the picture he has identified (see, for example, Neusner 2002).[52]

A Survey of Contemporary Approaches

A great deal thus remains to be done, but nonetheless, scholars of recent years have adopted various approaches to facilitate the use of rabbinic

---

[51] As we turn to late rabbinic works, probably already from the Muslim period, such as *Seder Eliyahu* and *Pirke de-Rabbi Eliezer*, the hand of one author seems a reasonable explanation for some of their novel literary characteristics. This observation, indeed, gives us a good means to shed light on the collective and much less unified character of rabbinic works of late antiquity.
[52] For some (mostly critical) treatments of Neusner's works see below n. 56. See also the sharp criticism of Poirier (1996, and the bibliography listed in n. 1).

literature as a historical source. First, they have used a broadened definition of 'history' to include not only events and politics but also social relations, daily life, economy, beliefs, and conceptual and hermeneutical developments. These perspectives have made rabbinic literature, with its relative indifference towards politics, into a rich and abundant source for contemporary historians. Though focusing on the unique characteristics of the Jews and Judaism, rabbinic literature describes a group that was also part of the larger cultural milieu of Roman society,[53] and thus serves as a source to depict Roman provincial society.[54]

Various approaches have been applied in an effort to make chronological sense of the disordered rabbinic literature. Some scholars have abandoned the goal of detailed reconstruction of developments of rabbinic themes, and have chosen a less ambitious path, presenting a composite picture of the majority views in rabbinic literature.[55] Similarly, the 'documentary approach', developed by Neusner and his students, presents themes and topics as documented in specific works; it is based on the estimated date of the end of the formation of a given work which then allows for dating ideas within the text, and ascribing ideological tendencies to the redactors of the works.[56] A refined version of this approach would further emphasise the unique voice of rabbinic compilations not as the voice of deliberate redactors who carefully shaped the text in accordance with their views, but rather as a reflection of prevailing tendencies in the specific time and place in which the work evolved and was transmitted. Other studies refer to rabbinic literature as constituting future norms, ideas and values. At the time of its creation a certain tannaitic text might have reflected the views of a marginal minority.

---

[53] See the introduction in Schäfer (ed. 1998). For the relation of rabbinic literature to Roman Law see Hezser (1998, ed. 2003); Mélèze Modrzejewski (2003); Hayes (2002a); Cohen (1999a: ch. 8). For a slightly different assessment, see Blidstein (1997).

[54] See Lapin (2003); Safrai (1995). Safrai argued that rabbinic literature is our only source written from within a Roman-dominated population and not from the point of view of governing Roman officials. As Schäfer (ed. 1998) comments, we are very far from applying to rabbinic literature the methods of Goitein (1967–93), in which Jewish society of the medieval Mediterranean served as an example for the wider society.

[55] See Stern (1994a). His introduction includes a justification of this approach, as well as a helpful survey of the methodological difficulties presented here. His method presents an overall account on the basis of the majority of rabbinic sources, and offers a cumulative picture of the rabbinic corpus up to the seventh century. Readers should, however, take into account that there is no guarantee that specific details represent late-Roman Palestine (not that Stern has claimed so), nor any other more specific milieu.

[56] This approach was advocated and repeatedly drawn upon by Neusner and his students. See, for example, Porton (1988, 1994). For a sample of the many (mostly critical) discussions of this approach see Burns (2007: 407–10 and additional bibliography in n. 17); Hezser (2002b: 128–31; 1997: 20–3). Gafni (2001: 216–20); Stern (1994a); Bakhos (2006a: 172–4); S. Schwartz (2001: 8–9).

However, in subsequent generations it would have been accepted as a normative part of the contemporary cultural fabric.[57]

At the same time, there have been developments in critical methodologies that have uncovered a sense of chronological development within rabbinic circles. Some scholars have explored the statistics of statements ascribed to Sages of various generations to reveal some coherent lines of development.[58] Others have utilised synoptic readings of rabbinic sources and compared versions of given traditions to identify the contributions of later transmitters and redactors in order to identify preserved traditions.[59]

Alongside such chronologically oriented methodologies, other studies offer suitable frameworks for setting the context of rabbinic sources, although they reject these sources as authentically representing specific events. Scholars have assessed the social relationships described in the texts as reflective of social relations and tensions. While it is improbable that R. Shimon B. Yoḥai and his son ever killed farmers for devoting themselves to farming and abstaining from Torah study, tensions over this issue appear to have been a prominent theme in the society that told such a story (see b.Shabbat 33b). According to this approach, one should also interpret rabbinic sources dealing with biblical figures or the Second Temple period as reflective of the Sages' own preoccupations, tendencies and concerns at the time they created these traditions.[60]

---

[57] Such studies should carefully consider the actual distribution of rabbinic literature at every stage. For a recent study advocating this model see Schremer (2007).

[58] This is as commented upon by Gafni (2001: 219) and demonstrated regarding the Bavli by Kalmin (1994b). For an intensive application of the method on Palestinian Talmud sources, see Lapin (2002).

[59] See Friedman (1987, 1993b, 2000) and Hayes (2000), and the other articles in Cohen's helpful volume (*The Synoptic Problem in Rabbinic Literature*). For a recent application, including some helpful methodological considerations, see Burns (2007). Recently, scholars have made attempts to elaborate upon this method and carefully distinguish between cases in which the redacted works manipulated their source material and cases in which they preserved earlier traditions as they were. This, for example, would have been an attempt to regain authenticity for some of the traditions in the Bavli. See Hayes (2000: 62). Similarly, Kalmin (2005: 206–7) claimed that 'sometimes, the layered nature of Talmudic discourse permits us to write the history of an idea or an institution, however, sometimes the process of editorial homogenization erases all or most evidences of such developments'. Kalmin and Hayes refer to the Babylonian Talmud. For a recent effort to distinguish between the early material (relevant for the study of Roman Palestine) and the later Babylonian addition (inspired by its Persian context of redaction) see Kalmin (2006). Our knowledge and understanding of editorial activity in Palestine is much weaker. The need to address this was already raised by Bokser (1990). Identification of two stages of editorial activity in Leviticus Rabbah was suggested by Visotzky (1990: 83, n. 1).

[60] This approach is used, in different ways, by Hezser (1997); Kalmin (1999: 1–5) applies it to rabbinic figures, biblical figures (ibid., pp. 15–22; 1998), and Second Temple figures (2002, 2004); for a similar approach in the study of daily life, see Eliav (1995: 8–12). For a recent effort to assess the ability of reading rabbinic history in exegetical materials see Fraade (2004).

Another approach claims that there was a set of practices and beliefs shared by most Jews of late antiquity, known as 'Common Judaism'. Accordingly, rabbinic literature is seen as the 'literary edge . . . of a far more broadly based movement'.[61] While not claiming that the majority of Jews responded to absolute rabbinic scrutiny, such an approach assumes that, in general, various customs and beliefs presented in rabbinic literature were part of a common Jewish way of life.[62]

A recent avenue of study considers the very creation, development and dissemination of rabbinic literature as a historical occurrence and accordingly assesses the social significance of rabbinic literary activity and the production of rabbinic literature.[63] This approach might shed light on issues such as the institutional structure that facilitated rabbinic literary activity (even if conveyed in an oral mode) and the gradual process that led to the dominance of rabbinic Judaism, if not during the period, at least as a consequence of it.

Lastly, cultural poetics advocates the reading of rabbinic literature as a cultural product of its times.[64] Such an approach also preaches a new understating of the historicity of rabbinic sources. According to this approach, the texts offer historical evidence for the perceptions of their narrators, authors, transmitters and redactors, as opposed to telling us historical and biographical information about the characters they present. Close reading and engaging in literary analysis sensitive to intertextuality has allowed scholars of this

[61] An expression borrowed from Lapin (1999: 206).

[62] The concept is offered here as a pragmatic framework, aimed at a description of common practices and beliefs. The concept of 'Common Judaism' was developed in studies of the Second Temple period. (See, for example, Meyers 2002: 152–7.) It was offered by Sanders, who was criticised for his essentialist approach, using it to define Judaism as 'covenantal nomism' (see Boccaccini 2002: 10). For an implication of this approach with regard to the question of mishnaic law, see Cohen (2007). See also Miller (2006: 12 n. 41, 21–8, 327–38). He defines as 'commoners' people who are designated as 'the people of place x'. Such a framework will enable us to evaluate common Judaism as perceived by rabbinic literature. For other applications of the concept in the context of rabbinic literature see Stern (1994a: 114).

[63] Lapin (2003: 162) claimed that 'the Mishnah and its study gave a measure of coherence to the rabbis as a movement'. See also ibid., p. 175, n. 38: 'The place of the Mishnah and other Tannaitic material in the development of an Amoraic tradition, as well as the development of such a "tradition" itself, implies, I am arguing, a greater degree of coherence.' Lightstone argued for the role of redaction of the Mishnah in the emergence of the rabbinic class. He proposed that with the rise of the Patriarchate in the days of Rabbi Judah haNasi the rabbinic guild (as he defines it) became a professional class in the administration of the Patriarchate. This change was supported by the promulgation of the Mishnah and led to a period of co-dependency of the Sages and the Patriarchate (Lightstone 2002: 188–9). For some initial considerations regarding the role of the redaction of the Yerushalmi and Palestinian Midrashim see Ir-Shai (2004: 82, n. 42).

[64] A leading advocate of this approach is Boyarin (1990, 1993a, 1993b, 2004a). See also Levinson (2000); Bakhos 2006a, and the survey and critique in S. Schwartz (2002).

school to present the texts as embedded in the historical whole in a way that produced values, reflected interests and constituted world views.[65]

Examples

I will conclude this essay with a few examples that demonstrate some of the issues concerning the applicability of rabbinic literature to the study of Judaism in late-Roman Palestine.

1. Obligatory Prayers

The development of obligatory prayers serves as a helpful example, demonstrating the question of dissemination of rabbinic customs, showing the image produced by early rabbinic texts, and raising typical doubts about the actual influence of the rabbis in that period. The importance of this issue is immense. If indeed the majority of Jews followed rabbinic practices and recited the prayers frequently, public exposure to the rabbinic world view was vast, and engaged many people on a regular basis (see Reif 2004). However, the literary inventory is confusing. On the one hand, we have early medieval prayer books that present canonised prayer, while on the other hand, a competing variety of practices persisted, as documented in Genizah findings. The core of obligatory prayer is, however, usually based on much earlier instructions in rabbinic literature, some of them ascribed to early second-century Sages. These instructions are presented in the earliest rabbinic document, the Mishnah, as valid and normative rules, as if it is apparent and accepted that they were commonly known and practised. Various prayers and benedictions are only mentioned by name, which appears to assume that their content is well known to the audience of the work (see Setzer 2005). Some sources ascribe the establishment of obligatory prayers to R. Gamliel, while others refer to it as a substitute for sacrifices. On the basis of this literary evidence, scholars have debated whether one should see the prayers as a successful revolutionary project established in the early tannaitic period, or a gradual development rooted in Second Temple days but not canonised until the end of the talmudic period (compare Heinemann 1977 with Fleischer 1990). As such, this case represents the inherent problem I discussed at the beginning of the essay: does rabbinic literature present Judaism as it was at the time of its redaction, or as later shaped by and on the basis of rabbinic literature?

---

[65] Here lies one of the shortcomings of this approach, usually pursued out of despair in our ability to reconstruct the reality of the past as it actually was. How can one explain a text as a product of its historical context if that context is irretrievable?

2. God-fearers: Non-Jewish Adherents of Judaism

In two aspects sources about God-fearers demonstrate basic methodological issues regarding the historicity of rabbinic sources. First, they reveal the potential of narrative and aggadic material as historical sources, as opposed to the rabbinic legal system that provided a theoretical framework which did not necessarily reflect social reality (and at times deliberately tried to shape it). The category of God-fearers appears only in non-legal rabbinic material, which concurs with non-rabbinic sources, while the rabbinic legal system lacks any category that fits the group.[66] Secondly, the Bavli shows no familiarity with God-fearers. It uses the Hebrew term for 'God-fearer' in a new understanding of a 'devoted Jew', and thus produces, as in many other cases, a picture at odds with the social structure of Jewry 'in the west' (a common term in the Bavli for the Land of Israel), that is, the Jewry of the Graeco-Roman region (Feldman 1993: 353).

3. The Image of God and Pagan Images in Synagogues

The subject of the image of God exemplifies the difficulties in approaching rabbinic theology. In many cases, works of late medieval thinkers, not to mention modern rationalistic trends, have shaped our understanding of rabbinic views. Many studies have called for a revision in our understanding of what was thought to be a key component of rabbinic monotheism—the incorporeality of God. Reconstruction of anthropomorphic ideas within rabbinic literature has uncovered some interesting parallels to pagan perceptions of icons as representative of divinities, though the representative icon of God is not a physical image—rather it is represented in the human body of all individuals.[67] Other studies have exemplified the manner in which Jews might have thought about their God through Graeco-Roman conceptual frameworks, such as shown, for example, in parables portraying the world as the arena and God as the Emperor (Grossmark 2004).

Arguments regarding the image of God should direct us to the lengthy debate about non-rabbinic ideas, thoughts and concepts, and thus to the question of non-rabbinic elements in Jewish society. The use of allegedly

[66] This is true unless we accept the speculative identification of *Ger Toshav*, a vague legal category used in rabbinic sources, with God-fearers. See Novak (1983: 23); Feldman (1993: 355). Goodman (1990b) offered the relevance of another category, the Noahides, which is used in rabbinic sources to regulate the legal obligations of non-Jews. Recently some rabbinic exegetical narratives have been analysed as hinting at the existence of the group: see Levinson (2000).
[67] See Lorberbaum (2004). The book includes a comprehensive survey of former literature. For a shorter bibliography see Goodman (2003: n. 10); Boyarin (2003: 3–23).

pagan imagery in synagogue art was one of the main arguments in favour of seeking to identify significant non-rabbinic elements in Judaism in the Diaspora, as well as in the Land of Israel.[68] Stern has recently pointed out that the rabbinic objection to the use of images in synagogues is only documented in the latest layers of the Babylonian Talmud (Stern 2000), and thus suggests a much more tolerant rabbinic approach to images in the Graeco-Roman milieu of earlier centuries. Thus, the assumption regarding Jewish avoidance of synagogue images might be another example of the tendency to perceive Judaism in the image projected by the Babylonian Talmud. Stern's observation corresponds with the argument for rabbinic anthropomorphism. Even if we do not go so far as to suggest that Palestinian rabbinic or other segments of Jewish culture related the synagogue images to the image of the Jewish God (Goodman 2003), at least we can portray their culture as less repelled by iconic imagery than might have been thought if our knowledge was based upon earlier scholarly views.

This case should serve as an important example for considering the subject of non-rabbinic or non-normative Judaism in late-Roman Palestine. It justifies a reconsideration of whether the phenomenon of synagogue images represents non-rabbinic avenues of society. What we have typically regarded as non-rabbinic might instead be based on our image of rabbinic Judaism as shaped by late materials in the Babylonian Talmud, if not even on later medieval Jewish perceptions. This might also be true of claims regarding non-rabbinic legal practices.[69]

4. Ignorance in Idolatry or Reflections of Jewish Customs?

My last example demonstrates the elusive nature of the historicity of rabbinic sources. I have mentioned that in many cases rabbinic representations of the 'other' are scarcely helpful for increasing our knowledge of any specific non-rabbinic social elements or practices. Goodman (2000: 6) has pointed to a talmudic source describing images worshipped twice in seven years in Rome, a practice unknown from any other source and probably not applicable for

---

[68] For a summation see Levine (1997; 2005: 605–10).

[69] Cotton (1998) argued for non-rabbinic practices as reflected in second-century marital contracts found in the Judaean Desert. Such arguments should also be reconsidered in this context. To a certain extent an image of rabbinic views as constructed in later layers of rabbinic literature served Cotton's claim for the non-rabbinic nature of much earlier documents. If we were able to reconstruct rabbinic views from the same time in which the document was produced, would they contradict the archeological findings? It is possible, in my view, that the assessment of the documents as non-rabbinic is a product of comparison with rabbinic norms that were regulated only later.

uncovering pagan practices at the time. However, this source should not be dismissed as totally non-historical. We learn that the rabbis had in mind a model of exercising certain cultic practices twice in seven years. A theory of the nature of the discourse about the 'other' would help us to utilise this piece of information. Depictions of the 'other' serve to differentiate the members of a group from other people by pointing to what seems to be estranged from 'our' culture, but in some cases another social dynamic is at work. Such a depiction might also reflect projections of the known and familiar, of the practices of the group itself. The 'other' is portrayed in a manner that fits what is common among 'us'. It is possible that in this case the rabbis, while portraying what they consider as Gentile practice, were influenced by their own customs. Indeed, Naeh (1998) has recently suggested that the cycle of Torah reading in Palestine occurred twice in seven years, not once in approximately three years, as had been formerly speculated. In an indirect way, this source might support this theory. The text may thus be relevant for depicting the rabbinic world, and in this case for supporting a reconstruction of a certain liturgical practice.

I consider this concluding example illustrative of my argument. Rabbinic literature can serve as a historical source, especially when read indirectly and through the lens of well-defined theoretical frameworks, and when perceived as a rabbinic cultural product that reflects delicate, sophisticated, and hardly recoverable relationships between text and reality.

Further Reading

Cohen (1999a); Horbury *et al.* (eds. 1999); Katz (2006); Urbach (1975).

Bibliography

Aderet, A. (1998), *From Destruction to Restoration: The Mode of Yavneh in Re-establishment of the Jewish People*, Jerusalem. [Hebrew]

Alexander, E. S. (2007), 'The orality of rabbinic writing', in C. E. Fonrobert and M. S. Jaffee (eds.), *The Cambridge Companion to the Talmud and Rabbinic Literature*, Cambridge, pp. 38–57.

Avery-Peck, A. J. (2006), 'The Galilean charismatic and Rabbinic piety: the holy man in the talmudic literature', in Amy-Jill Levine *et al.* (eds.), *The Historical Jesus in Context*, Princeton, pp. 149–65.

Bakhos, C. (2006a), 'Method(ological) matters in the study of Midrash', in idem (ed.), *Current Trends in the Study of Midrash*, Leiden, pp. 161–87.

Bakhos, C. (2006b), *Ishmael on the Border: Rabbinic Portrayals of the First Arab*, New York.

Baskin, J. R. (1983), *Pharaoh's Counselors: Job, Jethro, and Balaam in Rabbinic and Patristic Tradition*, Chico, CA.

Baskin, J. R. (2002), *Midrashic Women: Formations of the Feminine in Rabbinic Literature*, Hanover, NH and London.

Blidstein, G. J. (1997), 'Rabbinic Judaism and general culture: normative discussion and attitude', in J. J. Schachter (ed.), *Judaism's Encounter with Other Cultures*, Northvale, NJ, pp. 1–56.

Boccaccini, G. (2002), *Roots of Rabbinic Judaism: An Intellectual History from Ezekiel to Daniel*, Grand Rapids, MI and Cambridge.

Bohak, G. (2002), 'The Hellenization of biblical history in rabbinic literature', in Schäfer (ed.) (2002), Tübingen, pp. 3–16.

Bohak, G. (2003), 'Magical means for handling minim in rabbinic literature', in P. J. Tomson and D. Lambers-Petry (eds.), *The Image of the Judaeo-Christians in Ancient Jewish and Christian Literature*, Tübingen, pp. 267–79.

Bokser, B. M. (1983), 'Rabbinic responses to catastrophe: from continuity to discontinuity', *Proceedings of the American Academy for Jewish Research*, 50: 37–61.

Bokser, B. M. (1985), 'Wonder-working and the rabbinic tradition: the case of Hanina ben Dosa', *Journal for the Study of Judaism*, 16.1: 42–92.

Bokser, B. M. (1990), 'Talmudic studies', in S. J. D Cohen and E. L. Greenstein (eds.), *The State of Jewish Studies*, Detroit, pp. 80–112.

Boyarin, D. (1990), *Intertextuality and the Reading of Midrash*, Bloomington, IN.

Boyarin, D. (1993a), *Carnal Israel: Reading Sex in Talmudic Culture*, Berkeley.

Boyarin, D. (1993b), 'Midrash and praxis: on the historical study of rabbinic literature', in S. Friedman (ed.), *Saul Lieberman Memorial Volume*, Jerusalem, pp. 105–17. [Hebrew]

Boyarin, D. (2000), 'A tale of two synods: Nicaea, Yavneh, and rabbinic ecclesiology', *Exemplaria*, 12: 21–62.

Boyarin, D. (2003), *Sparks of the Logos: Essays in Rabbinic Hermeneutics*, Leiden.

Boyarin, D. (2004a), *Borderlines, Border Lines: The Partition of Judaeo-Christianity*, Philadelphia.

Boyarin, D. (2004b), 'The Christian invention of Judaism: the Theodosian Empire and the rabbinic refusal of religion', *Representations*, 85: 21–57.

Boyarin, D. (2005), 'The Yavneh-Cycle of the Stammaim and the invention of the rabbis', in Rubenstein (ed.) (2005), pp. 237–91.

Bregman, M. (1999), 'Pseudepigraphy in rabbinic literature', in E. G. Chazon, M. E. Stone and A. Pinnick (eds.), *Pseudepigraphic Perspectives*, Leiden, pp. 27–41.

Burns, J. (2007), 'The archaeology of rabbinic literature and study of Jewish–Christian relations in late antiquity', in J. Zangenberg (ed.), *Religions, Ethnicity and Identity in Ancient Galilee: A Region in Transition*, Tübingen, pp. 403–24.

Chernus, I. (1982), *Mysticism in Rabbinic Judaism: Studies in the History of Midrash*, Berlin.

Cohen, S. J. D. (1984), 'The significance of Yavneh: pharisees, rabbis and the end of Jewish sectarianism', *Hebrew Union College Annual*, 55: 27–53.

Cohen, S. J. D. (1992a), 'Was Judaism in antiquity a missionary religion?', in M. Mor (ed.), *Jewish Assimilation, Acculturation and Accommodation: Past Traditions,*

Current Issues and Future Prospects, Lanham, MD, New York and London, pp. 14–23.

Cohen, S. J. D. (1992b), 'The place of the rabbi in Jewish society of the second century', in L. I. Levine (ed.), *The Galilee in Late Antiquity*, New York, pp. 157–73.

Cohen, S. J. D. (1999a), *The Beginnings of Jewishness: Boundaries, Varieties, Uncertainties*, Berkeley.

Cohen, S. J. D. (1999b), 'The Rabbi in second century Jewish society', in Horbury *et al.* (eds.) (1999), pp. 922–90.

Cohen, S. J. D. (2003), 'A short history of Jewish circumcision blood', in M. E. Wyner (ed.), *The Covenant of Circumcision*, Hanover, NH and London, pp. 30–42.

Cohen, S. J. D. (2005), *Why Aren't Jewish Women Circumcised? Gender and Covenant in Judaism*, Berkeley.

Cohen, S. J. D. (2007), 'The Judaean legal tradition and the halakhah of the Mishnah', in C. E. Fonrobert and M. S. Jaffee (eds.), *The Cambridge Companion to the Talmud and Rabbinic Literature*, Cambridge, pp. 121–43.

Cotton, H. M. (1998), 'The rabbis and the documents', in M. Goodman (ed.), *Jews in a Graeco-Roman World*, Oxford, pp. 167–80.

Ehrlich, U. (2004), *The Nonverbal Language of Prayer: A New Approach to Jewish Liturgy*, Tübingen.

Ehrlich, U. and Langer, R. (2005), 'The earliest texts of the Birkat Haminim', *Hebrew Union College Annual*, 76: 63–112.

Eliav, Y. Z. (1995), 'What happened to R. Abbahu at the Tiberian Bath-House: the place of realia and daily life in the Talmudic Aggada', *Jerusalem Studies in Jewish Folklore*, 17: 7–20. [Hebrew]

Eliav, Y. Z. (1998), 'A "Mount without a Temple": The Temple Mount from 70 CE to the Mid-Fifth Century: Reality and Idea', Ph.D. dissertation, Hebrew University, Jerusalem.

Elman, Y. (2005), 'Torah Ve-Avodah: prayer and Torah study as competing values in the time of Hazal', in A. Mintz and L. Schiffman (eds.), *Jewish Spirituality and Divine Law*, Jersey City, NJ, pp. 61–124.

Elon, M. (1994), *Jewish Law: History, Sources, Principles*, Philadelphia.

Feldman, L. H. (1993), *Jew and Gentile in the Ancient World: Attitudes and Interactions from Alexander to Justinian*, Princeton.

Feldman, L. H. (2003), 'Conversion to Judaism in classical antiquity', *Hebrew Union College Annual*, 74: 115–56.

Fleischer, E. (1990), 'On the beginnings of obligatory Jewish prayers', *Tarbiz*, 59: 397–441. [Hebrew]

Fonrobert, C. E. (2000), *Menstrual Purity: Rabbinic and Christian Reconstruction of Biblical Gender*, Stanford, CA.

Fraade, S. D. (2002), 'Priests, kings and patriarchs: Yerushalmi Sanhedrin in its exegetical and cultural settings', in Schäfer (ed.) (2002), pp. 315–34.

Fraade, S. D. (2004), 'Moses and the Commandments: can hermeneutics, history, and rhetoric be disentangled?', in H. Najman and J. H. Newman (eds.), *The Idea of Biblical Interpretation: Essays in Honor of James L. Kugel*, Leiden, pp. 399–422.

Fraade, S. D., Shemesh, A. and Clements, R. A. (eds.) (2006), *Rabbinic Perspectives: Rabbinic Literature and the Dead Sea Scrolls*, Leiden.

Frankel, Y. (1981), *Readings in the Spiritual World of the Stories of the Aggada*, Tel Aviv. [Hebrew]

Frankel, Y. (1991), *The Ways of Aggadah and Midrash*, Ramat Gan. [Hebrew]

Frankel, Y. (2001), *The Aggadic Narrative: Harmony of Form and Content*, Tel Aviv. [Hebrew]

Friedman, S. (1987), 'Literary development and history in the Aggadic narrative of the Babylonian Talmud: a study based upon B. M. 83b–86a', in N. M. Waldman (ed.), *Community and Culture: Jewish Studies in Honor of the 90th Anniversary of the Founding of Gratz College*, Philadelphia, pp. 67–80.

Friedman, S. (1993a), 'The Holy Scriptures defile the hands: the transformation of a biblical concept in rabbinic theology', in M. Brettler and M. Fishbane (eds.), *Minha le-Nahum: Biblical and Other Studies Presented to Nahum M. Sarna*, Sheffield, pp. 117–32.

Friedman, S. (1993b), 'The historical Aggadah in the Babylonian Talmud', in idem (ed.), *Saul Lieberman Memorial Volume*, Jerusalem, pp. 119–64. [Hebrew]

Friedman, S. (2000), 'Uncovering literary dependencies in the Talmudic corpus', in S. J. D. Cohen (ed.), *The Synoptic Problem in Rabbinic Literature*, Providence, RI, pp. 35–57.

Gafni, I. M. (1989), 'The institution of marriage in rabbinic times', in D. Kraemer (ed.), *The Jewish Family*, New York, pp. 13–30.

Gafni, I. M. (1997), *Land, Center and Diaspora*, Sheffield.

Gafni, I. M. (2001), 'A generation of scholarship on Erez Israel in the Talmudic era: achievements and reconsideration', *Cathedra*, 100: 199–227. [Hebrew]

Gafni, I. M. (2004), *Center and Diaspora: The Land of Israel and the Diaspora in the Second Temple, Mishnah and Talmud Periods*, Jerusalem. [Hebrew]

Gafni, I. M. (2007), 'Rabbinic historiography and representations of the past', in C. E. Fonrobert and M. S. Jaffee (eds.), *The Cambridge Companion to the Talmud and Rabbinic Literature*, Cambridge, pp. 295–312.

Goitien, S. D. (1967–93), *A Mediterranean Society: The Jewish Communities of the Arab World as Portrayed in the Documents of the Cairo Geniza*, Berkeley.

Goodblatt, D. (1994), *The Monarchic Principle: Studies in Jewish Self-Government in Antiquity*, Tübingen.

Goodblatt, D. (2006), *Elements of Ancient Jewish Nationalism*, Cambridge.

Goodman, M. (1983), *State and Society in Roman Galilee*, Totowa, NJ.

Goodman, M. (1990a), 'Sacred Scripture and "defiling the hands"', *Journal of Theological Studies*, 41: 99–107.

Goodman, M. (1990b), 'Identity and authority in ancient Judaism', *Judaism*, 39: 227–45.

Goodman, M. (1992), 'The Roman state and Jewish patriarchate in the third century', in L. I. Levine (ed.), *The Galilee in Late Antiquity*, New York, pp. 127–39.

Goodman, M. (1994a), 'Sadducees and Essenes after 70 CE', in E. P. Porter, P. Joyce and D. E. Orton (eds.), *Crossing the Boundaries: Essays in Biblical Interpretation in Honour of Michael D. Goulder*, Leiden, pp. 347–56.

Goodman, M. (1994b), *Mission and Conversion: Proselytizing in the Religious History of the Roman Empire*, Oxford.

Goodman, M. (1996), 'The function of "minim" in early rabbinic Judaism', in H. Cancik, H. Lichtenberger and P. Schäfer (eds.), *Geschichte, Tradition,*

Reflexion: Festschrift für Martin Hengel zum 70. Geburstag, Tübingen, vol. 1, pp. 501–10.

Goodman, M. (1999), 'Galilean Judaism and Judaean Judaism', in Horbury *et al.* (eds.) (1999), pp. 596–617.

Goodman, M. (2000), 'Palestinian Rabbis and the Conversion of Constantine to Christianity', in P. Schäfer and C. Hezser (eds.), *The Talmud Yerushalmi and Graeco-Roman Culture*, vol. 2, Tübingen, pp. 1–9.

Goodman, M. (2003), 'The Jewish image of God', in R. Kalmin and S. Schwartz (eds.), *Jewish Culture and Society under the Christian Roman Empire*, Leuven, pp. 133–45.

Goodman, M. (2005), 'Jews and Judaism in the Mediterranean diaspora in the late Roman period: the limitation of evidence', in C. Bakhos (ed.), *Ancient Judaism in Its Hellenistic Context*, Leiden and Boston, pp. 177–203.

Green, W. S. (1978), 'What's in a name? The problematic of rabbinic "biography"', in idem (ed.), *Approaches to Ancient Judaism: Theory and Practice*, Missoula, MT, pp. 77–96.

Grossmark, T. (2004), 'This may be compared to an athlete who was wrestling with a royal prince: God and the arena in Jewish rabbinical literature', *Scripta Mediterranea*, 25: 3–24.

Habas-Rubin, E. (1999), 'Rabban Gamaliel of Yavneh and his sons: the patriarchate before and after the Bar Kokhva Revolt', *JJS* 50: 21–37.

Halbertal, M. (1997), *People of the Book: Canon, Meaning, and Authority*, Cambridge, MA.

Halivni, D. W. (1979–80), 'Doubtful attributions in the Talmud', *Proceedings of the American Academy for Jewish Research*, 56/57: 67–83. [Hebrew]

Harari, Y. (2006), 'The Sages and the occult', in S. Safrai *et al.* (eds.), *The Literature of the Sages*, Second Part: *Midrash and Targum . . .*, Assen, pp. 107–32.

Hasan-Rokem, G. (2000), *Web of Life: Folklore and Midrash in Rabbinic Literature*, Stanford, CA.

Hasan-Rokem, G. (2003), *Tales of the Neighborhood: Jewish Narrative Dialogues in Late Antiquity*, Berkeley.

Hauptman, J. (1999), 'Women and inheritance in rabbinic texts: identifying elements of a critical feminist impulse', in H. Fox and T. Meacham (eds.), *Introducing Tosefta: Textual, Intratextual and Intertextual Studies*, Hoboken, NJ, pp. 221–40.

Hayes, C. E. (1997), *Between the Babylonian and the Palestinian Talmuds*, New York.

Hayes, C. E. (2000), 'Halakha le-Moshe mi-Sinai in rabbinic sources: a methodological case study', in S. J. D. Cohen (ed.), *The Synoptic Problem in Rabbinic Literature*, Providence, RI, pp. 61–117.

Hayes, C. E. (2002a), *Gentile Impurities and Jewish Identities: Intermarriage and Conversion from the Bible to the Talmud*, Oxford.

Hayes, C. E. (2002b), 'Genealogy, illegitimacy, and personal status: the Yerushalmi in comparative perspective', in Schäfer (ed.) (2002), pp. 73–89.

Hayes, C. E. (2007), 'The "other" in rabbinic literature', in C. E. Fonrobert and M. S. Jaffee (eds.), *The Cambridge Companion to the Talmud and Rabbinic Literature*, Cambridge.

Hayward, R. (1999), 'Abraham as proselytizer at Beer-Sheba in the Targums of the Pentateuch', *JJS*, 49: 24–37.

Heinemann, J. (1977), *Prayer in the Talmud: Forms and Patterns*, Berlin and New York.

Hezser, C. (1993), *Form, Function, and Historical Significance of the Rabbinic Story in Yerushalmi Neziqin*, Tübingen.

Hezser, C. (1997), *The Social Structure of the Rabbinic Movement in Roman Palestine*, Tübingen.

Hezser, C. (1998), 'The codification of legal knowledge in late antiquity: the Talmud Yerushalmi and Roman law codes', in Schäfer (ed.) (1998), pp. 581–641.

Hezser, C. (2001), *Jewish Literacy in Roman Palestine*, Tübingen.

Hezser, C. (2002a), 'The social status of slaves in Talmud Yerushalmi and in Graeco-Roman society', in Schäfer (ed.) (2002), pp. 91–138.

Hezser, C. (2002b), 'Classical rabbinic literature', in M. Goodman (ed.), *The Oxford Handbook of Jewish Studies*, pp. 115–40.

Hezser, C. (2005), *Jewish Slavery in Antiquity*, Oxford.

Hezser, C. (ed.) (2003), *Rabbinic Law in its Roman and Near Eastern Context*, Tübingen.

Hirshman, M. (1996), 'Reflections on the Aggada of Caesarea', in A. Raban and K. G. Holum (eds.), *Caesarea Maritima: A Retrospective After Two Millennia*, Leiden, pp. 469–75.

Hirshman, M. (1999), *Torah for the Entire World*, Tel Aviv. [Hebrew]

Hirshman, M. (2006a), 'Torah in rabbinic thought: the theology of learning', in Katz (ed.) (2006), pp. 899–924.

Hirshman, M. (2006b), 'Aggadic Midrash', in S. Safrai *et al.* (eds.), *The Literature of the Sages*, Second Part: *Midrash and Targum . . .*, Assen, pp. 107–32.

Horbury, W., Davies, W. D. and Sturdy, J. (eds.) (1999), *The Cambridge History of Judaism*, vol. 3: *The Early Roman Period*, Cambridge.

Ilan, T. (1997), *'Mine and Yours are Hers': Retrieving Women's History from Rabbinic Literature*, Leiden.

Ir-Shai, O. (2004), 'The priesthood in Jewish society of late antiquity', in L. I. Levine (ed.), *Continuity and Renewal: Jews and Judaism in Byantine-Christian Palestine*, Jerusalem, pp. 67–106. [Hebrew]

Jacobs, L. (1971), 'Are there fictitious Baraitot in the Babylonian Talmud?', *Hebrew Union College Annual*, 42: 185–96.

Jacobs, L. (1991), 'How much of the Babylonian Talmud is pseudepigraphic?', in idem, *Structure and Form in the Babylonian Talmud*, Cambridge, pp. 6–17.

Jaffee, M. (1997), *Early Judaism*, Upper Saddle River, NJ.

Jaffee, M. (1998), 'The oral-cultural context of the Talmud Yerushalmi: Greco-Roman rhetorical paideia, discipleship and the concept of oral Torah', in Schäfer (ed.) (1998), pp. 27–61.

Jaffee, M. (2001), *Torah in the Mouth: Writing and Oral Tradition in Palestinian Judaism, 200 BCE–400 CE*, Oxford.

Jaffee, M. (2006), 'What difference does the "orality" of rabbinic writing make for the interpretation of rabbinic writings?', in M. Kraus (ed.), *How Should Rabbinic Literature be Read in the Modern World?*, Piscataway, NJ, pp. 105–35.

Jaffee, M. (2007), 'Rabbinic authorship as a collective enterprise', in C. E. Fonrobert and M. S. Jaffee (eds.), *The Cambridge Companion to the Talmud and Rabbinic Literature*, Cambridge, pp. 17–37.

Janowitz, N. (1998), 'Rabbis and their opponents: the construction of the "min" in rabbinic anecdotes', *Journal of Early Christian Studies*, 6.3: 449–62.

Kadushin, M. (2001a), *Worship and Ethics: A Study in Rabbinic Judaism*, New York; first published Evanston, IL, 1963.

Kadushin, M. (2001b), *Organic Thinking: A Study in Rabbinic Thought*, New York; first published New York, 1938.

Kadushin, M. (2001c), *The Rabbinic Mind*, New York; first published New York, 1952.

Kahana, M. (2006), '*Shes Moshzar*: the editing of Parashat *Bereshit Bara* in Midrash Gen. Rab.', in J. Levinson *et al.* (eds.), *Higayon l'Yona: New Aspects in the Study of Midrash, Aggadah and Piyut in Honor of Professor Yona Fraenkel*, Jerusalem, pp. 347–476. [Hebrew]

Kalmin, R. (1992), 'Talmudic portrayals of relations between rabbis: Amoraic or pseudepigraphic?', *AJS Review*, 17: 165–97.

Kalmin, R. (1994a), 'Christians and heretics in rabbinic literature of late antiquity', *HThR* 87: 155–69.

Kalmin, R. (1994b), *Sages, Stories, Authors, and Editors in Rabbinic Babylonia*, Atlanta.

Kalmin, R. (1998), 'Attitudes toward biblical heroes in rabbinic literature', in Schäfer (ed.) (1998), pp. 269–377.

Kalmin, R. (1999), *The Sage in Jewish Society of Late Antiquity*, New York.

Kalmin, R. (2002), 'Jewish sources of the Second Temple period in rabbinic compilations of late antiquity', in Schäfer (ed.) (2002), pp. 17–53.

Kalmin, R. (2004), 'Kings, priests, and sages in rabbinic literature of late antiquity', in Y. Elman, E. B. Halivin and Z. A. Steinfeld (eds.), *Neti'ot Ledavid: Jubilee Volume for David Weiss Halivni*, Jerusalem, pp. 57–92.

Kalmin, R. (2005), 'Between Roma and Mesopotamia: Josephus in Sasanian Persia', in C. Bakhos (ed.), *Ancient Judaism in Its Hellenistic Context*, Leiden and Boston, pp. 205–42.

Kalmin, R. (2006), *Jewish Babylonia Between Persia and Roman Palestine*, Oxford.

Katz, S. T. (ed.) (2006), *The Cambridge History of Judaism*, vol. 4: *The Late Roman-Rabbinic Period*, Cambridge.

Kimelman, R. (1999), 'Identifying Jews and Christians in Roman Syria-Palestine', in E. M. Meyers (ed.), *Galilee through the Centuries: Confluence of Cultures*, Winona Lake, IN, pp. 301–33.

Kimelman, R. (2001), 'The Shema' Liturgy: from covenant ceremony to coronation', in J. Tabory (ed.), *Kenishta: Studies of the Synagogue World*, vol. 1, pp. 9–106.

Kimelman, R. (2006), 'Rabbinic prayer in later antiquity', in Katz (ed.) (2006), pp. 573–611.

Klawans, J. (2000), *Impurity and Sin in Ancient Judaism*, Oxford.

Klein, S. (1977), *Sefer Ha-Yishuv*, Jerusalem; first published 1939. [Hebrew]

Kraemer, D. (1989), 'On the reliability of attributions in the Babylonian Talmud', *Hebrew Union College Annual*, 50: 175–90.

Kugel, J. L. (1998), *Traditions of the Bible: A Guide to the Bible As It Was at the Start of the Common Era*, Cambridge, MA.

Kugel, J. L (2006), *The Ladder of Jacob: Ancient Interpretations of the Biblical Story of Jacob and his Children*, Princeton.

Kulp, J. (2004), 'The participation of a court in the Jewish conversion procedure', *JQR* 94: 437–70.

Kulp, J. (2005), 'The origins of the Seder and Haggadah', *Currents in Biblical Research*, 4: 109–34.

Lapin, H. (1995), *Early Rabbinic Civil Law and the Social History of Roman Galilee: A Study of Mishnah Tractate Baba' Mesi'a'*, Atlanta.

Lapin, H. (1996), 'Jewish and Christian academies in Roman Palestine: some preliminary observations', in A. Raban and K. G. Holum (eds.), *Caesarea Maritima: A Retrospective After Two Millennia*, Leiden, pp. 496–513.

Lapin, H. (1999), 'Rabbis and cities in later Roman Palestine: the literary evidence', *JJS* 50: 187–207.

Lapin, H. (2000), 'Rabbis and cities: some aspects of the rabbinic movement in its Graeco-Roman enviroment', in P. Schäfer and C. Hezser (eds.), *The Talmud Yerushalmi and Graeco-Roman Culture*, vol. 2, Tübingen, pp. 51–80.

Lapin, H. (2002), 'Institutionalization, Amoraim and Yerushalmi Šebi'it', in Schäfer (ed.) (2002), pp. 161–82.

Lapin, H. (2003), 'Hegemony and its discontents: rabbis as a late antique provincial population', in R. Kalmin and S. Schwarz (eds.), *Jewish Culture and Society under the Christian Roman Empire*, pp. 319–47.

Lehnardt, A. (2002), 'The Samaritans (Kutim) in the Talmud Yerushalmi', in Schäfer (ed.) (2002), pp. 139–60.

Levine, L. I. (1989), *The Rabbinic Class of Roman Palestine in Late Antiquity*, Jerusalem.

Levine, L. I. (1997), 'The revolutionary effects of archaeology on the study of Jewish history: the case of the ancient synagogue', in N. A. Silberman and D. B. Small (eds.), *The Archaeology of Israel: Constructing the Past, Interpreting the Present*, Sheffield, pp. 166–89.

Levine, L. I. (2001), 'The status of the patriarchate in the third and fourth centuries: sources and methodology', in I. Gafni (ed.), *Kehal Yisrael: Jewish Self-Rule Through the Ages*, vol. 1: *The Ancient Period*, Jerusalem, pp. 103–38. [Hebrew]

Levine, L. I. (2005), *The Ancient Synagogue: The First Thousand Years*, New Haven and London.

Levinson, J. (2000), 'Bodies and bo(a)rders: emerging fictions of identity in late antiquity', *HThR* 93: 343–72.

Levinson, J. (2005), 'The cultural dignity of narrative', in Rubenstein (ed.) (2005), pp. 361–82.

Lightstone, J. N. (2002), *Mishnah and the Social Formation of the Early Rabbinic Guild: A Socio-Rhetorical Approach*, Ontario.

Lorberbaum, Y. (2004), *Image of God: Halakha and Aggadah*, Jerusalem. [Hebrew]

Mandel, P. (2000), 'Between Byzantium and Islam: the transmission of a Jewish book in the Byzantine and early Islamic periods', in Y. Elman and I. Gershoni (eds.), *Transmitting Jewish Traditions: Orality, Textuality, and Cultural Diffusion*, New Haven, pp. 74–106.

Mélèze Modrzejewski, J. (2003), '"Filios Suos Tantum": Roman law and Jewish identity', in M. Mor *et al.* (eds.) (2003), pp. 108–36.

Meyers, E. M. (2002), 'Jewish culture in Greco-Roman Palestine', in D. Biale (ed.), *Cultures of the Jews: A New History*, New York, pp. 135–80.

Milikowsky, C. (1991), 'Authority and conflict in post-destruction Roman Judea: the patriarchate, the rabbis, the people and the Romans', in D. J. Elazar (ed.), *Authority, Power and Leadership in the Jewish Polity*, Lanham, MD, New York and London, pp. 93–112.

Miller, S. S. (1984), *Studies in the History and Traditions of Sepphoris*, Leiden.

Miller, S. S. (1987), 'Intercity relations in Roman Palestine: the case of Sepphoris and Tiberias', *AJS Review*, 12: 1–24.

Miller, S. S. (1993), 'The Minim of Sepphoris reconsidered', *HThR* 86: 377–402.

Miller, S. S. (2006), *Sages and Commoners in Late Antique* 'Erez *Israel*, Tübingen.

Miller, S. S. (2007), 'Priests, purities, and the Jews of Galilee', in J. Zangenberg (ed.), *Religions, Ethnicity and Identity in Ancient Galilee: A Region in Transition*, Tübingen, pp. 375–402.

Moore, G. F. (1927–30), *Judaism in the First Centuries of the Christian Era: The Age of the Tannaim*, 3 vols., Cambridge, MA.

Mor, M. *et al.* (eds.) (2003), *Jews and Gentiles in the Holy Land*, Jerusalem.

Naeh, S. (1998), 'The Torah reading cycle in early Palestine: a re-examination', *Tarbiz*, 67: 165–86. [Hebrew]

Neusner, J. (1973), *Eliezer ben Hyrcanus: The Tradition and the Man*, 2 vols., Leiden.

Neusner, J. (1983), *Ancient Israel after Catastrophe: The Religious World View of the Mishna*, Charlottesville, VA.

Neusner, J. (1984), *In Search of Talmudic Biography: The Problem of the Attributed Saying*, Chico, CA.

Neusner, J. (1994), *The Judaism the Rabbis Take for Granted*, Atlanta.

Neusner, J. (2001), 'Introduction: the inquiry of Max Kadushin', in Kadushin (2001a), pp. ix–xvii.

Neusner, J. (2002), *Judaism When Christianity Began: A Survey of Belief and Practice*, Louisville, KY.

Newman, H. I. (2006), 'Closing the circle: Yonah Fraenkel, the Talmudic story and rabbinic history', in M. Kraus (ed.), *How Should Rabbinic Literature be Read in the Modern World?*, Piscataway, NJ, pp. 105–35.

Noam, V. (2005), 'Divorce in Qumran in light of early Halakhah', *JJS* 56.2: 206–23.

Noam, V. (2006), 'Traces of sectarian Halakhah in the rabbinic world', in Fraade *et al.* (eds.) (2006), pp. 67–85.

Noam, V. (2007), 'In the area of the laws of purification again', *Zion*, 72.2: 127–60. [Hebrew]

Novak, D. (1983), *The Image of the Non-Jew in Judaism: An Historical and Constructive Study of the Noahide Laws*, New York.

Oppenheimer, A. (1977a), 'The Jewish settlement in Iavne's period and Bar Kochba's revolution', *Cathedra*, 4: 51–66. [Hebrew]

Oppenheimer, A. (1977b), *The Am Ha-aretz: A Study in the Social History of the Jewish People in the Hellenistic-Roman Period*, Leiden

Oppenheimer, A. (1988), 'Jewish Lydda in the Roman era', *Hebrew Union College Annual*, 59: 115–36.

Oppenheimer, A. (1991), *Galilee in the Mishnaic Period*, Jerusalem. [Hebrew]

Oppenheimer, A. (1992), 'Roman rule and the cities of the Galilee in Talmudic literature', in L. I. Levine (ed.), *The Galilee in Late Antiquity*, New York and Jerusalem, pp. 114–25.

Oppenheimer, A. (1996a), 'Urbanisation and city territories in Roman Palestine', in I. M. Gafni, A. Oppenheimer, and D. R. Schwartz (eds.), *The Jews in the Hellenistic-Roman World: Studies in Memory of Menahem Stern*, Jerusalem, pp. 209–18.

Oppenheimer, A. (1996b), 'Tannaitic Benei Beraq: a peripheral centre of learning', in H. Cancik, H. Lichtenberger and P. Schäfer (eds.), *Geschichte, Tradition, Reflexion: Festschrift für Martin Hengel zum 70. Geburstag*, Tübingen, vol. 1, pp. 483–501.

Oppenheimer, A. (2001), 'The status of the Sages in the Mishnaic period: from model figures to national-spiritual leadership', in I. Gafni (ed.), *Kehal Yisrael: Jewish Self-Rule Through the Ages*, vol. 1: *The Ancient Period*, Jerusalem, pp. 85–102. [Hebrew]

Oppenheimer, A. (2007), *Rabbi Judah Ha-Nasi*, Jerusalem. [Hebrew]

Peskowitz, M. (1997), *Spinning Fantasies: Rabbis, Gender and History*, Berkeley.

Poirier, J. C. (1996), 'Jacob Neusner, the Mishnah, and ventriloquism', *JQR* 87: 61–78.

Porton, G. G. (1988), *Goyim: Gentiles and Israelites in Mishnah-Toseftah*, Atlanta.

Porton, G. G. (1994), *The Stranger Within Your Gates: Converts and Conversion in Rabbinic Literature*, Chicago.

Reif, S. C. (2004), 'The Bible in the liturgy', in Z. M. Brettler and A. Berlin (eds.), *The Jewish Study Bible*, pp. 1937–48.

Reiner, E. (1998), 'From Joshua to Jesus: the transformation of a biblical story to a local myth. A chapter in the religious life of the Galilean Jew', in A. Kofsky and G. G. Stroumsa (eds.), *Sharing the Sacred: Religious Contacts and Conflicts in the Holy Land*, Jerusalem, pp. 223–71.

Rosenfeld, B. (1997), *Lod and its Sages in the Period of the Mishnah and the Talmud*, Jerusalem. [Hebrew]

Rosenfeld, B. (1998), 'The settlements of the Sages in the Galilee, 70–400: periphery or center', *Hebrew Union College Annual*, 69: 40–103.

Rosen-Zvi, I. (2008), *The Rite that Was Not: Temple, Midrash and Gender in Tractate Sotah*, Jerusalem.

Rubenstein, J. L. (1999), *Talmudic Stories: Narrative, Art, Composition and Culture*, Baltimore and London.

Rubenstein, J. L. (2003), *The Culture of the Babylonian Talmud*, Baltimore.

Rubenstein, J. L. (2007), 'Social and institutional settings of rabbinic literature', in C. E. Fonrobert and M. S. Jaffee (eds.), *The Cambridge Companion to the Talmud and Rabbinic Literature*, Cambridge, pp. 58–74.

Rubenstein, J. L. (ed.) (2005), *Creation and Composition: The Contribution of the Bavli Redactors (Stammaim) to the Aggada*, Tübingen.

Rubin, N. (1995), *The Beginning of Life: Rites of Birth, Circumcision and Redemption of the First-Born in the Talmud and Midrash*, Tel Aviv. [Hebrew]

Rubin, N. (1997), *The End of Life: Rites of Burial and Mourning in the Talmud and Midrash*, Tel Aviv. [Hebrew]

Rubin, N. (2003), 'Brit Mila: a study of change in custom', in E. Wyner Mark (ed.), *The Covenant of Circumcision*, Hanover and London, pp. 87–97.

Rubin, N. (2004), *The Joy of Life: Rites of Betrothal and Marriage in the Talmud and Midrash*, Tel Aviv. [Hebrew]

Safrai, S. and Safrai, Z. (1998), *Haggadah of the Sages: The Passover Haggadah*, Jerusalem. [Hebrew]

Safrai, S. and Safrai, Z. (2005), 'Were the Sages a ruling elite?', in D. Gera and M. Ben Zeev (eds.), *The Path of Peace: Studies in Honor of Israel Friedman Ben-Shalom*, pp. 375–440.

Safrai, Z. (1995), *The Jewish Community in the Talmudic Period*, Jerusalem. [Hebrew]

Satlow, M. L. (2001), *Jewish Marriage in Antiquity*, Princeton.

Satlow, M. L. (2002), 'Fictional women: a study in stereotypes', in Schäfer (ed.) (2002), pp. 225–45.

Satlow, M. L. (2003), '"And on the earth you shall sleep": "Talmud Torah" and rabbinic asceticism', *Journal of Religion*, 83.2: 204–25.

Satlow, M. L. (2005), 'A history of the Jews or Judaism?', *JQR* 95.1: 151–62.

Schäfer, P. (ed.) (1998), *The Talmud Yerushalmi and Graeco-Roman Culture*, vol. 1, Tübingen.

Schäfer, P. (ed.) (2002), *The Talmud Yerushalmi and Graeco-Roman Culture*, vol. 3, Tübingen.

Schiffman, L. H. (1983), *Sectarian Law in the Dead Sea Scrolls: Courts, Testimony, and the Penal Code*, Chicago.

Schiffman, L. H. (1985a), 'The Samaritans in Tannaitic Halakha', *JQR* 75: 323–50.

Schiffman, L. H. (1985b), *Who was a Jew? Rabbinic and Halakhic Perspectives on the Jewish Christian Schism*, Hoboken, NJ.

Schiffman, L. H. (2003), *Understanding Second Temple and Rabbinic Judaism*, New York.

Schremer, A. (2003), *Male and Female He Created Them: Jewish Marriage in the Late Second Temple, Mishnah, and Talmud Periods*, Jerusalem. [Hebrew]

Schremer, A. (2005), 'Stammaitic historiography', in J. L. Rubenstein (ed.), *Creation and Composition: The Contribution of the Bavli Redactors (Stammaim) to the Aggada*, Tübingen, pp. 219–36.

Schremer, A. (2007), 'Midrash and history: God's power, the Roman empire, and hopes for redemption in tannaitic literature', *Zion*, 72: 5–36. [Hebrew]

Schwartz, J. J. (1991), *Lod (Lydda), Israel: From Its Origins through the Byzantine Period 5600 BCE–640 CE*, Oxford.

Schwartz, S. (1998), 'Gamliel in Aphrodite's bath: Palestinian Judaism and urban culture in the third and fourth centuries', in Schäfer (ed.) (1998), pp. 203–17.

Schwartz, S. (1999), 'The patriarchs and the diaspora', *JJS* 50: 208–22.

Schwartz, S. (2001), *Imperialism and Jewish Society, 200 BCE–640 CE*, Princeton.

Schwartz, S. (2002), 'Historiography on the "Talmudic period"', in M. Goodman, J. Cohen and D. Sorkin (eds.), *The Oxford Handbook of Jewish Studies*, Oxford, pp. 79–114.

Schwartz, S. (2004), 'Big-men or chiefs: against an institutional history of the Palestinian patriarchate', in J. Wertheimer (ed.), *Jewish Religious Leadership: Image and Reality*, vol. 1, pp. 155–73.

Setzer, C. (2005), '"Talking their way into empire": Jews, Christians and pagans debate resurrection of the body', in C. Bakhos (ed.), *Ancient Judaism in Its Hellenistic Context*, Leiden, pp. 155–75.

Shinan, A. (2004), 'The Bible in the synagogue', in Z. M. Brettler and A. Berlin (eds.), *The Jewish Study Bible*, New York, pp. 1929–37.

Siverstev, A. (2002), *Private Households and Public Politics in 3rd–5th Century Jewish Palestine*, Tübingen.

Stern, S. (1994a), *Jewish Identity in Early Rabbinic Writings*, Leiden, New York and Köln.

Stern, S. (1994b), 'Attribution and authorship in the Babylonian Talmud', *JJS* 45: 28–51.

Stern, S. (1995), 'The concept of authorship in the Babylonian Talmud', *JJS* 46: 183–95.

Stern, S. (2000), 'Pagan images in late antique Palestine synagogues', in S. Mitchell and G. Greatrex (eds.), *Ethnicity and Culture in Late Antiquity*, London, pp. 241–52.

Stern, S. (2003), 'Rabbi and the origins of the patriarchate', *JJS* 54: 193–215.

Sussman, Y. (1989), 'The history of Halakha and the Dead Sea Scrolls: preliminary observation on Miqsat Ma'ase ha-Torah (4QMMT)', *Tarbiz*, 59: 11–76. [Hebrew]

Sussman, Y. (1993), 'The scholarly oeuvre of Professor Ephraim Elimelech Urbach', in *E. E. Urbach: A Bio-Bibliography*, Supplement to *Jewish Studies*, 1, pp. 7–116. [Hebrew]

Sussman, Y. (2005), 'Oral law: literarily, the importance of the "dot on the iota"', in idem and D. Rosenthal (eds.), *Mehkerei Talmud: Talmudic Studies Dedicated to the Memory of Professor Ephraim E. Urbach*, vol. 1, Jerusalem, pp. 209–384. [Hebrew]

Tabory, J. (1933), *Jewish Prayer and the Yearly Cycle: A List of Articles*, Supplement to *Kiryat Sefer*, 64, Jerusalem; also available at: www.daat.ac.il/daat/bibliogr/tavori-2.htm [Hebrew]

Tabory, J. (1995), *Jewish Festivals in the Time of the Mishnah and Talmud*, Jerusalem. [Hebrew]

Tabory, J. (2006a), *Jewish Festivals in Late Antiquity*, in Katz (ed.) (2006), pp. 556–72.

Tabory, J. (2006b), 'The Passover Haggada', in S. Safrai *et al.* (eds.), *The Literature of the Sages*, Second Part: *Midrash and Targum . . .*, Assen, pp. 327–38.

Teppler, Y. (2007), *Birkat HaMinim: Jews and Christians in Conflict in the Ancient World*, Tübingen.

Urbach, E. E. (1975), *The Sages: Their Concepts and Beliefs*, Jerusalem.

Urbach, E. E. (1986), *The Halakhah: Its Sources and Development*, Tel Aviv.

Urbach, E. E. (1998), *Studies in Judaica*. [Hebrew]

Urbach, E. E. (2002), *The World of the Sages: Collected Studies*, Jerusalem. [Hebrew]

Valler, S. (2001), *Women and Womanhood in the Talmud*, Providence, RI.

Visotzky, B. L. (1989), 'Prolegomenon to the study of Jewish-Christianities in rabbinic literature', *AJS Review*, 14.1: 47–70.

Visotzky, B. L. (1990), 'Anti-Christian polemic in Leviticus Rabbah', *Proceedings of the American Academy for Jewish Research*, 56: 83–100.

Visotzky, B. L. (1995), *Fathers of the World*, Tübingen.

Visotzky, B. L. (2005), *Golden Bells and Pomegranates: Studies in Midrash Leviticus Rabbah*, Tübingen.

Wald, S. G. (2000), *BT Pesahim III: Critical Edition with Comprehensive Commentary*, New York and Jerusalem.

Walfish, A. (2001), 'The Literary Method of Redaction in Mishnah Based on Tractate Rosh Hashanah', Ph.D. dissertation, Hebrew University, Jerusalem. [Hebrew]

Walfish, A. (2006), 'The poetics of the Mishnah', in A. J. Avery-Peck and J. Neusner (eds.), *The Mishnah in Contemporary Perspective*, Part 2, Leiden, pp. 153–89.

Yadin, A. (2004), *Scripture as Logos: Rabbi Ishmael and the Origins of Midrash*, Philadelphia.

Yuval, I. J. (2006), *Two Nations in Your Womb: Perceptions of Jews and Christians in Late Antiquity and the Middle Ages*, Berkeley, CA.

19

Rabbinic Perceptions of Christianity and the History of Roman Palestine

WILLIAM HORBURY

WHAT DO RABBINIC TEXTS OFFER THE HISTORIAN OF CHRISTIANITY IN ROMAN PALESTINE? This may be the most well-worn of all the questions considered in the present volume. Other contributors have written substantially on it elsewhere (Alexander 1992, 2007; Kalmin 1994; Goodman 1996; Schäfer 2007). The roots of its current discussion go back to medieval Jewish–Christian controversy, and intertwine with the whole history of the reception of the Talmud in Europe and the western world.

The study of the rabbinic materials is sometimes broken into two parts, concerning Jesus and concerning the Christians. Here both parts must remain in view. Among recent authors, therefore, I am following in scope, but in much briefer compass, Johann Maier (1978, 1982), who wrote a book on each part; H. L. Strack (1910), who collected sources for both into one concise volume; and Travers Herford (1903), who brought both parts into one book. I keep in mind, however, others who have written simply on one part, including recently Peter Schäfer on Jesus and Philip Alexander (2007) on the Christians.

I

The problems of the sources are almost as famous as the sources themselves. Strack's title *Jesus, die Häretiker und die Christen nach den ältesten jüdischen Angaben* highlights one well-known difficulty with its mention of 'heretics'; some passages of the Talmud and Midrash which may speak of Christians deal expressly only with *minim*, the more general term conventionally rendered 'heretics'. This point of nomenclature recalls another problem, that the transmission of relevant passages has been affected in Europe since the late thirteenth century by censorship; the censor might expurgate—a process which saved the text from official destruction—but the internal response to this situation within the Jewish community could anticipate the censor

Proceedings of the British Academy **165**, 353–376. © The British Academy 2010.

through deliberate omissions and alterations by copyists and printers, especially as regards names.[1]

This enquiry also takes one beyond rabbinic texts in the strict sense, and beyond texts which belong to Roman Palestine. Strack's title spoke therefore not simply of Talmud and Midrash, as Travers Herford had done, but of the earliest Jewish statements, more generally. These include prayer-texts, especially the famous benediction concerning the *minim* in the Eighteen Benedictions; early piyyutim (nn. 52 and 54, below); and the Midrash-like and also polemical *Toledot Yeshu*, offering a narrative of the rise of Christianity.[2] Some sources take one beyond Roman Palestine chronologically, as with the piyyutim from the Byzantine age, or both chronologically and geographically, as with the Babylonian Talmud; but it is likely in all these cases that there is contact in some way with Jewish tradition and literature from Palestine in the Roman period, and it is more misleading to exclude this material than to include it. Lastly, the remarks on Christian origins ascribed to Jews in pagan and Christian sources from the Roman empire, mainly in Greek and Latin, need attention together with the Hebrew and Aramaic texts on Christianity transmitted in and in connection with rabbinic literature.

Almost all these Hebrew and Aramaic texts were being scrutinised by Jews and Christians in the thirteenth century, the first great age of Christian Hebrew study and the age when examination of the Talmud led on the one hand to the sentence of burning and on the other to a measure of ecclesiastical commendation. Some conflicting approaches which have remained influential can be detected in this medieval context.

First, there is the view taken by many Christians that the ostensible rabbinic references to Christianity are indeed meant as references to Christianity, but are often erroneous; put in its most negative form, as by Nicholas Donin in the Paris Disputation of 1240, this was one of the arguments for considering the Talmud both blasphemous and misleading. A more positive form of the same view can be seen in Travers Herford.

Secondly, there is the view advanced in medieval Jewish defence of the Talmud that these ostensible references really relate not to Jesus of Nazareth but to others, and not to Christians but to others. The ambiguity of the term

---

[1] Examples of these from sixteenth-century Talmud tractates and prayer-books printed by Geronimo (Gershom) Soncino and others are given in Popper (1899: 28–9); relevant phrases from censored and uncensored Babylonian Talmud manuscripts and early printed texts are collected in translation in Schäfer (2007: 131–44).

[2] Ehrlich and Langer (2006); on the *Toledot Yeshu*, with talmudic material, see E. Bammel (1966–67), reprinted together with several further studies of these texts in E. Bammel (1986). An Aramaic *Toledot Yeshu*, attested in Genizah fragments and probably current by the ninth century, is compared with more recently discovered Hebrew texts on the same lines by Deutsch (2000).

minim has already been noted; the argument for differentiating talmudic figures thought to be Jesus from the Jesus of the Gospels, which was fundamentally important, has rested partly on variations of name, notably when it is asked if ben Stada is a name for Jesus of Nazareth (b.Sanh. 67a, discussed below), and partly on chronology, as when Jesus (Yeshu ha-Noẓri) is presented as the pupil of Joshua ben Perahiah, *c*.100 BCE (b.Sanh. 107b). This defence was used by R. Jehiel of Paris in the Paris Disputation.[3] It is not without footholds in the texts, however, and in modern scholarship it is developed intensively in Johann Maier's two books; he urges concurrently that Christianity had little impact on the Jews of Judaea and Galilee before the Byzantine period.[4]

Thirdly, despite the perils of the times, it could be contended in the medieval Jewish community that the Talmud and other rabbinic texts did attest an early controversy against Christianity which it was a duty to continue. This line of argument is exemplified in the use made of b.Sanh. 43a, on the confutation of five disciples of Jesus before their execution, to introduce the Hebrew account of the Barcelona Disputation of 1263.[5] The suitability of rabbinic material for this purpose suggests that it has a polemical aspect, whereas Travers Herford, for instance, viewed it as careless and contemptuous legend. This polemical character of the rabbinic material has been re-emphasised in modern study especially by E. Bammel (1966–67: 318–20 (1986: 221–3)) and P. Schäfer (2007: 9).

Lastly, a trend in Christian thought represented by Raymund Martini and others accepted the principle that a revealed oral tradition going back to Moses lay behind rabbinic literature, although by no means everything in the literature reflected it. This approach could correspondingly find from a non-Jewish standpoint some truth as well as falsehood in the references to Christianity, as the use made of the Talmud on Jesus and the *Toledot Yeshu* as proofs for Christianity in Raymund Martini's *Pugio Fidei* strikingly shows (Horbury 1999: 19–21). Hence in the long term we find treatments of the passages on Christianity like that offered in a widely read eighteenth-century handbook by Christian Schoettgen (1733–42: vol. 2, 693–709), in which a chapter on talmudic charges against Jesus is followed by a chapter on things

---

[3] See the Latin record of the deposition of Magister Vivo (Jehiel): that the Talmud never lies, that Yeshu ha-Noẓri is Jesus of Nazareth, son of Miriam, but that he is not identical with 'our Jesus'— 'but he could not say who he was, whence it is sufficiently plain that he was lying'— *Dicit tamen quod alius fuit a nostro ihesu (sed nesciebat dicere quis ille fuisset, unde satis patet quod menciebatur)*. The text is printed from MS Paris Lat. 16558 in Merchavia (1970: 453).

[4] For a brief discussion of Maier's outlook see Horbury (1998: 19–20).

[5] Steinschneider (ed. 1860: 5), translated in Rankin (1956: 178–9), and discussed in Horbury (2001: 202–3).

which rabbinic authors have said well and truly concerning Jesus. Travers Herford is to some extent also an heir of this tradition.

Schoettgen's name brings us to the immediate background of the modern studies mentioned at the beginning. The medieval, early modern and modern Christian interpretation of these texts on Christianity was not unprepared to find aspects of truth in them, but it was also conditioned by ongoing discussion of the historical value of rabbinic literature in general. This question too has always accompanied modern study. In the early eighteenth century J. A. Fabricius, surveying recent debate, had tried to steer a middle course between the position that talmudic material is essentially from the fifth century and later, and is strongly influenced by Byzantine culture and Christian literature, and on the other hand the assertion that it preserves really old tradition.[6]

This early modern debate of course to some extent anticipates present-day discussion arising especially from emphasis on the late date and the formative character of the redaction of the great rabbinic corpora. In early fifth-century Galilee the Palestinian Talmud is likely to have come to completion, and at the same time the midrashim on Genesis, Leviticus and the Song of Songs were being compiled. The vast Babylonian Talmud, including much material which in Palestine entered the midrashim, was being edited in the East for perhaps two centuries after that (see Chapter 10, by Richard Kalmin, above). Much of the rabbinic material on Christianity was therefore brought together and edited well after the Roman empire had become Christian or, in the rabbinic phrase, had fallen into *minut*, 'heresy'.[7] Although the weight of the material on Jesus, and some material also on *minim*, is found in the Babylonian Talmud, there is also much on both Jesus and Christianity in the Palestinian sources, including those, like the Mishnah, Tosefta and some parts of the talmudic and midrashic texts, which reflect the second and third centuries—an important point for this enquiry focused on Roman Palestine. Moreover, it is likely that much of what is found in the Babylonian Talmud rests, like many other parts of its aggadic content, on Palestinian tradition.

On the other hand, with regard to Christianity it has been suggested that the Babylonian Talmud should indeed be singled out as the fullest source on Jesus, with the sharpest polemic concerning him overall, and that its passages on Christianity reflect Jewish controversy against Christianity beyond the Roman border, in Mesopotamia and Babylonia, as this controversy accompanied the long-lasting Persian conflict with the Christian Roman empire—a conflict which left its literary deposit from Christians under Persian rule

---

[6] Fabricius (1716: 6–8), considered more fully in Horbury (2010: 35–6).
[7] m.Sotah 9.15, 'the empire shall fall into heresy' (a late addition to the text), discussed with parallels in Simon (1986: 187) and Alexander (2007: 664, n. 14).

especially in the Syriac acts of the Persian martyrs.[8] This suggestion surely rightly affirms the polemical aspect of much rabbinic comment on Christianity, and well indicates one setting for such polemic. On the other hand, the tendency to contrast the material on Christianity in the Babylonian Talmud with that in Palestinian sources which is developed in this suggestion perhaps does less than justice to the overlap between these sources and to the interaction between rabbinic circles in Palestine and Babylonia. There are continuities between the source-material from the two regions on this subject both in content, as is often true of other aspects of aggadah, and in the polemical character of what is transmitted.[9] This character is by no means absent from the Palestinian material, and there was a Roman and Palestinian as well as a Babylonian setting for anti-Christian polemic.

The opposition to Christianity encouraged under Persian rule from the fourth century onwards continued that found in the Roman empire still in the fourth century, which brought Julian as well as Constantine, and found of course also earlier, especially but not only when reinforced by government in the second half of the third century. The change under Constantine affected Palestine especially from 324, when Constantine became sole emperor, not long after the time of Abbahu and other rabbinical teachers from whose circles polemical comment on Christianity is reflected in the Talmud and Midrash (see below). Some earlier rabbinic allusions considered below probably reflect conditions in the second and third centuries, and are likewise polemical.

Official protection for the Palestinian Jewish community continued after 324, as the institution of the Jewish patriarchate and many fourth-century synagogue buildings attest; but the patriarchate came to an end in the early fifth century. At the same time the need for polemic will not have lessened, despite the strength of the Palestinian Jewish community, given the Christian element in the population and the attempts to encourage Christianity epitomised by Epiphanius' narrative of Count Joseph's mission in Galilee under Constantine.[10]

Among the non-Jewish reports of Jewish remarks on Christian origins mentioned above, the earlier examples represent pre-Constantinian polemic. Under both Roman and Persian rule non-Jewish polemists are said to have cited statements which resemble material in the Talmud and the *Toledot*

---

[8] So Schäfer (2007: 115–22). The importance of Jewish–Christian polemic in this setting is also suggested by passages in Aphrahat, Ephrem Syrus and other Syriac writers.

[9] The contrast was also stressed in Kalmin (1994); on the other hand, that western (i.e. Palestinian) rabbinic traditions on Christianity are sometimes preserved only in eastern (Babylonian) texts is also the view taken in Alexander (2007: 688, 700).

[10] For a sober review of this narrative see Stemberger (2000: 71–81).

Yeshu.[11] The importance of such reports for this topic recalls, from the broader discussion of rabbinic literature as a historical source, G. Stemberger's indication (1999) of the need in this regard to consider the possible coherence of rabbinic with non-rabbinic material. In texts on Christianity such contact may highlight not only, on occasion, what may be historically significant convergences between rabbinic and non-rabbinic sources, but also influences of Christian writing or tradition on Jewish literature. For the history of Christianity in Roman Palestine, the latter may be important as well as the former.

A final preliminary consideration arises from Palestinian church history itself. The New Testament preserves in its early source-material some first-century Palestinian impressions of Jewish as well as specifically Christian life. Then Roman Palestine was the homeland or adopted home of a series of Christian authors who concerned themselves with the Jews and Judaism, notably Justin Martyr from Flavia Neapolis in the second century; Origen, who settled in Caesarea in the third century; Eusebius, bishop of Caesarea in the early fourth century; Epiphanius from Beth Zedek near Eleutheropolis in the fourth century; and Jerome, who settled at Bethlehem in the fourth century. All show some awareness of contemporary Jewish teaching, and their comments have been used for reconstruction of Judaean Jewish history and the history of the rabbinic movement. The extent of their Jewish knowledge must be assessed with care, but consideration of the significance of rabbinic texts for Palestinian Christianity should not neglect the fact that a series of Christian writers in or from Palestine, from the first to the fourth century, suggest Christian awareness of contemporary Judaism.

II

The beginnings of Christianity in Roman Palestine are related as a continuous story in the *Toledot Yeshu*, but glimpsed in rabbinic literature through a sometimes rather different series of detached sayings and anecdotes. These deal with the birth of Jesus, his teaching and disciples, his trial, death, and fate in the underworld, and teaching by his disciples after his death. The contrast between these passages and the *Toledot Yeshu* can be justly emphasised up to a point, but there is a good case for holding that an early form of the story which is later presented in the *Toledot Yeshu* lies behind much of the

---

[11] So Origen, *Contra Celsum*, 1.28–32, discussed below (Celsus quotes a Jew on Pantera); Elisha (Elisaeus) Vardapet, *History of Vardan and the Armenian War*, translated in Thomson (1982: 79, 90) (a letter of a fifth-century Persian governor to Armenia commending Mazdaism, and a reply from Armenian bishops and clergy, cite the Pantera story).

rabbinic material.[12] Justin Martyr in the second century holds that Jews had circulated a negative account of Jesus as a Galilean deceiver who was put to death (Justin Martyr, *Dial.* 17.1–2, 108.2). This statement is part of what is already a legendarily developed traditional Christian account of Jewish reaction, but its suggestion of a summary narrative with an emphasis on the charge of deception, which is also reflected in rabbinic tradition considered below (b.Sanh. 43a), is probably a pointer to the nature of contemporary Jewish comment.[13]

Clues to a narrative as it circulated in the second and third centuries are given by the statements on Jesus and the rise of Christianity which Celsus, writing against Christianity about 180 CE and quoted by Origen about sixty years later, ascribes to a Jew, especially when they are viewed in conjunction with other evidence. These statements at one point form a series from conception to early preaching which looks like part of a longer narrative (Origen, *C. Cels.* 1.28, 32); his mother was turned out by her husband, his father was a soldier named Panthera, he went to Egypt and learned magical powers, he came back and on account of these powers called himself a god. At the end of the third century a comparable series (expulsion by the Jews, gathering of followers, bandit-like existence) is offered in a pagan source rebutted by Lactantius.[14] Other individual points in the material ascribed by Celsus to the Jew find parallels in the *Toledot Yeshu* and in pagan anti-Christian polemic; the debt of pagan to Jewish polemic in antiquity has long been recognised.[15] The rabbinic texts as we have them influenced later forms of the *Toledot Yeshu* in many details, but the outline of the *Toledot* narrative in early forms seems itself to be presupposed in the rabbinic sources.[16]

A first important shared element is Jesus' patronymic: son of Pantera. This name presupposes the story of his descent as told by the Jew of Celsus: his mother was turned out by her husband, 'for she was convicted of fornication, and had a child by a soldier named Panthera' (Origen, *C. Cels.* 1.32). In Palestinian rabbinic sources Jesus is named as son of Pantera in two

---

[12] For the argument for an early connected narrative presented in the following paragraph see Horbury (1982: 188–92); evidence was more fully presented in my Ph.D. thesis, 'A Critical Examination of the Toledoth Jeshu' (Cambridge, 1970), ch. 3, summarised at pp. 431–7.

[13] On the passages from Justin and Christian tradition on Jewish reaction see Horbury (1998: 156–8).

[14] Lactantius, *Div. inst.* 5.3, 4, discussed in Horbury (1982); the unnamed pagan author was probably Sossianus Hierocles, governor of Bithynia in 303, against whose work Eusebius wrote.

[15] See especially Bauer (1909: 452–86), an appendix entitled 'Das Leben Jesu bei den jüdischen und heidnischen Gegnern des Christentums'.

[16] The influence of talmudic texts on versions of the *Toledot* is illustrated by Krauss (1902: 181–94). He set the origin of the *Toledot Yeshu* in the fifth century, but noted that much of their content was already attested through Celsus and others in the second and third centuries (Krauss 1902: 2–3, 246).

anecdotes in the Tosefta (Ḥullin 2.22–3, 24) and in parallel accounts in the later midrashic compilation Ecclesiastes Rabbah (1, on 1:8) and elsewhere, concerning encounters by Eleazar b. Dama and Eliezer b. Hyrcanos, respectively, with Christians: 'A story of R. Eleazar b. Dama, who was bitten by a snake, and Jacob of Kefar Sama came to heal him in the name of Jeshua ben Pantera . . .' (t.Ḥul. 2.22–3); 'Once when I [R. Eliezer ben Hyrcanos] was walking on the pavements (*istrataya*) of Sepphoris, I found Jacob of Kefar Sikhnin, and he told me a heretical saying (*davar shel minut*) in the name of Jeshua ben Panteri, and it pleased me . . .' (t.Ḥul. 2.24).[17]

The immediate context of these stories (t.Ḥul. 2.20–1) is a detailed prohibition of contact with *minim*, discussed in the following section. The two anecdotes are warnings not to infringe this rule. Thus ben Dama seeks to prove to R. Ishmael that it is indeed permissible to be healed in this name, but he dies before he can break down the fence set up by the Wise; Eliezer ben Hyrcanos is arrested and brought before a Roman magistrate on a charge of heresy (*minut*), but although he is set free he grieves at the accusation, and remembering his pleasure in the saying he heard confesses that he has transgressed the words of the Torah, 'Keep thy ways far from her [*minut*]' (Prov. 5:8, cf. 7:25–6, on the 'strange woman'). The Tosefta probably received its last major editing later than the Mishnah, but like the Mishnah, with which it is closely related in content, it reflects Palestinian teaching in the second and third centuries.

These texts belong also to discussion of rabbinic sources on Palestinian Christians. Their points of interest include the reference in the second anecdote to a saying transmitted orally in the name of Jesus. This may be compared with a story from the Babylonian Talmud (Shabbat 116a–b) in which a philosopher is said to put forward statements which he claims are written in the Gospel. In this legendary anecdote Rabban Gamaliel and his sister Imma Salome, wife of R. Eliezer b. Hyrcanos, from Judaea in the late first and early second centuries, show up a Christian philosopher as swayed to quote the Gospel successively in two opposite senses by successive bribes—a golden lamp and (still more valuable) a Libyan ass. Points which are consistent with a second- or third-century date for the story include the mention of a Christian philosopher (thus Justin Martyr (e.g. *Dial.* 1.1, 6) and Tatian (*Ad. Gr.* 42.1) present themselves as philosophers), and the punch-line

---

[17] For further parallels in the two Talmuds (for the first story) and the Babylonian Talmud (for the second) see the synoptic tables in Maier (1978: 182–6, 144–51), respectively. The significance of the occurrences of 'ben Pantera' in the (Palestinian) Tosefta is not discussed in the review of 'Palestinian versus Babylonian Sources', well noting the actuality and local colour of the former but suggesting that sharp adverse biographical comment is more typical of the latter, in Schäfer (2007: 113–15).

'the ass has overturned the lamp', which alludes to the anti-Christian charges of ass-worship and of incest after the lamp is upset by a dog, current from the time of Hadrian (Minucius Felix, *Oct.* 9.3, 6–7, citing Fronto).[18] The currency of sayings of Jesus in both oral and written forms is thus an aspect of Christianity attested in rabbinic literature. For the narrative of Jesus' origins and actions, however, the passages from the Tosefta are significant as Palestinian sources attesting the patronymic ben Pantera and suggesting knowledge of and perpetuation of the story behind it.[19]

The view that the name has nothing to do with Jesus of Nazareth is unlikely in view of the narrative ascribed by Celsus to a Jew.[20] Various suggestions that the name is simply emblematic (corresponding, for instance, to *parthenos*) or that it is derived from other names are also unlikely, for reasons including the attestation of the name Panthera.[21] This was a widespread Greek name known also in Latin transliteration. In connection with the eastern Roman provinces it figures in the first-century Latin epitaph of the Sidonian soldier Tiberius Julius Abdes Pantera, found at Bingerbrück, which gave rise to the speculation that the gravestone of Celsus' Panthera had been discovered by the Rhine, and in Greek in the name 'Anchorimphis son of Panther' in a papyrus list of *sitologoi*, including many Jewish names, from the Fayyum (101–2 CE).[22] The anecdotes of meetings with disciples of Jeshua ben Pantera as they are told in the Tosefta can be ascribed in origin to the second century, perhaps not far from the time when Celsus was writing. The Jewish story of Pantera itself was placed in the first century by D. Rokeah (1969–70), and this seems reasonable in view of the reflections of the accusation, without a father's name, in the Gospels of Matthew and John (Matt. 1:19—child thought to be the son of a man other than Joseph; John 8:41—in a reply to Jesus, 'we were not born of fornication').

---

[18] Palestinian origin therefore seems likely, as suggested by Safrai (2003: 257–8); but the 'philosopher' and the anti-Christian charges implied may suggest composition in the second or third century rather than (as he proposes) in the fourth. See E. Bammel (1982); Visotzky (1987); on Fronto, C. P. Bammel (1993).

[19] An understanding of the usage as early anti-Christian polemic is followed with a fresh discussion (not mentioning Maier's work) by Jaffé (2008). Professor Judith Lieu kindly brought this article to my notice.

[20] For this suggestion see Maier (1978: 264–6).

[21] See the concise but wide-ranging survey in Maier (1978: 266–7), with nn. 606–19; similarly Jaffé (2008: 260–3).

[22] Deissmann (1923: 57–8; 1910: 68–9) (in each case with a photograph of the gravestone); *Berliner Griechische Urkunden* 715, republished as *CPJ* 428 by Tcherikover and Fuks (1960: vol. 2, 215–16) (without discussion of this name). An occurrence of the Greek noun *pentheros* in a Jerusalem ossuary inscription (*CIJ* 1211) is viewed as probably a proper name by Ilan (2002: 301, s.v. *Pantheras*).

Later on, perhaps from the early fourth century, comes a tradition in the Babylonian Talmud showing that this story of Jesus' descent was known in Babylonia, but that the body of narrative concerning a figure called ben Stada, who brought magical texts from Egypt, as the Tosefta reports, had by this time been associated with that concerning the son of Pantera and taken likewise to refer to Jesus. 'Ben Stada is Ben Pandera. Rab Ḥisda [Sura, end of third century] said, The husband was Stada, the lover Pandera.'[23] Other possibilities are then mentioned. Among the Palestinian Christians, Eusebius in the early fourth century knows that Jews slanderously assert that the Saviour was born of Panther; here he seems not to be dependent on Origen's refutation of Celsus in the previous century.[24]

The *Toledot Yeshu* as we have them include the story in various forms. Commonly it has been 'Judaised', so that the husband (Johanan (John)) and the father (Pandera) are both Jewish. The name Pandera is combined with that of Joseph, probably for polemical reasons, because Joseph's paternity seemed to be demonstrable from the New Testament itself (Matt. 13:55 'is not this the carpenter's son?'). There are traces, however, of relatively old versions in which the father is a Gentile, and Maimonides was still aware of the story in this form.[25]

It seems likely that the ben Stada story was brought together with that of ben Pantera in the third century. In the Tosefta and the Talmud Yerushalmi, ben Stada brings magical spells from Egypt (a tradition ascribed to Eliezer b. Hyrcanos), is classified as a 'fool' (*shoteh*), and is stoned as a leader-astray into idolatry (*mesit*), in accord with Deut. 13:7–12 (6–11) and m.Sanh. 7.10, after witnesses have lain in wait for him at Lydda.[26] It is often held that ben Stada was from the beginning a name for Jesus, for each of them is said to

---

[23] b.Shab. 104b, b.Sanh. 67a, adding the suggestion that Stada was his mother's name; the first sentence can also be understood as a rhetorical question, 'Was he indeed ben Stada?', with its answer 'He was ben Pandera' (see Maier 1978: 238). The spelling of Pandera with dalet rather than tet became common.

[24] Eusebius, *Ecl. proph.* 3.10, on Hosea 5:14 LXX 'I am as a panther to Ephraim' and 13:7 LXX 'I shall be as a panther', in Gaisford (ed. 1842: 111); Eusebius argues that the Jews have misunderstood a mystical traditional interpretation of this verse, where the Lord names himself as a panther.

[25] So Amulo, *C. Iudaeos*, 40 (mid-ninth century), reprinted in Strack (1910: 17*) (they assert that our Lord is the son *nescio cuius ethnici, quem nominant Pandera*); Maimondies in Halkin (ed. 1952: 12–13) (his mother was Jewish, but his father was Gentile).

[26] t.Shab. 9.15 (ben Stada scratched spells on his skin), parallel with p.Shab. 12.4, 13d (he brought spells from Egypt by marking them on his skin), and b.Shab. 104b (he brought spells from Egypt by scratching them on his skin), all in the name of R. Eliezer b. Hyrcanos, who receives a reply describing ben Stada as a fool; t.Sanh. 10.11, parallel with p.Sanh. 7.16, 25c–d (they set witnesses to lie in wait for ben Stada at Lydda, and brought him to court and stoned him) and b.Sanh. 67a (thus they did to ben Stada at Lydda, and they hanged him on Passover eve). For synoptic tables of these texts see Maier (1978: 207–16).

have learnt magic in Egypt (Origen, *C. Cels.* 1.28) and each was viewed as a *mesit* (b.Sanh. 43a, discussed below).[27] On the other hand, the difference in name (in a compilation, the Tosefta, which includes unveiled references to Jesus son of Pantera) and the placing of the proceedings against ben Stada in Lydda suggest that originally the name belonged to another figure accused of magical practices learnt in Egypt, one who was known in the rabbinic circles of Lydda in the inter-war period (70–135) when Eliezer b. Hyrcanos taught there.[28] It has also been suggested that ben Stada was the apostle St Peter, who did indeed visit Lydda (Acts 9:32–43) and could have been viewed as a *mesit* (Schwartz 1995). Once again, however, the divergence of the narrative as well as the name from other traditions concerning Peter makes the identification unlikely. The name Stada can be associated, rather, with the Greek name Stadieus (Ilan 2002: 306).

In any case, the theme of bringing magic from Egypt will probably have figured in early versions of the *Toledot Yeshu* narrative, although later it was overtaken in these texts by the parallel story of the theft of the divine Name as inscribed in the Temple.[29] Coupled with the condemnation of ben Stada as a *mesit*, the Egyptian theme will have been instrumental in the identification of ben Stada with ben Pantera. This identification is attested in the Babylonian Talmud, but it was probably current in Palestine as well as Babylonia by the end of the third century.[30]

The theme of Egyptian magic is probably also the force attracting a mention of the figure of Jesus in the famous story of Joshua b. Perahiah's over-hasty rejection of his disciple Jesus as they were on their way back to Jerusalem from Alexandria, in the days of Alexander Jannaeus. This appears fully only in the Babylonian Talmud, but is paralleled in the Yerushalmi by a story of the slightly later Judah ben Tabbai and an unnamed disciple on the same journey.[31] It seems likely that a version of this story was associated with Jesus in amoraic Palestine (from the third to the fifth century) as well as in Babylonia.[32] Its fascination lies in its implied suggestion that Christians

---

[27] For the history of the treatment of ben Stada passages and an argument for the identification of ben Stada with Jesus see Catchpole (1971: 9–10, 35, 44–7, 61–4); for other sponsors of this view see also Maier (1978: 204 and nn. 385–7); similarly, with the focus on the Babylonian Talmud, Schäfer (2007: 15–18).

[28] So J. Derenbourg, S. Krauss and others cited and followed in Maier (1978: 204, n. 388). Discussion of the abundant rabbinic references to Lydda is reviewed in Oppenheimer (1988).

[29] For the charge of learning magic in Egypt see Origen, *C. Cels.* 1.28; Arnobius, *Adv. nat.* 1.42, in a form also recalling the *Toledot Yeshu* narrative of the Jerusalem Temple (pagans may say, he stole from the shrines of the Egyptians the names of powerful angels and arcane teachings).

[30] See the passages cited in n. 23, above; for synoptic presentations of the texts cited here and in n. 26 see Maier (1978: 207–16).

[31] b.Sanh. 107b, b.Sotah 47a; p.Hag. 2.2, 77d, discussed together by Maier (1978: 114–29).

[32] Alexander (2007: 700) inclines to the view that the story reflects Palestinian tradition.

might have been too hastily rejected in early days. Is this a response to views current in the second and third centuries which associated the disciples of Moses and of Christ, and to the phenomenon in this period of Christians wishing to become proselytes?[33]

Two last points from polemic concerned with the figure of Jesus relate to his teaching and his condemnation, respectively. The first is known simply from Palestinian tradition, the second is from a Babylonian tradition with, so I have suggested, a Palestinian core. The teaching of Jesus, envisaged with an emphasis on his own claims for himself which recalls both John's Gospel and the *Toledot Yeshu*, is rebutted in a saying ascribed to the late third-century Caesarean teacher Abbahu.[34] It is a pointed paraphrase and application of Balaam's prophecy (Num. 23:19), 'God is not a man, that he should lie; neither the son of man, that he should repent: has he said, and shall he not do it? or has he spoken, and shall he not make it good?' The application runs, 'If a man says to you, *I am God*, he is a liar; *I am the Son of man*, he will regret it; *I am going up to the heavens*, has he said? but he shall not make it good.'

Here the Gentile prophet is presented as foreseeing and disallowing the claims of Jesus, with a striking understanding of 'Son of man' as an exalted title which suggests that the Danielic background of the Gospel phrase is taken seriously, in line with the midrashic associations of Dan. 7 with the Davidic messiah.[35] The final reference to ascension rather than resurrection may reflect an early form of the narrative developed in the *Toledot Yeshu* concerning Jesus' promise of (magical) ascent through use of the divine Name and its frustration by a faithful Jew, perhaps already associated with the similar story told of Balaam himself (Targum Ps.-Jonathan Num. 31:8; Maier 1978: 73 and nn. 155–6). At the same time the passage recalls points where the New Testament itself emphasises ascent rather than resurrection, notably

---

[33] Galen, *De pulsuum differentiis*, 2.4; 3.3 in Walzer (1949: 14–15, 37–56) (followers of Moses and of Christ both show loyalty to undemonstrated presuppositions; note that Galen visited Palestine and was a friend of the governor Flavius Boethus); *Clementine Homilies*, 8.6–7, probably from a Syrian setting (for Jews and Christians respectively, Moses and Christ are equally valid teachers of the same truth); Justin Martyr, *Dial.* 47.4 (condemning Christians who pass over into Judaism); Eusebius, *Hist. eccl.* 6.12, 1 (Serapion of Antioch (bishop at the end of the second century) writes to Domnus, who had adopted Judaism in time of persecution) and *Mart. Pionii*, 13 (Smyrnaean Jews invite persecuted Christians into the synagogue), discussed with other texts by Simon (1986: 106–7).

[34] p.Ta'anit 2.1, 65b, discussed by Maier (1978: 76–82) (the saying was a protest against the imperial cult, and was later misunderstood as anti-Christian); Schäfer (2007: 107–9), shows that the Christian reference is far more likely to be original.

[35] Akiva on the 'thrones' of Dan. 7:9 as one of the Almighty, and 'one for David', according to b.Hag. 14a, b.Sanh. 38b; the one like a son of man coming with the clouds (*annene*) of heaven in Dan. 7:13 as the Davidic messiah, the Davidic descendant 'Anani' of 1 Chron. 3:24 (Targ. 1 Chron. 3:24, 'he is king messiah who shall be revealed'; Tanhuma Buber, Genesis, *Toledot*, 20, fo. 70b, justifying this interpretation of 1 Chron. 3:24 by quotation of Dan. 7:13).

in sayings of Christ in John 3:13 (descent and ascent, with a mention of the Son of Man) and 20:17 ('I ascend . . .'), and in the epistles in Eph. 4:9–10 (descent and ascent). Abbahu's saying is also contemporary with later Christian presentation of Christ as a second divine being who descended and ascended, as set out in Caesarea by Eusebius, following here in the footsteps of Justin Martyr.[36]

Lastly, the description of the trial of the disciples of Christ and then of their master in the Babylonian Talmud (Sanh. 43a) has been noticed already for medieval recognition of the passage on the disciples as a precedent for polemic against Christianity. Now the description of the condemnation of Jesus himself is mentioned especially for what appears to be its ancient core, the sentences 'on Passover eve they hanged Jesus . . . because he practised sorcery and deceived and led astray Israel'.[37] In Sanh. 43a as we have it these are linked by a sentence on the proclamation that he was to be stoned. Nevertheless, the first sentence is not wholly consistent in time with this sequel on the proclamation, which takes the hearer or reader back to an earlier period, and its substance—'they crucified him on Passover eve'—is found as a separate unit at the end of one of the traditions on ben Stada cited above (b.Sanh. 67a). Similarly, the second sentence, on the grounds of condemnation, is quoted as a separate saying at the end of the story in b.Sanh. 107b discussed above. It is likely that these sentences are older material which has been integrated secondarily with the description of the proclamation and the stoning. This description will have gained importance when the assumption was made that (as the practice laid down in the Mishnah would imply) the hanging (crucifixion) of Jesus must have been the hanging up of the dead body which follows a stoning.

Here then we have material which is probably older than its surroundings, and which corresponds to second-century statements that Jesus was crucified by the Jews (Justin Martyr, *Dial.* 108.2; Origen, *C. Cels.* 2.5, 9, quoting the Jew of Celsus) as a magician and deceiver of the people (Justin Martyr, *Dial.* 69.7, cf. 108.2 (deceiver)); compare, earlier, Mark 3:22, on sorcery, and Matt. 27:63, John 7:12, 47, on deception. It can be ascribed to second-century Palestine. It forms a grave summary of fundamental reasons for rejecting Christianity, on the lines of the legislation on sorcery in Deut. 18:9–14 and false prophecy in Deut. 13:2–12 (1–11), 18:15–22, as treated together in

---

[36] See Eusebius, *Dem. evang.* 6, introduction (257c), on the prophecies that one entitled Lord and God would descend to mortals and again ascend in their sight.

[37] For the argument summarised here, with a criticism of J. Maier's view that the passage does not refer to Jesus, see Horbury (1998: 104–7) (part of a corrected reprint of 'The benediction of the *minim* and early Jewish–Christian controversy' from *Journal of Theological Studies*, n.s. 33 (1982), 19–61).

m.Sanh. 7.10–11; in this movement people have been drawn away into idolatry by seeming prophecy, commended by works which have appeared to be signs and wonders, but must be in fact from below rather than above.[38]

This selection of material concerning Jesus has illustrated the importance of the subject of Christianity in Palestinian as well as Babylonian sources, from the second century onwards. For the historian of Palestine it attests Jewish encounters with Christians (t.Ḥul. 2.22, 24), with a specific mention of Sepphoris; Jewish awareness of Gospel exposition as it might be given by a Christian 'philosopher', a teaching figure typical of the second and third centuries; the currency of oral and written sayings of Jesus; and the early development of a rebuttal of Christianity with regard to the Christian narrative of Christ and its associated claims for his status as a prophet, messiah and divine being. Abbahu's saying on these claims is part of the rabbinic material which suggests a lively anti-Christian polemic as well as a shared Jewish–Christian engagement in biblical interpretation in late third-century Caesarea (Levine 1975: 80–4; de Lange 1976: 11, 27, 45–7, 54). The rabbinic material also reflects a more general account of Jesus which is an early form of the narrative found in the *Toledot Yeshu*, and rabbinic sources themselves are amplified in the amoraic period, not least by the incorporation of the ben Stada traditions.

Some divergences from the historical framework of the traditions handed down among the Christians begin to appear, notably in the references to Lydda and stoning and the association of Jesus with teachers of the Hasmonaean age; but the rabbinic polemic continues to cohere with Palestinian Christian impressions of Jewish polemic, as attested in the Gospels, Justin Martyr and Eusebius, and to fit the general presentation of Christianity as it is taken up from the Gospels in these authors. These passages then suggest that Christianity, including Christianity in Palestine, received considerable attention from Palestinian rabbinic teachers throughout the period from the second century to Constantine.

III

The study of rabbinic passages on Christians, like the study of passages on Christ, has been divided between the perception of anti-Christian polemic and the view that the texts are at best scanty and often of questionable relevance to Christianity. It has of course been possible for the same author to take differing overall views of the ostensible references to Christ and to the

---

[38] This view is presented more fully in Horbury (1999: 30–1).

Christians, respectively. Some at least of the references to *minim* clearly apply to Christians, and Christian arguments are often envisaged in indirect rabbinic polemic, in the view of scholars including S. Krauss (1996: 7–11), A. Marmorstein (1935), E. E. Urbach (1953: cols. 122–3, Eng. trans. in 1972: col. 191; 1971), who urged that many rabbinical texts which have been taken to be anti-Gnostic are really anti-Christian, and Marcel Simon (1986: 179–201). More recent writers who represent aspects of this position include Raphael Loewe (1966) and B. L. Visotzky (1995). Similarly, Christianity forms the main background of statements on the *minim* for Philip Alexander; he holds (2007: 663–4) that *minim* are often Jewish Christians, since it is reasonable to suppose that rabbinic teachers would have been especially concerned with Jews affected by Christianity, although in the later material it is likely that Christians in general are envisaged. For Yaakov Y. Teppler (2007: 164–348), mainly concerned with the earlier rabbinic material on *minim*, Christianity likewise forms its chief background, and Christians of Gentile as well as Jewish origin are envisaged.

The Hebrew term *minim*, 'kinds' or 'species', conventionally rendered 'heretics', a special use of the plural of *min*, may correspond to the special Greek term *genistai*, from *genos*, mentioned by Justin Martyr in a list of Jewish sects (*Dial.* 80.4). Two centuries later St Jerome seems to have known the Aramaic plural *minaé*, for in a response to St Augustine which has influenced interpretation of *minim* as Jewish Christians in a sectarian sense he asserts (associating Augustine's view that the Apostles might legitimately have observed the ceremonial law with contemporary Judaising heresy) that through all the synagogues of the East there is until today a Jewish school of thought called that of the Minaei, condemned by the Pharisees and more commonly called Nazaraei, who believe in Christ but wish to be both Jews and Christians (Jerome, *Ep.* 112.13).[39] Interpretation of the *minim* as a narrowly defined sect, however, seems not to suit the broad attestation within Christianity of many Christian characteristics which emerge from the rabbinic material. In any case, near Justin's time, in the second and third centuries, exegeses, regulations and prohibitions concerning *minim* are already prominent in the Mishnah and Tosefta, and evidently sometimes concern Christians.

Thus the biblical arguments ascribed to *minim* are often focused on the theme of 'Two powers in heaven', and a typical example occurs in t.Sanh. 8.7: Adam was created on the last day of the Hexameron 'lest the *minim* should say, God had a partner in his work' (see in general Segal 1977). Here the assertion ascribed to the *minim* is one typical of Justin Martyr and Eusebius,

---

[39] On the letter see Kelly (1975: 269 and n. 37).

that 'Let us make' in the first chapter of Genesis (1:26) is spoken by God to his offspring begotten before all created things, the Logos, the Son (Justin, *Dial.* 62.1–5; Eusebius, *Dem. evang.* 5.7). Justin represents himself as endeavouring to convince Trypho the Jew that there is 'another God besides the Maker of the universe' (*heteros*, or sometimes *allos*, *theos*).[40] Eusebius (*Praep. evang.* 7.12–13) argues likewise that, next to the being of the God of the universe, the Hebrew oracles introduce a second being and divine power. He quotes here a series of biblical passages on the divine word and wisdom, followed by texts which imply or mention two lords (Gen. 1:26, Ps. 33:9, Gen. 19:24, Ps. 110:1); then he quotes Philo on the Logos as 'second God' (*Qu. Gen.* 2.62, on Gen. 9:6 'in the image of God made he [the Logos] man') and as God's first-born son (*Agr.* 51, quoting Exod. 23:20 on the angel of the Lord; *Plant.* 8–10). Here the Christian contention rebutted in a number of rabbinic disputes with *minim* is summarised. The importance of this type of Christological argument for interpretation of passages on the *minim* was brought out especially by Marcel Simon (1986: 193).

To move from the Tosefta to a parallel passage in the Mishnah (Sanh. 4.5), here a single man was created lest the *minim* say 'there are many powers in heaven'. The connection of the 'many' with the creation of Adam recalls Philo's explanation of Gen. 1:26 as the divine Father conversing with his powers (*Fug.* 68–9, cf. *Conf.* 169, where 'let us make' signifies plurality), and the roots of the mishnaic formulation may well lie in pre-Christian inner-Jewish controversy; but again, apart from this connection, Justin's description of Christian piety might also be taken in a plural way: 'we worship and adore [God], and the son who came from him and taught us these things, and the army of other good angels who follow him and are like him, and the prophetic spirit' (Justin Martyr, *I Apol.* 6.2).[41]

These two rabbinic passages and others like them continue a biblical tendency to give the one God alone the glory (Deut. 32:39, Isa. 44:6), a tendency also followed in the 'Monarchian' stream of Christian thought in the second and third centuries. The rabbinic texts are rebutting, however, a view of the divine powers which is now associated with *minim*, but which also has biblical roots; in many Jewish writings of the Hasmonaean and Herodian ages the supreme deity had been envisaged in a divine assembly in association with

---

[40] Justin Martyr, *Dial.* 55.1; 56.4; 11; 14, 62.2–4, discussed with other passages by Bobichon (2003: vol. 2, 610–11 (on 11.1)).

[41] Gnostics and Jewish Christians are thought to be in mind in Segal (1977: 109–15), Gnostics (seemingly distinguished sharply from Christians) in many discussions cited by Maier (1982: 233, n. 309), but Justin's terminology suggests that members of the 'great church' could also create the impression reflected in the Mishnah, through a binitarian emphasis on the Father and the Son coupled with a view of the Son as greatest among a company of divine spirits.

other divine beings, termed as in the Qumran Songs of the Sabbath Sacrifice 'gods' (*elohim* or *elim*), in line with such biblical texts as Exod. 15:11, Job 1–2, Ps. 29:1, Ps. 82:1, Ps. 89:6–7, Ps. 95:3.[42] The angel of the Lord in such passages as Exod. 23:20 can readily be understood as the greatest of these divine beings. Philo too, as just cited, can be associated with this line of thought.

Early Christians could accordingly depict Christ as like but greater than the angelic powers or 'gods', as in Heb. 1:4–14 and Justin as just cited (*I Apol.* 6.2). Presentations of this kind were developed strikingly in the Christian writers usually designated as Gnostic, such as Basilides and Valentinus in the second century.[43] They were also central, however, as the passages from Justin Martyr just cited suggest, in the thought of those Christian writers who were later accepted as church fathers. The development towards a doctrine of the Trinity, as it is attested in Justin and Eusebius, has the strong binary or 'binitarian' ('two powers') aspect illustrated above, as well as a triadic one.[44]

A link between *minim* and Christians is suggested from another angle when the warning 'not to have dealings with *minim*' is set out with formidable fullness in t.Ḥul. 2.20–1; for it is followed and illustrated by the anecdotes concerning those put in peril by friendly contact with Christians, in t.Ḥul. 2.22–4, discussed above. Justin Martyr correspondingly says that the Jewish *didaskaloi* had laid it down that Jews should have no dealings or discussions with Christians (*Dial.* 38.1, 112.4). Later on the Christian side, in the third century, warning against Christian synagogue attendance is represented in the relatively moderate treatment of this subject by Origen (de Lange 1976: 86–7).

The famous benediction 'of the minim' can be viewed in the context of the prohibition in t.Ḥullin. It curses the *minim* in general, but probably became current not long before the period when the cursing of believers in Christ by Jews is repeatedly mentioned by Justin Martyr; this happens in the synagogues (*Dial.* 16.4, 96.2), he says, and in these assemblies the *archisyagogoi* also teach

---

[42] Qumran usage in this sense is registered in Clines *et al.* (eds. 1993: 253b, s.v. *el* 1a; p. 286a, s.v. *elohim* 3a). A 'binitarian' trend in Jewish thought before and at the time of Christian origins is brought out with reference to Philo, Justin and other sources by writers including Barker (1992) and (with discussion of the *minim*) Boyarin (2004: 112–47); see also Kirk (1928).

[43] The Jewish and Gnostic (or Gnostic Christian) backgrounds of the rabbinic remarks on two or more powers are rightly noted by Maier (1982: 196–8), but he stresses the lack of clearly Christian positions rebutted without doing full justice to the importance of binary statements in the development of Christian doctrine and in such early anti-Jewish polemic as that of Justin Martyr.

[44] The case for identifying a primarily binitarian outlook in much of the early development leading to the doctrine of the Trinity was vigorously presented in Kirk (1928: 199–219); for its importance in Christian Platonism from Justin to Eusebius see Stead (1994: 155–6).

mockery of Christ, 'after the prayer' (*Dial.* 137.2).[45] The benediction may well represent a specifically rabbinic move against 'heresy', as Philip Alexander suggests (2007: 673–5). The influence already being exerted by the rabbinic movement is then underlined by Justin Martyr's complaint, which confirms that this prayer-formula was widely adopted and had effects outside Palestine. From the Christian viewpoint, it supported some regretted contemporary and earlier measures of separation and exclusion mentioned in Justin (*Dial.* 38.1, 112.4, cited above) and, earlier, in the Gospels of Luke (6:22) and John (9:22, 12:42, 16:2). A Christian viewpoint also suggests, however, that at least in this case *minim* may refer to all Christians, not just those of Jewish birth; for Justin's complaint comes from a Gentile Christian well aware of the special position of Christian Jews (discussed in *Dial.* 47.1–5, 48.4), and he makes no suggestion that only they are envisaged in the curse.

With the history of Palestinian Christianity in view, an important upshot of the material considered so far was underlined by H. Graetz: at the time of the strict measures of separation from *minim* noted above, and the constant rebuttal of their exegeses, there was also a considerable tendency in the rabbinic movement towards friendly relations with *minim* in the form of Christians (Graetz 1846: 21–8). Eleazar ben Dama was prepared to receive a Christian healer, and Eliezer ben Hyrcanos was accused of *minut* because he talked with a Christian in Sepphoris and liked the saying of Jesus which he quoted (t.Ḥul. 2.22–4). The depiction of a premature rejection of Jesus by his teacher discussed already (b.Sanh. 107b, and parallel) might point in a similar direction, as noted above.

The *minim* continue to appear frequently in amoraic sources. As in the earlier texts, they are in close proximity to Jews. So the *minim* of Capernaum lead R. Ḥaninah into riding an ass on the Sabbath (EcclR 1.8). Sometimes they are clearly Jews themselves, as in the case of those who tempt R. Jonathan in the continuation of the passage just cited. Another recurrent feature is debate on biblical interpretation with *minim*. So a series of exegetical rebuttals of them is credited to the third-century R. Simlai, and preserved most fully in the Talmud Yerushalmi (Ber. 9.1–2, 12d–13a, partly paralleled in GenR 8.9).[46] Once again it is concerned with the theme of divine powers, first with the question of creation (Gen. 1:1, 26–7), where the background is likely to be binary, but then with the threefold names of God in Josh. 22:22

---

[45] See Horbury (1998: 8–11) (noting seven passages from Justin's *Dialogue* on the cursing of Christians, four more on the cursing or mockery of Christ, with two on the circulation of negative accounts of Christ, and two (cited already) on prohibition of converse); see also pp. 67–110.
[46] Visotzky (1988); his suggestion that 1 Cor. 11:11 is deliberately echoed in the rabbinic saying well allows for the possibility that Christian writings were known, although it may still be more likely that both texts draw on a common source.

and Ps. 50:1, where the focus is triadic. This combination of two types of argument is probably secondary, but it does correspond to the later mingling of binary and triadic discussion in Christian sources.[47]

Another much-discussed argument with a Christian background is preserved in the Babylonian Talmud (Sanh. 38b) and attributed to the fourth-century Palestinian teacher Idi.[48] A *min* quotes Exod. 24:1, 'he said to Moses, Come up to the Lord', noting that the Lord himself can hardly be the speaker. The unnamed speaker can be understood as a divine figure other than the Lord, probably the great angel of Exod. 23:20–1 who will go before the people and whom Philo identified with the Logos; Idi correspondingly replies that it is indeed this angel, Metatron (who is second only to God himself in later Hebrew mystical literature). The *min* will have wished to identify the figure of Exod. 23:20–21 with Christ, a conclusion reached by Justin Martyr (*Dial.* 75.1–3) through other means, his bearing of the name Joshua (Jesus).

The view that Christians are most often envisaged in the rabbinic references to *minim* is consistent with the likelihood that Christianity is envisaged in a number of rabbinic and targumic passages which do not mention *minim*. A much-discussed instance from the Midrash Pesikta Rabbati is formed by two brief Aramaic sayings given in the name of R. Ḥiyya bar Abba, a Babylonian scholar who taught in Palestine at about the same time as Abbahu.[49] 'If a son of whoredom says to you, There are two Gods, say to him, I am He of the Red Sea, I am He of Sinai . . . If a son of whoredom says to you, There are two Gods, say to him, Here (Deut. 5:4) there is written not: Face to face Gods spoke [plural], but: The Lord spoke with you.' The background of the suggested replies is a famous midrash on different appearances of the one God—as a young warrior at the Red Sea, an aged law-giver at Sinai, and so on.[50] The claims rebutted belong to the topic of 'Two Powers' and might easily have been attributed to *minim*, but here each is debited to 'a son of whoredom'.

In the light of the rabbinic attestation of the Pantera story noted above, this phrase suggests that Christianity is in view. Is it aimed at Christ in

---

[47] For the varied interpretation of the passage see Maier (1982: 196 and n. 648). Ps. 50:1, being rendered in the Septuagint simply as 'the God of gods, the Lord', was treated in the second and third centuries with binary emphasis on 'the Lord' as Christ; see Irenaeus, *Haer.* 5.35, 2 (the earth again summoned by Christ); Eusebius, *Dem. evang.* 6.3 (261d) (the Logos calls the earth).

[48] Krauss (1996: vol. 1, 11); Simon (1986: 195–6); Segal (1977: 68–73); Alexander (2007: 701–4).

[49] Friedmann (1880: fos. 100b–101a, part of ch. 21), discussed with a review of interpretation by Maier (1978: 244–7) (judging that one is not compelled to think of Christianity here).

[50] Mekhilta de-R. Ishmael, Shirata, 4, on Exod. 15:3, discussed with parallel texts in Williams (2000: 118–35).

particular or Christians as his followers?[51] There is in either case an allusion to Christ, but that the followers are primarily in view is suggested by comparison with a piyyut of Yannai, probably from the sixth century; here Christians are those who 'break out in bastardy according to their root principles'.[52] An earlier complaint of similar polemic against Christians is implied in a saying attributed to Jesus in the Coptic Gospel of Thomas (105): Whoever knows father or mother shall be called the son of a harlot.

Further examples of rabbinic biblical interpretations in which Christianity is implicitly envisaged include midrashic exposition and targumic rendering of the Song of Songs.[53] In Byzantine Palestine, as noted already from Yannai, some of the anti-Christian polemic already current in the pre-Constantinian empire is gathered and no doubt intensified in early piyyutim.[54]

Rabbinic literature, then, offers considerable traces of Palestinian Jewish contact with Christians and disputation with them, throughout the Roman period. This result is itself not unimportant for the historian of Palestinian Christianity. Thus it complements the view exemplified in Maier, that Palestinian Jews in the Roman period insulated themselves entirely from thought or discussion of Christianity. This attitude was probably sometimes taken, but it did not in practice preclude an appreciable amount of contact and disputation with Christians. Rabbinic evidence, therefore, coheres with the impression of the importance of Palestine as a Christian centre gained from early patristic texts and also from pagan authors such as Lucian of Samosata.[55]

To look back now over this short survey as a whole, some conclusions reached at earlier stages may be recalled as follows. The aggadah of the Babylonian Talmud includes much biographical comment on Christ and material too on the Christians, bearing a polemical character which has been rightly noted; but the material offered in Palestinian sources is connected with it and should not be underrated. Christianity has not been rigorously excluded from these Palestinian sources, and they too can be biographical

---

[51] For the former view see Schäfer (2007: 109–11), for the latter Williams (2000: 133), and Boyarin (2004: 137).

[52] Quoted from Zulay (1938: 339) and interpreted as a reference to Christianity by Rabinowitz (1965: 30–1); this interpretation is rejected by Maier (1982: 142–3) and as cited in n. 421, unconvincingly in view of the cluster of polemical terms connected with Christianity found in the context here.

[53] See Krauss (1996: 7–11), Marmorstein (1935), Urbach (1953: cols. 122–3, Eng. trans. in 1972: col. 191; 1971, repr. in 1999: 318–46), Simon (1986: 179–201), Loewe (1966) and Visotzky (1995).

[54] Sokoloff and Yahalom (1999: 216–17) (Purim poem on the crucifixion of Haman).

[55] Lucian, *De mort. Peregr.* 11 (Peregrinus learned Christianity in Palestine), discussed with other non-Christian comments on Palestinian Christianity by Horbury (2006: 34).

and sharply polemical. They suggest that Christianity was sufficiently prominent in Roman Palestine to evoke such a reaction, with its overtones of communal protection. They also show traces of relatively close contact with Christians. In the second and third century, however, a response was developed to the Christian narrative of Christ and its claims for his status as a prophet, messiah and divine being. Measures discouraging converse with Christians were associated with this. Yet rabbinic sources can offer glimpses of Palestinian Christianity itself: its representation in Sepphoris at the beginning of the second century, the self-presentation of its teachers as philosophers, the oral and written currency of sayings of Jesus, and the Caesarean Christian presence in the late third century.

The Christian piety which rabbinic sources indicate is close to the presentations of Christ as a second divine being in Justin Martyr and Eusebius. The series of contacts between rabbinic texts and a Christian author (Justin) who presents a literary debate with a Jew is striking. More generally, rabbinic literature can match Christian literature in subject-matter and sometimes in form; biblical debates with the *minim* correspond to Christian discussion of biblical testimonies *adversus Iudaeos*, and comments and anecdotes concerning Jesus compare more loosely with treatments of this subject in canonical and apocryphal gospels and in Origen's *Contra Celsum*. Christian Jews are certainly sometimes in view in rabbinic sources, but the doctrine reflected in these sources suggests the church of Jews and Gentiles rather than a particular sect.

Further Reading

Alexander (2007); E. Bammel (1966–67); de Lange (1976); Krauss (1902); Maier (1978, 1982); Schäfer (2007); Simon (1986); Visotzky (1995).

Bibliography

Alexander, P. S. (1992), '"The parting of the ways" from the perspective of rabbinic Judaism', in J. D. G. Dunn (ed.), *Jews and Christians: The Parting of the Ways AD 70 to 135*, Wissenschaftliche Untersuchungen zum Neuen Testament 66, Tübingen, pp. 1–26.

Alexander, P. S. (2007), 'Jewish believers in early rabbinic literature (2nd to 5th centuries)', in O. Skarsaune and R. Hvalvik (eds.), *Jewish Believers in Jesus: The Early Centuries*, Peabody, MA, pp. 659–709.

Bammel, C. P. (1993), 'Die erste lateinische Rede gegen die Christen', *Zeitschrift für Kirchengeschichte*, 104: 295–311.

Bammel, E. (1966–67), 'Christian origins in Jewish tradition', *New Testament Studies*, 13: 317–35; repr. in Bammel (1986), pp. 220–38.

Bammel, E. (1982), 'Schabbat 116a/b', *Novum Testamentum*, 24: 266–74; repr. in Bammel (1986), pp. 257–64.

Bammel, E. (1986), *Judaica: Kleine Schriften*, I, Wissenschaftliche Untersuchungen zum Neuen Testament 37, Tübingen.

Barker, M. (1992), *The Great Angel: A Study of Israel's Second God*, London.

Bauer, W. (1909), *Das Leben Jesu im Zeitalter der neutestamentlichen Apokryphen*, Tübingen; repr. Darmstadt, 1967.

Bobichon, P. (2003), *Justin Martyr, Dialogue avec Tryphon: Édition critique, introduction, commentaire*, Paradosis 47, 2 vols., Fribourg.

Boyarin, D. (2004), *Border Lines: The Partition of Judaeo-Christianity*, Philadelphia.

Catchpole, D. R. (1971), *The Trial of Jesus: A Study of the Gospels and Jewish Historiography from 1770 to the Present Day*, Studia Post-biblica 22, Leiden.

Clines, D. J. A. *et al.* (eds.) (1993), *The Dictionary of Classical Hebrew*, vol. 1, Sheffield.

Deissmann, A. (1910), *Light from the Ancient East: The New Testament Illustrated by Recently Discovered Texts of the Graeco-Roman World*, trans. L. R. M. Strachan, London; translation of *Licht vom Osten*, 2nd/3rd edn., Tübingen, 1909.

Deissmann, A. (1923), *Licht vom Osten: Das neue Testament und die neuentdeckten Texte der hellenistisch-römischen Welt*, 4th edn., Tübingen.

de Lange, N. (1976), *Origen and the Jews: Studies in Jewish–Christian Relations in Third-Century Palestine*, Cambridge.

Deutsch, Y. (2000), 'New evidence of early versions of *Toldot Yeshu*', *Tarbiz*, 69: 177–97. [Hebrew]

Ehrlich, U. and Langer, R. (2006), 'The earliest texts of the *Birkat Haminim*', *Hebrew Union College Annual*, 76: 63–80, 99–106.

Fabricius, J. A. (1716), *Bibliotheca Antiquaria*, 2nd edn., Hamburg and Leipzig.

Friedmann, M. (1880), *Midrash Pesiqta Rabbathi*, Vienna.

Gaisford, T. (ed.) (1842), *Eusebii Pamphili Episcopi Caesariensis Eclogae Propheticae*, Oxford.

Goodman, M. D. (1996), 'The function of minim in early rabbinic Judaism', in H. Cancik *et al.* (eds.), *Geschichte, Tradition, Reflexion: Festschrift für Martin Hengel zum 70. Geburtstag*, 3 vols., Tübingen, vol. 1, pp. 501–10.

Graetz, H. (1846), *Gnosticismus und Judenthum*, Krotoschin; repr. Farnborough, 1971.

Halkin, A. S. (ed.) (1952), *Moses Maimonides' Epistle to Yemen*, New York.

Horbury, W. (1982), 'Christ as brigand in early anti-Christian polemic', in E. Bammel and C. F. D. Moule (eds.), *Jesus and the Politics of his Day*, Cambridge, pp. 183–95.

Horbury, W. (1998), *Jews and Christians in Contact and Controversy*, Cambridge.

Horbury, W. (1999), *Christianity in Ancient Jewish Tradition*, Cambridge.

Horbury, W. (2001), 'Hebrew apologetic and polemical literature', in N. de Lange (ed.), *Hebrew Scholarship and the Medieval World*, Cambridge, pp. 189–209.

Horbury, W. (2006), 'Beginnings of Christianity in the Holy Land', in O. Limor and G. G. Stroumsa (eds.), *Christians and Christianity in the Holy Land: From the Origins to the Latin Kingdoms*, Turnhout, pp. 7–89.

Horbury, W. (2010), 'The New Testament and rabbinic study: an historical sketch', in R. Bieringer, D. Pollefeyt, P. J. Tomson and F. García Martinez (eds.), *The New Testament and Rabbinic Literature*, Supplements to the *Journal for the Study of Judaism*, 136, Leiden, pp. 1–40.

Ilan, T. (2002), *Lexicon of Jewish Names in Late Antiquity*, Part 1: *Palestine 330 BCE–200 CE*, Texte und Studien zum antiken Judentum 91, Tübingen.

Jaffé, D. (2008), 'Une ancienne dénomination talmudique de Jésus: Ben Pantera', *Theologische Zeitschrift*, 64: 258–70.

Kalmin, R. (1994), 'Christians and heretics in rabbinic literature of late antiquity', *HThR* 87: 155–69.

Kelly, J. N. D. (1975), *Jerome*, London.

Kirk, K. E. (1928), 'The evolution of the doctrine of the Trinity', in A. E. J. Rawlinson (ed.), *Essays on the Trinity and the Incarnation*, London, pp. 159–237.

Krauss, S. (1902), *Das Leben Jesu nach jüdischen Quellen*, Berlin; repr. Hildesheim and New York, 1977.

Krauss, S. (1996), *The Jewish-Christian Controversy: From the Earliest Times to 1789*, vol. 1: *History*, ed. and rev. W. Horbury, Texte und Studien zum antiken Judentum 86, Tübingen.

Levine, L. I. (1975), *Caesarea under Roman Rule*, Studies in Judaism in Late Antiquity 7, Leiden.

Loewe, R. (1966), 'Apologetic motifs in the Targum to the Song of Songs', in A. Altmann (ed.), *Biblical Motifs*, Cambridge, MA, pp. 159–96.

Maier, J. (1978), *Jesus von Nazareth in der talmudischen Überlieferung*, Darmstadt.

Maier, J. (1982), *Jüdische Auseinandersetzung mit dem Christentum in der Antike*, Darmstadt.

Marmorstein, A. (1935), 'Judaism and Christianity in the middle of the third century', *Hebrew Union College Annual*, 10: 223–63; repr. in idem, *Studies in Jewish Theology*, London, 1950, pp. 179–224.

Merchavia, Ch. (1970), *The Church versus Talmudic and Midrashic Literature (500–1248)*, Jerusalem. [Hebrew]

Oppenheimer, A. (1988), 'Jewish Lydda in the Roman Era', *Hebrew Union College Annual*, 59: 115–36; repr. in idem, *Between Rome and Babylon*, Texte und Studien zum antiken Judentum 108, Tübingen, 2005, pp. 47–65.

Popper, W. (1899), *The Censorship of Hebrew Books*, New York; repr. 1968.

Rabinowitz, Z. M. (1965), *Halakha and Aggada in the Liturgical Poetry of Yannai*, Tel Aviv. [Hebrew]

Rankin, O. S. (1956), *Jewish Religious Polemic*, Edinburgh.

Rokeah, D. (1969–70), 'Ben Stara is Ben Pantera: towards the clarification of a philological-historical problem', *Tarbiz*, 39: 9–18. [Hebrew]

Safrai, Z. (2003), 'The House of Leontis "Kaloubas": a Judaeo-Christian?', in P. J. Tomson and D. Lambers-Petry (eds.), *The Image of the Judaeo-Christians in Ancient Jewish and Christian Literature*, Wissenschaftliche Untersuchungen zum Neuen Testament 158, Tübingen, pp. 245–66.

Schäfer, P. (2007), *Jesus in the Talmud*, Princeton and Oxford.

Schoettgen, C. (1733–42), *Horae Hebraicae et Talmudicae*, 2 vols., Dresden and Leipzig, vol. 2 (1742).

Schwartz, Joshua (1995), 'Peter and Ben Stada in Lydda', in R. Bauckham (ed.), *The Book of Acts in its Palestinian Setting*, Carlisle and Grand Rapids, MI, pp. 391–414.

Segal, A. F. (1977), *Two Powers in Heaven: Early Rabbinic Reports about Christianity and Gnosticism*, Studies in Judaism in Late Antiquity 25, Leiden.

Simon, Marcel (1986), *Verus Israel: A Study of the Relations between Christians and Jews in the Roman Empire (135–425)*, trans. H. McKeating, Oxford; first published Paris, 1948; reissued with *Post-Scriptum*, Paris, 1964.

Sokoloff, M. and Yahalom, J. (1999), *Jewish Palestinian Poetry from Late Antiquity*, Jerusalem. [Hebrew]

Stead, C. (1994), *Philosophy in Christian Antiquity*, Cambridge.

Steinschneider, M. (ed.) (1860), *Nachmanidis Disputatio*, Berlin.

Stemberger, G. (1999), 'Rabbinic sources for historical study', in J. Neusner and A. J. Avery-Peck (eds.), *Judaism in Late Antiquity*, Part 3: *Where we Stand: Issues and Debates in Ancient Judaism*, vol. 1, Leiden, pp. 169–86.

Stemberger, G. (2000), *Jews and Christians in the Holy Land: Palestine in the Fourth Century*, trans. R. Tuschling, Edinburgh.

Strack, H. L. (1910), *Jesus, die Häretiker und die Christen nach den ältesten jüdischen Angaben*, Schriften des Institutum Judaicum in Berlin 37, Leipzig.

Tcherikover, V. and Fuks, A. (1960), *Corpus Papyrorum Judaicarum*, vol. 2, Cambridge, MA.

Teppler, Y. (2007), *Birkat haMinim*, Texte und Studien zum antiken Judentum 120, Tübingen.

Thomson, R. W. (1982), *Elishe: History of Vardan and the Armenian War*, Harvard Armenian Texts and Studies 5; Cambridge, MA and London.

Travers Herford, R. (1903), *Christianity in Talmud and Midrash*, London.

Urbach, E. E. (1953), 'Apologetiqah yehudit', *Encyclopaedia Hebraica*, vol. 5, Jerusalem, cols. 120–35.

Urbach, E. E. (1971), 'The homiletical interpretations of the Sages and the expositions of Origen on canticles and the Jewish-Christian disputation', *Scripta Hierosolymitana*, 22; repr. in idem, *Collected Writings in Jewish Studies*, ed. R. Brody and M. D. Herr, Jerusalem, 1999, pp. 318–46.

Urbach, E. E. (1972), 'Apologetics', *Encyclopaedia Judaica*, vol. 2, Jerusalem, cols. 188–201 (Eng. trans of Urbach (1953)).

Visotzky, B. L. (1987), 'Overturning the lamp', *JJS* 38: 72–80; repr. in Visotzky (1995), pp. 75–84.

Visotzky, B. L. (1988), 'Trinitarian testimonies', *Union Seminary Quarterly Review*, 42: 73–85; repr. in Visotzky (1995), pp. 61–74.

Visotzky, B. L. (1995), *Fathers of the World: Essays in Rabbinic and Patristic Literatures*, Wissenschaftliche Untersuchungen zum Neuen Testament 80, Tübingen.

Walzer, R. (1949), *Galen on Jews and Christians*, Oxford.

Williams, C. H. (2000), *I am He: The Interpretation of 'Anî Hû' in Jewish and Early Christian Literature*, Wissenschaftliche Untersuchungen zum Neuen Testament 2.113, Tübingen.

Zulay, M. (1938), *Piyyute Yannai*, Berlin. [Hebrew]

20

Politics and Administration

AHARON OPPENHEIMER

SOMETIMES ONE GETS THE FEELING THAT the more historical research advances, the more difficult it becomes to solve the problems of using the talmudic literature as a historical source. However, when we touch on the subject of politics and administration it is possible to reach a solution more easily. Here we have a chance of providing a basis for the historical significance of the talmudic sources by reference to external sources. It is sometimes possible to weave together talmudic and classical sources, which are, of course, not dependent on each other, providing us with some chance of finding an authentic historical route. Moreover, it is possible to learn in both directions: from the classical source, on historicity in the talmudic source, and from the talmudic source, about historical details which the classical source does not relate to. I shall confine myself to one example with a number of consequences: the relationship between Severan activities in the field of cities and urbanisation with the talmudic sources which include actions and rulings of Rabbi Judah haNasi.

* * *

Ulpian, the Roman legal writer, who was active in the first quarter of the third century, devotes one chapter of his work to the office of proconsul and his authority. This was written in the days of Caracalla and has been preserved in the *Digest*. Here Ulpian mentions legislation of Septimius Severus and Caracalla, in one of the years between 196 and 211, on the privileges and duties of Jews serving in civic functions. This legislation rules that Jews were allowed to take office in the government of the city, as long as this did not conflict with their religion.[1]

Two parallel episodes in the Babylonian and Jerusalem Talmuds demonstrate that members of the city leadership institutions, the *boule* and the *strategoi*, applied to Rabbi Judah haNasi for a ruling on the distribution of the burden of the crown tax (*aurum coronarium*) to which they were subject. It appears that the members of the *boule* asked for equal distribution from an

[1] Ulpian, *Digest* L 2:3:3, ed. Mommsen-Krüger, p. 896 (in Linder 1987: 103–7).

Proceedings of the British Academy **165**, 377–388. © The British Academy 2010.

institutional point of view, whereby the members of the *boule* would shoulder half the burden, and the two *strategoi* the other half. The *strategoi*, on the other hand, wanted equal distribution from a personal point of view, whereby every member of the *boule*, and each *strategos*, would take responsibility for the same sum. Rabbi Judah haNasi ruled on the side of the *boule*, for he decided that each institution should bear half the tax. The discrimination against the *strategoi* would be offset by the preferential status of their office, which gave them wider powers to extract the tax later from the inhabitants of the city.[2] These actions include a double novelty: the first is an urban elite which submits itself to the leadership of the patriarch, something which had not existed in the generations before Rabbi Judah haNasi. There can be little doubt that this phenomenon is due to the recognition of Rabbi by the Roman authorities, to Rabbi's own economic status, and his closeness to the urban elite. The second novelty is the very existence of a Jewish *boule* and *strategoi*, which links up with the legislation of Septimius Severus and Caracalla.

A further talmudic source, found in the Babylonian Talmud, provides evidence of a crown tax imposed on Tiberias, for representatives of the town came to ask Rabbi Judah haNasi for the rabbis not to be exempted from the payment of the tax. Rabbi Judah haNasi refuses this, which leads to the inhabitants of Tiberias leaving their city bit by bit, so that in the end the tax is abolished by the Roman authorities (b.Bava Batra 8a). This episode as a whole has a number of undeniably aggadic elements, but its main constituents have a measure of authenticity: first, the imposition of the crown tax itself; secondly, the exemption from some of the Roman taxes which is granted to the rabbis;[3] thirdly, the phenomenon of leaving settlements because of the burden of taxes (which is, in fact, better known from the time of the imperial crisis after the days of Rabbi Judah haNasi, but not in cities like Tiberias); fourthly, there is parallel evidence for cases of abolition of the crown tax, as, for example, the edict of Alexander Severus[4] where he announces the cancellation of the crown tax to mark his ascent to the throne. Incidentally, if indeed this source is talking about the cancellation of the crown tax, then, in Shmuel Safrai's opinion (1994), this provides a *terminus post quem* for Rabbi's being alive and active as patriarch. In my opinion there may have been other cases of exemption. Perhaps Macrinus did the same in

---

[2] b.Bava Batra 143a (compare the Munich MS); p.Yoma 1, 39a, ed. The Academy of the Hebrew Language, col. 564.

[3] The grandson of Rabbi, Rabbi Judah Nesiah, refused to exempt the rabbis from participation in the tax imposition for building a wall for Tiberias. Just like yeshiva students in present-day Israel, they had claimed that 'rabbis don't need guarding'. However, it must be remembered that this appears to have been a time of economic crisis.

[4] Papyrus Fayûm 20, from 24 June 222, see Grenfell *et al.* (1900: 116–23).

217, or Elagabalus when he ascended the throne in 218? After all, the information from PFayûm 20 is only known through a random discovery of a papyrus.

I would like to propose that the two sources which deal with the *boule* and *strategoi* applying to Rabbi are also related to Tiberias, perhaps even to the same case as the last source to which we referred. This is not just because all these three sources talk of the crown tax. The basis of these things is rooted in understanding the nature of the institution of the *strategoi*. Here there can be no doubt that this is a translation into Greek of the Latin term *duoviri*, which refers to the two highest officers of the city.[5] This institution is known from different cities in the eastern provinces, and Fergus Millar has shown us various examples: the duovirate existed in various different cities in the Roman provinces of Asia in that period. The term *strategos* is mentioned, for example, in an inscription from the city of Gerasa across the Jordan, as well as in an inscription from a basilica of the Severan period, found in Sebaste, the central city of the Samarian hills, to which Septimius Severus gave the status of *colonia*. When Palmyra, the oasis in the Syrian Desert, became a colony too, it took on the accepted practice of appointing *duoviri*, and during the years 224–62, the incumbents of these two highest offices in the city are referred to as *strategoi*. The institution of the *strategoi* is also mentioned in a bill of sale written in Edessa in northern Mesopotamia, which was found in the excavations at Dura Europus on the banks of the Euphrates, now in Syria near the Iraq border. *Strategoi* are also mentioned in the context of the cities of Petra and Gaza (see Millar 1990: 46–8).

In the talmudic literature there are several places where the number of *strategoi* is mentioned, and there are always two of them.[6] The *duoviri*, as their name implies, were always two, for the institution is parallel to the two consuls in the city of Rome. It is important to note that the institution of the duovirate existed only in cities with the status of *colonia*. Thus, if the *boule* and *strategoi* who applied to Rabbi Judah haNasi in these sources were the members of civic institutions, and if the *strategoi* are equivalent to the duovirate, then Tiberias must have had the status of a colony before the death of Rabbi Judah haNasi, for the institution of the duovirate existed only in *coloniae*. In general, we should note that the colonies in the provinces enjoyed many privileges of self-government, and their institutions were similar to

---

[5] For this office, see Waldstein (1967).

[6] 'They gave a parable: To what may we compare this matter? To a king who had two *strategoi* . . .' (p.Ber. 8, 12c, col. 63); 'R. Levi said: This can be compared to a friend of a king, who deposited by him an article. His son came to claim back the article deposited with him. The king said to him: Go and bring two *strategoi* and twelve members of the *boule* and through them I will return to you the article' (DeutR Ekev 3, ed. Lieberman (Oxford MS 147), p. 84).

those in the city of Rome. Tiberias is the only city which could possibly have become a colony in the time of Rabbi Judah haNasi. In the Babylonian Talmud, there is a collection of aggadot about Rabbi and 'Antoninus'. This collection also includes an account of an episode which at first glance appears to be an aggadah dealing with the transformation of Tiberias to a colony.[7]

There are about a hundred traditions in the talmudic literature which tell of the close relations between Rabbi Judah haNasi and 'Antoninus', the Roman emperor. On the one hand, these traditions have aspects in common with similar traditions about conversations between Rabbi Joshua b. Ḥananiah and Hadrian; Rabban Gamaliel and his colleagues with the nobles of Rome; and Rabbi Akiva and Tineus Rufus. On the other hand, these conversations do not only contain questions about Torah, halakhah and aggadah, they also contain some further elements. Scholarly consensus today accepts the identification of 'Antoninus' with Caracalla (Marcus Aurelius Antoninus), for there is a certain amount of evidence, both written sources and archaeological finds, which confirm this emperor's positive attitude to Jews. Caracalla also visited the East. However, all these traditions about conversations between him and Rabbi are no evidence that such conversations actually took place between them. It is possible that they took place with the governor of the province or some sort of high officials, but many of them consist of purely aggadic material.

We may see something of the closeness between Rabbi Judah haNasi and the nobles of Rome from the evidence that he preferred the natural science of non-Jewish scholars to that of the rabbis. This is found in a baraita in the Babylonian Talmud. The subject under discussion is where the sun hides at night:

> Our rabbis taught: the Sages of Israel say: . . . At night [the sun goes] above the firmament. But the sages of the peoples of the world say: . . . Below the earth. Rabbi said: their claim seems better than ours, for by day wells are cold, and at night they are warm. (b.Pesaḥim 94b)

An interesting anecdote informs us how great Rabbi's influence in astronomy was, even in modern times. Rabbi Israel Meir haCohen of Radin—the author of the *Ḥafeẓ Ḥayim*—wrote his work *Mishnah Berurah* exactly a

---

[7] 'Antoninus once said to Rabbi: It is my desire that my son Asverus should reign instead of me and that Tiberias should be declared a Colony. Were I to ask one of these things, it would be granted, while both would not be granted. Rabbi thereupon brought a man, and having made him ride on the shoulders of another, handed him a dove bidding the one who carried him to order the one on his shoulders to liberate it. The Emperor perceived this to mean that he was advised to ask [of the Senate] to appoint his son Asverus to reign in his stead, and that subsequently he might get Asverus to make Tiberias a free Colony' (b.Avodah Zarah 10a).

hundred years ago, and is still seen (by *mitnagdim*) as the decisive ruling in such things to this day. He writes:

> You should not knead [the dough for] *maẓah* in water that has stayed out [overnight] . . . This is because at night the sun goes underneath the ground and heats the wells. (*Hilkhot Pesaḥ* CDLV 1)

To return to Tiberias: the tradition about Tiberias which we are discussing tells of Antoninus seeking advice from Rabbi on how to ask the Roman senate to agree for his son to be emperor after him, and for Tiberias to become a colony. They would agree to one request, but not to two. Rabbi advises him to ask the senate for his son to succeed him as emperor, and then to tell his son to make Tiberias a colony.

This source is bathed in an aggadic atmosphere. It is quite clear that the tradition it quotes does not reflect anything of the spirit of the political processes at Rome. It is only logical to assume that it was, in fact, Rabbi Judah haNasi who asked the emperor to give Tiberias the status of a colony, and not 'Antoninus' who put this request to Rabbi. There is no basis for the supposition presented here, and attributed to 'Antoninus', that the Roman senators would not grant him two requests. However, it does fit in with what is known of a number of different cities in the eastern empire, to which emperors of the Severan dynasty granted the status of a *colonia*. Moreover, it also fits with some inscriptions which have been identified on coins of Tiberias from the time of Elagabalus—who was proclaimed emperor in 218 after Macrinus, following a rumour spread by his mother that he was the son of Caracalla. On these coins, the letters COL (for col[onia]) appear to have been added to the name of Tiberias. It should be noted that such a finding alone should have been enough to demonstrate that Tiberias did indeed become a colony, and that this happened in the time of Elagabalus. This, indeed, is the claim of Meshorer (1985: 35), based on the Latin letters COL, which he identifies on the reverse of the coins. However, these coins clearly bear Greek letters also, and coins do not generally have inscriptions in Latin on one side and Greek on the other. Indeed, Alla Stein has rejected Meshorer's claims, and denies that the letters COL appear on any coin of Tiberias.[8] Be that as it may, in a document written in 1035, found in the Genizah in Fustat, we find the words *medinta Tiberia colon[ia]* (= in the city of Tiberias Colon[ia]) (Friedman 1981: 207–12). We may assume, then, that this wording reflects a tradition that Tiberias was a colony in ancient times.

Accepting the possibility that Tiberias received colonial status in the days of Rabbi can throw light on the reasons and meaning for the move of the Jewish leadership institutions from Sepphoris/Ẓippori to Tiberias, in the first

---

[8] Personal communication.

half of the third century. The leadership institutions (the patriarch and the Beit haVa'ad), continued to increase in power from the time of their low-profile rehabilitation at Ushah (and Shefaram), following the repressive legislation in the wake of the Bar Kokhba revolt, through their move to Beit She'arim and Sepphoris in the days of Rabbi Judah haNasi. The move to Beit She'arim, indeed, which was a royal estate given to Rabbi, reflects the recognition of Rabbi by the Roman authorities, while the move to Sepphoris/Diocaesarea, which was a *polis*, shows the submission of the urban elite to his rule. The final station was Tiberias, which now became the most important of the cities of Galilee, once it had received colonial status. The move to Tiberias took place after the death of Rabbi, and the subsequent beginning of the process of separation between the patriarchate and the Beit haVa'ad. It was in the context of this process that the Beit haVa'ad moved first to Tiberias, in the middle of the third century, and Rabbi Yoḥanan b. Nafḥa served as its *av beit din*. Afterwards the patriarchate moved too, at the latest in the time of Rabbi Judah Nesiah II, the great-great-grandson of Rabbi. In any event, by the time of Diocletian, who became emperor in 284 CE, the patriarchate was already seated in Tiberias. Thus what the Babylonian Talmud calls the 'wanderings of the Sanhedrin', which lasted over a hundred years in Galilee, came to an end.[9] They had begun in the little town or village of Ushah, and ended in Tiberias, capital of Galilee, with colonial status. From now on, the patriarchate and rabbinical leadership did not move from Tiberias until the abolition of the patriarchate after the death of Rabban Gamaliel VI, in the middle of the first half of the fifth century.

The Severans were very active in raising the status of settlements in the eastern provinces and in North Africa to that of a *polis*, or *colonia*. The founder of the dynasty, Septimius Severus, gave the status of *polis* to Lydda/Lod in 199/200, as a result of which it received the name Diospolis,[10] and to Beit Guvrin, which received the name Eleutheropolis.[11] Apparently, he had earlier promoted Sebaste, which was already a *polis*, to the status of a *colonia*,[12] while, in contrast, the status of *polis* was temporarily removed from Neapolis/Shechem, which lost its status because it had supported his rival Pescennius Niger in the year 194.[13] The urbanisation policies of Severus can

---

[9] Genesis Rabbah 97, ed. Theodor-Albeck, pp. 1220–1; cf. b.Rosh haShanah 31a–b; Yalkut Shimoni, Genesis 161, ed. Hyman-Shiloni, pp. 844–5.

[10] See Hill (1914: 141, nos. 1–2); Rosenberger (1975–77: vol. 2, pp. 28–31; vol. 3, p. 80); Kindler and Stein (1987: 96–9).

[11] See Spijkerman (1972: pls. 1–4); Kindler and Stein (1987: 112–16).

[12] *Digesta* L 15:1:7. This occurred between the years 201 and 211, as can be seen from the numismatic findings, and most likely happened in the year 201/2. See Hill (1914: pp. xxxix, 80 and nos. 12–13); Kindler and Stein (1987: 222–9).

[13] Scriptores Historiae Augustae, *Severus*, 9.5.

also be seen in other cities, outside the borders of *provincia Syria-Palaestina*. Thus, for example, he gave the status of *colonia* to various cities in the new province of Mesopotamia, including Haran, Resaina and Nisibis.[14] Caracalla and Elagabalus carried on this policy. Caracalla granted the status of colony to Edessa. Colonial status was also granted to Emesa, and to Antioch in Syria.[15] Palmyra also became a colony, perhaps as early as the time of Septimius Severus himself.[16] In Syria-Palaestina, Elagabalus gave the status of a city to Emmaus, which was renamed Nicopolis, and to Antipatris.[17] As noted, it is possible that he made Tiberias a colony. He also gave the status of colony to Petra, and to Sidon and Caesarea (Acra in Lebanon).[18] In the days of Severus Alexander, Bostra also became a colony.[19]

The growth in the number of cities seems to have led to changes in the Roman administration of Palestine. In the days of the Second Temple, there was only one city in Judaea proper, Jerusalem, and even here there is no consensus among modern scholars about its actual status (see, for example, Tcherikover 1961). A further city was Jaffa, which Vespasian made into a *polis* called Flavia Ioppe. The country was divided into twenty-four toparchies (administrative divisions), centred around a settlement that did not hold city status. There is evidence of these toparchies in Josephus (*BJ* 3.54–5), Pliny the Elder,[20] and documents from the Judaean Desert from the days of the Bar Kokhba revolt (Lewis *et al.* eds. 1989: nos. 12, 16). A process of urbanisation had already begun in the days of the emperor Hadrian (117–38), who rebuilt Jerusalem as a pagan city, and gave it the status of a *colonia*, as a result of which the city received the name of Aelia Capitolina.[21] Hadrian also took steps to Hellenise the cities of Galilee, Tiberias and Sepphoris (which was reamed Diocaesarea on receiving the status of *polis*,

[14] Jones (1971: 220–1); Kindler (1982–83); on Nisibis see Oppenheimer *et al.* (1983: 319–34).
[15] For Edessa, see: Bellinger and Welles (1935); Goldstein (1966). For Emesa, see *Digesta* L 15:1:4; cf. L 15:8:6; Wroth (1899: 237–41). For Antioch, see *Digesta* L 15:8:5; Wroth (1899: pp. lviii–lxiii, 151–232).
[16] *Digesta* L 15:1:5; Schlumberger (1942–43).
[17] For Emmaus, see Jones (1971: 279 and n. 72); Schürer (1973–87: vol. 1, pp. 512–13, n. 142); Kindler and Stein (1987: 177–9). For Elagabalus' grant of city status to Emmaus, see: Stein (thesis 1990: 153–95). For Antipatris, seven kinds of coins are known, all of them from the days of Elagabalus. See Hill (1910: pp. xv–xvi, 11); Vliet (1950: 116–17, nos. 11–12); Meshorer (1985: 54, nos. 149–52); Kindler and Stein (1987: 41–2); Schürer (1973–87: vol. 2., pp. 167–8), see also *Inscriptiones Graecae ad Res Romanas Pertinentes*, I, no. 631, republished by Robert (1940: 103–4, no. 43); see also Robert (1940: 101–3, nos. 41–2).
[18] Petra: Ben Dor (1948–49); Spijkerman (1978: 218–19, 236); Sidon: Hill (1910: pp. lxxxvii–cxvi, 139–99); Nidejian (1971: 93); Caesarea: Seyrig (1959).
[19] Kindler (1983: 64); *Inscriptions greques et latines de la Syrie* XIII, no. 9057.
[20] *HN* 5.68–70 (ed. Ian-Mayhoff); Stern (1974–84: vol. 1, pp. 468–78).
[21] Cassius Dio, *Historia Romana* 69.12, 1. Cf. Stern (1974–84: vol. 2, no. 440) and Millar (1964: 60–2).

presumably from this emperor). In other words, he gave them a pagan identity, and put their local government in the hands of non-Jews (see Jones 1971: 278). The real drive towards a process of urbanisation occurred, however, as noted, in the days of the Severans, in other words in the days of Rabbi Judah haNasi. Unlike Hadrian, the Severans, as we have seen, legislated to allow Jews to become members of the city administration. We can learn about the Roman administrative organisation from the *Onomasticon* of Eusebius.[22] Unlike the situation we saw earlier with the toparchies, Eusebius' lists do not contain any record of a village which belongs to the territory of another village; his lists are all made up of towns and cities, together with the villages which are to be found in their territories.

The administrative development which led to there being a city in the centre of every territory appears to be rooted in the period of urbanisation in the days of the Severan dynasty. In other words, in the days of this dynasty, the process which created the toparchies, most of which were centred round a village, came to an end, and from now on the territories are concentrated round cities only.

There is a considerable degree of overlap between the urbanisation policy of the Severans in Syria-Palaestina and the policies and rulings of Rabbi Judah haNasi towards the cities. Rabbi Judah haNasi gave exemption from the *mizvot* dependent on the produce of the Land of Israel, such as the sabbatical year and tithes, to cities whose inhabitants were mostly non-Jews:

> Rabbi exempted Beit She'an [from *mizvot* dependent on the Land of Israel], Rabbi exempted Caesarea, Rabbi exempted Beit Guvrin, Rabbi exempted Kefar Zemaḥ. (p.Demai 2, 22c, col. 121)

Rabbi Judah haNasi stressed that there was no intent to remove these cities from the halakhic borders of the Land of Israel, and that they were still subject to the purity of the Land of Israel.[23] This step of his was intended to give an incentive to Jews to settle in these cities, like the present-day exemption from specific taxes given to the inhabitants of Eilat, or the tax reductions given to people living outside the main conurbations in present-day Israel. With these rulings, Rabbi joined in the urbanisation policies of the Severans.

Among the settlements listed above, which Rabbi Judah haNasi exempted from the *mizvot* dependent on the produce of the Land of Israel, only Kefar Zemaḥ was not a city. This village was probably included in the territory of the city of Susita/Hippos, which was originally one of the cities of the

---

[22] *Eusebius: Das Onomastikon der biblischen Ortsnamen*, ed. E. Klostermann, Leipzig, 1904 (repr. Hildesheim, 1966). See also Oppenheimer (2005).

[23] 'Cities surrounded by the Land of Israel, for example, Susita and the villages around it, Ashkelon and the villages around it, even though they are free of tithes and of the rule of the sabbatical year, are not subject to the law governing the land of the gentiles' (t.Ahilot 18.4).

Decapolis. Zemaḥ would seem to have been sited near wadi a-Samekh in the Golan, and to have received its name from this valley. It is possible to deduce the reason for the exemption of Kefar Zemaḥ from a baraita which is found in the continuation of the discussion in the Jerusalem Talmud, in its parallels, and in the Reḥov inscription.[24] In these three sources, the only place to be mentioned from the list of places which Rabbi exempted from the *miẓvot* dependent on the produce of the Land of Israel is Kefar Zemaḥ. The baraita lists the Jewish agricultural settlements on the periphery of the Jewish settlement in the area of Susita which were obliged to take tithes and observe the sabbatical year, in spite of the fact that they were sited in an area of pagan settlements. Kefar Zemaḥ is mentioned among these Jewish settlements, but, as we saw, eventually 'Rabbi exempted Kefar Zemaḥ' and released it from tithes and the sabbatical laws, apparently to make it easier for its Jewish inhabitants in their economic competition with their non-Jewish neighbours. It should be noted that Rabbi Judah haNasi is mentioned explicitly in the mosaic from Reḥov, in spite of the fact that all the evidence points to this being made in the Byzantine era, in other words, much later than Rabbi's own time.[25]

In the continuation of the discussion in the Jerusalem Talmud, it says that Rabbi Judah haNasi relied on a precedent of Rabbi Meir, the central tanna of the Ushah generation, for the exemption which he gave to Beit She'an.[26] This precedent is simply a support for the ruling of Rabbi which, as we have said, was political and economic in origin, stemming from his wish to encourage Jewish settlement in mixed cities.

The process of granting an exemption to Ascalon is to be found in the Tosefta and the Jerusalem Talmud.[27] Ascalon was also a city where most of the inhabitants were non-Jews, and it was sited on the halakhic border of the Land of Israel. The process of giving the exemption was carried out by a group of rabbis headed by Rabbi Judah haNasi, which met in Lydda/Lod, the most important Jewish centre in Judaea proper in those days. At first they ruled that Ascalon was not subject to the impurity of *ereẓ ha-amim*/Gentile territory abroad, and is thus included within the halakhic borders of the Land of Israel. In that case, the city would be subject to the *miẓvot* dependent on the produce of the Land of Israel, so that in the second stage, they gave Ascalon an exemption from tithes, and presumably also from the sabbatical laws.

[24] p.Demai 2.22d, col. 122; cf. t.Shevi'it 4.10, ed. Lieberman, p. 181; Sussman (1974, 1976).
[25] Another possibility of identification for Kefar Zemaḥ is the site of present-day Zemaḥ, on the southern shore of the Sea of Galilee.
[26] p.Demai 2.22c, col. 121; cf. b.Ḥullin 6b.
[27] p.Yevamot 7, 8a, col. 862; p.Shevi'it 4, 36c, cols. 197–8; t.Ahilot 18.18.

Note that Rabbi did not absolve Sepphoris, his place of residence, or Lod, or Tiberias, from the *miẓvot* dependent on the produce of the Land of Israel, because their population was mostly Jewish. From all this, it would seem that Rabbi's intention was to strengthen the Jewish settlement in those cities which he exempted from the *miẓvot* dependent on the produce of the Land of Israel, giving an incentive for Jews to settle there, and helping them in their daily and seasonal economic competition with their non-Jewish neighbours in those mixed cities.

To sum up, even though the Romans did not force, or even request it, Rabbi Judah haNasi joined in the Severan urbanisation policy, and exempted mixed cities from tithes and the sabbatical laws in order to strengthen the Jewish basis there. The result is well known, for example, in Caesarea. Not only did the number of Jewish inhabitants grow, but an important *beit midrash* was even founded there in the time of the amora'im. This became possible also as a result of processes within the Jewish community which led to the separation of the patriarchate from the Beit haVa'ad after the death of Rabbi Judah haNasi. Archaeological finds further indicate that there was quite a large Jewish settlement in and around Beit She'an. In other words, Beit She'an experienced a significant growth of its Jewish population as a result of the ruling of Rabbi Judah haNasi. The situation is similar in the other cities we have noted, which were also subject to Rabbi's rulings. Thus, in my opinion, it is possible to find a real connection between the urbanisation initiative of the Severans and the rulings of Rabbi Judah haNasi, whose goals were to encourage Jews to move from the villages to the city.

Further Reading

Alon (1980–84); Gafni (2008); Goodblatt (2006); Jones (1971); Kindler (1982–83); Kraemer (1999); Meshorer (1985); Millar (1990); Oppenheimer (2005); Stemberger (1999).

Bibliography

Alon, G. (1980–84), *The Jews in Their Land in the Talmudic Age: 70–640 CE*, 2 vols., Jerusalem.

Bellinger, A. R. and Welles, C.-M. (1935), 'A third century contract of sale from Edessa in Osrhoene', *Yale Classical Studies*, 5: 93–154.

Ben Dor, S. (1948–49), 'Petra Colonia', *Berytus*, 9: 41–3.

Friedman, M. A. (1981), *Jewish Marriage in Palestine*, vol. 2, Tel Aviv.

Gafni, I. (2008), 'Rabbinic historiography and representation of the past', in C. E. Fonrobert and M. S. Jaffee (eds.), *The Cambridge Companion to the Talmud and Rabbinic Literature*, vol. 3, Cambridge, ch. 13.

Goldstein, J. A. (1966), 'The Syriac bill of sale from Dura-Europos', *Journal of Near Eastern Studies*, 25: 1–16.

Goodblatt, D. (2006), 'The political and social history of the Jewish community in the Land of Israel', in S. K. Katz (ed.), *The Cambridge History of Judaism*, vol. 4: *The Late Roman-Rabbinic Period*, Cambridge, pp. 404–30.

Grenfell, B. P. *et al.* (1900), *Fayûm Towns and their Papyri*, London.

Hill, G. F. (1910), *British Museum Catalogue: Phoenicia*, London.

Hill, G. F. (1914), *British Museum Catalogue: Palestine*, London.

Jones, A. H. M. (1971), *The Cities of the Eastern Roman Provinces*, 2nd edn., Oxford.

Kindler, A. (1982–83), 'The status of cities in the Syro-Palestinian area as reflected by their coins', *Israel Numismatic Journal*, 6/7: 79–87.

Kindler, A. (1983), *The Coinage of Bostra*, Warminster.

Kindler, A. and Stein, A. (1987), *A Bibliography of the City Coinage of Palestine*, BAR International Series 374, Oxford.

Kraemer, D. (1999), 'Rabbinic sources for historical study', in J. Neusner and A. J. Avery-Peck (eds.), *Judaism in Late Antiquity*, Part 3, vol. 1, Leiden, Boston and Köln, pp. 201–12.

Lewis, N., Yadin, Y. and Greenfield, J. C. (eds.) (1989), *The Documents of the Bar-Kokhba Period in the Cave of Letters: Greek Papyri*, ed. N. Lewis; *Aramaic and Nabatean Signatures Subscriptions*, ed. Y. Yadin and J. C. Greenfield, Jerusalem, nos. 12, 16.

Linder, A. (1987), *The Jews in Roman Imperial Legislation*, Detroit and Jerusalem.

Meshorer, Y. (1985), *City-Coins of Eretz-Israel and the Decapolis in the Roman Period*, Jerusalem.

Millar, F. (1964), *A Study of Cassius Dio*, Oxford.

Millar, F. (1990), 'The Roman *coloniae* of the Near East: a study of cultural relations', in H. Solin and M. Kajava (eds.), *Roman Eastern Policy and Other Studies in Roman History*, Helsinki, pp. 7–58.

Nidejian, N. (1971), *Sidon Through the Ages*, Beirut.

Oppenheimer, A. with Isaac, B. and Lecker, M. (1983), *Babylonia Judaica in the Talmudic Period*, Wiesbaden.

Oppenheimer, A. (2005), 'Urbanisation and city territories in Roman Palestine', in *Between Rome and Babylon: Studies in Jewish Leadership and Society*, Tübingen.

Robert, L. (1940), *Les Gladiateurs dans l'orient grec*, Limoges.

Rosenberger, M. (1975–77), *City Coins of Palestine*, vols. 2 and 3, Jerusalem.

Safrai, S. (1994), 'On the chronological problem of the Patriarchs in the second and third centuries', in S. Safrai (ed.), *In Times of Temple and Mishnah*, Jerusalem, pp. 620–6. [Hebrew]

Schlumberger, D. (1942–43), 'Les Gentilices romains des Palmyréniens', *Bulletin d'Études Orientales*, 9: 53–82.

Schürer, E. (1973–87), *The History of the Jewish People in the Age of Jesus Christ*, rev. and ed. G. Vermes *et al.*, 3 vols., Edinburgh.

Seyrig, H. (1959), 'Une monnaie du Césarée du Liban', *Syria*, 36: 38–43.

Spijkerman, A. (1972), 'The coins of Eleutheropolis Iudaea', *Liber Annuus*, 22: 369–84.

Spijkerman, A. (1978), *The Coins of the Decapolis and Provincia Arabia*, ed. M. Piccirillo, Jerusalem.

Stein, A. (1990), 'Studies in Greek and Latin Coin Inscriptions on the Palestinian Coinage', Ph.D. thesis, Tel Aviv University.

Stemberger, G. (1999), 'Rabbinic sources for historical study', in J. Neusner and A. J. Avery-Peck (eds.), *Judaism in Late Antiquity*, Part 3, vol. 1, Leiden, Boston and Köln, pp. 169–86.

Stern, M. (1974–84), *Greek and Latin Authors on Jews and Judaism*, 3 vols., Jerusalem.

Sussman, Y. (1974), 'An Halakhic inscription from the Bet She'an Valley', *Tarbiz*, 43: 88–158. [Hebrew]

Sussman, Y. (1976), 'Baraita *di-Teḥumei Ereẓ Yisrael*', *Tarbiz*, 45: 213–57. [Hebrew]

Tcherikover, V. (1961), 'Was Jerusalem a Greek *polis* at the time of the Procurators?' in *The Jews in the Greek and the Roman World*, Jerusalem, pp. 199–216. [Hebrew]

Vliet, N. van der (1950), 'Monnaies inédites ou très rares du médaillier de Sainte Anne de Jérusalem', *Revue biblique*, 57: 116–17, nos. 11–12.

Waldstein, W. (1967), 'Duoviri', in K. Ziegler and W. Sontheimer (eds.), *Der Kleine Pauly*, vol. 2, Stuttgart, cols. 176–8.

Wroth, W. (1899), *British Museum Catalogue: Syria*, London.

21

Economy and Society

HAYIM LAPIN

RABBINIC LITERATURE IS AN IMPORTANT RESOURCE for social and economic
historians of the second through the fourth centuries and later, but only if
properly understood. The usual problems of composition, date and text
(see the several contributions to this volume) are aggravated if, for
instance, one wants to use rabbinic literature to document the history of
price fluctuation or currency values, since it is precisely exchange rates or
prices that are likely to be updated with successive handling, and technical
terms like the names of coins are subject to considerable corruption. Still, the
texts are undoubtedly the product of late-antique Roman provinces, or in the
case of the Babylonian Talmud from neighbouring Sasanian Mesopotamia,
and they reflect considerable concern in anecdote, sermon, legal proscription
and legal analysis, for the stuff of economic and social history, and they
do so from the perspective of conformist but fundamentally alienated
provincials.

Money

Rabbinic literature works with a currency system that is a hybrid of the 'standard' Roman gold and silver currency and a version of a local currency (see
Table 21.1; Ben David 1971; Lapin 1995: 122–34; Sperber 1966; Weiser and
Cotton 1996). At the lower end of the scale (between *ma'a* and *peruta*) there
are other denominations that appear rarely in rabbinic literature (m.BB 5.12).
The system is assumed by the Mishnah and early tannaitic corpora and thus
pre-dates the early third century. There are some clear parallels (the ratio of
sela to *denarius*, for example) in early second-century documents from the
Judaean Desert (Weiser and Cotton 1996), but the precise relationship to a
currency in use at a given moment remains unclear. Complicating matters,
there is some slippage for theoretical purposes: an *aureus* was valued at 25
denarii (as at m.BK 4.1), but valuing it at 24 (as at t.BB 5.11) allowed all
lower denominations to be considered fractions of it. In addition, there are
varying assessments of individual lower denominations (e.g. m.BM 3.13;
t.BB 5.12), also resulting in valuations of the *issar* (*as, assarion*) to the *dinar*

Proceedings of the British Academy **165**, 389–402. © The British Academy 2010.

Table 21.1. Rabbinic currency equivalencies.

Terminology			Rabbinic equivalents		
Rabbinic	Roman	Greek	Golden dinar	Sela	Dinar
Golden dinar	Aureus (denarius)	—	1	—	—
Sela	—	Tetradrachma	6	1	—
Shekel	—	Didrachma	12	2	—
Dinar	Denarius	Drachma	24	4	1
Ma'a	—	Obol	144	24	6
Pondion	Dupondius	—	288	48	12
Issar	As	Assarion	576	96	24
Peruta	—	—	4608	768	192

that are unattested elsewhere in the Roman empire (Howgego 1984–85). These differential valuations are presumably attempts to systematise a complex history of coinage production and terminology.

There are numerous citations of prices in both hypothetical and anecdotal traditions, although if Sperber's collection is representative considerably more are given in tannaitic literature than in later Palestinian texts (Sperber 1991: 101–6). It is tempting to try to reconstruct price series from this information, and a new critical review of this material is a desideratum. Nevertheless, given the historiographical problems posed by rabbinic texts, the data appear to give at best a sense of relative scale rather than firm data.

Rather more significant is the vantage point of provincial intellectuals that rabbinic literature provides for what money was and how it functioned. Rabbis inhabited a decidedly monetised sector of the society. Money sometimes is idealised as a fixed measure of value: a small neighbourly loan of a loaf of bread repaid in kind risks overpaying the lender, a form of usury; valuing the loaf as coin and repaying that value avoids this (m.BM 5.9). Despite a prohibition on interest, texts on dowry articulate and quantify the use value of money: the husband was to obligate himself to 150 per cent of the value of money brought in, but 80 per cent of the value of goods (m.Ket. 6.3–4).

Interestingly, gold coinage posed a problem, apparently in both theory and practice. Comments on the valuation of dowry raise the question of whether for that purpose gold coin is money or goods; one, assignable to the mid-second century if we may trust the attribution, states that it was local custom in some places not to make use of gold denarii (t.Ket. 6.5). Applying a definition of sale to the exchange of money, generally 'that which is less valuable' was 'commodity' (lit. 'produce') with respect to the other coin, which was 'money': bronze coinage was 'commodity' with respect to silver;

bad coin to good coin.[1] In the case of gold, however, an alternative tradition, seemingly attributable to about 200, treated gold as 'produce' with respect to silver (m.BM 4.1; t.BM 3.13–14; p.BM 4.1, 9c; b.BM, 44a–b). Arguably, this reversal of an earlier formulation is an inchoate formulation of Gresham's law in response to the deteriorating value of silver currency.

Coinage also *represents* a value that it does not necessarily intrinsically *possess*. A given coin may be short-weighted, worn, or, increasingly the case for silver currency from the late second century onwards, debased. An under-weight coin was deemed valid if it retained a specified proportion of its expected weight (m.BM 4.5; the precise proportion is disputed). Another passage, apparently dealing with visibly worn or clipped coins, rules that a coin that retained half its original weight could still be retained, and the passage may imply that even in the second century coins might be widely valued by weight rather than face value (m.Kel. 4.12 with t.BM 3.17–18). The rate of exchange for coins may have varied from place to place, and it was at least possible to imagine capitalising on the marginal difference (e.g. t.Ma'as. Sh. 3.14; not necessarily pre-dating the third century). An illustration in the Yerushalmi, unfortunately too corrupt to retain precise details, involves individual credit, transportation and clearance transactions (t.Ma'as. Sh. 3.14 with p.Ma'as. Sh. 4.1).

With the collapse of the denarius and the subsequent transformation of Roman currency, the classical rabbinic model of currency became entirely notional, much as the denarius it referred to did. Traditions reflecting the third and fourth centuries consequently give some insight into the way rabbis (and other provincials) perceived and handled a changing currency. The Palestinian Talmud and other roughly contemporary texts would now use earlier terminology in new ways: *dinar* might now refer to the current gold coin, aureus or solidus; *maneh*, in earlier terminology 100 *dinar*, to a subdivision of the (golden) *dinar* (Sperber 1991). The texts also provide evidence for local terminology for coinage, some conventional (e.g. *PWLR, follaris*; *QRT, keration*), others appearing only here (e.g. *RBN, LQN = leukon?*). As with the evidence of prices, a review of the few passages specifying rates of currency exchange relative to gold coinage is a desideratum, although the material is less likely to fill in gaps in numismatic knowledge than offer a perspective on monetary practice as it was understood locally (cf. Sperber 1991).

---

[1] The definition of sale (although not the rules of its completion) including the problem posed by barter is raised in *Digest* 18.1.1 (Paulus), roughly contemporary with the end of the tannaitic stratum.

Trade and Markets

Markets are presupposed in both the legal and the non-legal material in rabbinic literature. In general, our texts share with contemporary Greek and Latin writers a generally negative view of marketers (Rosenfeld and Menirav 2005: 171–209). For this reason traditions about rabbis undertaking *pragmateia*, presumably business affairs, are striking (GenR 77.2, 100.10, Theodor/Albeck 910, 1205; also p.Sotah 9.14, 24b, with emendation), as is a tradition commenting on life's five typical stages that lists 'when [a man] is in his prime and goes out to his *pragmateia*' (LevR 7.4, Margulies 94–5). There is a fair amount of discussion in the texts of market prices and exchange rates for currency, both of which are subject to fluctuation and local variation. These issues arise mostly in the context of specific ritual or legal concerns, but there is ample material for comparative law and economic or social thought, most notably in the development of *iustum pretium* and *laesio enormis*, in Roman Law (Jolowicz 1937; Sperber 1973).

For rabbinic texts, markets are a fundamental feature of collective life. Referring to the biblical 'city of refuge', the Palestinian Talmud specifies that it 'may be built only at (?) a marketplace; if there is no marketplace there they build a marketplace there' (p.Mak. 2.7, 31d; see also Sifre Num. 159, H. 221). Rabbinic literature has a range of terms for merchants and other market actors from money to peripatetic peddlers to shopkeepers to large-scale grain merchants (Rosenfeld and Menirav 2005: 71–136). In exceptional cases markets are discussed in the context of patronage and benefaction. The clearest, and most interesting, has Diocletian establishing an eight-day fair (*yarid*) at Tyre, a passage that draws attention to provincial reception of imperial endowments and the 'epigraphic habit' (p.AZ 1.4, 39c, with Lieberman 1959: 78–81; Rosenthal 1963: 23–8).

Marketplaces and marketing are identified with cities as a matter of course. *Shuk* (pl. *shevakim*) can mean 'street' as well as 'market', but in some cases a connection with marketing is clear, as with the 'grain-*shuk*' of Tiberias (GenR 79.6 Theodor/Albeck 943–4; cf. EcclR 10.8). For cities like Caesarea, Tiberias or Sepphoris, where rabbis were concentrated, there are traditions involving specified (and specialised?) markets such as the *sidki/sirki*[2] (p.BM 5.8, 1c) that could serve to set the price on which contracts for delayed delivery might be based. In connection with 'Gentile' cities such as Tyre or Scythopolis, traditions regarding markets cluster around two ritual issues: (1) Whether festivals, and their attached fairs—by definition periodic

---

[2] Perhaps Greek *sitike*, i.e. grain district, street or market; cf. *amphodou seitikes*, as in *SEG* VIII 43 (Scythopolis, first century CE). Alternatively: modifying an implied *plateia* or *agora*.

affairs—were idolatrous and hence prohibited, for example, the Saturnalia of Scythopolis (p.AZ 1.2, 39c); Diocletian's festival at Tyre, and the three exemplary fairs of Akko (Ptolemais), Gaza and Botna (p.AZ 1.4, 39d). In passing, traditions mention such matters as decorations and ancillary activities, kinds of items bought, locations travelled to, and networks of communication for evaluating distant markets. (2) Whether produce for sale in the marketplace was deemed to come from 'Jewish' territories subject to tithes and other biblical laws. The significance for economic and social historians is the regional sourcing of markets and claims to local information about such sources. Regarding Caesarea, for instance, rabbis claim to know that white bulbous onions come from 'Har Ha-melek' (i.e., the hill country of Judaea?) and not from either the immediate environs of the city or, seemingly, from its *territorium* (p.Dem. 2.1, 22c).

Outside the cities, markets are discussed as a feature of large villages, what tannaitic sources call *ayarot* (sing. *ir*, for clarity hereafter 'town'), that are also assumed to support synagogues and other features of communal organisation (Safrai 1995; with Lapin 1998). These are distinct from both *kefar*, 'village', and *kerak*, 'city'. Features addressed by the texts include market hierarchy and periodicity. A seller might fare better if he takes a jewel to the city or holds an animal for the *itliz*, a periodic animal market (m.Arak. 6.5). More significantly, because it articulates the connection between village markets and prices and those of cities, once a price is set in Tiberias itself, claims a tradition attributed to a late-third-century rabbi, the *ayarot* can use that price for their provisioning transactions (p.BM 5.6, 10c).

Texts dealing with certain ritual matters seem to presuppose markets with a Monday–Thursday period. In particular, the scheduling of the annual reading of the Scroll of Esther on the festival of Purim may reflect a theoretical articulation of markets and the flow of goods from villages to city (Lapin 2004). Nevertheless, the schema offers insight into how a regional geography might be understood. Elsewhere, 'town' markets are said to meet once weekly, on Friday or perhaps Thursday (t.BM 3.20; Sifra Behar par. 3.8, W. 107d). The context is interesting as well: the statement appears as a gloss to a rule that one who questions the quality of a coin received should be given, if in a city, enough time to show it to a moneychanger (*shulhani* = *tabellarius*, *trapezites*), 'but in the villages (*kefarim*) until Sabbath eves' (m.BM 4.6). As the glossator seems to have understood this passage, a villager may have access to coin, but not to an expert; for that a trip to a local market town (*ir*) was necessary, and one had to allow to the earliest Friday.

Periodic village markets are at the low end of the marketing hierarchy: they meet local demand and, *inter alia*, may help to funnel goods up the hierarchy into the city warehouses and markets. There are also larger-scale periodic fairs (*yarid*, pl. *yeridim*) mentioned above, connected with urban (e.g.

Gaza, Tyre, Scythopolis) or rural festivals (Botna, possibly Bet Ilanis (?),
both frequently identified with Mamre).[3] There has been renewed discussion
of the *itliz* (or *atliz*) in recent decades. The most plausible derivation of the
term is from Greek *ateles* (*sc. panegyris*), a festival free from customs
(Lieberman 1959: 76–7; for *ateleia* and marketing de Ligt 1993: 45–8, 229–34,
56–8) although taxes are never associated with its function. The context in
tannaitic corpora almost always presupposes some sort of animal market—
presumably seasonally inflected—but in later texts a more general market,
perhaps, in de Ligt's typology, a local rather than a regional fair (de Ligt
1993: 77–8). Rosenfeld and Menirav consider the *sidki* market a seasonal
grain exchange, but considering the ongoing necessity for grain for the urban
economy (and its political potency) a year-long market whose functions
change over the year may be a better guess (Rosenfeld and Menirav 2005: 48;
Safrai 1994: 247–8).

Finally, rabbinic texts offer some local, provincial reflection on markets
and orientation to markets. Produce is brought to market through various
means. Market professionals have already been mentioned: some (e.g. bakers)
are direct producers; others, such as the *tagar*, seem to have been wholesalers
who bought up produce to bring it to market (e.g. m.BM 4.12). But the texts
also know that householders may bring their own produce to market, and in
some cases may straddle the divide between producer or occasional marketer
and 'professional' marketer (m.Dem. 5.7; cf. p.Shevi. 7.4, 37c). Sale by producing households takes on a gendered cast in some texts. In some, setting up
one's wife as marketer is conventional (e.g. m.Ket. 4.3); in others it requires
special comment: 'for sometimes a man is ashamed to sit in front of his shop
and he gives it to his wife and she sells' (t.BK 11.7). On the consumer side,
rabbis can describe one of their own as, exceptionally, buying everything he
eats from the marketplace (p.Dem. 2.2, 22c; p.Shab. 2, 5b). Elsewhere, the
expectation is that one has sources other than the marketplace for one's grain:
'from here you learn that one who buys grain from the marketplace is of low
status' (GenR 91.6, Theodor/Albeck 1122). The alternative sources may not
be one's own small or large landholdings alone. Rabbis are also depicted as
making arrangements for provisions directly with producers (p.Dem. 2.2, 22c;
p.Shevi. 9.9, 39a).

---

[3] Botna, p.AZ 1.4, 39d, Lapin (2001: 135, n. 65); but cf. Amm. Marc. 14.3.3 (Batnae in
Mesopotamia). Bet Ilanis (text uncertain), Sifre Deut. 306, F. 339, Mader (1957); Safrai (1994:
253–4). Cf. Alon (1957: vol. 2, 98–9); Krauss (1910: 300–2); Sperber (1991: 89 and 232, n. 6).

Social Location and Hierarchy

Class, Status

The debates about the utility of class, order and status for stratification in the Roman empire have largely been left behind, unresolved since the 1970s and 1980s (see Garnsey and Saller 1987: 107–25). Still, the Roman empire and its provinces had elaborate terminologies and practices of hierarchy, and rabbinic literature illustrates some local manifestations. Class is not an object of direct analysis in rabbinic texts as such, certainly not in the formal Marxian sense, nor should we expect this (but cf. de Ste. Croix 1981: 19–30). The literature does, however, adumbrate the social implications of wealth and of the control of the means of production. This is sometimes seemingly beneficent (on festival eves workers turn to their employers for help to purchase what they need, RuthR 3.4); at others ominously influencing the decisions judges make with respect to the parties in a dispute ('Does anyone not know that everything that the tenant farmer has belongs to Bar Ziza [the landlord]?', p.BK 6.7, 5c; p.Shevu. 7.2, 37d).

Extortionate city councillors are said to force, and if necessary to falsify, the sale of the property of rural landowners who refuse to serve as city magistrates or councillors (p.Ta'an. 4.8, 69a; cf. LamR 4.4, and LamR B. 4, p. 102). The story is told about pre-70 Jerusalem, but must be read against the fourth-century history of the decurionate. In a clear, if jaded, reference to the poor as the objects of late-antique benefactions (cf. Brown 2002), one text imagines Esau in the form of estate managers (*epitropayya*, from Greek *epitropos*) who go out to the villages to exploit (*bazin*) the tenant farmers, and return to the cities where they gather up the poor to distribute alms (PRK 10.1, B. 95b–96a; M. 161). That it is *epitropoi*—someone else's agents—who are here stigmatised should remind us that the deployment of power that comes from the control of wealth is always in practice more complicated than any nomothetic application of Marx and Engels would be. Despite a recurrent egalitarian motif (e.g. *all* Israel are children of Abraham, Isaac and Jacob, m.BM 7.1) status and social power are rarely severed from wealth in rabbinic corpora. But as the exploitative *epitropoi* hoped, status appropriate to one's wealth was earned and manifested through performance (Lendon 1997). The most striking examples revolve in some measure around the Palestinian Patriarch (*nasi*), who is also remembered as a central figure in rabbinic circles. The *nasi* is depicted as a matter of course as appropriating the Roman *salutatio* (p.Shab. 12.3, 13c (p.Hor. 3.3, 48c); p.Ta'an. 4.2, 68a). In a famous story about the deposition of the Patriarch Gamaliel, the Patriarch is criticised for his high-handedness and his ignorance of the hardship under which at least one of his colleagues works. Although the story contains some status-levelling themes, Gamaliel's temporary replacement is a young upstart from a good family, much to the disappointment of Akiva the great sage (p.Ber. 4.1, 7c–d (p.Ta'an. 4.1, 67d); cf. b.Ber. 27b–28a).

As it turns out, the Patriarch is frequently presented as an important player in the one form of competitive preferment that rabbis directly address, *minnui* ('appointment', probably to ritual functions; discussion, literature in Hezser 1997: 79–93; Levine 1989: 139–45). Here too wealth was significant and it needed to be appropriately performed. 'Unless you have someone to serve you,' says Yoḥanan to Ḥaninah b. Sisi, whom he found chopping his own wood, 'you will never receive an appointment' (p.Sanh. 2.6, 20c). Appointment brought its own status performances: distinctive dress, people rising before the appointee and addressing him as 'my master' (i.e. *rabbi*) (p.Bik. 3.3, 65d). Rabbis themselves are sometimes described as cutting a visible social figure when walking in public, physically leaning on one or more disciples or attendants. The same is said of an aristocratic woman (*matrona*), leaning on her slave (GenR 45.10, Theodor/Albeck p. 458).[4]

Household, Kinship, Gender

In tannaitic corpora the household is imagined as organised in a series of radial relationships around an adult male property-owning head (Lapin 2003a, 2006). As in other ancient Mediterranean models of the household, the principal relationships are with wife or wives, sons and daughters, and slaves ('Gentile' or 'Hebrew'; see generally Hezser 2005). Lateral relationships—between, for example, wives, offspring of different wives, adult and minor offspring, or between sons and daughters—are the sites of conflict and competition. Legal discussions presuppose the permissibility of polygynous marriage and examples are attested in documents from the Judaean Desert, although anecdotes (as opposed to theoretical discussions) are rare in Palestinian rabbinic texts (Friedman 1986: 2–11; Satlow 2001: 188–92; Schremer 1997). This model of the household continues to be dominant throughout later rabbinic texts, although even in the earlier works there is considerable slippage between this 'ideal' and its exemplification. There is room here for comparative law and an intertwined history of law on several levels. One is rabbinic patriarchy and Roman *patria potestas*. Unlike the Roman family as described by the jurists, the authority of the rabbinic head of household lapses with a son's or daughter's attainment of majority, but

---

[4] The image is applied by analogy to Sarah and Hagar. For the gesture—leaning on attendants—compare the attended woman bathers depicted on a mosaic from Piazza Armerina and on the lid of the Projecta Casket.

this appears to be set, impractically, at puberty. For daughters, the legal traditions assume marriage by the father at or before puberty, but recent work on age at marriage suggests that this does not reflect the norm even within rabbinic circles (Satlow 2001: 104–11; Schremer 1995/96; cf. Katzoff 1997). Similarly, the texts do not spell out how or when sons establish independent households or property, short of inheritance at the death of the father. They do imagine situations in which adult sons are still part of the father's household or even collectively maintaining the father's undivided estate after his death (e.g. m.Eruv. 6.7; m.BB 9.4). As with Roman law, a relatively late age of marriage for men and a high rate of mortality may have levelled some of the peculiar effects of the legal system, if actually practised (Saller 1994; see also Tropper 2005, 2006).

Two further areas of comparative work involve the evolution of aspects of family law (dowry, maintenance of wives or children). For the Mishnah and related texts, juxtaposition to documentary texts, especially those from the Judaean Desert, point, for instance, to the ways in which scribal conventions regarding the clauses of a marriage document were modified as they were adapted by rabbis as 'Jewish' law. Second is the possible contribution to legal anthropology in Palestine (Gagos and van Minnen 1994). Rabbinic texts preserve hundreds of cases, anecdotes in which a rabbi gives a legal decision in a case brought before him. Taken together they suggest that rabbis served (at most) as arbitrators for adherents, but that in Palestine rabbis in the third and fourth centuries heard a much broader range of civil and marriage law cases than did their predecessors. The evidence, for all its problems, offers insight into processes of legal problem-solving and conflict resolution, and in particular the negotiation of the contracting and dissolution of marriage, and possibly its appropriation by (in this case) a religious and ethnic interest group (cf. Harries 1999: 172–90; Modrzejewski 1952).

Among the interesting developments between the fifth century BCE (if we may trust the books of Ezra and Nehemiah) and the Hellenistic period is the disappearance in Palestine of large kinship groupings (e.g. clans) as salient social formations. The stereotyped household discussed above is bi-generational, and it gives way to new marital and then bi-generational households. However, at the edges of legal discussions and narratives is a very loose invocation of kinship: 'relations' (*kerovim*, sing. *karov*) who can be counted upon to check out a potential wife in the bathhouse (m.Ket. 7.8) or negotiate for a woman in a case of divorce (p.Ket. 7.7, 31c). The Palestinian Talmud explains the term *keẓiẓa* in a tannaitic tradition (t.Ket. 3.3) as a ritual in which 'relations' publicly mark a man's sale of his ancestral landholdings or his marriage to or divorce from an inappropriate woman (p.Ket. 2.10, 26d; p.Kid. 1.5, 30c). The identity of the relations varies with context, narrowly including close agnatic kin, or expanding to include a surprisingly broad set of men linked through marriage (see e.g. m.Sanh. 3.4). The recurrence of 'relations' suggests networks of relations beyond the 'nuclear' patriarchal household (Lapin 2006).

Of the stories of *salutatio* before the Patriarchs, one involves the order of precedence of two *zara'in* ('seeds', i.e. families, lineage groups; p.Shab. 12.3, 13c (p.Hor. 3.3, 48c)). Unfortunately, they are named *bouleutai* and *paganoi*; neither, not even *bouleutai* of an imagined proto-feudal colonate, can be described as a lineage. The Patriarchs themselves claimed a genealogical succession. Bowersock (1998: 40–1) has noted the regular use of 'Patriarchs' in the plural in the Theodosian Code, and suggested the shared use by males of the household of the Patriarch of the title 'Patriarch'. If so, it would be attractive to suppose that Patriarchs and their relations formed a kinship group. Priests and levites constituted a special category of descent group, with some ritual perquisites and entitlement to tithes and other priestly gifts if Jews donated them. It is possible, however, that the renewed interest in priesthood in late antiquity, including a listing of 'courses' (i.e. patrilineal segments of the priestly lineage that according to earlier traditions had divided the ritual year between them) and their putative places of residence, already attested in the Palestinian Talmud (p.Ta'an. 4.5, 68d; Trifon 1989/90), were matched by the consolidation of new priestly lineage groups along these (archaising) lines.

An Urban, Provincial Sub-elite

We have had occasion several times to note the vantage point from which rabbis viewed the features of the high-imperial and late-antique Palestinian economy and society discussed above. The vantage point is one of a propertied, monetised, market-oriented group of men. Particularly in the Palestinian Talmud and other amoraic corpora, the vantage point is also decidedly urban. Whatever the 'real' geographical distribution of rabbis, the literature places them, their study houses, and their social connections overwhelmingly in cities (Lapin 1999, 2000; Levine 1989: 25; cf. Hezser 1997: 157–84). Cities, their fixtures and their institutions—statuary, markets, stoas, tetrapyla, councils, and above all baths—punctuate rabbinic stories. Rabbinic literature and the rabbinic movement that produced them are thus an object lesson in both Romanisation and its failures. The failures are most readily apparent to a classically trained historian of the later Roman empire, and they pre-date any putative state-sponsored Christian discourse of Jewish difference. Yet they can only be properly understood within the context of a deep and thoroughgoing enculturation. While a few in rabbinic circles may have been wealthy even by Roman standards—the Gamalielide Patriarch is the best candidate—'propertied' of rabbis means an ability to devote much to study and collegiality; to provide (and care about) an education for sons. One indication of the scale of their wealth is that some rabbis occupied the tertiary tier of provincial landowners upon whom curial duties began to devolve when wealthier men ceased to compete for the honour. Property, money, markets, baths, residence, all these identify rabbis as an urban sub-elite, precisely the sector of a provincial population where we expect pretensions to education and taste, in short aspirational Hellenisation or Romanisation.

Among such men, it is not entirely unexpected to find their movement described in terms familiar from Greek associations, or along the lines of the scholastic traditions of philosophical schools described by Diogenes Laertius or Eunapius; Roman legal tradition as described by Pomponius; or contemporary Christian self-fashioning as philosophy.[5] Moreover, some knowledge of Greek must be assumed (Lieberman 1942, 1950; cf. Lieberman 1963; Stern 1994: 170–81), as must some familiarity with, for example, contemporary Christian debates in the fourth century or later (e.g. Lapin 2003b). And yet on the level of conscious identification, Romanisation failed utterly (Stern 1994). Almost the only educational values the texts espouse are biblical and rabbinic, in Hebrew and Aramaic;[6] and the closest intellectual interlocutors are across the imperial boundaries in Sasanian Babylonia, where a branch of the rabbinic movement flourished with which Palestinians exchanged traditions. The explicit political engagement of rabbinic texts is utterly parochial: whether Samaritans' compliance with Diocletian's order of universal sacrifice made them 'Gentiles' (p.AZ 5.4, 44c); or whether in commanding desecration of the Sabbath, none other than Ursicinus wanted Jews' apostasy or merely warm bread for his troops (p.Shevi. 4.2, 35a (p. Sanh. 3.6, 21b); p.Beiẓah 1.6, 60c). There are two basic approaches we may take here. First, that rabbinic alienation with respect to the Roman world is symptomatic of the peculiar, essentially Jewish, history and stance. But we should take seriously a second possibility, that the process is symptomatic also of a broader failure of the later Roman state to co-opt its local elites, giving way to regionally and ethnically segmented society.

[5] Boyarin (2004: 74–86); Satlow (2003); Tropper (2004: 136–56); cf. Brent (1993); Glucker (1978); Lynch (1972); I develop this further in chapter 3 of a forthcoming book.
[6] See m.Sot. 9.14; t.Sot. 15.8; but note p.Shab. 6.1, 7d; p.Sot. 9.16, 24c, with the claim that Greek education improved the marriageability of daughters (and the claim that the tradition's tradent falsified the transmission to justify teaching daughters Greek). See also the view, formulated or preserved in Mesopotamia, b.BK 83a.

Further Reading

Baker (2002); Hezser (1997, 2005); Lapin (1995, 1999, 2001); Levine (1989); Safrai (1994); Satlow (2001); Sperber (1991).

Bibliography

(In addition to the works cited below, readers should consult the bibliography to Chapter 17, which includes references relevant to this chapter.)

Alon, G. (1957), *Studies in Jewish History in the Times of the Second Temple, the Mishna and the Talmud*, 2 vols., Tel Aviv. [Hebrew]

Baker, C. M. (2002), *Rebuilding the House of Israel: Architectures of Gender in Jewish Antiquity*, Stanford.

Ben David, A. (1971), 'Jewish and Roman bronze and copper coins: their reciprocal relations in Mishnah and Talmud from Herod the Great to Trajan and Hadrian', *Palestine Exploration Quarterly*, 103: 109–21.

Bowersock, G. B. (1998), 'The Greek Moses: confusion of ethnic and cultural components in later Roman and early Byzantine Palestine', in Hayim Lapin (ed.), *Religious and Ethnic Communities in Later Roman Palestine*, Bethesda, MD, pp. 31–48.

Boyarin, D. (2004), *Border Lines: The Partition of Judaeo-Christianity*, Philadelphia.

Brent, A. (1993), 'Diogenes Laertius and the apostolic succession', *Journal of Ecclesiastical History*, 44: 367–89.

Brown, P. (2002), *Poverty and Leadership in the Later Roman Empire*, The Menahem Stern Jerusalem lectures, Hanover, NH.

de Ligt, L. (1993), *Fairs and Markets in the Roman Empire: Economic and Social Aspects of Periodic Trade in a Pre-Industrial Society*, Amsterdam.

de Ste. Croix, G. E. M. (1981), *The Class Struggle in the Ancient Greek World: From the Archaic Age to the Arab Conquests*, Ithaca, NY.

Friedman, M. A. (1986), *Jewish Polygyny in the Middle Ages: New Documents from the Cairo Genizah*, Jerusalem. [Hebrew]

Gagos, T. and van Minnen, P. (1994), *Settling a Dispute: Toward a Legal Anthropology of Late Antique Egypt*, Ann Arbor, MI.

Garnsey, P. and Saller, R. P. (1987), *The Roman Empire: Economy, Society, and Culture*, Berkeley.

Glucker, J. (1978), *Antiochus and the Late Academy*, Hypomnemata: Untersuchungen zur Antike und zu ihrem Nachleben, Göttingen.

Harries, J. (1999), *Law and Empire in Late Antiquity*, Cambridge.

Hezser, C. (1997), *The Social Structure of the Rabbinic Movement in Roman Palestine*, Texte und Studien zum antiken Judentum 66, Tübingen.

Hezser, C. (2005), *Jewish Slavery in Antiquity*, Oxford.

Howgego, C. (1984–85), 'The relationship of the issar to the denar in rabbinic literature', *Israel Numismatic Journal*, 8: 59–64.

Jolowicz, H. F. (1937), 'The origin of laesio enormis', *Juridical Review*, 49: 50–72.

Katzoff, R. (1997), 'Age at marriage of Jewish girls during the Talmudic period', *Teudah*, 13: 9–18. [Hebrew]

Krauss, S. (1910), *Talmudische Archäologie*, 3 vols., Leipzig.

Lapin, H. (1995), *Early Rabbinic Civil Law and the Social History of Roman Galilee: A Study of Mishnah Tractate Baba' Mesi'a'*, Atlanta.

Lapin, H. (1998), 'Review: Z. Safrai, *The Jewish Community* [Hebrew]', *JQR* 89: 217–21.

Lapin, H. (1999), 'Rabbis and cities in later Roman Palestine: the literary evidence', *JJS* 50: 187–207.

Lapin, H. (2000), 'Rabbis and cities: some aspects of the rabbinic movement in its Greco-Roman environment', in P. Schäfer and C. Hezser (eds.), *The Talmud Yerushalmi and Graeco-Roman Culture*, vol. 2, Texte und Studien zum antiken Judentum 79, Tübingen, pp. 51–80.

Lapin, H. (2001), *Economy, Geography, and Provincial History in Later Roman Palestine*, Texte und Studien zum antiken Judentum 85, Tübingen.

Lapin, H. (2003a), 'Maintenance of wives and children in early rabbinic and documentary texts from Roman Palestine', in C. Hezser (ed.), *Rabbinic Law in Its Roman and Near Eastern Context*, Tübingen, pp. 177–98.

Lapin, H. (2003b), 'Hegemony and its discontents: rabbis as a late antique provincial population', in R. L. Kalmin and S. Schwartz (eds.), *Jewish Culture and Society under the Christian Roman Empire*, Leuven, pp. 319–48.

Lapin, H. (2004), 'Some observations on Mishnah Megillah 1:1–3', in Y. Elman, E. B. Halivni and Z. A. Steinfeld (eds.), *Neti'ot le-David: Jubilee Volume for David Weiss Halivni*, Jerusalem.

Lapin, H. (2006), 'The construction of households in the Mishnah', in A. J. Avery-Peck and J. Neusner (eds.), *The Mishnah in Contemporary Perspective*, Part 2, Leiden, pp. 55–80.

Lendon, J. E. (1997), *Empire of Honour: The Art of Government in the Roman World*, Oxford.

Levine, L. I. (1989), *The Rabbinic Class of Roman Palestine in Late Antiquity*, Jerusalem and New York.

Lieberman, S. (1942), *Greek in Jewish Palestine: Studies in the Life and Manners of Jewish Palestine in the II–IV Centuries CE*, New York.

Lieberman, S. (1950), *Hellenism in Jewish Palestine: Studies in the Literary Transmission, Beliefs and Manners of Palestine in the I Century BCE–IV Century CE*, New York.

Lieberman, S. (1959), 'Ten words', *Eshkolot*, 3: 73–89. [Hebrew]

Lieberman, S. (1963), 'How much Greek in Jewish Palestine?', in A. Altmann (ed.), *Biblical and Other Studies*, Cambridge, MA, pp. 123–41.

Lynch, J. P. (1972), *Aristotle's School: A Study of a Greek Educational Institution*, Berkeley.

Mader, E. (1957), *Mambre: Die Ergebnisse der Ausgrabungen im heiligen Bezirk Râmet el-Halîl in Südpalältina, 1926–1928*, Freiburg.

Modrzejewski, J. (1952), 'Private arbitration in the law of Greco-Roman Egypt', *Journal of Juristic Papyri*, 6: 239–56.

Rosenfeld, B.-Z. and Menirav, J. (2005), *Markets and Marketing in Roman Palestine*, Supplement to the *Journal for the Study of Judaism* 99, Leiden.

Rosenthal, E. S. (1963), 'Ha-moreh', *Proceedings of the American Academy of Jewish Research*, 31: 1–71.

Safrai, Z. (1994), *The Economy of Roman Palestine*, London.

Safrai, Z. (1995), *The Jewish Community in the Talmudic Period*, Jerusalem. [Hebrew]

Saller, R. P. (1994), *Patriarchy, Property and Death in the Roman Family*, Cambridge Studies in Population, Economy and Society in Past Time, Cambridge.

Satlow, M. L. (2001), *Jewish Marriage in Antiquity*, Princeton.

Satlow, M. L. (2003), '"And on the earth you shall sleep": "Talmud Torah" and rabbinic asceticism', *Journal of Religion*, 83: 204–25.

Schremer, A. (1995/96), 'Men's age at marriage in Erez Israel in the Second Temple and Talmudic periods', *Zion*, 61: 45–66. [Hebrew]

Schremer, A. (1997), 'How much Jewish polygyny in Roman Palestine?', *Proceedings of the American Academy for Jewish Research*, 63: 181–223.

Sperber, D. (1966), 'Palestinian currency systems during the Second Commonwealth', *JQR* 56: 276–301.

Sperber, D. (1973), 'Laesio enormis and the Talmudic law of ona'ah: a study in the social history of third century Palestine', *Israel Law Review*, 8: 254–74.

Sperber, D. (1991), *Roman Palestine, 200–400: Money and Prices*, 2nd edn., Bar-Ilan Studies in Near Eastern Languages and Culture, Ramat Gan.

Stern, S. (1994), *Jewish Identity in Early Rabbinic Writings*, Arbeiten zur Geschichte des antiken Judentums und des Urchristentums, Leiden.

Trifon, D. (1989/90), 'Did the priestly courses (*Mishmarot*) transfer from Judaea to Galilee after the Bar Kokhba revolt?', *Tarbiz*, 59: 77–93. [Hebrew]

Tropper, A. D. (2004), *Wisdom, Politics, and Historiography: Tractate Avot in the Context of the Graeco-Roman Near East* (includes the text of Avot in Hebrew with English translation), Oxford Oriental Monographs, Oxford.

Tropper, A. D. (2005), 'The economics of Jewish childhood in late antiquity', *Hebrew Union College Annual*, 76: 189–233.

Tropper, A. D. (2006), 'Children and childhood in light of the demographic of the Jewish family in late antiquity', *Journal for the Study of Judaism in the Persian, Hellenistic and Roman Period*, 37: 299–343.

Weiser, W. M. and Cotton, H. (1996), '"Gebt dem Kaiser, was des Kaisers ist . . .": Die Geldwährungen der Griechen, Juden, Nabatäer und Römer im syrisch-nabatäischen Raum', *Zeitschrift für Papyrologie und Epigraphik*, 114: 237–87.

Conclusion

MARTIN GOODMAN

THE STUDIES IN THIS VOLUME HAVE AMPLY DEMONSTRATED that a great deal of evidence preserved within the rabbinic tradition in medieval manuscripts originated in the Roman provinces of Palestine between *c*.200 and *c*.700 CE. They have not disguised the peculiar complexities inherent in accessing and evaluating this evidence because it was preserved within a living tradition in which sayings and stories were transmitted as much through oral as written transmission, but they have also indicated how the caution necessarily engendered by the special nature of rabbinic literature can be overcome by the techniques used by specialists to ensure that this evidence can be used with a degree of confidence by historians.

Part I of the volume has discussed the rich context, revealed especially by archaeology, epigraphy and Christian writings, against which the rabbinic evidence is to be understood, and it has examined the issues of principle in the study of the medieval manuscripts of rabbinic works about which all users of these texts need to take a view before their contents can be taken to say anything at all about late antiquity. The conclusion of the debate between Peter Schäfer and Chaim Milikowsky, in a modicum of agreement that there are good grounds to believe that some rabbinic texts are more likely than others to have undergone extensive changes after the end of late antiquity, reinforces the worth of the ten contributions to Part II, in which individual texts or types of text have been analysed to discover what historical information can and cannot be derived from them.

It is evident from these studies that rabbinic literature cannot be treated for this purpose as an undifferentiated corpus. Similar problems do indeed crop up in each of the chapters in Part II, but there are substantial differences in the ways that are suggested for treating these problems, ranging (in discussions of rabbinic works as a whole) from considerable confidence about the location and dating of the redaction of the Mishnah, in something like the form found in the medieval manuscripts, in Palestine in the early third century (Amram Tropper in Chapter 6) to much scepticism about whether the medieval manuscripts of Hekhalot texts have any value for late antiquity at all (Peter Schäfer in Chapter 15). A number of contributors recommend the

Proceedings of the British Academy **165**, 403–405. © The British Academy 2010.

labour-intensive strategy of judging separately not just every text but every story, saying and description in these texts, a procedure that seems inevitable (for instance) when using stories about Roman Palestine that are embedded in the Babylonian Talmud (so Richard Kalmin in Chapter 10), and Alexander Samely provides (in Chapter 11) a theoretical justification for breaking down much rabbinic literature into such smaller units, which may well have circulated independently of the larger compilations in which they are now embedded.

For extracting useful historical data from these texts, none of which were created originally with the preservation of such data in mind, the contributors to both Part II and Part III of the volume have demonstrated in case studies a number of fruitful techniques, from stripping away the halakhic and midrashic elements of rabbinic stories in the hope of uncovering a core element which reflects contemporary life (a procedure similar to the use of Christian saints' lives for social and cultural history), to seeking to relate rabbinic material directly to other types of evidence (especially archaeology and epigraphy). In such endeavours the vast extent of rabbinic literature and its repetitiveness, so that stories and sayings are often found in subtly different forms in different places, helps the process of winnowing the original version (if such a concept is deemed applicable) from the reworked additional material.

But not least important in Part III have been the demonstrations by each author that what the rabbinic texts can tell us, even at their most reliable, provides only a very partial glimpse of late-Roman Palestine. The rabbis, as Jewish religious enthusiasts, ignored much of the world of cities, churches and bishops described by Fergus Millar in Chapter 2. Those embedded in the 'rabbinic culture' analysed in Chapter 16 by Seth Schwartz both participated in and ignored the Roman culture by which they were surrounded. The rabbinic texts may therefore provide exceptionally useful information about mundane aspects of daily life such as the preparation of food (a topic of much importance in halakhic discussions because of the role of food taboos in Judaism), and Catherine Hezser in Chapter 17 has shown how closely rabbinic observations can be fitted to the archaeological record in many cases, but they will tell us much less about the theology and ideology of other groups in Palestine, not only pagans and Christians (generally treated by the rabbis as an undifferentiated mass of idolaters) but also (as Moshe Lavee shows in Chapter 18) non-rabbinic Jews of their own day, about some of whose ideas it is possible to glean a glimpse from the iconography of synagogue art and the wording of inscriptions. Aharon Oppenheimer has shown (in Chapter 20) how a combination of numismatic and other evidence with rabbinic texts can enlarge knowledge of a specific aspect of civic administration within Palestine in the early third century, but to write a political history of the late-Roman state based on rabbinic texts would be impossible—even the names of Roman emperors would hardly be known, and most of the names that are recorded would be very hard, if not impossible, to date.

For specialists in late-Roman studies, then, the rabbinic sources provide a precious insight into the lives of a very specific group in the eastern Roman empire. It will be rarely that great conclusions applicable to the whole Roman world can be deduced from rabbinic texts alone. But historians should ask themselves how many other groups within the Roman world inhabited, like the rabbis, their own separate ideological world in which the wider issues of the Roman state were kept at a distance, impinging on provincial life only at moments of high drama in times of war or, more mundanely, through the bureaucratic extraction of taxes. It is questionable whether the world of 'rabbinic culture' revealed through these texts would have been deduced from the other evidence for Roman Palestine preserved either in Christian manuscripts or through archaeology. The rabbinic texts of late antiquity survive only because the rabbis of the Middle Ages copied them. If the same had been true of other groups elsewhere in the empire, would a similar picture emerge for other provinces?

Index

The letter n indicates a footnote.